Television Courtroom Broadcasting Effects

The Empirical Research and the Supreme Court Challenge

Paul Lambert

University Press of America,® Inc.
Lanham • Boulder • New York • Toronto • Plymouth, UK

4501 Forbes Boulevard, Suite 200, Lanham, Maryland 20706
UPA Aquisitions Department (301) 459-3366

10 Thornbury Road, Plymouth PL6 7PP, United Kingdom

Printed in the United States of America
British Library Cataloguing in Publication Information Available

Library of Congress Control Number: 2012946769
ISBN: 978-0-7618-6005-1 (cloth : alk. paper)—ISBN: 978-0-7618-6006-8 (electronic)

The paper used in this publication meets the minimum requirements of American National Standard for Information Sciences Permanence of Paper for Printed Library Materials, ANSI/NISO Z39.48-1992.

I offer my thanks and appreciation to my mother and late father, Siobhán, Allison, Stephen, and Steve O'Connor, Deirdre, Eimear, Steve, Vinny, Joe, Mal, Séan, Derek, Pete, Ronan, Anartha, Morko, and also to Hon. Mr Justice Gerard Hogan, Dr. Eoin O'Dell, TJ McIntyre, David Linehan, Devorah Eisenberg, Elizabeth Loftus, Ronan Kennedy, Marie McGonagle and Liam O'Malley, whether for their kind assistance or inspiration. Special appreciation is extended to Dr. Eoin O'Dell for his kind suggestions and vision.

The publication of this book is kindly assisted with a grant from the National University of Ireland Galway

Television courtroom broadcasting arguments and research are inadequate. They need to define and recognise television courtroom broadcasting forms. Television courtroom broadcasting research needs to expand to overcome the many gaps and challenges. The following work seeks to highlight some of these challenges but also some of the solutions.

"The purpose of the court is not education and not spectacle or public entertainment, but justice." (G. Gerber)

"Social scientists measure the intelligence of monkeys more effectively than courts have attempted to ascertain the effects of television in the courtroom." (J. Hirschhorn)

Reviews

"The issue of television in the court room is as old as television itself. Within a decade of television's triumph, the issue reached the U.S. Supreme Court. Its ruling effectively barred television from the courtrooms for over a decade, and established the standard for ad hominum arguments against televising trials. This book is a corrective. First, it recounts the arguments for and against television in courtrooms, and reveals most of them to be self-serving assertions with next to no evidence to support them. Second, it takes the claims and counterclaims seriously, and sets out a sensible approach to replace hot air with hard evidence. This topic is timely. Courts are under pressure to revise their rules. It will become the indispensible read for everyone interested in the topic."

Malcolm M. Feeley, Claire Sanders Clements Dean's Professor Jurisprudence and Social Policy Program Boalt Hall School of Law University of California at Berkeley

"Paul Lambert questions many of the assumptions involved in television broadcasting of court proceedings, as well as raising several other issues that have not been extensively addressed. He also proposes an innovative methodology for studying these assumptions and issues that will add a new, interesting and useful perspective to the discussion and debate over the advisability and effects of the cameras in the courtroom."

Eric P. Robinson, Deputy Director Donald W. Reynolds National Center for Courts and Media Managing Editor Reynolds Courts and Media Law Journal

"In 1923 Lord Hewart the Lord Chief Justice of England and Wales bestowed upon the English language the aphorism, '...that it is of fundamental importance that justice should not only be done but should manifestly and undoubtedly be seen to be done.'

This oft cited maxim is the foundation stone of the principle, in respect of our criminal courts at least, that as a nation we subscribe to the open justice principle. In simple terms this is interpreted to mean that citizens should be free to enter courtrooms and observe trials without hindrance. It also means that restrictions should be placed on the media's ability to report on cases only in the most compelling of situations. Restrictions of course may be statutory or discretionary.

In October 2011 new [UK] Criminal Procedure Rules once again emphasised the important principle of open justice and this is deemed to be consistent with the jurisdiction's commitment to the freedom of expression principle contained in Article 10 of the European Convention on Human Rights. It is also deemed to be in the public interest. (See for example *R. v. Croydon Crown Court ex parte Trinity Mirror & Others* [2008] EWCA Crim 50).

I mention this to pose the question why do citizens physically have to attend court in order to observe judicial proceedings? In this advanced technological age surely television broadcasting from court is long overdue? In September 2011 [UK] Justice Secretary Kenneth Clarke announced the hardly radical news that the ban on televising court sentencing was to be overturned. The primary argument for doing so was that the public would benefit from knowing more about the justice system. Three years earlier the Liberal Democrat Autumn Conference decisively rejected a motion to support the televising of court proceedings. The proposer Jonathan Marks QC had argued that were broadcasting from court to be permitted there would be a wide range of beneficial effects for the British public. These included, • Contributing significantly to public understanding of the criminal justice system; • People would become more aware of the reasons for decisions; • Increasing confidence in the system i.e. it would be more transparent; • It would enhance the performance of judges and lawyers; • It would be an educational resource for young people; • Improve public scrutiny of the criminal justice system. Three years after the Justice Secretary's announcement shows that the debate about television broadcasting is proceeding at snail's pace in the UK.

How are our legislators to decide whether full broadcasting should be permitted? How is the public to know whether the benefits claimed in its name are not simply an excuse for commercial television to increase its advertising revenues? There is a need for detailed research to be carried out.

The publication of Paul Lambert's new book could not be better timed. It is the most comprehensive research based assessment of the pros and cons of television broadcasting available on the market today.

The author argues the case for more effects based research prior to the introduction of live or contemporaneous courtroom broadcasting. He identifies the overwhelming majority of issues that need to be further addressed and reviews the evidence to date particularly from research and experience in the United States.

It may come as a surprise to those of us following the debate in the UK that the United States Supreme Court has only considered broadcasting issues on three occasions in over half a century. What is perhaps even more surprising is that the debate still rages on in the United States.

All those of us with an interest in open justice will welcome this book as making a major contribution to the debate; being perhaps the only book on the market that provides a totally objective assessment of the evidence to date."

Professor Duncan Bloy, School of Journalism, Media and Cultural Studies Cardiff University Co-author of: Hadwin and Bloy: Law and the Media, second edition

"Paul Lambert offers a fascinating, lucid and comprehensive account of the effects, concerns and challenges of broadcasting in the courtroom, a notoriously neglected area of study that will undoubtedly benefit from this new, coherent, wholly accessible and empirically researched analysis. An essential read for anyone interested in justice and the media in the 21st century."

Dr Glen Creeber, Senior Lecturer in Television Studies Aberystwyth University Course leader of Television MA, Teaching "Television Analysis" and "Research Methods" Author of: The Television Genre Book; Fifty Key Television Programmes; Previously On: Television Drama in the Age of Serial Fiction; Studying Television: An Introduction

Contents

Chapter One

Introduction

INTRODUCTION

The core theme of this book is the research challenge posed by the Supreme Court and whether we currently know the effects of television courtroom broadcasting.[1]

The research challenge and this book highlight the necessity of undertaking substantial and ongoing empirical research in relation to the effects of television courtroom broadcasting (TCB) (including in-court television courtroom broadcasting cameras and camera operators).

It provides a critical analysis of television courtroom broadcasting *effects research*. For all of the discussion and interest in television courtroom broadcasting, there is no body of properly considered and scientific television courtroom broadcasting research in relation to the effects.

Issues such as courtroom broadcasting other than television courtroom broadcasting and the television courtroom broadcasting arguments are beyond the current focus.

The general non scientific research to date is *flawed* and in many instances *absent*. The general research is also wholly lacking in sophistication and methodology. The Supreme Court research challenge has not been addressed in any sustained research.

Some of these criticisms also apply to the empirical and scientific research. One commentator notes that "[s]ocial scientists measure the intelligence of monkeys more effectively than courts have attempted to ascertain the effects of television in the courtroom" (Hirschhorn). This book identifies many of these research flaws and challenges in the limited research to date. Significantly more sophisticated television courtroom broadcasting research is required.

As a starting point, the author identifies for the first time the Supreme Court challenge. There are only three main Supreme Court cases considering television courtroom broadcasting (TCB). One of the constant themes in these cases, if not the only constant theme, is the acknowledgement that there are research gaps and that more empirical and scientific research is called for. This is the Supreme Court research challenge.

There are many forms of courtroom broadcasting, and also many forms of television courtroom broadcastings. These are identified for the first time. We need to begin recognising the various different types of television courtroom broadcasting.

The book sets out an initial categorisation forms matrix for identifying and distinguishing the different types of television courtroom broadcasting. This forms matrix then assists us in beginning to address the research gaps and challenges. Many of these gaps and challenges are referred to below.

The book also identifies comparative studies and research tools which can also assist in correcting the deficiencies in the television courtroom broadcasting research to date. These include research from psychology and law (e.g. eyewitness identification; weapons focus) and media and communications studies (e.g. programme styles/genres; gatekeeping; media message and content analysis; audience research).

The author also looks at one of the suggested effects of television courtroom broadcasting, namely, in-court distraction effects of television cameras on the courtroom participants (also known as courtroom actors). This was also highlighted by the Supreme Court. The distraction effect can also encompass the camera operator in the courtroom. The author suggests, for the first time, that eye tracking technology can be used for empirically researching in-court cameras distraction effects.

Television courtroom broadcasting arguments are fundamentally flawed. They ignore the fact that there are different types and forms of television courtroom broadcasting. The forms matrix begins to identify and categorise these different forms. No argument is verified without research or applies (equally) across *all* forms of television courtroom broadcasting. An argument must be justified in the context of a particular form (or forms) of television courtroom broadcasting. Proponents/opponents fail to research, confirm or validate any of their arguments. For example, many advocate television courtroom broadcasting because it is, or will be, educational. Yet, proponents/opponents never say why, how, in what circumstances, for what forms, etc. it will be educational. Nor do proponents/opponents show any research or validation. There is no suggestion either as to which television courtroom broadcasting form(s) will be most educational. Also, none of the various proposed effects are adequately researched or verified. Generally a proposition or argument is only accepted once repeated and verified. This accepted method of study has not been recognised in the television courtroom broadcasting debate or research to date. Research going forward must: distinguish between the different forms of television courtroom broadcasting; identify in advance what exactly is being testing; involve those with knowledge and experience of conducting research; be properly conducted and recorded; be in such a manner that the research and methods may be critically examined by other researchers; be able to be replicated; and be validated by other research.

In summary, the book identifies for the first time the common theme and the *empirical research challenge* of the Supreme Court in relation to television courtroom broadcasting (TCB). It also refers to the flaws, gaps and challenges in television courtroom broadcasting arguments and research. It proposes how we may begin to address and rectify this in future, including with a first forms map or matrix and with some specific research examples, including in particular eye tracking technology, psychology and communications. Without expanding television courtroom broadcasting research, our understanding remains limited at best. The author's proposals and analysis in relation to the benefits of eye tracking technology for in-court effects research regarding the distraction effects of television cameras in courts is most novel. The author's successful in-court proof of concept demonstration experiment is the first such research.

Each chapter below is deserving of an entire research book on its own right. Indeed, this equally applies to many parts of individual chapters. The core theme throughout, however, remains the effects research issues and challenges and our knowledge of the effects.

This is significant internationally and not just in the US.

This also sets a challenge for the current second federal courts experiment which is just underway.

NOTE

1. Earlier versions of parts of chapters 2, 3, 4, 11 and 15 appeared in P. Lambert, Courting Publicity, Twitter and Television Cameras in Courts (West Sussex: Bloomsbury: 2011).

Chapter Two

The Supreme Court and the Research Challenge

INTRODUCTION

This work relates to television courtroom broadcasting (TCB) effects research issues. The legal starting point is the Supreme Court cases which refer to the research issues, and which set the Supreme Court effects research challenge. The identification of the Supreme Court effects research challenge is significant internationally.

The starting point for any discussion (including policy discussion and legal discussion) of TCB is the effects concerns and effects research challenges of the Supreme Court. In the end, while there are three Supreme Court cases, they vary substantially on what they are, and are not confirming, from a formal legalistic perspective. One could argue that they do not decide or establish any general legal rule per se. (This discussion, however, is beyond the scope of the current work.)The common theme in the three cases, however, is that they all refer to and recognise that the issue is an empirical legal one. They establish the Supreme Court empirical research challenge in relation to the effects of television courtroom broadcasting.

It is also necessary to point out that while the Supreme Court has set an empirical research challenge, and said that this research is necessary, it never defined or scoped how this research should occur. TCB is not defined. There are no frames, baselines or parameter factors established. Clearly there are concerns voiced by the Supreme Court, and many potential effects referred to. However, there is a lot going on in-between, and which must be expanded upon in order to address the research challenge and the concerns. It is this gap and interface in which this work is substantially focused and concerned. This work significantly develops our knowledge of how to support and develop our research, language, definitions, baseline and parameters of the research necessary to deal with the effects concerns that exist, and to deal with the Supreme Court research challenge.

Without doubt television courtroom broadcasting has occurred more frequently in the US than anywhere else, albeit in different forms. However, the debate in relation to the various television courtroom broadcasting effects issues continues, even in the US. While the issues surrounding television courtroom broadcasting are always topical, they have been given added impetus of late with legislative efforts to introduce television cameras into US federal courts, into the Supreme Court, as well as the advent of a form of television courtroom broadcasting in the new UK Supreme Court.[1] There are also calls to expand television courtroom broadcasting in the UK beyond the UK Supreme Court, in particular by Sky TV.[2] In addition, a second federal courts pilot experiment has begun, and which is expected to last three years.[3] It remains to be seen, however, what baseline research and data gathering will occur *prior to* the cameras being introduced, nor the full extent of the other research relating to the experiment.

The proposed "Sunshine in the Courtroom" is a bill to provide for television coverage access of Federal court proceedings in the United States. It was introduced for the first time in the 105 th Congress (1997-1998), and has been reintroduced in the 109 th (2005-2006), 110 th (2007-2008) and 111 th Congress (2009-2010). See H.R. 1280 (105th Congress), S. 829 (109th Congress), H.R. 2128 and S. 352 (110th Congress), and H.R. 3054 and S. 657 (111th Congress).[4]

Despite the importance of the effects issues raised, it is perhaps surprising that the Supreme Court has only referred substantially to television camera issues on three occasions. The two seminal cases are *Estes*[5] and *Chandler*.[6] The most recent case, which occurred in 2010, is *Hollingsworth*.[7] However, it is clear from these cases that the Supreme Court was and is aware that there are substantial research gaps. The common theme in each of these cases is the challenge by the Supreme Court that social science and empirical research be undertaken as part of addressing these research gaps.

The Supreme Court challenge identifying the need for proper research of these issues has not yet been fully taken up by social science researchers, the media nor the courts themselves. The gaps, concerns and effects are not addressed.

THE SUPREME COURT CHALLENGE

The most recent Supreme Court case was in January 2010 (*Hollingsworth*[8]) while the other two were in 1965 (*Estes*[9]) and 1981 (*Chandler*[10]) respectively. One would have thought that in the 48 years since the first substantive case in the Supreme Court, that substantial empirical research would have occurred to meet the challenge. Such research would have enhanced our knowledge and understanding of television courtroom broadcasting. This has not occurred.

There are various research problems. For example, there are many research gaps. Many studies are non scientific and non empirical. Too many rely on self reports, opinion reports and questionnaires only. The first reported television courtroom broadcasting case occurred in 1953.[11] Yet since then, there appears to have only been approximately twenty four scientific, methodical and empirical studies of television courtroom broadcasting issues identified in the literature (see below). These are welcome, but obviously insufficient.

The most recent case (*Hollingsworth*[12]) arguably avoids giving a definitive judgement, as the majority focused its decision on procedural issues. The majority opinion in *Estes*[13] (in 1965) clearly came out against television courtroom broadcasting and referred extensively to effects issues. The majority opinion in *Chandler*[14] (in 1981) has been accepted as permitting states to experiment with television courtroom broadcasting. (However, on a careful reading of *Chandler*, [15] it is arguably less pro-camera than camera advocates might feel[16]). It held that *Estes*[17] did not rule that there was a Constitutional rule that *all* television coverage of *criminal* trials was inherently a denial of due process[18] (emphasis added).

The Supreme Court set a challenge in these three cases of addressing the various research gaps — some of which it identified. The cases implicitly called for more research and in particular more social science and empirical research. Unfortunately, despite such a challenge being set as far back as 1965, there are relatively few attempts to address the research gaps empirically. The challenge remains — even for the current second federal experiment.

Indeed, it is ironic that while some of the Supreme Court's comments focused on how television technology may change in future, neither the Supreme Court nor commentators since, have recognised that research and research tools may also change. Indeed, the research tools have improved vastly since 1953. In the case of eye focus and eye tracking, the research and technology has significantly advanced (see below).

It is in this context, that it is suggested that today's technology and *eye trackers* (see below) have advanced to the extent that we can begin to empirically address some of the research issues and challenges set by the Supreme Court. While eye trackers can be used for both in-court and out-of-court research, it is perhaps most relevant to in-court research of effects on courtroom participants.

First, let us see what the Supreme Court said in relation to the lack of research, some specific research gaps, and the challenges it set.[19]

THE *ESTES* CASE

The *Estes*[20] case decided against courtroom broadcasting and effectively barred cameras from US courts for decades. It held that television courtroom broadcasting infringed the defendant's rights to a fair trial.[21] While it referred to out-of-courts effects issues, the comments in relation to in-court-effects are the most extensive. They are also the most interesting to eye tracking research. Addressing these is the challenge.

Mr Justice Clarke delivered the main opinion. It sets out many of the areas that should be addressed by a sustained body of empirical effects research. It should be noted, however, that not all potential effects issues were identified and set out in *Estes* and the other judgements.[22] This is an area deserving of research itself.

The *Estes* Research Challenge: Addressing the Gaps

The Supreme Court recognised that there was not enough proper and empirical research, and set a challenge that such research be undertaken to fill the substantial research gaps. It did not set out a definitive list of specific gaps, nor could it in a single case such as this.

Set out below are some of the effects comments of the Supreme Court as regards the research absences and gaps, and then subsequently in relation to the specific issue of the empirical research challenge.

"[O]ur empirical knowledge of its full effect on the public, the jury or the participants in a trial, including the judge, witnesses and lawyers, is limited."[23] The Supreme Court recognised that there is a distinct lack of empirical research, and a sustained body of such research. By referring to the public and the courtroom participants, the Supreme Court also acknowledges in-court effects research gaps and out-of-court effects research gaps. (It is not clear, however, if the reference to "public" means the viewing audience or whether the Supreme Court has considered potential effects on the viewing audience, as separate from potential effects on other groups or the public at large).

Clarke J added,

> The State would dispose of all these observations with the simple statement that they are for psychologists because they are purely hypothetical. But we cannot afford the luxury of saying that, because these factors are difficult of ascertainment in particular cases, they must be ignored. Nor are they 'purely hypothetical.' They are no more hypothetical than were the considerations deemed controlled in *Tumey*, *Murchison*, *Rideau* and *Turner*.[24] They are real enough to have convinced the Judicial Conference of the United States, this Court and the Congress that television should be barred in federal trials by the Federal Rules of Criminal Procedure; in addition they have persuaded all but

> two of our States to prohibit television in the courtroom. They are effects that may, and in some combination almost certainly will, exist in any case in which television is injected into the trial process.[25]

While the Supreme Court is saying that it does not always need to wait for tangible psychological or other effects, it is implicit that it wants research to be undertaken in the various effects research areas and is setting this challenge. It is also noted that the Supreme Court felt that some effects may be difficult to ascertain. Eye tracking now allows us to undertake empirical research, and in particular, empirical distraction effects research with eye tracking, as demonstrated for the first time by the author's proof of concept research.

Texas, in defending cameras, argued that no prejudice has been shown by *Estes*, that there were no distractions and that "psychological considerations are for psychologists, not courts, because they are purely hypothetical."[26] It also argued that the defendant had not established any "isolatable prejudice."[27] Therefore, to show effects and a sufficient quantity of effects to amount to (potential) prejudice, a party needs to be aware of when and where effects can occur. He or she can seek to find such effects in an instant case. However, are they properly trained and equipped to do this? Can they focus on finding effects and dealing with the core of their case at the same time? What can researchers and interested parties do in terms of general empirical research? Unfortunately, despite the challenge set by the Supreme Court, and indeed Texas itself, the various research challenges are not yet properly addressed. However, eye tracking now allows us to properly research in-court distraction effects.

The ABA Committee on Professional Ethics and Grievances was quoted by the Supreme Court as reporting that,

> courtroom photographing or broadcasting or both would impose undue police duties upon the trial judge[,] ... that the broadcasting and the photographing in the courtroom might have an adverse psychological effect upon trial participants, judges, lawyers, witnesses and juries[,] ... [and] that partial broadcasts of trials, particularly on television, might influence public opinion which in turn might influence trial results.[28]

The ABA House of Delegates, is reported as deciding to have a Special Committee study Canon 35 and to,

> conduct further studies of the problem, including the obtaining of a body of reliable factual data on the experience of judges and lawyers in those courts where either photography, televising or broadcasting, or all of them, are permitted. ... The fundamental objective of the Committee and of all others interested must be to consider and make recommendations which will preserve the right of fair trial.[29]

Harlan J added,

> Surely possibilities of this kind carry grave potentialities for distorting the integrity of the judicial process bearing on the determination of the guilt or innocence of the accused, and, more particularly, for casting doubt on the reliability of the fact-finding process carried on under such conditions ... To be sure, such distortions may produce no telltale signs, but in a highly publicized trial the danger of their presence is substantial, and their effects may be far more pervasive and deleterious than the physical disruptions which all concede would vitiate a conviction. [30]

Chief Justice Warren emphasised that,

> our condemnation of televised criminal trials is not based on generalities or abstract fears. The record in this case presents a vivid illustration of the inherent prejudice of televised criminal trials and supports our conclusion that this is the appropriate time to make a definitive appraisal of television in the courtroom. [31]

Warren CJ also stated that he believed that,

> it violates the Sixth Amendment for federal courts and the Fourteenth Amendment for state courts to allow criminal trials to be televised to the public at large. I base this conclusion on three grounds: (1) that the televising of trials diverts the trial from its proper purpose in that it has an inevitable impact on all trial participants; (2) that it gives the public the wrong impression about the purpose of trials; and (3) that it singles out certain defendants and subjects them to trials under prejudicial conditions not experienced by others. [32]

Warren CJ also added,

> It is common knowledge that 'television ... can ... work profound changes in the behaviour of the people it focuses on.' [33] The present record provides ample support for scholars who have claimed that awareness that a trial is being televised to a vast, but unseen audience, is bound to increase nervousness and tension, cause an increased concern about appearances, and bring to the surface latent opportunism that the traditional dignity of the courtroom would discourage. Whether they do so consciously or subconsciously, all trial participants act differently in the presence of television cameras. And, even if all participants make a conscientious and studied effort to be unaffected by the presence of the television, this effort in itself prevents them from giving their full attention to their proper functions at trial. Thus, the evil of televised trials, as demonstrated by this case, lies not in the noise and appearance of the cameras, but in the trial participants' awareness that they are being televised. To the extent that television has such an inevitable impact it undercuts the reliability of the trial process. [34]

In the dissenting opinions it was stated that,

> [w]e deal here with matters subject to continuous and unforeseeable change – the techniques of public communication. In an area where all the variables may be modified tomorrow, I cannot at this time rest my determination on hypothetical possibilities not present in the record of this case. There is no claim here based upon any right guaranteed by the First Amendment. But it is important to remember that we move in an area touching the realm of free communication, and for that reason, if for no other, I would be wary of imposing any *per se* rule which, in the light of future technology, might serve to stifle or abridge true First Amendment rights. [35]

However, while television and broadcasting technology may change, so too can research models, research techniques, research knowledge and research tools. One example of an advanced research tool is an eye tracker (see below).

Neither the Supreme Court, nor commentators, have recognised that as broadcasting technology may change, so too can the research tools available.

Stewart J states that,

> It is obvious that the introduction of television and news cameras into a criminal trial invites many serious constitutional hazards. The very presence of photographers and television cameramen plying their trade in a courtroom might be so completely and thoroughly disruptive and distracting as to make a fair trial impossible. Thus, if the scene at the September hearing had been repeated in the courtroom during this jury trial, it is difficult to conceive how a fair trial in the constitutional sense could have been afforded the defendant. And even if, as was true here, the television cameras are so controlled and concealed as to be hardly perceptible in the courtroom itself, there are risks of constitutional dimensions that lurk in the very process of televising court proceedings at all. [36]

Mr Justice White, dissenting, states that,

> [i]n my view, the currently available materials assessing the effect of cameras in the courtroom are too sparse and fragmentary to constitute the basis for a constitutional judgment permanently barring any and all forms of television coverage. As was said in another context, 'we know too little of the actual impact ... to reach a conclusion on the bare bones of the ... evidence before us.' White Motor Co. V. United States, 372 U.S. 253, 261. It may well be, however, that as further experience and informed judgment do become available, the use of cameras in the courtroom, as in this trial, will prove to pose such a serious hazard to a defendant's rights that a violation of the Fourteenth Amendment will be found without a showing on the record of specific demonstrable prejudice to the defendant. [37]

This later aspect of the judgement is seldom, if at all, commented upon.

White J adds,

> The opinion of the Court in effect precludes further opportunity for intelligent assessment of the probable hazards imposed by the use of cameras at criminal trials. Serious threats to constitutional rights in some instances justify a prophylactic rule dispensing with the necessity of showing specific prejudice in a particular case. [38]

"Here, although our experience is inadequate and our judgment correspondingly infirm, the Court discourages further meaningful study of the use of television at criminal trials. Accordingly, I dissent." [39] "[W]e are concerned here only with a criminal trial of great notoriety, and not with criminal proceedings of a more or less routine nature."[40] While not explicit, this is a partial acknowledgement of different forms of courtroom broadcasting (CB) and television courtroom broadcasting (TCB).

Harlan J adds,

> Permitting television in the courtroom undeniably has mischievous potentialities for intruding upon the detached atmosphere which should always surround the judicial process. Forbidding this innovation, however, would doubtless impinge upon one of the valued attributes of our federalism by preventing the States from pursuing a novel course of procedural experimentation. My conclusion is that there is no constitutional requirement that television be allowed in the courtroom, and, at least as to a notorious criminal trial such as this one, the considerations against allowing television in the courtroom so far outweigh the countervailing factors advanced in its support as to require a holding that what was done in this case infringed the fundamental right to a fair trial. [41]

Harlan J continues,

> [A]t its worst, television is capable of distorting the trial process so as to deprive it of fundamental fairness. Cables, kleig lights, interviews with the principal participants, commentary on their performances, 'commercials' at frequent intervals, special wearing apparel and makeup for the trial participants - certainly such things would not conduce to the sound administration of justice by any acceptable standard. [42]

Also "[w]ithin the courthouse, the only relevant constitutional consideration is that the accused be accorded a fair trial. If the presence of television substantially detracts from that goal, due process requires that its use be forbidden." [43]

Even the motion hearing to determine whether cameras be permitted at the trial, was broadcast live and with "considerable disruption."[44] "I cannot say at this time that it is impossible to have a constitutional trial whenever any part of the proceedings is televised or recorded on television film. I cannot now hold that the Constitution absolutely bars television cameras from every criminal courtroom, even if they have no impact upon the jury, no effect upon any witness, and no influence upon the conduct of the judge." [45]

Estes Effects/Actual Effects

The Supreme Court said that in the proceedings at hand there had been adverse effects and that there had been prejudice. For example, it stated that,

- "The videotapes of these hearings clearly illustrate that the picture presented was not one of that judicial serenity and calm to which the petitioner was entitled."[46] There were 12 camera men with television and photographic cameras[47] ;
- It was conceded that their activities "led to considerable disruption of the hearings"[48] ;
- "[T]he circumstances and extraneous influences intruding upon the solemn decorum of court procedure in the televised trial are far more serious than in cases involving only newspaper coverage"[49] ;
- The witnesses and jury "were undoubtedly made aware of the peculiar public importance of the case by the press and television coverage being provided, and the fact that they themselves were televised live and their pictures rebroadcast on the evening show"[50] ;
- "When he [i.e. the defendant] finally made his way into the courthouse it was reasonable for him to expect that he could have a respite from his merciless badgering and to have his case adjudicated in a calm atmosphere. Instead, the carnival atmosphere of the September hearing served only to increase the publicity surrounding petitioner and to condition further the public's mind against him."[51]

JUROR EFFECTS

The Supreme Court referred to various effects and potential effects. One of these was juror effects. It stated the following.

The potential impact of television on the jurors is perhaps of the greatest significance.[52]

The conscious or unconscious effect that this may have on the juror's judgement cannot be evaluated, but experience indicates that it is not only possible but highly probable that it will have a direct bearing on his vote as to guilt or innocence. Where pre-trial publicity of all kinds has created intense public feeling which is aggravated by the telecasting or picturing of the trial the televised jurors cannot help but feel the pressures of knowing that friends and neighbours have their eyes upon them. If the community be hostile to an accused a televised juror, realizing that he must return to neighbours who saw the trial themselves, may well be led 'not to hold the balance nice, clear and true between the State and the accused ...'[53]

[W]hile it is practically impossible to assess the effect of television on jury attentiveness, those of us who know juries realize the problem of jury 'distraction.' The State argues that this is *de minimis* since the physical disturbances have been eliminated. But we know that distractions are not caused solely by the physical presence of the camera and its telltale red lights. It is the awareness of the fact of telecasting that is felt by the juror throughout the trial. We are all self-conscious and uneasy when being televised. Human nature being what it is, not only will a juror's eyes be fixed on the camera, but also his mind will be preoccupied with the telecasting rather than with the testimony.[54]

Furthermore, in many States the jurors serving in the trial may see the broadcasts of the trial proceedings ... jurors would return home and turn on the TV if only to see how they appeared upon it. They would also be subjected to re-enactment and emphasis of the selected parts of the proceedings which the ... broadcasters determined ... and would be subconsciously influenced the more by that testimony ... they would be subjected to the broadest commentary and criticism and perhaps the well-meant advice of friends, relatives and inquiring strangers who recognised them on the streets.[55]

[N]ew trials plainly would be jeopardized in that potential jurors will often have seen and heard the original trial when it was telecast. Yet viewers may later be called upon to sit in the jury box during the new trial. These very dangers are illustrated in this case where the court, due to the defendant's objections, permitted only the State's opening and closing arguments to be broadcast with sound to the public.[56]

The Supreme Court added,

- Four jurors had seen the earlier (pre-trial) broadcasts[57] ;
- Pretrial hearings can hold difficulties for defendants[58] ;
- "The presence of television would certainly emphasize to the trial participants that the case is something 'special'"[59] ;
- "To increase the possibility of influence and the danger of a 'popular verdict' by subjecting the jurors to the view of a mass audience whose approach to the case has been conditioned by pretrial publicity can only make a bad situation worse. The entire thrust of rules of evidence and the other protections attendant upon the modern trial is to keep extraneous influences out of the courtroom "[60] ;

- "The knowledge on the part of the jury and other trial participants that they are being televised to an emotionally involved audience can only aggravate the atmosphere created by pretrial publicity." [61]

Stewart J adds,

> It is important to bear in mind the precise limits of the question before us in this case. The petition for a writ of *certiorari* asked us to review four separate constitutional claims. We declined to review three of them, among which was the claim that the members of the jury 'had received through the news media damaging and prejudicial evidence ...' We thus left undisturbed the determination of the Texas Court of Criminal Appeals that the members of the jury were not prejudiced by the widespread publicity which preceded the petitioner's trial. [62]

He continues,

> Some of those risks are catalogued in the *amicus curiae* brief filed in this case by the American Bar Association: '[P]otential or actual jurors, in the absence of enforceable and effective safeguards, may arrive at certain misconceptions regarding the defendant and his trial by viewing televised pre-trial hearings and motions from which the jury is ordinarily excluded. Evidence otherwise inadmissible may leave an indelible mark ... Once the trial begins, exposure to nightly rebroadcasts of selected portions of the day's proceedings will be difficult to guard against, as jurors spend frequent evenings before the television set. The obvious impact of witnessing repeated trial episodes and hearing accompanying commentary, episodes admittedly chosen for their news value and not for evidentiary purposes, can serve only to distort the jurors' perspective ... Despite the court's injunction not to discuss the case, it seems undeniable that jurors will be subject to the pressure of television-watching family, friends and, indeed, strangers. ... It is not too much to imagine a juror being confronted with his wife's television-oriented viewpoint ... Additionally, the jurors' daily television appearances may make them recognizable celebrities, likely to be stopped by passing strangers, or perhaps harried by intruding telephone calls ...' Constitutional problems of another kind might arise if a witness or juror were subjected to being televised over his objection. [63]

WITNESS EFFECTS

The Supreme Court also referred to witness effects, as follows,

> The quality of the testimony in criminal trials will often be impaired. The impact upon a witness of the knowledge that he is being viewed by a vast audience is simply incalculable. Some may be demoralized and frightened, some cocky and given to overstatement; memories may falter as with anyone speaking publicly, and accuracy of statement may be severely undermined. Embarrassment may impede the search for the truth, as may a natural tendency

> toward overdramatization. Furthermore, inquisitive strangers and 'cranks' might approach witnesses on the street with jibes, advice or demands for explanations of testimony.[64]

Clarke J adds,

> [W]itnesses would be able to go to their homes and view broadcasts of the day's trial proceedings, notwithstanding the fact that they had been admonished not to do so. They could view and hear the testimony of preceding witnesses, and so shape their own testimony as to make its impact crucial. And even in the absence of sound, the influences of such viewing on the attitude of the witness toward testifying, his frame of mind upon taking the stand or his apprehension of withstanding cross-examination defy objective assessment. Indeed, the mere fact that the trial is to be televised might render witnesses reluctant to appear and thereby impede the trial as well as the discovery of the truth.[65]

JUDGE EFFECTS

The Supreme Court also acknowledged effects on judges, namely,

- "A major aspect of the problem is the additional responsibilities the presence of television places on the trial judge. His job is to make certain that the accused receives a fair trial. This most important task requires his undivided attention. Still when television comes into the courtroom he must also supervise it"[66] ; This is very seldom recognised, recorded or researched;
- "Judges are human beings also and are subject to the same psychological reactions as laymen"[67] ; There is apparently no empirical research of this issue. This should be addressed by research in future.
- "Telecasting is particularly bad where the judge is elected, as is the case in all save a half dozen of our States. The telecasting of a trial becomes a political weapon, which, along with other distractions inherent in broadcasting, diverts his attention from the task at hand – the fair trial of the accused"[68] ;
- "[I]t is difficult to remain oblivious to the pressures that the news media can bring to bear on them both directly and through the shaping of public opinion."[69]

It continues,

> The State would dispose of all these observations with the simple statement that they are for psychologists because they are purely hypothetical. But we cannot afford the luxury of saying that, because these factors are difficult of ascertainment in particular cases, they must be ignored. Nor are they 'purely

> hypothetical.' They are no more hypothetical than were the considerations deemed controlled in *Tumey*, *Murchison*, *Rideau* and *Turner*.[70] They are real enough to have convinced the Judicial Conference of the United States, this Court and the Congress that television should be barred in federal trials by the Federal Rules of Criminal Procedure; in addition they have persuaded all but two of our States to prohibit television in the courtroom. They are effects that may, and in some combination almost certainly will, exist in any case in which television is injected into the trial process.[71]
>
> How much more harmful is a procedure which not only offers the temptation to judges to use the bench as a vehicle for their own ends, but offers the same temptation to every participant in the trial, be he defense counsel, prosecutor, witness or juror![72]
>
> The transcript of the trial belies any notion that frequent interruptions and inconsistent rulings communicated to the jury any sense that the judge was unable to concentrate on protecting the defendant and conducting the trial in a fair manner, in accordance with the State and Federal Constitutions ... What ultimately emerges from this record, therefore, is one bald question — whether the Fourteenth Amendment of the United States Constitution prohibits all television cameras from a state courtroom whenever a criminal trial is in progress.[73]

DEFENDANT EFFECTS

The Supreme Court also referred to defendant effects. It should be noted that, generally, defendant effects are one of the least researched areas of television courtroom broadcasting in both the general non-empirical studies and also the empirical studies to date. The Supreme Court states as follows,

> [W]e cannot ignore the impact of courtroom television on the defendant. Its presence is a form of mental — if not physical — harassment, resembling a police line-up or the third degree. The inevitable close-ups of his gestures and expressions during the ordeal of his trial might well transgress his personal sensibilities, his dignity, and his ability to concentrate on the proceedings before him — sometimes the difference between life and death — dispassionately, freely and without distraction of wide public surveillance. A defendant on trial for a specific crime is entitled to his day in court, not in a stadium, or a city or nationwide area. The heightened public clamor resulting from radio and television coverage will inevitably result in prejudice. Trial by television is, therefore, foreign to our system. Furthermore, telecasting may also deprive the accused of an effective counsel. The distractions, intrusions into confidential attorney-client relationships and the temptation offered by television to play to the public audience might often have a direct effect not only upon lawyers, but the judge, the jury and the witnesses.[74]

The Supreme Court noted that the original trial judge initially imposed no restrictions whatsoever.[75] However, as matters progressed,

> the trial judge himself was harassed ... he ... decided that a booth should be built at the broadcasters' expense to confine its operations; he then decided to limit the parts of the trial that might be televised live; then he decided to film testimony of the witnesses without sound in an attempt to protect those under the rule; and finally he ordered that defense counsel and their argument not be televised, in light of their objection. Plagued by his original error — recurring each day of the trial — his day-to-day orders made the trial more confusing to the jury, the participants and the viewers. Indeed it resulted in a public presentation of only the State's side of the case.[76]

Warren CJ noted that the defendant had objected to televising, but that the motion hearing actually had at least 12 cameramen and equipment present, and photographers roaming about and taking pictures from all angles.[77] The courtroom was relatively small and the cameras were fully visible to all present.[78] Also, "[t]hat is not to say that all participants in the trial would distort it by deliberately playing to the television audience, but some undoubtedly would. The even more serious danger is that neither the judge, prosecutor, defense counsel, jurors or witnesses would be able to go through the trial without considering the effect of their conduct on the viewing public."[79]

Warren CJ states,

> Our decisions in *White v. Maryland*, 373 U.S. 59, and *Hamilton v. Alabama*, 368 U.S. 400, clearly hold that an accused is entitled to procedural protections at pretrial hearings as well as at actual trial and his conviction will be reversed if he is not accorded these protections. In addition, in *Pointer v. Texas*, 380 U.S. 400, we held that a pretrial hearing can have a profound effect on the trial itself and effectively prevent an accused from having a fair trial. Petitioner clearly did not have a fair determination of his motion to exclude cameras from the courtroom. The very presence of the cameras at the September [pre trial] hearing tended to impress upon the trial judge the power of the communications media and the criticism to which he would have been subjected if he had ruled that the presence of the cameras was inconsistent with the petitioner's right to a fair trial. The prejudice to petitioner did not end here. Most of the trial participants were present at the September hearing — the judge, defence counsel, prosecutor, prosecution witnesses and defendant himself — and they saw for themselves the desecration of the courtroom. After undergoing this experience it is unrealistic to suppose that they would come to the October trial unaware that court procedures were being sacrificed in this case for the convenience of television. The manner in which the October proceedings were conducted only intensified this awareness. It was impossible for any of the trial participants ever to be unaware of the presence of television cameras in court for the actual trial. The snouts of the four television cameras protruded through the opening on the booth, and the cameras and their operators were not only readily visible but were impossible to ignore by all who were surveying the activities in this small courtroom. No one could forget that he was constantly in the focus of the 'all-seeing eye.' Although the law of

> Texas purportedly permits witnesses to object to being televised, it is ludicrous to place this burden on them. They would naturally accept the conditions of the courtroom as the judge establishes them, and feel that it would be as presumptuous for them to object to the court's permitting television as to object to the court reporter's recording their testimony. Yet, it is argued that no witnesses objected to being televised. This is indeed a slender reed to rely on, particularly in view of the trial judge's failure, in the course of his self—exculpating statements justifying his decision to allow television, to advise the witnesses or the jurors that they had the right to object to being televised. Defence counsel, however, stated forcefully that he could not concentrate on the case because of the distraction caused by the cameras. And the trial judge's attention was distracted from the trial since he was compelled to make seven extensive ruling concerning television coverage during the October proceedings alone, when he should, instead, have been concentrating on the trial itself. [80]

Again, the issue of court and court personnel having to deal with applications and camera issues is seldom researched or recorded at all.

OUT-OF-COURT EFFECTS RESEARCH

The Supreme Court also referred specifically to out-of-court issues (albeit not identifying them by this category description, and devoting significantly less consideration to it). It said the following,

> The televising of trials would cause the public to equate the trial process with the forms of entertainment regularly seen on television and with the commercial objectives of the television industry ... In addition, if trials were televised there would be a natural tendency on the part of broadcasters to develop the personalities of the trial participants, so as to give the proceedings more of an element of drama. This tendency was noticeable in the present case. Television commentators gave the viewing audience a homey, flattering sketch about the trial judge, obviously to add any extra element of viewer appeal to the trial. [81]

The research and the literature seldom refer to the out of court issues. It is really only in the seminal work by Susanna Barber[82] that there is a call for out—of—court effects research.

Warren CJ states,

> Broadcasting in the courtroom would give the television industry an awesome power to condition the public mind either for or against the accused. By showing only those parts of its films or tapes which depict the defendant or his witnesses in an awkward or unattractive position, television directors could give the community, state or country a false and unfavourable impression of the man on trial. Moreover, if the case should end in a mistrial, the showing of selected portions of the trial, or even of the whole trial, would make it almost impossible to select an impartial jury for a second trial ... To permit this

> powerful medium to use the trial process itself to influence the opinions of vast numbers of people, before a verdict of guilt or innocence has been rendered, would be entirely foreign to our system of justice.[83]

Warren CJ continues,

> The sense of fairness, dignity and integrity that all associate with the courtroom would become lost with its commercialization. Thus, the televising of trials would not only have an effect on those participating in the trials that are being televised, but also on those who observe the trials and later become trial participants.[84]

OUT-OF-COURT EFFECTS: EDUCATION

The Supreme Court also referred to out-of-court educational issues. This is seldom researched. The courts and the arguments do not properly consider this issue. The court said the following,

> It is argued that television not only entertains, but also educates the public. But the function of a trial is not to provide an educational experience; and there is a serious danger that any attempt to use a trial as an educational tool will both divert it from its proper purpose and lead to suspicions concerning the integrity of the trial process ... This divided effort undercut confidence in the guilt—determining aspect of the procedure, and, by so doing, rendered the educational aspect self-defeating.[85]

Harlan J adds,

> Many trials are newsworthy, and televising them might well provide the most accurate and comprehensive means of conveying their content to the public. Furthermore, television is capable of performing an educational function by acquainting the public with the judicial process in action. Albeit, these are credible policy arguments in favor of television, they are not arguments of constitutional proportions.[86]

The "propriety of closed circuit television for the purpose of making a court recording or for limited use in educational institutions obviously presents markedly different considerations."[87]

This implicitly acknowledges that there are different forms (see below also) of television courtroom broadcasting. The forms issue is not defined or addressed in the literature or the research to date. This is the first work to tackle the forms issues.

Warren CJ states,

> Finally, if the televising of criminal proceedings were approved, trials would be selected for television coverage for reasons having nothing to do with the purpose of trial. A trial might be televised because a particular judge has gained the fancy of the public by his unorthodox approach; or because the district attorney has decided to run for another office, and it is believed his appearance would attract a large audience; or simply because a particular courtroom has a layout that best accommodates television coverage. For the most part, however, the most important factor that would draw television to the courtroom would be the nature of the case. The alleged perpetrator of the sensational murder, the fallen idol, or some other person who, like petitioner, has attracted the public interest would find his trial turned into a vehicle for television. Yet these are the very persons who encounter the greatest difficulty in securing an impartial trial, even without the presence of television. This Court would no longer be able to point to the dignity and calmness of the courtroom as a protection from outside influences. For the television camera penetrates this protection, and brings into the courtroom tangible evidence of the widespread interest in a case — an interest which has often been fanned by exhaustive reports in the newspapers, television and radio for weeks before trial. The present case presents a clear example of this danger.[88]

Warren CJ also states,

> How is the defendant to prove that the prosecutor acted differently than he ordinarily would have, that defence counsel was more concerned with impressing prospective clients than with the interests of the defendant, that a juror was so concerned with how he appeared on television that his mind continually wandered from the proceedings, that an important defence witness made a bad impression on the jury because he was 'playing' to the television audience, or that the judge was a little more lenient or a little more strict than he usually might be? And then, how is petitioner to show that this combination of changed attitudes diverted the trial sufficiently from its purpose to deprive him of a fair trial? It is no answer to say that an appellate court can review for itself tapes or films of the proceedings. In the first place, it is not clear that the court would be able to obtain unedited tapes or films to review. Even with the cooperation of counsel on both sides, this Court was unable to obtain films of this trial which were in any sense complete. In addition time limitations might restrict the television companies to taking pictures only of those portions of the trial that are most newsworthy and most likely to attract the attention of the viewing audience. More importantly, the tapes or films, even if unedited, could give a wrong impression of the proceedings. The camera which takes pictures cannot take a picture of itself. In addition, the camera cannot possibly cover the actions of all trial participants during the trial. While the camera is focused on the judge who is apparently acting properly, a juror may be glancing up to see where the camera is pointing, and counsel may be looking around to see whether he can confer with his client without the close-up lens of the camera focusing on them. Needless to say, the camera cannot penetrate the minds of the trial participants and show their awareness that they may at that moment be the subject of the camera's focus. The most the camera can show is

> that a formally correct trial took place, but our Constitution requires more than form.[89]

This is most significant in terms of developing details and coding of empirical research. However, this particular part of the judgement has been ignored to date. It also goes to the balance and duty of whom should prove and research effects in particular cases, (whether in order to argue the issues in that instant case, on appeal, or generally).

Harlan states that "[w]e must take notice of the inherent unfairness of television in the courtroom, and rule that its presence is inconsistent with the 'fundamental conception' of what a trial should be." [90]

Harlan J also states that,

> The arguments advanced against the constitutional banning of televised trials seem to me peculiarly unpersuasive. It is said that the pictorial broadcasting of trials will serve to educate the public as to the nature of the judicial process. Whatever force such arguments might have in run—of—the-mill cases, they carry little weight in cases of the sort before us, where the public's interest in viewing the trial is likely to be engendered more by curiosity about the personality of the well-known figure who is the defendant (as here), or about famous witnesses or lawyers who will appear on the television screen, or about the details of the particular crime involved, than by innate curiosity to learn about the workings of the judicial process itself. Indeed it would be naive not to suppose that it would be largely such factors that would qualify a trial for commercial television 'billing,' and it is precisely that kind of case where the risks of permitting television coverage of the proceedings are at their greatest.[91]

FORMS

The Supreme Court also implicitly referred to form *issues*. However, it did not explicitly set out the different forms of courtroom broadcasting. The court did not mention "forms" nor did it refer to any form descriptions or categorisations by name. The research nor the literature to date has explicitly referred to this issue. Unfortunately, there is also no research or scoping of the implication of forms of television courtroom broadcasting to the general discussion. This is the first work to begin to do so.

The Supreme Court said the following,

- "The probable impact of courtroom television on the fairness of a trial may vary according to the particular kind of case"[92] ;
- "When the issue of television in a non-notorious trial is presented it may appear that no workable distinction can be drawn based on the type of case involved, or that the possibilities for prejudice, though less severe, are

nonetheless of constitutional proportions ... The resolution of those further questions should await an appropriate case."[93]

It added,

> I do not deem the constitutional inquiry in this case ended by the finding ... that no isolatable prejudice was occasioned by the manner in which television was employed in this case. Courtroom television introduces into the conduct of a criminal trial the element of professional 'showmanship,' an extraneous influence whose subtle capacities for serious mischief in a case of this sort will not be underestimated by any lawyer experienced in the elusive imponderables of the trial arena. In the context of a trial of intense public interest, there is certainly a strong possibility that the timid or reluctant witness, for whom a court appearance even at its traditional best is a harrowing affair, will become more timid or reluctant when he finds that he will also be appearing before a 'hidden audience' of unknown but large dimensions. There is certainly a strong possibility that the 'cocky' witness having a thirst for the limelight will become more 'cocky' under the influence of television. And who can say that the juror who is gratified by having been chosen for a front-line case, an ambitious prosecutor, a publicity-minded defense counsel, and even a conscientious judge will not stray, albeit unconsciously, from doing what 'comes naturally' into pluming themselves for a satisfactory television 'performance'?[94]

What is also significant is that as no forms of courtroom broadcasting and TCB are expressly set out by the Supreme Court. This gap and challenge needs to be fully considered in all future TCB discussions.

NEED TO SHOW ACTUAL PREJUDICE?

Mr Justice Harlan in *Estes*[95] states that the "petitioner has not asserted any isolatable prejudice resulting from the presence of television apparatus within the courtroom or from the contemporaneous or subsequent broadcasting of the trial proceedings." [96]

The State (Texas) argued that specific prejudice must have been shown for the constitutional due process and fairness clause to apply. [97] Warren CJ states that,

> I believe petitioner in this case has shown that he was actually prejudiced by the conduct of these proceedings, but I cannot agree with those who say that a televised trial deprives a defendant of a fair trial only if 'actual prejudice' can be shown. The prejudice of television may be so subtle that it escapes the ordinary methods of proof, but it would gradually erode our fundamental conception of trial. A defendant may be unable to prove that he was actually prejudiced by a televised trial, just as he may be unable to prove that the introduction of a coerced confession at his trial influenced the jury to convict

> him when there was substantial evidence to support his conviction aside from the confession. [98]

To the extent to which Texas is saying there are no effects shown, it beholds researchers to examine each of the separate effects issues. Too much of the general "research" has not identified and isolated an individual effect hypothesis. Many such studies cannot be said to have researched any actual or specific effect. To answer the Supreme Court, Texas, etc., research must be obtained through rigorous, demonstrated, replicable, verifiable, research of a specific effect hypothesis. In meeting this challenge, the standard and scope of the research needs to be expanded, more robust and empirical. If the overall standard and quality is not sufficient, it does not properly address the challenges set.

Also, "[t]here is no claim that the conduct of the judge, or that any deed or word of counsel, or of any witness, or of any juror, was influenced in any way by the presence of photographers or by television." [99] Other than a very manifest example, how is a defendant meant to review and research for such effects while his case is ongoing?

The research required is difficult and complex. The defendant is normally also focused on other issues, namely, the trial hearing itself. In addition, "[t]here is little wonder that the defendant cannot 'prove' the existence of such factors. Yet we all know from experience that they exist."[100]

The focus of whose responsibility it is to undertake effects research is also underrepresented in the literature.

SUBTLE AND DISCRETE EFFECTS

The Supreme Court recognised that there may be subtle and or discrete effects. It said the following, that "[t]elevision in its present state and by its very nature, reaches into a variety of areas in which it may cause prejudice to an accused. Still one cannot put his finger on its specific mischief and prove with particularity wherein he was prejudiced."[101] Television "amounts to the injection of an irrelevant factor into court proceedings. In addition, experience teaches that there are numerous situations in which it might cause actual unfairness — some so subtle as to defy detection by the accused or control by the judge."[102] Certainly in terms of eye attention and eye focus, we know that such effects are now no longer so subtle as to defy detection. The author's proof of concept demonstration of eye tracking in an actual courtroom shows this. The eye movements of simulated courtroom participants in test settings and in actual court settings, can be examined and recorded. There are many potential areas of courtroom actor eye tracking research that can now be carried out.

We

> should not be deterred from making the constitutional judgment which this case demands by the prospect that the day may come when television will have become so commonplace an affair in the daily life of the average person as to dissipate all reasonable likelihood that its use in courtrooms may disparage the judicial process. If and when that day arrives the constitutional judgment called for now would of course be subject to re-examination in accordance with the traditional workings of the Due Process Clause. At the present juncture I can only conclude that televised trials, at least in cases like this one, possess such capabilities for interfering with the even course of the judicial process that they are constitutionally banned. On these premises I concur in the opinion of the Court. [103]

THE *CHANDLER* CASE: EMPIRICAL DATA/EFFECT SHOWN

The Supreme Court in *Chandler*[104] again referred to research and empirical evidence research.

- It was held that "at present no one has presented empirical data sufficient to establish that the mere presence of the broadcast media in the courtroom inherently has an adverse effect on that process under all circumstances. Here, the appellants have offered nothing to demonstrate that their trial was subtly tainted by broadcast coverage – let alone that all broadcast trials would be tainted"[105] ;
- "No evidence of specific prejudice was tendered"[106] ;
- "Absent a showing of prejudice of constitutional dimensions to these appellants, there is no reason for this Court either to endorse or to invalidate Florida's experiment"[107] ;
- "Nor have the appellants shown either that the media's coverage of their trial — printed or broadcast — compromised the jury's ability to judge them fairly or that the broadcast coverage of their particular trial had an adverse impact on the trial participants sufficient to constitute a denial of due process"[108] ;
- "One is entitled to wonder if such a statement would be made in a court of justice by any state trial judge except as an appeal calculated to gain the favour of his viewing audience"[109] ;
- Because technology has changed since the *Estes*[110] case, it was argued that "many of the negative factors found in *Estes* ... are less substantial factors today than they were at that time"[111] ;
- The Supreme Court notes in a footnote that in the original experiment permitted by the Supreme Court of Florida, that court acknowledged that the research was "limited" and "non-scientific"[112] ;
- "Nonetheless, it is clear that the general issue of the psychological impact of broadcast coverage upon the participants in a trial, and particularly upon the defendant, is still a subject of sharp debate"[113] ;

- "Comprehensive empirical data are still not available — at least on some aspect of the problem"[114];
- It also adds that "... at present no one has been able to present empirical data sufficient to establish that the mere presence of the broadcast media inherently has an adverse effect on that process"[115];
- Even the *amici* briefs supporting Florida in the Supreme Court case, admit that more experimentation is needed to evaluate the potential psychological prejudice[116];
- "To demonstrate prejudice in a specific case a defendant must show something more than juror awareness that the trial is such as to attract the attention of broadcasters"[117];
- "The appellants have offered no evidence that any participant in this case was affected by the presence of cameras."[118]

THE *HOLLINGSWORTH* CASE

The most recent Supreme Court case was in early 2010. The Supreme Court was asked to stay the television broadcast of a trial. The Californian District Court had issued an order permitting broadcasting live via streaming video to a number of courts.[119] The defendants objected.[120] They sought a stay, which was granted by the Supreme Court.[121]

The origin of the case is the same sex marriage law proposal (Proposition 8)(or Prop 8) in California. Those supporting it submitted that they had been harassed as a result of their support, which included receiving death threats.[122] They appear to have anticipated these threats continuing or increasing if the case was televised.

The Californian court had envisaged this case as an experiment of television courtroom broadcasting in California's federal courts[123] (as opposed to its state courts which already permit certain broadcasting). This necessitated changing a local law which banned such broadcasting.[124] It is also interesting in that the transmission was to other courthouses – and apparently not a push television broadcast to a public audience.

Hollingsworth: Camera and Effects Issues Avoided

The Supreme Court, however, resolved the "question without expressing any view on whether such trials should be broadcast. We instead determine that the broadcast in this case should be stayed because it appears the courts below did not follow the appropriate procedures set forth in federal law before changing their rules to allow such broadcasting."[125]

The Supreme Court majority did not expressly consider courtroom broadcasting argument or effects issues. It states that its

> review is confined to a narrow legal issue: whether the District Court's amendment of its local rules to broadcast this trial complied with federal law. We conclude that it likely did not and that applicants have demonstrated that irreparable harm would likely result from the District Court's actions. We therefore stay the court's … order to [which] permits the live streaming of court proceedings to other federal courthouses. We do not address other aspects of that order, such as those related to the broadcast of court proceedings on the Internet, as this may be premature.[126]

Therefore, arguably, the case does not have a wider significance for television courtroom broadcasting.

Hollingsworth: Reference to Camera Issues

However, while not being of any wider significance, the case does refer to camera issues and research issue. The Supreme Court, for example, referred to the Judicial Conference, which it said has a restrictive position on the broadcast of court proceedings.[127] The Supreme Court again referred to effect issues, and it can be seen that the research challenge is reiterated and remains.

Hollingsworth: Reference to Witness Effects Issues

The Supreme Court, referred to witnesses and stated that the,

> Applicants also *have shown* [emphasis added] that irreparable harm will likely result from the denial of the stay. Without a stay, the District Court will broadcast the trial. It would be difficult — if not impossible — to reverse the harm from those broadcasts … This Court has recognized that witness testimony may be chilled if broadcast[128] ... Some of the applicants' witnesses have already said that they will not testify if the trial is broadcast, and they have substantiated their concerns by citing incidents of past harassment ... (71 news articles detailing incidents of harassment related to people who supported Proposition 8). These concerns are not diminished by the fact that some of applicants' witnesses are compensated expert witnesses. There are qualitative differences between making public appearances regarding an issue and having one's testimony broadcast throughout the country. Applicants may not be able to obtain adequate relief through an appeal. The trial will have already been broadcast. It is difficult to demonstrate or analyze whether a witness would have testified differently if his or her testimony had not been broadcast. And witnesses subject to harassment as a result of broadcast of their testimony might be less likely to cooperate in any future proceedings.[129]

HOLLINGSWORTH: EVIDENCE OF HARM/EFFECTS

It is interesting that the Supreme Court said that the applicants against broadcast, had established effects and harm if broadcast. Perhaps more noteworthy is the comment that the respondents have not demonstrated any harm if there was no proposed broadcast. The court states that the "balance of equities favors applicants. While applicants have demonstrated the threat of harm they face if the trial is broadcast, respondents have not alleged any harm if the trial is not broadcast. The issue, moreover, must be resolved at this stage, for the injury likely cannot be undone once the broadcast takes place."[130]

Hollingsworth: Considered Rules Are Required

In terms of court rules, the Supreme Court reiterated that the,

> Court's interest in ensuring compliance with proper rules of judicial administration is particularly acute when those rules relate to the integrity of judicial processes. The District Court here attempted to revise its rules in haste, contrary to federal statutes and the policy of the Judicial Conference of the United States. It did so to allow broadcasting of this high-profile trial without any considered standards or guidelines in place. The arguments in favor of developing procedures and rules to allow broadcast of certain cases have considerable merit, and reasonable minds can surely differ over the general and specific terms of rules and standards adopted for that purpose. Here, however, the order in question complied neither with existing rules or policies nor the required procedures for amending them.[131]

Even if the local law had been validly amended, that was not the end of the matter. The Supreme Court felt that even if it "had been validly revised, questions would still remain about the District Court's decision to allow broadcasting of this particular trial, in which several of the witnesses have stated concerns for their own security."[132]

Hollingsworth: Publicity Effects

The Supreme Court also noted that,

> courts ... have allowed the broadcast of their proceedings on the basis that those cases were not high profile,[133] ... or did not involve witnesses,[134] ... Indeed, one District Court did not allow the broadcasting of its proceedings because the case 'involv[ed] very sensitive issues.'[135] ... This case, too, involves issues subject to intense debate in our society. The District Court intends not only to broadcast the attorneys' arguments but also witness testimony ... *Sony BMG*, 564 F. 3d, at 11 ... (distinguish[ed] broadcast of attorneys' arguments from other parts of the trial). This case is therefore not a good one for a pilot program. Even the studies that have been conducted thus far have

not analyzed the effect of broadcasting in *high-profile*, divisive cases.[136] (Emphasis added).

Hollingsworth: No Empirical Data

The dissent opinion could,

> find no basis [that] the applicants would suffer irreparable harm.[137] Certainly there is no evidence that such harm could arise in this nonjury civil case from the simple fact of transmission itself … Neither the applicants nor anyone else 'has been able to present empirical data sufficient to establish that the mere presence of the broadcast media inherently has an adverse effect on [the judicial] process,' *Chandler* v. *Florida*, 449 U. S. 560, 578–579 (1981). Cf. M. Cohn & D. Dow,[138] Cameras in the Courtroom: Television and the Pursuit of Justice 62–64 (1998) (canvassing studies, none of which found harm, and one of which found that witnesses 'who faced an obvious camera, provided answers that were more correct, lengthier and more detailed'). And, in any event, any harm to the parties, including the applicants, is reparable through appeal. Cf. *Chandler, supra*, at 581.[139]

The dissent minority do not cite or refer these studies however. In any event, Cohen and Dow[140] only found four (4) social science studies (see below). This could hardly be definitive or acceptable as a sufficient body of research. However, that the minority sought to refer to social science research at all, is some acceptance and endorsement that social science research is worthwhile and required. The challenge remains.

Cohen and Dow,[141] in *Cameras in the Courtroom: Television and the Pursuit of Justice*, in 2002, refer to four (4) social science studies. These are,[142]

- Ernest H. Short, and Associates, Evaluation of California's Experiment with Extended Media Coverage of Courts, submitted to Administrative Office for the Courts; the Chief Justice's Special Committee on the Courts and the Media, and the California Judicial Council (1981);
- M.T. Johnson and C. Krafka, Pilot Program Involving Electronic Coverage in Six US District Courts and Two Appeal Courts (Federal Judicial Centre, 1994);
- J. Hoyt, Courtroom Coverage: The Effects of Being Televised, Journal of Broadcasting 21 (1977): 489-495;
- E. Borgida, K. Debono and L. Buckman, Cameras in the Courtroom: The Effects of Media Coverage on Witness Testimony and Juror Perceptions, Law and Human Behavior 14 (1990): 489-508.

In context, therefore, they found only four studies between 1953 and 2002.

The literature and searches of the author identifies the following methodical and empirical research,

1. James Hoyt. Courtroom Coverage: The Effects of Being Televised, Journal of Broadcasting 21 (1977): 487 – 495 [Wisconsin];
2. Ernest H. Short, and Associates, Evaluation of California's Experiment with Extended Media Coverage of Courts, submitted to Administrative Office for the Courts; the Chief Justice's Special Committee on the Courts and the Media, and the California Judicial Council (1981) [California];
3. Donald Lewis Shores, Jr, The Effects of Courtroom Cameras on Verbal Behaviour: An Analysis of Simulated Trial Witness Testimony in Courtrooms Using Television Cameras (Ph.D diss. University of Florida, 1981);
4. Steve Robert Pasternack, The Effects of Perceived Community Pressure on Simulated Juror Guilt Attributions: A Study (Ph.D diss., University of Tennessee, Knoxville, 1982);
5. Saul M. Kassin. TV Cameras, Public Self-Consciousness, and Mock Juror Performance, Journal of Experimental Psychology (1983/4): 336–349;
6. Anna R. Paddon, Television Coverage of Criminal Trials with Cameras and Microphones: A Laboratory Experiment of Audience Effects (Ph.D diss., University of Tennessee, Knoxville, 1985);
7. E. Borgida, K. Debono and L. Buckman, Cameras in the Courtroom: The Effects of Media Coverage on Witness Testimony and Juror Perceptions, Law and Human Behaviour 14 (1990): 489-508 [Minnesota];
8. Alan Punches, The Cognitive Effects of Camera Presence on the Recall of Testimony in a Simulated Courtroom Setting (Ph.D diss., Colarado State University, Fort Collins, 1991);
9. M.T. Johnson and C. Krafka, Pilot Program Involving Electronic Coverage in Six US District Courts and Two Appeal Courts (Federal Judicial Centre, 1994) [in part only];
10. New York State Committee to Review Audio-Visual Coverage of Court Proceedings, An Open Courtroom: Cameras in New York Courts (New York: Fordham University Press, 1997) [in part only];
11. Kermit Lyol Netterburg, Cameras in the Courtroom: Is a Picture Worth a Thousand Words? (Ph.D diss., University of Minnesota, 1980);
12. Allen Bukoff, The Effects of Video Camera Techniques on the Pre-Deliberation Judgements and Perceptions of Role-Playing Jurors (Ph.D diss., Kent State University, 1984);

13. SL Alexander, "Mischievous Potentialities": A Case Study of Courtroom Camera Guidelines, Eight Judicial Circuit, Florida (Ph.D diss., University of Florida, 1989);
14. Steve Anthony Esposita, OJ TV: A Narrative Analysis of Television's Pretrial Coverage of the OJ Simpson Case (Ph.D diss., Wayne State University, 1996);
15. William Petkanas, Cameras on Trial: An Assessment of the Educational Affect of News Cameras in Trial Courts (Ph.D diss., New York University, 1990);
16. Paul E. Thaler, The Impact of the Television Camera on Courtroom Participants: A Case Study of the Joel Steinberg Murder Trial (Ph.D diss., New York University, 1990)
17. Theresa D. Keller, Cameras in Courtrooms: An Analysis of Television Court Coverage in Virginia (Ph.D diss., University of Tennessee, 1992);
18. Roberta Enter, The Image of the Judiciary: A Semiotic Analyse of Broadcast Trials to Ascertain its Definition of the Court System (Ph.D diss., New York University, 1993);
19. Steven Arthur Kohm, I'm Not a Judge But I Play One On TV: American Reality Based Courtroom Television (Ph.D diss., Simon Fraser University, 2004);
20. Ruthie Elizabeth Reeves Stewart, The Changing Relationship Between Camera and the Courts (MA diss., Florida Atlantic University, 1998);
21. Jessica Ossinger, Electronic Access to Courtrooms: Television as an Educational Socializing Agent on the Judiciary (MA diss., The University of Maine, 2006);
22. UMR Research Limited, Media Coverage of Court Proceedings: Summary Report (1998);
23. Kimberly Allan, Professor Judy McGregor and Susan Fountaine, The Impact of Television, Radio and Still Photography Coverage of Court Proceedings, Final Report, A Report for the Department for Courts, (Massey University, April 1998)(New Zealand);
24. Alves, Hon. Nathan Braverman, Chaor, Baron, Hon. Jean Szekeres, Groton, Hon. Thomas C. III, Leasure, Hon. Diane O., Plitt, Hon. Emory A., Jr., Report of the Committee to Study Extended Media Coverage of Criminal Trial Proceedings in Maryland, Committee to Study Extended Media Coverage, a Subcommittee of the Legislation Committee of the Maryland Judicial Conference (2008).

Of course, while welcome, this is hardly a sufficient body of research to be determinative of effects issues and queries in television courtroom broadcasting.

The *Hollingsworth* dissent further states that the,

> applicants also claim that the transmission will irreparably harm the witnesses themselves, presumably by increasing the public's awareness of who those witnesses are. And they claim that some members of the public might harass those witnesses. But the witnesses, although capable of doing so, have not asked this Court to set aside the District Court's order … And that is not surprising. All of the witnesses supporting the applicants are already publicly identified with their cause. They are all experts or advocates who have either already appeared on television or Internet broadcasts, already toured the State advocating a 'yes' vote on Proposition 8, or already engaged in extensive public commentary far more likely to make them well known than a closed-circuit broadcast to another federal courthouse. The likelihood of any 'irreparable' harm is further diminished by the fact that the court order before us would simply increase the trial's viewing audience from the occupants of one courtroom in one courthouse to the occupants of five other courtrooms in five other court-houses (in all of which taking pictures or retransmissions have been forbidden). By way of comparison literally hundreds of national and international newspapers are already covering this trial and reporting in detail the names and testimony of all of the witnesses. … I see no reason why the incremental increase in exposure caused by transmitting these proceedings to five additional courtrooms would create any further risk of harm, as the Court apparently believes ... Moreover, if in respect to any particular witness this transmission threatens harm, the District Court can prevent that harm. Chief Judge Walker has already said that he would keep the broadcast 'completely under the Court's control, to permit the Court to stop it if [it] proves to be a problem, if it proves to be a distraction, [or] if it proves to create problems with witnesses.' ... The Circuit Council confirmed in a press release that the District Court 'will fully control the process' and that 'Judge Walker has reserved the right to terminate any part of the audio or video, or both, for any duration" or to terminate participation in the pilot program 'at any time.' [143] ... Surely such firm control, exercised by an able district court judge with 20 years of trial-management experience, will be sufficient to address any possible harm, either to the witnesses or to the integrity of the trial. [144]

Hollingsworth: Education

The dissent referred to,

> the public's interest in observing trial proceedings to learn about this case and about how courts work [145] ... [and the] statement of Chief Judge Walker ... '[I]f the public could see how the judicial process works, they would take a somewhat different view of it.' 'I think the only time that you're going to draw sufficient interest in the legal process is when you have an issue such as the issues here, that people think about, talk about, debate about and consider.' [146]

It is unclear if the Supreme Court was attempting to refer to education issues and educational effects.

Hollingsworth: Dissent - No Harm Identified

The dissent felt that the "majority ... identifies no real harm, let alone 'irreparable harm,' to justify ... this stay ... And the public interest weighs in favour of providing access to the courts."[147] There is only "potential harm to witnesses — harm that is either nonexistent or that can be cured through protective measures by the District Court as the circumstances warrant." [148]

SOME OTHER CASES

While this work is not about the general arguments or the caselaw per se, given that the focus relates to effects research issues, there are some cases other than the three Supreme Court camera cases we can refer to.

In *Sheppard* the Supreme Court reversed the denial of a *habeus corpus* petition by Sam Sheppard, whose murder trial was conducted in what the Court described as a "carnival atmosphere" of saturation media coverage.[149] "Since the state trial judge did not fulfill his duty to protect Sheppard from the inherently prejudicial publicity which saturated the community and to control disruptive influences in the courtroom," the Court concluded, "we must reverse the denial of the habeas petition."[150] The Court's decision focused on the media excesses during Sheppard's trial, and the trial judge's failure to control the media. In light of such evident fair trial violations, the majority did not discuss the availability or need for empirical research into the effects of media coverage on trials.

The New Hampshire Supreme Court in *Petition of WMUR Channel 9* suggests that the "psychological effects on participants in the trial of having cameras in the courtroom is not greater than where reporters wait on the courthouse steps with cameras."[151] The Court is also reported as saying that the studies found that a courtroom camera "improves public perceptions of the judiciary and its processes, improves the trial process for all participants and educates the public about the judicial branch of government."[152] However, upon examination, the said court opinion does not properly identify or cite the actual studies and findings it refers to.[153] There are no definitions, forms or research referred to.

In *State v Langley*[154] the defendant was unsuccessful in appealing his trial verdict, arguing in part that he was prejudiced and had objected to the taking of photographs during the trial. The appeal court felt that the issue was "whether the record discloses that the taking of the photographs during the trial of this case influenced the jury."[155] This was despite various rules having been broken in the process of allowing such photography.[156] However, the issue of televising over a person's objections to televising appears not to have been researched thus far. It also ignores whether it is tenable for an active party to research and record affects in the own case.

There is also a German case (albeit in 1964) which barred cameras on the basis of awareness of the significant wider television audience and the psychological effects. It held that "the awareness that filming will be used to produce a programme which will be seen by an audience of thousands of people creates in the parties and witnesses a sort of psychological state that will induce them to restrain their statements or to make a declaration more suited for a theatre performance than a trial. This distorting effect could impair the main purpose of the trial: to obtain evidence and ascertain the truth."[157]

This is not meant to be a definitive review however.

NEW YORK STUDY

The New York study of television broadcasting issues, claimed, in part, that while the distraction effects issues "have been laid to rest," and what "remains very much alive are the concerns about the psychological impact of the camera: how will the realization that their every word or gesture is being transmitted to a vast, unseen audience the behaviour of trial participants."[158] This is incorrect, as is demonstrated for example, by the continued existence of the Supreme Court challenge, and indeed the author's research and demonstrations in relation to eye tracking and camera distraction effects. The New York study is generally presumptive and opinion based. The New York study did not address the Supreme Court challenge. The only aspect of the study which was potentially empirical was an outsourced public survey.[159] It, therefore, ignores the lack of sufficient research evidence thus far.

THE SUPREME COURT ISSUES AND EYE TRACKING

We see from the three cases above that the Supreme Court referred to a large number issues and concerns relating to television courtroom broadcasting, and which should be the focus of empirical research.

In terms of applying eye tracking technology, for example, to the Supreme Court challenge, one of the options is to research the effect issues identified by the Supreme Court.

The effects issues identified by the Supreme Court are summarised and also set out in full in Appendix 2. The full set of effects concerns are seldom mentioned in the literate, which is why it is useful to list these in full in the Appendices. The headline effects categories are,

- Lawyers
- Juries (In–Court)
- Prospective Juries (Out–of–Court)

- Judges
- Defendants
- Parties
- Witnesses
- Court Personnel
- Courtroom Participants' (Actors') Effects Generally
- Other In-Court Issues
- Audience
- Public
- Other Effects Issues.

CONCLUSION

It is clear that the effect issues are not researched or answered in the small number of empirical studies to date. The challenge set by the Supreme Court still remains. They are not properly addressed in the small number of empirical studies nor in the general non empirical studies thus far. For one, there is no baseline research to measure any changes. Very few studies have sought to examine in–court effects with observers and sophisticated code measurements. Eye tracking technology offers the best avenue for examining some of the effect concerns raised by the Supreme Court, in particular distraction and divided attention. There is also potential to examine some of the other effects raised by the Supreme Court challenge.

The author highlights the importance of television camera location and actor/participant location in carrying out effects research. It is noted also that there is one reference to location by the Supreme Court. However, this is not a recognition by the Supreme Court of the major significance of the location issue to researching the effects of television cameras in court. It is pointed out elsewhere herein that effects will depend upon where the television cameras are located and where the courtroom participants are located.[160] This is not part of the Supreme Court challenge but is equally important in terms of designing adequate and robust TCB effects research.

It is important to point out that in addressing the TCB research challenges and in developing TCB effects research studies, we often need a level of sophistication which can only be obtained through cross disciplinary research. The research questions and the research tasks demand this. Interdisciplinary research is not unique. In one example, three distinguished law professors undertook detailed empirical interdisciplinary research to address an issue posed as a result of a Supreme Court case. The results were published in the Harvard Law Review.[161] The law professors were from Yale, Temple and George Washington universities respectively.

Various legal and interdisciplinary research is recommended by the author. One of these areas relates to distraction effect research in relation to the courtroom participants in court, caused by the television cameras in court. This is the distraction effect challange. The author proposes for the first time that eye tracking technology be used for effects research of the distraction effects on courtroom participants caused by television cameras in the courtroom. This is most novel, but such interdisciplinary research is not without comparison. Eye tracking has been used to research the effects of videotaped confessions.[162] Eye tracking is also proposed in relation to mandated health advertisements/warnings on tobacco products and related litigation.[163] This interdisciplinary research and the above legal interdisciplinary research published in the Harvard Law Review all support the author's approach and suggestions.

NOTES

1. See, for example, UK Department for Constitutional Affairs in Great Britain consultation, Broadcasting Courts (2004), consultation paper available at www.dca.gov.uk/consult/courts/broadcasting-cp28-04.pdf , accessed 13 August, 2012.
2. See, for example, J. Ryley, Justice Must Be Televised, Allowing TV Cameras in Court Would Greatly Help to Restore Public Faith in Criminal Proceedings, Guardian online,www.guardian.co.uk/commentisfree/2010/dec/05/justice-television-cameras-court-mps-expenses, accessed 13 August, 2012.
3. Courts Selected for Federal Cameras in Court Pilot Study, June 8, 2011, http://www.uscourts.gov/News/NewsView/11-06-08/Courts_Selected_for_Federal_Cameras_in_Court_Pilot_Study.aspx , accessed June 26, 2010.
4. All available at www.govtrack.us/congress/bill.xpd?bill=s111-657&tab=related , (last accessed on August 19, 2012).
5. *Estes v Texas*, 381 US, (1964), 532–616.
6. *Chandler v Florida*, 449 US, (1981), 560–589.
7. *Hollingsworth v Perry*, 558 US _ 2010, available at www.supremecourt.gov/opinions/09pdf/09A648.pdf , accessed 13 August, 2012. See "US Judge Overturns Gay Marriage Ban," Irish Times online, www.irishtimes.com , accessed 13 August, 2012, regarding ultimate trial decision.
8. *Hollingsworth v Perry*, ibid.
9. *Estes v Texas*, above.
10. *Chandler v Florida*, above.
11. Referred to by Barber as being the case of Billy Eugene Manley in Oklahoma City which occurred in 1953, see S. Barber, News Cameras in the Courtroom: A Free Press – Fair Debate (Ablex: New York, 1987), 10-11. It appears cinema or movie courtroom broadcasting occurred before TCB. There does not appear to be any effects research however.
12. *Hollingsworth v Perry*, above.
13. *Estes v Texas*, above, 532–616.
14. *Chandler v Florida*, above.
15. *Ibid.*
16. See R.K. Sherwin, When Law Goes Pop: The Vanishing Line Between Law and Popular Culture (Chicago: The University of Chicago Press, 2000).
17. *Estes v Texas*, above, 532-616.
18. *Chandler v Florida*, above. Headnote (a).
19. See Appendices.
20. *Estes v Texas*, above, 532–616.

21. Ibid, 535.
22. The research and literature does not appear to refer to or acknowledge this point.
23. *Estes v Texas*, above, 541. Clarke, J.
24. *Tumey v Ohio*, 273, US 510 (1927) [year omitted in original]; *In re Murchison*, 349, US 133 (1955); *Rideau v Louisiana*, 373, US 723 (1963); *Turner v Louisiana*, 379, US 466 (1965). Chief Justice Warren referring to *Tumey* states that "the Court found the procedure so inconsistent with the conception of what a trial should be and so likely to produce prejudice that it declared the practice unconstitutional even though no specific prejudice was shown." Referred to in *Estes v Texas*, ibid, 562.
25. *Estes v Texas*, ibid, 550. Clarke, J. Obviously certain equipment matters have changed over time. However, this is the context of the challenge, the challenge still remains nonetheless, and was in fact reiterated in the most recent case of *Hollingsworth v Perry*, above, in 2010.
26. Referred to at *Estes v* Texas, ibid, 541. Clarke, J.
27. Ibid, 542. Clarke, J.
28. Referred to ibid, 599. At 645 in ABA Journal 42 (1956). Also ABA Rep. 83 (1958) 790-791. Harlan J.
29. Ibid, 599, referring to ABA Rep. 83 (1958) 284. Harlan J.
30. Ibid, p. 592. Harlan J.
31. Ibid, p. 552. Warren, CJ.
32. Ibid, p. 565. Warren, CJ.
33. Ibid, 569, referring to [first name not given], Keating, Not 'Bonanza,' Not 'Peyton Place,' But the U.S. Senate, New York Times Magazine, April 25, 1965, 67, 72. Keating commented in relation to a stockholders meeting that "[s]ome stockholders seemed very much aware that they were on camera." Ibid, n. 24, 569. Warren, CJ.
34. Ibid, 569-570. Chief Justice Warren. Footnote omitted. In footnote 24, at 569, he refers to R.P. Tinkham, Should Canon 35 be Amended? A Question of Proper Judicial Administration, ABA Journal 42 (1956): 843–845, and p. 884, at 845, who refers to examples of how people react when they know they are on television. He also refers to [no first name given] Gould, New York Times, March 11, 1956, S2, p. X 11, col. 2, who states that even experienced performers can be affected, and that this "psychological and emotional burden must not be placed on a layman whose testimony may have a bearing on whether, in a murder trial, another human being is to live or die." Referred, to ibid, 569. Warren, CJ.
35. *Estes v Texas*, *ibid*, 603–604. Stewart, J. Minority opinion.
36. Ibid, 611–612. Stewart, J. Minority opinion.
37. Ibid, 616. White, J. Minority opinion.
38. Ibid, 616. White, J. Minority opinion.
39. Ibid, 616. White, J. Minority opinion.
40. Ibid, 587. Harlan J.
41. Ibid, 587. Harlan J.
42. Ibid, 588. Harlan J.
43. Ibid, 589. Harlan J.
44. Ibid, 604. Stewart, J. Minority opinion.
45. Ibid, 615. Stewart, J. Minority opinion.
46. Clarke, J., in *Estes*, ibid, 536.
47. Ibid, 536. Clarke, J.
48. Ibid, 536. Clarke, J.
49. Ibid, 548. Clarke, J.
50. Ibid, 536–537. Clarke, J.
51. Ibid, 578. Warren, CJ. Note also the analysis of Sherwin of the differing judicial intentions behind the *Estes* and *Chandler* cases. See R.K. Sherwin, When Law Goes Pop: The Vanishing Line Between Law and Popular Culture (Chicago: The University of Chicago Press, 2000), 140 et seq, and 247–248; and R.K. Sherwin, The Jurisprudence of Appearances, New York Law School Law Review 43 (1999–2000): 821–842.
52. *Estes v Texas*, ibid, 545. Clarke, J.
53. Ibid, 545. Clarke, J.
54. Ibid, 546. Clarke, J.

55. Ibid, 546. Footnote omitted. Clarke, J.
56. Ibid, 546-547. Clarke, J.
57. Referred to ibid, 551. Clarke, J.
58. Ibid, 536. Clarke, J.
59. Ibid, 592. Harlan J.
60. Ibid, 592. Harlan J.
61. Ibid, 593. Harlan J.
62. Ibid, 609-610. Stewart, J. Minority opinion.
63. Ibid, 612-613. Stewart, J. Minority opinion.
64. Ibid, 547. Clarke, J.
65. Ibid, 547. Clarke, J.
66. Ibid, 548. Clarke, J.
67. Ibid, 548. Clarke, J.
68. Ibid, 548. Clarke, J.
69. Ibid, 548–549. Clarke, J.
70. Ibid, referring to *Tumey v Ohio*, 273, US 510 (1927) [year omitted in original]; *In re Murchison*, 349, US 133 (1955); *Rideau v Louisiana*, 373, US 723 (1963); *Turner v Louisiana*, 379, US 466 (1965). Chief Justice Warren referring to *Tumey* states that "the Court found the procedure so inconsistent with the conception of what a trial should be and so likely to produce prejudice that it declared the practice unconstitutional even though no specific prejudice was shown." Referred to ibid, 562.
71. Ibid, 550. Clarke, J.
72. Ibid, 565. Warren, CJ.
73. Ibid, 614. Stewart, J. Minority opinion.
74. Ibid, 549. Clarke, J.
75. Ibid, 551. Clarke, J.
76. Ibid, 551. Clarke, J.
77. Ibid, 552–553. Warren, CJ.
78. Ibid, 555. Warren, CJ.
79. Ibid, 566–567. Warren, CJ.
80. Ibid, 567-569. Warren, CJ.
81. Ibid, 571. Warren, CJ.
82. S. Barber, News Cameras in the Courtroom: A Free Press – Fair Trial Debate (Norwood, New Jersey: Ablex, 1987).
83. *Estes v Texas*, above, 547. Warren, CJ.
84. Ibid, 574. Warren, CJ.
85. Ibid, 575. Warren, CJ.
86. Ibid, 589. Harlan J.
87. Ibid, 590. Harlan J.
88. Ibid, 576–577. Footnote omitted. Warren, CJ.
89. Ibid, 579–580. Warren, CJ.
90. Ibid, 580. Warren, CJ.
91. Ibid, 594-595. Harlan J.
92. Ibid, 590. Harlan J.
93. Ibid, 590. Harlan J.
94. Ibid, 591. Footnote omitted. Harlan J.
95. Ibid, 532–616.
96. Ibid, 587. Harlan J.
97. Ibid, 593. Harlan J.
98. Ibid, 578. Warren, CJ.
99. Ibid, 613. Stewart, J. Minority opinion.
100. Ibid, 547. Clarke, J.
101. Ibid, 544. Clarke, J.
102. Ibid, 545. Clarke, J.
103. Ibid, 595-596. Harlan J.
104. *Chandler v Florida*, above, 560–589.

105. Ibid, 561.
106. Ibid, 568.
107. Ibid, 560-589.
108. Ibid, 560-89.
109. Ibid, 566. Chief Justice Warren.
110. *Estes v Texas*, above, 532–616.
111. See *Chandler v Florida*, above, 576.
112. Ibid, at n.11, at 576, referring to *In re Petition of Post-Week Stations, Florida, Inc.*, 370 So. 2d, 764, 781 (1979).
113. Ibid, 578.
114. Ibid, 578.
115. Ibid, 559–560.
116. See ibid, n. 12, at 560.
117. Ibid, 560.
118. Ibid, 581.
119. *Hollingsworth v Perry*, above, 1.
120. Ibid, 2.
121. Ibid.
122. Ibid.
123. Ibid, 4.
124. Ibid, 9.
125. Ibid.
126. Ibid, 7. Neither does this research, given the time and resources available, the wider issues of courtroom broadcasting and is rather limited to television courtroom broadcasting, in particular the research and effect issues.
127. Ibid, 11.
128. Ibid, 12–13, referring to *Estes* v *Texas*, above, at 591 (Harlan, J., concurring).
129. Ibid, 12–13.
130. Ibid, 13.
131. Ibid, 14.
132. Ibid, 15.
133. Ibid, 15, referring to *E*Trade Financial Corp.* v *Deutsche Bank AG*, 582 F. Supp. 2d 528, 535 (SDNY 2008).
134. Ibid, 15, referring to *Marisol A.* v *Giuliani*, 929 F. Supp. 660, 661 (SDNY 1996); *Katzman* v *Victoria's Secret Catalogue*, 923 F. Supp. 580, 586–587 (SDNY 1996).
135. Ibid, 15, referring to *Schoeps* v *Museum of Modern Art*, 599 F. Supp. 2d 532, 534 (SDNY 2009).
136. Ibid, 16.
137. So apparently, the first eight lives do not count as irreparable?
138. Referring to M. Cohn and D. Dow, Cameras in the Courtroom: Television and the Pursuit of Justice (New York: Rowman & Little, 1998, and 2002).
139. *Hollingsworth v Texas*, above, dissent, 6–7.
140. Referring to M. Cohn and D. Dow, above.
141. M. Cohn and D. Dow, above.
142. *Ibid*, 62 et seq.
143. *Hollingsworth v Texas*, above, 7 – 8, referring to News Release, Federal Courthouses to Offer Remote Viewing of Pro-position 8 Trial (January 8, 2010), www.ca9.uscourts.gov/datastore/general/2010/01/08/Prop8_Remote_Viewing_Locations.pdf (accessed on 13 August, 2012, and referred to as available in Clerk of Court's case file).
144. *Hollingsworth v Texas*, ibid, 7–8.
145. Ibid, 7–8, referring to *Nebraska Press Assn.* v *Stuart*, 427 U. S. 539, 587 (1976) (Brennan, J., concurring in judgment); see also Exh. 2, at 42, Application To Petition.
146. Ibid, 7–8. Referring to Walker, CJ, in *Nebraska Press Association* v *Stuart*, 427 U. S. 539.
147. Ibid, 7–8.
148. Ibid, 7–8.

149. Sheppard v Maxwell , 384 U.S. 333 , 355 (1966).
150. Ibid, at 363.
151. New Hampshire Supreme Court, Petition of WMUR Channel 9, (December 13, 2002), www.courts.state.nh.us/opinions/2002/0212/wmur156.htm as referred to in Stepniak, D., above, 101. Accessed by author on June 8, 2010.
152. Referred to ibid, 101.
153. Referred to ibid, 101. Page 8 of court opinion. The opinion refers to the *Chandler* case, above, at n. 5, 565.
154. *State v Langley*, 214 Ore. 445, 323 P.2d 301 (1958), as referred to in The Special Committee on Radio and Television of the Association of the Bar of the City of New York, Radio, Television, and the Administration of Justice: A documented Survey of Materials, New York and London: Columbia University Press, 1965), pp. 99-100. This appeal was decided by the Supreme Court of Oregan. Also referred to ibid, 179.
155. *Hollingsworth v Texas*, above, at 320-321, 323 of judgement, and as referred to ibid, 98. Note also E. Greene, Media Effects on Jurors, Law and Human Behavior 14 (2005): 439–450.
156. Ibid, 99–100, 179.
157. German Fed. Ct., 19 BGHSt 45; see also 10 BGHSt 202 and BGHSt 111, as referred to in A. Biondi, TV Cameras Access into the Courtroom: A Comparative Note, Yearbook of Media and Entertainment Law (YMEL), (1996): 140–141.
158. The Special Committee on Radio and Television of the Association of the Bar of the City of New York, Radio, Television, and the Administration of Justice: A documented Survey of Materials (New York and London: Columbia University Press, 1965), 53, as referred to in D. Stepniak, above, 366.
159. Television Cameras in the Courts, A Survey of New York State, December, 1996, Marist Institute for Public Opinion Poll, as contained in New York State Committee to Review Audio-Visual Coverage of Court Proceedings, An Open Courtroom, Cameras in New York Courts (New York: Fordham, 1997), 113–123.
160. The author also refers to location issues at P. Lambert, Effects Research Issues in Television Courtroom Broadcasting: Getting Past Monkey, 10th European Conference on eGovernment, University of Limerick, 17–18 June, 2010; P. Lambert, Time to Leave the Monkey Behind?: How Eye Tracking and Psychology Can Contribute to Television Courtroom Broadcasting Effects Research, British Psychological Society, BPS Cognitive Psychology Section Annual Conference, 27th Annual Cognitive Psychology Section Conference, Cardiff University, September 6–8, 2010; P. Lambert, Eye Tracking Technology and Television Courtroom Broadcasting, Computers and Law, August 11, 2010, www.scl.org/site.aspx?i=ed16965 , accessed 13 August, 2011; P. Lambert, TCB Effects: Eye Tracking and Camera Distraction in Court, Irish Association of Law Teachers Annual Conference, Strand Hotel, Limerick, November 26-28, 2010; P. Lambert, Monkey Magic: Problems With Effects Research of Television Courtroom Broadcasting, Irish Law Times 18 (2010): 278–280; P. Lambert, A Candid Camera, Eye Tracking Technology Could Transform Courtroom Broadcasting, New Law Journal, 10 December, 2010, 1699–1700.
161. D.M. Kahan, D.A Hoffman and D. Braman, Whose Eyes Are You Going to Believe? *Scott v Harris* and the Perils of Cognitive Illiberalism, Harvard Law Review 122 (2008–2009): 837–906. The research was funded by the National Science Foundation, and funds at Yale and Temple Universities.
162. See, for example, G. Lassiter, A. Geers, P. Munhall., I. Handley and M. Beers, Videotaped Confessions: Is Guilt in the Eye of the Camera?, in M. Zanna, ed., Advances, in Experimental Social Psychology, 20 (San Diego, CA: Academic Press, 2001): 189–253.
163. P. Smith, Evaluating the Corrective Statements Proposed in the Court Case *US Department of Justice vs Philip Morris U.S.A. Inc., et al*, M.S., State University of New York at Buffalo, 2009.

Chapter Three

Camera Developments in US

INTRODUCTION

Television courtroom broadcasting remains controversial — even in the US. It is also very much a contemporary issue of debate. Unfortunately, in the US, the Supreme Court effects research challenge is ignored. Significant ongoing research is yet required.

Having said that, it is useful to look at what else is happening at the moment in the US. It will assist in emphasising the importance of addressing the Supreme Court research challenge with future research.

There have been many attempts to expand TCB to federal courts. An initial pilot programme in the federal courts was discontinued in 1994, partly because only brief snippets were used on television. However, recently a second federal pilot programme has been announced. Certain legislators attempts to expand TCB to the Supreme Court also continue.

In addition, the Supreme Court has recently been called upon to deal with a courtroom broadcasting case. The court in *Hollingsworth*[1] effectively prevented the form of TCB being proposed. It also referred again to the issue of the lack of sufficient empirical research. The Supreme Court challenge remains.

What do we know about the effects of such broadcasting? Still relatively little. The Supreme Court challenge for a sustained body of empirical effects research has not been properly addressed. This challenge occurred in the seminal cases of *Estes*, *Chandler* and more recently in *Hollingsworth* (2010).

THE LEGISLATIVE EFFORTS

Federal Rule of Criminal Procedure 53, adopted in 1946, prohibits photography in courtrooms. There have been various attempts to enact legislation which would mandate TCB in federal courts.[2] A number of politicians are strong advocates of legislating for federal television courtroom broadcasting.[3] Obviously others oppose it, which explains in part the failure of the US legislative proposals to date.[4] The judicial Conference also opposes the federal legislative proposals.[5] A representative of the Judicial Conference, Chief Judge Edward R. Becker, US Courts of Appeals, Third Circuit, conveyed the judiciarys' opposition to TCB and Bill S.721.[6] He referred to the report after the first federal pilot experiment, where 64 percent of participating judges reported that, to some extent, the cameras made witness more nervous than they would otherwise be, make witnesses less willing to appear in courts and further that 41 percent (of judges) found that to some extent witnesses were distracted.[7] A content analysis of 90 stories covered by TCB during the experiment, showing that there was an average of 56 seconds of courtroom footage per story and that most footage was voiced over.[8]

Judge Tunhein also spoke for the Judicial Conference in opposition to the proposed federal legislation.[9] The judiciary feel that the "perceived benefit for allowing cameras is outweighed by the potential for harm to an individual involved in the litigation process."[10] The effects and concerns "are far from hypothetical."[11] He also indicated that the proposed legislation does not address the complexities of TCB.[12] This includes ignoring funding issues.[13]

The National Association of Criminal Defense Lawyers states that any TCB should be subject to the consent of the parties.[14] This was in a presentation in relation to proposed federal TCB legislation.

THE LEGISLATIVE EFFORTS

One of the legislative proposals is the bill S. 829 To Allow Media Coverage of Court Proceedings.[15] The bill makes no reference to research or the mandating of research if enacted, nor to the media form of such TCB broadcasting.

When Judge Becker pointed out at one of the Senate hearings that the first federal pilot research found that the average footage use by the media was 56 seconds, one of the panellists (another judge) asked if the federal experiment was civil or criminal cases. It was civil cases only. The questioner felt that this explained why only 56 seconds were used by the media.[16] He stated that there "are very few civil cases that draw much attention."[17]

Another Senate hearing witness, Professor of Law, Lynn D. Wardle, is introduced as having "done extensive research on media coverage of court proceedings."[18] Wardle states that the "experience" of 48 courts with TCB, 35 allowing criminal TCB, cannot be ignored.[19] However, Wardle does not address the issue of research nor empirical research. Wardle does not refer to validation of the suggested positive or negative effects.

The author Ronald Goldfarb also testifies at the Senate hearing. He refers to "all" of the research studies, in particular the official studies.[20] He states that in all states "all of the perceived problems of the impact or potential impact of television"[21] did not occur. This is not correct as the research leaves many gaps. In any event, Goldfarb then states that the research only refers to witness, jury and lawyer courtroom participants.[22]

Goldfarb then states that "in every one of those studies, the result ... found that the presence of the television camera, generally unseen, had no impact."[23] This misrepresents and misinterprets even the general studies. Most studies do not document and record the camera location. The Short Report, often cited as one of the main studies, does not record the camera location in most of the case studies it researched. It is, therefore, a misrepresentation to state that the cameras were "generally unseen." In terms of the studies he refers to, these are not cited. The empirical studies referred to in his book, which he cites as his main source (titled TV Or Nor TV), he only identifies eight (8) social science studies regarding courtroom broadcasting. That is eight (8) studies in 45 years. He is also implicitly accepting uncriticised, all of the general studies and equates a general sophistication and generalisability to the general studies which they do not uniformly deserve. The suggestion that all of the studies, or specific studies if cited, "found" that there was "no [adverse] impact" at all is also incorrect. It ignores that some adverse effects were found, and also that even the self report, opinion report and questionnaires do refer to some adverse effects. It also makes an assumed, but incorrect, generalisation that there are therefore no adverse effects whatsoever.

Goldfarb also states that he looked at "every study that had ever been made" empirically.[24] He then states that "[e]very one of those studies, as well, indicated that what might have seemed to be rationale conclusions really has no basis."[25] This accepts, or at least implies, positive findings of there being no adverse effects. This is not correct and misrepresents the nature of the research, and also misrepresents and ignores that some adverse effects have been found.

Goldfarb continues that the consensus is that cameras are forgotten within "30 or 40 seconds."[26] No research study is cited, nevermind a consensus across a broad basis of studies with similar methodologies.

Media arguments in cases and policy debates arguing for access have also misrepresented and generalised the research. Courtroom View Network, for example, argues that all of the studies are "consistent and unambiguous: electronic coverage of trial court proceedings – not merely oral argument, but trials, including jury trials – simply does not impede the fair administration of justice, compromise the dignity of the court, or impair the orderly conduct of proceedings."[27] The author sought to obtain copies of the studies from the source cited. Unfortunately, the studies cited (footnote 8, page 10) were unavailable from the source, and in some instances also were unavailable from court offices in the jurisdictions referred to.[28] The general studies have not sought to empirically research, in some instances, any effects issues. They also rely on self reports, opinion reports and questionnaires. As the author points out, if one is testing a hypothesis, that that hypothesises effect is not shown in an instant study does not allow one to generalise from the test, that there is conclusively and generally no such effect at all. The general research, and the Courtroom View Network Memorandum, all fail to attempt identify research in relation to each potential effect, and list the studies pertinent to that effect, and compare the results and methodologies of those particular studies. There is no such rigour. It is interesting also, that the Courtroom View Network Memorandum highlights effect issues such as administration of court and dignity of the court, and omits or backgrounds reference to courtroom actor effects, including defendant effects.[29] The same Memorandum also misinterprets the California Short Report finding by saying that Short answered the "effect" questions negatively.[30] In fact the most that can be said when an effect hypothesis is not found to a significant degree, is that the effect was not found or that there was a nil effect result. This on its own does not allow generalisation or conclusions that there is not and cannot be an effect. Indeed, the Short Report did find adverse answers in some of its research. None of the flaws, carveouts or the caution expressly present in the Short report are not referred to. The Memorandum also refers to the first federal pilot experiment as "a success,"[31] but without referring to the actual media usage of the footage and empirical content analysis highlighted in the federal report, and noted separately as one of the factors leading to the TCB discontinuance in federal courts.

There is also academic misrepresentation. One recent paper states that many of *Estes* statements in relation to the impact upon the courtroom participants "have since been debunked by empirical research."[32] No studies or empirical research is cited. The only support for the statement is Marjorie Cohn and David Row's book at pages 62 - 64.[33] Cohen and Dow, only refer to four (4) social science studies between 1953 and 2002, namely,

- Ernest H Short and Associates, Evaluation of California's Experiment with Extended Media Coverage of Courts (1981) [California];
- Federal Judicial Centre, Pilot Program Involving Electronic Coverage in Six US District Courts and Two Appeal Courts (1994);
- J. Hoyt, Courtroom Coverage: The Effects of Being Televised, Journal of Broadcasting 21 (1977): 489 [Wisconsin];

- E. Borgida, K. Debono and L. Buckman, Cameras in the Courtroom: The Effects of Media Coverage on Witness Testimony and Juror Perceptions, Law and Human Behavior 14 (1990): 489, [Minnesota].

This is hardly a significant body of research, and certainly not sufficient to reach firm general conclusions. The first Federal pilot study was only partly empirical, namely the outsourced audience research. This was partly responsible for the discontinuance of the first Federal experiment. The Federal study apparently did not undertake any in-court empirical effects research.

None of these studies research all of the courtroom participants and out-of-court effect issues. Most commentators also ignore all of research gaps (including with the four studies referred to), and also the other empirical research studies.

HOLLINGSWORTH BACKLASH

Given that the Supreme Court effectively prevented the form of courtroom broadcasting proposed in *Hollingsworth*, it is not surprising that there is criticism beginning to emerge.[34] It has been suggested that the *Hollingsworth* decision raises the bar for future TCB, and is a return to the *Estes* position.[35] A senior judge is reported to have responded to and criticised the Supreme Court decision — which prevented the proposed filming. Judge Alex Kozinski, Chief Judge of the Ninth Circuit Court of Appeals, is reported to have said that TCB will increase public respect for the justice system and possibly also improve trials.[36] The points reported by Judge Kozinski are all arguments and none appear to refer to any evidence or empirical research. There is no reference to the Supreme Court challenge. Judge Kozinski and Johnson's article, "Of Cameras and Courtrooms,"[37] in the Fordham Intellectual Property Media & Entertainment Law Journal is reported as being a response to the Supreme Court in *Hollingsworth*.[38]

However, while criticising the Supreme Court and being a "fierce advocate of cameras in the courtroom,"[39] Judge Kosinki implicitly reflects the author's point, that there are different forms of television courtroom broadcasting. He is reported as advocating (1) stationary television cameras; (2) no zooming in and out; and (3) TCB which does not dramatize the courtroom events.[40] While Judge Kosinki may not have intended it, his position demonstrates that there are different TCB forms and more importantly that if a jurisdiction decides to permit TCB, it has a choice to make in relation to which form of TCB it wishes to allow.

It does not appear that any US jurisdictions which have experimented with TCB have empirically recognised the forms and choices available. This is a significant omission.

FEDERAL COURTS: THE FIRST PILOT EXPERIMENT

There is a divergence between many different forms of TCB in the US. There is then further divergence between many state courts which allow some form of TCB or TCB experimentation on the once hand, and the federal courts on the other which generally prohibit TCB.[41] The federal courts undertook a three year experiment with certain TCB in civil cases, which began in 1991 and ended in December 1994.[42] The federal circuits which participated in the pilot experiment all volunteered.[43] It is also overlooked that criminal cases were not included in the experiment.[44] Commenting on the federal experimental report, Judge Tunheim states that the report may even have downplayed some of the negative TCB statistics, including distraction effects, making courtroom participants more nervous.[45]

The experiment in the Federal Courts was discontinued by federal judges, deciding by a margin of 2-1 against continuing or permitting TCB. This was reported to be on the basis that generally only snippets of court proceedings were used by the media and there was not, or not enough, educational TCB.[46]

There was one particular aspect of the initial pilot experiment which can be described as empirical research. The pilot review researchers engaged professional outsourced research of audience issues. (It remains to be seen what will happen with the second federal pilot experiment).

It is noted that the official review was initiated near the end of the experiment, and there was no prior baseline research. In terms of the footage that was filmed and broadcast, at least one commentator refers to it as being boring.[47]

FEDERAL COURTS: A SECOND PILOT EXPERIMENT

Judge Sentelle of the federal courts announced on September 14, 2010 that there was a decision made by the federal judges in the US to initiate a second period of pilot experimentation.[48] This is the Judicial Conference of federal judges, which Judge Sentelle is the current Chair. It appears however, that lots of the details still have to be worked out, and also that the parties may object in a given case.[49]

The second pilot, approved by the Judicial Conference of the United States, will be national and will last three years, with “interim” and final reports.[50] There does not appear, therefore, to be any consideration of baseline issues and effects research. What is interesting in term of TCB form issues, is that the pilot will encompass recording by the court, and not third parties, such as television networks.[51]

The decision of the Judicial Conference is reported as being to "evaluate the effects of cameras in federal courtroom."[52] It is not clear if the Supreme Court challenge will be addressed.

PLANNING FOR THE SECOND FEDERAL PILOT

The recent announcement by Judge Sentelle that the federal courts are planning a second experimental period is fortuitous. If properly planned, it will allow for sustained empirical research to begin addressing the Supreme Court challenge. The vast majority to date are inadequate as they are ill planned, leave unrecorded data and are non empirical.

Those planning the second federal courts experiment should bear in mind a number of empirical issues.

Most previous effects studies fail to record any prior baseline data. Once it is decided to introduce cameras to specific courtrooms, a period of data collection should be undertaken prior to the cameras being allowed in. This allows us to compare for effects before and after cameras are introduced. This has been ignored in the general and empirical studies to date. Will the second Federal experiment incorporate baseline data?

The Supreme Court cases dealing with cameras note that communications technologies can change over time. Ironically, however, the Supreme Court did not recognise that research technologies and methods can also improve. Let us consider just one example already highlighted above.

It is interesting that the Recording Industry Association of America (RIAA) objected to TCB internet broadcasting of one of its cases, fearing that the footage would be manipulated and edited by third parties after broadcast.[53] It would be useful to consider recording objection issues in the federal and other pilots.

Interestingly also, Judge O'Scannlain also speaking against legislated federal courtroom broadcasting, makes a statement which hints at more empirical research. He states that even modern miniture technology and cameras "does nothing to reduce the significant and *measurable* negative impact that cameras coverage can have on the trial participants themselves."[54] (Emphasis added).

EYE TRACKING

One of the arguments often cited is that the courtroom participants, or courtroom participants, will be affected by the cameras. Modern eye tracking technology can help to answer part of this challenge. Eye trackers monitor and record where a person is actually looking, and for how long. The author's research on television courtroom broadcasting effects research, proposes eye tracking to test for in–court camera effects. We can use eye trackers to see if mock courtroom participants in real and simulated courtrooms, are distracted by the cameras (and camera operators where present).

Eye trackers are already used successfully in the internet, marketing, advertising, medical, aeronautics and automobile industries, to name but a few. Why should they not be used for courtroom camera effects research?

LOCATION

Another issue generally ignored in the research to date is location. Generally, the studies do not record where the television camera is located in the courtroom, nor where the respective courtroom participants are located. In assessing and comparing effects studies, we need to know exactly where cameras and participants are located. If the camera is at the back of the courtroom, then the lawyers are unlikely to be visually distracted by it, whereas the judge might be. In considering distraction effects on each respective courtroom actor in a given case, we need to know where they are located and where the camera is located. This assists us in comparing one study with another study. Generally, this is not possible with the limited research so far. The location issues need to be incorporated into the data collection in the proposed federal experiment.

FOOTAGE MATERIAL FOR RESEARCH

In the previous federal experiment it appears that not all of the requests for broadcast footage were satisfied by the media. This was requested so as to undertake content analysis. It might be an idea to formalise or mandate access to such copy during the second experiment.

FEDERAL COURTS CHOSEN

The courts have now been chosen for the second federal experiment. The courts announced[55] are as follows,

- Middle District of Alabama;
- Northern District of California;
- Southern District of Florida;
- District of Guam;
- Northern District of Illinois;
- Southern District of Iowa;
- District of Kansas;
- District of Massachusetts;

- Eastern District of Missouri;
- District of Nebraska;
- Northern District of Ohio;
- Southern District of Ohio;
- Western District of Tennessee;
- Western District of Washington

The pilot experiment is meant to commence from 18 July, 2011 and last a period of three years. However, the effects research effort remains to be seen, and in particular what baseline research will be undertaken *prior to* cameras being introduced.

SUPREME COURT

There are also attempts to enact legislation to allow TCB in the Supreme Court.[56] The *Hollingsworth* decision, and certain comments by Supreme Court judges,[57] could be viewed as an indicator that Supreme Court TCB will not happen any time soon. In the general discussions and arguments, there is no reference to forms or the undertaking of empirical effects research.[58] Karen Aho asks if such coverage would be delivered seriously by the media.[59] Other commentators argue strongly for access,[60] but say nothing in terms of the forms and effects. Supreme Court Justice Kennedy, also made a presentation to senators at a Senate Judiciary Committee calling for no TCB legislation for the Supreme Court.[61]

One commentary in relation to proposals for Supreme Court TCB notes the "lack of depth of studies" and the fact that "most studies focus on cameras' effects on jurors and witnesses. The Supreme Court, of course, has neither. No research seems to focus solely on the effects of camera coverage on appellate arguments"[62] and issues.

Just as Dolores K. Sloviter notes that the *Estes* court realised that that case was not the "the last word on this issue,"[63] it is now suggested that we have not reached the last word on the large variety of research issues to be addressed and researched. Both proponents and opponent of TCB,[64] as well as other interested parties, need to begin effects research in support of their arguments and each research hypothesis.

CONCLUSION

Clearly many issues have been referred to above. Each is deserving of an entire book in and of itself. Equally, each is desirous of substantial research. While this is true, the focus of this research has remained strictly focused upon illuminating and advancing the importance of addressing the Supreme Court research challenge.

Without expanding our research and data gathering methods, our knowledge and policy decisions regarding effects of courtroom broadcasting remain limited. We will also continue to ignore the Supreme Court challenge.

It is hoped that the second Federal pilot experiment will raise the bar in terms of its empirical research and meet part of the Supreme Court research challenge. This needs to begin prior to the cameras rolling.

NOTES

1. *Hollingsworth v Perry*, 558 US _ 2010, available at www.supremecourt.gov/opinions/09pdf/09A648.pdf (accessed 13 August, 2012).

2. See, for example, Glassley Pushes for Cameras in Federal Courts, in *Des Moines News*, March 20, 2009, www.kcci.com/news/18975176/detail.html (accessed 13 August, 2012); www.opencongress.org/bill/110-s352/show (accessed 13 August, 2012). Grassley Pushes for Cameras in Federal Courts, KCCI8, www.kcci.com/news/18975176/details.html, accessed April 5, 2009. Cameras in Courtroom Bill Moves in Senate, The Third Branch, www.uscourts.gov/ttb/2008-04/article07.cfm , accessed April 22, 2009. 110th Congress Acts on Judiciary Initiatives, The Third Branch, (2008)(40), www.uscourts.gov, accessed 13 August, 2012. Also, Sunshine in the Courtroom Act of 2009, S. 657, 111th Congress (2009), www.govtrack.us/congress/bill.xpd?bill=s111-657 , accessed 13 August, 2012; Sunshine in the Courtroom Act of 2009, HR 3054, 111th Congress (2009), www.govtrack.us/congress/bill.xpd?bill=h111-3054 , accessed 13 August, 2012. These efforts will no doubt continue.

3. Ibid. Generally note, for example, E.M. Hodgkins, Throwing Open a Window on the Nation's Courts by Lifting the Ban on Federal Courtroom Television. (The Impact of the Mass Media Revolution), Kansas Journal of Law & Public Policy (1995): 89-103.

4. See, for example, D. Hatch, Focus is on Courtroom Cameras, Electronic Media 19 (2000): 2, referring to Orrin Hatch, Chairman of the Senate Judiciary Committee. Also, D. Hatch, Cameras in Court, Electronic Media 17 (1998): 38.

5. Judicial Conference Opposes Bill to Bring Cameras into Federal Courts, News Release, Administrative Office of the US Courts, September 6, 2000, www.uscourts.gov/Press_Releases/press_090600.html , accessed April 24, 2009.

6. Referred to ibid.

7. Referred to ibid.

8. Ibid.

9. J. Tunhein, Judicial Conference of the United States, Statement of the Honorable John R. Tunheim, Judge, United States District Court for the District of Minnesota, For the Committee on the Judiciary of the United States House of Representatives, Hearing on Cameras in the Courtroom: The 'Sunshine in the Courtroom Act of 2007,' HR 2128, September 27, 2007 (Washington: Administrative Office of the US Courts, 2007).

10. Ibid, Introduction, ii.

11. Ibid, 2.

12. Ibid, 14-15.

13. Ibid, 14.

14. B.E. Bergman, Written Statement of Barbara E. Bergman, on Behalf of the National Association of Criminal Defense Lawyers, Before the Senate Committee on the Judiciary, Re: 'Cameras in the Courtrooms,' November 9, 2005, 2.

15. Proposed by Senator Grassley on April 18, 2005. Cited as the Sunshine in the Courtroom Act of 2005, 109th Congress 9 (2005).

16. Allowing Cameras and Electronic Media in the Courtroom, Wednesday, September 6, 2000, US Senate, Subcommittee on Administrative Oversight and the Courts, Committee on the Judiciary, Washington, DC, 38, referring to testimony and questions of Judge Zobel.
17. Ibid.
18. Ibid, 40 and 46.
19. Ibid.
20. Ibid, 55 et seq.
21. Ibid, 55.
22. Ibid.
23. Ibid.
24. Ibid, 56.
25. Ibid, 56.
26. Ibid.
27. J. Sherman and D. Kawamoto, Boies, Schiller & Flexner LLP, Memorandum: Prepared for the Committee on Court Administration and Case Management (Hon. John R. Tunheim, Chair), The Judicial Conference of the United States, submitted on behalf of Courtroom View Network, June 6, 2009, at 9.
28. Correspondence with author.
29. J. Sherman and J. D. Kawamoto, above, see 8 – 10 for example.
30. Ibid, 12.
31. Ibid, 15.
32. L.J. Myers, Hollingsworth v Perry: The Supreme Court's Renewed Hostility Toward Cameras in the Courtroom, Michigan State University College of Law (Spring 2010), www.law.msu.edu/king/2009-2010/Myers.pdf , accessed 13 August, 2012, 27.
33. M. Cohn and D. Dow, Cameras in the Courtroom: Television and the Pursuit of Justice (New York: Rowman & Little, 2002).
34. One academic example is L.J. Myers, *Hollingsworth v Perry*: The Supreme Court's Renewed Hostility Toward Cameras in the Courtroom, *ibid.* Media examples include Editorial, Discrimination on Trial, But Not on TV, New York Times, January 14, 2010, www.nytimes.com/2010/01/14/opinion/14thu3.html?_r=1 , accessed 13 August, 2012; D. Lithwick, How the Supreme Court Managed to Insult Both the Law and the Public, Sodahead, January 16, 2010, www.sodahead.com , accessed 13 August, 2012.
35. L.J. Myers, ibid, 23.
36. Reported in B. Egeilko, Let Cameras in Courts, Chief Judge Says, San Francisco Chronicle, October 8, 2010, C-3. It refers to an article in the "Fordham University Law Review," co-authored by Judge Kozinski. A. Kozinski, (Judge) and R. Johnson, Of Cameras and Courtrooms, Fordham Intellectual Property Media & Entertainment Law Journal 10 (2010): 1107-1134.
37. A. Kozinski and R. Johnson, above, 1110.
38. Reported in B. Egeilko, Let Cameras in Courts, Chief Judge Says, San Francisco Chronicle, October 8, 2010, C-3.
39. K. Hill, A New Argument in Favor of Cameras in the Courtroom: Bloggers Suck, Above the Law.com, http://abovethelaw.com/2010/04/a-new-argument-in-favor-of-cameras-in-the-courtroom-bloggers-suck/ , accessed 13 August, 2012.
40. Referred to ibid.
41. See general description section, Section 3: Federal Courts Articulate the Cons: Bases for Opposition to Cameras in the Courtroom, in Cameras in the Courtroom, Part 1: Louisiana Approach (Introduction), www.louisianainsurancelitigation.com/2008/03/cameras_in_the_courtroom.html , accessed 13 August, 2012.
42. H.J. Reske, No More Cameras in Federal Courts: Judicial Conference Ends Experiment Despite Few Complaints from Judges, ABA Journal, (November, 1994): 28. Also H.J. Reske, Rally for Court Cameras Falls Short: Judicial Conference Committee Rejects Judge's Plea to Keep Broadcasting, ABA Journal, (March, 1995): 30; D. Kiesel, Federal Court Ban Requests, ABA Journal (November, 1984): 29.

43. H.J. Reske, Cameras Experiment One Year Old: Retired Justice Marshall Among the Judges Who Refused Broadcast Requests, ABA Journal (July, 1992): 28. Also, J. Tunhein, above, n. 1, at 4.

44. See J. Tunhein, above, 4, 17.

45. Ibid, 17-19.

46. S.F. Chance, Considering Cameras in the Courtroom, Journal of Broadcasting and Electronic Media 39 (1995): 555-562, at 559. Also, E. Rodriquez and R. Schmidt, US Judicial Conference Tries a Little Openness: From Cameras to Protective Orders to Itself, Legal Times, March 27, 1995, p. 1, referred to in S.F. Chance, ibid. The judges were also concerned by potential jury and witness effects, see H.J. Reske, No More Cameras in Federal Courts: Judicial Conference Ends Experiment Despite Few Complaints from Judges, ibid. D. Kiesel, No To Cameras: Federal Ban Remains, ABA Journal (November, 1984): 29.

47. H.J. Reske, Ground-Breaking But Boring: Few Cameras Expected in Federal Courts as Broadcast Experiment Gets Underway, ABA Journal (September, 1991): 26.

48. Associated Press, U.S. Judges Agree to Pilot Study of Cameras in Court, First Amendment Centre, www.firstamendmentcenter.org/news.aspx?id=23378, accessed October 18, 2010.

49. See ibid.

50. Judiciary Approves Pilot Project for Cameras in District Court, www.uscourts.gov , accessed October 14, 2010.

51. Ibid.

52. R. Longley, Judiciary Approves Cameras in Courtroom Test, Robert's US Government Info Blog, September 21, 2010, www.usgovtinfo.about.com, accessed October 14, 2010.

53. RIAA Fears 'Manipulation' of Courtroom Web Broadcasting, Privacy Digest, January 21, 2009, www.privacydigest.com, accessed April 3, 2009.

54. D. O'Scannlain, J., Statement of Judge Diarmuid O'Scannlain on Behalf of the Judicial Conference of the United States Regarding S. 829 as Applied to Federal Trial Courts, November 9, 2005, Exhibit 4, 48. (Online copy http://judiciary.senate.gov/hearings/testimony.cfm?id=1672&wit_id=4799, accessed October 31, 2010). He also states that the judges feel that the proposed law, S. 829, fails to adequately protect the right to a fair trial. Ibid, 50.

55. Courts Selected for Federal Cameras in Court Pilot, June 8, 2011, http://www.uscourts.gov/News/NewsView/11-06-08/Courts_Selected_for_Federal_Cameras_in_Court_Pilot_Study.aspx , accessed June 25, 2012.

56. T. Romm, Judiciary Panel Advances Bill to Compel Supreme Court to Televise Proceedings, The Hill.com, http://thehill.com , accessed May 11, 2010. Also, E.F. Daniels, Cameras May Yet Cover the Supremes, Multichannel News (November 20, 2000): 84; Can Congress Mandate Cameras in the Courtroom?, Scotus, Supreme Court of the United States Blog, www.scotusblog.com/wp/can-congress-mandate-cameras-in-the-courtroom/, accessed May 15, 2009.

57. Ernest Svenson refers to comments of Chief Justice Roberts and Judge Souter against TCB, in E. Svenson, Cameras in the Courtroom? Between Lawyers, http://betweenlawyers.corante.com, accessed August 13, 2012. Justice Brennan was also in favour of TCB, while Justice Marshall was against. See S. Stern, Brennan's Conversation on Cameras in Court, at The Justice Brennan Blog, http://justicebrennan.com/blog/?p=312, accessed August 13, 2012.

58. An example of the general discussion is R.L. Brown, Essay: Just A Matter of Time?, Video Cameras at the United States Supreme Court and the State Supreme Courts, Journal of Appellate Practice and Process 9 (2007): 1–17. An example of arguments is M. Cohn, Let the Sun Shine on the Supreme Court, Hastings Constitutional Law Quarterly 35 (2008): 161-168.

59. K. Aho, TV and the Supreme Court: Broadcasters Want Access, But Will They Deliver Serious Coverage? Columbia Journalism Review, (September/October, 2003): 63.

60. Example being, Why Have Cameras Been in Katie Couric's Colon But Not the Supreme Court?, Reason, August 4, 2010, available at http://reason.com/blog/2010/08/04/reasontv-why-have-cameras-been, accessed August 13, 2012. Generally, see also T. Mauro, Court, Cameras, Action!, USA Today, May 27, 2009; D. Wolf and B. Guttentag, Cameras in Camera, Wall Street Journal, July 9, 2003, A14.

61. J. Biskupic, Justice Pleads with Senate: No Cameras in High Court, USA Today, February 15, 2007.

62. Would Cameras Change the Court?, The News Media & The Law (May 1, 2006): 22.
63. D.K. Sloviter, If Courts Are Open, Must Cameras Follow? Hofstra Law Review 26 (1998): 873-889, at 883.
64. Ibid, 889.

Chapter Four

Cameras

The UK Perspective

INTRODUCTION

The Supreme Court effects research challenge, and how we go about addressing this challenge, are significant issues for any consideration of TCB. It is useful not only to consider the discussion and introduction of a limited form of television courtroom broadcasting in the UK as this is a new development, but also because there is no significant effects research in the UK whatsoever. The UK TCB discussion has not yet considered the US Supreme Court effects research challenge.

The most recent development in the UK is the introduction of television courtroom broadcasting in the recently created UK Supreme Court. Television courtroom broadcasting previously only occurring in limited once off instances in the UK. There was and is no regularly permitted television courtroom broadcasting, outside of the UK Supreme Court. Neither is there any extended pilot experiment with television courtroom broadcasting, besides the Supreme Court. No empirical effects research appears to have yet occurred or been prepared in the UK.

The general rule remains that television courtroom broadcasting is not permitted (see below). Given the general prohibition and some discussion and debate on the issue,[1] the UK Supreme Court TCB development is somewhat surprising. Until the introduction of TCB in the new UK Supreme Court, it was not at all clear that TCB would be introduced in the UK. It was equally unclear what form any such broadcasting would take. One of the more surprising suggestions was to try and broadcast UK cases in the US before introducing them to UK audiences.[2] Recently television cameras have been permitted into the new UK Supreme Court. There are already calls by Sky TV to expand this further.[3]

THE LEGAL BACKDROP

The UK legal background remains the Criminal Justice Act 1925. It prohibits television courtroom broadcasting. Section 41 Criminal Justice Act 1925 prohibits the taking of photographs or the making of sketches in or around the court as well as the publishing of such photographs or sketches.[4] This is interpreted as including cinematic and television filming.[5] This is still the current legal position[6] in the UK, notwithstanding the separate position as regards the recent UK Supreme Court.

Section 41of the Criminal Justice Act is titled "Prohibition on taking photographs, etc, in court." It states that no person shall,

> take or attempt to take in any court any photograph or with a view to publication make or attempt to make in any court any portrait or sketch, of any person, being a judge of the court or a juror or a witness in or a party to any proceedings before the court, whether civil or criminal.

Section 20 of the Criminal Justice (Northern Ireland) Act 1945 also applies similar restriction in Northern Ireland in relation to prohibiting photography and sketching.[7]

Section 9 of the Contempt of Court Act 1981 refers to "Use of tape recorders." It states that it is a contempt of court "to use in court, or bring into court for use, any tape recorder or other instrument for recording sound, except with the leave of the court."

DOCUMENTARIES AND APPLICATIONS (THE TRIAL (1993))

The first filming in a UK courtroom occurred on 31 May 1993, when a shoplifting and assault case was filmed by Nick Catliff and the BBC in Edinburgh's Sheriffs Court.[8] The Trial was shown on BBC 2 as a one off example of a documentary type programme which included in-court television footage of a real case. This is reported as the first such broadcast in Britain.[9] It was shown in five episodes and contained footage of criminal trials.[10]

One of the reasons for how this was permissible was that the footage was from Scotland, which was not subject to the England and Wales Criminal Justice Act 1925 prohibition.[11] Mark Stephens, a media lawyer, feels that the participants in The Trial acted up and were "playing to the unseen gallery."[12]

It is also noted that there was reported to be three cameras with camera operators used in the filming of The Trial.[13]

The producer of The Trial also feels that the Simpson criminal case set back the cause of TCB in the UK.[14] He also feels that serious newspaper reporting of the courts is retreating.

It also appears that there was a controlled experiment in Scotland in 1992, and also a separate report.[15] This may have led to a somewhat more liberal attitude to some forms of TCB in Scotland. Live TCB does not appear to be permitted.[16] It is understood to be infrequent however.

CNN applied to film the Harold Shipman inquiry in the UK.[17] Apparently there was filing of the Marchioness sinking inquiry and also closed circuit filming of the first General Pinochet extradition hearing.[18] Various media outlets also applied unsuccessfully to cover all of the Hutton inquiry regarding Dr. David Kelly.[19]

In 2005 Sky TV obtained permission to broadcast live a transmission from the in-court stenography in the retrial of Sion Jenkins.[20]

CAPLAN REPORT 1989

The Televising the Courts: Report of a Working Party of the Public Affairs Committee of the General Council of the Bar [of England and Wales],[21] or Caplan Report as it has become known, is often seen as one of the main UK discussion documents and recommendations in the UK on the issue of television courtroom broadcasting.

The authors of the report travelled to the US for a fact find mission. However, Brian McConnell notes that they only travelled to two US states.[22]

It recommends television courtroom broadcasting pilots in the UK.[23] Interestingly, while Recommendations 7.1 (i) and 7.1 (iii) recommends an Advisory Committee be established to report to the Lord Chancellor and the Home Secretary and which should include psychologists, the next recommendation is arguably unclear.[24] Recommendation 7.1 (iv) recommends that the Advisory Committee "devise and monitor pilot projects involving research and the actual broadcasting of civil and criminal trials and of appellate proceedings."[25] It is unclear if it is saying that empirical effects research and psychology research is recommended and should be carried out.

Jonathan Caplan is quoted as saying that "[i]t is surprising that it [i.e. TCB] has not been examined before."[26] One of the other authors, Michael Kalisher QC, is also reported as agreeing that defendants would suffer from more publicity.[27] The third author, Anthony Speaight, refers positively to the New York experiment.[28] However, the New York experiment referred to was subsequently discontinued. Brian McConnell also separately criticises some of the evidence which the Caplan Report and Bar Council ignored or failed to find, such as so called cheque book journalism and TCB in the New York Steinberg case.[29] This also became an issue in the Simpson criminal case. Alisdair Logan, the solicitor who represented the Guildford Four and Maguires, refers to his visit to the US where he indicates that he found that judges did not want TCB.[30] McConnell notes that the judge in the Steinberg case did not prohibit the jurors from watching television reports of the ongoing case.[31] The issue of TCB and different jurisdictions has been referred to previously. It is interesting, therefore, that McConnell states that "American justice is not British justice."[32] He refers also to elected officials, pre-trial prosecution media statements, and media statements made by both sides during the course of US trials.[33]

It is clear, however, that the Caplan Report has not recommended any effects baseline research and effects research be carried out before any actual pilot filming and or pilot broadcasting.

The Caplan Report without discussing or referring to any effects issues or any effects research, states that in the US "the anticipated risks remained, capable of being controlled."[34] It later acknowledges that it is "not aware of any clear empirical evidence which demonstrates the educative value of televising the courts, but that is not perhaps surprising since it might be thought logically to follow."[35] No educational effects research on television courtroom broadcasting is referred to. It is not explained why educational effects should "logically ... follow."[36]

The report does refer to one UK study[37] which the report states found that respondents "claimed to have learned from what they saw."[38] However, it is unclear what research was undertaken or how applicable it is to television courtroom broadcasting effects issues. Indeed, the exact numbers of "educated" respondents not clear. Caplan refers to 500 viewers being surveyed, one fifth having seen the programme [i.e. exactly 100], and that "those who had seen five or more episodes [no number given]"[39] claimed an educative effect.

The report is emphatic in stating that "intrusion and disruption can be *entirely* eliminated" (emphasis added).[40] This seems somewhat sweeping – especially given the point that the report has not referred to any empirical effects research or general research of television courtroom broadcasting effects to this stage.

The report does refer to the apparent self reports and opinion reports in *In re Florida in Post-Newsweek.*[41] The Florida Supreme Court is referred to as stating that there was "absolutely no adverse effect upon the participants' performance or the decorum of the proceedings."[42] However, this is not based upon any empirical or effects research other than opinion reports and self reports. The Supreme Court of Florida does also add, however, that the concerns,

> are but assumptions unsupported by any evidence. No respondent has been able to point to any instance during the pilot programme period where these fears were sustained. Such evidence as exists would appear to refute the assumptions. The *survey* reflects that the assumed influences upon participants during the experimental period were perceived to vary in degree from not at all to slightly (emphasis added).[43]

The Caplan Report refers to a two year experiment in Massachusetts which was positive but relied upon "survey data."[44]

Caplan then refers to the California research, presumably the Short Report, but this is not stated.[45] Caplan states that the result of this "survey demonstrated yet again that the feared adverse effects did *not* occur. In particular, there was *no* evidence that the witnesses became more *nervous*, or that they became less *responsive* or *decisive*, when filmed"[46] (emphasis added).

The James Hoyt research is purportedly referred to in a footnote on page 33.[47] There is no express reference to Hoyt in the text. Caplan refers to a case in New York, but without naming or referencing it, where a witness refused to testify because of television cameras.[48]

The Caplan Report states that it reviewed "hundreds" of surveys and reports - but only refers to Short and Hoyt as (empirical) effects research.[49] It states that it only found one adverse study. It was,

> a report in 1979 of an ad hoc committee of the Bar Association of Greater Cleveland, and we did not find it impressive. It did not state the questions asked in the questionnaires distributed. It did not fully analyse the responses. It was based on only three trials and the participants were very small in number. Yet it claimed the spectacular finding of 'a chilling psychological effect' on all participants, including judges and lawyers.[50]

The report is not referenced or cited in the Caplan Report. However, subsequently this is tempered to an "absence of adverse conclusions."[51]

While the report favours television courtroom broadcasting, it has been describe as "cautious" in the level of such broadcasting to be permitted.[52] Subsequent, and possibly as a result of the Caplan Report, a private members bill was introduced. This was the Courts (Research) Bill 1991. The bill was not successful however.[53]

ENGLAND AND WALES PILOT

There appears to have been an experiment in England and Wales already[54] which occurred on or about 16th November 2004.[55] The footage was not broadcast.[56] It appears that the in–court effects research consisted of questionnaires and no empirical research.[57]

The then Lord Chancellor, Lord Falconer, announced at the Edinburgh Television Festival on August 29 2004 that the Court of Appeal would allow television cameras on a demonstration basis.[58] The footage was for internal judicial consideration only.[59] Apparently, the experiment used small remote controlled cameras and focused on judges and counsel only, and apparently with consent required.[60] It is understood that the judges evaluating the project were to be shown mock broadcasts with the in-court footage and "traditional" broadcasts without the footage.[61] A separate report indicates that the pilot lasted six weeks.[62]

BROADCASTING COURTS CONSULTATION PAPER 2005

The Department of Constitutional Affairs launched a consultation entitled Broadcasting Court[63] in November 2004.[64] The consultation period closed on February 28, 2005.[65] The consultation was unusual. It was not a report, contained "no proposals,"[66] draft changes or possible changes. The consultation consisted mainly of a seminar (on January 10, 2005) and an online questionnaire.[67]

The Lord Chancellor launching the "consultation paper"[68] on the November 15, 2004 indicated that there would be no changes adversely affecting victims, witnesses or jurors.[69] He acknowledged attitudes had changed since the restriction introduced in Section 41 of the Criminal Justice Act 1925 (CJA). Calling for a public debate, he stated that we "have to make sure that any such step would benefit justice, not burden justice."[70] The CJA prohibits the taking of photographs in or around the court. In addition, "[n]o change to make our courts more open and accessible should worsen or jeopardise in any way the position of witness and victims or make witnesses reluctant to appear."[71] Lord Falconer also stated that he could "see no case for televising cases involving children and I think we will need to consider very carefully the question of broadcasting criminal trials."[72] He also stated that he was "concerned at overseas research showing that people believe that if their evidence might be televised that would reduce the likelihood of their coming forward as a witness."[73] He concluded that "[j]ustice should be seen to be done. But our priority must be that justice is done."[74]

The executive summary refers to the argument of beneficial educational effects and increased "confidence in the judicial system."[75] It also refers to the "needs of participants" especially "those most likely to be vulnerable."[76] "If permitting broadcasting was likely to have an impact on people's willingness to take part in proceedings, or to make participation even more of an ordeal, there would need to be very strong arguments in its favour."[77]

The highest appeal court in England and Wales was the House of Lords. By virtue of also being attached to parliament, it was televised similar to parliament.[78] Clause 37 of the Constitutional Reform Bill proposed amending the restriction in Section 41 of the Criminal Justice Act 1925 by adding the carveout of "apart from the [new] Supreme Court." [79] As the highest appeal court was already broadcast, the filming of the new Supreme Court was permitted.[80]

The consultation paper notes that,

> the Government are particularly concerned with the role of witnesses in increasing the number of criminal cases are successfully resolved. A range of current initiatives aims to make court appearances less daunting, and to encourage witnesses to feel more secure giving evidence. In view of this, the potential impact of broadcasting courtroom proceedings is one of the most important considerations in relation to this topic, and the one which argues most strongly against permitting the broadcasting of first instance trials.[81]

Also,

> potential witnesses may refuse to appear if they know that their testimony if going to be broadcast, which could lead to delays, cracked trials, or miscarriages of justice.[82]

The consultation document recognised the there were potential in-court effects and out-of-court effects.[83] It also recognised that depending on the broadcasting techniques adopted, participants could feel under greater "scrutiny."[84] In addition, "[t]here are often difficulties in persuading people to testify, for example if they fear intimidation, ... a case being broadcast would be a further obstacle."[85]

Indeed, it does refer to the professional public opinion poll undertaken as part of the New York study. The consultation paper raises concerns with the findings. The New York public survey "indicates that people may be deterred from acting as witnesses by the presence of cameras ... 54% of those surveyed said they would be less willing to testify if cameras were present."[86] It also refers to New Zealand, where "58% of respondents in a representative sample of adults said that cameras would have an impact on their willingness to appear as a witness in a criminal trial."[87]

Even where witnesses were not discouraged, "testifying can be a nerve-racking experience, which the presence of recording equipment could compound. 87% of trial and appellate judges surveyed in California reported that witnesses were more nervous or self-conscious when giving testimony before cameras."[88] The consultation paper also refers to the decision in the Shipman Inquiry deciding against television cameras based on the addition effect it would have on witnesses.[89]

While the New York study was opinion report, self report and questionnaire based, the consultation paper refers to the result which it finds "disturbing" that "37% of these [351] judges said that television coverage causes judges to render a ruling they otherwise might not issue."[90]

The consultation report does refer to the content analysis undertaken for the first federal pilot experiment, which found that on average, the television courtroom broadcasting footage examined made up 56 seconds of the news story.[91]

Annex E of the consultation paper refers to other jurisdictions and research.[92] However, most of the references refer to "opinion" reports only.[93] This includes the federal experimental pilot study, the California Task Force report, the New York report in 1996 and Canada.[94]

However, research is referred to in New Zealand where a "case-by-case evaluation found that most judges were distracted by cameras."[95]

BROADCASTING THE COURTS RESPONSE TO CONSULTATION 2005

The responses to the Consultation Paper were compiled and released on June 30, 2005.[96] Again it was noted that the Consultation paper "made no proposals but sought views on the complex and sensitive issues around broadcasting court proceedings."[97] Again it is noted that there are potentially different forms, including reference to different courts, proceedings and stages of this proceedings.[98] There was a seminar and a website forum used as part of the consultation. However, all of the responses were opinions and responses to a questionnaire and or free comment. "[S]upport for widespread broadcasting is limited, and that there is grave concern about the potential impact on participants, especially witnesses and jurors, and on the trial process."[99] There is no reference to effects research.

THE BARRISTERS, 2008

A further documentary type programme called The Barristers was shown in 2008. It was described as a fly-on-the-wall type documentary, as was a previous solicitor's office documentary called No Win, No Fee from the BBC in 2008.[100]

The Barristers programme focused mainly on student and recently qualified barristers, how they qualify and their role and progress in court. It was produced by the BBC who described it as a series "where raw emotion meets centuries-old tradition" and also capturing reactions to "what they [i.e. the barristers in general] perceive as an attack from Government, which wants to curb their earnings and open up the legal profession to others."[101] It was also billed as describing, amongst other things, "a glamorous job which produces Prime Ministers, millionaires and the judges who shape our law."[102] While it is clearly a documentary type programme, it is also clearly being "sexed up" to some extent. Apparently, the programme took eight years of negotiations to get to filming stage.[103]

The programme makers apparently had "years of negotiation" before being permitted to film the programme.[104] Unfortunately, it does not describe what structures, discussions, restrictions, intended formatting style, etc. were discussed or indeed agreed upon. It is also unclear who exactly the years of negotiation took place between. If there were any procedures or rules (agreed or otherwise) these were not evident, and therefore cannot be examined in this instance nor in considering any other potential programmes.

There was also another UK docudrama programme called Criminal Justice which was fiction based. However, it has received criticism from the (some of) the barrister profession for portraying barristers as being "underhand, unprincipled and overly aggressive."[105]

PRIVY COUNCIL 2006

It is reported that the Judicial Committee of the Privy Council Pitcairn appeal hearing was videotaped and sent to the islanders, but only to be seen by them.[106]

UK SUPREME COURT 2009

The UK Supreme Court, takes over from the House of Lords judicial appeal function. TCB is prohibited in England and Wales. In order to introduce TCB in the Supreme Court, the Criminal Justice Act 1925 needed to be amended.

The Constitutional Reform Bill introduces a Clause 37 to maintain the current status quo of the currently televised House of Lords/Supreme Court.[107] The section reads,

> In section 41 of the Criminal Justice Act 1925 (c.86)(prohibition on taking photographs etc. In court), for subsection (2)(a) substitute —
> '(a) the expression 'court' means any court of justice (including the court of a coroner), apart from the Supreme Court.'

This clause is "simply to replicate the existing arrangements. It is not an indication of a Government position on the wider issue of courts broadcasting considered."[108]

The new Supreme Court was eventually established by the Constitutional Reform Act 2005.[109] The Supreme Court has three courtrooms, each with four fixed cameras.[110] Joshua Rozenberg, however, refers to there being two Supreme Court courtrooms.[111] The court opened in October 2009.[112] As highlighted above, Sky TV is already calling to expand UK TCB beyond the new Supreme Court into other courts.

COURT OF APPEAL AND SENTENCING DECISION 2011

Following on foot of the UK Supreme Court experiment, there has been lobbying by certain broadcasters to expand TCB in England and Wales. There are reports that the UK government is receptive. Public statements by Prime Minister Cameron and Justice Secretary Kenneth Clarke indicate that they wish to move ahead with the broadcasting of sentencing decisions, and later still Court of Appeal decisions.[113] Witnesses and other courtroom actors will not be shown. There is no indication, however, of what if any effects research or baseline research may be carried out.

DISCUSSION

If UK TCB is expanded beyond the Supreme Court what might it look like and what forms would it take? The General Counsel for TruTV when speaking about previous discussion about TCB in the UK in 2004, said that if they got permission to film they "would be delighted to show interesting cases."[114] The criteria of TruTV for filming a case are that there is "something unique."[115] The TruTV editors make a decision as to what is "newsworthy."[116]

James Morton feels that the public will not be interested in normal cases, which can be mundane and will rather be interested only in "the English equivalent of the O.J. Simpson trial."[117] There will also be only a "market" for "major trials."[118] He also notes that most cases are "incomprehensible without a commentator."[119] Anthony Speaight, a barrister, argues in favour of TCB broadcasting, but without referring to forms or research issues.[120] Others argue in favour of criminal case TCB, such as William Harbage QC.[121] Sir Hugh Laddie separately calls for webcam internet TCB.[122]

Without knowing that TCB would later be permitted in the new Supreme Court, Morton states that cases in the precursor to the Supreme Court (the House of Lords), would not grab attention, were incomprehensible to most and were a "switch-off."[123]

Defendants are one of the seldom consulted and researched areas of the television courtroom broadcasting discussion. Morton notes that defendants appear not to have been consulted in the UK official discussion.[124] He also makes the same point in relation to the police.[125]

There have been recent calls after the Supreme Court development, to expand cameras to other courts. The new DPP, interviewed on Channel 4 News, was positive towards TCB subject to appropriate safeguards.[126] Mark

Stephens, a media solicitor, predicts TCB being introduced in stages, appellate courts, then civil cases and then finally criminal cases.[127] The Ministry of Justice (in 2009) is reported as saying the Ministers are not convinced of the case for TCB and that there are no plans currently to change current arrangements.[128]

The Bar Council is again quoted as saying that the advantages of TCB outweigh the disadvantages and that TCB "*will* enhance the public's *understanding* of *and confidence* in our legal system"[129] (emphasis added). It would be useful, therefore, to have had a research programme in place to examine these propositions before and during the TCB project in the UK Supreme Court (and indeed in the second federal pilot experiment). It does not appear that the Bar Counsel countenances any such research. C.H. Rolph comments that while educational TCB may be one of the stated intentions, this will not occur in practice as the media are more concerned with ratings and profit.[130]

One of the issues not addressed is that of costs and the form of any TCB that may be expanded beyond the Supreme Court. C.H. Rolph notes that "someone has to provide the apparatus, the know-how, and the hordes of technicians."[131] This issue has not been discussed or considered. Neither is there any suggestion from the media that they are willing to cover the fit out and or running costs of any of the possible forms of TCB that potentially could be expanded. Lord Hailsham is also referred to as being concerned about how the media would edit the courtroom footage.[132] (Apparently, at least some federal judges are also concerned, in that the first federal experiment was not continued).

Martin Dockray[133] refers to the basis for the original restriction in the Criminal Justice Act 1925, namely, to prevent distraction from the cameras and operators/photographers and to protect courtroom participants.

IRELAND

While there is no television courtroom broadcasting in Ireland, the author carried out judicial research in 1996 and 2010. The 2010 judicial survey was conducted during February and March 2010 in relation to judicial attitudes in the Republic of Ireland to television courtroom broadcasting. This repeated and expanded upon the seminal related research of the author in 1996.

Judges in Ireland were asked if they were in favour, in principle, of permitting courtroom broadcasting in Irish courts. 77.50% responded negatively, while 22.50% were in favour (Part Question A-3)(2010). The full results remain to be published.

In 1996, 66.6% of Irish judges responded negatively to this question.[134] Therefore, if we approximate the figures against television courtroom broadcasting in Ireland, the 67% of judges in 1996 increased to 78% in 2010. The judicial opposition to TCB in Ireland has increased. A majority of Irish judges continue to oppose TCB.

CONCLUSION

The then UK Lord Chancellor, Lord Falconer, when introducing the UK consultation states that "[c]ameras in the courtroom would be a big step. We have to make sure that any such step would benefit justice, not worsen it." Very detailed literature reviews of the courtroom broadcasting literature and comparative literature is required. In addition, it is critical that empirical research is properly planned and undertaken.

It is unfortunate that legislatures and the judiciary did not avail of the opportunity to undertake and arrange for ongoing empirical research once a decision was made to introduce TCB with the new UK Supreme Court.

However, the debate in relation whether to expand TCB in the UK needs to consider the forms and effects of such broadcasting. It also needs to make transparent proposals in relation to what empirical research is being proposed as part of such experiment(s) and pilot(s). Baseline issues still remain.

There will undoubtedly be costs involved in researching, rolling out and running television courtroom broadcasting. Who will cover these costs? This issue has yet to be properly discussed and researched, apart from one comment that this offers an opportunity for the media "funding" the courts through charges.[135] Even before the current recession, there was acknowledgement that there was a lack of UK government funding for court and legal innovations.[136] While there have been calls to roll out court IT which is interactive and remote, such as conferencing, internet, Skype, etc., the focus of IT budgets appear aimed more at cost saving than service provision.[137] Sir Hugh Laddie, speaking to the Society of Computers and Law, states that the UK courts do not do IT well.[138] Will it do TCB well? Will it refer to the US Supreme Court research challenge?

In relation to courtroom IT generally, there is an acknowledgement that little is known of the effects.[139] As regards the form of expanded TCB, if permitted, Professor Jeremy Barnett, advocates that the courts or court service undertake the filming and arrangements.[140] This is somewhat similar to the second federal experimental pilot.

The Caplan Report is noted as recommending limited courtroom broadcasting with strict rules of coverage, and excluding certain types of proceeding and courtroom participants.[141] The Bar Council stressed it was recommending an experimental period only.[142] A Law Society committee chairman feels that an experiment may be the "best test."[143] However, any experiment and test must be based on proper research and research data gathering methodologies — including baseline data. The research challenge remains — even in the UK. It is interesting that Henry Hodge, the above Law Society member, feels that TCB may well cause changes in how cases are conducted.[144] It is critical, therefore, to address the research issues at the same time as making any proposal to permit TCB. This aspect of the debate has been wholly missed in the UK.

The UK discussion and policy considerations need to avoid the misunderstandings and misrepresentation which have occurred elsewhere. Discussions such as Henry Schleiff,[145] where he suggests that TCB in the US has increased public confidence in the justice system, but without referencing any research or statistics whatsoever, are not to be recommended.

NOTES

1. For example, Television on Trial, The Economist, December 19, 1998; J. Pritchard, Should Cameras be Allowed in the Courtroom? Legal Business (January – February, 1992), 3-5; J. Pritchard, Televising the Courts: Some Second Thoughts, Legal Business (May, 1995): 11-12.

2. See R. Verkaik, Cameras Cross the Atlantic: The USA's Trial Broadcasters Are Making A Pitch to Televise UK Hearings, Gazette (17 May, 1995): 14, referring to a TruTV (then CourtTV) proposal.

3. A. Laughlin, Sky News Calls for Courtroom TV Cameras, Digital Spy, December 6, 2010, last accessed on January 18, 2010.

4. Department of Constitutional Affairs [UK], Broadcasting Courts, Consultation Paper, CP 28/04 (November, 2004) 13.

5. Ibid, referring to *Re Barber v Lloyds Underwriters* [1987] 1 QB 103, 105; and *R v Loveridge, Lee and Loveridge* [2001] 2 Cr. App. Rep. 29, CA.

6. Martin Dockray raises the issue of whether the state and judiciary bound by the Section 41 restrictions. See M. Dockray, Cameras at the Door of the Court, New Law Journal 20 (1990): 548.

7. Department of Constitutional Affairs [UK], Broadcasting Courts, Consultation Paper, CP 28/04 (November, 2004): 13.

8. N. Catliff, On Camera Not In Cameras, New Law Journal 144 (1994): 1597.

9. R. Verkaik, above.

10. Department of Constitutional Affairs [UK], Broadcasting Courts, Consultation Paper, CP 28/04 (November, 2004): 18.

11. R. Verkaik, above.

12. Referred to ibid.

13. Referred to in G. Langdon-Down, Cameras In Court: American Lawyers Switch On To Living Life Through A Lens, Law Society Gazette (September 30, 2004): 24.

14. Nick Catliff, referred to in S. Ward, Fights, Cameras, Action, Law Society Gazette 18 (2001): 22.

15. Department of Constitutional Affairs [UK], Broadcasting Courts, Consultation Paper, CP 28/04 (November, 2004): 18. It is unclear if they are generally available.

16. Ibid.

17. Ibid.

18. Ibid.

19. Department of Constitutional Affairs [UK], Broadcasting Courts, Consultation Paper, CP 28/04 (November, 2004): 17.

20. Falconer Close to Rejecting TV Trials as Sky Breaks New Ground in Jenkins Case, Law Society Gazette (July 7, 2005), www.lawgazette.co.uk , accessed August 13, 2011.

21. J. Caplan, M. Kalisher and A. Speaight, Televising the Courts: Report of a Working Party of the Public Affairs Committee of the General Council of the Bar [of England and Wales] (London: Bar Council of England and Wales, 1989).
22. B. McConnell, above, 1622.
23. Ibid, 50.
24. Ibid.
25. Ibid.
26. Bar Recommends TV in Courts, New Law Journal, May 26, 1989, 706.
27. Ibid.
28. Ibid.
29. B. McConnell, Cameras in Court, New Law Journal, November 16, 1990, 1622.
30. Referred to in R. Verkaik, above, 14.
31. B. McConnell, above, 1622.
32. Ibid.
33. Ibid.
34. J. Caplan, M. Kalisher and A. Speaight, above, at 26.
35. Ibid, para 4.2, 28.
36. Ibid.
37. Ibid, 28, referring to a study by Dr. Mallory Wober of the Independent Broadcasting Authority who carried out a viewers survey in relation to an apparent non-court case programme called Case on Camera. J.M. Wober, Case on Camera: An Audience Verdict (IBA Research Department, February, 1986).
38. J. Caplan, et al, above, 28.
39. Ibid, 28.
40. Ibid, 29.
41. Ibid, 31 – 32, referring to *In re Post-Newsweek Stations*, 370 Southern Reporter, 2nd Series, 766-769.
42. Ibid, 32, referring to *In re Post-Newsweek Stations*, 370 Southern Reporter, 2nd Series, 766-769, at 769.
43. Ibid, 32, referring to *In re Post-Newsweek Stations*, 370 Southern Reporter, 2nd Series, 766-769, 775-776.
44. Ibid, 32, referring to Report of the Advisory Committee to Oversee the Experimental Use of Cameras and Recording Equipment in Courtrooms, indicated as being available from the National Centre of the State Courts, Williamsburg, Virginia.
45. Ibid, 32, the reference given is Evaluation of California's Experiment with Extended Media Coverage (1981), and available from the National Centre for State Courts.
46. Ibid, 32.
47. Ibid, 33, referring to J. Hoyt, Courtroom Coverage: The Effects of Being Televised, Journal of Broadcasting 21 (1977): 487–495.
48. Ibid, 33.
49. Ibid, 34.
50. Ibid, 34.
51. Ibid, p. 34.
52. D. Stepniak, Audio–Visual Coverage of Courts (Cambridge: Cambridge University Press, 2008), 14.
53. Department of Constitutional Affairs [UK], Broadcasting Courts, Consultation Paper, CP 28/04 (November, 2004), 15. Also M. McKeone, Defeat for TV Courts Bill, Law Society Gazette (1991): 88. The McKeone article notes that understanding that Lord Lane opposes TCB while Lord Taylor appears to support TCB, ibid. Sir Thomas Bingham, Master of the Rolls, is also reported as having favoured a TCB experiment. Referred to in The Thoughts of Sir Thomas, New Law Journal 144 (1994): 593.
54. D. Stepniak, Audio–Visual Coverage of Courts (Cambridge: Cambridge University Press, 2008), 60; n. 280, at 60; 61; and 56 et seq. Also referred to in Pros and Cons of Courtroom Cameras Set Out, 15 November, 2004, www.number10.gov.uk/Page6578 , accessed March 2, 2010.

55. Also referred to in Pros and Cons of Courtroom Cameras Set Out, 15 November, 2004, www.number10.gov.uk/Page6578 , accessed 2 March, 2010.

56. D. Stepniak, above, 60; n. 280, 60; 61; and 56 *et seq*. See also Department of Constitutional Affairs, Broadcasting Courts, Consultation Paper, CP 28/04 (November, 2004): 19-20.

57. D. Stepniak, above, 60; n. 280, at 60; 61; and 56 et seq.

58. J. Morton, Court TV – the Cameras Are Switched on Again, Criminal Law Legislation Update 68 (2004): 451–453.

59. Ibid, 451.

60. Grania Langdon-Down, Lights, Cameras, Law, Law Society Gazette (September 30, 2004) www.lawgazette.co.uk , accessed August 13, 2011.

61. Ibid.

62. Why Right to Switch Off Camera Is Central to Granting Court TV, LexisNexis News Analysis, 2005 but no date given, www.lexisnexis.com.elib.tcd.ie/uk/legal/delivery/PrintDoc.do?fromCart=false&dnl ..., accessed May 9, 2009.

63. Department of Constitutional Affairs [UK], Broadcasting Courts, Consultation Paper, CP 28/04 (November, 2004).

64. See www.dca.goc.uk/consult/courts/broadcasting-cp28-04.htm , accessed December 14, 2009.

65. Ibid. Note generally, Cameras May be Allowed in Court: But Safeguards Will Remain, Daily Post, February 8, 2005. Also, for example, R. Rothwell, Lights, Camera, Court, Law Society Gazette 18 (2004): 5.

66. Ibid.

67. Ibid.

68. See summary at www.number10.gov.uk/Page6578 , accessed March 2, 2010.

69. Ibid.

70. Ibid.

71. Ibid.

72. Department of Constitutional Affairs, Broadcasting Courts, Consultation Paper, CP 28/04 (November, 2004): 5.

73. Ibid.

74. Ibid.

75. Ibid, parag. 2, at 6.

76. Ibid, parag. 5, at 6.

77. Ibid, parag. 5, at 6.

78. Ibid, parag 12, at 15.

79. Ibid, parags 13 and 14, at 15.

80. Ibid.

81. Ibid, parag. 10, at 44.

82. Ibid, parag. 11, at 45.

83. Ibid, parag 1, at 43.

84. Ibid, parag 2,at 43.

85. Ibid, parag 11, at 45. Indeed, there have been some "gangland" type cases in Ireland where this appears to have been an issue.

86. Ibid, parag. 12, at 45, referring to the Cameras in New York Courtrooms, and the Marxist Institute for Public Opinion Poll, December, 1996, contained therein.

87. Ibid, parag. 12, at p. 45, referring to UMR Insight Limited, Media Coverage of Court Proceedings: A Summary Report (February, 1998).

88. Ibid, parag. 13, at 45, referring to Report Summary of the California Judicial Task Force on Photographing, Recording and Broadcasting in the Courtroom.

89. Ibid, parag. 14, at 45 – 46, referring to Decision on Application by Cable News Network (CNN), October 25, 2001. The consultation paper also refers to Lord Irvine of Lairg, the then Lord Chancellor, who commented after the Woodward case in the US that there "is a serious risk that witnesses might be influenced in the evidence they give, or find undue pressure being placed on themselves or their families as a consequence of live coverage." In Reporting the Courts: The Media's Rights and Responsibilities, 4th RTE/UCD Media Lecture, University College Dublin, April 14, 1999.

90. Ibid, parag. 28, at 49, referring to New York State Committee to Review Audio-Visual Coverage of Court Proceedings.

91. Ibid, parag. 27, at 61, referring to quote of same contained in the New York study (1997).

92. Ibid, at 100.

93. Ibid, at 100 et seq.

94. Ibid.

95. Ibid, at 109, referring to UMR Insight Ltd., Media Coverage of Court Proceedings: Summary Report (February, 1998) and The Impact of Television, Radio and still Photography on Coverage of Court Proceedings – Final Report; A Report Prepared for the Department of Courts by a research team from the Department of Human Management, Massey University (April, 1998). This is the New Zealand research.

96. Department of Constitutional Affairs, Broadcasting Courts, Response to Consultation, CP(R) 28/04 (June 30, 2005), Response to Consultation Carried Out by the Department for Constitutional Affairs. 259 responses were made in total, see 7.

97. Ibid, parag. 1, at 4. Interestingly, one of the consultation criteria was to be clear on the proposals, see, parag 2, at 44.

98. Ibid, parag. 6, at 5.

99. Ibid, parag. 1, at 42.

100. C. Baksi, Court on Camera, Law Society Gazette 13 (2008): 50.

101. See, BBC Two Unveils its Autumn 2008 highlights, www.bbc.co.uk/pressoffice/pressreleases/stories/2008/07_july/10/bbctwoXXXl, accessed April 4, 2009. See also comments of Daithí Mac Síthigh in his blogs "Barred," www.rhymeswithporridge.com/2008/10/barred/, accessed April 4, 2009 and "The Barristers: An Update," at www.rhymeswithporridge.com/2008/12/the-barristers-an-update/, accessed April 4, 2009. Daithí Mac Síthigh may have moved his blog to www.lexferenda.com/, accessed on August 13, 2011.

102. See Open University, The Barristers, About the Series, www.open2.net/about_the_barristers.html , accessed April 4, 2009.

103. C. Baksi, above.

104. See ibid.

105. See S. Jones, Objection: BBC Drama is Unfair on Us, Says Barristers, The Guardian online, www.guardian.co.uk/media/2008/jul/03/television.law , accessed August 13, 2011, and also commented upon by Daithí Mac Síthigh in his blog, Barred, www.rhymeswithporridge.com/2008/10/barred/ , accessed April 4, 2009.

106. J. Rozenberg, Sending the Right Message, Law Society Gazette 25 (2008): 8.

107. Department of Constitutional Affairs [UK], Broadcasting Courts, Consultation Paper, CP 28/04 (November, 2004): 15.

108. Ibid, 15.

109. M. White, New Supreme Court Puts Cases On Camera, British Legal History Has Been Made With the New Supreme Court Taking Over from the House of Lords as the Highest Court in the Land, October 1, 2009, http://news.sky.com , accessed November 16, 2009.

110. Details at Chancery Bar Association, www.chba.org.uk/news/?a=79844 , accessed August 13, 2011.

111. J. Rozenberg, Sending the Right Message, Law Society Gazette 25 (2008): 8.

112. TV Cameras To Capture New Era For Law Lords, TimesOnline, http://business.timesonline.co.uk/tol/business/law/article6827863.ece , accessed August 13, 2011. U.K. Supreme Court's Ahead of its American Cousin, October 23, 2009, www.star-telegram.com/242/story/1707301.html , accessed November 16, 2009.

113. See, for example, N. Morris, Cameron Backs Move to Put Cameras in Court, Independent (UK), September 6, 2011; Ban on Filming in Law Courts to be Lifted, Guardian, September 6, 2011.

114. Referred to in G. Langdon-Down, Cameras in Court: American Lawyers Switch On To Living Life Through A Lens, Law Society Gazette (30 September, 2004): 24.

115. Ibid.

116. Ibid.

117. J. Morton, above, 451.

118. Ibid, 452.
119. Ibid.
120. A. Spreaight, Let the Cameras In, Law Society Gazette 38 (2001): 16. See also, Court TV Deterrent, New Law Journal 16 (1988): 906, referring to deterrent effects.
121. W. Harbage, QC, Camera in Court, Counsel (February, 2005): 13.
122. Management/IT: Court on Camera, Law Society Gazette (March, 2007): 13.
123. J. Morton, above.
124. Ibid, 453.
125. Ibid.
126. Referred to in C. Baksi, News: Starmer Wades Into TV Trials Debate, Law Society Gazette (January 15, 2009): 2.
127. Ibid.
128. Ibid.
129. Referred to in C.H. Rolph, C.H., In Camera, New Law Journal 16 (1990): 382.
130. Ibid.
131. Ibid.
132. Ibid.
133. M. Dockray, Cameras at the Door of the Court, New Law Journal 20 (1990): 548.
134. P. Lambert, Judicial Questionnaire on Courtroom Broadcasting, Irish Law Times 15 (1997): 50-57; also P. Lambert, Courtroom Television Broadcasting, Communications Law 2:5 (1997): 180-187.
135. "[H]as the Lord Chancellor not realized the potential for funding the courts by charging the media for the privilege of obtaining highly marketable footage," Reality Television, Criminal Law and Justice Weekly (2003): 917.
136. Management/IT: Court on Camera, Law Society Gazette (March, 2007): 13. On court IT generally, note A. Oskanp, A. Lodder, A., and M. Apistola, Eds., IT Support of the Judiciary, Australia, Singaport, Venezuala, Norway, The Netherlands and Italy (The Hague: Asser Press, 2004). Note also comments of Lord Justice Brooke in, Poor [IT] Technology 'Lets Down' UK Courts, BBC News, 20 June, 2002.
137. Ibid, referring to statements of Jeremy Barnett, Vice Chairman of the Bar Council IT Panel.
138. R. White, Courts Web-Cam Call, Law Society Gazette 10 (2007): 4.
139. See Court21 Project and home page description, www.court21.ac.uk/ , accessed August 13, 2011. The Court21 Project is now known as The Center for Legal and Court Technology, www.legaltechcenter.net/default.aspx , accessed August 13, 2011.
140. Referred to in Management/IT: Court on Camera, Law Society Gazette, (March, 2007): 13. He also voices concern in relation to media editing, *ibid.* In relation to US courts and IT, see one case study, E.C. Pradao and L.S. Hyman, "Technological Advances in the Courtroom," Issues in Democracy: The Changing Face of U.S. Courts 8 (2003): 32-36.
141. Bar Paves Way for TV Courts, Law Society Gazette (1990): 87.
142. Ibid.
143. Referring to Henry Hodge, Chairman of the Law Society Council Courts and Legal Service Committee, see ibid.
144. Ibid.
145. H. Schleiff, Cameras in Courts, New Law Journal, 154 (2004): 1745.

Chapter Five

What Exactly Is Courtroom Broadcasting?

SCOPE

The core theme of this book is the research challenge posed by the Supreme Court and our current knowledge. There is a need to undertake substantial ongoing empirical research in relation to the effects of television courtroom broadcasting (TCB).

The book provides a critical analysis of television courtroom broadcasting *effects research* relating to television courtroom broadcasting. For all of the discussion and interest in television courtroom broadcasting, there is no body of properly considered and scientific research in relation to the effects of television courtroom broadcasting. Hence, the effects research issues and the Supreme Court challenge remain real considerations. This is significant internationally and not just in the US.

We should be concerned with the effects research issues and challenges. That is distinct from commentary or general research in relation to courtroom broadcasting (CB) per se. We need to define television courtroom broadcasting, to define and set out baselines and parameters for television courtroom broadcasting in order that we might begin to research the effects issues and challenges effectively. This enables us to advance beyond the limited and circumspected "research" to date. Why do we need to do this? Why is it important? It is important because only defined and delineated effects research properly and adequately informs our understanding and policy discussions in relation to courtroom broadcasting and television courtroom broadcasting. This work, and the implications of this work, offer valuable and important contributions to our consideration of television courtroom broadcasting.

In focusing on the effects research issues and challenges, however, a very fundamental question arises. This is the question raised in the heading above. What exactly is courtroom broadcasting? What is television courtroom broadcasting? Despite the apparent obviousness and simplicity of these questions, they have never been addressed in the literature or research to date. As the research and the scoping exercise below make clear, however, the answers to these questions require greater analysis than commentators have afforded. Only after considerable research, scoping and baseline parameter setting, was the author able to develop the first considered definition of what television courtroom broadcasting (TCB) is. This defines and delimits what television courtroom actually is. *Television courtroom broadcasting is television cameras in the courtroom, filming courtroom proceedings for live and or contemporaneous television push broadcast to the general public.*

This definition is then critical in scoping what is and is not encompassed within television courtroom broadcasts concerns, such as the effects research issues and the Supreme Court research challenge. The benefit of this definition is that it also enables the current research, and future research, to begin distinguishing the different categories within television courtroom broadcasting. Why is this important? This is important because once we see that there are different forms of television courtroom broadcasting, we must consider whether there are different effects for different categories and forms of television courtroom broadcasting. We can also ask what are the different effects for different forms of courtroom broadcasting generally. For example, will radio courtroom broadcasting differ from television courtroom broadcasting? Is one category or form of television courtroom broadcasting better at educating? Consider, for example, the proposition that (television) courtroom broadcasting will educate. Do we know? Do we know which TCB form will educate best?

Proper scoping, parameters and definitions makes it abundantly clear that we need new research and that many challenges, including the Supreme Court challenge, remain to be addressed. It is equally clear that these issues require significantly more attention than at first meets the eye. Vast amounts of the general discussion, and what has passed as "research" previously, is in fact superficial and without any research foundation or research validation.

It will be evident from reading this work that our research, use of language and our research effort each require a new level of detail, as compared with the discussion heretofore.

It is important to point out that in addressing the TCB research challenges and in developing TCB effects research studies, we often need a level of sophistication which can only be obtained through cross disciplinary research. The research questions and the research tasks demand this. While parts of the current research may well be novel recommending interdisciplinary research, is not unique.[1]

Various legal and interdisciplinary research is recommended by the author. One of these areas relates to in-court distraction effects research in relation to the courtroom participants in court, caused by the television cameras in court. The author proposes for the first time that eye tracking technology be used for effects research of the distraction effects on courtroom participants.

The starting point is to begin the scoping and parameter setting.

There are many types of courts, as well as many different types of television programmes. Equally, there are many different styles of presentation, filming and editing which focus on law and the courts. Beyond the courtroom, there are many different ways to view courtroom broadcasting footage and many different types of viewing audience. The boundaries of courtroom broadcasting are wide. Arguably the boundaries are still expanding. This is the context of this work in relation to television courtroom broadcasting (TCB)[2] effects research issues.

Before we begin, however, some scoping of the parameters of this work is necessary. The overall topic of courtroom broadcasting is extensive and emotive. This work cannot cover all aspects of all courtroom broadcasting. It is, therefore, necessary to confine it. This work is confined to one aspect of *television* courtroom broadcasting, namely, the effects research and in particular the empirical effects research. It is also necessary to set out what aspects will and will not be covered.

Focusing on the general issues or on the arguments to any significant extent, would take the present work in a different direction than the research effects focus.

SCOPE EXCLUSIONS

At a headline level, this work focuses on one aspect of *television* courtroom broadcasting, namely, the effects *research* issues.

Therefore, the book is not about the general topic of courtroom broadcasting, which implies all courtroom broadcasting. It will not summarise the extensive and varied literature about courtroom broadcasting. There is already an extensive general literature available elesewhere.[3]

Court proceedings can be broadcast on radio, both live and recorded. Radio courtroom broadcasting, while interesting and deserving of research, is excluded from this work.[4] There also appears to have been no research focus on the effects of radio courtroom broadcasting. This particular form is arguably complicated by "real" radio courtroom broadcasting of court proceedings, as opposed to real participants/actors reading from a transcript of the actual proceedings. Radio courtroom broadcasting would also appear to be less popular or frequent than television courtroom broadcasting. This also limits, to some extent, the scope for radio effects research. There is simply less radio courtroom broadcasts to examine. Therefore, radio courtroom broadcasting is excluded from the scope of this work. Arguably, however, the topic of television courtroom broadcasting deserves greater definition and research.

Court proceedings can be broadcast on the internet, which has occurred in some limited instances. Again, this can be live or recorded. The task of covering internet courtroom broadcasting is beyond the scope of this work. In addition, the instances of internet courtroom broadcasting are relatively limited. The author is also unaware of any research into the effects of internet courtroom broadcasting, which reduces the scope for analysis. Therefore, internet courtroom broadcasting is excluded from the scope of this work. However, this is an area which deserves to be defined and researched in future. Internet courtroom broadcasting can be referred to as ICB or iCB. It is also important to appreciate that this can also be described and differentiated from television courtroom broadcasting (TCB) as it can be a "pull" facility. The public audience can search and look up whatever ICB they wish (so long as it is uploaded to the internet by, for example, the court service). It is more "user" friendly than TCB which is "pushed" by television broadcasters to the pre-selected audience(s) or pre-selected audience scheduling slots.

It also appears that the first courtroom footage was shown in movie theatres. This is now more or less historic only. There does not appear to be any definitions or effects research in relation to such broadcasting.

Courtrooms can also be broadcast or relayed on closed circuit television to predefined locations, such as other rooms, courts or buildings. Examples include, relay to larger spillover areas to accommodate additional physical attendees or relays to other courthouses. Technically this is television filming and coverage. However, this is relayed, and is not generally (push) broadcast. It is also closed and limited to viewing at fixed predefined locations only. Such filming or relaying is not publically broadcast. It is not "pushed" or made available to a general public television viewing audience.[5] There is very little general literature on relayed or closed circuit television courtroom broadcasting. The author has found no research on relayed or closed television courtroom broadcasting effects. It occurs significantly less frequently than public push television courtroom broadcasting. This work, therefore, does not cover relayed or closed circuit courtroom broadcasting.[6]

Courtroom cases are, on occasion, recorded and made available, generally for purchase, on electronic recording media (e.g. videos, tapes, CDs and DVDs). However, the effects of these do not appear to have been researched or analysed. It does feature on occasion in the educational arguments for permitting courtroom broadcasting. However, recording media issues are beyond the scope of this work. Most of the discussion and effects research (where it exists) relates almost entirely to push television courtroom broadcasting. It is further justified by the fact that television courtroom broadcasting is more frequent than other forms of courtroom broadcasting. There is equally a greater general literature available relating to television courtroom broadcasting. However, this issue is deserving of definition and research in future.

This work, by necessity, also excludes the recent advent of juryroom courtroom broadcasting. This is a very recent activity. There does not appear to be a significant literature yet available and the author is unaware of any significant effects research focus on juryroom courtroom broadcasting.[7] It is also questionable whether this form of courtroom broadcasting will extend beyond the US. Indeed, it is questionable whether it will ever become popular across US states. It is, therefore, beyond the scope of the current work. Again, it is deserving of definition and research in future.

Court activity can also be captured via still camera photography. These pictures can feature in television courtroom broadcasting or publication in newspapers, magazines and journals. Such instances may be infrequent. There appears little, if any, dedicated literature to such photography, nor its effects. Still photography is outside the scope of this work. However, it deserves to be defined and researched in future.

This work also excludes courtroom filming for purposes other than contemporaneous push television broadcast. This would exclude, for example, reconstruction or dramatised reconstruction of courtroom proceedings for contemporary television broadcast. This could occur, for example, in a celebrity trial if television cameras were not permitted into the actual courtroom. Again, this area is lacking definition and research as of yet.

Courtroom cases can also be filmed for historical, archival and record purposes. It is not intended for contemporaneous broadcast to the public. Such courtroom filming is not within the focus of this work. Such activities do not appear to be defined or researched thus far.

Some television courtroom broadcasting uses television cameras that belong to the television station (or producer). In other instances, the cameras belong to the state, court or court service. The general literature, and effects research, does not adequately address nor differentiate these distinctions as of yet. This is not addressed as a stand alone issue as it is beyond the scope of the present work. However, it is deserving of definition and research in future.

While I shall refer occasionally to the position elsewhere in terms of what (if any) television courtroom broadcasting is permitted, such a cross jurisdictional review of TCB law and practice is not the purpose of, nor within the scope of, this work.

Therefore, the following are not covered within the scope of this work, namely,

- Courtroom broadcasting (CB) generally;
- History of television courtroom broadcasting (TCB);
- General literature on television courtroom broadcasting;
- General television courtroom broadcasting arguments (legal or otherwise);
- Movie theatre courtroom broadcasting;
- Radio courtroom broadcasting (RCB);
- Internet courtroom broadcasting (ICB or iCB);
- Closed circuit courtroom broadcasting (CCB);
- The relay of courtroom broadcasting footage other than through a pushed television broadcast to the public (RYCB);
- The distribution and use of courtroom broadcasting footage on CD, DVD or other electronic media recording or storage devices (recording media courtroom broadcasting (MCB));
- Still photography of courtroom proceedings (PCB);
- Juryroom (television) courtroom broadcasting (JCB);
- Television courtroom broadcasting for archival or record keeping purposes (record keeping television courtroom broadcasting (ACB).

Some of these can be considered as distinct forms of courtroom broadcasting. This is the first occasion where such forms are differentiated and identified in the literature, at least as far as the author can identify. These need to be properly defined and researched for all courtroom broadcasting discussion and research in future. The lack of definitions to date is unfortunate, if not remiss.

This work is not about the history of the general topic of courtroom broadcasting (TCB). This has been summarised elsewhere already, particularly in the US.[8] It will instead focus on effects research issues with *television* courtroom broadcasting. It also advocates that significant television courtroom broadcasting definition and research be undertaken to address the effects research gaps and challenges.

Neither is this work about the various arguments of proponents and opponents of television courtroom broadcasting (whether legal, constitutional[9] or otherwise). It does not examine or assess the various television courtroom broadcasting arguments. To the extent that these shall be referred to, it is only to highlight the lack of television courtroom broadcasting definition, research and validation of any of the arguments, for or against, television courtroom broadcasting. The arguments continue to be strongly ventilated. That the arguments continue, suggests that no conclusions have yet been reached.

There are significant amounts of commentary in relation to (television) courtroom broadcasting. While this is much wider and more divergent from the focus of this work, it is worth mentioning at least in passing. Some of the literature[10] relates to general commentary, historical issues, description, (briefly) comparative, significantly argumentative (in terms of advocating or arguing for or against courtroom broadcasting, or some type of courtroom broadcasting), referring to specific cases or applications, particular courtroom participants, rights, media rights/right of access, defendant or party issues, rules, regulations and exceptions, facilitation or adaptation for courtroom broadcasting, or referring to peripheral but related issues. It is surprising how little definition and empirical effects research appears in the general literature. Media reporting issues are also beyond the focus of this work, as are the media arguments specific to TCB.[11] While referred to, the different forms of media and television reporting are not the core or specific focus of this work.[12] Generally, contempt of court issues are beyond the scope of this work.[13] General media effects, other than in relation to TCB, are not the main focus of the work.[14] The general issues in relation to pre-trial publicity are also outside the focus of this work.[15] There is also a general commentary in relation to the images and portrayal of law.[16] While crossing with the current work, it is not the main focus. Legal documentaries and reconstructions are also beyond the core focus of the present work.[17] None of the general literature thus referred to, refers to television courtroom broadcasting (TCB) or the definitions or forms of courtroom broadcasting. None of it refers to empirical research. However, there is some discussion and argument in relation to general effect issues.[18] While referred to in various instances, this work is not about the advantages and disadvantages of courtroom broadcasting, nor of television courtroom broadcasting per se.[19]

NEW/EXPANDED TCB

The idea of opening up courtrooms to television courtroom broadcasting is certainly one which interests lawyers, broadcasters and the public in general. Television courtroom broadcasting arguments receive particular media attention at times of celebrity trials.[20] The Simpson[21] (criminal) case is a particular example. It is arguably unfortunate that examples of popular[22] and or celebrity television courtroom broadcasting, often accused of being "voyeuristic entertainment,"[23] come to represent television courtroom broadcasting generally.

Should television courtroom broadcasting be permitted outside of the US, in federal courts, the Supreme Court? The arguments, whether for and against, occur in many jurisdictions. Examples of the arguments include that television courtroom broadcasting will be educational (or not) or that television courtroom broadcasting will/will not adversely effect the courtroom participants (often referred to in the general literature as "courtroom actors") e.g. distraction. However, have the arguments been properly defined, researched and proven? Are there educative effects? Are there distraction effects? Has the research proven any of these effects? This work answers the later question in the negative. There are too many, flaws, gaps and challenges. Significantly, we have too few definitions. The author proposes the first considered definition of television courtroom broadcasting (TCB).

NO SIDE ADOPTED

It is important to point out also that, this work does not seek to advocate the acceptance or rejection of television courtroom broadcasting *per se*. No particular view or argument on either side of the debate is adopted.

WHAT IS TELEVISION COURTROOM BROADCASTING?: SCOPE AND DEFINITION

What is courtroom broadcasting? "Courtroom broadcasting" is not properly defined in the literature. What is television courtroom broadcasting? This is a lack of definition in the literature. However, this work will seek to describe and define at least generally, what is meant by "*television* courtroom broadcasting" in the context of legal and judicial proceedings. This assists in further scoping what is and is not covered by television courtroom broadcasting, and indeed the focus of this work. It is also necessary to encapsulate such definitions in order to clarify the research effort, the research challenges, and ultimately the wider discussion and debate in future.

This work is limited to the author's definition of TCB: *television courtroom broadcasting is television cameras in the courtroom, filming courtroom proceedings for live and or contemporaneous television push broadcast to the general public.* This definition excludes relayed or closed circuit television courtroom broadcasting (in other courts or similar locations). It also excludes radio, pull internet, recording media, juryroom, still photography and archival recording courtroom broadcasting. The term *television courtroom broadcasting*, is therefore used throughout in relation to this effects research work (and the abbreviation TCB).

Defining courtroom broadcasting should the starting point to effects research. It is then necessary to scope and define the baselines and parameters of television courtroom broadcasting so that the effects research challenges may be addressed. For example, only proper definitions, baselines and parameters allow us to isolate a particular effect issue to be researched. The author will refer, *inter alia*, to one effect issue specifically, namely distraction or distraction of the participants in court (courtroom participants) from the television cameras in the courtroom. This is part of the Supreme Court effects research challenge, namely, detailing important issues such as scoping distraction effects, baselines and location issues, and to suggesting a specific solution to undertaking particular distraction effects research. The author recommends, for the first time, that eye tracking technology be used to conduct effects research experiments to measure eye focus and in-court distraction effects. Furthermore, the author undertakes research which incorporates a successful proof of concept demonstration of eye tracking technology in an actual criminal courtroom (in Ireland). This demonstrates that eye tracking can be used to research, measure and record TCB distraction effects on courtroom participants in the courtroom. The insight of the author in making this recommendation, and furthermore in carrying out the successful proof of concept demonstration are both original. (See chapters 12 and 17). The obvious consequence of the author's research is to now proceed to research, develop and undertake a series of eye tracking experiments in relation to TCB distraction effects issues. A significant research effort, as well as funding, will be required.

This aspect of the research is therefore significant internationally.

SCOPE: GENERAL

"Courtroom broadcasting" is generally not defined in the literature. Hence, television courtroom broadcasting and other forms of courtroom broadcasting are not defined either. This is the first research identified, which defines its scope in terms of one form of courtroom broadcasting over others, and which then seeks to examine a specific aspect (namely, effects research challenges) in relation to that specific form of courtroom broadcasting. The focus of this work is the television courtroom broadcasting form. Specifically, this work examines the effects research challenges of the television courtroom broadcasting form, and how we might address (some of) the effects research challenges.

It is argued that there is no sufficient body of empirical effects research of television courtroom broadcasting, nor of television courtroom broadcasting arguments, sufficient to answer the arguments. First, there is not enough research *per se*. Secondly, any research to date is either limited, flawed or unverified.[24] None of the arguments are sufficiently defined, established or verified, whether generally or empirically.

The television courtroom broadcasting arguments are also generally presumptive. One example, is the presumption that television courtroom broadcasting will be educational. This has not been properly defined or researched. It has not yet been proven to be correct. (Chapters 14 and 15 explore the educational issues).

There is no proper evidence of positive or negative effects because we have not properly defined such effects nor researched for such effects. No body of replicated research has properly set out any particular effect it is seeking to investigate in relation to any particular form of courtroom broadcasting. It is difficult, therefore, to arrive at properly valid, and generalisable, research conclusions. There is a general absence of research which has been subsequently replicated and verified.

It follows that there can be a critique of the naive view that any one of the arguments in favour of, or against, television courtroom broadcasting is correct or (more) legitimate (than others). In fact, both sides in this debate are naive in assuming that they have sufficiently defined, examined, researched and verified their own arguments in any properly considered manner. No body of research currently validates any of the arguments whatsoever.

The varied and diverse issues which are involved in television courtroom broadcasting have received less than considered analysis. The different forms of courtroom broadcasting, and television courtroom broadcasting, have not been defined. The author's definition (above) is the first properly considered definition. Effects are generally not defined. The overall body of effects research into television courtroom broadcasting is surprisingly small. This work reviews and critiques the research, and indeed lack of defined research. It focuses on some of the challenges and the pertinent alternative avenues for future research into television courtroom broadcasting effects.

The sophistication of research needs to develop. In addition, all research going forward needs to define and identify which television courtroom broadcasting form, and sub-form, it is investigating, and for which issue or effect. There is a requirement for an overall map of courtroom broadcasting forms.

This work highlights some of the main challenges involved in advancing proper television courtroom broadcasting research generally, and some of the particular avenues available for particular future television courtroom broadcasting research. An example is distraction effects of in-court television courtroom broadcasting distraction. One of the most obvious avenues for effects research in relation to television courtroom broadcasting is through psychology research. A cursory review of the eyewitness identification perception literature[25] (in psychology), indicates how much we have yet to define and investigate in terms of courtroom actor effects. This points the way for much of the future television courtroom broadcasting research. The author proposes for the first time, definitions and form categories for television courtroom broadcasting. The Supreme Court research challenge (see below) is also identified for the first time. This sets the scene for the research that needs to be undertaken. The author also identifies for the first time how eye tracking technology can be applied to the Supreme Court research challenge, in particular, distraction effects. Eye tracking is already used in many fields, including, internet, advertising, marketing, security, psychology, communications, aircraft design, vehicles, etc. The author shows that eye tracking also points the way for much future research of TCB effects. It is noted that the Supreme Court was not, and is still not, aware of eye tracking. Eye tracking research of TCB will also go beyond the expectations of the Supreme Court judges when they said that certain effects may be beyond properly measurable effects investigation. We can now track, record and measure actual distraction effects in relation to television cameras in courts. The author also disagrees with suggestions that the in-court effects discussion is effectively over.[26] It is far from over. In addition, we are now able to properly address the distraction effects challenge with comparative research fields and comparative research tools, one example being eye tracking technology (see below).

FORMS OF COURTROOM BROADCASTING

It is important that future research addresses the absence of an overall map or matrix of (television) courtroom broadcasting to date. Future research needs to be located on such a map. Research must start from such a definitional map of television courtroom broadcasting (see Chapter 6). The map allows research to identify which particular form of courtroom broadcasting is being researched in any given instance. Within the particular form in question, we can then identify which particular effect we are researching within that form. For example, we could examine and research educational effects of the radio courtroom broadcasting (RCB) form and the educational effects of the television courtroom broadcasting (TCB) form, and then compare them. Such a global map also assists our formation of definitions.

No discussion or argument can be sufficiently considered, or compared, unless it identifies the television courtroom broadcasting form (and or subform) to which it relates. Are trial cases different from appeal cases? Are criminal cases different from civil cases? Does showing brief snippets differ from showing extended coverage? Significant research challenges remain to be addressed.

If we are considering effects on courtroom participants, we must say which actor is being investigated, and how. It is important to say what camera types are involved, where the camera is located, etc. (This also ties in with eye tracking distraction research). Even a brief review of the literature to date, indicates that even some of these simple points on the map of television courtroom broadcasting are absent. This is unfortunate. The implication is that much of the research to date is fundamentally flawed. It is incomplete. We do not know where on the map such research is. We realise also that particularly relevant factors have not been gauged, coded and incorporated into particular research studies. It also means the replication of such research is not possible. A map of courtroom broadcasting clarifies our understanding of the research issues. We can also gauge its quality.

The debate and research to date is so basic and limited (in definitions, methods and in what is ignored), that no firm conclusions whatsoever can be drawn. This is the first research that the author is aware of which seeks to identify and map the different *forms of* television courtroom broadcasting. Future discussion, and research, needs to appreciate and address the different forms of courtroom broadcasting. Equally, no argument in future, whether in favour of television courtroom broadcasting or against television courtroom broadcasting, can be considered to have merit without addressing and defining the different courtroom broadcasting forms. Current TCB research is limited in focus, technique and methodology. Comparisons to other research fields indicate how basic the television courtroom broadcasting research has been to date — if and where it exists.

Many people are already aware of most of the headline general television courtroom broadcasting arguments, and equally some of the Constitutional legal "rights" issues. No one, however, is able to say how, why or which of any of the respective arguments have been substantiated and validated. In fact, none have been validated. Many people would have difficulty defining and differentiating different forms of television courtroom broadcasting.

For example, take the proposition that (all[27]) television courtroom broadcasting will educate. How will it educate? Why will it educate? Who will it educate? What forms will educate? What forms educate best? How do we know some, or any, of them will educate? What amount (or standard) of educative value is required for television courtroom broadcasting to be legitimised as being educational, or alternatively for any of the countervailing arguments to be outweighed? Frequently, complex and competing legal and constitutional rights must be weighed and balanced against each other. How do we define "education" and measure "educational TCB"?

SUB-FORMS OF TELEVISION COURTROOM BROADCASTING

All research, and all arguments, need to identify which form of (television) courtroom broadcasting it relates too. After that, the research should identify if it relates to criminal or civil cases, appeal or trial cases. These could be considered as sub–forms of courtroom broadcasting. There are many other sub–forms. Greater granularity of the issues is needed. Without this, the research is much too wide and general. This is particularly so with the definition and research of effects on those inside the courtroom. This is referred to as in-court effects research.

OUT-OF-COURT EFFECTS RESEARCH

If we want a full discussion on the many issues and complexities of television courtroom broadcasting, we also need to move outside of the courtroom — and bring a robust research focus with us. There has been no proper body of research into effects on the viewing (and non viewing) public.[28] Out-of-court research also needs to be located on the map of courtroom broadcasting. This focuses on the actual courtroom broadcasting television audience, as well as the wider audience as may discuss and consider cases covered by television courtroom broadcasting. Why is this relevant? Consider, for example, what the public might learn from a televised celebrity murder case or from a televised commercial law case or from an environmental law case. Are they equal? Is the audience equally educated? No courtroom broadcasting argument has sought to distinguish the types of cases and legal issues which occur. This work critiques the research to date, and indeed the lack of research, and proposes how we may begin to bridge the research gaps and challenges with, for example, definitions, eye tracking and a first map of the forms of television courtroom broadcasting.

COMPARISONS AND TOOLS

Our definitions and research methods for researching the effects of television courtroom broadcasting need to draw on wider research disciplines and methods. Subjects at law schools also indicate that there are ample avenues to begin comprehensive research of television courtroom broadcasting, particularly the effects. Criminology and legal-psychology are just two examples of cross disciplinary research subjects. We cannot limit ourselves solely to narrow legal pigeon holes, such as a non-specific general legal literature, legal constitutional literature, legal contempt principles, etc., when considering TCB. We need to broaden our horizons and embrace cross disciplinary research opportunities.

The book relies heavily on existing legal-psychology research into crimes, witnesses and eyewitness identification to show how existing research and research tools in these areas can also aid television courtroom broadcasting research. This work also argues that research into the effects of television courtroom broadcasting, should adapt the research, and methodologies, of eyewitness identification research. This work also advocates communications and media research, and research tools, for television courtroom broadcasting research.[29]

Critically, television courtroom broadcasting arguments lack credibility, sophistication, and substance, because they lack definition, empirical research, validation and ignore the forms and sub-forms categories. The various arguments also ignore pertinent and relevant research and research tools from established comparative research.

We need to rely more heavily on social science and empirical research if we are to address the Supreme Court challenge. Let us not forget that this is not just an issue of concern for the US. It interests us all.

OPINIONS AND SELF REPORTS

Most of the research to date is general (non-empirical) subjective research. It almost solely asks a few courtroom participants how they subjectively feel. To rely on questionnaires and self reports (i.e. asking a person if they have been affected by in-court cameras) as the sole indicator of whether there are effects or not, is wholly inadequate. Unfortunately, too much of the current research relies on own self reports of effects upon oneself, and opinion self reports of perceived effects on other courtroom participants.

While television courtroom broadcasting has existed in certain jurisdictions[30] for some time, the amount of research is diminutive. Few studies of television courtroom broadcasting have been willing to go beyond the limited scope of opinion surveys. These studies have been described by one commentator as "qualitatively inadequate."[31] It is hoped and suggested that a wider range of research, and with wider comparative research tools and comparators, will be used in future in an effort to better consider the full implications of television courtroom broadcasting for the legal justice system, the public, and to also address the Supreme Court challenge. This work criticises television courtroom broadcasting arguments, on both sides, in that they are not adequately empirically researched or validated. Wider research possibilities are available – but ignored thus far. Some, as is the case of eye tracking, are only now identified for the first time.

All of this is significant. It goes beyond the mere "self report" personal views of certain courtroom participants in relation to themselves. They are asked questions on whether they feel that they have been affected by television courtroom broadcasting. These opinion surveys are on their own limited and unreliable. Thus far, most television courtroom broadcasting effects research is almost solely confined to these limited self reports of certain individuals in the court process.[32]

Only certain people are asked and not across all categories of persons in court. The study population is statistically limited. The quality of the questions vary from study to study. Typically the self report studies are not repeated and or replicated. They are, therefore, not validated by peer research. Typically the public in court are not asked. In effect, therefore, it appears that all of the courtroom participants who give self reports are professionally trained or experienced. Defendants are typically not asked to undertake self report research studies).

Also, such studies generally appear not to be drafted by the persons most qualified to draft such research and or appreciate the issues involved, nor the ample additional research fields and techniques available for television courtroom broadcasting research. Judges and court personnel (alone) are also arguably not the best qualified to conduct this research, as appears to occur in many instances.

A BRIEF HISTORY OF COURTROOM BROADCASTING AND RESEARCH

While focusing on the effects research of television courtroom broadcasting, some reference to the origins of courtroom broadcasting is necessary. Television was first demonstrated in 1928.[33] The first reported television courtroom broadcast occurred in Oklahoma in 1953, where a camera was placed in a special booth[34] at the back of the courtroom.[35] Courtroom footage was previously filmed and then shown in cinemas.[36] Television courtroom broadcasting continues to be debated,[37] and is still a "controversial and dividing issue,"[38] even in the US. The arguments in relation to effects are still "ongoing."[39] These debates are enhanced during the latest celebrity trials, such as Simpson, Kennedy Smith, Menendez, Woodward, Jackson, Dr Murray, etc. Most televised cases in the US are under local state rules, not national or federal rules. Indeed, a pilot scheme undertaken in federal courts was discontinued,[40] as was a pilot scheme in New York.[41]

Despite the longstanding debates, there is still no conclusion to the effects-debates, be it in the US or elsewhere. The substantial point in terms of this work, is that there is no substantive and sufficiently detailed definitions and or body of research to decide any of the effects-debates.[42]

No body of research examines audience effects. This is the out-of-court effects arena. We need many more studies to research the impact of television courtroom broadcasting content and forms. The only specific empirical audience effects research appears to be Anna R Paddon and in part the first federal pilot experiment, the New York study and the New Zealand study.[43]

In terms of many aspects of television courtroom broadcasting, there is no research at all. We will see some of the gaps below. The creation of an overall map of courtroom broadcasting will assist us in revealing (some of) the gaps in research.

Large amounts of "research" of television courtroom broadcasting must be discounted. This includes much of the general effects research. There are various reasons, some being that the research source appears no longer available; it does not record any statistics or sources whatsoever; it does not define its method or methodology of investigation – or such methodology is faulty or unsound; there is no link between the investigation and the conclusions suggested; many rely solely on self report questions. The latter ask individuals if they themselves were affected. In terms of relying on self reports, and self report conclusions, this cannot be strongly relied upon and is often criticised. While self reports of observations of others is worth undertaking (if undertaken and recorded properly), again sole or overreliance on third party self reports is suspect. Unfortunately, significant amounts of what is purported as "research" of effects cannot be relied upon. One of the challenges is to overcome this problem. Eye tracking (see below) provides one of the solutions.

What research is left is diminutive in comparison to: the issues at stake, the importance of the effects debates over the decades, and in comparison to the length of time that forms of television courtroom broadcasting have been around, (albeit without definition until now). The research is surprisingly small. In terms of empirical research there are just over twenty studies since 1953. The Supreme Court challenge to carry out empirical research remains.

It is important to distinguish types of research into television courtroom broadcasting effects. One can have generally court administered in-court surveys of effects, which are designed, recorded and reported on, to varying degrees of sophistication. Some of these are self reports and third party self reports. In addition, or alternatively, one can have scientifically or social science designed and recorded research of, specifically identified effect issues. These latter studies are typically the most rigorous and more considered of effects research studies. Unfortunately, these type of effects research studies are the ones least frequently undertaken. For example, there are few scientific or social science research studies into television courtroom broadcasting effects. The volume of empirical research needs to be vastly increased.

That is not the whole research picture however. The bigger picture is that vast areas of television courtroom broadcasting and effects issues have not yet been defined and researched. A small number of previous commentators have from time to time suggested an effect research issue to be researched, or a set of research issues to be researched. Only rarely have they sought to undertake that research. This is partly understandable as such research can be complex, time consuming, expensive and cannot be undertaken individually or with only a small number of people. It is important to point out also that the research expertise may not rest with one individual or one school of research expertise. The best research will be cross disciplinary. However, only with proper definitions and a global TCB map or matrix can we begin to contemplate all of the research effects gap and challenges.

One of the main points this work identifies for the first time, is that we must begin our research study from definitions and a holistic map of the court process and the television courtroom broadcasting process. We must do this in order to identify all of the areas and issues within those areas which need to be researched for effects and other issues. Only by looking at the whole map can we start to see what particular issues and what particular areas have been researched to date. By doing this we then see how many areas have not been defined and have not been researched. We see how many studies, research a particular issue and can try to compare these; try to verify these; and seek to replicate and validate these studies. No official or officially supported studies have been identified which seek to replicate and or validate any specific previous research.

By mapping the issues and the research effort to date, we can also see what complimentary research and research methods from other disciplines can be applied to the television courtroom broadcasting research challenges. When we do this we start to see where existing research can be complimentary to the challenges, as well as see comparative research tools which can also be adapted or applied.

It is, therefore, possible to say that in many areas there is no body of television courtroom broadcasting research. In the areas where there is research, it is still very limited. A further point is that the research effort does not seek to map the tapestry of courtroom broadcasting. It does not distinguish or define the different types of (television) courtroom broadcasting. The research effort does not focus on the potential different effects of different forms of courtroom broadcasting and television courtroom broadcasting.

The general or non-social science research is almost random and ad hoc. It is often very basic and simplistic in methodology. It does not consider in advance what effect is being examined nor how best to examine that effect. It is not carried out to a standard which might be replicated or validated by further studies. As this present work continues, the focus is increasingly the empirical and social science research issues (as opposed to the general research).

EDUCATION

There is frequent reference to (and belief in) the educational effect of television courtroom broadcasting. However, there is no indication of what is meant by "education," "educational" and the "message" conveyed via television courtroom broadcasting. For example, is the aim to educate the public on the details (or result)(or arguments) of a specific case or is it to educate generally? If the later, what general principles, issues, etc., is it aiming to impart? Is the educational effect to be one of civic information? Is the message that offenders will be pursued and prosecuted (deterrence)? Is the message that we respect the rights of victims?[44] Is the aim to help inform citizens as to what they will face, or may see, should they ever be in court? (somewhat like a user's manual approach). Is it to legitimise the court system? (For example, do (new) international tribunals[45] feel a (greater) need to publicise and legitimise themselves? Do they feel a need to court publicity?). Equally, how does existing educational and communications research impact upon or change the argument that television courtroom broadcasting will be/is educational? Unpicking the different strands of the educational effect(s) issues is not just useful, but is a necessity if we are to properly understand television courtroom broadcasting (TCB) issues.

THE RESEARCH AND ARGUMENTS INTERFACE

Without proper and adequate definition and research into television courtroom broadcasting, it is not possible to enter a fully informed debate of the advantages, disadvantages, policy, legal issues and the constitutional "rights" principles.

The basic headline arguments, on both sides, are naive because they have not incorporated proper and full definition and research. For example, they do not consider the different forms of television courtroom broadcasting. (See Chapter 6).

This work suggests significant amounts of research needs to be undertaken to *begin* a serious consideration of this important topic. Without such research, neither side in the debate can claim justification. Even this dichotomy is over-simplistic.

Yet, there are many opportunities available for such investigation, and which are evident in various other research fields, such as law-psychology, media, communications, social scientific research, and eye tracking.

We can only truly appreciate the overarching legal and constitutional principles once we have asked much more detailed questions. For example, what do courtroom broadcasting arguments past and present tell us about the justifications for and against television courtroom broadcasting? What television courtroom broadcasting arguments have been defined, validated, or indeed researched at all?

The Constitution provides fundamental principles, albeit headline principles. However, these are too general to be instantly applied (or relevant) in every instance. We must ask specific and detailed questions in addition to looking at such headline guiding principles when considering (a) whether television courtroom broadcasting can or should be permitted, (b) under what circumstances and in what situations, (c) under what conditions, rules, procedures and or regulations, and (d) in relation to which television courtroom broadcasting form(s).

If it is shown that there are different forms of television courtroom broadcasting (and or different effects for each, and or more/less enhanced effects), we see that the headline policy, legal and constitutional principles are better informed and the legal debate changes. The rights arguments may have to be recalibrated. We are no longer looking at a provision of the Constitution[46] in isolation. For example, would a publicity rule based on publicity and volume of audience carry a different weight than a publicity rule based on the quality of the form, content or audience? It also differs in respect of whether we are talking about so called media publicity-rule rights or public-rights. Is it the case that *any* television courtroom broadcasting audience is good and the bigger the audience better?

FORMS OF TELEVISION COURTROOM BROADCASTING

This work shows that there are indeed numerous different forms of television courtroom broadcasting.[47] Despite these various forms, there has been no definition, differentiation or investigation of these forms thus far. This work contributes the first explicit categorisation of the television courtroom broadcasting forms. The outcome of any legal and constitutional argument may well differ depending on what form or forms are being looked at. Equally, depending on research and analysis into the effects of television courtroom broadcasting, the policy, legal and constitutional argument/principle may also differ, as well as the result of such arguments. New effects research issues may arise, depending on the television courtroom broadcasting form being instantly examined.

This work shows that there are indeed different television courtroom broadcasting forms. Each of the different arguments proposed, for and against, in relation to television courtroom broadcasting are affected by the type and form being discussed. Depending on the form, particular arguments can become stronger or weaker. It is over-simplistic in the extreme to suggest that all arguments can apply equally to all forms of television courtroom broadcasting. This is one of the major flaws with the television courtroom broadcasting discussion, and arguments, to date. It is surprising that nobody has ever sought to make this categorisation before.

The author's forms categorisation is not complete. It is a beginning. However, even this initial forms categorisation highlights the fact that not all television courtroom broadcasting is the same and therefore by logical assumption, not all television courtroom broadcasting arguments (whether for or against) apply equally to every form. It is wrong to generalise all issues and effects equally to every form.

For example, some forms will lend themselves more to being educational and others will not.[48] It is possible to carry out research to identify which are more educational – and critically why. This knowledge should feed into and enhance the level of debate and (political and judicial) policy making in relation to decisions regarding *permissible* television courtroom broadcasting and *permissible* television courtroom broadcasting forms (if so permitted).

There is no overall definitions and categorisation of courtroom broadcasting. Neither is there any overall definitions and categorisation of different television courtroom broadcasting forms. Within television courtroom broadcasting itself, there is no identification of the many issues which impact upon and help to decide which particular form of television courtroom broadcasting applies. These are discussed below. The issues include the following, namely, who grants permission?, is an application required?, who makes the application?, to whom?, what (formal) controls or rules apply?, what in particular can be filmed by the cameras?, type of programming?, who makes the recording?, what type of camera(s) and location?, which media categories apply?, etc.

There has equally been no proper body of empirical research and examination of the effects of television courtroom broadcasting, and television courtroom broadcasting forms, on the courtroom case participants and public participants.

Television courtroom broadcasting has always been a contentious and emotive subject. There are many arguments, advanced by either side. It is not necessary in this work to report all of the arguments and the related literature, which is significant, but some of these arguments are briefly categorised and summarised in the Appendices.[49] It is noteworthy that debates seldom refers to the research studies undertaken, nor those which should be undertaken. Definitions are equally lacking but deserving of research.

NEED FOR RESEARCH

The question of whether television courtroom broadcasting should be permitted cannot yet be answered. We do not know the effects. We cannot know. There is no sufficient body of empirical research or validation. Of course there are many arguments in favour, and equally against, television courtroom broadcasting — but the central point is that too many gaps and challenges remain.

Why can we say this? We can say this because none of the proponents, for or against, substantiate their arguments with a body of research — in particular forms and effects research. None of the arguments are demonstrably verified. Neither is there any replication research, whether by repeat studies or third party studies. Again, this work suggests that eye tracking, eyewitness identification studies, and media and communications studies, pave the way for effects research in relation to courtroom actor effects (*in-court* effects research).

Appreciating the form is crucial. Only by seeing and comparing television courtroom broadcasting systematically can we begin to fully appreciate all of the issues and arguments of television courtroom broadcasting. It is also the only way that we can properly begin effects research into television courtroom broadcasting and see the results of courtroom broadcasting. Only by beginning to consider an overall map for television courtroom broadcasting do new issues, not previously considered, come to light.

The rules relating to television courtroom broadcasting which already exist, suffer from the same flaws, namely, that they do not identify any particular form of television courtroom broadcasting and is thus flawed in scope. This is another area deserving of research.

Other than referring to the arguments vaguely, there is no systemised analysis or definition. To be effective, the research and definitions needs to be more precise and enumerated. None of the television courtroom broadcasting arguments really address the fact that there are different ways to film courtroom proceedings, that there are different ways to present and edit it and different ways to broadcast it to the public. The body of television courtroom broadcasting arguments has not addressed the different television courtroom broadcasting forms.

SUMMARY

This book proposes, for the first time, the important and significant question: what is television courtroom broadcasting? Only by answering this question; arriving at a definition of television courtroom broadcasting; and by defining and scoping its baselines and parameters, can we then proceed to address TCB effects research. Only by doing the foregoing, can we address the Supreme Court effects research challenge.

The research, therefore, proceeds with a definition for television courtroom broadcasting (TCB), which is new; identifying the Supreme Court challenge; identifying and categorising the television courtroom broadcasting forms; examining and suggesting valuable research avenues in relation to providing substance to those various arguments, in particular, distraction effects of eye tracking. The author also successfully undertook the world's first proof of concept demonstration of eye tracking technology for in-court distraction effects research caused by television cameras and or camera operators in the courtroom. The addition of eye tracking adds a significant new solution to the Supreme Court challenge.

NOTES

1. D.M. Kahan, D.A. Hoffman and D. Braman, Whose Eyes Are You Going to Believe? *Scott v Harris* and the Perils of Cognitive Illiberalism, Harvard Law Review 122 (2008–2009): 837–906. The research was funded by the National Science Foundation, and funds at Yale and Temple Universities.

2. The term television courtroom broadcasting and the abbreviation TCB will be used interchangeably throughout.

3. See generally S. Barber, News Cameras in the Courtroom: A Free Press – Fair Debate (Ablex: New York, 1987); W. Freedman, Press and Media Access to a Criminal Courtroom (New York: Quorum Books, 1988); D. Stepniak, Audio-Visual Coverage of Courts, (Cambridge: Cambridge University Press, 2008).

4. Note, however, experiments with digital recordings of cases in certain US federal courts. See, Project Expanded: More Courts Offering Digital Audio Recordings Online, US Courts, The Federal Judiciary, www.uscourts.gov/newsroom/2009/digitalAudio.cfm , accessed April 22, 2010.

5. "Push" means pushing or making media content available to the public viewing audience over a public television network. The content is pushed out to the public, in this case television courtroom footage pushed over publically available television network channels. This is to be differentiated from "pull" content which is more audience focused. With pull content the individual is more active and seeks and pulls the content they want, such as from the internet or mobile communications devices. The pull content is more relevant and interesting to the user. Telecommunications and broadcasting regulations generally focus on push content as opposed to pull content.

6. It is understood that certain criminal courts in the new criminal courts complex in Dublin, when facilitating jury selection, utilises closed circuit television cameras between the courtroom and the jury waiting room. While this would not initially appear to fall within the author's definition of TCB, it is a subject which may well be deserving of consideration.

7. However, see P.A. Joy and K.C. McMunigal, Clients, Lawyers, and the Media, Criminal Justice 19 (2004-2005): 77. A TV station also sought access to an execution, see D.J. DeBenedictis, Cameras Banned, Pens Allowed: San Francisco Judge Refuses TV Station's Request to Tape Inmate Execution, ABA Journal (August, 1991): 16.

8. See, for example, S. Barber, above; D. Stepniak, above.

9. Thaler also explicitly makes the distinction between constitutional and legal issues on the one hand, and the television and its psychological impact. See P. Thaler, The Impact of the Television Camera on Courtroom Participants: A Case Study of the Joel Stenberg Murder Trial (Ph.D diss., New York University, 1990): 5.

10. See Appendix 1 for a sample of this general literature.

11. Generally, see for example, R.D. Rotunda, Reporting Sensational Trials: Free Press, a Responsible Press, and Cameras in the Courts, Communications Law and Policy 3 (1998): 295–313.

12. Generally see, for example, C.A. Tuggle and S. Huffman, Live Reporting in Television News: Breaking News or Black Holes?, Journal of Broadcasting & Electronic Media 45 (2001): 335–344; J. Katz, What Makes Crime 'News'? Media Culture and Society 9 (1987): 47–75;

13. However, it is referred to briefly when discussing Irish sections subsequently.

14. See Appendices.

15. Ibid.

16. Ibid.

17. However, see D.M. Glatt, Trial by Docudrama: Fact or Fiction? Cardoza Arts and Entertainment Law Journal 9 (1990): 201-230; M. Reith, Viewing of Crime Drama and Authoritarian Aggression: An Investigation of the Relationship Between Crime Viewing, Fear, and Aggression, Journal of Broadcasting & Electronic Media 43 (1999): 211-—221.

18. See Appendices.

19. On that topic, note for example, D.F. O'Scannlain, Some Reflections on Cameras in the Appellate Courtroom, Journal of Appellate Practice and Process, (2007): 323–330;

20. Most of this media and public attention occurs in the US, partly due to the fact that many US states permit courtroom broadcasting.

21. The OJ Simpson (criminal) case where he was charged and acquitted of a double murder.

22. "Popular" is used in its media analysis context e.g. popular tabloid versus more considered broadsheet. Popular in effect means tabloid dumbed down for mass market. This is one element of the different forms of courtroom broadcasting.

23. P. Mason, Court on Camera: Electronic Broadcast Coverage of the Legal Proceedings, www.usfca.edu/pj/camera-mason.htm . Note also references in footnote 2. Accessed August 13, 2011.

24. See below.

25. See, for example, Chapters 8.

26. D. Stepniak, Audio-Visual Coverage of Courts (Cambridge: Cambridge University Press, 2008).

27. Most arguments in favour of courtroom broadcasting on educational grounds refer to courtroom broadcasting generally and ignore any reference to or considerations of the different forms and sub-forms of courtroom broadcasting.

28. There is only a limited number of stand alone studies.

29. See Chapters 5, 6 and 16.

30. Courtroom broadcasting has not occurred (apart from selective background shots) in Ireland albeit the Law Reform Commission briefly commented on the issue of courtroom broadcasting in its Report on Contempt of Court, (Dublin: Government Publications, 1994): 22–25. Kieron Wood has also called for court and tribunal broadcasting, see for example, Calls for Live TV of Tribunals, Sunday Business Post, April 30, 2000. Note also a paper presented by Mr. Justice Carney to Dublin University entitled "Restrictions on the Media Other Than Defamation," (date unavailable). See also, O.R. Goodenough, Retheorising Privacy and Publicity, Intellectual Property Quarterly 1 (1997): 37–70, at 39.

31. See D. Slater, and V.P. Hans, Methodological Issues in the Evaluation of 'Experiments' with Cameras in the Courts, Communications Quarterly, 30:4 (1982): 376–380. Indeed, this is part of the reason for the Supreme Court challenge. For a non TCB reference see A. Evans, Lawyers' Perceptions of Their Values: An Empirical Assessment of Monash University Graduates in Law, 1980–1998, Legal Education Review 12 (2001): 209–266. See also Chapters 5 – 7.

32. It is also particularly difficult to gauge one's own non verbal communications, as noted in T–R Valikoski, The Criminal Trial as a Speech Communication Situation (Tampere, Finland: University of Tampere, 2004), and references therein.

33. A. Durant and M. Lambrou, Language and Media (London: Routledge, 2009), 244.

34. Indeed, one of the criticisms when trying to distinguish one courtroom broadcast form from another, or trying to compare them, is that the rules and procedures which may be applied are ad hoc and not recorded (properly).

35. Referred to in S. Barber, above, 10. The first live broadcast was in 1955.

36. Cinema courtroom broadcasting would appear to be historic at this stage. It is also beyond the scope of the current work.

37. See, for example, recent application for permission to broadcast in the case of *Sony Warner, Atlantic, Arista and UMG*, Court of Appeals For the First Circuit, No. 09–1090, Amicus Brief, January 29, 2009, www.eff.org/files/filenode/inresonybmgetal/CVNMotionOralArgument.pdf . Accessed August 13, 2011.

38. P.E. Thaler, The Impact of the Television Camera on Courtroom Participants: A Case Study of the Joel Steinberg Murder Trial (Ph.D diss., New York University, 1990), 176.

39. R.E.R Stewart, above, 9.

40. See, for example, G. Comstock, *et al*, Television and Human Behaviour, (New York: Columbia University Press, 1978), as referred to in D. McQuail and S. Windahl, Communications Models: For the Study of Mass Communication (London: Longman, 1993), 67; D. Stepniak, above, 102. Note, however, that there is a recent proposal for a second federal pilot experiment. See Judiciary Approves Pilot Project for Cameras in District Court, www.uscourts.gov , accessed October 14, 2010.

41. See D. Stepniak, above, 102; also O'Brien et al, Chapter Eight: Cameras in the Courts, Media Law Handbook, available at www.isba.org/newscenter/medialawhandbook/CHAPTER%2008%20-%20Cameras%20in%20the%20Courtroom.pdf and also Lee, "Cameras in the Courtroom," First Amendment Centre, available at www.firstamendmentcenter.org/Press/topic.aspx?topic=cameras_courtroom , accessed September 11, 2010.

42. See Chapters 3, 4, 5 and 6.

43. This does not include rating penetration figures. A.R. Paddon, Television Coverage of Criminal Trials with Cameras and Microphones: A Laboratory Experiment of Audience Effects (Ph.D diss., University of Tennessee, Knoxville, 1985); Johnson, M.T., and Krafka, C., Pilot Program Involving Electronic Coverage in Six US District Courts and Two Appeal Courts, (Federal Judicial Centre) [in part only]; New York State Committee to Review Audio-Visual Coverage of Court Proceedings, An Open Courtroom: Cameras in New York Courts (New York: Fordham University Press, 1997) [in part only]; Kimberly Allan, Professor Judy McGregor and Susan Fountaine (Massey University), The Impact of Television, Radio and Still Photography Coverage of Court Proceedings, Final Report, A Report for the Department for Courts (April 1998)(New Zealand).

44. Note the current debates as to victim impact statements and also notification rights for victims. Also note P. Lambert, Time to Leave the Monkey Behind?: How Eye Tracking and Psychology Can Contribute to Television Courtroom Broadcasting Effects Research, British Psychological Society, BPS Cognitive Psychology Section, Annual Conference, 27th Annual Cognitive Psychology Section Conference, Cardiff University (September 6–8, 2010). Also P. Lambert, TCB Effects: Eye Tracking and Camera Distraction in Court, poster regarding the first in-court proof of concept demonstration of eye tracking technology for TCB effects research, at the Irish Association of Law Teachers, Annual Conference (November 26–28, 2010).

45. Genenrally see, K.N. Calvo–Goller, The Trial Proceedings of the International Criminal Court, ICTY and ICTR Precedents (Leiden: Martinus Nijhoff, 2006); M Cherif Bassiouni, The Legislative History of the International Criminal Court (New York: Transnational Publishers, 2005); B. Broomhall, International Justice and the International Criminal Court: Between Sovereignty and the Rule of Law (Oxford: OUP, 2003).

46. Generally, see for example, L. Tribe, American Constitutional Law (Foundation Press, 1999); G. Hogan and G. Whyte, JM Kelly: The Irish Constitution (Dublin: Lexis Nexis, Butterworths, 2003).

47. Indeed, there are different forms of courtroom broadcasting.

48. Note Chapters 3, 11 and 12.

49. Also see generally S. Barber, Press and Media Access to a Criminal Courtroom, above; W. Freedman (New York: Quorum Books, 1988); D. Stepniak, above.

Chapter Six

What Is *Television* Courtroom Broadcasting (TCB)?

INTRODUCTION

In order to consider the Supreme Court challenge, and then to research and address it, we need to define what television courtroom broadcasting actually is. As pointed out above, TCB is defined as television cameras in the courtroom, filming courtroom proceedings for live and or contemporaneous television push broadcast to the general public.

We then need to build on that definition. It is imperative that we separate and categorise the different types of television courtroom broadcasting. We must recognise that there are different forms of courtroom broadcasting (CB) and television courtroom broadcasting (TCB). Why is this relevant? It is important because there can be different effects from different forms of television courtroom broadcasting. Our research needs to be sophisticated enough to distinguish different issues, forms and effects of TCB.

When we identify and research a particular form or a particular effect, we need a similar pattern of analysis in each repeated study of that issue. This builds up our understanding of the general repeated effects; we can generalise. We need similar baselines, frames of definition, understanding and patterns of analysis to research each form and each effect. We need sophisticated levels of baseline research prior to television cameras being introduced, and then sophisticated research once television cameras are introduced.

What are the different forms, and sub–forms, of television courtroom broadcasting? What are the effects of television courtroom broadcasting? Are all forms and sub-forms of television courtroom broadcasting the same? If not, why not? Do different sub–forms of television courtroom broadcasting have different quality and content of information?

As it currently stands today, nobody has any proper understanding of television courtroom broadcasting effects — because there are no global definitions, so many gaps and challenges are not addressed, and there is no replication research. There were three Supreme Court camera cases, yet the issues and concerns are not properly researched as of yet.

This work identifies, and then categorises in the first overall matrix of the different television courtroom broadcasting forms. This appears to be the first time that such a forms matrix has been suggested.

The research needs to define and examine the different forms of television courtroom broadcasting. It should examine effects on the television courtroom actors or participants (*in–court effects*) for each of the different forms. Another set of effects-research should examine effects on the audience (or audiences) and the public (*out-of-court effects*). Strictly speaking, out-of-court effects can be wider than just the viewing audience for a particular case. This is another research gap.

Do different television courtroom broadcasting forms have different audience and or the public effects? Do different television courtroom broadcasting forms and sub–forms have different audiences? If there are different forms of television courtroom broadcasting, some being diverse, would any legal and constitutional arguments[1] in relation to the permissibility, or necessity, of television courtroom broadcasting differ according to each? If there are different effects of television courtroom broadcasting, then would legal and constitutional (and "rights") arguments also differ? If there are different forms (and this work shows there are), should proponents not be promoting particular television courtroom broadcasting forms over others?

Slotnick and Segal while calling for the televising of Supreme Court cases, caution that "this should be accomplished on a limited and experimental basis. There are many *ways*, of course, in which such a major change could be implemented."[2] This is because, as the author points out, there are different forms of television courtroom broadcasting.

NO GLOBAL PICTURE

Another overall flaw in existing research, and one which should be borne in mind particularly when television courtroom broadcasting may be permitted in new courts or new jurisdictions, is that there has been a small amount of research. The research is diminutive, flawed, limited, basic and at no stage seeks to outline a global picture of all of the potential issues and effects. Neither does it describe how each of these may be tested for, nor how to go about examining and researching challenges at a global level. That is not to suggest that each and every study has to examine and research all potential issues and effects. Equally, it would be foolish and blinkered to discontinue conducting (limited) courtroom actor self report effects type research. However, relying on such a limited approach alone in the future would be a serious mistake and would call into question the seriousness, if not the integrity, of those arguing in relation to television courtroom broadcasting access. Also generally ignored, is a focus on those permitting TCB, and the tasks of administering the daily procedure of TCB.

VALIDATION OF ARGUMENTS

Many of those who are proponents and opponents of television courtroom broadcasting state their arguments in favour or against in absolute terms e.g. it *will be* educational; it *will* enable democracy; it *will have* adverse effects on courtroom participants; it *will not* have adverse effects on courtroom participants; it *will* educate; it *will not* seek to educate, it *will only* seek to entertain or be an extra pictorial facility to pre-existing news programming forms; etc. All of these comments, and others, state that something definitive is the case or that something definitive will be the case.

No one states that it is their view that "if permitted television courtroom broadcasting may have the effect of 'X'" and that if permitted, they will seek to demonstrate this by adopting particular (recognised and tested) research methodologies to support or prove their proposition. New research is needed. The limited existing research is flawed and limited. It is one dimensionally focused purely on certain courtroom participants' opinions. Such research is not capable of proving proponent or opponent arguments. Validity needs to be addressed in TCB effects research. This is an accepted norm in general and scientific research.[3] This is a significant challenge for TCB.

GENERALISATION IGNORES FORMS

It is also true to say that while both proponents and opponents of television courtroom broadcasting are frequently absolute in the arguments they propose, they are also being overly generalistic. For example, in saying that television courtroom broadcasting will be educational, such proponents are implying that all television courtroom broadcasting will be educational. There is no regard or differentiation being made for different television courtroom broadcasting forms, different effects of different forms, and different messages and effects within each form.

One form may, for instance, have its primary effect of education, and have information or entertainment as its second effect. Another may have information as its primary aim and effect, while another still may have information as its only effect. Furthermore, the form which may be most educational may have the least audience.

Therefore, we have issues in terms of identifying and classifying the most educational and most informative forms of television courtroom broadcasting. Is it best to have the form with the greatest audience, even though educational effects are backgrounded or minor in comparison to other forms? New research is needed to enable a properly advised policy debate.

We need to be considering these types of issues when developing new research studies and methodologies for television courtroom broadcasting. Otherwise television courtroom broadcasting research will continue to suffer the flaw of being behind the times in terms of the results which it produces. Respect for its methodologies and integrity will be diminished. Rights issues and policy considerations are also diminished.

THE STARTING POINT

It has already been indicated that one of the substantial challenges with television courtroom broadcasting research and debate, is that there has been no identification and analysis of the different television courtroom broadcasting forms.[4] Without identifying and incorporating the television courtroom broadcasting forms into the research and debate, arguably no valid conclusions are achievable.

Most television courtroom broadcasting arguments and research to date, start without reference to any television courtroom broadcasting form(s). Without identifying and starting with a television courtroom broadcasting form, it is not possible to begin proper research of the issues involved in television courtroom broadcasting. Television courtroom broadcasting forms must be the centre point for all discussions, arguments and research into television courtroom broadcasting in future. We cannot make proper and considered conclusions without undertaking proper and sustained research.

FORMS OF TELEVISION COURTROOM BROADCASTING

This work identifies and summarises many of the different television courtroom broadcasting forms in the first map or matrix of television courtroom broadcasting (TCB) categories. This is a novel and necessary contribution because no one appears to have identified, and defined, that there are indeed different categories and forms courtroom broadcasting which we need to appreciate globally. There are also different arguments, different justifications and different forms and sub-forms of television courtroom broadcasting. It is ridiculous to suggest and presume, as proponents and opponents do, that all types of television courtroom broadcasting are the same and that they all have the same effects on everyone. This is a major challenge for the television courtroom broadcasting discussion to date.

The form diagrams and descriptions are not complete. It is the first effort in the literature to document and map the forms of courtroom broadcasting (CB) and television courtroom broadcasting. Television courtroom broadcasting (TCB) discussions, arguments and research should incorporate, define and reference these forms in future.

IMPORTANCE OF IDENTIFYING PARTICULAR FORMS

Some forms may be potentially more educational than others. One cannot say (television) courtroom broadcasting per se is educational, without identifying which form of television courtroom broadcasting one is discussing. One cannot properly research educational television courtroom broadcasting without identifying in advance the form of television courtroom broadcasting. One cannot purport to research courtroom broadcasting generally and say it is educational if, for example, one was researching radio courtroom broadcasting only. One would not have researched anything whatsoever about internet courtroom broadcasting, television courtroom broadcasting, etc.

One cannot assess the overall issues of television courtroom broadcasting without understanding that there is no one single form of television courtroom broadcasting. We need to map the various forms. Debate, and research, needs to begin with understanding that there are different forms. Discussion and debate needs to then refer to which form in particular it is proposed to research, how, and why. Not every argument applies to every form (and or equally). The research of television courtroom broadcasting is much more complex than the general literature suggests. However, the flaws and challenges can be addressed.[5]

FORMS AND THE TCB LITERATURE

None of the CB literature or cases explicitly indicate that there are different forms and, therefore, potentially different effects. No research or commentary to date suggests that we can only properly consider and understand the effect issues once we understand the forms from a global holistic level. The author is the first to do so. Let us consider the literature.

Short and Associates state that electronic media coverage of courts "does not occur in a singular manner. Rather, the 'amount' of coverage occurs across a broad range." [6] No authorative forms and definitions are included.

Daniel Stepniak acknowledges that there are differences to consider in terms of the manner of introducing television courtroom broadcasting, by whom, and "the basis upon which it is regulated and controlled."[7] Stepniak's book is described as relating to "television camera recording and broadcast of courtroom proceedings," but he acknowledges other issues such as still photography, audio recording by radio broadcasters and courts' own webcasting.[8] He interchangeably uses the term "courtroom televising," "broadcasting of proceedings," "audio-visual coverage," etc. Stepniak acknowledges that there are "factors distinguishing various forms of media, nature of recordings and broadcast formats."[9] "For example, live broadcasts may be distinguished from delayed transmissions; audio recordings and broadcast from video recordings; civil proceedings from criminal proceedings; first instance hearings from appeal hearings; overlay footage from actual excerpts of hearings; the recording and broadcast of segments of hearings from 'gavel to gavel' coverage; edited from unedited broadcasts; and broadcast from commentary from broadcasts without commentary."[10] While Stepniak favours courtroom broadcasting, he "does not advocate a particular minimum level of access."[11] Indeed "the impact of audio-visual recordings and broadcasts may warrant additional restrictions with respect to certain categories of cases, or segments of proceedings."[12] It can be seen that Stepniak has the tentative background for differentiating and separating different TCB forms. These now need to be fully distinguished and defined. This book is a first step.

NEWS

Some research distinguishes different news types. This is relevant to TCB form issues.

Steve Anthony Esposito in his research, refers to television news and to three "subgenres" within television news. [13] The three subgenres are,

- Nightly news;
- Television networks primetime news magazines (e.g. ABC's PrimeTime Live);
- Syndicated tabloid television programmes.[14]

These subgenres can be focused on the same case, yet each can "tell the same story in potentially different ways."[15] Also creating impacts are close-ups, wide shots, graphics, music, length of shots, editing styles.[16] He also highlights differences between "real and represented" time, where real time is "collapsed into two or three micro-narratives."[17]

Television news incorporates "a complex process of visual and narrative presentation."[18] It should not be assumed, as is the case with so many of the television courtroom broadcasting arguments, that the same programming and effects apply equally across all footage broadcast. Choosing the image, language, camera locations, lights and story line all impact upon the end product footage which is eventually broadcast.[19] The raw in-court footage also has to be moulded. "[P]resenting events exactly as they occur does not fit with the requisites of television news."[20] Television news programming must also adhere to and fit within specific time frames and schedules.[21] Narrative examination research reveals that "the taken-for-granted 'language' of television empowers television journalists to 'objectively' present the Simpson story in a sometimes biased, judgemental, often prejudicial manner."[22]

The tabloid news programmes use shock, close-ups, drama, entertainment, which "do little more than excite, anger, and titillate viewers with a heavy dose of sex, violence, and celebrity."[23] It contains little factual information and acts to trivialise.[24]

Critics feel that the snippets of 15 – 30 seconds are chosen on "high visual intensity, rather than of legal significance,"[25] effectively "entertainment news."[26] Murder or homicide is "relatively rare, but the seriousness of the crime and sensationalism by the press"[27] can give a disproportionate impression.

Esposito identifies footage items which are negative for the defendant, including close ups, linking to weapons and an out-of-court crime scene videos.[28]

ENTERTAINMENT, DAYTIME TV, ETC.

The Simpson (criminal) case shown on prime time newsmagazines is entertainment, and involved dramatic angles and themes.[29]

The way in which certain programmes are produced, with music, still photographs, zoom ins, lighting, and camera angles and space, create bias and infer guilt.[30] They "shed no factual light"[31] and trivialise the proceedings.[32] There is also a tendency towards exclusives, hype and self promotion.[33]

The three sub-genres "all structure their narratives from a particular perspective that reinforces a set of preferred meaning."[34] Of the three news subgenres, tabloid television devoted most coverage to the Simpson (criminal) case.[35]

Certain programmes also incorporate re-enactments.[36] These may or may not be correct, but are certainly created out-of-court material.

Esposito adds that "[s]pecific attention should be given to the stylistic influences that 'trash TV' has had on traditional television news' pre-trial coverage. Such an application could provide an answer to the question of whether television news is becoming more of a threat to a defendant's Constitutional rights."[37]

We also need to consider and distinguish between forms of television courtroom broadcasting, for example, to determine which forms best protect existing rights, advance education, etc. Esposito calls for research comparing the Simpson (criminal) case with other non-televised celebrity cases to compare effects, such a length and stages of the cases.[38] There may well be "options" as to which "best serves" the defendant's constitutional rights.[39]

Short and Associates found that their surveys did not point to "a single, overall attitude; rather there were attitudes towards"[40] television courtroom broadcasting. There is no research of what, if any, form(s) of television courtroom broadcasting courtroom participants and the public prefer. Therefore, a single general question such as, are you in favour of television courtroom broadcasting, does not help us to distinguish between attitudes between the forms.

In terms of the screen footage, Allen Bukoff refers to different screen formats and differentiates between full-screen formats and spit-screen formats.[41]

Steve Anthony Esposito also refers to increasing entertainment and infotainment. He states that types of coverage are converging and that television courtroom broadcasting must be "presented within [media] themes, formats, and explanations originally found solely in entertainment programs."[42] Dramatic and out-of-court extralegal issues are frequently highlighted.[43]

A representative of TV3 in Ireland has indicated that television is about entertainment, its role is to entertain and is ratings driven.[44]

Richard K. Sherwin offers a critical assessment of the blurring of law, film, television and entertainment in When Law Goes Pop, The Vanishing Line Between Law and Popular Culture.[45] He asks "What happens when law becomes just like film and TV?"[46] He also refers to a *feedback loop*, whereby actions inside the courtroom are influenced by the media footage outside.[47] When law goes pop, the normal procedural and institutional rules breakdown or fail to function.[48]

Sherwin highlights how TruTV (previously Court TV) competes with CNN and afternoon soaps.[49] The images on TruTV are "disproportionately violent and eroticized."[50] Lawyers have also taken part in docudramas.[51] The Law Society Gazette (UK) refers to an impromptu survey in the US which found that six out of thirty afternoon shows where "'People's Court' – type programmes."[52] The same article also refers to a programme called The Law Firm which is similar to The Apprentice format for young lawyers.[53]

Given that certain television courtroom broadcasting is scheduled as or at the same time as, daytime television, this is a topic deserving of research. The "format of all of these [daytime TV] shows is essentially the same."[54] Sports news[55] is also deserving of analysis to the extent that is can be shown at the same time as courtroom broadcasting. The representation of witnesses and parties is generally not researched in terms of TCB output filmed and broadcast.[56] Helene A. Shugart refers to the genre of popular television reality shows.[57] Few studies examine how the media frame the courts in their coverage.[58]

Simon Gallant and Jennifer Epsworth refer to different forms of editing for specific types of media.[59]

David Goldberg, Gavin Sutter, and Ian Waden also refer to television formats, and in particular the issue of intellectual property protection for the formats of certain television programmes.[60]

Live broadcasting of media events[61] is also relevant as certain courtroom broadcasting can be live. However, it does not yet seem to have been empirically researched. Kenneth Creech also refers to the lack of scientific research and evidence of the concerns.[62]

One media book states that "oral arguments on appeal are seldom well suited to broadcast news."[63] Does this effect what is chosen for filming or broadcast from the court? Does research need to examine what occurs in courts normally and then how TCB uses and portrays this?

CATEGORISING THE FORMS

The following categorisations are the first considered identification and categorisation for each of the various courtroom broadcasting (CB) and *television* courtroom broadcasting (TCB) forms. Set out below is a more detailed forms wheels[64] or sub components of television courtroom broadcasting. These are called the Wheels of Television Courtroom Broadcasting. Global categorisation is required to get an overall appreciation for the television courtroom broadcasting issues and also to be able to start the process of meaningful and co-ordinated effects research.

FORMS OF COURTROOM BROADCASTING (CB)

While, the following are not covered within the scope of the book, it is essential to identify that there are different forms of courtroom broadcasting, namely,

- Courtroom broadcasting (CB) generally;
- Movie theatre courtroom broadcasting (MCB);
- Radio courtroom broadcasting (RCB);
- Internet courtroom broadcasting (ICB or iCB);
- Closed circuit courtroom broadcasting (CCB);
- The relay of courtroom broadcasting footage other than through a pushed television broadcast to the public (RYCB);

- The distribution and use of courtroom broadcasting footage on CD, DVD or other electronic media recording or storage devices (recording media courtroom broadcasting (MCB);
- Still photography of courtroom proceedings (PCB);
- Juryroom (television) courtroom broadcasting (JCB); [a sub-form of TCB?];
- Television courtroom broadcasting for archival or record keeping purposes (record keeping television courtroom broadcasting (ACB)[a sub-form of TCB?].

The author seeks to overcome the lack of definition to date, by proposing a definition of television courtroom broadcasting (TCB). This work is limited to the author's definition of TCB: *television courtroom broadcasting is television cameras in the courtroom, filming courtroom proceedings for live and or contemporaneous television push broadcast to the general public.*

TCB WHEELS OF JUSTICE

The wheels categorisation below is the first attempt at a global or holistic categorisation of all forms of television courtroom broadcasting. None of the general research or caselaw explicitly acknowledges that there are different forms of TCB and that there can be different effects. Generally, the empirical effects research fails to do so also – with the exception of perhaps Reality Television Courtroom Broadcasting (RTCB)(see below).

In the form wheels below, the form is referred to in the top line. The variables within that form wheel are listed below the heading. In the Law wheel, we see that the law can be civil law or criminal law. This applies similarly to other wheels. The term "unknown" is included because a particular factor or data set may not be recorded in some contemporary and historical examples of TCB. In some other instances it may not be made available.

Slot 3 (Levels of Courts) will change from country to country/jurisdiction to jurisdiction. The Slot 3 above refers to the Irish courts. The Slot 3 below refers to England and Wales.

THE REALITY TCB FORM

The existence of the Reality Television Courtroom Broadcasting supports the forms analysis. Steven Arthur Kohm identifies one of the most obvious, but seldom discussed, forms of television courtroom broadcasting, namely, US reality-based television courtroom broadcasting.[65] While this identification is very useful from the point of view of supporting the forms analysis, the TCB Reality Courtroom Broadcasting Form is not the core focus of this work.

Law	Stage	Level	Timing	Footage	By	Purpose
↑	↑	↑	↑	↑	↑	↑
Unknown	Unknown	Unknown	Unknown	Unknown	Unknown	Unknown
Civil	Pretrial	Supreme	Live	All (G2G)	Court	Educate public
Criminal	Trial	High	Recorded	Any	Station	
	Hearing	Circuit	Delay	Sections	Stations	Educate students
	Appeal	District	Redact		Pool	Inform
		Small Claims				Confidence
		Childrens				Media Rt
		Criminal Appeal				Public Rt
						Record
		Special Criminal				History
		Central Criminal				Other
		[Tribunals]				
		[Court martials]				
↓	↓	↓	↓	↓	↓	↓

Figure 6.1. Wheels of Television Courtroom Broadcasting: Court Form Wheel.

Kohm examines the Judge Judy and People's Court reality programmes. This form of programming is found to be entertainment, or a "use of judgement as a form of entertainment."[66]

Interestingly, while we frequently have commentators saying that (television) courtroom broadcasting is real and shows exactly what goes on in the courtroom, Kohn notes that even reality based television courtroom broadcasting claims to be "real."[67] However, reality television is the "most unrealistic of all television genres."[68]

These reality based courtroom programmes are also different and distinct from fictional drama courtroom programmes, in that they claim to portray reality, real people and not participants.[69] The essential features of reality television are an emphasis on real, non participants and a focus on the unusual or extraordinary.[70]

Level
↑
Unknown
Supreme
Court of Appeal
High Court
Appeal
High Court
Queens Bench
Admin.
Family
Divisional
Chancery
Crown Court
County Court
Magistrates Court
Tribunals
↓

Level
Supreme
↑
Unknown
Supreme
Court of Appeal
High Court
Queens Bench
Admin.
Family
Divisional
Chancery
Crown Court
County Court
Magistrates Court
Tribunals
↓

Figure 6.2. Wheels of Television Courtroom Broadcasting: Court Level Slot. Note: Slot 3 (levels of courts) for England and Wales.

He also describes the "close cousin" of reality television courtroom broadcasting as trash television shows such as Oprah and Jerry Springer.[71]

Law	Stage	Actor	Consent	Blocking	Camera Location	Camera Man	Focus	In-Court Effect
↑	↑	↑	↑	↑	↑	↑	↑	↑
Unknown	Unknown	Unknown	Unknown	Unknown	Unknown	Unknown	Unknown	Unknown
Civil	Pretrial	Judge	Notified	Can show any participants	Static	Yes	Anyone	Gen distraction
Criminal	Trial	Juror	Not notified		Moving	No	Only some	
	Hearing	Lawyer	Asked	Can show some participants	Location Height	1+	Pan	Actor distraction
	Appeal	Prosecutor	Not asked				Sweep	Attention
		Defender	Needed	Must block certain participants			Focus	Camera focus
		Court staff	Not needed				Zoom	
		Witness					Reaction	Act different
		Expert						Psychol.
		Defendant Party						(various)
		Public						Looping
		(in court)						
		Press						
↓	↓	↓	↓	↓	↓	↓	↓	↓

Figure 6.3. Wheels of Television Courtroom Broadcasting: In-Court Effect Form Wheel. Note: Does not refer to type of camera; camera location; actor location, all of which are also relevant.

Other day time television programmes include soap operas, game shows and tabloid talk shows.[72] Reality TCB competes with these.

Kohn refers to mainstream news genres, documentary genres,[73] and the reality television genre.[74] He also refers to the "tabloid [television] talk show format"[75] and the elements making up the talk show television genre.[76] Such programmes are designed for a mainly female audience.[77]

He adds that programmes,

> featuring elements of real cases, real lawyers and the re-enactments of participants would be akin to the recreated crime scenes of America's Most Wanted. However, just as America's Most Wanted is less 'real' than the video verite style of COPS, courtroom programs that mix participants and real lawyers and judges clearly law more toward the fictional end of our continuum of reality.[78]

Kohn, while referring to Nicole Rafter and Charles Alexander Hahn, refers to a general "courtroom film genre."[79] However, this includes practically all

Law	Stage	Camera Location	Focus	Programme Genre	TV Consent	Actor	Non Actor	Out of Court Effect
↑	↑	↑	↑	↑	↑	↑	↑	↑
Unknown	Unknown	Unknown	Unknown	Unknown	Unknown	Unknown	Unknown	Unknown
Civil	Pretrial	Static	Anyone	News	Main	Judge	Audience	
Criminal	Trial	Moving	Only some	Current affairs	Backdrop	Juror	Friends	
	Hearing	Location Heights	Pan	Document.	Film+voice	Lawyer	Groups	
	Appeal		Sweep	Reality	Film only	Prosecutor	Students	
			Focus	Peak	Length	Defender	Public	
			Zoom	Off peak	Lead-in	Witness	Future parties	
			Reaction	Ct TV	C'mentary	Expert		
				Public TV	Trailer	Defendant Party		
				Commercial public TV	Presenter	Public		
				Other	Expert	(in court)		
					Main story	Press		
					Body story			
					End filler			
					No music			
					Music type			
					Scheduling			
↓	↓	↓	↓	↓	↓	↓	↓	↓

Figure 6.4. Wheels of Television Courtroom Broadcasting: Out-of-Court Effect Form Wheel.

courtrooms contained in moving pictures. Significantly smaller, albeit no less complex, is what is referred to herein as television courtroom broadcasting.

There is a "dearth" of research on reality based television courtroom broadcasting – despite it being around for decades.[80] This applies to TCB generally.

While referring to the website iCourthouse.com, Kohn acknowledges "the reality-based courtroom TV format."[81] He also refers to "media forms."[82] He acknowledges that there is overlap and borrowing of "formats and structures among ... reality court TV shows."[83] He labels People's Court as the progenitor of "the reality-based courtroom television format."[84]

He undertakes content analysis of Judge Judy and indicates that it "follows a consistent and predictable format."[85] It is also "a highly visual, commercially driven media format."[86]

Rules	Application	Consent	Blocking	Camera Location Specified	Focus	Research/ Stats	Use/ Purpose	Effect
↑	↑	↑	↑	↑	↑	↑	↑	
Unknown	Unknown	Unknown	Unknown	Unknown	Unknown	Unknown	Unknown	
Yes	Needed	Asked	Can show any participants	Yes	Anyone	Yes	Educate public	
No	Not needed	Needed	Can show some participants	No	Only some	No	Educate students	
Rule	In advance	Not needed	Must block certain participants	Law	Pan	Req'd	Inform	
Regs	No hearing	Judge	Law	Rules	Sweep	Not req'd	Confidence	
Rule & regs	Hearing	Juror	Rules	Judge	Focus		Media Rt	
Presumption	At trial	Lawyer	Judge	Ct service	Zoom		Public Rt	
	Appeal	Prosecutor	Ct service	Station	Reaction		Record	
	Ct office	Court staff	Station	Cameraman			History	
	Judge	Witness	Cameraman				Other	
		Expert						
		Defendant Party						
↓	↓	↓	↓	↓	↓	↓	↓	

Figure 6.5. Wheels of Television Courtroom Broadcasting: Control Form Wheel.

Later Kohm states that more research is required in relation to the audience(s) of reality-based courtroom television broadcasting "genre."[87]

Jessica Ossinger[88] indicates that TruTV is infotianment programming, that is "educational programming told through an entertainment medium." Ossinger also contrasts TruTV with public service broadcasting.[89] She also refers to drama and fictional court programming such as Judge Judy and Law & Order.[90]

US

The US commentary also supports the forms thesis. While Ronald L. Goldfarb is in favour of TCB, he is not advocating a free for all where the media is able to choose and undertake any and all potential forms of TCB. Rather he seeks to "find a sensible solution to ... '...How can we best blend new media technologies with our traditional and revered commitment to democracy and justice?'"[91] Goldfarb concludes that TCB in the US should be a "publicly run, non commercial channel" run according to strict legal rules and procedures.[92] He is clearly favouring more considered forms of TCB, and not the more entertainment leaning forms.

Law	Stage	Level	Timing	Footage	By	Purpose
Criminal	Pretrial	LA County Superior Court	Live	All (G2G) Sections	Pool	Unknown

Figure 6.6. Wheels of Television Courtroom Broadcasting: Court Form Wheels of OJ Simpson (Criminal) Case.

Steven Kohn[93] refers to People's Court and Judge Judy as two "models" of "American Reality-Based Courtroom TV" daytime TCB. He sees significant difference between each of these programme styles.[94]

C-SPAN, the US cable network, has a standing offer to cover cases in full if permitted to televise Supreme Court cases.[95] C-SPAN is another model.

Courtroom View Network (CVN) provides gavel to gavel (G2G) coverage of cases.[96] It does not use commentators or editing techniques.[97] CVN covers civil cases almost exclusively.[98] Therefore, it is quite a different type of TCB than that under TruTV (formerly Court TV).

Judge Tunheim refers to state rules in the US, and describes that,

> [w]hile most US states permit some use of cameras in their courts, such access by the media is not unlimited. The majority of states have imposed restrictions on the use of cameras in the court or have banned cameras altogether in certain proceedings. Although it is somewhat difficult to obtain current information, it appears that approximately 31 states that permit cameras have restrictions of some kind written into their authorizing statutes, such as allowing coverage only in certain courts, prohibiting coverage of certain types of proceedings or of certain witnesses, and/or requiring the consent of the parties, victims of sex offenses, and witnesses. Thirteen states, including the District of Columbia, do not allow coverage of criminal trials. In nine states, cameras are allowed only in appellate courts. The District of Columbia prohibits cameras altogether. Utah allows only still photography at civil trials. In fact, only 19 states appear to provide the presiding judge with the type of broad discretion over the use of cameras contained in this [proposed] legislation.[99]

He also states that "[p]resently, two of the 13 appellate courts, the Second and Ninth Circuits, have decided to permit coverage in appellate proceedings. This decision was made by the judges of each court. As for cameras in district courts or have acknowledged that the district court in that circuit already have such a prohibition."[100]

The judge concludes that it "is clear from the widely varying approaches to the use of cameras that the state courts are far from being of one mind in

Law	Stage	Actor	Consent	Blocking	Camera Location	Cameraman	Focus	In-Court Effect
↑	↑	↑	↑	↑	↑	↑	↑	↑
Criminal	Trial	Unknown	Unknown	Unknown	Unknown	Unknown	Unknown	Unknown
		Judge	Notified	Can show any participants	Static	Yes	Only some	Gen distraction
		Juror	Not notified	Can show some participants	Moving		Pan	Actor distraction
		Lawyer	Asked	Must block certain participants	Location Height		Sweep	Attention
		Prosecutor	Not asked				Focus	Camera focus
		Defender	Needed				Zoom	Act different
		Court staff	Not needed				Reaction	Psychol.
		Witness						(various)
		Expert						Looping
		Defendant Party						
		Public						
		(in court)						
		Press						
↓	↓	↓	↓	↓	↓	↓	↓	↓

Figure 6.7. Wheels of Television Courtroom Broadcasting: In-Court Effect, Form Wheel of OJ Simpson (Criminal) Case.

the approach to, or on the propriety and extent of, the use of cameras in the courtroom."[101]

Judge Diarmuid O'Scannlain, refers to the Simpson (criminal) case, and suggest that no one "believes that the presence of cameras in that courtroom did not have an impact on the conduct of the attorneys, witnesses, jurors, and judge – almost universally to the detriment of the trial process."[102] He also distinguishes trial and appellate courts.[103]

Ronald Goldfarb also indicates that there are different "forms" of TCB and TCB permission.[104] Goldfarb states that "[e]very State before they adopted their rule had a press-bar-media-wiseman/wise woman committee that ran for from a year to 3 years to study all of the perceived problems of the impact or potential impact of television on witnesses, on jurors, on lawyers, and all the participants to the administration of justice."[105] "[I]n every one of those studies, the result was once sceptical lawyers and judges found that the presence of the television camera, generally unseen, had no impact, and that the real disturbances in the justice system were what went on outside the courtroom as opposed to what went on in the courtroom."[106] No definitions and no body of empirical research is referred to.

Law	Stage	Camera Location	Focus	Programme Genre	TV Content	Actor	Non Actor	Out of Court Effect
↑	↑	↑	↑	↑	↑	↑	↑	↑
Criminal	Trial	Static	Unknown	Unknown	Unknown	Unknown	Unknown	Unknown
		Location Heights	Only some	News	Main	Judge	Audience	
			Pan	Current affairs	Backdrop	Juror	Friends	
			Sweep		Film+voice	Lawyer	Groups	
			Focus	Peak	Film only	Prosecutor	Students	
			Zoom	Commercial public TV	Length	Defender	Public	
			Reaction		Lead-in	Court staff	Future parties	
					C'mentary	Witness		
					Trailer	Expert		
					Presenter	Defendant Party		
					Expert	Public		
					Main story	(in court)		
					Body story	Press		
					End filler			
					No music			
					Music type			
					Scheduling			
↓	↓	↓	↓	↓	↓	↓	↓	↓

Figure 6.8. Wheels of Television Courtroom Broadcasting: Out-of-Court Effect, Form Wheel of OJ Simpson (Criminal) Case.

Goldfarb continues. "In addition to the studies by the States and the Federal Judicial Centre, I went to the Lexis–Nexis machinery and found every study that had ever been made by sociologists, pollsters, and other social scientists to try and determine scientifically, such as you can under these circumstances, whether there really is something to be said for the fact that the presence of an unseen eye would somehow or other disrupt the participants."[107] "[A]fter 30 or 40 seconds one failed to even notice" the television cameras.[108] He does not refer, for example, to in-court distraction effects. Nor does he refer to methodologies such as eye tracking.

However, Goldfarb is not in favour or uncontrolled TCB forms, rather, he is in favour gavel to gavel (G2G) coverage.[109]

Ellia Thompson also confirms that television cameras "continue to be banned in most American courtrooms — state and federal."[110] Ellia Thomp-

Rules	Application	Consent	Blocking	Camera Location Specified	Focus	Research/ Stats	Use/ Purpose	Effect
↑	↑	↑	↑	↑	↑	↑	↑	
Yes	Judge	Judge	Can show some participants	Unknown	Only some	No	Unknown	
No				Yes	Pan			
Rule			Judge	No	Sweep			
Regs				Judge	Focus			
Rule & regs				Ct service	Zoom			
Presumption				Station	Reaction			
				Cameraman				
↓	↓	↓	↓	↓	↓	↓	↓	

Figure 6.9. Wheels of Television Courtroom Broadcasting: Control OJ Simpson Form Wheel.

son also refers to the Simpson (criminal) case backlash."[111] In 1989, 44 US states permitted video and or audio coverage on a permanent or experimental basis.[112] Federal courts were also experimenting with videoing for record keeping purposes.[113] In 1998 one media text refers to thirteen states requiring defendant consent for TCB.[114] Apparently, Ohio and Iowa adopted more restrictive forms of TCB after the experimental periods.[115] Other media texts confirms that the TCB rules are "diverse"[116] and the TCB "laws vary from state to state."[117]

> [M]any difficult questions remain unanswered, they are not mainly legal questions. How does editing of proceedings affect the perceptions of the audience? Does broadcast coverage actually educate the public about the judicial system, as broadcasters have argued when seeking camera coverage? Does broadcast coverage affect the fairness of trials? Can photojournalists function with quiet dignity? Did televising of the O.J. Simpson criminal trial turn out to be a setback for cameras in the courtroom?[118]

UK

While never explicitly mentioned, some of the UK literature also supports the forms thesis. Henry Schleiff states that the prospect of a "British model following that of Court TV is highly unlikely."[119] The same article quotes Lord Falconer when he announced a UK TCB pilot, where states that the form of the pilot will be in non jury courts, with few witnesses, and a right to object to the TCB.[120] Witnesses will not be filmed.[121] Lord Falconer continues that "[w]e don't want our courts turned into US-style media circuses. We will not have OJ Simpson–style trials in Britain."[122]

Henry Schleiff, who is Chairman and CEO of CourtTV (as it then was) suggests that in the US, cameras in the courtroom are becoming the norm.[123] This is a misrepresentation, as it ignores the different forms of TCB in the US and also suggests that there is uniform and general adoption of TCB.

Henry Schleiff makes the interesting point that trials have a wider impact on the public than in previous years.[124] However, there are many counter arguments to this, such as enhanced fragmentation of the media and ever increasing numbers of channels, including news channels.

An article in the New Law Journal agrees that there is no uniform TCB, TCB form or guidelines in the US.[125] The same article also acknowledges the point that there are different audiences, by referring to the potential deterrent effect of sentencing TCB, as younger people watch more than they read.[126]

While the UK official consultation does not expressly refer to the form issues, it provides ample evidence that form issues exist and are live concerns. The UK Department of Constitutional Affairs consultation entitled Broadcasting Courts,[127] launched in November 2004[128] even attempts definitions distinguishing different form type issues of courtroom broadcasting, in particular, text only, sound only, still pictures and moving pictures plus sound.[129]

The consultation is relevant in relation to the forms issue. For example, Lord Falconer in the statement launching the consultation document, clearly sees differences between different types of cases. He states that he can see "no case" for TCB "involving children" and also feels the issue of whether TCB should include criminal cases requires careful consideration.[130] The position of witnesses should not be worsened or "jeopardise[d]."[131] How much empirical research refers to witness issues? Very little, and none of which is replicated research.

The executive summary states that the "complexity of the [TCB] issues is increased by the number of different types of proceedings which would be affected, the stages each case go through, and the different participant involved."[132] This refers to *form* issues aswell as *process* issues and actor effect issues.

It adds that "[i]nternational experience, and the experience of televising Parliament, offer various models."[133]

It points out that an option could be to proceed with radio courtroom broadcasting, as occurred with initial Parliamentary broadcasting.[134] The consultation further refers to and distinguishes TCB, internet courtroom broadcasting and even a dedicated TCB channel.[135]

The Protocol Governing Pilot Filming in the Appellate Jurisdiction of England and Wales, Royal Courts of Justice 2004 also refers to forms, where it states that "[t]he audio-visual images made during the appellate pilot filming project may *only* be used in a format laid down by the heads of division in support of the pilot project."[136] (Original emphasis).

The consultation also states that "Section Three gives details of the different types of court proceedings, and information relevant to the question whether they might be broadcast."[137] Section Three refers, inter alia, to different types of hearings in criminal courts, civil courts, family courts, coroners courts and also tribunals.[138] It also differentiates the many different potential participants in the different court settings.[139] It also differentials some of the different parts of the respective cases, such as opening statements, closing statements, cross examination of witnesses, judicial summing up of the case, decision delivery, sentence delivery.[140] It also refers to the press and public as attendees in court proceedings,[141] which does not appear to be referred to in any of the US research.

This reiterates (implicitly) the point made by the author that different issues and different considerations arise depending on each respective form of court and form of TCB.

The author highlights the fact that there is not just one all encompassing form of TCB. This is reiterated again by the UK consultation when it states that "broadcasting" covers "a range of options."[142]

It adds that "[b]efore any decision could be taken whether to change current provisions, close attention needs to be paid to the needs to be paid to the needs of the participants in court proceedings – particularly ... witnesses and litigants in person ... impact on people's willingness to take part in proceedings ... more of an ordeal."[143]

There are also various arguments, and some of these can even vary depending on the form.[144] A large issue is how any proposed TCB would be regulated and controlled.[145] "Most jurisdictions where broadcasting (particularly via television) [hence acknowledging, as the author has pointed out, different forms of courtroom broadcasting] is allowed apply strict rules."[146]

The rules, the consultation points out, can govern what may be recorded, what may be shown, allocating control decisions, etc.[147] It also refers to different stages of the proceedings, different types of media, the amount of editing, editing and mandated minimum content amounts, broadcasting delays, subsequent follow on use of footage, etc.[148]

Many organisations could be responsible for undertaking the TCB filming.[149] This is seldom considered or researched, nor its effects.

The UK consultation notes that the Scottish Practice Note of Lord Hope (of August 6, 1992) prohibited live TCB.[150] As regards the first TCB broadcast from Scotland, a documentary, it notes that The Trial programme was a "dramatic and educative entertainment" form.[151]

While the UK consultation implicitly agrees with the different forms of TCB, and indeed courtroom broadcasting, it falls short. For example, it implies an acceptance of the view that TCB in the US states (with the exception of New York) is the same.[152] This is not correct, there is huge variety between the states, and even within states.

ADDITIONAL FORM CONSIDERATIONS

Once we delve into the different forms, we also need to consider additional general issues.

Criminal/Civil

The New York study found that 94% of applications for camera access were for criminal trials.[153] A subset was analysed to show the following sub-breakdown, 59% violent crime, 7% sex crimes, 34% non violent crimes.[154] The research to date does not seek to distinguish effects as between civil and criminal TCB.

Presentation

The order of presentation is very important. The framing and sequential presentation of questions and evidence are as much a part of the legal process and advocacy[155] as the importance of the legal concepts at play.[156] Courts and legal practitioners throughout the world appreciate the dangers of bias and "leading questions." It is recognised that it is legitimate to have rules and procedures to address what, and how, matters may be presented in court. This order of presentation at trial has equivalent parallels in both print journalism and media programming. It is difficult, therefore, to convincingly argue that the different forms of television courtroom programming should not be issues for consideration and research. In addition, it cannot reasonably be argued that there should be no rules in place influencing the final television courtroom broadcast product or form.

Consent

The original Florida experiment proceeded on the basis of allowing filming even over the objections of the defendants.[157] The case of *Zamora v Florida* is one such example.[158] The New York experimental law also provided for filming over participant objections.[159]

In terms of broadcasting the jury, Steve Robert Pasternack's empirical research found that there could be adverse community pressure on jurors if they were broadcast, and therefore recommended that states should prohibit the broadcast of jurors.[160] Are the jury asked to consent in advance? Should their consent be required? The US National Association of Criminal Defense

Lawyers advocated for TCB being subject to consent of the parties in a presentation in relation to proposed legislation for federal TCB.[161]

Rules

S.L. Alexander in the observational part of the research, notes that the media covering trials had a "great deal of freedom."[162] The amount of freedom, the restrictions, the predefined rules or regulations, and what a particular judge may impose, all combine to ensure that the form of gathering broadcast footage can differ significantly. In one case the judge indicated in an interview afterwards that he granted more flexibility to the media because there was no jury and because he understood that the case may have national interest.[163] The rules and regulations governing television courtroom broadcasting have an important impact on the form ultimately broadcast. William Petkanas agrees that in the US the various state laws relating to television courtroom broadcasting are "extremely diverse."[164] Short and Associates also refer to the state rules as being "diverse."[165] Many states are "still formulating policies."[166] Kermit Lyol Netteburg also acknowledges "the wide variation in types of coverage" rules (or as he says, "plans").[167] The literature does not recognise how the rules change and impact the form of in-court filming and also the end product footage that is broadcast. Neither does it recognise that the forms of in-court filming and rules each impact upon the gatekeeping, selection and production and editing processes. Netterburg does acknowledge, however, three themes of variation, namely, types of courts covered; the how access rules are changed; and whether courtroom actor consent is needed.[168] Theme one refers to camera access to trial courts only; appeal courts only; or both.[169]

Gavel to Gavel (G2G)

Short and Associates found that full or gavel to gavel (G2G) cases were seldom shown.[170] The original Florida experiment used gavel to gavel (G2G) cases.[171] Sometimes television programmes will broadcast the testimony of certain witnesses gavel to gavel (G2G).[172] In the Steinberg case in New York, WCBS broadcast the case gavel to gavel (G2G), while competing stations WABC and WNBC broadcast hours of coverage but not full gavel to gavel (G2G).[173]

LIVE/RECORDED

Cases can also be included for later programming or televised live. The first live broadcast occurred as far back as 1955 (Washburn case in Waco, Texas).[174]

FOOTAGE ANGLES/SHOTS/ZOOMS

Roberta Enter notes that television courtroom broadcasting visual content involved two elements, namely, the event and how it is shot or filmed.[175] The television directors "guides" the audience through the camera angles and perspectives they choose.[176] The cameras angles and camera distance are significant.[177] Zooming is also important.[178]

CLOSED CIRCUIT COURTROOM BROADCASTING

It is surprising that there was a closed circuit trial relay as long ago as the 1950's, when a relay was permitted from the courtroom to an auditorium in the Oklahoma case of Gene Leroy Hart.[179]

TRIBUNAL FORMS

While tribunals are not the direct focus of this work, there have been various tribunals in Ireland, the UK and elsewhere. There is no televising of such proceedings but there has been interest.[180]

NEW FORMS

Karmen Erjavec and Melita Poler Kovacic make two points in relation to genres.[181] Firstly, they argue for a more expansive understanding of genre forms.[182] Secondly, they categorise mobi news (or news using mobile phone cameras), as a new genre.[183] They also refer to the process of production issues,[184] as well as produce a mobi new [production] genre chain.[185]

PERMISSION

Who/What grants access permission?

There is no uniform form or model of television courtroom broadcasting. In terms of access, this can vary between a number of access situations. A judge can allow an access request on a case by case basis within their own decision making power and discretion (so long as there is no higher rule preventing them). On the other hand, courts or higher courts can establish the ground rules which permit and provide for television courtroom broadcasting. It is also possible for politicians as legislators to provide a statutory framework permitting and providing for television courtroom broadcasting.[186]

APPLICATION

Do the media have to apply for access in each instance? If so, to whom?

We have no clear understanding if most instances of television courtroom broadcasting are conditional on a prior application by the media? If there is an application, is this under some predefined procedures set out by a superior court, judges, the court services, policy makers? Is the procedure, application form, and decision recorded? What is the ultimate result of the filming and broadcasting? Is this also recorded? What are the trends and implications evident? If there are frequent instances where judges individually are being asked to permit television courtroom broadcasting, in the absence of a superior ruling or policy on the issue, how beneficial is it to permit such undocumented practices?

Where there are application procedures, are they sufficiently documented? For example, it there a reference to the type and style of programming to be used? Is there a reference to what can and cannot be done with the footage for the intended courtroom broadcast? Is there a reference to secondary uses of the footage? The issue of access applications is an area ripe for research and comparison, partly because in some instances we can identify some application procedures.

CONTROL RULE

Do any procedures, controls or restrictions apply? If so, from where?

There are many controls and restrictions which may be imposed, from checks and balances in terms of safety of jurors to application procedures. Equally, there have been many television courtroom broadcasts where there has been no predetermined formal procedural controls in place, such as where a judge is asked to permit access and grants the request. While such a judge may (or may not) provide certain limited and loose formalities, they are seldom if at all documented. Such ad hoc case by case television courtroom broadcasting is undesirable in that it contributes to uncoordinated television courtroom broadcasting and television courtroom broadcasting practice. Equally, it is much more difficult to document and to research the issues involved in such instances. In terms of where there are some controls, these may be very basic and general, or may be more considered and involved, for example, associated research.

RESTRICTIONS/CONTROL IMPOSED BY?

Who and what can control or restrict the access and filming?

Not all television courtroom broadcasting has had documented procedures. In those that have, there is again a disparity. Some can be imposed by individual judges, higher courts or higher judges, or alternatively by a legal statute. Differences are also apparent between court codes and legal statutes which are television courtroom broadcasting specific, media specific or more general[187] with, for example, an amendment added to cater for television courtroom broadcasting or media reporting. Obviously depending on the basis of the primary document permitting television courtroom broadcasting, the level of consideration and or detail involved may vary. Also, the more detailed the document and the more consideration given to its drafting, the more considered will be its provisions, and in particular any associated research and also the restrictions and regulations encompassed within it. The Michigan Model Guidelines[188] is an example of court rules and procedures for courtroom broadcasting. It would be difficult for a judge, on his own, to be expected to think of all of the issues involved with cameras. (However, as is pointed out later, there are many more issues and considerations which even the Michigan Model Guidelines etc. need to encompass[189]).

LENGTH/TIME

What is permitted/required to be filmed and or broadcast?

The examples of television courtroom broadcasting to date vary considerably. However, it is clear that some are broadcast on a full length of the case basis, known as gavel to gavel (G2G). Sometimes this has been required by the judge or the rule or statute catering for television courtroom broadcasting. Other television courtroom broadcasts can vary according to what the broadcast producer decides in a particular instance. Effectively the case is edited according to the decisions of the television station. The length of broadcast footage can also vary according to the broadcast use/form (see below) in a given instance. In each form the television producer decides what they want to leave in or leave out and accordingly on the length of the broadcast footage ultimately used. Sometimes also a judge may impact upon the length of a case. For example, judges sometimes are able to delay the feed of a court broadcast if they decide something needs to be edited or redacted out from the footage actually broadcast to the public.[190] Similarly a judge may need to halt footage, which again impacts on the length of the case. In the *Simpson* (criminal) case Judge Ito halted footage when jurors were shown on television, which was not permitted. It is unclear if anyone has undertaken research into how frequently such issues arise and or the amount of (additional) administrative efforts required. Where the full length of a case must be shown, whether live or relayed subsequently, this can impact on whether the case is shown at all, or indeed where it is shown e.g. peak or off peak times.

RELAY AND FILMING FORM

What are the different types of filming courtroom broadcasting?

How court scenes are captured on film varies considerably across a number of scenarios. It can be live, recorded, delayed, edited by court, etc. Again there is no categorisation, definition and research across the instances of courtroom broadcasting, thus preventing an overall appreciation and understanding of courtroom broadcasting *per se*.

PROGRAMME-USE GENRE

What is the style of programme that the footage is used for?

There are many instances of courtroom broadcasting and many different programmes which use television courtroom broadcasting footage. Yet, we still do not know what these are or their individual prevalence. It is very clear that we need to start research into all of the different types of programmes, and channels, which use television courtroom broadcasting footage.

This is required so that we can properly see the extent of television courtroom broadcasting and which forms predominate. Such research also interfaces with consideration of the various arguments used in relation to television courtroom broadcasting. Of these, the most important is possibly the educational arguments and issues. We also need to understand the different forms of television courtroom broadcasting programmes that exist, before we can consider the use of the court footage in each of these programme forms.

BROADCAST CONTENT USE

How is the broadcast content used?

The broadcast use and broadcast forms of television courtroom broadcasting is perhaps where we get most differences. There as many uses and forms of television courtroom broadcasting as there are forms of broadcasting and forms of television programming. These can vary from a number of parts of a case relayed as part of a headline news programme item (which differs from something backgrounded or shown later in the broadcast) to, for example, still shots taken from courtroom film used as a backdrop to a news story on a case, to current affairs programmes to documentaries. Across these multitude of forms of television courtroom broadcasting there is also a variety in scope for presenters to make comments and or introduce the case, or alternatively for a third party (e.g. expert, witness, party, police, etc.) to comment on the case also.[191] In any discussions and research of television courtroom broadcasting we need to be cognisant of the form employed and thereby appreciate the potentially different issues and different effects pertinent to that form. Not all forms are the same, and we should not presume that they are. Equally we should not presume that all effects of television courtroom broadcasting are the same. Research needs to be specific and tailored to the form of television courtroom broadcasting involved. (Note the potential for the courts to undertake filming in the second federal experiment pilot).

BROADCASTER/PRODUCER

Who broadcasts it?

Just as much as television courtroom broadcasting forms can have effects, or different effects, so too can different television courtroom broadcasters. Indeed, certain broadcasters may be more/less inclined towards certain television courtroom broadcasting forms. The main traditional broadcasters are public[192] and commercial broadcasters.[193] However, we also have to consider the programme makers. These may be in house or independent film makers.[194] In addition, the programme maker can be a dedicated regular court programmer or on occasion also a court dedicated courtroom broadcast channel.

FILM CAPTURE FORM

Who films the case?

In the context of television courtroom broadcasting there is an additional category whereby sometimes the actual court staff will be responsible for the courtroom filming. They will then relay this to the interested television networks. More frequently however, it will be filmed by the broadcaster themselves when they have been permitted access. Other filming forms include filming by each television station who is interested or who has requested access. On other occasions the permitted form may require a single camera or a single operator and their film footage will be pooled[195] or given to other television networks, thus reducing the number of camera and television in the actual courtroom.

CAMERA FORM

What rules, if any, apply to the type of camera(s) used?

One of the obvious areas where different forms are visible is when different forms of television courtroom broadcasting camera are involved. Obviously in forms where the court personnel are involved in organising the footage, the filming may be more regular and may permit wall mounted cameras. These may or may not be fixed in that they may be allowed to move or pan about. They may also be allowed or forbidden from zooming in and out. In media focused forms, the cameras can vary between hand held (on shoulder) and fixed locations. Obviously a camera operator may feel more inclined to move about in the courtroom when they are not limited to a fixed camera or fixed location. On occasion, courts have said that camera can be present but that they must be at the back of the court, in a special booth or even on a balcony.[196]

LOCUS

Where can/must the camera be?

There are different types of cameras and sometimes these have been specifically referred to by the court or court procedures. Various cases have also referred to location issues. There is a very uneven field across camera location issues and we do not have any general or overall impression or understanding of when, how or why cameras must be located in particular locations, and the reasons and justifications. There is no research and also no guidance to other courts or interested parties. The literature does not refer to definitions, location, forms or eye tracking.

EQUIPMENT

What equipment is or is not allowed?

There is no overall picture of what equipment is and is not allowed across the various examples of courtroom broadcasting. We need to start recording this and referencing it in an overall perspective.

PURPOSE/AIM OF COURTROOM BROADCASTING FORM

What is the purpose of the courtroom broadcasting?

There have been many arguments in favour of television courtroom broadcasting and equally many legal arguments and judicial comments in relation to television courtroom broadcasting. However, there are no definitions, comparison, analysis or research of these. By continuing to ignore the gaps in research in this regard, we are condemning our discussion and consideration of television courtroom broadcasting to repeat these flaws and gaps. There is no definitive compendium of all of the various proponent and opponent argument, nor of the judicial and policymaker justifications for permitting or refusing, as the case may be, courtroom broadcasting. This is certainly needed and called for. We equally need a means by which we can understand television courtroom broadcasting, and trends in courtroom broadcasting, by which we easily see and compare the various categorised decisions for allowing and refusing access in individual cases. This needs to be referenced according to location, level, type of court, type of case and the justifications and evidence relied upon. We need to expand this also, across national boundaries to get an overall understanding also.

BROADCAST TIME

How is courtroom broadcasting scheduled?

There are many forms of television courtroom broadcasting. One item which distinguishes them is scheduling. When is the television courtroom broadcasting programme, or the programme with some television courtroom broadcasting footage, actually shown? The ultimate television courtroom broadcast aired may depend on whether the television courtroom filming is live or relayed for later use. For example, certain forms are viewed as more media friendly or attractive to broadcasters. In an instance where a court case may only be broadcast where it is shown live, certain broadcasters may decide or feel there is no programming slot available for it. It is therefore ignored. Similar issues may arise if there is a requirement that the case can only be broadcast in full — even if relayed later. This has clear implications as to the form of television courtroom broadcasting, its effects, its audience, etc. It also impacts on what type of presentation and trailers will be used for the television courtroom broadcasting footage. These very important issues have not been researched or analysed.

BROADCAST AUDIENCE

Who watches courtroom broadcasting?

So many of the arguments and discussions in relation to television courtroom broadcasting refer to the audience. Yet there is a distinct lack of research into who the television courtroom broadcasting audience is. Equally, we do not know how the audience, or audiences, differ across different television courtroom broadcasting forms, television programmes, jurisdictions, etc. Critical to many of the proponents' arguments in favour of television courtroom broadcasting, is the view that it is or will be educational. Yet, they never go into any detail on why or how the audience, or the wider public, will be educated? The audience needs to be considered and involved in the examination and research of television courtroom broadcasting issues generally, and in particular in terms of education, effects, motivation, learning, recall, usage, etc.

COURT FORM

What courts can be accessed?

We do not currently know what courts and types of courts are accessible to television courtroom broadcasting other than on an individual case by case basis. There is no overall recording and comparison of which courts across the US, and across other jurisdictions, allow or restrict television courtroom broadcasting according to courts, judges, per individual decision and under a predetermined policy document of some sort. We do not even have simple comparisons such as whether it is appeal courts, trial courts, what exclusions may apply, etc. across the instances of television courtroom broadcasting.

CASE FORM

What cases can be shown?

All of the literature on television courtroom broadcasting indicates that there is a very uneven field in terms of what cases and types of cases are, and are not, amenable to courtroom broadcasts. Why are they all not compared? How can we hope to get a proper understanding and appreciation for television courtroom broadcasting overall, if we are not even undertaking basic court form comparisons?

CONSENT FORM

What consent(s), if any, are required? How are they obtained? When?

It is very curious that there are no records or comparison of who can and cannot consent (in the sense of not requiring consent) across the various locations where television courtroom broadcasting is permitted. Consent raises many important issues in term of permission, ultimate forms(s), etc. and really needs to be properly documented, compared, researched and considered. It also has import in terms of the content of television courtroom broadcasting programmes and the technologies used.

RESEARCH

Does any research occur, or sufficient research?

Very few of the cases broadcast are compared, nor the justification for broadcasting. There is also little comparison of the different procedures, rules and restriction across different courts, jurisdictions and forms. There is also little comparison between jurisdictions. We do not have a clear picture of who imposes rules and for what purpose.

Wherever there is courtroom broadcasting, the forms, details and justifications vary. Critically, there is no forms matrix by which we can begin to locate and compare different courtroom broadcasting and different jurisdictions. Undermining all television courtroom broadcasting discussion is the lack of definition, research and sophisticated empirical research. We need to address this. We also need to consider the issue of requiring or mandating research in all instances of television courtroom broadcasting and certainly in all pilot experiments of television courtroom broadcasting.

CONCLUSION

There are many form issues. In the first instance, we need to define and categorise the different types of television courtroom broadcasting (TCB) in order to properly research and code them, and to undertake properly considered effects research. While even the Supreme Court referred to this issue in passing, it has called for more empirical research.[197] This has not occurred to date. This is the first work to attempt to undertake a definition, identification and categorisation exercise in relation to television courtroom broadcasting (TCB).

All of the literature on television courtroom broadcasting indicates that there is a very uneven field in terms of what cases and types of cases are and are not amenable to courtroom broadcasts. Why are they all not compared? How can we hope to get a proper understanding and appreciation for television courtroom broadcasting overall if we are not undertaking comparative research.

NOTES

1. The legal and constitutional issues are not the focus, and are beyond the scope, of the current work. The arguments are also beyond the scope of this current work.
2. E.E. Slotnick and J.A. Segal, Television News and the Supreme Court: All the News That's Fit to Air? (Cambridge: Cambridge University Press, 1998), 242. Emphasis added.
3. For example, V. Stodden, Enabling Reproducible Research: Licensing for Scientific Innovation, International Journal of Communications Law and Policy 13 (2009), 1–25, at 2.
4. See for example S. Barber, News Cameras in the Courtroom (New Jersey: Ablex, 1997), which is one of the more detailed books on this topic, and which does not distinguish or categorise different courtroom broadcasting forms.
5. See suggestions in Chapters 16 and 17 to address the flaws in the research to date.
6. E.H. Short and Associates, Evaluation of California's Experiment with Extended Media Coverage of Courts, Submitted to: The Administrative Office for the Courts, The Chief Justice's Special Committee on the Courts and the Media and The California Judicial Council (September, 1981) 53.
7. D. Stepniak, Audio–Visual Coverage of Courts (Cambridge: Cambridge University Press, 2008), 6.
8. Ibid, 9.
9. Ibid, 9.

10. Ibid, 9–10.
11. Ibid, 10.
12. Ibid, 47–48.
13. S.A. Espositio, OJ TV: A Narrative Analysis of Television's Pretrial Coverage of the O.J. Simpson Case (Ph.D diss., Graduate School of Wayne State University, Detroit, Michigan, 1996): 27.
14. Ibid, 27.
15. Ibid, 33.
16. Ibid, 34.
17. Ibid, 35.
18. Ibid, 54.
19. Ibid, 55.
20. Ibid.
21. Ibid, 59.
22. Ibid, 62.
23. Ibid, 204.
24. Ibid, 220.
25. To use the words of P. Thaler, The Impact of the Television Camera on Courtroom Participants: A Case Study of the Joel Steinberg Murder Trial (Ph.D diss., New York University, 1990): 7. Note also the first federal study, which also refers to short snippets.
26. Ibid, 8.
27. J. G. Peterson-Manz, Copycats: Homicide and the Press, Dissertation Abstracts International: Section B: The Sciences and Engineering 63 (2002): 591 *et seq*. For a more historical discussion see, D. Domke, The Press, Race Relations and Social Change, Journal of Communication 51 (2001) 317–344.
28. S.A. Esposito, above, 85-87, 129.
29. Ibid, 198.
30. Ibid, 274. See also W. Petkanas, Cameras on Trial: An Assessment of the Educational Affects of News Cameras in Trial Courts (Ph.D diss., New York University, 1990): 68 regarding different types of filming shots used.
31. Ibid.
32. Ibid, 275.
33. Ibid, 276.
34. Ibid, 271. On the separate topic of courtroom sketches, note Krupp, K., Journalism Meets Art, Media Studies Journal (1998): 71.
35. S.A. Esposito, ibid, 278.
36. Ibid, 273–274.
37. Ibid, 303.
38. Ibid, 304.
39. Ibid.
40. E.H. Short and Associates, above, 173.
41. A. Bukoff. The Effect of Video Camera Techniques on the Pre-–Deliberation Judgements and Perceptions of Role-Playing Jurors (Ph.D diss., Kent State University, 1984).
42. S.A. Esposito, above, 19.
43. Ibid.
44. Interviewed on the Fionn Davenport show on Newstalk, on November 26, 2010.
45. Sherwin also offers an insightful and critical analysis of the differing intentions behind the *Estes* and *Chandler* cases. See R.K. Sherwin, above, 140 et seq, and 247–248. Also, R.K. Sherwin, The Jurisprudence of Appearances, New York Law School Law Review 43 (1999–2000): 821-842. He identifies, in particular the rule whereby whatever the media highlights will bear the mark of the reality/fiction confusion, and the corollary of the rule that once one enters into the jurisprudence of appearances it is difficult to control how the image will be spun. See ibid.
46. R.K. Sherwin, above, 17.
47. Ibid, 27.
48. Ibid, 36.

49. Ibid, 163.
50. Ibid, 165.
51. One such docudrama, Born With Two Mothers, is referred to in Lawyers Keep It Real in Court Battle, Law Society Gazette (April 28, 2005), www.lawgazette.co.uk , accessed August 13, 2012.
52. The Verdict Is In: And You're Out, Law Society Gazette (August 4, 2006), www.lawgazette.co.uk , accessed on August 13, 2011.
53. Ibid.
54. W.B. Carney, Prime Time Law in America, New Law Journal, 147 (1997): 1845.
55. One reference is B. Hutchins and D. Rowe, Reconfiguring Media Sport for the Online World: An Inquiry Into 'Sports News and Digital Media, International Journal of Communication 4 (2010), 696–718.
56. One article along this theme is H.A. Shugart, Ruling Class: Disciplining Class, Race, and Ethnicity in Television Reality Court Shows, Howard Journal of Communications 17 (2006): 79–100.
57. Ibid.
58. R.A. Clawson, H.C.N. IV Strine and E.N. Waltenburg, Frame Supreme Court Decisions: The Mainstream Versus the Black Press, Journal of Black Studies, 33 (2003): 784–800.
59. S. Gallant and J. Epsorth, Media Law, A Practical Guide to Managing Publication Risks (London: Sweet and Maxwell, 2001): 344 et seq.
60. D. Goldberg, G. Sutter and I. Walden, Media Law and Practice (Oxford: OUP, 2009): 194 et seq. The main UK cases of *Green v Broadcasting Corporation of New Zealand* [1989] RPC 469; and appeal at [1989] RPC 700; and *Norowzian v Arks* (No 2) [2000] FSR 363, were each unfavourable to IP format protection in those particular cases. See ibid. Note also 224, ibid, referring to IP trade mark protection issues for programme name formats.
61. D. Dayan and E. Katz, Media Events: The Live Broadcasting of History (Cambridge: Harvard University Press, 1992).
62. K. Creech, Electronic Media Law and Regulation (Burlington, MA: Focal Press/Elsevier, 2007), 396.
63. D.M. Gillmor, J.M. Barron and T.F. Simon, Mass Communication Law, Cases and Comment (Belmont, CA: Wadsworth, 1998), 415.
64. While the author chose the term wheel of justice in relation to this first representation of the forms of television courtroom broadcasting, the author subsequently found the following reference, "[t]he wheels of justice must not stop merely because as accused is of such prominence that he and his alleged misdeeds have been publicized throughout the state," unreported decision of Texas Court of Criminal Appeals, (1964), apparently in *Estes v Texas*, referred to in K.L. Netteburg, Cameras in the Courtroom: Is a Picture Worth a Thousand Words? (Ph.D diss., University of Minnesota, 1980): 17.
65. S.A. Kohm, I'm Not A Judge But I Play One On TV: American Reality-Based Courtroom Television (Ph.D diss., Simon Fraser University, 2004).
66. Ibid, iv.
67. Ibid, 4.
68. Ibid, 26.
69. Ibid.
70. Ibid, 42.
71. Ibid, 16.
72. Ibid, 407.
73. Ibid, 30.
74. Ibid, 32.
75. Ibid, 64, referring to J.M. Shattuc, The Talking Cure: TV Talk Shoes and Women (New York: Routledge, 1997).
76. Ibid, 65, again referring to Shattuc, above.
77. Ibid, 65, 408, 409.
78. Ibid, 82.
79. Ibid, 89, referring to N, Rafter and C.A. Hahn, Courtroom Files, in N. Rafter, Shots in the Mirror: Crime Films and Society (Oxford: Oxford University Press, 2000).

80. Ibid, 90.
81. Ibid, 100.
82. Ibid, 118.
83. Ibid, 123.
84. Ibid, 126, 190.
85. Ibid, 137.
86. Ibid, 138.
87. Ibid, 398.
88. J. Ossinger. Electronic Access to Courtrooms: Television as an Educational Socializing Agent on the Judiciary (MA diss., The University of Maine, 2006): 1. But note carveouts at 24 as regards unrealistic infotainment and its effect of creating low confidence in the court system.
89. Ibid, 31–32.
90. Ibid, 37.
91. Referred to in book review, R.P. Matsch, "Television in the Courtroom: Mightier Than The Pen?" Michigan Law Review 97 (1999): 2037-2041. Referring to R.L. Goldfarb, TV or Not TV: Television, Justice, and the Courts (New York: New York University Press, 1998).
92. R.P. Matsch, ibid.
93. S.A. Kohm, The People's Law Versus Judge Judy Justice: Two Models of Law in American Reality-Based Courtroom TV, Law and Society Review, 40 (2006): 693-–727.
94. Ibid.
95. See E.F. Daniels, Cameras May Yet Cover the Supremes, Multichannel News (November 20, 2000): 84.
96. J. Herman and D. Kawamoto, D., Memorandum, Prepared for the Committee on Court Administration and Case Management (Hon. John R. Tunheim, Chair), the Judicial Conference of the United States, submitted on Behalf of Courtroom View Network, (June 6, 2009), 22.
97. Ibid.
98. Ibid.
99. Judicial Conference of the United States, Statement of the Honourable John R. Tunheim, Judge, United States District Court for the District of Minnesota, For the Committee on the Judiciary of the United States House of Representatives, Hearing on Cameras in the Courtroom: The 'Sunshine in the Courtroom Act of 2007,' H.R. 2128, (September 27, 2007): 6–7.
100. Ibid, 6.
101. Ibid, 7.
102. J. O'Scannlain, (Exhibit 4) Statement of Judge Diarmuid O'Scannalain On Behalf of The Judicial Conference of the United States Regarding S.892 As Applied to Federal Courts, 63.
103. Ibid, 64–65.
104. R. Goldfarb, in Statement of Ronald Goldfarb, Allowing Cameras and Electronic Media in the Courtroom, US Senate Subcommittee on Administrative Oversight and the Courts, Committee on the Judiciary, Washington DC (September 6, 2000): 55.
105. Ibid.
106. Ibid.
107. Ibid, 56.
108. Ibid.
109. Ibid, 58 and 59.
110. E. Thompson, Courtroom Cameras: Issue Moves in and Out of Focus, Quill Magazine (September, 2004): 7–9, at 7.
111. E. Thompson, ibid, 7–9, at 8. Also, M.A. Franklin, D.A. Anderson, and L.B. Lidsky, Mass Media Law Cases and Materials (New York: Foundation Press, 2005), 702.
112. D.M. Gillmor, J.M. Barron and T.F. Simon, Mass Communication Law, Cases and Comment (Belmont, CA: Wadsworth, 1998), 416.
113. Ibid.
114. Ibid, 417.
115. Ibid, 417.
116. Ibid.
117. R.L. Sadler, Electronic Media Law (Thousand Oaks, CA: Sage, 2005), 367.

118. D.M. Gillmor, J.M. Barron, and T.F. Simon, above, 419.
119. H. Schleiff, Cameras in Courts, New Law Journal, 154 (2004): 1745.
120. Ibid.
121. Ibid.
122. Ibid. Lord Falconer concluded that "[j]ustice should be seen to be done. But our priority must be that of justice." Referred to ibid.
123. Ibid.
124. H. Schleiff, Cameras in Courts, New Law Journal 154 (2004): 1745.
125. Court TV Deterrent, New Law Journal 138 (1988): 906.
126. Ibid.
127. Department of Constitutional Affairs [UK], Broadcasting Courts, Consultation Paper, CP 28/04 (November, 2004).
128. See www.dca.goc.uk/consult/courts/broadcasting-cp28-04.htm , accessed on December 14, 2009.
129. Department of Constitutional Affairs [UK], Broadcasting Courts, Consultation Paper, CP 28/04 (November, 2004): 41.
130. Ibid, 5.
131. Ibid.
132. Ibid, 6.
133. Ibid, 7. Also, 20.
134. Ibid, 6.
135. Ibid, see 42 for example.
136. Referred to ibid, 99.
137. Ibid, 6.
138. Ibid, see 21 et seq.
139. Ibid.
140. Ibid, and 23
141. Ibid, 24.
142. Ibid, 6. Also 40 et seq.
143. Ibid.
144. Note parag. 6, ibid, 7.
145. Ibid, 7.
146. Ibid.
147. Ibid.
148. Ibid, 67.
149. Ibid, 7.
150. Ibid, 18.
151. Ibid, referring to Liz Green in the Australian Law Journal. Full citation not given. Australian Law Journal 69 (1995): 477.
152. Ibid, parag. 38, 20.
153. New York State Committee to Review Audio-Visual Coverage of Court Proceedings, An Open Courtroom: Cameras in New York Courts (New York: Fordham University Press, 1997): 37 and 37, n. 43.
154. Ibid.
155. However, there are also critics of the Common Law adversarial system of justice. See J.D Jackson, Law's Truth, Lay Truth and Lawyers' Truth: The Representation of Evidence in Adversary Trials, Law and Critique III (1992): 29—49.
156. See, for example, L. Walker, J. Thibaut and V. Andreoli, Order of Presentation at Trial, Yale Law Journal 82 (1972): 216–226. This work also involved an interesting and insightful experiment.
157. S.L. Alexander. "Mischievous Potentialities": A Case Study of Courtroom Camera Guidelines, Eight Judicial Circuit, Florida, 1989 (Ph.D diss., University of Florida, 1990), 18, 22, 23, 13, 136.
158. *Zamora v Florida*, 372 So. 2d 473, 1979, 1979; 77; 77-25123-A, 11/30/77, referred to S.L. Alexander, ibid, 82.
159. W. Petkanas, above, 16-17.

160. S.R. Pasternack, The Effects of Perceived Community Pressure on Simulated Juror Guilt Attributions: An Experimental Study (Ph.D diss., University of Tennessee, Knoxville, 1982): iv.

161. B.E. Bergman, Written Statement of Barbara E. Bergman, on Behalf of the National Association of Criminal Defense Lawyers, Before the Senate Committee on the Judiciary, Re: 'Cameras in the Courtrooms,' November 9, 2005, 2.

162. S.L. Alexander, above, 115.

163. Referred to ibid, 115.

164. W. Petkanas, above, 41.

165. E.H. Short, and Associates, above, 1, n. 3.

166. S.R. Pasternack, above, iv.

167. K.L. Netteburg, Cameras in the Courtroom: Is a Picture Worth a Thousand Words? (Ph.D diss., University of Minnesota, 1980): 4.

168. Ibid, 4-5.

169. Ibid, 5.

170. E.H. Short and Associates, above, 54.

171. P. Thaler, above, 9.

172. Ibid, 103, giving the example of the testimony of Hedda Nussbaum in the Steinberg case in New York.

173. Ibid, 116.

174. R. Enter, The Image of the Judiciary: A Semiotic Analysis of Broadcast Trials to Ascertain Its definition of the Court System (Ph.D diss., New York University, 1993), 15.

175. Ibid, 26.

176. Ibid, 27.

177. Ibid, above, 28.

178. Ibid, above, 78.

179. P. Thaler, above, 21, referring to S. Barber, above, but without page citation.

180. One of the few general texts is C. Vismann and S. Ogger trans, Tele-Tribunals: Anatomy of a Medium, Grey Room 32, 10 (2003): 5–21. This is an MIT Press Journals publication.

181. K. Erjavec and P. Kovacic, A Discursive Approach to Genre, Mobi News, European Journal of Communication 24 (2009): 147–164.

182. Ibid.

183. Ibid.

184. Ibid, 148.

185. Ibid, 153.

186. There is an example of such a measure at the moment where some US politicians are trying to introduce a law allowing for television cameras in federal courts. See "Glassley Pushes for Cameras in Federal Courts," in Des Moines News, March 20, 2009, www.kcci.com/news/18975176/detail.html (accessed August 13, 2011). Also see www.opencongress.org/bill/110-s352/show , accessed August 13, 2011.

187. An example of general rules is the California Rules of Court (Revised 1 January, 2009).

188. See Chapter 12.

189. See Chapter 12, and elsewhere throughout.

190. For example, some of the international tribunals and courts which are broadcast. Indeed, this also occurred as far back as 1962 in the case of *State v Manley*, Docket Number 22092, Oklahoma County District Court, as referred to in W. Freedman, above, 42–43.

191. The later is particularly evident in dedicated channel courtroom broadcasting in the US.

192. Such as the BBC in the UK or RTE in Ireland.

193. Examples being TV3 in Ireland and TruTV in the US.

194. The recent The Barristers programme and Legal Eagles appear to be examples of independent producers.

195. See the example of State of Connecticut Judicial Branch, protocol for Broadcasting, Televising, Recording or Photographing Appellate Court Oral Arguments, www.jud.state.ct.us/EXTERNAL/supapp/protocol_ap_oral_argu.htm , accessed August 13, 2012.

196. Indeed, some of the camera footage from the Irish courts is from a balcony. *State v Manley* (1962) also has a special booth, as referred to in W. Freedman, Press and Media Access to a Criminal Courtroom (New York: Quorum Books, 1988), 42–43

197. See Chapter 2.

Chapter Seven

Are There TCB Genres and Formats?

INTRODUCTION

Further form issues arise for consideration with television courtroom broadcasting (TCB), in particular those arising from the media and communications literature. The question which arises is whether there is a "genre" or a "format" of television courtroom broadcasting. Indeed, might there be "genres" and or "formats" of TCB? Another alternative to consider is whether television courtroom broadcasting fits within any of the pre-existing forms of media genres and formats. This is a large and significant research challenge to be addressed. This is not explicit in the Supreme Court challenge.

Richard K. Sherwin emphasises the need to educate ourselves in relation to media consumption.[1] Michael Foley, in a stronger tone, states that the public has a right to know how news organisations make their decisions.[2] Sherwin also asks if we "adequately appreciate how TV formats skew political and legal matters toward exaggerated and simplistic ('stereotypical') meanings for ease of assimilation and heightened emotional impact?"[3] These comments highlight the need for increased media literacy.[4] This arises also in relation to our understanding of courtroom broadcasting and courtroom broadcasting forms. Much of these comments relate to the end product courtroom footage i.e. out-of-court.

Valikoski[5] also refers to a model of communications in-court.[6]

There does not appear to be any process-research in relation to television courtroom broadcasting. However, there are occasional articles in relation to trail venue process issues.[7] There is also a study in Cork in relation to domestic violence and the criminal-process.[8]

In terms of media attention and courtroom broadcasting, Andrea Biondi refers to two categories of trial, namely, the sensational trial and the general

Table 7.1. Valikoski Matrix of In-Court Criminal Hearing Communications. From Valikoski.

Monologue 1 Monologue 2 Monologue 3 Question-Answer-Discussion	Parties' information and obstacles to processing the case	Stage 1
Monologues	Stating the claim/defense • Proposals 1 and 2 and the groundings for the argument	Stage 2
Dialogue, Discussion	Description of the matter Testimony • Interview • Debate • Negotiation	Stages 3 and 4
Monologues	Closing arguments 1 and 2 and justified, evaluated and re-evaluated proposals	Stage 5
Monologue	Justified conclusion/judgment	Stage 6

Discussion in a courtroom can be seen as an argumentation, a definition, and alteration and suggestions for solving a problem. A solution to the problem, then includes a justified proposal with conclusions and consequences in the subject-matter.

interest trial.[9] He defines or describes sensational trials as being those involving famous people, sex offence cases, violence and "cruel acts." He defines general interest cases in terms of their wide social interest and relevance for the whole community. The first category of trials frequently involve the disclosure or examination of very personal details. There is an argument that courtroom broadcasting of such details can violate individuals rights, including human rights, not to be humiliated, disadvantaged or caricatured — regardless of it being for education or educational purposes.[10]

Yet, we know very little about how TCB works in-court and out-of-court. We need an increased media literacy in terms of TCB. This includes how TCB media decisions are made; how TCB is made; and the different filming processes and communications processes in TCB courtrooms. This includes, across the different TCB forms. Is the courtroom communications process changed by the introduction of TCB?

GENRES AND FORMATS: IS TCB A GENRE?

Media and communications studies recognise many categories of television broadcasting programme/content. The main categories are television genres and television formats. Yet, no model has been researched or proposed for TCB or TCB effects. Might media and communications research assist in understanding and categorising TCB forms?

A media genre "means a kind or type and is often loosely applied to any distinctive category of cultural product … In relation to most mass media content … the concept of genre is useful and not especially controversial …. Genre can refer to any category of content that has [four] … characteristics."[11] The four characteristics are,

- Its collective identity is recognized more or less equally by its producers (the media) and its consumers (media audiences);
- This identity (or definition) relates to purposes (such as information, entertainment or subserviants), form (length, pace, structure, language, etc) and meaning (reality reference);
- The identity has been established over time and observes familiar conventions; cultural forms are preserved, although these can also change and develop within the framework of the original genre;
- A particular genre will follow an expected structure of narrative or sequence of action, draw on a predictable stock of images and have a repertoire of variants of basic themes.[12]

Genres "refers to a type of text and ... 'can be defined as patterns/forms/styles/structures which transcend individual ... products, and which supervise both their construction ... and their reading by audience.'"[13] The audience uses genres to categorise programmes.[14]

Also, a "[f]ormat ... describes a particular variant on a generic form; it is also used to describe ... [particular] technology ..., for example, VHS [format]."[15]

WHY IS THIS IMPORTANT?

It helps us to understand TCB, how TCB is formed, what it may mean, and how it might be used by the audience and or the public. It might also help us to understand how courtroom participants may use TCB. It also helps us to research and consider effects.

Nick Lacey emphasises that it is important to identify which genres apply to a text, and furnishes a model and matrix to assist genre categorisation.[16] It relies on identifying the setting, character, narrative, iconography, style and stars[17] (participants/actors). With the possible limited exception of Reality TCB, this has not been attempted for TCB.

This is important because this enables us to understand and appreciate television courtroom broadcasting and its effects. Genres (and sub-genres)(and formats) are recognised categories of media programming. Genres and formats are also referred to in communications research.[18] Are there genres and sub-genres of television courtroom broadcasting? Are there different effects across different genres and formats of television courtroom broadcasting? Are some more emphasised? Are some more preferable?

The additional importance of this, is that there is not just one constant form of television courtroom broadcasting. Nor is there one single constant effect of television courtroom broadcasting across all forms and genres/formats of television courtroom broadcasting.

Clearly, we need to begin this research. We need to be much more active in our approach to the research of television courtroom broadcasting. The detail and volume of research must also improve. Indeed, this approach is also supported by recent research which examines blogging and blawging (legal blogs) under the categories of genres and sub genres.[19]

TELEVISION GENRES

First, let us look at television genre issues and how they may apply to television courtroom broadcasting. Genre simply means a type or kind of television programme.[20] A fundamental issue is definition and what constitutes a "genre" and a genre in television.[21] Detailed research of whether TCB is a genre is required.

Genres "are metalanguages, they 'suggest' to an audience how to read a text."[22] The scheduling of a programme can also affect how the audience will receive and understand it.[23] Genres refers to "shared understandings between producers and audiences about forms and the purposes they serve."[24]

At a general level, genre "means a sort, or type, of text: horror movie, musical, autobiography, tragedy, etc."[25] If something can be categorised into an existing genre category it means we can then see what other texts it resembles[26] or competes with. We can also more easily distinguish it from other genres.[27] We also have "expectations"[28] about a programme once we know what genre category it is in. What do we expect of TCB? What do we expect of different forms of television courtroom broadcasting (TCB)?

Genres can be classified according to the properties that distinguish different text types:

1. Classification on the basis of formal arrangement …
2. Classification on the basis of theme or topic …
3. Classification on the basis of mode of address: genre is identified by how the text addresses its audience …
4. Classification on the basis of attitude or anticipated response …[29]

Marie Gillespie and Jason Toynbee add that,

> We never engage with media in a vacuum. Rather, we enjoy and make sense of particular media texts in relation to other texts of a similar type. In media studies these types of a text are known as genres (from the French for 'type' or 'kind'). They include westerns, comedy, sci–fi, horror, thrillers, soaps, news and 'reality TV.' Of course, we can classify media texts according to different criteria: by director, actor, style or some other system of categorisation. But genre is one of the principal ways in which audiences, producers and critics routinely classify media. Our cultural knowledge of media genres is woven into the very texture of our everyday lives and shapes the media choices we make, as well as the expectations and assumptions that we bring to understanding and enjoying media texts.[30]

How do we classify TCB, and different forms of TCB?

Genres helps us to recognise and distinguish different programmes from each other.[31] We can also consider genres as "maps."[32] Media classification systems also serve to "establish hierarchies of values."[33] In addition,

[g]enre labels (... news, etc.) are used to categorise media by:

- media audiences seeking the pleasures of the familiar and the reassurance involved in knowing broadly what might happen in a particular media text;
- media industries aiming to avoid risk and ensure profitable differences;
- media critics, and others with power to classify media, in establishing.

Genres "are characterized by their own ... formats and languages."[34] This implies that genres are wider than and or superior to media formats. The crime series has for decades been one of the most popular television genres.[35] The "news interview" genre is also "familiar and readily recognizable."[36] Glen Creeber[37] variously refers to numerous examples of genres. There are 222 television genres listed on one website.[38] It describes television genres as "a way of classifying TV programs by format or type of content. Some genres will be shared with other media (such as science fiction); others are specific to television."[39] In terms of courtroom broadcasting, the potentially most relevant genres include (in particular the categories highlighted in italics),

> *Reality Television*; *News*; Documentary (e.g. Police, Camera, Action!; Great Crimes and Trials; COPS; Crime Invasion: Britain's New Underworld; Police Stop; The Police Tapes; Crime's Children: Crime's Carousel); *Live Television*; *News Broadcasting*; *News Program*; *Current Affairs*; Educational Television; *Evening News*; True Crime; Docudrama; Legal Drama; Police Procedural; Police.[40]

GENRE ELEMENTS

Genres also have a large repertoire of different elements and a programme with a given genre combines some of the elements from that genre repertoire.[41] Some of the elements of the cinema and television genre include,

- Audio–visual elements;
- Narrative;
- Ideological relations.[42]

Audio visual elements include stars, personalities, presenters, set, camera style, lighting, edited style, music, voices and other sound effects are associated with particular genres.[43] Lacey states that the elements which constitute and identify a genre are character types, setting, iconography, narrative and style.[44] With one exception, these are ignored in TCB research. How do we break down the various elements of TCB? Have we attempted to do so to date?

Infotainment also suggests that news is moving beyond "serious, sober remit into the area of entertainment … hybridity … using elements of entertainment, celebrities or film clips, often unacknowledged, in many ways television news stories, newspapers will often seek to make headlines more exciting by triggering genre resonances."[45] Is TCB evolving? Are different forms of television courtroom broadcasting (TCB) evolving?

How much audience research[46] of TCB occurs, at all, or on an ongoing basis? After a genre is assigned, we can also carry out discourse analysis to examine the different types of meaning in each.[47] How is "time" structured on television and in news television?[48] "Narratives organise and represent time in different ways, and it is important to analyse how they do so."[49] The order of events "can shape, in quite powerful ways, the build up of dramatic tension, the climax and the closure of a narrative."[50] Viewers put the story narrative together by,

- Formulating, testing and revising hypotheses based on incoming information;
- Making causal connection and inferences;
- Reconstructing the temporal order and duration of the events;
- Gap filling in narrative time or logic;
- Assessing the spatial frame of reference in which the story occurs;
- Considering how space, décor, lights, framing and the other elements of style express human relationships.[51]

The "narrative … is designed to engage imaginatively."[52] "When we think of different types of media discourse, such as those found in tabloid newspapers, adverts, television soaps, or gossip magazines, we are thinking about different genres or text types."[53] So genres are categories of text type. "Each type is identifiable because of specific features commonly associated with both its form and function."[54]

Let us look at some specific genre examples in a little more detail.

STATION GENRES

Cable television or pay television channel itself can be a genre.[55] "The development of pay TV, in fact, has been structured around niche-marketing to audience genre preferences for sports, music video, lifestyle programming, documentary and so on."[56] Glen Creeber[57] states that television genres create an order or index of television content. Genre categories help us to make sense of the volume of television content.[58] If we are looking to laugh, we may go to the Comedy Channel; if we want news updates, we might go to CNN; or if we want music, we may go to MTV.[59] These are examples of channel genres or categories of types of television content. If we are not sure of what exactly we want to see, there are "mixed genre" channels such as the BBC which contain a variety of different genre programming.[60] Genre categorisation "enables us to make sense of a large number of choices by separating them into smaller and easily recognisable generic categories."[61] Generic channels include Comedy Central, Sci-Fi Channel, MTV, CNN News.[62] Therefore, we could say that TruTV (previously Court TV), like CNN or MTV, is a television genre of television. No one in the literature identified to date has categorised TruTV as a television genre. This appears to be the first mention of TCB as a genre issue in the literature.

PROGRAMME GENRES

Genres are "conceptual categories used to link together a number of television programmes, but they also articulate a range of cultural assumptions that become linked to the category beyond the programme itself."[63]

That content may be legal-subject based does not equate to a legal genre. However, if we say court or court programming is the content, we might say that there is a genre of courtroom programming or a courtroom broadcasting genre. However, "[n]early every television programme is explicit in its genre identity, clearly branded by its channel, promotional campaign, narrative form and iconography."[64] Therefore, we need to consider the programme and the content, not just the channel. The programme can have a genre, not just the channel. This is more complex. Individual TruTV programmes could, therefore, be said to be examples of a courtroom television broadcasting genre, depending on their form and style.

The audience, critics, networks aswell as the programme text also help to define the genre of a particular programme or channel.[65] Programmes and genres can also be interpreted differently in different communities and cultures.[66] Fintan Maguire of TV3 recently also referred to "an American format."[67] Do US content, formats and genres translate, and transfer, to other countries? Is US style TCB transferrable elsewhere? All of these issues need to be considered in terms of television courtroom broadcasting.

NEWS GENRE

TV news is recognised as a genre.[68] The news genre is "widely understood; and instances of broadcast news are instantly identifiable as such to audiences. Indeed, news has claims to be the most widely ... understood ... genre ... However, even within this genre, there are generic variations ... subgenres such as the news report, the news interview, or the news headline."[69]

When we begin to analyse the news we are initially "required" to understand the process which is involved in the making of television news.[70] The producers of news make decisions in relation what news to cover and what not to cover.[71] (This also relates to the news "gatekeeping" research).

"Since TV news is still one of the prime sources of information in the process of democratic decision-making, the study of the genre remains a critical issue."[72]

Again, there can be genre/format crossover. For example,

> [N]ews and current affairs formats inevitably hybridised. Editors tried to make their talking heads appealing ... The format was occasionally revamped to maintain viewer interest.[73]
> [N]ews circulates mainly through moving images, let alone where news circulates mainly through moving images, let alone where news is subject to ratings pressures in an entertainment filled environment yet these fictional shapings may angle our feelings about events in quite powerful ways, so it is important to be aware of how these processes occur.[74]

However, the globalisation of television news[75] and the arrival of continuous rolling news and rolling updates[76] makes research and categorisation more difficult.

> In current affair shows the gravitational pull of infotainment was much more pronounced. Emotional scenes, such as a sporting victory or a homecoming, might be rendered with music and slow motion. Private conflicts were dramatised (often literally via 're-enactments') to produce public narratives. Facts were still routinely respected, but their status was subordinated to the mythic or symbolic resonance of a story.[77]

TCB AS NEWS

Overall there are a remarkably small number of themes which dominate the news.[78] In addition, the genesis of most news stories is limited to the symbiotic relationship between journalists and official sources.[79] Much of modern newsprint and programming comes from official sources and even officially printed copy. Arguably, less and less independent investigation and writing are carried out, thus limiting the number of topics and agendas covered in the news.

The advent of continuous rolling news and world news stories means that the same content is repeated over and over and that the actual quality of what is shown arguably diminishes and or is condensed. Television genres, styles and forms vary significantly. For example, one study presented the same content to research groups which differed in terms of fragmentation of spaces, logical gaps, close-ups and zooming in and out.[80] No one has focused on these issues as they occur with television courtroom broadcasting. These are valid areas of research as between different types of television courtroom broadcasting (TCB).

It is necessary to be aware of and differentiate between messages, codes and forms used by television news broadcasting and television courtroom broadcasting in particular. Zooming in and out can have different affects on the audience. The changing of cameras can have effects, as can de–coupling camera and audio signals. Long and short shots and different angle shots also have an impact. So too with voiceovers. Indeed, this was an area of concern in the first federal pilot experiment.

The form of the presentation of news stories has been found to have a strong impact upon news information retention.[81] This should be considered when asking, what is the purpose of television courtroom broadcasting, and on focusing courtroom broadcasting research.

Stuart Hall writes that,

> Journalists speak of 'the news' as if events select themselves. Further, they speak as if which is the 'most significant' news story, and which 'news angles' are most salient are divinely inspired. Yet of the millions of events which occur every day in the world, only a tiny portion ever become visible as potential news stories; and of this proportion, only a small fraction are actually produced as the day's news in the news media. We appear to be dealing, then, with a 'deep structure' whose function as a selective device is un-transparent even to those who professionally most know how to operate it.[82]

Often television courtroom broadcasting research may be criticised for involving only basic and cursory research methodologies, in particular self reports.[83] Frequently, no aim or underlying hypothesis is established. This means that the research effort overall is varied and unfocused. The amount and types of data gathered in many cases is limited. Few television courtroom broadcasting studies can be directly compared (if at all). There is no body of reception analysis or research of the effects of television courtroom broadcasting on the audience or study of content or content types for television courtroom broadcasting. What information is portrayed in television courtroom broadcasting and how is this comprehended? Studies are rarely carried out in a systematic manner. Frequently, television courtroom broadcasting research does not identify an aim or purpose in advance. Therefore, what effect can it actually be researching? The studies that do exist often rely on untrained court personnel to carry them out and only focus upon limited observational or self report questionnaires.[84]

The way in which people form news information is extremely complex.[85] This is as true about news broadcasting as it is about television courtroom broadcasting research. News events are certainly about reality but the way in which we structure, and experience, events on television plays a role in our comprehension.[86] This is one of the reasons why further research is required. We need to ask who produces media texts; why? and for whom?[87] How do the media create "expectations" and assumptions in the audience? How do the media sell, advertise and promote television courtroom broadcasting? How do these differ across television courtroom broadcasting forms?[88] Why has TCB media research been so limited?

TCB NEWS CONTENT

One point also overlooked in most TCB debates is that regardless of news TCB, much information the public gets about the justice system, is from entertainment programming.[89] This needs to be researched.

NEWS SNIPPETS AND SOUNDBITES

Time is critical in news selection, and the importance varies across the different types of news, namely, hard news, soft news, spot news, developing news and continuing rolling news.[90] Obviously there are other factors too involved in news selection.[91]

However, that the media will only broadcast the briefest of snippets of actual in-court footage, is often argued as a reason against TCB, or against particular forms of TCB. The first federal pilot experiment found that there was an average broadcast length of 56 seconds of courtroom footage per court story.[92]

In New Zealand[93] what was broadcast was a mix of courtroom footage, out of court footage and re–cut file footage.[94] There was also editing, splicing, re–ordering and a "mixture of visual elements."[95] This "has implications if a purpose of the cameras in court pilot was to promote public understanding of the court procedure and the justice system."[96] The study found that "[n]one of the 149 stories evaluated contained film continuously shot in the court. Instead stories were generally a mixture of visual film gathered inside the court, outside the court and re–cut with file footage."[97] There can, therefore, be a large difference between what is filmed and what may be broadcast.

In 1968 the average sound bite was 43.1 seconds.[98] By 1988 it was reduced to 8.9 seconds.[99] Television provides adults with at least 70 per cent of their news.[100] However, if content is reduced to snippets and soundbites, what is the effect on education and informative value? We need to research this from a television courtroom broadcasting perspective. We also need to recognize that research methods are evolving too.

What impact does the competing media environment have on television courtroom broadcasting and the effort to produce educative form television courtroom broadcasting? We need to begin considering more nuanced television courtroom broadcasting research.

NEWS SCHEDULING

News scheduling restraints and practices in relation to television programming are factors which do not exist (or exist in the exact same way) for popular broadsheet newspapers.[101] This is another issue which exemplifies the difference between print and broadcasting. There are also different scheduling arrangements between different forms of print and broadcasting. These differences affect the form of material which is presented to the reader or audience. This impacts upon the eventual form of television courtroom broadcasting. Part of this may be referred to as filtering or gatekeeping in media research.

NEWS PRODUCTION, SOURCES AND PROCESS

Obtaining other peoples' opinions is also an exercise in creating supportive evidence. We tend to seek opinions which assist our pre-existing theories. Gaye Tuchman[102] also writes that reporters choose between competing facts subjectively when making "news judgements" about particular facts. They are deciding what is "more important or interesting to highlight and this reflects the content of the story and also those stories which are actually printed."[103]

Some court participants also provide information for newspaper reporters. Frequently reporters fail to verify or corroborate general information they receive.[104] It would be interesting to see what effects this would have on television courtroom broadcasting if the information they receive from party opponents, or "experts," was less than accurate or biased. The presentational style of journalism relies overwhelmingly or "official sources" without serious challenge.[105]

Context and importance attached to news items can often depend upon where items in the story are presented. A charge placed at the beginning of the story (because it appears more newsworthy or important) might receive more attention than the denial placed towards the bottom of the story.[106] As Piyah Haldar states in a different context, "the frame ... becomes just as much of a sign as the photograph is itself."[107] Haldar continues that "what the camera frames, and what the law frames, it controls and configures — but what must also be understood is that the question of form (con-conformion) cannot be separated from the question of the frame."[108]

Generally, newspaper writers seeking to justify their "reports" rely on,

- present conflicting possibilities in relating to truth claims;
- present supplementary evidence to support a "fact";
- using quotation marks to indicate that the reporter is not making a true claim;
- before presenting the most "material facts" first;
- carefully separating the facts from opinions by using the labels analysis.[109]

Isrolowitz states that the,

> process of reporting and writing news entails subjective decisions such as choosing the lead and angle of the story, selecting individuals to interview and quote, and assigning value laden adjectives to events and institutions. These decisions 'are all influenced by the personal history [the reporter] brings to this work.' Ironically, the techniques associated with objectivity may provide a means of cover for reporters who seek to promote a certain viewpoint in their accounts. For example, several editors and reporters have acknowledged the practice of 'shopping' for opinions consistent with their own. In the course of this process, '[information] that is inconsistent with the slant of their stories is discarded.' This practice illustrates how an article that purports to be free from a reporter's personal biases may subtly embody those biases.[110]

The process, sources and production values in TCB have yet to be examined.

There has been various research of the communication process and of the process of selecting and producing a media story. Indeed, there are calls for more knowledge and research in this area. Michael Foley indicates that the public has a right to know how news organisations make their decisions.[111] Slotnick and Segal call for better understanding of the flow of information between judicial elites and the public,[112] as does Newton Emerson.[113] However, there is no research of how a television courtroom broadcasting story has been selected, produced, created, edited and ultimately broadcast. In considering the meaning and effects of television courtroom broadcasting, we need to begin the research of the legal and justice process. We need to consider the process of, and how, TBC fits within that process and the process of and how TCB stories are created.

News denotes events but is also used to describe

> a constructed representation of such events or actions … Language in news media structures how whatever goes on in the world is represented,
>
> - How stories are selected,
> - How they are organised, and
> - How they are presented.[114]

Alan Durant and Marina Lambrou state that,

> It might seem that 'news' (as media presentation) should simply reflect 'news' (as actions and events). Such reflection would give news objectively and truthfulness. If, on the other hands, you consider that reported 'news' reshapes news events and actions to a significant extent, then 'news' appears not so much direct reporting of events as the output of a media agenda for news-making. In between the events and reports or stories, there would be a set of creative and editorial processes for giving form to whatever events and actions are depicted. News, in this second view, serves an agenda. It can use its own framing and storytelling techniques to highlight issues, to campaign, to criticise, to celebrate, to promote forthcoming events, or to attract attention to or distrust attention from *other* events. This view of news is essentially that news language serves rhetorical purposes as much as it reflects how things are or what has happened. News, in such a perspective, may even offer only a distorted and distorting account of how the world is. To understand the language of news, accordingly, would be to understand its capability for bias, manipulation and possibly deception as well as its potential to inform.[115]

What constitutes news?[116] and what is the meaning of newsworthiness?[117] Alan Durant and Marina Lambrou refer to news categories by reference to two lists, namely, a list of new topic areas and newsworthiness features.[118] The two lists,

> represent two dimensions of the genre of a news story: its field (what it's about) and its function (here, the function of gaining attention, having an impact, or achieving some other effect such as entertaining, frightening or shocking). A news story is always about *some* particular area. Its language is adapted to expectations associated with that area (e.g. a sport of personal interest story will differ from an international news story is also adapted to *highlight* its newsworthiness (in this way, it justifies or maximises the attention it will be given).[119]

What are news sources?[120] Is courtroom broadcasting a new "source"? Norman Fairclough states,

> With respect to production, it is important to be aware that what we read in a newspaper or see on the television screen is not a simple and transparent representation of the world, but the outcome of specific professional practices and techniques, which could be and can be quite different with quite different results. It is also important to be aware that the practices which underlie texts are based in particular social relations, and in particular relations of power. With respect to consumption, important issues are the diversity of practices of reading, listening and viewing (and their social conditions), and the potential for divergent interpretations and uses of any given text by different sections of a readership or audience.[121]

Fairclough continues,

> Part of critical media literacy is an overall sense of the practices of media and of the media order of discourse, and a sensitivity to significant tendencies of charge. This question assumes that any given media text will shed some light upon these issues, in that it will be a product of a particular state and evolution of the order of discourse. Particular questions here include,
>
> - Is the text indicative of stable or unstable relationships, fixed or shifting boundaries, between discursive practices within the order of discourse, and between the media order of discourse and socially adjacent orders of discourse?
> - What particular choices (inclusions/exclusions, of genres or discourses) in this text associated with?
> - What chain relationships across the media order of discourse and/or socially adjacent' orders of discourse in this text situated within?
> - What particular tendencies of change (e.g. commodification or conversationalization of media discourse) does this text exemplify?[122]

NARRATIVE GENRES

Nick Lacey refers to game shows as an example of narrative genres. They can be defined with reference to a standard setting (television studio), standard set of characters (e.g. studio audience and host), narrative (prize questions or prize tasks), iconography (e.g. "glitzy set") and style ("basic 'live' television").[123] News programmes can also be examples of "non-narrative genres."[124]

MIXED GENRES

However, the use of genre is not always easy to describe. "Not all categories are easily identifiable, genres do not always remain the same and some ... are ... hybrid ... genres."[125] Genre hybrids or "generic hybrids"[126] can combine a number of styles or elements. Yet in one of the more important media books in the US, there is no mention of the word or term "genre."[127] Often "[t]elevision genres and programming formats are notoriously hybridised … [and are] becoming more so."[128] Increasingly today it could be said that it is almost impossible to think of a programme without more than one genre.[129] Yet genres remain the "primary framework to create and understand new programming."[130] Increased hybridisation and "additions with ongoing formats, also means audiences are subject to increasingly complicated generic content."[131] So there might be more than one genre category of television courtroom broadcasting.

SUB GENRES

There are also "subgenre"[132] issues to consider. Denis McQuail states that

> [o]ne of the strengths of the genre idea is its capacity to adapt and extend to cope with dynamic developments. This is well represented in the even more recent rise of the 'talk show' genre, which began as entertainment interviews with celebrities and as 'breakfast television' format and has expanded luxuriously throughout the world in manifestations that range from the sensationalist knockabout to very serious occasions for political participation.[133]

Is it time to expand to a new TCB genre?

Martin Montongomery adds,

> [B]roadcast news interviews are themselves not all of a single type. We may distinguish four principal sub-genres: (1) interviews with correspondents (reporting and commenting); (2) interviews with ordinary people affected by, or caught up in, the news (witnessing, reacting and expressing opinion); (3) interviews with experts (informing and explaining); and (4) interviews with 'principles' – public figures with some kind of responsible role in relation to news event (accounting). The four sub-genres may be defined — as here — by characterising the social identity and role of the person being interviewed and their characteristic contribution to the interview; but they could really be described in terms of the kinds of lead-in that set the agenda of the interview or the kinds of questions that form its spine. For instance, a prototypical question to a correspondent is 'Can you tell us more about what is going on?' … A prototypical question to an ordinary witness or bystander is 'What could you see …?', or 'What did/does it feel like …?'. And the question to an expert

> explores the implications of a situation: 'Given X, can you explain its implications?' [134]

In addition, Martin Montegomery also provides a news interview matrix.[135] Alan Durant and Marina Lambrou add that despite the matrix classification, sometimes an interview starts as one type but finishes as another, and can also be a hybrid of matrix types.[136] There is a "repertoire" of different types of news interviews.[137] Bulletin news programmes routinely use edited fragments, thus providing "perspectival sound-bites."[138]

Durant and Lambrou refer to Martin Montgomery's news interview matrix and indicate that similar models can be created for features of related media genres.[139] Does this include TCB? They state,

> Studying the news interview requires a distinctive mode of analysis appropriate to its distinctive character. To clarify this point, it is useful to begin by considering, by way of contrast, how news is typically analyzed when it appears in story form. Traditional content analyses tend to focus on matters such as the themes that predominate within a given range of stories, and the balance and diversity of viewpoints represented therein. For example, studies of election news are concerned with the proportion of coverage devoted to each candidate, and the tendency for stories to concentrate on the theme of the horse race (e.g. who's ahead, campaign strategy, publicity efforts, etc.) to the exclusion of more substantive matters (e.g. the candidates' qualifications, issue positions, policy proposals, etc.). Studies of political news beyond the confines of the campaign have revealed a similar emphasis on political strategy over policy substance.[140]

We can see that many research challenges remain for TCB. For example,

> [E]verything which is seen on TV screen arrives there only after a complex process of mediation involving many people and institutions and a great deal of technology and artifice. TV news is expected to provide a window which is more transparent than most, but it is no different from other TV genres in these respects. Its transparency and perceived factuality is a testament to the extent to which its conventions of representation have been naturalized. Understanding the semiotics of factuality is perhaps one of the most important literacy skills required by readers and viewers in the modern industrial world. But the ways in which information and entertainment have become inextricably linked in most TV genres means that the task of identifying and evaluating claims to factuality has become more complex than ever before.[141]

FORMATS

Television formats provide a "framework of understanding."[142] In addition, they help to show how news is constructed.[143] Denis McQuail refers to David Altheide and Robert Snow[144] who developed a "mode" of media analysis which utilised the terms "media logic" and "media format." Media formats are described by Denis McQuail as "essentially subroutines for dealing with specific themes within a genre."[145] He refers to an example, namely that of David Altheide[146] who refers to a "format for crisis" in television news. The main condition for regular news handling of a crisis are accessibility, visual quality, drama and action, relevance to audience and thematic unity.[147] Doris Graber[148] also states that "television journalists have developed repertoires – another possible term for frames, logic or sub-genre formats of highly stereotyped cues for many specific situations in politics." She makes the point also that there is an essential difference between encoding and decoding of audiovisual language from verbal language. It is more associational, connotative and unstructured and less logical, clearly defined and delimited.[149] Denis McQuail also adds that the "systematic analysis of audiovisual languages is, nevertheless, still at an early stage."[150] It would be premature to say there can be no TCB genres and or no TCB formats, or that none will develop.

The above comments again supports the contention that research of effects of audiovisual [non spoken] language needs further research in particular the effects of audiovisual language in the courtroom and of courtroom television broadcasting needs to begin. It is not possible to say there are no effects in a particular area when one has not even begun research of that area.

References to formats appear less frequently in the literature than genres. Some distinguish between,

> genres and other categories ('modes', 'formats', 'forms' and the like) and thus to understand the extent to which multiple generic participation is as much a feature of television as it is of other media. (Just as Friends (NBC, 1994 – 2004) could be said to participate in the genres 'television programme', 'television series', 'fictional narrative', 'comedy', and so on, so most breakfast shows could be said to participate in the genres 'television programme', 'actuality' and, depending on the nature of the programme, 'news' and or 'topical variety' and perhaps even 'daytime' or 'morning' TV.)[151]

The following reference further suggests that "format" relates more to content specifically while overall style is referring to genre, namely that "[i]n some cases, the cumulative effect of repeated tweaking of the format and content amounts to a change in genre … Often this shift is accompanied by a move downmarket, both in storylines and production values."[152]

Functional media research is used particularly in relation to the "media in new forms."[153] Yet it has not been considered in relation to TCB.

Most media categorisation is undertaken with the descriptive term genre. However, formats is also used. Glen Creeber refers to formats as "in some ways [a] competing, term" to genres.[154] "[U]nlike genre, format is widely used within the industry and among consumers as a way of describing the kind of programme they are watching. Formats can be original and thus copyright, franchised under licence, and traded as a commercial property. Genres, by definition, are not original. Format is a production category with relatively rigid boundaries that are difficult to transgress without coming up with a new format."[155]

He adds that "[g]enre is the product of a text – and audience-based negotiation activated by the viewer's expectations. Genre is the larger, more inclusive category and can be used to describe programmes that use a number of related formats, such as the game show."[156]

In addition, "some television formats actively challenge the idea of genre. The 'liveness' of television, its investment in immediacy and provisionality, is in direct conflict with the regulated production imperatives implied by genre and format."[157]

The series 24 is described as changing the action series by "changing 'the rules of television making format central to a drama'" with its real-time nature.[158] The Walking with Dinosaurs series "format" is indicated to follow the educational television genre.[159] Yet, it seeks to be entertaining too. It merges traditional nature documentary and the spectacle effect of film.[160]

Programmes and styles change so we cannot think of a genre as being static and "stable elements."[161]

Many issues arise for television courtroom broadcasting (TCB) from the above.

INFORMATION FORMATS

Television developed "information formats along the following lines,"[162]

This has not been considered in research of TCB.

DRAMA/DOCUMENTARY/DOCUDRAMA FORMATS

Television forms include documentaries. These include "fly–on–the–wall formats"[163] of documentaries. "'Drama-documentary' is the label most often used in Britain and parts of Europe to indicate the combination of dramatic and documentary elements in a programme. In the USA, the term 'docudrama' has been the preferred term. Rather than a distinct subgenre of programme, it is best to see the classification as pointing to a very wide range of different mixtures."[164] Some also see the development of categories such as drama–documentary" as blurring boundaries and misinforming the public.[165] Increasingly television drama seeks to portray its programme content as being (more) realistic.[166]

Table 7.2. Television Information Formats. Adapted from Creeber.

A talking medium	Words were heard one at a time, so a given current affairs show could only contain so many words, as opposed to a newspaper, where many more words could be printed, even if only a minority of them were read by any one reader
A video medium	Moving pictures were more telegenic than talking heads. Having videotape of an event to hand tended to determine its inclusion in a news show, over and above any assessment of its overall importance in a news story. Conversely, events of great significance for which there was no footage were less likely to reach the top of the news agenda.
A hybridised medium	TV was very prone to evolution by spin off. Successful formats were compulsively copied. In this very active semiotic environment, "information" could never be "pure" – it would always be presented via the techniques and generic formats that were regarded as most appealing at the time.
A porous medium	TV contained an unusual mixture of incommensurable types of progressing, especially fact and fiction, rubbing up against each other. Its formats were very porous to each other. News was constantly borrowing generic characteristics from non-news formats.

REALITY TV

Reality TCB may be the most popular and identifiable TCB format, or at least certain programme formats within Reality TCB e.g. Judge Judy. Reality television is an example of "factual" television.[167] It is a hybrid version taking many aspects from other styles and is now often generically described as infotainment, a combination between information and entertainment.[168] Originally in the 1990's it was used to describe "the particular genre of magazine–format programmes based on crime, accident and health stories, what we might call 'trauma TV.'"[169] Some examples listed for this type of programming include Unsolved Mysteries, Rescue 911, Cops, America's Most Wanted, Emergency 999, Crimewatch UK, Police Camera Action, Blues and Twos.[170] The makeup of reality TV is set out in Table 7.4.

Like a "magazine format" such programming will have a set number of scripted stories per programme episode.[171] The content is carefully packaged. For example,

> [T]he disparate elements are strongly narrativised in ways that conform to conventional fictional police dramas or to the form of melodrama. In turn, the individual stories are structured within an overarching public service narrative address. In the case of 'trauma TV' we are given to understand that our viewing pleasures are safely contained by an explicit appeal to a communitarian logic of security (that is to say, how to avoid becoming a victim of crime or

Table 7.3. Infotainment Formats (Examples). Adapted from Creeber.

1	Lifestyle	Cooking, gardening, travel, house improvement, antiques
2	Reality	Traffic camera shows, home video shows, neighbours from hell, street interviews. This format has evolved into "survival" shows
3	Tabloid	Consumer stories, crime, celebrities, scandal, hidden cameras and chequebook journalism
4	Investigative	Most popular where the reporters put themselves in physical danger of assault by the subjects of the investigation
5	Talk	Including celebrity chat shows, Oprah and Springer, late night variety shows [e.g. confessional]
6	Animal	Vet shows, nature documentaries; environmental stories

> how to participate in crime-detection processes) … argued that this narrative structure is reflected strongly in audience responses to reality TV programmes based in the work of the emergency services. Here the fear occasioned by exposure to crime or ill health is balanced by the resolution offered in the outcomes of the featured cases. In the case of programmes constructed around a drama of everyday life we may be offered the interpretation of psychologists to lend general insight into the particular experiences being represented (for example, Big Brother …). In either case, the 'public service' utility of the programme is often awkwardly at odds with the entertainment–based drive of the narrative structure.[172]

The range of reality and factual programming has also expanded greatly.[173] Reality TV is now a,

> genre description of any factual programme based on an aesthetic style of apparent 'zero-degree realism' – in other words a direct, unmediated account of events, often associated with the use of video and surveillance-imaging technologies. During the 1990s the low-gauge video imaging, grainy, under-lit and often unsteady, became the pre-eminent televisual signifier of truthfulness. After a hundred years of moving-image culture we can now understand how each epoch has its own privileged style for the delivery of visual evidence. For the first 'actuality' audiences, the flickering images of everyday street scenes were astonishingly truthful and accurate … the widespread success of programmes based in this appeal to authenticity occurs at the same time as the widely acknowledged triumph of simulation and spectacle … An image-saturated culture appears to have produced a greater hunger than ever before for an astringent aesthetic of visual realism.[174]

Reality TV describes a variety of "hybrid genres – particularly factual entertainment content. It is a useful term that instantly says this television programme is a hybrid of non-fiction and entertainment elements. Reality TV is also a value–laden term, and its association with entertainment, information,

Table 7.4. Characteristics of Reality TV. Adapted from Creeber.

1	Camcorder, surveillance or observational 'actuality footage'
2	First-person participant or eyewitness testimony
3	Reconstructions that rely upon narrative fiction styles
4	Studio or to-camera links and commentary from 'authoritative' presenters
5	Expert statements from emergency services personnel or psychologists

authenticity, performance and other conceptual values ensures it means different things to different people."[175]

There is no one definition of the Reality TV genre.[176] Reality TV or "popular factual" is a catch all category for a variety of different one off type programmes, series,

> and formats that follow real people and celebrities and their everyday or out of the ordinary experiences. Reality TV subcategories include infotainment about crime or emergency services; docusoaps about institutions or groups of people; lifestyles, often about how to do gardening, or making over someone's home or personal appearance; life-experiment programmes where people experiment with different social experiences; reality game shows where a game element is introduced to a group of people in a controlled situation; reality talent shows where members of the public or celebrities audition for and perform music, or other artistic endeavours; and the reality hoax, a mock situation that usually mocks those deceived by an elaborately staged set-up. There are other emergent categories within reality TV, such as reality business series like The Apprentice (BBC, 2005-), and the wide range of formats shows how all-encompassing this type of hybrid content can be.[177]

Reality TV also has audience interactive elements, such as giving opinions and voting.[178] The Reality TV form is also disruptive and interferes with the scheduling, and programming, of other television genres and formats.[179] It also uses "fast paced editing."[180] It can also include "observational documentaries."[181]

EDUCATIONAL PROGRAMMES

In 1995 the Roper Starch Global Consumer asked respondents what were most important attributes of television programmes they watched.[182] The first was "interesting" and the second was "educational." However, what is educational and educational television in particular, is not "as self-explanatory as it seems."[183] The "whole conception of education has changed over the years along with television itself."[184] If the genres and formats of television are changing, why should we assume that the education values and forms of what are educational television programmes, are not also changing?

Is television courtroom broadcasting (TCB) educational? If certain television courtroom broadcasting (TCB) programmes are educational at one stage, will they remain so indefinetly?

Public service broadcasting "rests partly"[185] on the concept of education. It is said that the US has significantly less public service broadcasting than Europe.[186] While there is limited public service broadcasting (PSB) in the US, there have been some calls for PBS to be disbanded.[187]

It also appears to be clear that most examination of educational programming refers to childrens' television programmes[188] and no adult "educational" programming. "[E]ducational television has always targeted children."[189] When we think of adult educational programming, there is in fact very little. It is in the main Open University type programmes. These programmes are mostly scheduled at non popular hours. They are scheduled in "graveyard slots."[190]

In addition, the content of educational programming needs to be considered. "[T]he proliferation of 'infotainment' has increasingly become the preferred form of educational television, or informational television at the turn of the millennium."[191] The Discovery Channel moved away from traditional "education" form to "merge learning and enjoyment."[192]

Glen Creeber adds,

> Educational programmes that court a general audience, of both adults and children, have adopted the modes of 'infotainment', marking the union of informational and entertainment programming. Programmes are made as engaging as possible, and in an audiovisual language that spectacularises what a few years earlier might have been fairly dry discourses of information. The final product is educational television that uses an audiovisual language originally associated with mainstream entertainment television, such as sensationalism, fact pace, spectacle, enhancing music and narrativisation.[193]

GENRE/FORMAT OF TELEVISION COURTROOM BROADCASTING

Nick Lacey refers to the various elements and components of the game show genre, in particular, setting, characters, narrative, iconography and style.[194] This exercise has not been undertaken for the different forms of TCB. "However, game shows are also formats."[195] This "format" can be commercialised through licensing to other jurisdictions.[196]

Not all genres are actually researched in depth or for any length of time.[197] What are the texts of courtroom broadcasting programmes? How is it promoted and described? In addition, we can also rely on media commentary to ask the following questions.[198] What do courtroom broadcasting programmes mean? How do we define courtroom broadcasting? How do we define courtroom broadcasting programmes? What do courtroom broadcasts mean for a specific community? What is the audience? If we are considering television courtroom broadcasting, we need to examine the category of the channel and the programme. David A. Harris describes TruTV as a "twenty-four hour a day format."[199] What TCB formats are there?

NEED FOR RESEARCH

Companies undertake communications audits, horizontally and vertically, to examine what is transmitted, passivity, direction (one way or two way), technologies, purpose, etc.[200] Do we need an audit of television courtroom broadcasting? What would it reveal?

Researching a television genre category requires analysis of the way in which institutions and people talk about and how they use genre categories, and then to chart the shifts in discourse about a particular genre category through historical contexts.[201]

Even media studies have and continue to be interdisciplinary, using for example social studies.[202] Glen Creeber notes that,

> formal markers that confirm to us that what we are watching (which might be a 'fly-on-the-wall' documentary or a sequence from, say, a current affairs programme) is a record of an ongoing, and at least partly media–independent, reality. Important here will be a sense of spontaneity of action and a movement of camera that presents us with something which is perceptually coherent but which is following developments beyond the control of the crew. Some observational sequences will be shot in a 'raw' style, gaining their realism from their lack of smoothness and of immediate significance when compared with television fiction. However, others may be shot in such a way television fiction. However, others may be shot in such a way as to imitate at least some of the scopic range and lucid continuity of fictional sequences ...[203]

The flow of documentary production has been summarised as follows: planning, shooting, editing, transformation/reception by audience.[204] Fly-on-the-wall documentaries are described as "real people in undirected situations."[205] How different is TCB? Is extended TCB just another documentary?

SUMMARY

Clearly, forms and sub-form issues need to be considered in future television courtroom broadcasting discussions and research. The research needs to incorporate these form distinctions in the design of the research studies. This is one of the ways of overcoming the flaws in the arguments which currently exist.

The forms descriptions show how little we really know about television courtroom broadcasting and how little we have researched the issues. In considering any of the arguments, whether for or against, we see that they do not seek to base themselves in any particular style or forms and sub-forms of television courtroom broadcasting. They thus assume that all such broadcasting is the same, regardless of court, type of case, the rights issues, broadcaster, programme forms, scheduling, location, etc. Such an assumption and approach is no longer tenable. Equally, different rights arguments can be recalibrated depending on the television courtroom broadcasting forms being considered.

NOTES

1. R.K. Sherwin, When Law Goes Pop: The Vanishing Line Between Law and Popular Culture (Chicago: The University of Chicago Press, 2000). D.M. Gillmor, J.M. Barron and T.F. Simon, Mass Communication Law, Cases and Comment (Belmont, CA: Wadsworth, 1998), 415.
2. M. Foley, in a radio interview on Lunchtime with Eamon Keane, Newstalk, December 28, 2009.
3. R.K. Sherwin, above, 251.
4. Ibid, 252.
5. T-R Valikoski, The Criminal Trial as a Speech Communication Situation (Tampere, Finland: University of Tampere, 2004), 199, and throughout.
6. Ibid, 150.
7. For example, the second session of the Irish Conference on Criminal Jurisdiction in November 2002 related to The Criminal Trial Process. See the Judicial Studies Institute Journal 3:1 (2002): 39–71. See also articles in relation to Trial Venue and Process: the Victim and the Accused, by I. O'Donnell, Dr. (103-112); M. O'Briain, (113–119); and K. Mulkerrins, (120-129). Note also R. Horgan, Domestic Violence and Civil Harassment: Some Issues Which Arise when the Case Comess to Court, Judicial Studies Institute Journal 4:1 (2004): 79–107.
8. See C. Fennell and A. Ryan, A Cork Study on 'Domestic' Violence and the Criminal Process: Tentative Conclusions from the Policing Perspective, Judicial Studies Institute Journal 4:1 (2004): 79–107.
9. A. Biondi, TV Cameras Access into the Courtroom: A Comparative Note, Yearbook of Media and Entertainment Law (YMEL) (1996): 133–150, at 146.
10. See J. Pritchard, Editorial, Should Cameras be Allowed in the Courtroom?, Legal Business magazine, (1992): 3, referred to in A. Biondi, above, 146.
11. D. McQuail, McQuail's Mass Communication Theory (London: Sage, 2005), 370.
12. Ibid.
13. Ibid, 132.
14. Ibid, 134.
15. N. Lacey, Narrative and Genre, Key Concepts in Media Studies (London: MacMillan Press, 2000), 206.
16. Ibid, 136-137.
17. Ibid, 137.
18. See J.H. Power, On the Intellectual Structure of the Human Communication Discipline, Communication Education 44 (1995): 191—222, at 198, where he refers to genres and formats in the context of complex, multi-unit discourse.

19. J.M. Cornett, The Ethics of Blawging: Genre Analysis, Loyola University Chicago Law Journal 41 (2009): 221–262.
20. G. Creeber, ed., The Television Genre Book (London: Palgrave MacMillan, 2008), 3. See also M. Briggs, Television, Audiences and Everyday Life (Maidenhead: Open University Press and McGraw Hill), foreword, xiii.
21. See ibid, 5.
22. Ibid, 248.
23. Lacey, N., above, 245.
24. M. Montgomery, above, 26-27, as referred A. Durant and M. Lambrou, Language and Media (London and New York: Routledge Taylor & Francis Group, 2009), 78.
25. A. Durant and M. Lambrou, Language and Media (London and New York: Routledge Taylor & Francis Group, 2009), 21.
26. Ibid.
27. See ibid.
28. See ibid, 22.
29. M. Montgomery, A. Durant, N. Fabb, T. Furniss and S. Mills, S., Ways of Reading (London: Routledge, 2006), as referred to in A. Durant and M. Lambrou, above, 23.
30. M. Gillespie and J. Toynbee, Analysing Media Texts (Maidenhead: Open University Press and McGraw Hill, 2006), 44.
31. See ibid, 44.
32. Ibid, 47.
33. See ibid, 48.
34. See Figure Box 14.1, in McQuail, D., above, 374.
35. See G. Creeber, above, 29.
36. A. Durant and M. Lambrou, above, 204.
37. Glen Creeber refers to the following genres, namely, Drama; *News*; Comedy; Science fiction; Melodrama; Talk shows; Religious; Variety; Situational comedy; Television programme; Television series; Docusoap; *Reality TV*; Soap opera; Crime drama; Crime series; Gangster genre; Police series; Police drama; Hospital drama; Westerns; Action series; Spy genre; Reality television; Horror; Detective; Triller; Docu drama; *Documentary*; Sport; Mini series; Costume drama; Postmodern drama; Music; Childrens' television; *Infotainment*; *Educational*; *Reality TV*; Animation; Popular entertainment; Quiz show; Celebrity talk show; Confessional talk show; Talk show; *Daytime TV*. The categories highlighted in italics are the ones potentially most relevant to analysing TCB content or programmes. Creeber, G., above, 29 and throughout.
38. See Freebase, www.freebase.com/view/tv/tv_genre , accessed August 13, 2012.
39. See ibid.
40. See ibid.
41. See M. Gillespie and J. Toynbee, above, 52.
42. Ibid, 52-53.
43. Ibid, 52.
44. N. Lacey, above, 133, as referred to in G. Creeber, above, 5.
45. M. Gillespie, and J. Toynbee, above, 74.
46. See, for example, ibid, 154.
47. See ibid, 153.
48. See comments in ibid, 93.
49. Ibid, 93.
50. Ibid, 93.
51. Ibid, 102.
52. G. Creeber, above, 127 – 128.
53. See A. Durant and M. Lambrou, above, 8.
54. Ibid.
55. G. Creeber, above, 7.
56. Ibid, 7.
57. Ibid, 1.
58. Ibid.

59. Ibid.
60. Ibid,
61. Ibid.
62. Ibid, 6.
63. See G. Creeber, ibid, 12 and referring to J. Mittell, Genre and Television: from Cop Shows to Cartoons in American Culture (London and New York, Routledge, 2004).
64. See G. Creeber, ibid, 10. It lists the programme Lost, Twin Peaks and Buffy the Vampire Slayer as a rare exceptions.
65. See G. Creeber, ibid, 10.
66. Ibid, 12-13
67. Fintan Maguire, interviewed on Orla Barry, The Green Room, Newstalk, November 15, 2010.
68. See D. McQuail, above, 37 et seq. A. Durant and M. Lambrou, above, 224. G. Creeber, above.
69. M. Montgomery, The Discourse of Broadcast News: A Linguistic Approach (London: Routledge, 2007), 26 – 27, as referred to in A. Durant and M. Lambrou, above, 77.
70. G. Creeber, above, 108.
71. Ibid. In commercial and non commercial television stations there is also constant pressure to get, maintain an increase ratings, for example, to justify funding. Creeber, ibid.
72. Ibid, 111.
73. See ibid, 117.
74. See M. Gillespie and J. Toynbee, above, 74. See generally, H.M. Beville, Jr., Audience Ratings: Radio, Television, and Cable (Hillside, NJ, Erlbaum, 1988).
75. See G. Creeber, ibid, 117 et seq.
76. See for instance ibid, 119.
77. Ibid, 117.
78. This is also pointed out by W.L. Bennett, L.A. Gressett and W. Haltom, Repairing the News: A Case Study of the News Paradigm, Journal of Communications 35 (1985): 50 -– 68, at 52.
79. Ibid, 50-51. See also M. Schudson, The Sociology of New Reporting, above, 271.
80. See G. Solomon and A.A. Cohen, Television Formats, Mastery of Mental Skills, and the Acquisition of Knowledge, Journal of Educational Psychology 69 (1977): 612–619.
81. B. Findahl and O. Hoijer, above, 392, and passim.
82. S. Hall, The Determination of News Photographs, in C. Cohen and J. Young, The Manufacture of News: a Reader (Beverly Hills: Sage, 1983), referred to in M. Schudson, The Sociology of News Production, Media, Culture and Society 11 (1989): 263–282, at 277.
83. See Chapters 5, 6 and 7.
84. See ibid.
85. This point is made by B. Findahl and O. Hoijer, above, 292.
86. Ibid, 390.
87. Question posed by A. Hart, above, 5.
88. See discussion in relation to expectations and research in social cognition in J.J. Skowronski, A.L. Betz, C.B. Thompson and L. Shannon, Social Memory in Everyday Life: Recall of Self-Events and Other-Events, Journal of Personality and Social Psychology 60 (1991): 831–832.
89. D.A. Harris, The Appearance of Justice: Court TV, Conventional Television, and the Public Understanding of the Criminal Justice System, Arizona Law Review 35 (1993): 785–827, at 797.
90. See D. McQuail, above, 314 et seq.
91. Ibid, 318.
92. M.T. Johnson and C. Krafka, Electronic Media Coverage of Federal Civil Proceedings, An Evaluation of the Pilot Program in Six District Courts and Two Courts of Appeal (Federal Judicial Centre, 1994), 34.
93. Media Coverage of Court Proceedings Pilot Evaluation Committee, Media Coverage of Court Proceedings, Introduction and Research Findings (August, 1998): 8.
94. Ibid.

95. Ibid.
96. Ibid.
97. Ibid, 12.
98. J. Caplan, Televising the Courts - Case For Reform, Media Law and Practice 13:2 (1992): 176. This figure is also used by J. Caplan, M. Kalisher, and A. Speaight, Televising the Courts: Report of a Working Party of the Public Affairs Committee of the General Council of the Bar [of England and Wales], (London: Bar Council of England and Wales, 1989).
99. Ibid.
100. Ibid.
101. Ibid, 409.
102. G. Tuchman, Objectivity as Strategic Ritual: Examination of Newsmen's Notions of Objectivity, American Journal of Sociology 77:4 (1972): 660-–679, at 663.
103. Ibid, 670. See also G. Millerson, The Technique of Television Production (London: Focal, 1989, 1990).
104. Ibid, p. 665.
105. J.P. Isralowitz, Reporter as Citizen: Newspaper Ethics and Constitutional Values, University of Pennsylvania Review 141 (1992): 242.
106. G. Tuchman, above, n. 9, 665.
107. P. Haldar, The Evidencer's Eye: Representations of Truth In the Laws of Evidence, Law and Critique 2 (1991): 171–189, at 181.
108. Ibid, 181–182.
109. G. Tuchman, above, 676.
110. J.P. Isralowitz, above, 241, (references omitted).
111. M. Foley, above.
112. E.E. Slotnick and J.A. Segal, Television News and the Supreme Court: All the News That's Fit to Air? (Cambridge: Cambridge University Press, 1998), 2–3.
113. N. Emerson, The Importance of Being Able to Spot a Calculated Media Story, Irish Times, September 8, 2010.
114. A. Durant and M. Lambrou, Language and Media (London and New York: Routledge Taylor & Francis Group, 2009): 85.
115. Ibid, 85–86. Emphasis in original.
116. Ibid, 86.
117. Ibid, 88.
118. Ibid, 89.
119. Ibid, 89.
120. See ibid, 89.
121. N. Fairclough, Media Discourse (London: Arnold, 1995), 201-205, referred to in A. Durant and M. Lambrou, above, 215.
122. N. Fairclough, referred to ibid, 216.
123. N. Lacey, above, 206, as referred to in G. Creeber, above, 5.
124. For example, J.G. Butler, Television: Critical Methods and Applications (Belmony: Wadsworth, 1994), as referred to in G. Creeber, ed., above, 5. Note also J.G. Butler, Television: Critical Methods and Applications (New York: Routledge, 2006).
125. G. Creeber, above, 1.
126. See ibid, 4–5. Generally also note W. Hawes, Television Performing: News and Information (Boston, Mass., Focal, 1991).
127. See ibid, 7, referring to E.T. Vane and L.S. Gross, Programming for TV, Radio and Cable (Boston, MA and London: Focal Press, 1994).
128. See ibid, 8 and references therein.
129. See ibid, 11.
130. See ibid.
131. See ibid, 137. Altman also refers to a "generic audience" to identify those sections of the public "sufficiently familiar with the genre to participate in a fully genre-based viewing" and also about "generic frustration" when "the emotion generated by ... a failure to respect generic norms." R. Altman, Cinema and Genre, in G. Nowell–Smith, ed., The Oxford History of World Cinema (Oxford: Oxford University Press, 1996): 280, as referred to in G. Creeber, above, 3.

132. See G. Creeber, ibid, 28. See D. McQuail, above, for example, 372.
133. See D. McQuail, above, 372.
134. M. Montgomery, The Discourse of Broadcast News: A Linguistic Approach (London: Routledge, 2007): 145-148, as reprinted in A. Durant and M. Lambrou, above, 201–202.
135. Ibid, 145–148, as reprinted in A. Durant and M. Lambrou, above, 203.
136. A. Durant and M. Lambrou, above, 203.
137. M. Montgomery, above, 145–148, as reprinted in A. Durant and M. Lambrou, above, 202.
138. Ibid.
139. A. Durant and M. Lambrou, above, 203.
140. Ibid, 204.
141. D. Graddol, The Visual Accomplishment of Factuality, in D. Graddon and O. Boyd-Barrett, eds., Media Texts: Authors and Readers (Clevedon: Multilingual Matters/Open University, 1994), 136–142, reprinted in A. Durant and M. Lambrou, above, 222–223.
142. To use the words of G. Creeber, above, 110.
143. Ibid.
144. See D.L. Altheide and R.P. Snow, Media Logic (Beverly Hills, CA: Sage, 1979), as referred to in D. McQuail, above, 374.
145. See D. McQuail, above, 374.
146. D.L. Altheide, Media Power (Beverly Hills, CA: Sage, 1979).
147. See D. McQuail, above, 374.
148. D. Graber, Political Language, in D. Nimmo, and K.R. Sanders, eds., Handbook of Political Communication (Beverly Hills, California: Sage, 1981).
149. As referred to in D. McQuail, above, 374.
150. Ibid, 374.
151. See G. Creeber, above, 6.
152. See ibid, 8.
153. See, for example, N. Luhmann, The Reality of the Mass Media (Cambridge: Polity, 2000), as referred to in D. McQuail, McQuail's Mass Communication Theory (London: Sage, 2005), 97.
154. G. Creeber, above, 9.
155. Ibid.
156. Ibid.
157. Ibid.
158. See ibid, 26.
159. See ibid, 132.
160. See ibid.
161. See M. Gillespie and J. Toynbee, above, 52.
162. G. Creeber, above, 116.
163. See ibid, 123.
164. See ibid, 42.
165. See commentary in ibid, 43, 44.
166. See comments and references in ibid, 33, and 30—36.
167. Ibid, 134.
168. See ibid.
169. Ibid, 134.
170. See ibid, 134.
171. See ibid, 134.
172. Ibid, 135-136.
173. See ibid, 136.
174. Ibid, 136
175. See ibid, 136.
176. Ibid, 136.
177. Ibid, 137.
178. See, for example, ibid, 138.
179. Ibid, 138.

180. Using the words of G. Creeber, ibid, 139.
181. Phrase used in ibid, 139.
182. Roper Starch 1995 Global Consumer Survey, as referred to in G. Creeber, ibid, 131.
183. See G. Creeber, ibid, 131.
184. See ibid.
185. See ibid.
186. See for example ibid.
187. See references in ibid.
188. See, for example, comments in ibid, 131.
189. Ibid.
190. See ibid, 132.
191. See ibid, 131.
192. See ibid, 132.
193. Ibid.
194. N. Lacey, above, 206.
195. Ibid.
196. Ibid.
197. G. Creeber, above, 4, referring to comedy drama.
198. See Mittell, above, 14, as referred to in G. Creeber, above, 12.
199. D.A Harris, The Appearance of Justice: Court TV, Conventional Television, and the Public Understanding of the Criminal Justice System, Arizona Law Review 35 (1993): 785-827, at 805.
200. A. Durant and M. Lambrou, above, 127.
201. See G. Creeber, above, 12, and references therein.
202. See for example, ibid, 123.
203. Ibid, 127.
204. See ibid, 125.
205. S. Mamber, Cinema Verite in America, Screen 13:3 (1972): 79, as referred to in G. Creeber, above, 128.

Chapter Eight

General (Non Social Science) Research Literature

INTRODUCTION

Examining all of the general literature, and indeed all of the references to the various arguments, is beyond the parameters of the current work. A literature review of the general courtroom broadcasting effects research of courtroom television broadcasting is referred to below. (Occasionally some social science effects research is also referred to).

The first courtroom television broadcast occurred in 1953.[1] We would, therefore, expect a significant amount of research and social science research from 1953 to date. What does the literature reveal? Appendix 3 also lists the general non scientific studies referred to in the literature. Set out below is an analysis of the references to research in the general literature.

BARBER

Susanna Barber,[2] News Cameras in the Courtroom: A Free Press – Fair Trial Debate, lists the courtroom broadcasting research to 1987 as consisting of seventeen (17) non-scientific research studies and two (2) scientific or social science research studies.[3]

If we recall, the first television courtroom broadcast was in 1953.[4] Barber, therefore, indicates that during the period 1953 - 1987 there were only seventeen (17) (non scientific) studies (see Appendix 3). Worse still, she indicates that there are only two (2) empirical social science research studies between 1953 and 1987. In the thirty four years of courtroom broadcasting to 1987, we only have two attempts to seriously or properly analyse (certain) effects of courtroom broadcasting in a scientific and properly recorded manner. The two (2) scientific or empirical studies are referred to as,[5]

- Hoyt, Courtroom Coverage: The Effects of Being Televised, Journal of Broadcasting 12(4) (1977): 487;
- Ernest H Short and Associates, Evaluation of California's Experiment with Extended Media Coverage of Courts, submitted to Administrative Office for the Courts; the Chief Justice's Special Committee on the Courts and the Media, and the California Judicial Council (1981).

STRICKLAND AND MOORE

In 1994 Strickland and Moore,[6] "Cameras in State Courts: A Historical Perspective," refer to "successful experiments with television in the ... courts." (See Appendix 3). They make no distinction between scientific and non scientific research. They do, however, refer to the Short Report and the New York research. However, some of their research sources appear to be newspaper stories. No definitions, forms or specific effects are referred to.

GOLDFARB

Ronald Golfarb[7] published his book, TV or Not TV: Television, Justice, and the Courts, in 1998. He is frequently referred to in discussions regarding courtroom broadcasting, particularly by those favouring courtroom broadcasting. His review indicates that during the period 1953 – 1998 there were eight (8) empirical social science studies in relation to courtroom broadcasting.

Therefore, since 1953 Goldfarb is only able to identify eight (8) social science studies regarding television courtroom broadcasting. That is eight (8) studies in 45 years. The first two of these are already listed in Barber, so he only lists an additional six (6) studies.

The social science studies were listed as,[8]

- James L. Hoyt, Courtroom Coverage: The Effects of Being Televised, Journal of Broadcasting 24 (1977): 487;
- Ernest H Short and Associates, Evaluation of California's Experiment with Extended Media Coverage of Courts, submitted to Administrative Office for the Courts; the Chief Justice's Special Committee on the Courts and the Media, and the California Judicial Council (1981);
- Donald Lewis Shores Jr, The Effects of Courtroom Cameras on Verbal Behaviour: An Analysis of Simulated Trial Witness Testimony in Court-

rooms Using Television Cameras, (Ph.D diss., University of Florida, 1981);

- Steve Robert Pasternack, The Effects of Perceived Community Pressure on Simulated Juror Guilt Attributions: A Study (Ph.D diss., University of Tennessee, Knoxville, Dec 1982);
- Saul M Kassin, TV Cameras, Public Self–Consciousness, and Mock Juror Performance, Journal of Experimental Psychology (1984): 336 - 349;
- Anna R Paddon, Television Coverage of Criminal Trials with Cameras and Microphones: A Laboratory Experiment of Audience Effects (Ph.D diss., University of Tennessee, Knoxville, (1985);
- E. Borgida, K. Debono and L. Buckman. Cameras in the Courtroom: The Effects of Media Coverage on Witness Testimony and Juror Perceptions, Law and Human Behavior 14 (1990): 489 – 509;
- Alan Punches. The Cognitive Effects of Camera Presence on the Recall of Testimony in a Simulated Courtroom Setting (Ph.D diss., Colarado State University, Fort Collins, 1991).

He states that in-court effects and changed behaviour are "unprovable."[9] This is not correct. To take one example, modern eye tracking technology can track and record where courtroom participants are looking and can record distraction effects. Distraction effects can be researched empirically. Ronald Goldfarb does not refer to any definitions, nor expressly recognise the form distinctions.

COHEN AND DOW

Cohen and Dow,[10] Cameras in the Courtroom: Television and the Pursuit of Justice, refer to four (4) empirical social science studies. These are,[11]

- Ernest H Short and Associates, Evaluation of California's Experiment with Extended Media Coverage of Courts, submitted to Administrative Office for the Courts; the Chief Justice's Special Committee on the Courts and the Media, and the California Judicial Council (1981);
- Federal Judicial Centre, Pilot Program Involving Electronic Coverage in Six US District Courts and Two Appeal Courts (the first federal pilot experiment);
- James L. Hoyt, Courtroom Coverage: The Effects of Being Televised, Journal of Broadcasting 21 (1977): 489 [Wisconsin];
- Borgida, DeBono and Buckman, Cameras in the Courtroom: The Effects of Media Coverage on Witness Testimony and Juror Perceptions, Law and Human Behavior 14 (1990): 489, [Minnesota].

Therefore, between 1953 – 2002 they can only find four (4) social science studies. No definitions or forms are referred to.

RESEARCH CITED BY COURTROOM VIEW NETWORK

A legal submission brief (promoting camera access) which was filed on behalf of Courtroom View Network[12] in 2009 aims to list the US State research findings to date.[13] There was no distinction made between scientific and non scientific research in the 18 studies or sources they refer to (see Appendix 3). Nor were definitions or forms referred to.

FREEDMAN

Warren Freedman,[14] Press and Media Access to the Criminal Courtroom (1988), does not address any specific social science research studies of courtroom participants and effects.[15] No definitions or forms are referred to. He mostly concentrates on First and Sixth Amendment issues. However, Chapters 5 and 7 do refer to courtroom cameras. There is a reference to a 1987 questionnaire sent to 1,000 television subscribers.[16] 25 percent of whom responded and 94 percent of those watched a particular trial on television.[17] 84 percent of the 25 percent agreed with the guilty verdict.[18]

HIBER

Amanda Hiber,[19] Should Cameras be Allowed in Courtrooms? (2008), nor contributors, cite or address the effects research. The book is a collection of essays by various contributors arguing particular opinions in relation to certain neat specific topics in relation to courtroom broadcasting generally. These include chapters on: Cameras Should/Should Not be Allowed in Courtrooms; Cameras Should be Allowed in Criminal Trials with Consent of All Parties; Cameras Should/Should Not be Allowed in the Supreme Court; Supreme Court Proceedings Should be Recorded but Not Televised; Cameras in Courtrooms Would Lead to a More Educated Public; Cameras Should/ Should Not be Allowed at High Profile Trials.[20] One contributor states that the US "Supreme Court has never made its arguments public."[21] No definitions or forms are referred to.

DERSHOWITZ

Alan Dershowitz, one of the lawyers involved in the OJ Simpson criminal case, wrote about the case and some of the wider legal issues.[22] However, while he refers to television courtroom broadcasting generally,[23] he does not refer to any of the empirical effects research nor any definitions.

SHERWIN

Richard K. Sherwin[24] in When the Law Goes Pop: The Vanishing Line Between Law and Popular Culture, while referring to Simpson, Estes, Chandler and important media issues, does not directly refer to television courtroom broadcasting effects research, definitions nor forms.

NEW YORK SPECIAL COMMITTEE ON RADIO AND TELEVISION

A New York report, Radio, Television, and the Administration of Justice: A documented Survey of Materials,[25] referred extensively to court reporting issues, including courtroom broadcasting, but it did not refer to effects, effects research, definitions nor forms.

IRELAND: RTE

Radio Telefis Eireann (RTE), the Irish national broadcaster, referred to the issue of television courtroom broadcasting in 1995 in a discussion paper.[26] However, there is no discussion of research issues, effects research nor forms.

The author has also undertaken, and repeated, initial baseline data research in relation to judicial opinions and public opinions regarding television courtroom broadcasting issues in Ireland. This has yet to be published however.

UK: CAPLAN REPORT

Televising the Courts: Report of a Working Party of the Public Affairs Committee of the General Council of the Bar [of England and Wales],[27] or Caplan report as it has become known, is often seen as one of the main UK discussion documents in the UK. It recommends certain television courtroom broadcasting for the UK.

It specifically recommends television courtroom broadcasting pilots in the UK.[28] Recommendation 7.1 (iv) recommends that the Advisory Committee "devise and monitor pilot projects involving research and the actual broadcasting of civil and criminal trials and of appellate proceedings."[29] The Caplan Report does not refer to definitions or forms.

There is no express reference to the empirical research.

The Caplan report states that it reviewed "hundreds" of surveys and reports - but only (possibly) implicitly refers to Short and Hoyt as (empirical) effects research.[30]

UK: BROADCASTING COURTS CONSULTATION PAPER 2005

The Department of Constitutional Affairs launched a consultation entitled Broadcasting Courts[31] in November 2004.[32] The consultation consisted mainly of a seminar (on 10th January 2005) and an online questionnaire.[33]

The Lord Chancellor stated that he was "concerned at overseas research showing that people believe that if their evidence might be televised that would reduce the likelihood of their coming forward as a witness."[34] He concluded that "[j]ustice should be seen to be done. But our priority must be that justice is done."[35] The executive summary refers to the argument of beneficial educational effects and increased "confidence in the judicial system."[36] It also refers to the "needs of participants" especially "those most ... vulnerable."[37] Also, "[i]f permitting broadcasting was likely to have an impact on people's willingness to take part in proceedings, or to make participation even more of an ordeal, there would need to be very strong arguments in its favour."[38]

Concerns are also raised in relation to witnesses, and whether they are willing to testify in a television courtroom broadcasting context.[39]

Even where witnesses were not discouraged, "testifying can be nerve-racking experience, which the presence of recording equipment could compound. 87% of trial and appellate judges surveyed in California reported that witnesses were more nervous or self-conscious when giving testimony before cameras."[40] The consultation paper also refers to the decision in the Shipman Inquiry which decided against television cameras based on the additional effect it would have on witnesses.[41]

The New York study comprised of an opinion report, self report and a questionnaire based. The UK consultation paper finds "disturbing" that "37% of these [351] judges said that television coverage causes judges to render rulings they otherwise might not issue."[42]

The consultation report does refer to the content analysis undertaken for the first federal pilot study, which found that on average, the television courtroom broadcasting footage examined, made up 56 seconds of the television story.[43]

Annex E of the consultation paper refers to other jurisdictions and research.[44] However, most of the references refer to "opinion" reports only.[45] This includes the first federal study, the California Task Force report, the New York report in 1996 and research in Canada.[46]

However, research is referred to in New Zealand where a "case–by–case evaluation found that most judges were distracted by cameras."[47] No explicit definitions and forms are properly distinguished in the UK consultations.

UK: BROADCASTING THE COURTS RESPONSE TO CONSULTATION 2005

The responses to the Consultation Paper were compiled and released on June 30, 2005.[48] Again it was noted that the Consultation paper "made no proposals but sought views on the complex and sensitive issues around broadcasting court proceedings."[49] It is implicitly noted that there are potentially different forms, including reference to different courts, proceedings and stages of these proceedings.[50] There was a seminar and a website forum as part of the consultation. However, all of the responses were either opinion responses to a questionnaire or free comment. "[S]upport for widespread broadcasting is limited, and that there is grave concern about the potential impact on participants, especially witnesses and jurors, and on the trial process."[51] There is no reference to effects research, forms or definitions.

ENGLAND AND WALES PILOT

There appears to have been an experiment in England and Wales already[52] which occurred on or about November 16, 2004.[53] The footage was not broadcast. [54] It appears to consist of questionnaires and no empirical research.[55]

SLOTNICK AND SEGAL

Elliot E. Slotnick and Jennifer A. Segal[56] refer to the television news media and Supreme Court in their book Television News and the Supreme Court: All the News That's Fit to Air? They acknowledge that there is only very "limited research" in relation to the wider issue of the courts, the judiciary and media reporting.[57] There is still less in relation to the narrower issue of television courtroom broadcasting. While not primarily directed to the issue of television courtroom broadcasting (TCB), Slotnick and Segal note that media court reporting "has received somewhat mixed evaluations, ranging from very poor to, at best, adequate."[58] In terms of general media court reporting there is only a "smattering of empirical research conducted on this relationship as well as on the nature of the coverage television affords the Court."[59] Some of the research found that the media reported reactions to Supreme Court decisions, rather than what the Supreme Court said or the details of its decision, and that some reports differed between the newspaper types.[60]

Part of Chapter 3 refers to "The Issue of Cameras in the Supreme Court."[61] The television courtroom broadcasting arguments, issues and some various useful and interesting interviews are referred to. However, the empirical research to date nor the extent of the research is referred to.[62] There is no reference to definitions or forms.

STEPNIAK

One of the most recent courtroom broadcasting books is Audio-Visual Coverage of Courts.[63] It notes that the early television courtroom proceedings, with lots of equipment, bulky cameras, television personnel and novelty, was "undoubtedly disruptive and distracting to participants."[64] However, it assumes "[t]echnological advances have ensured that audio-visual recording of court proceedings need not distract nor disrupt proceedings."[65]

Daniel Stepniak states that over 40 US states have "formally assessed the effect of courtroom televising"[66] yet he does not distinguish which of these are general and which are empirical studies, nor which studies can be relied upon. He also refers to "countless" and "vast" studies, experiments and literature on effects.[67] The author found just over twenty, which is hardly a reliable body of evidence. However, Stepniak only refers to a limited number of social science studies - in a footnote, namely,

- S.L. Alexander, Cameras in the Courtroom: A Case Study, Judicature, 74 (1991): 307;
- E. Borgida, K. Debono and L. Buckman, Cameras in the Courtroom: The Effects of Media Coverage on Witness Testimony and Juror Perceptions, Law and Human Behaviour 14 (1990): 489;
- Ernest H. Short and Associates, Evaluation of California's Experiment with Extended Media Coverage of Courts, submitted to Administrative Office for the Courts; the Chief Justice's Special Committee on the Courts and the Media, and the California Judicial Council (1981);
- Judicial Council of California, Report of Task Force on Photographing, Recording and Broadcasting in the Courtroom (February, 1996). [Arguably this is not empirical at all].

He later refers to the New York report,[68] and the first federal pilot experiment report.[69] The New York report is only empirical to the extent that there was a professional public opinion survey incorporated into it. The federal report is only empirical to the extent that there was limited content analysis of certain television courtroom broadcasting footage. There is no reference to

Susanna Barber's book nor the empirical studies referred to by her. He, therefore, refers to only there (3) studies and two (2) part studies which are empirical social science studies.

He refers to other problems. There are other potential effects apart from equipment distraction. The "mere knowledge of being recorded may still have an effect on participants."[70] Unfortunately, the general research relies almost entirely on opinions and "experiences."[71] In the first federal courts pilot experiment, "most participants *believe*" there are no, or minimal, effects.[72] (Emphasis added). In addition, pilot studies and experiments are generally only conducted after a particular jurisdiction is persuaded on the desirability or proceedings with television coverage.[73] The "function of such experiments is ... to reassure those unconvinced of the desirability of such coverage, to acclimatise courtroom participants and the public, and to determine the most appropriate and effective methods of regulation."[74] A New Hampshire case is noted as referred to state studies finding no or little adverse psychological effects, and instead finding certain positive effects.[75] However, upon examination, the studies are not cited in the case and there is no distinction between general opinion studies and empirical studies. The California studies he refers to in 1996 and 2000, each appear based on opinions and questionnaires only.[76]

Overall, the effects research is "inconclusive."[77] There is an "inconclusiveness of ... effect[s] ... on participants."[78] This applies equally to "detrimental and beneficial effects."[79] He does not access the quality, level and amount of general and empirical research undertaken. He only acknowledges that the "methodology and conclusiveness of the findings" have been questioned.[80]

His section "Inconclusiveness of research findings" states that "the extensive evaluation of experiments and courts' experiences with audio–visual coverage has not produced a consensus on the beneficial or detrimental effects of audio-visual coverage."[81] "[D]etrimental and beneficial effects ... [are equally] incapable of being established conclusively."[82] The author's eye tracking proof of concept demonstration research indicates that this is not correct. Stepniak argues that the "inconclusiveness" is due in part to "the fact that the effects which are being evaluated have been shown not to be capable of conclusive scientific evaluation as they rely on the subjective perceptions of courtroom participants and observers.[83] The effects are, he feels, "incapable of being established conclusively."[84] They are "intrinsically incapable of being conclusively established."[85] He states that the research and studies are "inevitably deemed inconclusive."[86] He seems to accept that opinions and self reports can be the only effects research. It is, he suggests, an "inescapable fact that effects can only be measured in terms of perceptions."

The author respectfully disagrees with the dismissal of the utility of undertaking considered and empirical research. (See eye tracking, psychology and communications research references below). It is also noted that Stepniak does not refer to definitions or forms.

NEW YORK STATE COMMITTEE TO REVIEW AUDIO–VISUAL

One of the most influential studies was the 1997 New York State Committee to Review Audio-Visual Coverage of Court Proceedings report, entitled An Open Courtroom: Cameras in New York Courts.[87] There was a majority report (in favour of broadcasting) and a minority report (against). However, the report was opinion survey and non–empirical (with the exception of professional public opinion survey research section).

While Stepniak compliments the level of endeavour and research involved in the report[88] he fails to note that the report did not seek to evaluate empirically, or otherwise, what it was tasked to do by the legislature, namely, examining if, inter alia, there is enhanced public understanding, familiarity and benefits with the courts.[89] This did not occur.

> The Legislature directed this Committee to evaluate the efficacy of the experimental program and to assess whether:
>
> 1. Any public benefits accrue from the experimental program;
> 2. Any abuses occurred during the program;
> 3. The extent to which and the way in which the conduct of participants in court proceedings changes when audio-visual coverage is present;
> 4. The degree of compliance by trial judges and the media with the requirements of Section 218 of the Judiciary Law;
> 5. The effect of audio–visual coverage on the conduct of trial judges both inside and outside the courtroom.[90]

Apart from engaging a third party professional firm to undertake public polling and interviews, all of the "comprehensive"[91] research was opinion based. While extensive, the research was not comprehensive, was not empirical (apart from the professional public opinion survey) and did not do what it was tasked to do. Stepniak states that the report "records studies undertaken to ascertain perceptions as to the effects of televising."[92] He also describes the minority report as being "the most comprehensive and persuasive case against televising of trial proceedings."[93] The minority report states that the "experiment has failed to prove that cameras in the courts provide a public benefit, significantly enhance public understanding of the judicial process or help to maintain a high level of public confidence in the judiciary."[94]

Stepniak states that the New York experiment "revealed substantial evidence of both beneficial and detrimental effects" including on victims and witnesses.[95]

CONCLUSION

This review indicates at least that there is more issues to be considered than the basic presumptive type arguments to date, would have us believe. However, the above literature is also remiss in avoiding definitions and form issues. Definitions are a basic requirement for effects research in future, whether in relation to courtroom broadcasting or television courtroom broadcasting.

NOTES

1. Listed by S. Barber, News Cameras in the Courtroom: A Free Press – Fair Trial Debate (Norwood, New Jersey: Ablex, 1987), as being the case of Billy Eugene Manley in Oklahoma City which occurred in 1953, see S. Barber, above, 10-11. See also W. Freedman, Press and Media Access to the Criminal Courtroom (New York: Quorum, 1988), 42-43.
2. S. Barber, ibid.
3. Ibid, in particular 70 et seq.
4. Listed by S. Barber, ibid, as being the case of Billy Eugene Manley in Oklahoma City which occurred in 1953, see ibid, 10-11.
5. Ibid, 71.
6. R.A. Strickland and R.H. Moore, Cameras in State Courts: A Historical Perspective, Judicature 78 (1994): 128—135, at n. 52, at 135.
7. R.L. Goldfarb, TV or Not TV: Television, Justice, and the Courts (New York: New York University Press, 1998), in particular 116 et seq.
8. Ibid, 116–123.
9. Ibid, n. 3, at 162, as referred to in D. Stepniak, Audio-Visual Coverage of Courts (Cambridge: Cambridge University Press, 2008), 365.
10. M. Cohn and D. Dow, Cameras in the Courtroom: Television and the Pursuit of Justice (New York: Rowman & Little, 2002).
11. Ibid, pp. 62 et seq.
12. Boies, Schiller and Flexner LLP, Memorandum, Prepared for the Committee on Court Administration and Case Management (Hon. John R Tunheim, Chair), The Judicial Conference of the United States, Submitted on Behalf of Courtroom View Network, June 6, 2009. Available www.google.ie/url?sa=t&source=web&cd=1&ved=0CBMQFjAA&url=http%3A%2F%2F www.courtroomview.com%2Fnews%2FCVN%2520White%2520Paper%2520(6%25206%252009)%2520(with%2520exhibits).pdf&ei=Gb2MTOuSFMOV4gbL2uWnCg&usg=AFQjCNEdysCcE_qaIlKgbw3EvomZW_7DTg&sig2=UJyaEtrpo493UfAhGO9kSw , accessed September 12, 2012.
13. Ibid, 10 et seq, n. 8, at 10.
14. W. Freedman, Press and Media Access to the Criminal Courtroom (New York: Quorum, 1988), apart from referring to an incompletely referenced audience questionnaire study, which was carried out by a university, 46.
15. Freedman does refer to empirical research being referred to in *Post-Newsweek Stations, Florida, Inc. v US* (370 So2d 764 (Fla., 1979), at 768–760, but Freedman does not identify, cite or consider such purported research. See W. Freedman, *ibid,* 83.
16. Study by Journalism Department at the University of Arizona, New Law Journal (30 November, 1987): 13 et seq, as referred to in W. Freedman, ibid, 46.
17. Ibid.
18. Ibid.
19. A. Hiber, ed., Should Cameras be Allowed in Courtrooms? (New York: Gale, 2008)
20. Ibid.

21. S. Grady, Cameras in Courtrooms Would Lead to a More Educated Public, in A. Hiber, ibid, 61.

22. A. Dershowitz, Reasonable Doubts: The Criminal Justice System and the O.J. Simpson Case (New York: Touchstone, 1996, 1997). Alan Dershowtz is also a notable legal academic in the US.

23. For example, ibid, 27, 29, 32, 33, 145, 146, 147, 148, 203.

24. R.K. Sherwin, When Law Goes Pop: The Vanishing Line Between Law and Popular Culture (Chicago: The University of Chicago Press, 2000). Note C. Parker, What Do They Learn When They Learn Legal Ethics?, Legal Education Review 12 (2001): 175–2008.

25. The Special Committee on Radio and Television of the Association of the Bar of the City of New York, Radio, Television, and the Administration of Justice: A Documented Survey of Materials (New York and London: Columbia University Press, 1965): 99–100.

26. K. Woods, Televising the Courts: A Radio Telefis Eireann Discussion Paper (Dublin: RTE, 1995). Prepared by Kieron Wood, the then RTE Legal Affairs Correspondent.

27. J. Caplan, M. Kalisher and A. Speaight, Televising the Courts: Report of a Working Party of the Public Affairs Committee of the General Council of the Bar [of England and Wales], (London: Bar Council of England and Wales, 1989).

28. Ibid, 50.

29. Ibid.

30. Ibid, 34.

31. Department of Constitutional Affairs [UK], Broadcasting Courts, Consultation Paper, CP 28/04 (November, 2004).

32. See www.dca.goc.uk/consult/courts/broadcasting-cp28-04.htm , accessed December 14, 2009.

33. Ibid.

34. Ibid.

35. Ibid.

36. Ibid, parag. 2, at 6.

37. Ibid, parag. 5, at 6.

38. Ibid, parag. 5, at 6.

39. Ibid, parag. 11, at 45. Ibid, parag. 12, at 45, referring to the Cameras in New York Courtrooms, and the Marxist Institute for Public Opinion Poll, December 1996, contained therein. Ibid, parag. 12, at 45, referring to UMR Insight Limited, Media Coverage of Court Proceedings: A Summary Report, (February 1998).

40. Ibid, parag. 13, at 45, referring to Report Summary of the California Judicial Task Force on Photographing, Recording and Broadcasting in the Courtroom.

41. Ibid, parag. 14, at 45—46, referring to Decision on Application by Cable News Network (CNN), October 25, 2001. The consultation paper also refers to Lord Irvine of Lairg, the then Lord Chancellor, who commented after the Woodward case in the US that there "is a serious risk that witnesses might be influenced in the evidence they give, or find undue pressure being placed on themselves or their families as a consequence of live coverage." In "Reporting the Courts: The Media's Rights and Responsibilities," 4th RTE/UCD Media Lecture, University College Dublin, April 14, 1999. See also Paul Lambert, article forthcoming in the Reynold's Courts and Media Law Journal, volume three.

42. Ibid, parag. 28, at 49, referring to New York State Committee to Review Audio-Visual Coverage of Court Proceedings.

43. Ibid, parag. 27, at 61, referring to quote of same contained in the New York study (1997).

44. Ibid, at 100.

45. Ibid, at 100 et seq.

46. Ibid.

47. Ibid, at 109, referring to UMR Insight Ltd., Media Coverage of Court Proceedings: Summary Report (February, 1998), and The Impact of Television, Radio and Still Photography on Coverage of Court Proceedings – Final Report, A Report Prepared for the Department of Courts by a research team from the Department of Human Management, Massey University (April, 1998). This is the New Zealand research.

48. Department of Constitutional Affairs, Broadcasting Courts, Response to Consultation, CP(R) 28/04, 30/06/2005, Response to Consultation Carried Out by the Department for Constitutional Affairs. 259 responses were made in total, see 7.

49. Ibid, parag. 1, at 4. Interestingly, one of the consultation criteria was to be clear on the proposals, see, parag 2, at 44.

50. Ibid, parag. 6, at 5.

51. Ibid, parag. 1, at 42.

52. D. Stepniak, Audio-Visual Coverage of Courts (Cambridge: Cambridge University Press, 2008), 60; n. 280, 60; 61; and 56 et seq. Also referred to in Pros and Cons of Courtroom Cameras Set Out, 15 November, 2004, www.number10.gov.uk/Page6578 , accessed on March 2, 2010

53. Also referred to in Pros and Cons of Courtroom Cameras Set Out, November 15, 2004, www.number10.gov.uk/Page6578 , accessed March 2, 2010.

54. D. Stepniak, above, 60; n. 280, 60; 61; and 56 et seq. See also Department of Constitutional Affairs, Broadcasting Courts, Consultation Paper, CP 28/04, November, 2004, 19-20.

55. D. Stepniak, ibid.

56. E.E. Slotnick and J.A. Segal, Television News and the Supreme Court: All the News That's Fit to Air? (Cambridge: Cambridge University Press, 1998).

57. Ibid, 2.

58. Ibid, 8.

59. Ibid, 8.

60. Ibid, 10 et seq., and references therein.

61. Ibid, 54 et seq.

62. The authors also provide very useful examination and case studies of media reporting of the Supreme Court as well as analysis of some of the types of cases covered by the court. See ibid, 89 et seq. Part of the media reporting analysis revealed that 82% of stories in the sample of particular types/stages of cases were "inaccurate." Ibid, 209. "The picture that emerges of network news coverage of Supreme Court docketing decisions is not a very happy one." Ibid.

63. D. Stepniak, above.

64. Ibid, 1.

65. Ibid, 3.

66. Ibid, 353.

67. Ibid, 69.

68. Ibid, 102 et seq.

69. Ibid, 130 et seq.

70. Ibid, 3.

71. Ibid, 8.

72. Ibid, 100–101.

73. Ibid, 8–9.

74. Ibid, 9.

75. New Hampshire Supreme Court, Petition of WMUR Channel 9 (December 13, 2002), www.courts.state.nh.us/opinions/2002/0212/wmur156.htm referred to in D. Stepniak, ibid, 101. Accessed by author on June 8, 2010.

76. D. Stepniak, above, 114 et seq, referring to Administrative Office of the Courts of California, Task Force on Photographing, Recording and Broadcasting in the Courtroom, Report Summary (1996), and Administrative Office of the Courts, Cameras in the Courtroom: Report on Rule 980 (May, 2000).

77. Ibid, 351.

78. Ibid, 4.

79. Ibid, 8.

80. Ibid, 100. Also 403–405.

81. D. Stepniak, above, 403.

82. Ibid, 8.

83. D. Stepniak, above, 403.

84. Ibid, 6.

85. Ibid, 6.

86. Ibid, 70
87. New York State Committee to Review Audio–Visual Coverage of Court Proceedings, An Open Courtroom: Cameras in New York Courts (New York: Fordham University Press, 1997).
88. D. Stepniak, above, 103.
89. See New York State Committee to Review Audio–Visual Coverage of Court Proceedings, above, xv-3; and D. Stepniak, above, 105.
90. New York State Committee to Review Audio-Visual Coverage of Court Proceedings, An Open Courtroom: Cameras in New York Courts (New York: Fordham University Press, 1997), 1-2.
91. D. Stepniak, above, 105.
92. Ibid, 103.
93. Ibid, 103. Also, 107.
94. New York State Committee to Review Audio-Visual Coverage of Court Proceedings, An Open Courtroom: Cameras in New York Courts (New York: Fordham University Press, 1997), 206, as referred to in D. Stepniak, above, 108.
95. Ibid, n. 25, at 58; 39–40; 61, as referred to in D. Stepniak, above, 369.

Chapter Nine

General (Non Social Science) Research Themes

INTRODUCTION

Examples of the general studies, and some of the flaws and issues with them, are highlighted below.

FLORIDA

One Florida experiment only commissioned (certain) courtroom actor surveys after the experiment period ended.[1] This is not unique. The research also had methodological flaws and was extremely simplistic.[2]

Various Florida studies had methodological flaws[3] and sometimes the subject population is too low for significant conclusions.[4]

One Florida study[5] sought to gauge responses from courtroom participants, but after an extended period, sometimes *up to a year after* the case and made no account of the time differences.[6] Two thirds of participants refused to respond.[7] No account was taken of self report issues, and particularly over time.[8] It is surprising, therefore, that the study "concluded" that there were few adverse effects.[9] At best, the most that could have been said, despite the faulty research, was that no or few adverse effects were found to be shown in that particular survey. This is a significant difference. It is a fundamental flaw to misrepresent the research findings as the study referred to appears to do, and indeed as other studies have also done.

Keller points out that Florida presented the first long term opportunity to research the effects of television courtroom broadcasting.[10] The pilot programme was established in 1975.[11] This would mean that between 1953 –

1975 various television courtroom broadcasts occurred, but without seeking to examine any long term effect. In fact the Florida experiment only really began in 1977,[12] which extends the period further to 1953 - 1977.

CALIFORNIA/SHORT REPORT

Paul Thaler describes this as follows,

> One of the most comprehensive studies was the year-long California survey-experiment in 1981, which adopted a diversified data collection method. In that experiment, researchers combined data from interviews from participants in specific trials, with general attitudinal responses gathered from questionnaires. They also confirmed interview responses with observations made by researchers attending a trial. Changes in participants' attitudes before being involved in a televised trial on well as during and after a trial were also noted.[13]

There were even issues with the Short Report study.[14] The Short Report acknowledges that there is an importance attached to where the television equipment is located in the courtroom as well as the placement of the television personnel.[15] Yet, these are frequently ignored and not recorded in most studies. The Short Report does not say that effects must be considered in terms of where television equipment is located and where the participants are located. This must be encompassed within future effects research, including the second federal pilot experiment.

The Short Report concludes that the relatively positive results "thus far should not be taken as licence to grant carte blanche access by extended media or to ignore the guidelines in the rules."[16] It continues that "California's experiment thus far with cameras in the courts has not been tainted by an *Estes* or a *Hauptman*,"[17] which is arguably prophetic in terms of the subsequent Simpson (criminal) case. It also adds that there should be no general access, and also that any access "should be done carefully."[18]

The Members of the Chief Justice's Special Committee on the Courts and the Media, The Judicial Council of California expressly did not adopt or agree with the Short Report, its finding or conclusions.[19] Ephraim Margolin's Memorandum dated October 16, 1981, attached to the above Memorandum of The Members of the Chief Justice's Special Committee, adds that "any report which fails to evaluate or even consider the use made by the media of the coverage obtained from observation of the courts leaves us with only a partial evaluation insufficient for a final determination of the wisdom of the project."[20] Indeed, few empirical studies since seek to review the media use of TCB footage. There is as yet no general picture.

The Cameras in the Courtroom: Report on Rule 980 Reports of 2000 does not refer to any effects research carried out. It does gather statistics on types of application the media applied to cover, as well as response questionnaires. However, it is noted that many media applications contained incomplete information.[21] The rule provisions in relation to the media being responsible for increased court costs do not appear to have been developed or used in practice.[22] They appear to have been ignored.

BAKER REPORT (FLORIDA)

The Baker Report was instrumental in Florida's move to allow cameras. It reported that there were no physical disruptions, which appears based on Judge Baker's views as the trial judge in a particular case (Zamora).[23] It also concluded that jurors were not hindered in their ability to follow the case, based on his interviews with them.[24]

VIRGINIA

The Virginia Association of Broadcasters research report on a broadcasting experiment included 35 interview data report sheets, but no analysis of these.[25]

BARTLETT

Possibly the first reference to "research" was the observations and comments of Judge Bartlett in a televised case in 1955.[26] However, it appears that there were no formal definitions, research, questionnaires, interviews, coding or documented research of any type.[27]

COLORADO

Donald Shores refers to the introduction of television cameras to Colorado courts, and notes that there was no controlled research, experiments or surveys.[28] There was equally no reference to definitions or formats.

RHODE ISLAND

The Rhode Island research study of its pilot programme refers to various research undertaken, but none appears to be listed nor the methodologies.[29] While the research apparently also included a political science academic and a psychology academic, these appear on a limited "volunteer"[30] basis, and were presumably limited by funding. No documented record is provided. In addition, it also appears that at least some of the research occurred after the pilot period expired.[31]

WASHINGTON

Kermit Netteburg identifies the first effects research as being the Washington experiment of television courtroom broadcasting which was shown to judges but not broadcast. However, there appears to be no written report or record of the research, the questions, nor the interviews undertaken.[32] It appear to be opinion and self report based only.[33] Donald Shores refers to (possibly the same) Washington experiment with cameras in 1974, which only had an "informal survey" of witnesses.[34]

FLAWS IN COURTROOM BROADCASTING RESEARCH

There are numerous flaws in the courtroom broadcasting research to date, in particular the general non scientific, non empirical research. These flaws are many and varied. Any future research must address these flaws.

There has been far too little research carried out into this important subject (i.e. effects). The existing research is less than comprehensive, which is perhaps surprising given the important issues at stake. For this reason, the author outlines some of the research avenues which should be pursued in future. The basis for many of these suggestions come from extensive research in related disciplines.[35]

There are far too little research studies. The existing research is not comprehensive. It is also frequently unscientific and unmethodical. Therefore, little reliance can be placed upon much of the research in terms of making any conclusions or determinations. Seldom do research studies extend over a long period of time. This means that it is difficult if not impossible to make any overall conclusions or determinations regarding the extended effects of television courtroom broadcasting. Few studies are compared with each other. None apparently attempt to replicate and/or verify the results of earlier studies. Therefore, there is a strong argument that none of the research has been conducted in any meaningful or scientific manner.

Susanna Barber[36] has written one of the few books on television courtroom broadcasting. In part of it, she examines the available US studies into television courtroom broadcasting.[37] Having carried out her examination, she concludes that a number of fundamental questions remain unresolved and unanswered. Some of the questions she raises[38] are included in the following questions, namely,

- Does television, as opposed to print [journalism], better inform the public about a particular case?
- Can gavel to gavel (G2G) broadcasts educate the public about the administration of justice? [or better educate the public?]
- Do time constraints imposed on many broadcast news stories mean that a case is treated either unfairly or inadequately?
- Does the public get a distorted picture of the judicial system, or a biased view of a particular trial, if stories are edited to highlight sensational testimony, cross-examination, or simply the opening and closing arguments?
- How does the public's understanding of courts and specific cases differ when broadcast rather than print is the medium of communication?
- What type or form of news coverage has consistently provided the most balanced coverage of legal issues, trial participants and court administration?

These and many other questions remain to be addressed in any meaningful, considered, logical and scientific manner as part of an examination of television courtroom broadcasting.

Television courtroom broadcasting research, and indeed legal research generally, has frequently ignored highly relevant literature and research from other (related) disciplines for too long. Television courtroom broadcasting issues cannot remain isolated and considered only in terms of conventional or traditional legal principles and legal texts.[39] Of course conventional legal materials remain relevant to the topic being discussed but the legal community and the general public should be aware of the wider research opportunities available. To do otherwise would be to remain precluded from better understanding how and why the courtroom operates in the context of media attention.[40] Research in other disciplines should be allowed to assist our understanding and assessment of television courtroom broadcasting generally.

It is important to remember that we should base our judgement and assessment of television courtroom broadcasting on the greatest amount of research, and best research, into the issues involved. We should not ignore whole areas which offer a greater potential for understanding the effects of television courtroom broadcasting.

Decisions in relation to television courtroom broadcasting in the past were sometimes based upon the level of knowledge and research, if any, available at that time. Currently, there are significantly more avenues for research, many of which provide a scientific basis for assessing actual effects on courtroom participants and on the general audience (i.e. the public) of television courtroom broadcasting.[41] They should not continue to be ignored. The author's proof of concept demonstration research of eye tracking technology in a courtroom to research camera distraction effects, points the way for some of this research in future. This proposal addresses part of the Supreme Court challenge.

SELF REPORT RESEARCH

One of the major flaws with the effects research to date is the nature of the opinion or self report studies themselves. (Particular) courtroom participants are asked to indicate whether they themselves have been affected, or sometimes adversely affected, by television courtroom broadcasting in a particular case they were just involved in. The nature of such questions automatically means that most courtroom participants are going to say that they themselves have not been affected. Sometimes they will say that it is their opinion that certain others have been affected, but certainly not them. Similarly, an eyewitness[42] may be very confident, even certain, but still be wrong or not notice or be aware of one of the many eyewitness identification and recollection factors hampering a correct identification. Another inherent flaw is that even when relying on such self report or opinion questionnaires, there seldom appears to be a cross comparison compiled between the answers on the effects on a person and the effects perceived by other people on the same person.

Many studies today employ various methodologies and techniques of observing and documenting actual effects and reactions on particular individuals to stimuli. Sometimes these stimuli involve a particular scene, a film, a video clip, a photograph, a written description or story, etc. In these instances it is possible to observe and test effects. Employing similar methodologies and techniques can bring television courtroom broadcasting research out of the dark ages. Firstly, these methodologies and techniques can be used to test effects of television courtroom broadcasting on courtroom participants and on the general viewing audience. However, they can also be utilised in the context of validating or contradicting, as the case may be, opinion self report studies. The new methodologies and techniques can be used to see, for example, whether a particular courtroom actor actually was distracted by or looked over at a television courtroom broadcasting camera, while in their answer to the questionnaire they may have indicated that they were not, or did not.

One of the main arguments of critics of courtroom broadcasting is that it (may) adversely affect courtroom participants. However, self report studies and questionnaires alone cannot hope to establish or even properly research this argument. That no one had sought to expand research beyond these limited studies is striking.

OPINIONS/SELF REPORTS

The official state and other studies rely too "heavily"[43] on opinion surveys and questionnaires alone. Yet "[e]ven with the self-reported system and its inherent bias, these studies all revealed that a significant minority of jurors, attorneys, and witnesses reported that cameras in the courtroom had significant impact on their role in the trial. This finding alone points to the indisputable point that a trial cannot be conducted fairly if all of the participants are unable to properly perform their parts."[44] Can we rely on these today? Not with modern research.

The 1991 Criminal Justice Section of the New York Bar Association is also criticised for having a "limited self-report" methodology and "self-reporting flaws" like other research.[45] When "examining psychological impact it may be necessary to abandon the simplistic self-reporting surveys and delve deeper into the issues."[46] The surveys are also described as "subjective" and are "based solely on the trial participant's viewpoints as to their personal opinions and feelings … Self-diagnosis is by its very nature problematic and distorted …"[47]

In addition the courtroom participants "are set up to be impartial and truthful and when asked if effected by the influence of television, they are apt to remind the sceptical and themselves that they are indeed impartial"[48] and not affected.

When "examining psychological impact it may be necessary to abandon the simplistic self-reporting surveys and delve deeper into the issues."[49] Opinions and self reports, are often based on "intuitive judgements."[50]

The perceptions of individuals as recorded in interviews often provide conflicting views.[51] In addition to the self report problem with respondents, one is not sure if replies are being made honestly.[52] A further problem is that replies may be made which the respondent hopes will please the questioner.[53]

Saul M. Kassin also notes the self report problems and the fact that it is widely referred to in the psychology literature.[54] He also refers to a manifest example of the problem in a courtroom broadcasting survey in a Florida Supreme Court study. The jurors, witnesses and lawyers all reported their belief that the cameras had a greater effect on the other courtroom participants than on themselves.[55]

Donald Shores also refers to the self report bias of the research to date.[56] He further states that "[m]any of the responses are personal estimations and speculations about contexts in which no variables were experimentally controlled."[57]

"As Warden[58] noted, 'A survey of judges and lawyers on their opinion of the validity of the Pythagorean Theorem would not change its true nature.' Opinion must give way to fact, and propositions must be tested against reality."[59] As the author variously points out, our research must expand.

MIXED OPINIONS

Some of the studies when they gauge opinions of judges, include some judges with experience of courtroom broadcasting and some without. Teresa Keller raises this as an issue.[60] This can also be an issue with other courtroom participants.

Also, the "concentration on fear [of effects] … has diverted attention from other important questions pertaining to the presence of cameras in the courtroom."[61]

LITTLE RESEARCH/FEW STUDIES

There is clearly not enough research. *Estes*, *Chandler* and *Hollingsworth* also note the lack of effects research effects.[62] Steve Pasternack also notes the "lack of data" and calls for not just more research but an "ongoing program of research."[63] Anna R. Padden also calls for ongoing research.[64]

Steve Esposito also describes televised justice as being "relatively unexplored."[65]

A majority of judges in the Rhode Island research felt that the pilot period "produced insufficient empirical experience upon which to base a permanent conclusion."[66]

Kermit Netterburg (in 1980) acknowledges that many effects questions are not answered.[67] He continues as follows,

> [p]erhaps the most crucial question yet unanswered is whether the surveys and case studies conducted … can be replicated with greater controls. … [Also,] what types of trials if any should be excluded from coverage … the frequency with which courts will be covered and the long-term effects on the court system.[68]

Netteburg notes that while research is beginning, many specific themes have not yet been researched, including some of the specific themes referred to in *Estes*.[69] No research address all issues and concerns. A follow on point is that research must be categorised. Then specific research on specific issues can then be compared, tested and improved upon. As the author points out, there are no definitions or description of TCB forms.

NO RESULTS

The "arguments about the effect ... on the judicial process continues."[70] The issue of different effects is still "unresolved."[71] The research that is there is "[i]nconclusive."[72] Evidence in relation to the various arguments "has not been systematically produced."[73] "Crucial questions still remain"[74] and the debate continues.[75] In terms of benefits, Kohm notes that we are still referring to only "presumed benefit[s]."[76] Alexander notes that the (general) research to date still leaves only "speculation" and no conclusions on the effects issues.[77]

CONFIDENCE

There is no evaluation of confidence issues in the general research.[78] How does television courtroom broadcasting effect public confidence in individual courtroom participants, courts and the justice process generally? Generally there is little research, and where there is, it is generally non-comparative and non-longitudinal.

GENERAL RESEARCH METHODS/METHODOLOGY

The effects debate is still ongoing[79] and in some respects the arguments and basis for propositions has not changed much since *Estes* in 1965.[80] Practically all of the US states' research involved unrepresentative samples and "anecdotal evidence."[81]

It has been argued that US states have made "policy decisions"[82] that there are no adverse effects, rather than having actual research findings, or rather than undertaking proper, controlled, replicated and validated empirical research.

Studies are limited in only adopting one method of study. Only the Short study is referred to as adopting a multimodal method.[83] In one instance a law firm was engaged to assess effects of certain in-court effects.[84] D.P. Killian also recognised the flawed methodology of the general research.[85] Catherine M. Boggs undertook a review of the research in 1981 and felt of 72 general studies at least 20 had methodological flaws undermining their reliability and validity.[86] Edna Einsiedel did not attend the case she was researching, relying on interviews.[87]

Netteburg criticises one of the early Florida studies, and which criticism is quoted in the Short Report, as having "methodological flaws, including extreme simplicity in instrumentation and the rush which the Florida's court deadline imposed on the researchers."[88] The studies lack proper methodology and have "no controls, disproof, or evaluation."[89] Teresa Keller acknowledges that there is no clear methodology referred to in the Terry article/ research.[90]

LONGITUDINAL

There is almost no longitudinal research over any extended period of time. Obviously, it undermines any long terms discussion of effects.

REASONS FOR LIMITED EFFECTS RESEARCH

Effects research has been "hampered."[91] There is uncritical research, no definitions, nor forms, etc. The psychological effects, or some of them, may not be "easily detectable."[92] Researching the effects issues, particularly in the courtroom environment, is also very complex.[93] Yet, more sophisticated research is required. We need to examine the reasons why there is limited research, in order to improve upon it.

SPECIFIC EFFECT/SPECIFIC HYPOTHESIS

Many arguments exist.[94] Yet the general studies overall are not specific in researching and testing individual effects arguments, nor in a manner which ensures each potential effect is isolated, nor ensuring that a specific "result" is not influenced by some other factor.[95]

NON DEFINED AND NON SPECIFIC STUDIES

Many "research" studies purport to research an issue, but do not define what they are specifically researching, nor how the proposed research method will test for a particular effect. If there is an effect, can it be demonstrated that the hypothesis or proposed effect is the result of the "cause" (e.g. camera; a camera filming; a camera operator, etc.) identified or some other cause?

MISINTERPRETING RESULTS

Many general studies are generalised beyond the validity and data.[96] "Reports" claim, for example, that particular research "demonstrated that audio-visual coverage does not adversely affect judicial proceedings."[97] However, this is wholly incorrect and mistaken. A research proposition may be that there is Y affect on person(s) A from cause X. If no positive result is demonstrated, or statistically demonstrated (or proven), then established research methods dictate that the conclusion is only that Y effect was not demonstrated. The research proposition was not established. It may also be that even if there is a minor Y effect shown in results, this may be so statistically insignificant that even still, the research proposition is not proven. Many suggestions of "conclusions" that there are no effects are, therefore, incorrect.

SMALL SAMPLES

Many of the state research studies rely on "a very small sample."[98] Virginia had 57 responses, California 56, Nevada 31 and New Jersey only "a relatively small number of respondents surveyed."[99] James L. Hoyt's study, while often cited, only had 12 subjects in each of the three video conditions.[100] The courtroom participants surveyed for the Short Report were limited to judges, attorneys and jurors.[101] Only a subset of these were then interviewed.[102]

Paul Thaler refers to a New York study by the Office of Court Administration after the Steinberg case. However, of the 1,095 people surveyed, only 32 were witnesses, of which only 1 witness was from New York City. He also criticises the fact that no convicted television courtroom broadcasting defendant was included in the survey or interviews.[103]

LOW RESPONSE RATES

One of the other problems is that there has been a low response rate for some of the post case survey questionnaires.[104] Shores refers to one survey of five trials in Florida in 1977-1978 which only had responses from nine witnesses (two of whom referred to detrimental effects).[105] The response rate for judges in the Florida and Wisconsin studies is indicated to be low.[106] The methodical witness studies to date also have relatively small subject numbers and responses.[107]

LITTLE ANALYSIS

It is noted that "[e]arly efforts included reactions from judges and surveys of participants. These methods continue, joined by more experimental methods."[108] To the extent that this suggests that there is significant and frequent experimental research, the record shows otherwise.

CONTAMINATION

In one instance at least, participants in a given case were interviewed on their experience of courtroom broadcasting but while being videotaped.[109] The interviews apparently elicited "glowing testimonials to the journalistic prowess of the media."[110] There does not appear to be any consideration of whether the interview filming, or questions may have had an affect on the responses.

JUDICIAL PROCESS/PROCEDURE

Teresa Keller states that until the time of her study in 1992 the research has focused "primarily on whether courtroom decorum and the defendant's right to a fair trial are adversely affected. Repeatedly, surveys, experiments and legal analyses fail to find clear evidence that the judicial procedure is harmed."[111]

CAMERA EFFECT/EMPIRICAL/NO RESEARCH

Donald Shores agrees that "little factual evidence exists to support either side of the question as to what effects the camera has" on witnesses communication behaviour.[112] "The effects of cameras on witnesses will never be known until systematic research efforts probe the question."[113] Burger J in *Chandler* also agrees that "[f]urther experimentation is necessary to evaluate the potential psychological prejudice associated with broadcast coverage of trials."[114] The impact is "unknown" according to another judge.[115] The literature acknowledges that the effects research is "sparse."[116]

POOLING

Where pooling arrangements have been in place, it does not appear that there has been any comparative research of the footage from the different networks.[117] This issue requires to be researched.

CAMERA SHOTS

There is generally no comparison or research of the effects of different types of camera shots in television courtroom broadcasting footage.[118] This requires to be researched.

DISTRACTION, ATTENTION AND OTHER EFFECTS

One theme in many surveys is that courtroom participants may see and notice the cameras, but will soon forget about them.[119] However, if a witness for example notices the camera(s) but says they forgot about the camera(s) once they began to be questioned, could there still remain a subconscious effect? The general research does not properly investigate this point.

On Netteburg's research, 59% incorrectly remembered that the defendant was guilty of both charges, only 5% correctly recalled that the defendant was found guilty of only one charge,[120] which was described as disturbing.[121] He suggests further research of defendants who are acquitted in televised trials.[122]

Kermit Netteburg finds "little evidence *to support*" some of the *Estes* decisions; "[o]ther research *fails to confirm* … detrimental effects … survey data … in Washington, Ohio, Florida and Wisconsin have *failed to demonstrate* [distraction effects]."[123] (Emphasis added). It is clear, therefore, that such research is *not* saying that effects do not exist. It is unfortunate, therefore, that so many commentators make the wholly incorrect assumption that these and other studies have found that there are no effects or no adverse effects. Such assumptions misrepresent the research and incorrectly advance conclusions which are in fact not founded.

CASE STUDIES

Case studies are useful but should not be generalised.[124] They have a "lack of generalizability."[125] In terms of considering case studies and general conclusions from these, the Short Report points out that a "representative sample of cases within an experimental period must be studied before general conclusions may be drawn."[126]

Just "because one trial can be conducted fairly under the camera's scrutiny does not mean that others can."[127] Also, a "one time survey … cannot support the inference that television *causes* prejudice and such was not the purpose of this study."[128] A "survey of public opinion cannot establish causal inference, either; we cannot prove that TV causes prejudice simply because people believe it does."[129]

Also,

> While the [Florida[130] and Wisconsin[131] study] surveys are more generalizable than case studies, they still cannot be used as evidence to draw causal conclusions. For instance, we might argue that the juror who has participated in only a televised trial has no knowledge of courtroom decorum in a non-televised trial setting and little basis for deciding whether the new situation is more fair or unfair.[132]

FORMS

The timelines and histories of television courtroom broadcasting is not located and compared with the developments, phases, genres and formats of television, television programming and television content generally.[133]

Kohm notes surprise at the lack of research of reality based courtroom television broadcasting, despite the first show of this kind, *Peoples Court*, dovetailing the California Judicial Council's decision to permit television courtroom broadcasting in the late 1970's.[134] Kimberly Podlas also notes the lack of research into the impact of reality television courtroom broadcasting, in particular *Peoples Court* and *Judge Judy*.[135] Podlas used surveys of those attending for jury service regarding their viewing habits of reality based syndicated TCB.[136] She found that reality TCB viewing influenced the jurors views and expectations of how active and proactive judges would be, and in addition influenced what opinions judges would have.[137] Frequent viewers tended to look for clues as to the judge's opinion, including interpreting judicial silences.[138] Podlas also refers to TCB mis-education effect issues.[139]

While "there is a marked difference between sensational trials such as O.J. Simpson's (criminal) 'trial of the century' and the more mundane kinds of disputes shown on a typical episode of Peoples' Court of 'Judge Judy.'"[140]

Rebecca Stuart refers to empirical studies (supporting courtroom televised broadcasting) but does not cite them.[141] While she states that results are overall positive, both civil and criminal media case coverage showed "small side effects."[142] These are not expanded upon.

Different forms are not distinguished in the research. Nor are there definitions. It is not possible to say which forms and patterns across those forms, are most favourable towards television courtroom broadcasting. Generally the studies do not even distinguish television courtroom broadcasting from other potential forms of courtroom broadcasting.

PRIVACY

Privacy, even in the courtroom setting, has been ignored in terms of research and evaluation, and is only addressed in comment and argument only. Can TCB infringe upon privacy rights? Within privacy, we have subsets of defendant privacy,[143] party privacy, juror privacy, witness privacy, lawyer privacy, judge privacy, court personnel privacy, public attendee privacy. These concerns are rarely considered. To what extent does mass or maximum publicity exposure on television courtroom broadcasting conflict with legitimate privacy issues?

CONTROLS

The general (non empirical) studies, with possibly one exception, failed to have adequate controls.[144]

COURTROOM PARTICIPANTS: DEFENDANTS

Very few of the general questionnaires and interviews involve the defendants.[145] This is a large omission in the research. Equally, there appears no empirical research of definition issues.

AUDIENCE

Susanna Barber highlights the need to focus on audience effects of television courtroom broadcasting.[146] There is little audience research of television courtroom broadcasting. More research is needed.

CONCLUSION

Despite the first courtroom television broadcast occurring in 1953,[147] the literature reveals a scant amount of overall general research being carried out. It is particularly concerning also, that there is even less references to quality or social–science research identified in the literature on the topic. One would have expected significantly more, given the general interest in the judicial and court process and in particular in terms of the justice issues at stake.

As has already been mentioned, there is actually a scant amount of even general research available on the effects of courtroom television broadcasting. Upon examination, a number of problems and shortcomings can be identified. These include,

- Not all of the research is available and or easily accessible. Hence it is difficult to review and is difficult for researchers in future to consider in their own research;
- Not all of the research is properly cited which hinders its availability to future researchers;
- Some of the research is not properly documented or methodical in terms of, for example, identifying who in particular undertook the research, their qualifications and expertise to do so, the exact numbers of people who were interviewed, what if any statistical recording and or analyses was recorded;
- There is no systematisation of research such that it may be compared with other research;
- There is no accurate or scientific recordal of such a nature as to make any wider effect general conclusions as to courtroom television broadcasting generally;

- Generally, we cannot tell what the courtrooms looked like and where exactly the camera(s) were located, thus making comparisons impossible;
- There is no clear theory or hypothesis presented, and thus examined in the general studies, so while some of them are indeed interesting, it is unclear what, if anything, they prove.

Indeed, some of the existing courtroom broadcasting studies are not even questionnaires and contain no quantifiable data and also do not even indicate how many people participated.[148]

Again Susanna Barber[149] notes that certain types of case tend to predominate in television courtroom broadcasting, in particular "notorious or sordid" cases. Studies further reveal that few trials are broadcast "in any substantial detail" and fewer still gavel to gavel (G2G) over the whole length of the case.[150]

Overall, we need definitions, consideration of forms and significantly more empirical research.

NOTES

1. A Sample Survey of the Attitudes of Individuals Associated with Trials Involving Electronic Media and Still Photography Coverage in Selected Florida Courts between July 5, 1977 and June 30, 1978, available from the Florida Supreme Court, as referred to in K. Netteburg, Does Research Support the Estes Ban on Cameras in the Courtroom, Judicature 63 (1980): 467–475, at 472.
2. K. Netteburg, Does Research Support the Estes Ban on Cameras in the Courtroom, Judicature 63 (1980): 467–475, at 472.
3. S.L. Alexander, 'Mischievous Potentialities': A Case Study of Courtroom Camera Guidelines, Eight Judicial Circuit, Florida, 1989 (Ph.D diss., University of Florida, (1990), 83.
4. S.L. Alexander, ibid, 84.
5. Courts of Florida, (1978). Referred to ibid, 491.
6. Referred to in E. Borgida, K. DeBona and L.A. Buckman, Cameras in the Courtroom, The Effects of Media Coverage on Witness Testimony and Juror Perceptions, Law and Human Behaviour 14:5 (1990): 489–508, at 491.
7. Ibid, 491.
8. Ibid.
9. Ibid.
10. T. Keller, Cameras in Courtrooms: An Analysis of Television Court Coverage in Virginia (Ph.D diss., The University of Tennessee, 1992), 52.
11. Ibid, 52.
12. Ibid.
13. P. Thaler, The Impact of the Television Camera on Courtroom Participants: A Case Study of the Joel Steinberg Murder Trial. (Ph.D diss., New York University, 1990), 178.
14. Some of which are referred to in E. Borgida, K. DeBona, K., and L.A. Buckman, above, 489–508, at 492.
15. E.H. Short and Associates, Evaluation of California's Experiment with Extended Media Coverage of Courts, Submitted to: The Administrative Office for the Courts, The Chief Justice's Special Committee on the Courts and the Media and The California Judicial Council (September 1981), (Short Report), above, 22.
16. Ibid, 244.
17. Ibid, 244.

18. Ibid, 244-245.

19. See Memorandum to Members of the Court Management Committee from Administrative Office of the Courts, Michael A. Fisher, Attorney Regarding Cameras in Court Experiment (Rule 980.2), 11.

20. Ibid.

21. Administrative Office of the Courts, Research and Planning Unit, Cameras in the Courtroom, Report on Rule 980 (May, 2000): 3. The report later says that "[e]very media request form received was missing at least one piece of requested information." Ibid, 13.

22. Ibid, 9.

23. See P. Thaler, above, 26. The author unsuccessfully sought to obtain a copy of the original study. Correspondence with author.

24. See P. Thaler, ibid.

25. VAB Assessment Report to the [Virginia] Supreme Court, 1989, as referred to in T. Keller, above, 12.

26. A.E. Blashfield, The Case of the Controversial Canon, American Bar Association Journal 48 (1962): 429-434, as referred to in D. Shores. The Effects of Courtroom Camera on Verbal Behaviour: An Analysis of Simulated Trial Witness Testimony in Courtrooms Using Television Cameras (Ph.D diss., The University of Florida, 1981), 19.

27. A.E. Blashfield, ibid.

28. D. Shores, The Effects of Courtroom Camera on Verbal Behaviour: An Analysis of Simulated Trial Witness Testimony in Courtrooms Using Television Cameras (Ph.D diss., The University of Florida, 1981), 19.

29. J.R. Weisberger, Cameras in the Courtroom: The Rhode Island Experience, Suffolk University Law Review XVII: 2 (1983): 299–311.

30. Ibid, 302.

31. Ibid, 302-303.

32. There are apparently recorded interviews on film. As referred to in K. Netteburg, above, 470 and 470, n. 1.

33. See K. Netteburg, above, 470.

34. D. Shores, above, 20.

35. See generally P. Lambert, Courtroom Television Broadcasting, Communications Law 2:5 (1997): 180–187; P. Lambert, Courtroom Television Cameras and the Media, Journal of Media Law and Practice 16:4 (1995): 139-144 as examples. On the context of open justice and court reporting generally see M. McGonagle, A Textbook on Media Law (Dublin: Gill and MacMillan, 1997), and the follow up Media Law (Dublin: Sweet and Maxwell, 2006); W. Freeman, Press and Media Access to the Criminal Courtroom, (New York: Quorum, 1988); N.T. Gardner, Cameras in the Courtroom: Guidelines for State Criminal Trials, Michigan Law Review 84:3 (1985): 475–516; and references throughout this present work. Also, P. Lambert, Effects Research Issues in Television Courtroom Broadcasting: Getting Past Monkey, 10th European Conference on eGovernment, University of Limerick (June 17-18, 2010); P. Lambert, Time to Leave the Monkey Behind?: How Eye Tracking and Psychology Can Contribute to Television Courtroom Broadcasting Effects Research, British Psychological Society, BPS Cognitive Psychology Section Annual Conference, 27th Annual Cognitive Psychology Section Conference, Cardiff University (September 6-8, 2010); P. Lambert, Eye Tracking Technology and Television Courtroom Broadcasting, Computers and Law (August 11, 2010), www.scl.org/site.aspx?i=ed16965 , accessed August 13, 2011; P. Lambert, TCB Effects: Eye Tracking and Camera Distraction in Court, Irish Association of Law Teachers Annual Conference, Strand Hotel, Limerick (November 26-28, 2010); P. Lambert, Monkey Magic: Problems With Effects Research of Television Courtroom Broadcasting, Irish Law Times 18 (2010): 278–280; P. Lambert, A Candid Camera, Eye Tracking Technology Could Transform Courtroom Broadcasting, New Law Journal (December 10, 2010), 1699–1700.

36. S. Barber, above.

37. These studies were carried out during the period between 1975 and 1981.

38. Ibid, 92-93.

39. Note an interesting chapter by R. Cranston, The Rational Study of Law: Social Research and Access to Justice, which discusses changing legal course subjects, in A.A.S. Zuckerman

and R. Cranston, Reform of Civil Procedure: Essays on Access to Justice (Oxford: Clarendon, 1995), 31–59.

40. One should also note that the Law Reform Commission has explored the separate (but related) area of contempt of court. See Law Reform Commission, Consultation Paper on Contempt of Court (Dublin: Government Publications, 1991) and the subsequent Law Reform Commission, Report on Contempt of Court (Dublin: Government Publications, 1994).

41. See comments of K. Mannheim, Ideology and Utopia (London: Routledge and Keegan Paul, 1936), regarding meaning and reference frames (within which to contextualise meaning and content) being historically located.

42. See eye tracking proof of concept demonstration and related issued referred to in Chapter 8.

43. P. Thaler, above, p. 34.

44. R.E.R. Stuart, The Changing Relationship Between Camera and the Courts (MA diss., Florida Atlantic University, 1998), 57.

45. Ibid, 58.

46. Ibid, 60.

47. Ibid, 56.

48. Ibid, 56–57.

49. Ibid, 60.

50. To use the words of J.R. Weisberger, above, 305.

51. See Short Report, E. Short and Associates, above, 19.

52. W. Petkanas, Cameras on Trial: An Assessment of the Educational Affects of News Cameras in Trial Courts (Ph.D diss, New York University, 1990), 113.

53. Ibid, 113.

54. S. Kassin, TV Cameras, Public Self-Consciousness, and Mock Juror Performance, Journal of Experimental Social Psychology 20 (1984) 336–349, at 337.

55. Ibid, 336–349, at 337, with references to N. Davis, Television in Our Courts: The Proven Advantages, The Unproven Dangers, Judicature, 64 (1980): 85–92; and also J. Wisenand, Florida's Experiment, American Bar Association Journal 64 (1978): 1860–1863.

56. D. Shores, The Effects of Courtroom Camera on Verbal Behaviour: An Analysis of Simulated Trial Witness Testimony in Courtrooms Using Television Cameras (Ph.D diss., The University of Florida, 1981), 29.

57. Ibid, 29.

58. K.P. Warden, Canon 35: Is There Room for Objectivity?, Washburn Law Journal 4 (1965): 211.

59. K. Netteburg, above, 473.

60. T. Keller, above, 24.

61. Ibid, 26.

62. S. Kassin, TV Cameras, Public Self-Consciousness, and Mock Juror Performance, Journal of Experimental Social Psychology 20 (1984): 336–349, at 337.

63. S.R. Pasternack, The Effects of Perceived Community Pressure on Simulated Juror Guilt Attributions: An Experimental Study (Ph.D diss., The University of Tennessee, Knoxville, 1982), 3.

64. A.R. Paddon. "Television Coverage of Criminal Trials with Cameras and Microphones: A Controlled Experiment of Audience Effects," Radio-television Journalism Division, AEJMC Montreal, Que, Canada, August 7, 1992, 14. Also, A.R. Paddon, Television Coverage of Criminal Trials with Cameras and Microphones: A Controlled Experiment of Audience Effects. (Ph.D diss., University of Tennessee, 1985).

65. S.A. Esposito, OJ TV: A Narrative Analysis of Television's Pretrial Coverage of the O.J. Simpson Case (Ph.D diss., Wayne State University, Detroit, Michigan, 1996), 26. See also D.P. Killian, The Propriety of Restrictive Guidelines for Cameras in the Court, Communications and the Law 9 (1987): 27–43, as described in S.L. Alexander, 'Mischievous Potentialities': A Case Study of Courtroom Camera Guidelines, Eight Judicial Circuit, Florida, 1989 (Ph.D diss., University of Florida, 1990), 72.

66. J.R. Weisberger, above, 303.

67. K. Netteburg, 467–475, at 469.

68. Ibid, 469, n. 11.
69. Ibid, above, 469.
70. P. Thaler, above, 16, referring also to W. Freedman, Press and Media Access to the Criminal Courtroom (New York: Quorum, 1988). Thaler does not refer to any page numbering in Freedman.
71. P. Thaler, above, 68.
72. Ibid, 34.
73. J. L. Hoyt, Courtroom Coverage: The Effects of Being Televised, Journal of Broadcasting (1977): 487–495, at 489.
74. P. Thaler, above, 70.
75. D. Shores, The Effects of Courtroom Camera on Verbal Behaviour: An Analysis of Simulated Trial Witness Testimony in Courtrooms Using Television Cameras (Ph.D diss., The University of Florida, 1981), 1.
76. S.A. Kohm, above, 357.
77. S.L. Alexander, 'Mischievous Potentialities': A Case Study of Courtroom Camera Guidelines, Eight Judicial Circuit, Florida, 1989 (Ph.D diss., University of Florida, 1990), 39–40.
78. J. Ossinger, Electronic Access to Courtrooms: Television as an Educational Socializing Agent on the Judiciary (MA diss., University of Maine, 2006), 21.
79. Ibid, 9.
80. Ibid.
81. E. Borgida, K. DeBona and L.A. Buckman, L.A., Cameras in the Courtroom, The Effects of Media Coverage on Witness Testimony and Juror Perceptions, Law and Human Behaviour 14:5 (1990): 489–508, at 491.
82. Ibid, 489-508, at 492.
83. As referred to ibid, 489–508, at 491.
84. D. Shores, referring to a one year experiment approved by the California Supreme Court beginning in June 1980, D. Shores. The Effects of Courtroom Camera on Verbal Behavior: An Analysis of Simulated Trial Witness Testimony in Courtrooms Using Television Cameras (Ph.D diss., The University of Florida, 1981): 26.
85. D.P. Killian, above, as referred to in S.L. Alexander. 'Mischievous Potentialities': A Case Study of Courtroom Camera Guidelines, Eight Judicial Circuit, Florida, 1989 (Ph.D diss., University of Florida, 1990): 72.
86. C.M. Boggs, Television Cameras in the Courtroom: An Examination of Studies and Their Value to Court Policy–Making (MA diss., University of Pennsylvania, 1981), as referred to in S.L. Alexander. 'Mischievous Potentialities': A Case Study of Courtroom Camera Guidelines, Eight Judicial Circuit, Florida, 1989 (Ph.D diss., University of Florida, 1990): 90.
87. E. Einsiedel, Television in the Courtroom: An Ohio Experiment, Association for Education in Journalism, Seattle, (1978), as referred to in S.L. Alexander. 'Mischievous Potentialities': A Case Study of Courtroom Camera Guidelines, Eight Judicial Circuit, Florida 1989 (Ph.D diss., University of Florida, 1990): 87.
88. K. Netterburg, Does Research Support the Estes Ban on Cameras in the Courtroom? Judicature 63 (1980): 467–475, at 472, as referred to in the Short Report, above, 12.
89. G. Gerbner, Trial by Television: Are We At The Point Of No Return?, Judicature 63 (1980): 416–426, at 426, as referred to in T. Keller, above, 70–71.
90. T. Keller, above, 52.
91. P. Thaler, above, 34.
92. Ibid, 68.
93. Ibid, 34.
94. Ibid, 27.
95. Ibid, 27.
96. T. Rimmer, Electronic Media in the Courtroom: Legal and Social Science Perspectives (Portland OR: American Association for Education in Journalism and Mass Communication, 1988); S.L. Alexander, above, 90.
97. M. Crosson, chief administrator of the courts in New York State, public report, as referred to in P. Thaler, above, 30–31.

98. R.E.R. Stuart, above, 57.
99. Ibid, 57.
100. J.L. Hoyt, above, 487-195, at 493.
101. Short Report, above, 19.
102. Ibid, 21.
103. P. Thaler, above, 178.
104. D. Shores, above, 22-23.
105. B. Pryor D. Strawn, R. Buchanan and M. Meeske, The Florida Experiment: An Analysis of the On-the-Scene Responses to Cameras in the Courtrooms, Southern Speech Communications Journal 45 (1979: 12–26, as referred to in D. Shores, above, 22-23.
106. K. Netteburg, above, 472.
107. D. Shores, above, 29.
108. T. Keller, above, 51.
109. See T. Keller, above, 52, referring to the John Gilbert Graham trial and the research reported in H.B. Terry, Electronic Journalism in the Colorado Courts, Journalism Quarterly 34 (1957): 341–348, at 354.
110. H.B. Terry, ibid, 348.
111. T. Keller, above, 71.
112. D. Shores, above, 37.
113. Ibid.
114. J. Berger, in *Chandler v Florida*, at 4146, as referred to in D. Shores, above, 38.
115. J. Fatzer, former Chief Justice of Kansas Supreme Court, in H.R. Fatzer, Cameras in the Courtroom: The Kansas Opposition, Washburn Law Journal 18 (1978): 230–243, as referred to in D. Shores, above, 38.
116. D. Shores, above, 39, and references to the general literature therein.
117. Note comments in Petkanas, regarding same in one jurisdiction, W. Petkanas. Cameras on Trial: An Assessment of the Educational Affects of News Cameras in Trial Courts (Ph.D diss., New York University, 1990), 63.
118. W. Petkanas, ibid, 68, regarding different types of camera angles.
119. See, for example, E. Einsiedel, Television in the Courtroom: An Ohio Experiment, paper presented to the Association for Education in Journalism, (August, 1978), as referred to in Netteburg, above, 470.
120. K. Netteburg, above, 474.
121. Ibid, 475.
122. Ibid.
123. Ibid.
124. See Short Report, above, 11.
125. K. Netteburg, above, 471.
126. See Short Report, above, 11.
127. K. Netteburg, above, 471.
128. Ibid, 471. Original emphasis.
129. K. Netteburg, above, 471.
130. A Sample Survey of the Attitudes of Individuals Associated with Trials Involving Electronic Media and Still Photography Coverage in Selected Florida Courts between 5 July, 1977 and 30 June, 1978, available from the Florida Supreme Court, as referred to in K. Netteburg, above, 472.
131. Report of the Supreme Court Committee to Monitor and Evaluate the Use of Audio and Visual Equipment in the Courtroom (April 1, 1979), as referred to in Netteburg, above, 472.
132. K. Netteburg, above, 472-473.
133. Note references to some of the different period and developments of television generally in S.A. Kohm, I'm Not a Judge But I Play One on TV: American Reality-Based Courtroom Television (Ph.D diss., Simon Fraser University, 2004), 87 et seq.
134. S.A. Kohm, ibid, 90. Also K. Podlas, Please Adjust Your Signal: How Television's Syndicated Courtrooms Bias Our Juror Citizenry, American Business Law Review 39 (2001) 1–24.
135. K. Podlas, ibid, 1–24.

136. Ibid, 1-2.
137. Ibid, 2.
138. Ibid.
139. Ibid.
140. S.A. Kohm, above, 90–91.
141. R.E.R. Stuart, above, 47–48.
142. Ibid, 47.
143. See P. Thaler, above, 159.
144. E. Borgida, K. DeBona and L.A. Buckman, above, 489-508, at 491.
145. Ibid, 92.
146. Ibid, 95 et seq.
147. Listed by S. Barber, as being the case of Billy Eugene Manley in Oklahoma City which occurred in 1953, see S. Barber, above, 10–11.
148. See ibid, 68.
149. Ibid, 80–81.
150. Ibid, 81.

Chapter Ten

Empirical Research and Themes

INTRODUCTION

The empirical studies referred to in the literature are identified above. However, how extensive are the issues and questions being examined in the limited number of empirical studies that exist? The figure below highlights many of the different effect concerns and issues highlighted for research in the empirical studies. The number of blanks emphasises (a) the limited number of empirical studies, (b) the many gaps that exist, and (c) the lack of verification via repeat studies of the actual studies being undertaken.

Furthermore, the three Supreme Court cases and the effects and research issues highlighted in those cases, also emphasises that there are significant issues and areas of concern which are not researched or researched adequately.

AUTHOR: ADDITIONAL SOCIAL SCIENCE STUDIES

In addition to the studies evident in the literature, there were also additional social science studies located by the author, namely,

- New York State Committee to Review Audio-Visual Coverage of Court Proceedings, An Open Courtroom: Cameras in New York Courts (New York: Fordham University Press, 1997) [in part only];
- Kermit Lyol Netterburg, Cameras in the Courtroom: Is a Picture Worth a Thousand Words? (Ph.D diss., University of Minnesota, 1980);
- Allen Bukoff, The Effects of Video Camera Techniques on the Pre–deliberation Judgements and Perceptions of Role-Playing Jurors (Ph.D diss., Kent State University, 1984);

- S.L. Alexander, "Mischievous Potentialities": A Case Study of Courtroom Camera Guidelines, Eight Judicial Circuit, Florida (Ph.D diss., University of Florida, 1989);
- Steve Anthony Esposita, OJ TV: A Narrative Analysis of Television's Pretrial Coverage of the OJ Simpson Case (Ph.D diss., Wayne State University, 1996);
- William Petkanas, Cameras on Trial: An Assessment of the Educational Affect of News Cameras in Trial Courts (Ph.D diss., New York University, 1990);
- Paul E. Thaler, The Impact of the television Camera on Courtroom Participants: A Case Study of the Joel Steinberg Murder Trial (Ph.D diss., New York University, 1990);
- Theresa D. Keller, Cameras in Courtrooms: An Analysis of Television Court Coverage in Virginia (Ph.D diss., University of Tennessee, 1992);
- Roberta Enter, The Image of the Judiciary: A Semiotic Analyse of Broadcast Trials to Ascertain its Definition of the Court System (Ph.D diss., New York University, 1993);
- Korni Swaroop Kumar, Murder and the News Media (Ph.D diss., Temple University, 1993) [Not a full TCB study];
- Steven Kohm, I'm Not a Judge But I Play One On TV: American Reality Based Courtroom Television (Ph.D diss., Simon Fraser University, 2004);
- Tarika Daftary–Kapur, The Effects of Pre– and Post–Venire Publicity on Juror Decision Making (Ph.D, The City University of New York, 2009) [Not a full TCB study];
- Kimberly Allan, Professor Judy McGregor and Susan Fountaine, The Impact of Television, Radio and still Photography Coverage of Court Proceedings, Final Report, A Report for the Department for Courts (Massey University, April 1998) (New Zealand);
- Alves, Hon. Nathan Braverman, Chaor, Baron, Hon. Jean Szekeres, Groton, Hon. Thomas C. III, Leasure, Hon. Diane O., Plitt, Hon. Emory A., Jr., Report of the Committee to Study Extended Media Coverage of Criminal Trial Proceedings in Maryland, Committee to Study Extended Media Coverage, a Subcommittee of the Legislation Committee of the Maryland Judicial Conference (Maryland).

EFFECT ISSUES IDENTIFIED BY SUPREME COURT

The Supreme Court, in *Estes*, *Chandler* and *Hollingsworth*, referred to a large number effect issues and concerns regarding television courtroom broadcasting, and which should be the focus of empirical research.

The court identified, in its own words, the following effect concerns, namely, distraction; distortion; disruption; general distraction; actor distraction; psychological effects; adverse psychological effects on judges, lawyers, witnesses, jurors; duties of the trial judge; influence on public opinion; influence on verdicts; further studies; body of reliable factual data; experience effects research; the integrity of judicial process; highly publicised trials; criminal trials; prejudice; diverting the trial; impacting on all participants; giving the public the wrong impression about the trial process; singling out certain defendants; prejudicial conditions not experienced by other defendants; changing behaviour because of awareness; increasing nervousness; increasing tension; opportunism; acting differently; effort of trying not to be effected; not giving full attention; noise of cameras; appearance of cameras; awareness of being televised; undercutting reliability of the trial process; techniques of public communication; future technology; process of televising; probable hazards; criminal trial with notoriety versus a routine trial; effects on the normal detached atmosphere; distorting the trial process; effects of commercials and intervals; detracting from the trial, justice and constitutional functions; undermining or effecting the serenity, calm and decorum of the court; decorum; witnesses and jury awareness; no longer calm; increasing publicity; conditioning the public; prejudicing the public; prejudice of actual and potential jurors; inadmissible evidence leakage; juror television viewing during trial; editing; commentary; peer pressure; courtroom actor objections ignored; conscious or unconscious effects; voting decisions; pre-trial publicity; community pressure; awareness; focus; attention; TV viewing; re-trial effects; pre-trial effects; emphasising that the case is special; popular verdicts; pre-trial publicity; bias; extraneous influence; knowledge of being televised; emotional audience; aggravation/escalation; jury prejudice by media; witness effects; witness TV viewing; amending testimony; attitude to testifying; apprehension; reluctance; quality of the testimony; impact of being filmed and broadcast; demoralized; frightening; cocky; overstatement; public speaking; accuracy; over dramatization; public recognition/harassment of witnesses; judge effects; additional responsibility; undivided attention; politics and elected judges; diversion; psychological effects and reactions; direct news media pressure; influence of public opinion by news media; psychology research; various effects; personal acting up; interruptions; rulings ; inconsistency; concentration; defendant effects; harassment; close ups; sensibilities; dignity; concentration; wide publicity; heightened publicity; effective counsel; intrusions; acting up; restrictions; objection by defendant; acting up; awareness; prejudice; out-of-court effects; entertainment; commercial objectives; developing the personalities of the courtroom participants; dramatisation; conditioning the public against the defendants; edited and selected programming; make an impartial jury for a re-trial impossible; influencing opinions before verdict; undermining fairness; effects on courtroom participants; effect of the audience who may become jurors, witnesses; effects in re education; entertain; diverting the process; leading to suspicions concerning integrity of trial process; dividing actor efforts; undercuting integrity of trial process; television as the most accurate and comprehensive means of conveying to the public; educational by acquainting with the judicial process; educational institutions; only selected trials; only courts with amenable layouts selected; sensational cases predominate; dignity and calmness; effects on other media; act differently; acting up; more lenient;

> playing to audience; playing to potential clients; change attitudes; editing; biasing editing; effects even on unedited film footage; wrong impression; television cannot cover everything and all actions in court, only where focused; lawyers will look to see if they can confer with their client without, or out of, close-ups; unfairness; educate as to nature of judicial process; personality, famous and celebrity; kind of case; non-notorious trial; subtle effects; effect on timid or reluctant witness; unconscious effects; effect of television performance; effects of constitutional dimensions; prejudice; jury ability to judge fairly; limited and non scientific research; prejudice; something more than juror awareness; threats; harassment; death threats; harm irreparable harm; live streaming; internet; effect of witness testimony chilling; unwillingness to testify; qualitative differences; adequate remedies to effects through an appeal; altered testimony; unwillingness to cooperate with future cases; integrity of trial process; high profile trials; considered standards and guidelines; witness security; non high profile cases; cases with witnesses; cases without witnesses; sensitive issue cases; all or parts of cases being broadcast; good and bad cases for television courtroom broadcasting experiments; high profile publicly divisive cases; effects of harm in non jury cases; adverse effects from presence of camera; all harm rectifiable on appeal; effect of increasing public awareness of witnesses; reasonable or feasible for witnesses to object; trial management; integrity of trial; protective measures; actual prejudice; subtle prejudice; slippery slope; coerced confession; jury influence.

Obviously some would appear to be repeated, or at least very similar. However, no one has researched whether there is actual duplication, or whether the Supreme Court may have been variously differentiating discrete effects. If the court was, then we should be reluctant to delete perceived duplication.

THE ISSUES COVERED IN THE EMPIRICAL RESEARCH

The following issues have been covered in the empirical research identified to date.

Table 10.1. Matrix of Empirical Studies

	Effects	
1	Disruption	
	• General; Ct Pers;	
	• Judge; Jury;	
	• Lawyers;	
	• Witness; Defendant;	
	• Parties; Public in ct	
2	Distraction	
	• General	16, 12
	• Ct Pers	

	• Judge	
	• Jury	
	• Lawyers	
	• Witness	
	• Defendant	
	• Parties	
	• Public in ct	
3	Role/Speech	
	• General	
	• Ct Pers	
	• Judge	
	• Jury	
	• Lawyers	
	• Witness	
	• Defendant	3
	• Parties	
	• Public in ct	
4	Role/Activity	
	• General	
	• Ct Pers	
	• Judge	
	• Jury	5
	• Lawyers	
	• Witness	7
	• Defendant	
	• Parties	
	• Public in ct	
5	Role/Encoding	
	• General; Ct Pers;	
	• Judge; Jury;	
	• Lawyers;	
	• Witness; Defendant;	
	• Parties; Public in ct	
6	Role/Memory	
	• General	
	• Ct Pers	
	• Judge	

	• Jury	8	
	• Lawyers		
	• Witness		
	• Defendant		
	• Parties		
	• Public in ct		
7	Being Filmed		
	• General; Ct Pers;		
	• Judge; Jury;		
	• Lawyers;		
	• Witness; Defendant;		
	• Parties; Public in ct		
8	Being Broadcast		
	• General; Ct Pers;		
	• Judge; Jury;		
	• Lawyers;		
	• Witness; Defendant;		
	• Parties; Public in ct		
9	Pressure		
	• General		
	• Ct Pers		
	• Judge		
	• Jury	4	
	• Lawyers		
	• Witness		
	• Defendant		
	• Parties		
	• Public in ct		
10	Camera location		
11	Camera height		
12	Camera type		
13	Rules	3	
14	Forms		
	• Reality	19	19
	• Push TV		
	• Radio		
	• Internet		

15	Education		
	• General		15
	• Audience		
	• Public		
	• Educ. Re?		
	• Judge		21
16	Information		
	• General		6
	• Audience		
	• Public		
	• Judge		18
17	Confidence		
	• General		
	• Audience		
	• Public		
18	Consent		17
19	Narrative analysis		14
		In-Court Effects	Out-of-Court Effects
		Social Science Research Studies	Social Science Research Studies

Note 1: S1 James L. Hoyt, Courtroom Coverage: The Effects of Being Televised, Journal of Broadcasting 21 (1900): 487–495.

S2 Ernest H Short and Associates, Evaluation of California's Experiment with Extended Media Coverage of Courts, submitted to Administrative Office for the Courts; the Chief Justice's Special Committee on the Courts and the Media, and the California Judicial Council (1981).

S3 Donald Lewis Shores, Jr., The Effects of Courtroom Cameras on Verbal Behaviour: An Analysis of Simulated Trial Witness Testimony in Courtrooms Using Television Cameras (Ph.D diss., University of Florida, 1981).

S4 Steve Robert Pasternack. The Effects of Perceived Community Pressure on Simulated Juror Guilt Attributions: A Study (Ph.D, University of Tennessee, Knoxville, 1982).

S5 Saul M. Kassin, TV Cameras, Public Self-Consciousness, and Mock Juror Performance, *Journal of Experimental Psychology* (1983/4): 336.

S6 Anna R. Paddon. Television Coverage of Criminal Trials with Cameras and Microphones: A Laboratory Experiment of Audience Effects (Ph.D diss., University of Tennessee, Knoxville 1985).

S7 E. Borgida, K. Debono and L. Buckman, Cameras in the Courtroom: The Effects of Media Coverage on Witness Testimony and Juror Perceptions, Law and Human Behaviour 14 (1990).

S8 Alan Punches, The Cognitive Effects of Camera Presence on the Recall of Testimony in a Simulated Courtroom Setting (Ph.D diss., Colarado State University, Fort Collins, 1991).

[S9] M.T. Johnson and C. Krafka, Pilot Program Involving Electronic Coverage in Six US District Courts and Two Appeal Courts (Federal Judicial Centre, 1994) [in part only].

[S10] New York State Committee to Review Audio-Visual Coverage of Court Proceedings, An Open Courtroom: Cameras in New York Courts (New York: Fordham University Press, 1997)[in part only].

S11 Kermit Lyol Netterburg, Cameras in the Courtroom: Is a Picture Worth a Thousand Words? (Ph.D, University of Minnesota, 1980).

S12 Allen Bukoff. The Effects of Video Camera Techniques on the Pre-Deliberation Judgements and Perceptions of Role-Playing Jurors (Ph.D diss., Kent State University, 1984).

S13 S.L. Alexander. "Mischievous Potentialities": A Case Study of Courtroom Camera Guidelines, Eight Judicial Circuit, Florida (Ph.D diss., University of Florida, 1989).

S14 Steve Anthony Esposita, OJ TV: A Narrative Analysis of Television's Pretrial Coverage of the OJ Simpson Case (Ph.D diss., Wayne State University, 1996).

S15 William Petkanas, Cameras on Trial: An Assessment of the Educational Affect of News Cameras in Trial Courts (Ph.D diss., New York University, 1990).

S16 Paul E. Thaler, The Impact of the Television Camera on Courtroom Participants: A Case Study of the Joel Steinberg Murder Trial (Ph.D diss., New York University, 1990).

S17 Theresa D. Keller, Cameras in Courtrooms: An Analysis of Television Court Coverage in Virginia (Ph.D diss., University of Tennessee, 1992).

S18 Roberta Enter, The Image of the Judiciary: A Semiotic Analyse of Broadcast Trials to Ascertain its Definition of the Court System (Ph.D diss., New York University, 1993).

S19 Steven Kohm, I'm Not a Judge But I Play One On TV: American Reality Based Courtroom Television (Ph.D diss., Simon Fraser University, 2004).

S20 Ruthie Elizabeth Reeves Stewart. The Changing Relationship Between Camera and the Courts (MA diss., Florida Atlantic University, 1998).

S21 Jessica Ossinger, Electronic Access to Courtrooms: Television as an Educational Socializing Agent on the Judiciary (MA diss., The University of Maine, 2006).

S22 Kimberly Allan, Professor Judy McGregor and Susan Fountaine, The Impact of Television, Radio and still Photography Coverage of Court Proceedings, Final Report, A Report for the Department for Courts (Massey University, April, 1998) (New Zealand).

S23 Alves, Hon. Nathan Braverman, Chaor, Baron, Hon. Jean Szekeres, Groton, Hon. Thomas C. III, Leisure, Hon. Diane O., Plitt, Hon. Emory A., Jr., Report of the Committee to Study Extended Media Coverage of Criminal Trial Proceedings in Maryland, Committee to Study Extended Media Coverage, a Subcommittee of the Legislation Committee of the Maryland Judicial Conference.

Note 2: Not including general, self or opinion reports.

The empirical studies, as identified in Table 10.1, make it transparent that only the following issues raised by the Supreme Court have had any examination in the empirical research, namely, two distraction studies of a limited courtroom participants; the role of select courtroom participants; the memory/recall of one category of courtroom actor; pressure issues on one courtroom actor; one study relating to form type issues; two studies relating to education issues.

It is clear, therefore, that both the general research and the empirical research attempts have left many areas not yet addressed and or validated. The challenge set by the Supreme Court still remains. Validation and replication issues are significant concerns.

What has been covered in the limited empirical research to date? This is referred to below, as this assists in visualising how many gaps there are, and how little verification has occurred.

THEMES AND ISSUES

The first television courtroom broadcast was in 1953.[1] Susanna Barber (1987) indicates that during the period 1953 - 1987 there were only seventeen (17) (non scientific) studies. Worse, she indicates that there are only two (2) social science research studies between 1953 and 1987. In those particular thirty four years of courtroom broadcasting, therefore, we only have two attempts to seriously or properly analyze (certain) issues and effects of television courtroom broadcasting.

The Supreme Court in both *Estes* and *Chandler*, the main US cases in relation to television courtroom broadcasting, "lamented the absence of hard data."[2] "The overall controversy about cameras in courtrooms in unusual for the lack of specific data which have been brought to bear on the questions raised."[3] "In view of the practical importance of this problem for the judiciary and the Supreme Court's repeated plea for behavioural research on the matter, it is surprising that, to date, the only relevant data available are anecdotal case studies, public opinion surveys, and the verbal reports of those who had participated in television trials."[4]

Since 1953 Ronald Goldfarb (1998) is only able to identify eight (8) social science studies regarding courtroom broadcasting. That is eight (8) studies in 45 years. The first two of these are already listed in Barber. So he only lists an additional six studies.

Susanna Barber lists James L Hoyt's study in 1977, Courtroom Coverage: The Effects of Being Televised,[5] as the first social science study of courtroom television broadcasting. The Hoyt study was "attempting to experimentally test [the] speculation, to determine if, in fact, individuals are affected by the awareness that they are being televised."[6] The

> study simulated some of the pressures placed on witnesses in the courtroom setting while at the same time maintaining experimental control so that the results could be meaningfully analyzed. Subjects were shown a brief film containing rather detailed information, then were asked specific questions about the content of the film. While answering the questions they were either facing a conspicuous television camera purportedly recording their answers to be viewed by a large number of people, or an unobtrusive camera hidden being a mirror, or no camera at all. … Based on the assumption obvious in the reasoning of Justices Clark and Warren [in *Estes*] it was predicted that they were televised (whether by an obtrusive or unobtrusive camera) the participants would recall significantly less correct information about the film than when they were not being televised. Because a number of the recent proposals for courtroom coverage by television have mentioned that cameras would be camouflaged, the unobtrusive camera condition was included to determine the effects of hiding the camera.[7]

SOCIAL SCIENCE RESEARCH

The author examined the social science research identified earlier by Barber, Goldfarb and the author.

FORMS

None of the research studies identified, referred to the different forms of courtroom broadcasting, at least explicitly, nor an overall map or framework for courtroom broadcasting, nor television courtroom broadcasting. Only one (S19) can be identified as a specific type or form of television courtroom broadcasting, namely, American reality television courtroom broadcasting.

Without identifying an overall map/matrix (which obviously may change and be expanded upon over time), it is almost impossible to fully contemplate the full breath and landscape of courtroom broadcasting sector issues. Neither is it possible to identify easily, what research has been undertaken so far, what has been replicated and fundamentally, what remains to be researched.

TYPE

A map of courtroom broadcasting also enables us to see what types of research have been undertaken and where existing research compliments TCB research of the same type. The present review indicated that in the above studies there were,

- 9 experiments;
- 9 surveys (S16 (case study));
- 4 reviews;
- 5 incorporated interview;
- 4 observations of court (live case);
- 1 Court (non live case).

RECORDED/QUANTIFIED

Twenty (20) studies were recorded or quantified, thus enabling further analysis and potential follow on studies by other researchers.

AIM/HYPOTHESIS

Fifteen (15) studies set out aims or hypothesis which were being tested or investigated.

CONTROLS/CONDITIONS

Eleven (11) had controls and conditions, thus trying to ensure that specific effects were being tested for or quantified.

VALIDATION/REPLICATION POSSIBLE

It appears that in at least eighteen (18) cases, there is insufficient detail to be able to try and retest, replicate and validate[8] these studies.

NUMBER OF SUBJECTS

Eighteen (18) identify how many subjects were being tested, which was a flaw present in much of the non social science research previously.

SUBJECT DESCRIPTION

Eighteen (18) referred to or identified the type of subjects involved, which is frequently important in assessing research.

METHOD

Twenty (20) referred to and set out the method and detail of study undertaken, thus ensuring it can be properly assessed and hopefully replicated subsequently.

EFFECTS

Sixteen (16) referred to one or more effects.

CAMERA LOCATION

Only six (6) referred in any specific detail as to where the camera was located, some with a map. Height was not referred to.

RULES

Few referred to or incorporated an examination of rules and rule effect issues.

EDUCATION

Only two (2) referred to any meaningfully investigated education issues and arguments.

QUESTIONNAIRES

Fifteen (15) used questionnaires. This emphasises the need to blend questionnaires with additional empirical research methods.

AUDIENCE EFFECT FOCUS

Only six (6) undertook research with an audience effect focus.

EYEWITNESS RESEARCH

None referred to or incorporated the literature and research in the eyewitness field.[9]

AGENDA SETTING

Only one (1) referred to or undertook media agenda setting type research in the context of courtroom broadcasting.

ADVANTAGES AND DISADVANTAGES

The positive and negative aspects of the non-social science research of television courtroom broadcasting is referred to above. Here, the author highlights some of the positives and negatives of the social science based research, and which point to where further research should focus.

DISCUSSION

This section sets out some of the questions and issues which should be addressed in future television courtroom broadcasting research studies.[10] Then it will highlight some of the various research tools and methodologies that can be used, and are being used in other fields of research. It will also outline at a headline level suggestions for specific television courtroom broadcasting research projects in future. This is on foot of the backdrop of having identified flaws with television courtroom broadcasting arguments and television courtroom broadcasting research up to this point. There are significant gaps in our knowledge and appreciation of all aspects of television courtroom broadcasting. However, that does not have to remain the position indefinitely. We can and should advance our knowledge of television courtroom broadcasting now that we have distinguished that there are different definitions and forms of television courtroom broadcasting. These forms are the backdrop and baseline for all considerations and discussions going forward.

What we also have to do in future is address the research gaps and research flaws that currently exist. While many of these have been highlighted, so too have some of the comparators and tools we may adopt and utilise for more considered research of television courtroom broadcasting in future. That we can have the benefit of other research and other research fields is of great assistance, as it means we do not have to start wholly from scratch. Neither do we have to proceed with research which is without comparative research results.

We are, therefore, somewhat fortunate as we consider and address the gaps and questions involving television courtroom broadcasting research. What specifically do we have to do? We need to consider some of the various research issues which arise for television courtroom broadcasting, some of the comparative research and research tools we can utilise, and then look at some of the specific research we can carry out and also the areas we need to identify to be researched.

INADEQUATE RESEARCH

There is practically no meaningful research into any of the many aspects of television courtroom broadcasting. Very few studies of television courtroom broadcasting can actually be described as research or qualitative research as we know it. Most of it amounts to study, reviews, observations, arguments and opinions (see above). In terms of what might be described as qualitative research, it is limited in its scope and focus. For example, it examines only self reports for some of the courtroom participants actually present. The above table shows many gaps. Many courtroom participants are ignored in current research. This means that this research is per se limited in scope. The audience are not researched in terms of watching, effects or adverse effects.

In addition, almost invariably effects type research is based upon survey type research. This utilises and relies solely upon the opinions of certain courtroom participants. Sometimes these courtroom participants may be interviewed but generally the courtroom participants are requested to fill in a questionnaire asking them for their opinions to various pre-defined issues. As with any survey or questionnaire, the questions asked can vary in number and sophistication. However, the main flaws with this approach are twofold. Firstly, this is not the most reliable means of gauging effects of television courtroom broadcasting on courtroom participants. Other more scientific methods are available. Secondly, these studies are once off. Therefore, there are no internal or external checks or validations.

OTHER POTENTIAL AVENUES FOR RESEARCH

This work is not meant to be a complete and comprehensive examination of all those areas which provide models for research into television courtroom television broadcasting and the effects thereof. Neither does the work profess any view on the arguments in favour of or against television courtroom broadcasting in the first instance – other than that both are inadequate.

However, it is meant to introduce areas which can assist future television courtroom broadcasting research. These have been unduly ignored for too long by the broadcasting, legal and judicial communities. What follows below is a brief description of some other potentially fruitful areas for research.

ADMINISTRATION

When studies are being undertaken it would be advisable to specify within the terms of reference, that the amount of time taken up by the court itself in administering television courtroom broadcasting should be recorded. This would include preparatory work, applications for access, as well as supervision at the hearing itself.

It might be useful also to document the instances where a judge uses his or her discretion,[11] if any, to prohibit coverage. Other statistics to be recorded are the number of applications to broadcast, the cases, type of cases applied for, etc. Such statistics would prove immensely useful in painting a more complete picture of the issues involved.

COMPARISONS

One also has to attempt to ascertain whether the court process is trivialised in some way because of television courtroom broadcasting or the manner of such broadcasting. For instance, whether because of television courtroom broadcasting being scheduled against programmes of lesser seriousness or even entertainment value and thus forced to compete with them. Therefore, the competing programmes may influence the style of television courtroom broadcasting. The apparent increase in the use made by lawyers of the media should also be looked at.[12] It has also been suggested that a study should be designed to compare trials which do have cameras and trials covered by the traditional media.[13] While there may be difficulties in such a proposal, in theory such a study could go a long way towards indicating whether or not the effects are advantageous or otherwise.

Another comparison would be cases covered by the press (television, radio and newspaper) and those cases not covered at all. This would of course involve a tremendous amount of work. But these *are* the issues which must be considered before properly evaluating and examining the whole question of television courtroom broadcasting.

Another study might inquire into what issues place stress upon the various courtroom participants, both in situations with courtroom cameras and without cameras present.[14] Equally, the courtroom participants could be tested for their accurate recall of events and details both with and without cameras present.

Sometimes television courtroom broadcasting is contingent upon courtroom actor consent. One wonders what the effect may be when a participant does object but, as in some US States, broadcasting is permitted over such an objection. There does not appear to be any comparative research of when, where and in what circumstances consent is and is not an issue for courtroom broadcasting. Such comparative research would be very useful.

A number of people make arguments in favour of television courtroom broadcasting in countries where such broadcasting is not presently permitted or is permitted only on an insignificant scale. Such people, almost without fail, make the same generic and headline level arguments as are always made. They do not make legal comparisons and contrasts between their own country and other countries. Neither do they examine the existing effects research in any great detail. This point is even more pronounced when those advocating television courtroom broadcasting emanate from the media. At no stage do media advocates stop and ask what are the issues and flaws with the research to date. Can anything be learnt from such research? Is there a need for further consideration of those jurisdictions which permit some form of television courtroom broadcasting? If television courtroom broadcasting is permitted in a new jurisdiction, are research resources dedicated to effects, monitoring, etc.?

COMPARATIVE RESEARCH

Studies also need to be compared to each other (and replicated). Without doing so it is arguable that no individual study can be relied upon as giving a genuine answer or reflection of whatever research proposal is studied. This is particularly so in terms of effects research. Cross referencing is also one of the methods of discovering mistakes in research and also of finding opportunities for further research.

An obvious and important area of study is a cross comparison of the various restrictions which apply in each jurisdiction (where courtroom broadcasting is permitted), and a comparison of the restrictions and rationales which apply in each jurisdiction.

MANY QUESTIONS EXIST

One author in particular, Susanna Barber, identifies a number of concerns in relation to (television) courtroom broadcasting but which also serve as areas for future research.[15] She asks: if the public is better informed, or even adequately informed, by electronic versus conventional media coverage of a case? Can gavel to gavel broadcasts serve to educate the public about the administration of justice in general? Do time constraints imposed on many broadcast news stories mean that a case is treated either unfairly or inadequately? Does the public get a distorted picture of the judicial system, or a biased view of a particular trial, if stories are edited to highlight sensational testimony, cross-examination, or simply the opening and closing arguments? How does public understanding of the courts and specific cases differ when broadcast versus printed news is the medium of communication. Which type of news coverage has consistently provided the most balanced coverage of legal issues, trial participants, and court administration? What kinds of legal news coverage are "educationally" valuable to the public at large? Do viewers primarily perceive televised trials as a form of entertainment programming? Are televised trials viewed primarily for their voyeuristic value? What kind of attitudes about defendants and other trial participants are generated by televised trial coverage and are these attitudes different from those formed by print coverage? Unfortunately, television courtroom broadcasting research and debate has not advanced since the initial broadcasts.

Dan Slater and Valerie P. Hans state that while continued use of attitude surveys is beneficial, other methods of scientific study also exist. They also state that comparing trials in which broadcast access is granted with trials where no media interest is present, is clearly insufficient. Comparisons must also be made among the subset of trials for which request for extended media coverage is made. These trials must then be randomly assigned to "extended coverage" and "conventional coverage" groups.[16] Overall, they suggest that the heretofore use of surveys should continue but only in conjunction with observational and expirical research.[17] This emphasises the point of this work, which is that the research conducted to date in relation to television courtroom broadcasting effects, is limited both in volume but also in its scope and methodology. None of it, nor the television courtroom broadcasting arguments, have been defined or verified.

EFFECTS RESEARCH

Since its inception courtroom broadcasting has been highly controversial, not least due to what is at stake at each court hearing. Much of the debates have centred on perceived dangers such as adverse effects upon witnesses, lawyers and jury members. It has to be admitted that no definitive evidence of these effects have been emerged. This, however, is due more to the diminutive amount of the research effort and the limits of the studies themselves. One commentator has said that "[s]ocial scientists measure the intelligence of monkeys more effectively than courts have attempted to ascertain the effects of television in the courtroom."[18] Susanne Barber also makes a similar point in relation to the lack of research available.[19] She also raises questions which should be addressed in any future research (referred to above).

COURTROOM PARTICIPANT RESEARCH

In terms of courtroom participant effects there are many research tools which can be used. Obviously one of these is self reports and questionnaires. However, given the inherent limits with such research we have to use other research tools in addition.

As with any research, before we decide on a specific tool or tools we have to define carefully what it is we are researching. In terms of television courtroom broadcasting we have to define what we mean by effects, and decide what amounts to a significant effect. This can be in terms of a significant effect upon an individual courtroom actor and/or over a statistical mean. One of the most obvious effects to test for is whether courtroom participants are distracted by and look at the courtroom cameras (obviously these are not necessarily always the same thing).

There are many other effects to test for, however. For example, Clark J in the *Estes* [20] case described four examples of how television courtroom broadcasting could prejudice a jury. It is possible to conduct research studies to examine each of these separate effects. The examples he gave include pressure to conform to a community verdict; distraction by cameras which result in missing case details; and non sequestered juries seeing courtroom broadcasts. This is why it is important to define in advance what is being tested for.

DEFENDANTS

Defendants may have more at stake than anyone else involved in the court process but they seem to be asked less frequently than other participants for their views regarding television courtroom broadcasting. This needs to be addressed in future research.

There are also other considerations. Defendant research may be addressed before court hearings but also at other non adversarial stages. One reason for this is to obtain their views at a time less stressful than at a court appearance. A decision as to whether to consent to camera access or a decision in relation to the principle of camera access may be more thoughtful and considered, if not less pressured, in a situation where there is no imminent court appearance.[21]

DIFFERENT RESTRICTIONS

Is it practical or possible to differentiate between different broadcasting or newspaper organisations in terms of access? Even if not, this does not mean that those permitting television courtroom broadcasting cannot legislate or provide in some way for differentiations between different television courtroom broadcasting forms.

This already occurs invariably through the different types of rules, restrictions and guidelines which apply to television courtroom broadcasting. Parliament also made a distinction. In Ireland, for example, it is only possible to have live broadcasts of parliament if it is presented in full. This has obvious implications in terms of the types of broadcasters interested in television courtroom broadcasting, as well as the forms of television courtroom broadcasting produced. However, the point being made here is that it is possible, and is already the case, that television courtroom broadcasting forms can be influenced by the broadcasting rules which apply. This directly or indirectly does discriminate and affect broadcasters differently. Indeed, in the Irish context the parliamentary rules applicable to parliamentary broadcasting only permit certain uses of the material filmed. It may not be used for light entertainment, political satire, party political broadcasts or advertising. Therefore, parliament can discriminate between what parliamentary proceedings footage is used for. This too can be managed in the television courtroom broadcasting context. As indicated elsewhere, certain courts also discriminate (indirectly) by having an accreditation/application process for broadcasters. These are valid areas of research and comparison.

REPLICATION

Not one courtroom broadcasting proponent or opponent that the writer is aware of, has ever said that their argument is supported by direct research and that such research has been replicated by subsequent research, or that the research they rely upon is supported by any other form/methodology of research (other than self reports/questionnaires). This is a significant research flaw.

Generally, research propositions are not accepted until they are defined, outlined and researched, and subsequent research (generally by others) replicates and verifies it.

VALIDATION

The research to date is not comprehensive. It is not scientific and methodologically based. It is not replicated in secondary studies. All of the studies to date appear to be stand alone studies. In all other areas of methodological and scientific research, a study must be logical and not undermined on its face. In addition, it must be validated[22] which means that a subsequent or follow up study must validate or at least support the results of the study. This does not happen with the courtroom broadcasting studies. Without this, while each study is interesting of course, no definitive conclusions as to the effects can be drawn from the research. The research is so limited that one cannot say, on the basis of such research to date, that there is any conclusive evidence of adverse effects upon courtroom participants, or on the opposite side, that there are positive effects.

One means of validating and supplementing research conclusions is to carry out a study over a period of time. Sometimes such studies can continue over decades with results being published on an interim ongoing basis. This does not mean that all television courtroom broadcasting studies need to continue for years. However, it is recommended that some of the studies be carried out over an extended period other than the once off, brief moment in time studies as are presently carried out.

LONGITUDINAL RESEARCH

Regardless of what methodology is uses in a specific research study, one of the tools used for verification and to enhance the global picture of the overall body of research is to conduct research over a long period of time. This means examining similar studies carried out over a considerable period of time. If also means that some of the studies should be longitudinal in nature or be repeated over the course of a specific period or television courtroom broadcasting project. In addition, there can be follow up studies on the same courtroom and/or experimental participants as well as replication studies (on new subjects). Television courtroom broadcasting research has not sought to use this accepted method of research.

EMPIRICAL RESEARCH DESIGN

Paul Thaler states that,

> Research into the camera debate has also been criticized for 'the lack of well-planned, comprehensive survey instruments' and for 'unstructured data collection methods' (Barber, 1987). Susanna Barber, a leading investigator in the field, calls for new research that uses a 'qualitative difference test' to measure two types of variables within a courtroom setting that are potentially prejudicial. Her methodology is similar to the type proposed by Slater and Hans (1982). Field experiments using randomly selected trials have been proposed.

They compare the behaviour of participants in trials covered only by 'traditional' media with those involved in 'electronic' media coverage.[23]

LACK OF EMPIRICAL RESEARCH

The Short Report in 1981 identifies only two empirical social science studies, namely Netteburg and Hoyt.[24] However, the Short report acknowledges that both of these are narrowly defined and "focus on specific issues" only.[25] According to the Short Report by "mid–1980, not enough research had been published to formulate comprehensive conclusions."[26] Anna R. Paddon in her study is referring to and relying on research in information processing theory.[27] The research needs to expand and incorporate other disciplines.

Chandler called for stringent guidelines and more effects research.[28] The case law "speculates" on the effects and call for empirical research.[29] There has been "little gathering of empirical data regarding actual behaviour of broadcast journalists."[30] The Supreme Court research challenge has not yet been addressed.

In the Californian study, incorporating the Short Report research, it was recognised as "essential to gather observational data in the courtroom."[31] Surprisingly few other studies have sought to do likewise. In addition, the Short Report while conducting certain observational research was limited to two areas of focus only, namely, obstrusiveness (disruption, distraction) and participant behavioural changes.[32]

The Short Report, in the seminal California study in 1981, acknowledges that "there still exists little scientific research responding to Justice Clarke's observations" [in the *Estes* case[33]].[34]

There are various references in the *Chandler*[35] case to empirical research and the need or utility for such research.[36] "How else are we to discover what is and is not fact about the effects of electronic and photographic court coverage?" asks the Short Report.[37] The Short Report reiterates that "little systematic and rigorous evaluation of electronic and photographic coverage of court proceedings had been carried out."[38] While there was scientific evaluation in parts of the Short Report, this was conducted concurrently with the pilot experiment,[39] thus without any analysis or statistical gathering prior to the introduction of television courtroom broadcasting. The Short Report indicates that up to its study in 1981, only two other US States undertook statewide evaluations of their own pilot experiments, and each of these "relying on after–the–fact surveys."[40] Thus they are after the experiment has occured and also appear to rely entirely or heavily upon self reports and questionnaires. The research prior to the Short Report is described as being of "varying degrees of methodological soundless and generalizability."[41] The Short Report[42] refers to certain prior studies on page 11 but does not properly cite these.

EMPIRICAL

S.L. Alexander's literature review on 1990 also finds few empirical studies, particularly regarding coverage of actual trials, and only a "handful" of out-of-court experiments.[43]

Cohen also concludes more social science research is needed.[44]

Estes, *Chandler*, Hughes, Cohen, Gerbner and others lament the lack of empirical research, case studies, etc.[45]

Donald Shores describes some of the psychological arguments as having an element of "abstractness."[46] There is a need, therefore, for significantly more research of all of these issues. Shores continues that "methodical investigation is needed to determine what effects cameras have on witnesses."[47]

Sophistication is needed because "the discovery and the objective measurement of this possible distortion"[48] requires more detailed research than has been planned and undertaken previously. Shores identifies two particular fields which are relevant to television courtroom broadcasting.[49] These fields are the effects of videotaping on the oral performance and attitudes of individual; and the effect of communication apprehension on verbal behaviour.[50] Shores notes not only that there is little television courtroom broadcasting effects research, but also that when choosing a particular aspect of courtroom broadcasting to research, one should look at similar and related fields.[51] "By conducting carefully-controlled experimental research, the media, jurists, and the general public can begin to perceive what effects cameras have on trial participants."[52]

OUT-OF-COURT: AUDIENCE

The out-of-court effects on society are generally ignored by social science research.[53]

There is little content analysis of actual courtroom broadcasting footage.[54]

In relation to the Simpson (criminal) case, Steve Esposito states that the general media buildup to the case contained the "underlying message of this avalanche of pretrial coverage was that Simpson was guilty."[55] What expectations[56] are set by television courtroom broadcasting and presenters is not investigated. There is little examination of how television, nor television courtroom broadcasting, contributes to pretrial publicity.[57]

How accurate is TCB? Is it accurate or an "optical illusion of truth"[58] ? Paul Thaler also noted that audience effects research is also neglected.[59] He suggests that further studies should research the relationship between media coverage and public opinion and effects on the court process.[60] He refers to Susanna Barber who describes the audience research to date as anecdotal.[61]

MEDIA EFFECTS

Few studies say what rules and local media landscape exist, and which are relevant in considering any courtroom broadcasting research study. However, Netteburg does indicate that in Wisconsin the media at that stage enjoyed greater freedom in Wisconsin courtroom "than in almost any other jurisdiction."[62] Other studies do not even make such a brief headline comment.

EDUCATIONAL

There is no proof that television courtroom broadcasting is educational.[63] If there is an argument that education, information, the public impression of the courts or judges will be improved or enhances, then it is necessary to examine in the first instance how the court system informs, educates or creates an impression currently.[64] Yet, these baseline points do not appear to have been examined in the general research. Generally, the positive educational effects arguments are not examined or validated. The research does not test the confidence of the public and the audience before and after television courtroom broadcasting. Have public perceptions changed in relation to the courts after television courtroom broadcasting?

LITTLE CONTENT ANALYSIS/FOOTAGE

There is now significant amounts of television courtroom broadcasting trial footage available. However, little has been analysed and used for effects research purposes. No proper research goes into content and production details, such how each courtroom actor is represented in courtroom footage; camera distance; camera angle(s); how the elements of the frame are used and arranged; if and how the camera(s) move; what type of editing was involved; if and how the subject move; if and how facial expressions and close up appears; courtroom participants; details of the sequence of shot; etc.[65]

PARLIAMENTARY BROADCASTING

There is generally no comparisons and distinctions with parliamentary broadcasting.

OTHER MEDIA

There is generally no comparison of newspaper and television courtroom broadcasting reports. Stephen Nevas also called for effects research to see if print and television coverage differed.[66] A separate flaw of research of media court reporting research is that it examined in most instances print media and not television.[67] This is additionally significant because it is believed that television can be more damaging to a defendant than newspaper media.[68]

MEDIA PROCESS/FOOTAGE USE

The research ignores questions such as how television news departments approach television courtroom broadcasting, for example, does courtroom access influence whether a story is actually covered; how does access change courtroom coverage; does coverage increase because of access.[69] Previous research has not examined how the media use courtroom footage and the meaning of and signs within such coverage.[70] No research appears to indicate how much media lobbying occurs nor on how many occasions the media have litigated in an effort to obtain television courtroom access and or to enhance such access.

MEDIA PROCESS

There is no study of the conventions[71] used by television courtroom broadcasting footage. Significant avenues exist for research in this area.

MEDIA (ETC.) SELECTION

There appears to be no research of why the media choose certain cases over others for television courtroom broadcasting. Again, significant research opportunities exist.

LITTLE EMPIRICAL RESEARCH ON EACH ISSUE

Donald Shores (1981) for example, seeks to examine camera effects on verbal behaviour of witness, and states that the only similarly focused research was Hoyt in 1977.[72]

EMPIRICAL CONTROLS

James L. Hoyts experiment in 1977 failed to provide controls for important variables affecting the responses of subjects.[73] Various issues could have contaminated his results.[74] There were also issues raised with the Kassin study.[75] Significant opportunity exists for research.

CONCLUSION

We now examine the specific research flaws to see how we may produce scientific and empirical results in television courtroom broadcasting effects research and seek to address the Supreme Court research challenge.

NOTES

1. Listed by S. Barber, above, as being the case of Billy Eugene Manley in Oklahoma City which occurred in 1953, see S. Barber, News Cameras in the Courtroom: A Free Press – Fair Trial Debate (Norwood, New Jersey: Ablex, 1987), 10–11.
2. S.M. Kassin, TV Cameras, Public Self-Consciousness, and Mock Juror Performance, Journal of Experimental Social Psychology (1984): 337–349.
3. J.L. Hoyt, Courtroom Coverage: The Effects of Being Televised, Journalism of Broad-casting (1977): 487–495, at 489.
4. S.M. Kassin, above, 337.
5. J.L. Hoyt, above, 487–495.
6. *Ibid*, 490–491.
7. *Ibid*, 490. Internal footnote reference omitted.
8. For example, V. Stodden, Enabling Reproducible Research: Licensing for Scientific Innovation, International Journal of Communications Law and Policy 13 (2009): 1–25, at 2.
9. See A. Heaton–Armstrong, E. Shepard, G.H. Gudjonsson and D. Wolchover, eds., Witness Testimony: Psychological, Investigative and Evidential Perspectives (Oxford: OUP, 2006).
10. Even in S. Barber, only Part 3 of the book is devoted to research issues, and even that does not recognise different forms of courtroom broadcasting. See S. Barber, above.
11. That is, where such a discretion exists. This is because not all systems allow judicial discretion in relation to permitting broadcasting. Other systems limit the discretion to an extent.
12. While this may indeed be so, some may point out that far more apparent is the use of lawyers by the media, be it print, radio or television.
13. D. Slater and V.P Hans, Methodological Issues in the Evaluation of 'Experiments' with Cameras in the Courts, Communications Quarterly 30:4 (1982): 376–380.
14. See S. Spacapan and S. Cohen, Effects and After Effects of Stressor Expectations, Journal of Personality and Social Psychology 45:6 (1983): 1243–1254.
15. Ibid, 92-93.
16. D. Slater and V.P. Hans, above, 379.
17. Ibid, 379.
18. J. Hirschhorn, Cameras in the Courtroom? No, Barrister 7:3 (1980) 6, 8.
19. S. Barber, above.
20. 381 US 532 (1965), referred to in W. Freedman, Press and Media Access to a Criminal Courtroom (New York: Quorum Books, 1988), 82.
21. Here appearance is used generally and can include appearing at the hearing of a case.
22. For example, V. Stodden, Enabling Reproducible Research: Licensing for Scientific Innovation, International Journal of Communications Law and Policy 13 (2009): 1–25, at 2.

23. P. Thaler. The Impact of the Television Camera on Courtroom Participants: A Case Study of the Joel Stenberg Murder Trial (Ph.D diss., New York University, 1990): 177–179.

24. E.H. Short and Associates, Evaluation of California's Experiment with Extended Media Coverage of Courts, Submitted to: The Administrative Office for the Courts, The Chief Justice's Special Committee on the Courts and the Media and The California Judicial Council (September 1981): 12–13. (Short Report).

25. Ibid, 12.

26. Ibid, 13.

27. A.R. Paddon, "Television Coverage of Criminal Trials with Cameras and Microphones: A Controlled Experiment of Audience Effects," Radio-television Journalism Division, AEJMC Montreal, Que, Canada (August 7, 1992): 1. Also A.R. Paddon. Television Coverage of Criminal Trials with Cameras and Microphones: A Controlled Experiment of Audience Effects (Ph.D diss., University of Tennessee, 1985).

28. S.L. Alexander, 'Mischievous Potentialities': A Case Study of Courtroom Camera Guidelines, Eight Judicial Circuit, Florida, 1989 (Ph.D diss., University of Florida, 1990): 19.

29. Ibid, 39.

30. Ibid.

31. Short Report, above, 22.

32. Ibid.

33. *Estes v Texas*, 381, US 533 (1965).

34. Short Report, above, 5.

35. *Chandler v Florida*, 449 US 560 (26 January, 1981).

36. See Short Report, above, 5.

37. Ibid, 5.

38. Ibid, 5.

39. Ibid, 5 and 19.

40. Ibid, 5, n. 9.

41. See ibid, 11.

42. See ibid, above, 11.

43. S.L. Alexander, above, 54.

44. J. Cohen, Cameras in the Courtroom and Due Process: A Proposal for a Qualitative Difference Test, Washington Law Review 57 (1982): 277-–291, as referred to in S.L. Alexander, above, 69.

45. As referred to in Alexander, S.L., above, 85.

46. D. Shores, The Effects of Courtroom Camera on Verbal Behaviour: An Analysis of Simulated Trial Witness Testimony in Courtrooms Using Television Cameras (Ph.D diss., The University of Florida, 1981), 2.

47. Ibid, 5.

48. Ibid.

49. Ibid, 16.

50. Ibid.

51. Ibid, 16.

52. Ibid, 39.

53. E. Borgida, K. DeBona and L.A. Buckman, Cameras in the Courtroom, The Effects of Media Coverage on Witness Testimony and Juror Perceptions, Law and Human Behaviour 14:5 (1990) 489–508, at 490.

54. See comments of S.A. Esposito. OJ TV: A Narrative Analysis of Television's Pretrial Coverage of the O.J. Simpson Case (Ph.D diss., Wayne State University, Detroit, Michigan, 1996), 34 *et seq*.

55. Ibid, 63.

56. Ibid, 67.

57. Ibid, 269.

58. To use the words of Esposito, ibid, 53.

59. P. Thaler, above, 179.

60. Ibid.

61. Ibid.

62. K. Netteburg, above, 469.

63. See W. Petkanas. Cameras on Trial: An Assessment of the Educational Affects of News Cameras in Trial Courts (Ph.D diss., New York University, 1990): 3.

64. Entner makes a similar point, see R. Entner, The Image of the Judiciary: A Semiotic Analysis of Broadcast Trials to Ascertain its Definition of the Court System (Ph.D diss., New York University, 1993), 25.

65. See R. Entner, ibid, 38 – 39.

66. S. Nevas, Case for Cameras in the Courtroom, Judges Journal, (Winter 1981): 22–24, and 49-50, as referred to in S.L. Alexander, above, 66, but title and page range ommited.

67. S.A. Esposito, OJ TV: A Narrative Analysis of Television's Pretrial Coverage of the O.J. Simpson Case (Ph.D diss., Wayne State University, Detroit, Michigan, 1996), 24–25.

68. Ibid, 24-25, and 269.

69. T. Keller, above, 72.

70. R. Entner, above, see Abstract, 4 and 12.

71. Esposito, above, 62.

72. D. Shores, above, 27.

73. Ibid, 28.

74. D. Shores, above, 28 – 29, again referring to Hoyt. Borgida et al also refer to shortcoming in the Hoyt study, E. Borgida, K. DeBona and L.A. Buckman, Cameras in the Courtroom, The Effects of Media Coverage on Witness Testimony and Juror Perceptions, Law and Human Behaviour 14:5 (1990): 489–508, at 490.

75. E. Borgida, K. DeBona and L.A. Buckman, *ibid*, 489–508, at 491.

Chapter Eleven

The Psychology Challenge

INTRODUCTION

Our interdisciplinary research needs to refer to psychology. This is necessary in order to address the Supreme Court research challenge. We must separate the different *in-court* and *out-of-court* issues, and then review the existing psychology research. Psychology is very relevant for courtroom broadcasting research.[1] Reviewing the psychology literature reveals many areas of psychology which will apply to courtroom broadcasting. To date, these have been missed opportunities.

Television courtroom broadcasting research often seeks to answer questions and issues by relying upon self reports and opinions reports. It also relies upon the expressed confidence of (some) courtroom participants. The issues of opinion reports, self reports[2] and confidence appear extensively in the existing psychology literature. Courtroom broadcasting research can and should refer to this extensive literature and research.

Another area of psychology investigations is eyewitness identification research. The models and tools of such research are very relevant to courtroom broadcasting. For example, psychologists research the factors involved in identification. On occasion they recommend improved procedures and on some occasion they also testify in court on these issues.[3] Many psychologists have testified in courts as to eyewitness identification factors.[4] Cases include *US v Amaral*[5] and *Estate v Galloway.*[6] Oliver P. Holtenson also refers to cases.[7]

A recent eyewitness research study indicates that 75% of people exonerated through the use of DNA evidence were originally convicted due largely to erroneous eyewitness identifications.[8] Calvin J. TerBeek strongly recommends using empirical and scientific based research in relation to eyewitness identification issues.[9] He also notes that the courts have not been shy to refer to and use statistical evidence in other instances.[10] Research also suggests that not all courtroom participants are familiar with psychology research findings. For example, research in Sweden involving police officers, prosecutors and judges found that a number of wrongful beliefs and understandings existed.[11] It also found that there were some differences between the subject groups.[12]

Eye tracking research can also be utilised, and is referred to in the next chapter. It is increasingly used for applications in many different fields. However, eye tracking tools have been used in psychology research too. It should now be applied to television courtroom broadcasting.

No body of research has sought to investigate effects and distraction effects on courtroom participants, other than by opinion reports and self reports. This is, in terms of the research capabilities available today, a glaring failure of courtroom broadcasting research. Can we seriously continue to rely wholly upon propositional, limited and flawed research and research methodologies, such as have been used in the past?

OUT-OF-COURT RESEARCH

One of the flaws to date is that much television courtroom broadcasting research focuses on potential effects inside the courtroom (*in-court*). It ignores any substantial or sustained reference and consideration of audience effects and effects on persons outside of the courtroom (*out-of-court*).[13] This means we have only begun research into one half of the television courtroom broadcasting spectrum. Can we, therefore, stand over the research effort to date? Psychology, media and communications studies should be applied to television courtroom broadcasting issues.

IN-COURT RESEARCH

In terms of the in-court research, this is limited. It focuses on some but not all of the courtroom participants. In addition, it is flawed because it relies on limited models of research. Primarily it uses questionnaires to ask (some) courtroom participants if they themselves have been affected (self-reports). Sometimes, but not always, researchers will ask a courtroom actor if they feel other courtroom participants have been affected (opinion-reports). Such reports and self report studies are limited, flawed and ignore an abundance of other opportunities for research.

The psychology research is very relevant to in-court television courtroom broadcasting issues.

IN-COURT SELF REPORTS AND OPINION REPORTS

The majority of studies into television courtroom broadcasting are limited to self report and opinion report studies. People in actual cases (or in mock cases) are asked for their opinions on whether they feel that they have been affected by the television cameras filming in the courtroom. While gathering such opinions is in itself a worthwhile exercise, self reports are not the most accurate indicator of an individual being affected by television cameras in the courtroom. Self report studies should not be relied upon as the sole indication of the in-court effects of television courtroom broadcasting. It may cost more to undertake wider ranging, more reliable and cross disciplinary research. However, this is an insufficient reason for limiting the scope of research into such an important social and legal issue as television courtroom broadcasting.

PSYCHOLOGY EYEWITNESS RESEARCH

Eyewitness research and eyewitness identification research tools in psychology are potentially very useful for effects research into television courtroom broadcasting.[14] Courts and the public have long recognised that there can be flaws with identifications and eyewitness identification evidence. In court, certain eyewitness identification requires additional corroboration evidence. Sometimes judges also give a warning to the jury in relation to such evidence.[15] Many psychologists who are familiar with such evidence and research, have assisted the courts in understanding these issues more fully.[16]

Wells and Murray state in their review of thirty-one psychology studies, that "the eyewitness accuracy-confidence relationship is weak under good laboratory conditions and functionally useless in forensically representative settings."[17] Eyewitness recall (or, perhaps recall by a participant in a televised trial, or a television viewer of a televised trial) may not be the most reliable indicator.

Eyewitness evidence is highly malleable and subject to influence by many factors.[18] Post event factors are one category of influence, such as questions, briefings, personal anticipation, cross examination and feedback or alleged feedback, from other witnesses or participants.[19] Psychology research examines the context of questions to witnesses, information given to witnesses, the replies and the effects of the context, questions and information. Generally, no similar examination occurs with television courtroom broadcasting research. Indeed, the context of the research, and sometimes the questions themselves, are not recorded. This makes it impossible for later researchers to examine these studies or to attempt to make comparisons across studies. It is important to record the questions asked, the context, all of the results and to describe how the research was carried out.

IDENTIFICATION EVIDENCE/WARNINGS

There have been many notorious examples of eyewitness unreliability.[20] Trained observers can give wrong identifications. Even "the most positive identification made by a confident witness may be wrong."[21]

In 2005 Georgia's Supreme Court warned judges about the unreliability of eyewitness identifications.[22] Lord Justice Scarman in *R v Dunne*,[23] states that "there is no branch of human perception more fallible than identifying a person." Heffernan also comments that "[e]yewitness testimony, however sincere and persuasive, is notoriously unreliable and the courts have long recognised that the frailties of human observation and memory may lead to mistaken identity and ultimately wrongful conviction."[24]

Courts, aware of the potential unreliability of visual identification evidence, frequently warn juries about such evidence and also advise juries of the importance of having supporting collaborative evidence. Kingsmill Moore J in *People (AG) v Casey (No 2)*, for example, referred to the need for cautions and warnings.[25]

The courts afford certain safeguards and warnings against eyewitness identification, particularly when uncorroborated by additional evidence.[26] The warnings attempt to restrict instances of bias, mistake, etc. Legal appeals are also possible.[27] No such general warnings are given in relation to television media presence in court.[28]

While there is no research on this point, the disparity between television courtroom television rules (where they exist), appear to be greater than differences between approaches to court warnings regarding identification. This arguably deserves further research.[29]

TELEVISION COURTROOM BROADCASTING FACTORS

Many different reasons and factors contribute to mistaken identification. One flaw with television courtroom broadcasting is that it frequently assumes that limited and basic courtroom actor questionnaires are not undermined by bias, drafting, self reports, confidence, etc., issues. Frequently these issues are left unanswered and even unconsidered.

A review of existing psychology research confirms that we must start to address the research flaws in courtroom broadcasting. We cannot continue to assume that courtroom participants and their replies, are better than eyewitnesses accounts, or better in all instances. They should at least be similarly tested and researched.

Similarly psychology, media and communications can assist out–of–court effect issues e.g. research of TCB effects while multi-tasking.

PSYCHOLOGY: MISTAKEN EYEWITNESS IDENTIFICATION FACTORS

Psychology research identifies many of the factors which contribute to incorrect identifications.[30] This research is already applicable to the many gaps in the courtroom broadcasting research. For example, how do we as courtroom participants see cameras in the courtroom? How do we identify them? What do we see? What do we see, and not see, in the courtroom? How does the process of viewing, recall and identification work in the courtroom setting?

> In the High Court of Australia, Evatt and McTiernan JJ. ... analysed the elements which underlie an assertion by a witness that he recognises a certain person. In a joint judgement they stated 'An honest witness who says "the prisoner is the man who drove the car"' whilst appearing to affirm a simple clear and impressive proposition, is really asserting: (1) that he observed a driver; (2) that the observation became impressed upon his mind; (3) that he still retains the original impression; (4) that such impression has not been affected, altered or replaced ... and (5) that the resemblance between the original impression, and the prisoner is sufficient to base a judgement, not of resemblance, but of identify.
> In recent years psychologists have undertaken research which reveals that each of the stages listed by Evatt and McTiernan JJ. is subject to factors which may weaken the value of the final identification and lead to a wrongful conviction.[31]

Many of the various factors identified as being applicable to eyewitness identification and eyewitness evidence can apply to research of the courtroom broadcasting issue. L. Re for example,[32] identifies many acquisition stage factors, event stage factors, witness factors, recollection factors, post event information factors, displacement factors, context importance factors, etc. Elizabeth F. Loftus and James M. Doyle[33] also identify many factors. The research processes through which psychology investigates and identifies various factors is important to courtroom broadcasting, given that courtroom broadcasting has not yet been so rigorous in its research.

Another point is that some studies have asked opinion report questions on, for example, whether the particular courtroom actor saw the witness or judge acting up or in some way being affected by the courtroom cameras. While this may be useful, it should not be the sole definitive evidence and form of study. For one thing, courtroom participants may be able to give their opinions and experience to a certain extent. However, they are arguably not qualified in all aspects and areas where a change may be effected and or visible. The television courtroom broadcasting research and research tools need to be expanded.

In addition, asking courtroom actor A about his or her opinion on whether courtroom actor B was affected or changed in some way (e.g. distraction) due to the cameras, ignores the fact that courtroom actor A was actually busy doing something in court as their primary task. Therefore, their task was not to observe meticulously everything that courtroom actor B may, or may not, have been doing. Equally, this applies to observing what the cameras, equipment and cameraman were doing. Such questions are also focused on main perceivable effects, and not more internal or non–observable effects. As previously pointed out, self reports and opinion reports are limited in that they may not on their own demonstrate in–court effects. In addition, they are not corroborated by any further or additional set of research techniques and studies. Again, we need to cast a wider net and involve more than one type of research technique to properly evaluate television courtroom broadcasting (TCB) effects.

Tim Valentine *et al*[34] points out that in the UK, the Turnball guidelines[35] enshrine "some" of the factors needed to be considered in assessing eyewitness identifications, but that other factors need to be taken into account also. Graham Davies and Laurence Griffiths[36] suggest that despite our history of knowing that mistaken identifications occur, procedural changes following the 1976 Devlin Report, and more recently CCTV and DNA evidence, mistakes till arise. They call into question the continued use of a single confident witness as being sufficient to convict an accused person.[37]

TELEVISION COURTROOM BROADCASTING SAFEGUARDS

In terms of television courtroom broadcasting research, there are generally no comparable safeguards. The courtroom broadcasting research does not identify or research the flaws of relying solely upon self reports and opinion reports. It appears some researchers may not be even aware of these issues. There are no suggestions made as to how to address the self report and opinion report issues.

In addition, not all courts which permit television courtroom broadcasting have procedures and restrictions, whether in place or documented. Judges are not generally aware of or advised on all of the issues involved in media, communication, production, editing, selection, etc., and generally have no direct input or control over what happens the footage once it is filmed and leaves the court.

One could refer to contempt of court rules as a court mechanism to protect and regulate proceedings in relation to cameras. However, is relying on contempt of court rules alone, a sufficient safeguard? Do contempt rules cover every issue which may arise in court and out of court in relation to television courtroom broadcasting? Contempt rules were developed prior to the advent of television courtroom broadcasting. Does contempt law reflect modern communications technologies such as courtroom broadcasting?

Surprisingly, no research has been carried out into in–court safeguards, or out–of–court safeguards, for television courtroom broadcasting. While there are "use" rule restrictions in relation to parliamentary broadcasting, there is no research of use issues and use safeguards in relation to courtroom television broadcasting.

PSYCHOLOGY RESEARCH ON EFFECTS

Elizabeth Loftus and Katherine Ketcham[38] point out that that human memory is extremely fragile and malleable. It can be "supplemented, altered or even reconstructed by as simple an instrument as a strong verb, embedded unnoticed in a question ..."[39] Individuals in studies have said that certain objects existed at a crime scene.[40] However, none of the objects in fact existed.[41] In one study 175 of those who received false information, identified a nonexistent barn. In experiments to test later recall, 805 people gave incorrect information as the period was prolonged.[42] Other examples of false recall include the fact that an assailant had curly hair, when in actuality he had straight hair; that broken glass was present when there was none at the accident; and giving incorrect colours of objects.[43]

CONFIDENCE REPORTS

It is noted that "any relations between identification accuracy, confidence, and event factors are complex."[44] However, in the context of the courtroom broadcasting research it is generally assumed that the confidence and self reports of courtroom participants are always accurate. No research effort to date investigates them. Why should we accept such giant assumptive leaps?

The (professionally trained) police officers in the Hulse and Mermon study tended to downplay their emotional responses.[45] The study found that there were significant differences in self report arousal and recorded arousal.[46] The police officers recall may be susceptible to the same arousal biases as other people.[47]

According to psychology research, juries are impressed by confident eyewitness identifications.[48] Courtroom broadcasting research predominantly relies on confidence reports. This occurs in the self reports, opinion reports and limited interviews of courtroom participants. These are useful but cannot be overly relied upon. Nor should they be solely relied upon.

Psychology research suggests that third parties largely accept eyewitness testimony based upon the *confidence* of the eyewitness and the degree of detail given in the eyewitness testimony.[49] Unfortunately, a person's individual confidence cannot be overly relied upon.

In the context of television courtroom broadcasting, for somebody involved in a trial to admit that they were affected by cameras could be tantamount to an admission that, but for the cameras they may have acted differently or perhaps rendered a different decision. It is not altogether surprising for them to express any affect upon themselves in the negative. Even if they were aware of cameras during a case, any decision reached by a courtroom actor should be clearly reached without influence from the cameras present. One might also add that it should also be without the appearance of such influence. Yet, official research almost invariably ignores these issues and leaves research questions unaddressed.

We should not be uncritical in our assessment of confidence in self report studies. Additional research and research tools need to be applied to this important topic in and of themselves, but also as a verification and additional test of opinion reports and self report studies.

That a witness, or courtroom actor, indicates confidence that they were not affected, is not conclusive. Psychology research has found jurors equally willing to believe an incorrect witness as a correct witness.[50] Interestingly, many of the questionnaire and self report studies of television courtroom broadcasting do not appear to code or rate courtroom actor confidence. Confidence is rated in psychology research as one of the two least important factors in testing accuracy of eyewitness identifications.[51]

It would be possible to introduce some confidence type tests to television courtroom broadcasting research. For example, testing of courtroom participants felt they were affected by cameras; testing if others thoughts so; and testing the confidence of each. Additional objective criteria can also be imposed, e.g. recording the event. Also, carefully arranging the different elements of what will be seen, recording and tested it is an important control mechanism.

CONSENT

Some of those involved in courtroom self-–report studies were initially asked if they consent to the use of television courtroom broadcasting. If they initially agreed and gave some tacit support to the presence of courtroom cameras, it may be inconsistent for them later to say that they were adversely affected by the use of cameras.[52] This has not been researched. Clearly this is relevant. Again, psychology research can be applied to investigating of this problem.

Other courtroom participants may not have consented, or at least have become heavily involved in the process. Given any acceptance, they could be less likely to disagree with courtroom broadcasting or identify any negative effects, if subsequently asked. This issue has not been researched to date. Psychology research can assist the consideration and investigation of this issue.

Courtroom broadcasting studies do not appear to gauge views of those actual and potential courtroom participants who objected to courtroom broadcasting. This would be very useful and would also assist comparison. Psychology research can also assist in designing such research.

INCONSISTENT

An individual courtroom actor may feel that others may be affected by cameras in the courtroom, but that they *themselves* are not so affected. Many of the opinion report studies concentrate on asking whether individuals feel that they themselves or other participants were or were not affected. Psychology research should be used to assess how correct or credible this is.

Psychology also shows us that people often reject information inconsistent with views they have of themselves.[53] If a courtroom actor feels everyone else is positive about television courtroom broadcasting if and when asked, this potentially affects their own replies. Another issue is the extent to which we can, or should, rely on opinion reports of effects on others as a sole validation for testing effects.

It is feared that incorrect information is most likely to be accepted when it comes from a position of authority or so called impartiality.[54] Again, this raises issues for television courtroom broadcasting research to date. Could it be biased or prejudicial against recording negative effects because of who asks the questions?

If television courtroom broadcasting is described as having no adverse effects or as being educational, responsible or impartial, it may be more difficult for courtroom participants to disagree – even when they do feel affects.[55] The psychology research emphasises the point that courtroom broadcasting studies need to become more sophisticated in focus.

AROUSAL

Arousal research suggests that once aroused, our focus narrows.[56] Therefore, potentially arousal, stress or excitement at television courtroom cameras could lead to more focus on the camera and less on the overall events, testimony, etc. It does not appear that we have properly considered or investigated issues such as stress and arousal on the different categories of courtroom participants, and how the introduction of cameras and television courtroom broadcasting may impact this. While investigating weapons focus issues, Lynn M. Hulse and Amina Memon[57] found that even professionally trained police officer recall performances, can be affected both qualitatively and qualitatively when they witness an arousing type event e.g. a shooting. Can it be assumed that television cameras in courts will not have some effect on professional police officer witnesses? What about other courtroom participants, both professional and otherwise?

WEAPON FOCUS AND CAMERA FOCUS

Psychology research into the weapons focus effect is relevant. Weapons focus is the phenomena whereby victims or witnesses of crimes involving a weapon are sometimes less able to identify the attacker because they were focusing on the weapon. The focus on the weapon "impairs"[58] the ability to see and remember other accurate information. Studies show that with a weapon present, recall for and identification of the face of the person holding the weapon is "impaired."[59] Studies also show correct identifications are reduced and incorrect identifications increase with a weapon present.[60] This has also been shown to be the case for adults and children.[61] Nancy Steblay[62] provides a general review of the weapon focus research.[63]

Opponents and proponents of television courtroom broadcasting should use weapons focus research methodologies to conduct research into whether courtroom participants may be distracted by, or may look at, television courtroom broadcasting cameras. Similarly, effects could occur because of other equipment and or cameras operators.

Why is it implicitly assumed that everyone in the courtroom will react the same? Research should examine whether some courtroom participants may be more affected than others.

In one of the psychology studies, Elizabeth Loftus, Geoffrey Loftus and Jane Messo[64] showed individuals a series of slides showing a crime being committed. The researchers then monitored subjects' eye movements with the use of a video camera. The study found that the subjects focused more often, and for longer periods of time, on the weapon as opposed to other objects that appeared in the scene. This does not mean that facial, clothing or other details are completely ignored, rather that the weapon is given a disproportionate amount of focus. The point is that because subjects pay less attention to the details of the criminal or other details in the scene, they may then be less likely to be correct in a subsequent identification. In another study, twenty six (26) per cent of individuals who saw a video where a weapon was present, gave a correct identification at a later test. Fourty six (46) percent of subjects who saw the weapon-hidden video gave correct decisions, which is significant.[65]

Video technology can be used to carry out experiments for effects of courtroom broadcasting.

Some of the weapons focus research also refers to arousal levels.[66] This highlights that potentially courtroom cameras, or television courtroom broadcasting, may have different affects and or arousal levels on different courtroom participants. This needs to be considered. For example, could the defendant or the parties be more prone to be affected than other courtroom participants? If so, what does that mean for television courtroom broadcasting issues and rights arguments? Arousal and weapons focus may not be the only areas of psychology of interest to television courtroom broadcasting effects research. Hulse and Memon[67] note that "[p]erceptual and attentional narrowing during encoding is unlikely to be the only explanation for the effects of arousal and weapon presence on memory." More complex research issues arise for television courtroom broadcasting than have been examined before.

Kerri L. Pickel et al found that control witness in their study reported fewer correct and more incorrect details when the subject carried a weapon versus a book.[68] However, they found some differences as between "educated" witness subjects.[69] They also refer to discussions and research which looks at why someone focuses on the weapon, e.g. that it is threatening.[70] So for example, could different courtroom participants be threatened in different ways by cameras and television courtroom broadcasting? Could some be threatened but not others? Consider that certain forms of television courtroom broadcasting can occur even if one of the courtroom participants has objected. Consider further, that some courtroom participants may on occasion object not to the cameras, but to being shown in the footage. What effect does this have? Are there different effects as between, a courtroom actor who knows that the camera(s) cannot focus or point at them, as opposed to a courtroom actor who is filmed but will have their face digitally blocked? Is this out of site "safeguard" different from an in-court "safeguard?" One study also found that weapon focus effect can occur even in personal states of low anxiety level.[71] This offers much for television courtroom broadcasting to consider.

L. Hope and D. Wright found that subject reaction times in dealing with a second task were impaired in the weapon present group and unusual object present groups, as compared to the control group.[72]

Jo Saunders[73] refers to the issues of introducing post event questioning (PEQ) and post event narratives (PENs) after the witnessed event and the influence these can have on recall and retrieval. This also ties in with television courtroom broadcasting effects research which rely upon and do not properly record the manner of how views, opinions and self reports of courtroom participants are obtained. Without proper examination and scrutiny, yet another challenge arises for the current body of research.

Courtroom proceedings involve many complex visual and aural elements. Introducing television cameras and television courtroom broadcasting brings more complexity. Courtroom participants have roles and tasks to undertake, both visually and aurally. Kerri L. Pickel et al[74] undertook research to see if a weapon's presence impairs memory for auditory information, similar to the way it does for visual information. They found diminishing memory accuracy when the task has more demanding auditory content.[75]

Certainly weapons focus raises many questions, but also opportunities, for television courtroom broadcasting effects research.

PSYCHOLOGY EYEWITNESS TOOLS

Modern high speed video and film techniques and other tools are currently being used in a variety of research forms. Psychology uses videos and high speed cameras for research of, amongst other things, attention, weapons focus and eyewitness focus issues. This is referred to below. These technologies and techniques are an obvious avenue of research into television courtroom broadcasting. These tools can permit accurate research into where courtroom participants are actually looking and also for how long. So far, they have been ignored. High speed cameras are very beneficial tools for carrying out television courtroom actor effects research.

While self report questionnaires are useful, it is possible with cameras and high speed cameras to see where a person is actually looking, for how long, and how frequently. These can be cross referenced with the questionnaire answers. They can also be used in laboratory settings. It is not necessary to get access to actual courtrooms to undertake such research. The use of high speed cameras has application in relation to in-court effects. High speed cameras can also be used for certain out-of-court research studies of the audience.

Many experiments involve test participants in a mock trial jury, as part of research into various factors involving eyewitness identification and testimony issues.[76] These can be repeated, both with more demanding effects research.

Elizabeth F. Loftus[77] indicates that many studies have examined how malleable eyewitness memory can be, and also how, affected by post event factors or post event information. She indicates that the procedures of some research can be quite straightforward.[78] The participants of the study are shown an event. Half of the participants are then given new misleading information regarding the event. The other half of the participants do not receive any new information.[79] Both groups are then tested in relation to the original event they witnessed. It would not be difficult to expand such models of research by introducing cameras to the event situations, and to test different effects.

A large variety of studies have researched and tested eyewitness identification issues.[80] Some of these could be followed in a courtroom setting. As well as testing courtroom participants in relation to identification of recall of participants such as a policeman or other witness, research could also test their identification and recall of a cameraman. Similar research could test recall and identification of various pieces of evidence. Research could also examine the camera type and model. Someone saying that they were not affected, could be asked to identify pieces of evidence and the camera. What are the implications if they can correctly identify the camera, but not one or more pieces of important evidence?

Other experiments into television courtroom broadcasting can also involve filmed events which are then shown to subject participants in the study. Subjects are divided into two or more study groups. Then each group is tested and examined in relation to the particular matter or effects hypothesis being researched.[81]

Lynn M. Hulse and Amina Memon in their study, used a novel system of live action realtime events shown on screen, and required officers to interact with and respond to the scenes.[82] They also tested anxiety and arousal levels before the experiments.[83] Then, during the experiments they monitored participants with wireless heart monitors.[84] This raises very important possible research possibilities for television courtroom broadcasting.

DISTRACTION EFFECTS TOOLS

The various tools utilised in weapons focus research can be used to actually see whether or not courtroom participants are distracted by or look at cameras. Some tools have a research subject look at a particular pre-recorded scene and examine eye movements to see which objects and part of the film the subject watches most. Therefore, it is possible to construct a similar study where subjects watch a particular court case with a camera present and to see if, how frequently, and for how long they focus on the courtroom camera. One of the results of some of the weapons focus research is that subjects focus on the weapon for longer than other objects in a scene. Is this true of some of the courtroom participants? This is something we can test for. Other studies can have two subject groups, one with a camera present and the other with none. The focus of such a study would be to examine the effects of courtroom cameras, specifically on how courtroom cameras influence what information is taken in by a courtroom actor, and how their recall for pertinent details of a case are affected. It is also possible to have follow up studies at medium and long term intervals.

PSYCHOLOGY AND SALIENCE

In some psychology studies regarding eyewitnesses, there is examination of salience[85] or importance. Applying such studies to courtroom broadcasting, we can stage a trial, film a trial, etc., and list all of the items that each actor category would have seen. Then we get them to list or rate these in order of importance. For example, it might be the most important items that they saw, one of which would have included a courtroom camera.

CAMERAS

Further testing can be undertaken into courtroom broadcasting forms by varying the type, size, colour, movement, location, noise, etc. of the camera or cameras. Research regarding recall and identification of central versus peripheral details[86] would also be relevant here. Additional research should also investigate the effects of cameras appearing only for certain witness testimony. Does the camera presence enhance the importance and or credibility of that witness in the eyes of the jury?

Research can focus on how long each courtroom actor may focus on the courtroom camera, and compare this to their opinion as to whether they saw or looked at the camera, and if they did, for how long.

The research can also involve pictures and drawings,[87] some of which for example, may have a courtroom camera present and a courtroom camera absent. This would also be somewhat easier to arrange than live or pre-recorded filming of a mock courtroom scene.

Research studies can be both laboratory based and more realistic field studies.[88] They can also be court based. Typical of such studies should be research examination of one isolated factor in television courtroom broadcasting filming. As with all research, one needs to define and describe the effect or test being carried out. This is not always evident in television courtroom broadcasting research. It is a significant flaw of courtroom broadcasting research studies that no hypothesis is generally proposed and identified, and then tested for. Arguably no effect of courtroom broadcasting is show.

Ewing et al have found that gaze direction affects judgements of facial attractiveness.[89] Clearly research is needed into the effects of different in-court camera positions, heights, angles and directions, and how this affects the audience when they see the footage. Douglas Martin and C Neil Macrae[90] also refer to how different processing strategies can be "primed," which also suggests that research is required of cameras and camera footage for television courtroom broadcasting. They also refer to research demonstrating that specific processing orientations impacts performance for face recognition.[91]

Sara Landstrom et al[92] found evidence in their study to show that different effects were obtained from using three differently located cameras to film the same interview. They found camera perspective bias. They also refer to concurring previous research.[93] They also state that "the camera should not be considered a passive bystander, objectively recording what is said and done. Instead, factors such as camera shot (i.e. the distance between the camera and the suspect; ... and the camera focus (e.g. if the camera is focused on the suspect alone or on both the suspect and the interrogator; ... can contribute to biased assessments."[94] Also, "[r]esearch has shown that ... particular camera focus can bias judgements on the suspect's guilt, voluntariness, and credibility."[95]

Martin Safer *et al*[96] found that when shown four pictures, taken from different standpoints in the same witnessed event scene, participants chose the close up picture. This emphasised critical details matching their memory if the event was emotionally arousing versus neutral.[97]

STRESS

Stress is meant to have a large influence of witnesses.[98] However, television courtroom broadcasting research has never looked at this issue. New research should add stress as a factor to be researched. Again, there is psychology research which can be helpful in designing and contextualising such research. Researchers also report that participant viewers relied heavily on verbal cues.[99]

CONTEXT

Psychology research has recognised the stages of recall and identification (namely, acquisition, retention and retrieval[100]). Can these be co-related or followed (as appropriate) in courtroom broadcasting research? To date, there is no effort to examine how and when different courtroom participants can be effected. Nor does research examine or contextualise (when research is carried out) the time and context of any possible argued effect.

It is important to also refer to when questions are asked of courtroom participants. Psychology research indicates that the longer the time between the event and the questions and recall, the more inaccurate and incomplete the witness will be.[101] This point is not always recognised in the research

Equally, post event information, discussions and questions[102] can alter, change or influence a witness as much as a courtroom actor. These issues are beyond the current study.

W. Oue *et al*[103] found that the visual features of the weapons affected the witnesses memory suggesting the shape of the weapon is a factor attracting witness attention. The types, models, size, locations, etc., of cameras need to be considered in television courtroom broadcasting effects research. This is another missed opportunity.

Similarly, it is most important to be careful that the questions or queries do not taint or influence the answer. Many television courtroom broadcasting studies, however, are conducted by people who would not otherwise draft questionnaires or experiments and who may not be aware that their queries, although well intentioned, may be influencing the reply.

Timing of post event information can be very relevant in a number of studies.[104] So, for example, if a camera is already present, or indeed permanently in the courtroom, this is potentially less relevant, obvious, affecting, etc. It is potentially less disrupting than a camera moving about in the courtroom. It is also potentially less disruptive than a camera and cameraman coming into the courtroom (a) after the case starts or (b) after many or all of the courtroom participants have come into and prepared themselves in the courtroom. Again, these issues are ripe for research.

There are also interesting differences in the form of retrieval. For example, differences have been found between asking subjects what they saw, versus asking them to reply to a predetermined set of list of questions.[105] Also, who is asking the questions is not always neutral.[106] Consider a judge after a televised courtroom trial asking jury members if they were affected by the camera broadcasting? Many potential bias issues arise.[107] Yet this is what has occurred in some televising courtroom research. Gary Wells and Amy Bradfield[108] amongst others, have been researching confirmations and feedback given to witness and found that it does influence the witness.

Melissa L.-H. Vo and W.X. Schneider also make the point that in looking at a given scene or carrying out a given task, we also rely on our existing knowledge and experience, which they refer to as "implicit knowledge."[109] Again, this appears not to have been considered or researched in the literature to date.

PSYCHOLOGY RECALL RESEARCH TOOLS

Another avenue for examination is to carry out studies with cameras present in the courtroom and with cameras absent. Then each group would be tested for the recall accuracy for details in the courtroom scene. Is there better and more detailed recall in the camera absent scenario? Does camera presence affect recall of central and peripheral details? Equally, these tests could be replicated in different courtroom broadcasting forms.

One tool is to test jurors or mock jurors for their recall and retention. The jurors are shown a particular case or take part in a case. One group has cameras present and the other does not. Thus, it is possible to compare results and see what the possible effects of the cameras were. Research can be conducted in such a way that if the camera present group recalls less pertinent details of the case that this effect can be isolated to the cameras present. One of the advantages of conducting these types of studies is that it can be possible for the juries not to know what is actually being tested for, thus avoiding bias. This is extremely difficult to do in a real courtroom broadcasting setting with real courtroom participants. In terms of medium and long term retention it is also possible to conduct follow up studies on both sets of jurors.

The videotaping of courtroom scenes or interviews of subjects after seeing or recalling events can be used in research studies.[110] Another study method is to stage a mock crime, then conduct interviews of the subject witnesses, and later arrange a mock trial where the witnesses are cross examined. Various factors can be tested for.[111]

BLOCKING

It is possible to study the effects of digital image blocking. Do witnesses (or indeed other courtroom participants) who have been able to have their image digitally blocked react any differently than those who know that their image will be shown? Is there any difference between those whose image is automatically blocked by a pre-existing court broadcasting rule or those who are asked for their preference or have to apply to have their image blocked? Similar studies can be used to test effects of those who may have objected to the television courtroom broadcasting but were overruled. Cameras can also be used, whether in a real television courtroom broadcasting context or a mock trial situation, to test for accuracy of self reports and third party reports of effects. A study could use (miniature) cameras to examine effects of broadcast cameras on courtroom participants and compare these to self reports *and* third party reports.

CONCLUSION

Psychology provides an abundance of relevant research opportunities. Sole reliance upon limited self report studies does not answer any of the arguments in the television courtroom broadcasting debate. The extensive literature of psychology research shows that we should not rely on self reports and opinion studies alone. What is required is more robust and scientifically based research following the lead of other fields of research, such as psychology. Existing research and developments within the area of psychology and law (not forgetting language and sociology) provides a wealth of material which should have a bearing on any serious effort to investigate television courtroom broadcasting effects.

NOTES

1. This not meant to be a summary or review of psychology or psychology literature, as such would be beyond the scope of this book. It does serve to highlight how parts of the literature and research in psychology can be the basis for or compliment research filling the gaps in courtroom television broadcasting research.

2. Even Mason's research in Europe is limited to self report type research. P. Mason, Court on Camera: Electronic Broadcast Coverage of the Legal Proceedings, available at www.usfca.edu/pj/camera-mason.htm . Last accessed on August 13, 2012.

3. L. Re refers to a case where the warning to jurors was not sufficient See L Re, Eyewitness Identification: Why So Many Mistakes?, Australian Law Journal 58 (1984), 519. While many factors may be already within the knowledge of jurors and other courtroom actors, the extent to which case factors or all of these factors are known to the public, i.e. jurors, is less certain. Holtenson strongly argues that judicial warnings are insufficient. O.P. Holtenson, The Admission of Expert Evidence of Opinion as to the Potential Unreliability of Evidence of Visual Identification, Melbourne University Law Review 16 (1988) 521–547. Judges are not experts in the mental processes which occur during the identification process and are not in the best placed position to advise on identification evidence and Holtenson therefore advocates expert psychological testimony.

4. See A. Heaton-Armstrong, E. Shepard, G.H. Gudjonsson and D. Wolchover, D., eds., Witness Testimony: Psychological, Investigative and Evidential Perspectives (Oxford: OUP, 2006).

5. *US v Amaral*, 488 F.2d 1148 (1973).

6. 275 N.W. 2d 736 (Iowa) (1979).

7. O.P. Holtenson, The Admission of Expert Evidence of Opinion as to the Potential Unreliability of Evidence of Visual Identification, Melbourne University Law Review 16 (1988): 521-547, at 542 et seq. Note also A. Roberts, Eyewitness Identification and Expert Insight: *R v Forbes*, International Journal of Evidence & Proof 14 (2010): 57–62.

8. G.L. Wells and A.L. Bradfield, Good, You Identified the Suspect: Feedback to Eyewitnesses Distorts their reports of Witnessing Experience, Applied Psychology 83 (1998): 360–376, at 360, as referred to in C. TerBeek, A Call or Precedential Heads: Why the Supreme Court's Eyewitness Identification Jurisprudence is Anachronistc and Out-of-Step with the Empirical Evidence, Law & Psychology Review 31 (2007) 21–51, at 21–22.

9. G.L. Wells and A.L. Bradfield, above, 21–51.

10. *Ibid*, 51, referring to the case of *Roper v Simmons*, but no citation given.

11. P.A. Granhad, L.A. Stromwall and M. Hartwig, Eyewitness Testimony: Tracing the Beliefs of Swedish Legal Professionals, Behavioral Sciences and the Law 23 (2005) 709–727.

12. Ibid.

13. There was, however, one study found where viewer reaction to a particular case was gauged via a questionnaire in Arizona. One thousand questionnaires were used with a twenty five percent response rate. 95% watched the trial more than once and 84% agreed with the guilty verdict. See New Law Journal (30 November, 1987) at 13 *et seq.*, as referred to in W. Freedman, Press and Media Access to the Criminal Courtroom (New York: Quorum, 1988), 46.

14. See generally A. Heaton-Armstrong, E. Shepard, G.H. Gudjonsson and D. Wolchover, above.

15. There are increasingly strong arguments in psychology to suggest that these may be insufficient. For example, not every judge or every juror is familiar with the research identifying the process through which witnesses make identification, recall what they witnessed, and the various factors which effect witness perception and recall. Note also C. TerBeek, above, 21–51.

16. E. Loftus, E. is just one such example. See also O.P. Holtenson, above, 521–547.

17. Referred to in C. Hollin, Psychology and Crime: An Introduction to Criminological Psychology (London: Routledge, 1989), 161. Also G.L. Wells, *et al*, Accuracy, Confidence, and Juror Perceptions in Eyewitness Identification, Journal of Applied Psychology 64:4 (1979): 440–448.

18. *Ibid.* See also See also D. Martin, and C.N. Macrae, Processing Style and Person Recognition: Exploring the Face Inversion Effect, Visual Cognition, 18: 2 (2010)161–170, at 163.

19. B. Culter and S. Penrod, Mistaken Identification: The Eyewitness, Psychology, and the Law (New York: Cambridge University Press, 1985), 195. Also B.E. Bell and E.F. Loftus, Trivial Persuasion in the Courtroom: The Power of (a Few) Minor Details, Journal of Personality and Social Psychology 56:5 (1989): 669–679.

20. See example in L. Re, above, 509 – 520, at 509.

21. L. Re, ibid, 510.

22. As referred to in C. TerBeek, A Call or Precedential Heads: Why the Supreme Court's Eyewitness Identification Jurisprudence is Anachronistic and Out-of-Step with the Empirical Evidence, Law & Psychology Review, 31 (2007): 21–51, at 47.

23. *R v Dunne* (English Court of Appeal) October 4 1976, (unreported), referred to in L Re, ibid, 516. This may not be the leading case as there are indeed many cases which have had to touch on these issues. Note also *People (AG) v Casey (No 2)* [1963] IR 33.

24. L. Heffernan, Evidence: Cases and Materials (Dublin: Thomson Round Hall, 2005), 284, and also Chapters 4 and 7, ibid, regarding expert evidence. See generally Chapter 7 therein on visual identification evidence.

25. Ibid, 284, case at [1963] IR 33. See also related cases referred to therein.

26. See L. Re, above, 517. See generally Cross and Tapper on Evidence, (Oxford: OUP, 2007), for example 578 et seq, and commentary in A. Keane, The Modern Law of Evidence (Oxford: OUP, 2008), 549 et seq.

27. *People (AG) v Stafford* [1983] IR 165, is an example of where an appeal was successful on the basis that the trial judge misdirected the jury in his summation and warnings to the jury. Note also *R v Turnbull* [1976] 3 All ER 549. Cutler and Penrod note that jurors do not/cannot assess the detrimental impact that reading or seeing media reports may be having upon them, and thereby cannot guard against it. It has also been found, they note, that the judge's warning to a jury does not do away with jury prejudice. "The only certain safeguard against the effects of pretrial publicity is to impanel a jury which has not been exposed to pre-trial publicity." B.L. Cutler and S.D. Penrod, above. Note also references to warnings, corroboration, etc. in Chapter 10. Also note references to Twining under the heading Witness in this Chapter, post. Twining also points out that warning the jury about the perils of convicting on identification evidence alone is not a sufficient safeguard. W. Twining, Rethinking Evidence, Exploratory Essays (Oxford: Blackwell, 1990), 152–175.

28. A warning may be of little use if it is given after the information has been given to the subjects and is thus processed by the brain. However, warnings before the information is received seems to ensure that they read the information slower and increase their resistance to suggestion.

29. This is currently beyond the scope of the present work.

30. However, as previously pointed the courts have long held the view that eye witness identification must be considered very carefully.

31. L. Re, above, 510, referring to Evatt and McTiernan, JJ., in *Craig v The King*, High Court, Australia. No citation given. *Craig v R* [1933] HCA 41; [1933] CRL 49 (1933) (29 August, 1933), www.austlii.edu.au , accessed on January 30, 2013.

32. Ibid.

33. E.F. Loftus and J.M. Doyle, Eyewitness Testimony: Civil and Criminal (New York: Kluwer, 1987), Chapter 2. Note also second edition/supplement published in 1994 by Lex Law Publishing.

34. T. Valentine, A. Pickering and S. Darling, Characteristics of Eyewitness Identification that Predict the Outcome of Real Lineups, Applied Cognitive Psychology 17 (2003): 969-993, at 989.

35. *R v Turnball* [1976], 3 All ER 549. Note also A. Roberts, Eyewitness Identification and Expert Insight: *R v Forbes*, International Journal of Evidence & Proof 14 (2010): 57–62.

36. G. Davies and L. Griffiths, Eyewitness Identification and the English High Courts: A Century of Trial and Error, Psychiatry, Psychology and Law, 15:3 (2008): 435–449.

37. Ibid.

38. E.F. Loftus. and K. Ketcham, The Malleability of Eyewitness Accounts, in S. Lloyd-Bostock and B.R. Clifford, eds., Evaluating Eyewitness Testimony (New York: Wiley, 1985): 159–170; W. Twining, Identification and Misidentification in Legal Processes: Redefining the Problem, in S. Lloyd–Bostock and B.R. Clifford, eds., ibid, 255–280, and other sections therein. Also E. Loftus, Eyewitness Testimony (Cambridge MA: Harvard University Press, 1979, 1996). Also, E. Loftus, A 30-year Investigation of the Malleability of Memory, Learning and Memory 12 (2005): 361–366.

39. Ibid.

40. Ibid.

41. Ibid.

42. Ibid.

43. See E.F. Loftus and K. Ketcham, above; W. Twining, above, in Legal Processes: Redefining the Problem," in S. Lloyd-Bostock and B.R. Clifford, ibid, 255–280, and other sections therein. Also E. Loftus, Eyewitness Testimony (Cambridge MA: Harvard University Press, 1979, 1996).

44. L.M. Hulse and A. Memon, Fatal Impact? The Effect of Emotional Arousal and Weapon Focus on Police Officer's Memories for a Simulated Crime, Legal and Criminal Psychology 11 (2006): 313–325, at 322.

45. Ibid, 323.

46. Ibid.

47. Ibid.

48. See L. Re, above, 515

49. B. Culter and S. Penrod, above, 195; C. Hollin, Psychology and Crime: An Introduction to Criminological Psychology (London: Routledge, 1989), 165. See also C. TerBeek, above, at 24 et seq, and 40 et seq.

50. Ibid, 19, referring to G. Wells et al in 1978, G. Wells, Applied Eyewitness-testimony Research: System Variables and Estimator Variables, Journal of Personality and Social Psychology 12 (1978): 1546–1557, also E. Loftus, 177.

51. See B. Cutler and S. Penrod, 112.

52. Also when people are questioned or surveyed they arguably pay greater attention and may be less likely to be confused e.g. in trade mark litigation surveys for instance. This point is made in J. Jacoby, Survey and Field Experimental Evidence, in S. Kassin and L. Wrightsman, eds., The Psychology of Evidence and Trial Procedure (Beverly Hills: Sage, 1985): 194. Some commentators also make a similar point with regard to courtroom broadcasting. They feel courtroom actors will be more responsible when being filmed. Whether this is true or not, something which has not been shown either way, it remains a fact that only a very small percent of cases will be covered. This is so even with a whole channel devoted to courtroom broadcasting.

53. D. McQuail and S. Windahl, Communications Models: For the Study of Mass Communication (London: Longman, 1993), 47. Generally also E. Loftus, Eyewitness Testimony (Cambridge MA: Harvard University Press, 1979, 1996); A. Heaton-Armstrong, E. Shepard, G.H. Gudjonsson and D. Wolchover, eds., Witness Testimony: Psychological, Investigative and Evidential Perspectives (Oxford: OUP, 2006).

54. See E.F. Loftus and K. Ketcham, above; W. Twining, above. Also E. Loftus, Eyewitness Testimony (Cambridge MA: Harvard University Press, 1979, 1996).

55. See G.S. Goodman and A. Hahn, Evaluating Eyewitness Testimony, in I. Weiner and A. Hess, Handbook of Forensic Psychology (New York: Wiley, 1987), 258–283.

56. L.M. Hulse and A. Memon, Fatal Impact? The Effect of Emotional Arousal and Weapon Focus on Police Officer's Memories for a Simulated Crime, Legal and Criminal Psychology 11 (2006): 313–325, at 314.

57. Ibid, 313-325. There are also other parallels with courtroom broadcasting and the instant study. Defendants in the courtroom broadcasting context have been seldom researched. Also, there is no apparent television courtroom broadcasting arousal research. Note comments ibid, 313.

58. See references and definition in K.L. Pickel, D.B Narter, M.M. Jameson and T.T. Lenhardt, The Weapon Focus Effect in Child Eyewitnesses, Psychology, Crime and Law 14:1 (2008): 61–72, at 72. Also L. Hope and D. Wright, Beyond Unusual? Examining the Role of Attention in the Weapon Focus Effect, Applied Cognitive Psychology 21 (2007): 951–961, at 957–958.

59. L.M. Hulse and A. Memon, above, 314. This is also discussed in the findings of their study, ibid, 321.

60. Ibid.

61. See, for example, G.M. Davies, S. Smith, and C. Blincoe, A 'Weapon Focus' Effect in Children, Psychology, Crime and Law 14:4 (2008): 19-28.

62. N. Steblay, A Meta–analytic Review of Weapon Focus Effect, Law and Human Behavior 16 (1992): 413–424.

63. Note also E. Loftus, G. Loftus and J. Messo, Some Facts About Weapon Focus, Law and Human Behavior 11 (1987): 55–62; A. Maass and G. Kohnken, Eyewitness Identification: Simulating the Weapon Effect, Law and Human Behavior 13 (1989): 379–408; R.T. McCraty, M. Atkinson and J Sundram, Impact of the HeartMath Self-Management Skills Program on Physiological and Psychological Stress in Police Officers, (Boulder Creek, CA: Institute of HeartMath), HeartMath Research Centre Publications No. 99–075)(1999); K.L. Pickel, Unusualness and Threat as Possible Causes of Weapon Focus, Memory, 6 (1998): 277-295; M. Safer, S–A Christianson, M. Autry and K. Osterlund, Tunnel Memory for Traumatic Events, Applied Cognitive Psychology 12 (1998): 99–117; S. Sporer, S. Penrod, D. Read and B. Cutler, Choosing, Confidence and Accuracy: A Meta-analysis of the Confidence–Accuracy Relation in Eyewitness Identification Studies, Psychological Bulletin 118 (1995) 315–327; P. Woolnough and M. MacLoud, Watching the Birdie Watching You: Eyewitness Memory for Actions Using CCTV Recordings of Actual Crimes, Applied Cognitive Psychology 15 (2001): 395–411; J. Yuille and J. Cutshall, A Case Study of Eyewitness Memory of a Crime, Journal of Applied Psychology, 71 (1986) 291–301; J. Yuille, G. Davies, F. Gibling, D. Marxsen and S Porter, Eyewitness Memory of Police Trainees for Realistic Role Plays, Journal of Applied Psychology 79 (1994): 931–936; K.L. Pickel, T.A. French, and J.M. Betts, A Cross-modal Weapon Focus Effect: The Influence of a Weapon's Presence on Memory for Auditory Information, Memory 11 (2003): 277–292; K.L. Pickel, S.J. Ross, and R.S. Truelove, Do Weapons Automatically Capture Attention?, Applied Cognitive Psychology, 20 (2006): 871–893; W. Oue, W., Y. Hakoda, N. Onuma, N., The Effects of Visual Features of a Weapon on Eyewitnesses' Cognitive Processing, Japanese Journal of Psychology, 77:5 (2006) 443–451.

64. E. Loftus, G Loftus, G., and J. Messo, *ibid.* Referred to in B. Cutler and S. Penrod, Mistaken Identification: The Eyewitness, Psychology and the Law, (New York: Cambridge University Press, 1995), pp. 101-102. Generally see also R.C.L. Lindsay, D.F. Ross, J.D. Read and M.P. Toglia, eds., The Handbook of Eyewitness Psychology, (Mahwah, NJ: Erlbaum, 2007).

65. B. Cutler and S. Penrod, ibid, 102, referring to Brian L. Cutler, Steven D Penrod, and T.K. Martens, "The Reliability of Eyewitness Identifications: The Role of System and Estimator Variables," Law and Human Behavior 11 (1987): 223–258.

66. Husle, L., and Memon, A., Fatal Impact? The Effects of Emotional Arousal and Weapon Presence on Police Officers' Memories for a Simulated Crime, Legal and Criminal Psychology 11 (2006): 313–325 at 313.

67. Ibid, 314.

68. K.L. Pickel, S.J., Ross and R.S. Truelove, Do Weapons Automatically Capture Attention, Applied Cognitive Psychology 20 (2006): 871–893, at 871.

69. Ibid.

70. Ibid, 871.

71. T.H. Kramer, R. Buckhout and P. Eugenio, Weapons Focus, Arousal, and Eyewitness Memory, Attention Must be Paid, Law and Human Behaviour 14:2 (1990): 167–184, as referred to in K.L Pickel, S.J. Ross and R.S. Truelove, Do Weapons Automatically Capture Attention, Applied Cognitive Psychology 20 (2006) 871–893, at 872.

72. L. Hope and D. Wright, Beyond Unusual? Examining the Role of Attention in the Weapon Focus Effect, Applied Cognitive Psychology 21 (2007): 951–961.

73. J. Saunders, Memory Impairment in Weapon Focus Effect, Memory and Cognition 37:3 (2009) 326–335, at 326, and references therein.

74. K.L. Pickel, T.A., French and J. Betts, A Cross-modal Weapon Focus Effect: The Influence of a Weapon's Presence on Memory for Auditory Information, Memory 11:3 (2003): 277–292.

75. Ibid.

76. See B. Cutler and S. Penrod, Mistaken Identification: The Eyewitness, Psychology and the Law (New York: Cambridge University Press, 1995), 9, 101–102.

77. E. Loftus, Eyewitness Testimony (Cambridge, Ma.: Harvard University Press, 1996), vii.

78. Ibid.

79. Ibid.

80. See A. Heaton-Armstrong, E. Shepard, G.H. Gudjonsson and D. Wolchover, eds., Witness Testimony: Psychological, Investigative and Evidential Perspectives (Oxford: OUP, 2006).

81. See example reference to such experimentation in E. Loftus, Eyewitness Testimony, above, 25.

82. L.M. Hulse and A. Memon, above, 316.

83. Ibid, 317.

84. Ibid.

85. See references in, for example, *ibid*, p. 26. Note also references in M. L-H. Vo and W. Schneider, A Glimpse is Not a Glimpse: Differential Processing of Flashed Scene Previews Leads to differential Target Search Benefits, Visual Cognition 18:2 (2010): 171–200, at 173.

86. See ibid, p. 63. See also B. Cutler and S. Penrod, above, 183.

87. See, for example, the many examples of drawings in E. Loftus, Eyewitness Testimony, above.

88. See references in for example B. Cutler and S. Penrod, above, 10.

89. L. Ewing, G. Rhodes and E. Pellicano, Have You Got the Look? Gaze Direction Affects Judgements of Facial Attractiveness, Visual Cognition 18:3 (2010): 321-330. See also D. Martin and C.N. Macrae, Processing Style and Person Recognition: Exploring the Face Inversion Effect, Visual Cognition 18:2 (2010): 161–170.

90. D. Martin and C.N. Macrae, Processing Style and Person Recognition: Exploring the Face Inversion Effect, Visual Cognition 18:2 (2010): 161–170, at 163.

91. Ibid, 167.

92. S. Landstrom, E. Hjelmsater and P. Granhag, The Camera Perspective Bias: A Case Study, Journal of Investigative Psychology and Offender Profiling 4 (2007): 199–208.

93. They give the example of G. Lassiter, A. Geers, P. Munhall., I. Handley and M. Beers, Videotaped Confessions: Is Guilt in the Eye of the Camera?, in Zanna, ed., Advances, in Experimental Social Psychology, Vol. 20, (San Diego, CA: Academic Press, 2001), 189-253, referred to ibid, 205.

94. Landstron et al, above, 200.

95. *Ibid.*

96. M. Safer, S-A. Christianson, M. Autry and K. Osterlund, K., Tunnel Memory for Traumatic Events, Applied Cognitive Psychology 12 (1998): 99–117, as referred to in L.M. Hulse and A. Memon, above, 314–315.

97. Ibid.

98. See E. Loftus, Eyewitness Testimony, above, 33.
99. Ibid, 199.
100. See, for example, ibid, 50, 113, 114.
101. See ibid, 53.
102. See ibid, 54, 94.
103. W. Oue, Y. Hakoda and N. Onuma, The Effects of Visual Features of a Weapon on Eyewitnesses' Cognitive Processing, Japanese Journal of Psychology 77:5 (2006): 443–451.
104. See ibid, 64.
105. See ibid, 90.
106. See ibid, 97.
107. The judge is not necessarily a neutral party on this issue. He may have considered an application to allow cameras and decided in favour – possibly in sight of the jury or they are aware of the decision. The judge may have made some positive comments by the judge. The jury before being asked are aware of the views of the judge in terms of reinforcing acceptance of the cameras and a view of no adverse effects.
108. G. Wells and A. Bradfield, 'Good, You Identified the Suspect': Feedback to Eyewitnesses Distorts Their Reports of Witnessing Experience, Applied Psychology 83 (1998): 360-376, at 360, as referred to in C. TerBeek, above, 25–26.
109. M, L.– H. Vo and W. X. Schneider, A Glimpse is Not a Glimpse: Differential Processing of Flashed Scene Previews Lead to Differential Target Search Benefits, Visual Cognition 18:2 (2010). 171–200, at 172.
110. See references in ibid, 183.
111. See example referred to ibid, 185.

Chapter Twelve

The Distraction Challenge

EYE TRACKING AND TELEVISION COURTROOM BROADCASTING

Eye tracking (the study of eye movement and gaze) was not directly considered in the Supreme Court decisions. Neither has it been considered, as far as the author can find, in the vast general literature in relation to television courtroom broadcasting. However, eye tracking technology is significantly advanced. It is now so sophisticated that it can greatly assist in conducting research of effects of television courtroom broadcasting, and in such way as the Supreme Court may not have even considered possible.

Eye tracking can greatly assist in addressing the research challenge set by the Supreme Court. Indeed, it has been suggested that the Supreme Court decisions only "speculates on effects."[1] S.L. Alexander also notes the lack of empirical research.[2]

It is now clear that the Supreme Court was not aware of eye trackers and did not refer to eye tracking in any way whatsoever. Eye tracking can be used for conducting in–court effects research, in particular research of distraction effects.

The basis of the arguments in the television courtroom debate are largely unchanged since 1965.[3] While psychological, media and communications research has also advanced, eye tracking technology in particular provides definite avenues for examining the actual in–court and audience effects gaps referred to by the Supreme Court. Now, more than at any stage previously, we are in a position to begin research of actual effects issues without having to rely solely on limited self reports and opinion reports. Let us consider some of these avenues below.

While eye tracking technologies are relatively recent, the study of gaze has existed since the eighteenth century.[4] Visual attention has been studied for a considerable time.[5] Eye tracking research and techniques[6] have been used successfully in advertising, marketing, psychology, eyewitness accuracy studies, internet usage research, health, etc. The literature on eye tracking is constantly growing[7] and increasingly recognised.[8]

While William Petkanas suggests that recordings of television courtroom broadcasting may be shown to audience subjects, and that they may then be interviewed afterwards e.g. in terms of what they found informative and interesting,[9] no reference is made to eye tracking. (Definitions and forms are also ignored). He further suggests that another study might have one group viewing film footage, while the other reads reports of the same case.[10]

Eye tracking also helps with other research issues. For example, Tuula–Riitta Valikoski[11] notes that many responses to in–court research questions of attentional focus issues (in this instance prosecutors) do not provide evidence of cognitive processes, only reported indications of attentional effects. Eye tracking provides direct and recorded accurate measurement of eye movement and eye focus.

ADVANTAGES OF EYE TRACKING

Eye tracking "provides a more direct and continuous measure of attention" than manual measurements.[12] It also overcomes the limitations of opinion reports and self reports. Furthermore, it can be used to test and validate opinion reports and self reports. "[E]ye movements are a direct indicator of overt attention" and provide "a highly direct measure of visual attention, eye systems also allow continuous measurement of eye movements."[13] We should be researching this in the context of television courtroom broadcasting. Eye tracking permits testing and direct observation of eye fixation, focus and attention on television cameras.[14] Eye tracking research also has the advantage that is tracks and documents exactly what people see.[15] It can also be recorded.

EYE TRACKING AND PSYCHOLOGY

Eye trackers are increasingly used in psychology and eyewitness identification research. Sheree Josephson and Michael E. Holmes used eye trackers recently to examine whether eyewitness use scanpaths to recognise suspects in photograph lineups.[16] Elizabeth Loftus in seeking empirical evidence for the weapons focus effect,[17] used a corneal reflection device[18] to discover where and for how long individuals would focus their attention. A corneal reflection device is one of the types of eye trackers that can be used.[19]

However, while there has been psychology and eye focus research on particular legal issues, primarily eyewitness identification issues, the issue of television courtroom broadcasting effects is largely, if not entirely, ignored.

More recently there is also increasing use of eye tracking in relation to psychology research into the effects of cameras and camera perspective in recorded police interviews and confessions.[20] This is partly driven by the knowledge that there can be false convictions, and erroneous and false confessions captured on video recordings of suspect interrogations. One result of this research is that it has been found that different camera angles and focus orientations of the interview camera can alter significantly how viewers of such film footage rate the genuiness and voluntariness of the recorded "confessions." The manner in which the evidence is filmed, i.e. the confession footage, can influence judgements of guilt.[21] Mock jurors have been found to be influenced by the camera angle from which the interrogation is filmed.[22] This is now known as *camera perspective bias*.[23] This is additionally significant since the Innocence Project which applies DNA technology and techniques to past cases. It found that a quarter of the DNA exoneration cases originally relied strongly on false confessions.[24]

Most criminal investigation interviews that are recorded, adopt a suspect focused angle only. This is as opposed to focusing on the police officer or focusing on both of them at the same time. This also enhances the salience of the suspect and also the perceived voluntariness of any confession.[25] G. Daniel Lassiter and Audrey A. Irvine[26] showed the same interview recorded on different cameras to show suspect only, police officer only, and both equally focused. The research study subjects then viewed one of the videos, depending on which group they were in. The ones who saw the suspect only video, perceived less coercion.[27] Other research also confirmed that suspect focus only videos yielded significantly higher ratings for perceived guilt and voluntariness.[28] As a result of the Lassiter and Irvine study, the police in New Zealand changed their practice to ensure that there was no suspect only video recordings, and that suspect and questioner were always in frame.[29] Pressure is increasing to change policies elsewhere also.

Lezlee J. Ware[30] also examined camera perspective bias and used eye trackers to monitor visual attention. She also refers to studies and the literature which shows that suspect-focus-only camera perspective, creates a bias for judgements of voluntariness and guilt.[31]

EYE TRACKING RESEARCH

The device used in an eye tracking study is known as an eye tracker. One of the initial stages in designing eye tracking experiments is formulating a hypothesis to research.[32] So it is not possible to properly research effects, if one does not say what effect hypothesis one is attempting to test and research. This applies to social science and science research generally as it does to television courtroom broadcasting research. Frequently, this basic step is absent in television courtroom broadcasting research.

The aim of eye tracking research is to study the eye position and eye movements of the subject. The main eye tracking measures and metrics[33] include,

- Fixation;
- Fixation (gaze) duration;
- Fixation rate (overall);
- Fixation duration mean (overall);
- Number of fixations (overall);
- Scanpath (fixation sequence);
- Area of interest (AOI);
- Gaze percentage (proportion of time) per AOI;
- Number of fixations per AOI;
- Gaze duration mean per AOI.

Eye tracking allows researchers to examine,[34]

- Fixation count/duration/order;
- Areas of interest (per region);
- Transitions between regions;
- Time to fixation (first);
- Counting of visits and re–visits;
- Task completion duration.

However, such studies can be expensive, complex and require collaboration and expertise across research fields.[35] The eye tracking hardware and software can be expensive too. Notwithstanding that, we need to apply eye tracking to the problems of gaps in television courtroom broadcasting research. The Supreme Court challenge needs to be addressed.

EYE TRACKING FORMS: INTERACTIVE AND DIAGNOSTIC

Andrew Duchowski refers to various eye tracking case studies[36] and applications.[37] At a headline level, the two headline application categories are interactive (input) applications and diagnostic applications.[38]

Diagnostic eye tracking can be used in the fields of psychology, marketing, advertising, human factors and ergonomics.[39] It is also used in law enforcement and policing security.[40]

Interactive applications include using eye tracking to input instructions to or interact with a (technology) device of some sort using eye focus.[41] For example, a person's gaze can be used to give instructions or input instructions. Quadriplegics, for example, can use their eyes to move a pointer or cursor.[42] Such applications include the fields of human computer interaction, visual displays and computer graphics.[43]

EYE TRACKING APPLICATIONS

Companies and researchers use eye tracking research to track displays. For example, companies using or advertising on the internet can use eye tracking to test an advert or the location of an advert. Do viewers look at the advert, for how long, or do they miss the advert entirely because of its location? Where is the best location for the advert? Eye tracking addresses these important commercial issues.

Andrew Duchowski refers to various eye tracking examples in neuroscience and psychology,[44] industrial engineering and human factors (e.g. aviation, driving and visual inspection),[45] marketing and advertising (e.g. advert design and placement, label and product design and placement, television, internet),[46] and computer science.[47]

SMI refer to eye tracking applications in medical research, diagnostics, surgery, psychology, sports and performance, human machine interactions, market research, neuroscience research, psycholinguistics, opthatmology, ergonomics, etc.[48]

Further eye tracking applications exist in visual systems and linguistics. Other eye tracking applications include uses in relation to gaming machines, medical instruments, vehicles, vehicle safety, computer interaction, medical diagnostics, security, law enforcement, video conferencing, information kiosks, interactive advertising, etc.[49] "Eye movements are the only means of communication for some severely disabled people."[50] Mercedes use eye tracking technology for driver fatigue alert systems.[51] There are also potential applications in security and computer security.[52] We also have many market research applications.[53]

Computer games development is another area where eye tracking is utilised.[54]

Eye tracking might also be used to develop more general mass market applications, such as gaze controls for heating, lighting[55] or perhaps television. Overall, there are many current applications[56] and many more promised.

There are various eye tracker manufactures. Examples include Tobii,[57] EyeTracking Inc,[58] SMI,[59] Arrington Research,[60] Asley,[61] SensoMotoric Instrument (SMI),[62] and Polhemus.[63] There are increasing numbers of international conferences relating to eye tracking. One is the Fixational Eye Movements and Visual Stabalisation conference.[64] Another is Eye Tracking Research and Applications (ETRA).[65] Lund University Humanities Lab is one university to offer courses in eye tracking technology.[66] Various other universities and university departments use eye tracking as a valuable tool of research.[67]

However, there does not appear to be any reference in the literature or conference papers to some of the eye tracking legal applications in relations to television courtroom broadcasting. This is the first research to explore these possibilities. Indeed, the in-court proof of concept demonstration undertaken by the author, is the first such research in relation to TCB and eye tracking anywhere. Eye tracking and psychology research can begun to address the research gaps in television courtroom broadcasting effects research. The Supreme Court has been calling for empirical research and has set a challenge. The three Supreme Court cases highlight some of the avenues for empirical research. Some of the potential eye tracking research is referred to below.

EYE TRACKING IN-COURT

Some of the research gaps referred to in the cases, and where eye tracking may be applied to television courtroom broadcasting, are referred to below,

- We should apply eye tracking to the various courtroom participants. Do they look at the television camera? If so, for how long?;
- What is the effect?;
- What difference does the location of the camera have on the different courtroom participants?;
- Are there different effects for camera only versus camera and cameraman?;
- Are there different effects for different types of camera?;
- How do in–court television cameras effects differ for courtroom participants while undertaking tasks?

The literature to date does not incorporate an analysis of the different tasks of the different courtroom participants into discussion or research of the different effects issues being examined.

We should employ eye tracking to examine distraction, attention, etc. of courtroom participants in the context of task analysis.[68] A "critical variable in information space is the task that the user is expected to carry out."[69]

Almost invariably the literature and limited research ignores reference to and consideration of camera location and frame issues. We need to be able to describe and represent descriptively and diagrammatically the various camera issues.[70]

Distraction and distraction research needs to examine the camera location issues. While eye tracking can assist in this, we also need to start recording where the camera is located in the courtroom, so that different research studies can be compared.

It is important in studies to know where the different courtroom participants are located and which direction they are facing, and how this compares with the camera location. For example, are the courtroom participants facing straight on, left or right when they look at the camera? We need to be able to compare this across research findings.

"In the [*Estes*] case construction of a television booth in the courtroom made it necessary to alter the physical layout of the courtroom and to move from their accustomed position to benches reserved for spectators."[71]

In most research, the location and height of the cameras is not considered or even documented, so we cannot look back to assess and compare different cases or research studies on these points.

Different angles and frames can have different effects and meanings.[72] We need to begin examining the various issues in the television courtroom broadcasting field.

Different frames can have different costs and benefits, advantages and disadvantages.[73] We need to begin examining and contrasting these for television courtroom broadcasting.

Many issues of confidence and ratings come up in relation to television courtroom broadcasting research. Many opportunities arise in terms of examining these issues with eye tracking technology. For example, an eye tracker and an observer could both look at a particular courtroom actor and try to examine how many times they focus their attention or look at the television camera in the courtroom. The observer could press a button to record each time they perceive the courtroom actor to look at the camera.

Indeed, a second observer could also look at the courtroom actor and try and record their perceptions during the case or after the case (e.g. the Short report, above).

The various results would then be compared. The observers would also be tested for their confidence ratings.[74] This would assist in dealing with the problem of most television courtroom broadcasting research, namely, of relying solely upon self report, opinion reports and questionnaires.

There are various types of eye trackers. One avenue for in–court research is to use eye trackers which are incorporated into lightweight glasses.[75] This type of research allows itself to be adopted to different courtroom participants and also in realistic settings and in real court settings. There are also various types of head mounted eye tracking tools.[76]

Other studies can use a variety of eye trackers where subjects can view pictures or videos of court scenes on a PC, laptop or projection screen.

In considering different television courtroom broadcasting forms, and in particular long extended footage versus short or snippet footage, we need to research what is viewed, for how long, eye movement behaviour and visual processing speeds.[77]

EYE TRACKING OUT-OF-COURT

Various studies can be undertaken with eye trackers in relation to out–of–court effects. Just some of the potential studies can involve the following.

The actual footage and segments broadcast potentially have effects. One aspect we need to begin research of, is the use and integration of different footage segments; presenter discussion, analysis, etc. Is there continuity, discontinuity, visual momentum[78] effects on the viewer?

We should ask "what do you think you see?"[79] in the context of the audience of television courtroom broadcasting. There is significant scope for research in this area.

Eye trackers can help us to see what the audience focuses upon in a given TCB picture or broadcast.

Is television courtroom broadcasting designed best to educate? Are certain forms of television courtroom broadcasting best to educate? Some researchers[80] refer to preparation and deliberate design of multimedia presentations in order to enhance learning and education.

How and what do the audience learn from television courtroom broadcasting? We can now at least track what they are looking at and what they see, and for how long, in television courtroom broadcasts and pictures of television cameras in courts. Eye tracking now permits this research.[81]

We should also begin to research camera focus issues in terms of witnesses. Just as research has found that there are problems and biases created by police interviews which only record the suspect being interviewed, issues arise with TCB in–court also. If a television camera focuses on a witness or suspect being examined or cross–examined, does this create different impressions and effects that the television camera focusing on the questioner and the person being questioned? Psychology studies and eye tracking[82] can assist in starting this research.

Some television courtroom broadcasting seeks to focus on the defendant for a reaction shot when a witness is being interviewed. The witness testimony, if carried as audio, is played over a closeup of the defendant. What issues does this raise? For one, there may be effects. It would appear that the research referred to above in relation to videotaped confessions and eye tracking may assist in investigating these issues for the first time.

The video confession research is also concerned that "as the salience of the suspect in the video is increased" perceived voluntariness may also increase.[83] Does this hold relevance for television camera zooming in the courtroom? Research of these issues could involve eye tracking, as well as confidence research and research of judgements, awards, verdicts, etc.

How useful are news snippets of television courtroom broadcasting? Are they educational? Eye tracking research can begin to assist us in addressing these questions. Consider, for example, the eye tracking research undertaken by Melissa L.–H. Vo and W.X. Schneider[84] into the information we obtain from mere glimpses. They found "strong evidence for the influence of flashed scene previews on the guidance of eye movements which indicated that participants were able to generate, store, and make use of initial scene representation for subsequent target search ... the results ... add to the growing evidence that initially generated scene representations can be stored across saccades continuously exhibiting their influence on eye movement control."[85] However, one group was found to process information faster than the other group.[86] Does this have implications for television courtroom broadcasting?

Carrick C. Williams also used eye tracking in his research, finding that target memory was influenced by the number of target objects presentations, not the number of searches for the target(s).[87] In one experiment, the number results showed that the more times the target object was presented, then the better the visual memory.[88] He concludes that "the present study demonstrates that when looking for car keys multiple times, memory for car keys is impacted by how many times they are found. However, memories for other objects encountered in the search are tied to how much those objects are viewed."[89]

Complex issues such as emotions and emotional content in the footage also need to be examined. Reiko Graham et al[90] found that during longer presentations "validity and emotion interacted such that cuing by emotional faces, fearful faces in particular, was enhanced relative to neutral faces. These results converge with a growing body of evidence that suggests that gaze and expression are initially processed independently and interact at later stages to direct attentional orienting." In Graham *et al*'s study the participant subjects were asked to perform a task and then tap a spacebar on a computer.[91] This assisted in recording time spent reacting to the stimulus. Different subject groups can be compared.

Helena Rutherford and Jane Raymond[92] also refer to research which found that,

> presenting negative versus neutral targets in short alternating blocks and examining [inhibition of return (IOR)] on the first trial of each new block, we show that the emotional modulation of IOR stems from the affective context in place before visual orienting is initiated, not by perceptual processing of the targets after cue effect.[93]

Newspaper reports consist of different layouts, articles, texts, headlines, photographs, captions, "tickers, drop quotes, fact boxes, maps, diagrams, tables, etc."[94] Television programming contains some of these plus many additional elements. How does the audience interact with, use, and (possibly) learn from television courtroom broadcasting and different forms of such broadcasting? What viewing, learning and cognitive processes are involved? Significant research has yet to be undertaken in relation to audience effects issues in television courtroom broadcasting. Eye tracking tools can clearly assist in examining these issues.

Jana Holsanova et al used eye tracking to research the effects of reading information graphics in a newspaper study.[95] They found that different spatial layouts had a significant effect on readers' eye movement behaviour.[96] They indicate that the results are important in contributing to the study of "attentional guidance in printed media."[97] Research identifies different reading and scanning speeds with different tasks and purposes.[98] We need to start undertaking research into attention, education, information, etc., in relation to the television courtroom broadcasting audience.

Holsanova *et al* also refer to research regarding cognitive load[99] and the cognitive theory of multimedia learning.[100] In term of suggesting effects for television courtroom broadcasting, e.g. education, educational across all forms of television courtroom broadcasting, we need to incorporate additional factors such as competing programmes, forms, task, dual–tasks being undertaken, environment, etc. into the research Arguably, research of television courtroom broadcasting is more complex because it is multi media and multimodal[101] based. Considerations such as distraction, priming, negative priming, attentional capture, attentional orientation, visual search, divided attention also arise.[102]

That, however, is no reason to avoid such research. In order to research such suggestions and also in terms of making such research more realistic, various methods of eye tracking can assist in undertaking such types of research.

Eye tracking can be used to carry out many types of the TCB effects research of TCB effects.

DESIGN

In terms of designing television courtroom broadcasting, and forms of TCB (obviously without presuming that there should be TCB), we should consider how to get the best broadcast footage for educational purposes, and the optimum scenario for filming without adverse effects upon courtroom participants. Considerations which have not been considered before are how best to tailor initial design features[103] to try and accomplish these aims. Additional design features, both in terms of in–court and out–of–court effects, are camera type, height and location. These design features have not been addressed in the general television courtroom broadcasting literature nor in the limited effects literature. Wickens et al, for example, refer to and examine issues involved with framing issues with design applications and visual spacing[104] and refer to different effects.[105]

Adapting, in even a very general manner, the frames referred to by Wickens et al,[106] to television courtroom broadcasting, we might consider the following frames in television courtroom broadcasting research (including eye tracking),

- Courtroom frame, details of the parameters of the instant courtroom setting and environment;
- Actor head frame, defined in terms of their orientation of head;
- Trunk frame, if different from head (e.g. a juror may have to look left or right to see the witness stand, camera, etc.);
- Camera location frame;
- Camera focus frame, orientation and direction of camera focus;
- Camera control frame, e.g. details of the camera operator;
- Glasses[107] can incorporate eyetrackers, so it is possible for one or all courtroom participants in a research experiment to wear eye trackers.

Christopher D. Wickens et al[108] also suggest that the interaction of the different frames and the effort necessary to deal with same will vary in cognitive demand, time, workload, etc. between frames. They also note that in particular high risk systems, giving the examples of vehicle control and medical operations, and the premium put on reducing driving errors.[109] Schmidt also refers to the high stakes of criminal cases and investigations. [110] Many would agree that court cases, and especially certain types of court cases, are equally important and high risk systems.

EYE TRACKING AND DUAL TASKING

The issue of dual tasking and multi tasking in courtroom has not been researched or addressed yet. What are the effects on a courtroom actor of doing various tasks at once? These complex issues have yet to be considered in the courtroom broadcasting context. While there is some eye tracking research referring to this issue in other fields, this is a complex issue which needs consideration in the courtroom broadcasting context. The issue of carrying out dual tasks simultaneously appears in eye tracking research.[111]

Viewer strategies and tactics may also be involved. For example, in terms of reading and eye tracking research, Khosla et al[112] (depending on whether the subjects perceive a forthcoming task as difficult or not), subjects adopt different strategies and which can influence their fixation times.

In terms of television courtroom broadcasting numerous research possibilities arise. Various types of research experiments can be conducted with eye tracking monitoring different camera and courtroom "photographic stimuli." [113]

One could have separate subject groups who also have to perform tasks and tap a spacebar. Reaction times and eye movement can be tracked and coded. The groups might in one scene have to tap the space bar as soon as the judge arrived into the courtroom. In one group, the scene may have a camera and camera operator moving; in another a camera and camera operator with no movement; another with camera only; and a final control group with no camera at all. In each the judge arrives in (after introducing the camera focus element). The research can then be compared.

Jaana Simola et al[114] state that,

> [t]he finding that eye movement patterns differ when different processing demands are encountered can be used for developing an interactive information search application that learns and adapts to users' goals and intentions. For example, by examining which parts of a search engine results are read in different states, such as *reading* or *decision* states, it is possible to infer about the intentions and interests of the user (original emphasis).

Should we not research audience viewing of television courtroom broadcasting? Take a gavel to gavel (G2G) criminal trial for example. How does the intention, tasks and load on the viewer affect what they see, how their eyes fixate and for how long? Does this change during different segments of the trial, (e.g. opening, testimony, arguments and motions, closing), and or between different courtroom participants (e.g. judge, witness, expert witness)? Eye tracking can assist us in the task of beginning to unlock the answers to these queries.

EYE TRACKING AND DISTRACTION

One of the concerns with television courtroom broadcasting is that the cameras in court "might be so completely and thoroughly disruptive and distracting as to make a fair trial impossible." [115] Mr Justice White states that,

> the currently available [research] materials assessing the effect of cameras in the courtroom are too sparse and fragmentary ..., 'we know too little of the actual impact ... to reach a conclusion ... evidence before us.' It may well be, however, that as further experience and informed judgment do become available, the use of cameras in the courtroom, as in this trial, will prove to pose such a serious hazard to a defendant's rights that a violation of the Fourteenth Amendment will be found without a showing on the record of specific demonstrable prejudice to the defendant. [116]

Again, one of the concerns with television courtroom broadcasting has been the distracting effect on the courtroom participants. Up until now, however, the Supreme Court has not realised that research tools actually exist to examine these issues. Eye tracking provides tangible methods for examining actual distraction of courtroom participants caused by television cameras in court.

We should apply eye tracking to the various courtroom participants who are involved in televised cases. Do they look at the television camera? If so, for how long? What is the effect? Eye trackers allow us to begin this research.

Are there different effects for camera only versus camera plus cameraman? Are there different effects for different types of camera? Again, eye trackers allow us to begin the research.

Many issues of confidence and ratings come up in relation to television courtroom broadcasting research. Many opportunities arise in terms of examining these issues with eye tracking technology. For example, an eye tracker and an observer could both look at a particular courtroom actor and examine how many times they focus their attention or look at the television camera in the courtroom. The observer could press a button to record each time they perceive the courtroom actor to look at the camera. The observer in court can be tested against what is recorded by the eye tracker. Thus far, the use of observers in court to record the effects of television courtroom broadcasting has not been independently assessed.

The various results would then be compared. The observers would also be tested for their confidence ratings. [117] This would assist in dealing with the problem of most television courtroom broadcasting research, namely, that of relying solely upon opinion self report, opinion reports and questionnaires.

There are various types of eye trackers. One avenue for in–court research is to use eye trackers which are incorporated into lightweight glasses. [118] With eye tracking glasses[119] it is possible for one or all courtroom participants in a research experiment to be tested for distraction. This type of research allows itself to be adopted to different courtroom participants and also in realistic settings and in real (non live) court settings. There are also various types of head mounted eye tracking tools.[120] These can also be used for television courtroom broadcasting effects studies.

Other studies can use a variety of eye trackers where subjects can view pictures or videos of court scenes on a PC, laptop or projection screen. This particular method may allow for examination of greater numbers of test subjects.

In terms of television courtroom broadcasting numerous research possibilities arise. Various types of research experiments can be conducted of eye tracking monitoring of different camera and courtroom "photographic stimuli."[121]

One could have separate subject groups who also have to perform tasks and tap a spacebar. Reaction times and eye movement can be tracked and coded. The groups might in one scene have to tap the space bar as soon as the judge arrives into the courtroom. In one group, the scene may have a camera and camera operator moving; in another a camera and camera operator with no movement; another with camera only; and a final control group with no camera at all. In each the judge arrives in. The research can then be compared.

FIRST IN-COURT DEMONSTRATION

Some of the one off in–court television broadcasts in the UK took literally years of negotiation before approval and agreement was reached. As noted above, the Supreme Court (and most other courts elsewhere) are not aware of the existence of eye trackers when discussing TCB issues, particularly effect issues. No commentator has discussed or identified the utility of eye tracking of TCB effects research. It is, therefore, very novel to suggest and recommend, as the author does, eye tracking in order to address (parts of) the Supreme Court research challenge.

It is useful and would assist in scoping eye tracking experiments of TCB in–court effects, to bring an eye tracker into an actual courtroom. This will assist in scoping actual eye tracking experimentation, deciding upon which eye trackers to use, developing hypothesis and models of examination for effects, etc. (See Chapter 17 for more details of the eye tracking in–court proof of concept demonstration research of the author).

One of the advantages of an eye tracker is that whatever the subject looks at, can be monitored, but also recorded. Therefore, the demonstration of where the subject is looking, and can look (their cone of vision) can be recorded in relation to their position in the courtroom. Location issues should be incorporated in future research.

CONCLUSION

Researchers use eye tracking and content analysis to examine education, etc.[122] Why should we not use eye tracking in addressing the many effects gaps posed by television courtroom broadcasting and the Supreme Court?

Kari–Jouko Raiha, Professor of Computer Science at the Finnish University of Tampere and project coordinator of the Communication by Gaze Interaction (COGAIN) project states that we should "think of all of the other potential applications for this technology that we just haven't thought about, or imagined yet."[123] Eye tracking in the context of examining certain effects of television courtroom broadcasting is recommended by the author as one such application. To use the description of Tom Armstrong and Bunmi Olatunji in a different eye tracking context, it "provides a more direct and continual measure of limitations in more manual measurements."[124] It also has potential to overcome the limitations of opinion reports, opinion self reports and opinion observer reports. Furthermore, it can be used to test and validate opinion reports. "[E]ye movements are a direct indicator of overt attention" and provides "a highly direct measure of visual attention, eye systems also allow continuous measurement of eye movements."[125] We should be researching this in the context of television courtroom broadcasting.

We should also not automatically accept common sense views just because they appear to be logical or common sense. We should still seek to weigh them, analyse and research them. That many commentators and proponents may feel that many of the in–court effects issues are moot because we now no longer have the very large and bulky cameras, cables and equipment as were initially used in courts, does not mean we should stop research. In fact, the contrary should be the case, because the research tools available have now increased so much. We now have significantly advanced research tools with eye trackers which the Supreme Court never thought possible. We should avail of the opportunity presented.

H.C. Schmidt also states that the current research in psychology into videotaped confessions is motivated by the Supreme Courts treatment of confession evidence cases.[126] It is surprising that more research has not been undertaken into the effects of television courtroom broadcasting, given that the Supreme Court first called for empirical research studies as far back as the *Estes*[127] case in 1965.

One of the advantages of eye tracking is that it permits testing and direct observation of fixation, focus and attention.[128] Eye tracking research also has the advantage that is tracks and documents exactly what people see – and what they ignore.[129]

The time has come to address the research challenge set by the Supreme Court and also to ensure that the research effort into the effects of television courtroom broadcasting advances beyond the criticism that "[s]ocial scientists measure the intelligence of monkeys more effectively than courts have attempted to ascertain the effects of television in the courtroom."[130] It is time to move beyond limited opinion self reports and opinion reports and embrace eye tracking research.

Eye tracking can be particularly beneficial in addressing distraction effect research. We should embrace the opportunity. This involves expanding upon the initial proof of concept demonstration work of the author (see Chapter 18), and also the suggestions of the author that eye tracking can address part of the Supreme Court challenge.

NOTES

1. S.L. Alexander, "Mischievous Potentialities": A Case Study of Courtroom Camera Guidelines, Eight Judicial Circuit, Florida, 1989 (Ph.D diss., University of Florida, 1990), 39.
2. Ibid.
3. R.E.R. Stewart, The Changing Relationship Between Camera and the Courts (MA diss., Florida Atlantic University, 1998), 9.
4. See Overview, www.fixation2010.se/overview, last accessed on April 30, 2010.
5. For a brief review and introduction to visual attention research, see A. Duchowski, Eye Tracking Methodology, Theory and Practice (London: Springer, 2007), 3 –13.
6. See ibid regarding eye tracking techniques generally, 52–86.
7. J. Nielsen and K. Pernice, Eyetracking Web Usablility (Berkely, CA: New Riders, 2009); M. Wedel and R. Pieters, Eye Tracking for Visual Marketing (Hanover, MA: now Publisher, 2008), Foundations and Trends in Marketing, vol. 4; J.M. Spector, Handbook of Research on Educational Communications and Technology (New York: Lawrence Erlbaum Associates, Taylor and Francis, 2008). See also J.M. Henderson, ed., Real–world Scene Perception (New York: Psychology Press, Taylor and Francis, 2005); G. Hatfield, Perception and Cognition: Essays in the Philosophy of Psychology (Oxford: Clarendon Press, 2009); C. Bundesen and T. Habekost, Principles of Visual Attention: Linking Mind and Brain (Oxford: Oxford University Press, 2008); P. Shah and A. Miyake, The Cambridge Handbook of Visuospatial Thinking (Cambridge: Cambridge University Press, 2005).
8. S.F. Davis, Handbook of Research Methods in Experimental Psychology (Oxford: Blackwell, 2003), 367, 378.
9. W. Petkanas, Cameras on Trial: An Assessment of the Educational Affects of News Cameras in Trial Courts (Ph.D diss., New York University, 1990), 118.
10. Ibid.
11. T–R Valikoski, The Criminal Trial as a Speech Communication Situation (Tampere, Finland: University of Tampere, 2004), 178.
12. T. Armstrong and B.O. Olatunji, What They See Is What You Get: Eye Tracking of Attention in the Anxiety Disorders, American Psychological Society, March, 2009, www.apa.org/science/about/psa/2009/03/science–briefs.aspx, accessed August 13, 2012.
13. Ibid.
14. See L.J. Ware, Monitoring Visual Attention in Videotaped Interrogations: An Investigation of the Camera Perspective Bias (MSc diss., Ohio University, 2006), 11.
15. See www.prsresearch.com/prs–tools/, May 25, 2010, accessed August 13, 2012.

16. An example is S. Josephson and M. Holmes, Have You Seen Any of These Men? Looking at Whether Eyewitnesses Use Scanpaths to Recognize Suspects in Photo Lineups, ETRA, Proceedings of the 2010 Symposium on Eye–Tracking Research & Applications, Austin, Texas (22 – 24 March, 2010).

17. E. Loftus, G. Loftus and J. Messo, Some Facts About 'Weapon Focus,' Law and Human Behaviour 11:1 (1987) 55–62, at n. 43 at 55. More recently, see for example, J.Y. Kwak. Remembering Faces: Using Eye Movement Measures to Investigate Differences Between True and False Memory (Ph.D diss., University of California, 2009).

18. As originally used by G.R. Loftus and N.H. Mackworth, Cognitive Determinants of Fixation Location during Picture Viewing, Journal of Experimental Psychology 4:4 (1978) 565–572.

19. See description in L.J. Ware, above, 34–35.

20. This is also noted ibid, 35.

21. H.C. Schmidt, Effects of Interrogator Tactics and Camera Perspective Bias on Evaluations of Confession Evidence (MSc diss., Ohio University 2006), 3.

22. G.D. Lassiter and A.A. Irvine, Videotaped Confessions: The Impact of Camera Point of View on Judgements of Coercion, Journal of Applied Social Psychology 16 (1986) 286–276. Referred to in H.C. Schmidt, above, 9–10.

23. The author refers to camera perspective bias issues in Ireland, see P. Lambert, Confessions and Camera Perspective Bias, Bar Review (December, 2010), 128–130.

24. See www.innocenceproject.org, and as referred to in H.C. Schmidt, above, 11.

25. See H.C. Schmidt, above, 25–26.

26. G.D. Lassiter and A.A. Irvine, above, 286–276. Referred to in H.C. Schmidt, above, 26.

27. Ibid.

28. See for example G.D. Lassiter, P.J. Munhall, R.J. Ploutz–Snyder and D.L. Breitbecher, Illusory Causation: Why It Occurs, Psychological Science 13 (2002), 299–305, as referred to in H.C. Schmidt, above, 28.

29. See H.C. Schmidt, above, 31.

30. L.J. Ware, above.

31. W.A. Geller, Police Videotaping of Suspect Interrogations and Confessions: A Preliminary Examination of Issues and Practices, A Report to the National Institute of Justice, Washington, DC: US Department of Justice (1992); S.M. Kassin, The Psychology of Confession Evidence, American Psychologist 52 (1997), 221–233; and G.D. Lassiter, Illusory Causation in the Courtroom, Current Directions in Psychological Science 11 (2002): 204–208; each as referred to in L.J. Ware, above, 10.

32. Overview, www.fixation2010.se/overview, accessed April 30, 2010, above, 157. There are also different types of research design, see ibid, 159 et seq.

33. R.J.K. Jacob and K.S. Karn, Eye Tracking in Human–Computer Interaction and Usability Research: Ready to Deliver the Promises, in J. Hyona, R. Radach and H. Deubel, eds., The Mind's Eye: Cognitive and Applied Aspects of Eye Movement Research (Amsterdam: The Netherlands: Elsevier Science, 2003), 573–605, referred to ibid, 173. Such research relies on sophisticated software (see reference ibid, 88–91. Detailed experience and expertise with software, computers, computer science and statistics can also be a prerequisite to undertaking such studies. Note also, ibid, 171), and hardware tools, as well as calibration of those tools (see comments in relation to calibration issues, ibid, 87–99, and 301).

34. Also V. Sundstedt, Eye Tracking in User Studies, SIGGRAPH 2009, New Orleans, www.siggraph.org/s2009/, accessed August 13, 2011, and also www.scss.tcd.ie/Veronica.Sundstedt/, accessed June 12, 2010.

35. Ibid.

36. See A.T. Duchowski, above, 181 *et seq*. See also C. Morimoto and M.R.M. Mimica, Eye Gaze Tracking Techniques for Interactive Applications, Computer Vision and Image Understanding 98:1 (2005): 4–24.

37. A.T. Duchowski, ibid, 203 et seq.

38. Ibid, 205. Also V. Sundstedt, Eye Tracking in User Studies, SIGGRAPH 2009, above.

39. Ibid, 205. Also, M. Bingemann, Eye–tracking Device Watches You Watching Ads, PC World Business, 10 May, 2007, www.pcwprld.idg.com.au/article/182716/eye–tracking_device_watches_watching_a... , accessed 30 April, 2010.

40. See, for example, www.setcan.com/eyelock.html, referring to the EyeLock training system which comprises a forward focus camera and two eye trackers, all of which are encompassed in a pair of glassed that a combat or police trainee wears, accessed August 13, 2012.

41. See A.T. Duchowski, above, 205.

42. A.T. Duchowski, *ibid*, 206. One enterprising father also wrote his own iPhone application, called the iComm, to allow his disabled daughter to point instructions of the iPhone screen using her eyes. Reported in (Irish) Metro, May 11, 2010, 8.

43. A.T. Duchowski, ibid.

44. Ibid, 207 et seq.

45. Ibid, 241 et seq.

46. Ibid, 261 et seq. K. Lillington, IBM Plots the Future at Tech Summer Camp, Irish Times, July 29, 2005, referring to IBMs Webgaze Analyser for research how people read internet pages.

47. Ibid, 275.

48. See www.smi.com, accessed June 5, 2010.

49. Referred to by Tobii, at www.tobii.com, accessed April 30, 2010.

50. J.S. Agustin, as referred to in the eye tracking blog of Martin Tall, Martin Tall on Gaze Interaction, A Blog on Research and Developments in Eye Tracking and Gaze Interaction, http://gazeinteraction.blogspot.com/2009/04/research–paper–on–itu–gaze–tracker–that.html, accessed August 13, 2012.

51. See Eye Tracking, at the blog http://jeffnolan.com/wp/2010/03/25/eye–tracking/, accessed April 30, 2010. Note also Q. Ji and X. Yang, Real–Time Eye, Gaze, and Face Pose Tracking for Monitoring Driver Vigilance, Real–Time Imaging 8:5 (2002): 357–377.

52. D. Silver and A. Biggs, Keystroke and Eye–Tracking Biometrics for User Identification (2008), http://citeseerx.ist.psu.edu/viewdoc/summary?doi=10.1.1.88.4306. Accessed June 5, 2012.

53. See www.eyetracking.com, accessed April 30, 2010.

54. For example, see V. Sundstedt, Eye Tracking in User Studies, SIGGRAPH 2009, above.

55. See An Affordable Future for Eye Tracking in Sight, www.physorg.com/news63294534.html, accessed April 30, 2010.

56. See also D. Richardson and M. Spivey, Eye Tracking: Research Areas and Applications, in G. Bowlin and G. Wnek, Encyclopedia of Biomaterials and Biomedical Engineering, August 31, 2004.

57. See www.tobii.com, accessed April 30, 2012.

58. See www.eyetracking.com, accessed April 30, 2012.

59. See www.smivision.com/en/gaze–and–eye–tracking–systems/home.html, accessed June 5, 2010.

60. See www.arringtonresearch.com/, accessed June 5, 2012.

61. See www.asleyetracking.com/Site/, accessed June 5, 2012.

62. See www.smi.com, accessed June 5, 2012.

63. See www.polhemus.com, accessed 5 June 5, 2012.

64. Fixation 2010, Stockholm, Sweden, June 21–22, 2010. See www.fixation2010.se/, accessed April 30, 2010. Note also the Communication by Gaze Interaction (COGAIN) eye tracking project, which aims, inter alia, to advance the technologies, and attempt to reduce the substantial cost of eye trackers. See An Affordable Future for Eye Tracking in Sight, www.physorg.com/news63294534.html, accessed April 30, 2010.

65. See http://etra.cs.uta.fi/, accessed June 12, 2010.

66. See Lund Eye Tracking Academy (LETA), www.humlab.lu.se/en/edciation/leta, accessed June 5, 2012.

67. For example, the Image Synthsis Group, Computer Science Department, Trinity College, Dublin, and the Department of Psychology, University College Dublin. The ISG was also involved in organising workshops in relation to eye tracking, see http://isg.cs.tcd.ie/iwet/Ab-

starct14.htm, last accessed on May 25, 2010. There are numerous researchers using eye trackers in the US.

68. Wickens et al refer to task analysis issues and research, see C.D. Wickens, M. Vincow and M. Yeh, Design Applications of Visual Spatial Thinking: The Importance of Frame of Reference, in P. Shah and A. Miyake, The Cambridge Handbook of Visuospatial Thinking (Cambridge: Cambridge University Press, 2005), 383–425, at 385 et seq. See also P. Shah, E. Freedman and I. Vekiri, The Comprehension of Quantitative Information in Graphical Displays, in P. Shah and A. Miyake, The Cambridge Handbook of Visuospatial Thinking (Cambridge: Cambridge University Press, 2005), 426–476, at 450 et seq regarding task demands.

69. C.D. Wickens, M. Vincow and M. Yeh, Design Applications of Visual Spatial Thinking: The Importance of Frame of Reference, in P. Shah and A. Miyake, above, at 415

70. See generally discussion of frame representation issues in C.D. Wickens, M. Vincow and M. Yeh, ibid, 387 et seq.

71. *Estes v Texas*, 381 US 532 (1965), 572. Warren, CJ.

72. See C.D. Wickens, M. Vincow and M. Yeh, ibid, 398 et seq.

73. Ibid, at 401.

74. Note that the Short Report in California did attempt to have observers in court to ascertain if the courtroom actors were effected by the cameras. However, they did not have the benefit of eye trackers, nor do they appear to have been tested for confidence. Indeed the test recording sheet does not appear to rate whether or how many times a particular courtroom actor is (a) distracted by and (b) focuses at the television camera. Schmidt used a press button system once the subject perceived a target effect. See H.C. Schmidt, above, 30.

75. See example reference to same at www.eyetracker.co.uk/, accessed 12 June, 2012.

76. In terms of head mounted display applications see discussion in C.D. Wickens, M. Vincow and M. Yeh, ibid, 406 et seq.

77. Note recent research by M, L.–H. Vo and W., X. Schneider, A Glimpse is Not a Glimpse: Differential Processing of Flashed Scene Previews Lead to Differential Target Search Benefits, Visual Cognition 18:2 (2010): 171–200.

78. See C.D. Wickens, M. Vincow, and M. Yeh, ibid, above, 383–425, at 402.

79. See SMI article of this heading available at www.smi.com, last accessed on 5 June, 2010.

80. See E.E. Mayer, Multimedia Learning: Guiding Visuospatial Thinking with Intructional Animation, in P. Shah and A. Miyake, above, 477–508, at 479.

81. Of course we also have other issues to consider in dealing with measuring audience education and information gain, such as understanding, coding, differences between pictures, videos, text and audio, different channels and different speeds. See general comments in E.E. Mayer, E.E., Multimedia Learning: Guiding Visuospatial Thinking with Intructional Animation, *ibid*, 477–508, at 479–481.

82. See H.C. Schmidt, above, generally, and 39, and also references therein.

83. See L.J. Ware, above, 18–19, and references therein.

84. M, L.–H. Vo and W., X. Schneider, above, the EyeLink eye tracker described at 179.

85. Ibid, 187.

86. Ibid, 191. The information shown to the groups was different, see 192, ibid.

87. C.C. Williams, Not all Visual Memories Are Created Equal, Visual Cognition 18:2 (2010): 201–228.

88. Ibid, 224.

89. Ibid, 226.

90. R. Graham, C.K. Friesen, H.M. Fichtenholtz and K.S. LaBar, Modulation of Reflexive Orienting to Gaze Direction by Facial Expressions, Visual Cognition 18:3 (2010): 331–368.

91. Ibid, 339.

92. H. Rutherford and J. Raymond, Effects of Spatial Cues on Locating Emotional Targets, Visual Cognition 18(3) 2010, 389–412.

93. Ibid, 389.

94. J. Holsanova, N. Holmberg and K. Holmqvist, Reading Information Graphics: The Role of Spatial Contiguity and Dual Attention Guidance, Applied Cognitive Psychology 22 (2008) 1–12, at 1.

95. Ibid, 1–12. The main measures of online reading compared were reading order; reading time; and text–graphic integration. Ibid, 8.

96. Ibid, 1, 10.

97. Ibid, 1.

98. See references in R. Khosla, J. Simola, J. Salojarvi and I. Kojo, Using Hidden Markov Model to Uncover Processing States from Eye Movements in Information Search Tasks, Cognitive Sytems Research 9 (2008): 237–251, and 238. R. Khosla, et al researched different instructional tasks, namely, word search, question – answer task and finding subjectively most interesting answer, and tracking time for the various tasks. Ibid, 238–240. They also refer to different subject states, namely, scanning, reading and decision state. Ibid, 245–246, and 249. The decision state suggested a more careful analysis, Reading Information Graphics: The Role of Spatial Contiguity and Dual Attention Guidance, Applied Cognitive Psychology 22 (2008): 1–12, at 248.

99. See for example P. Chandler and J. Sweller, Cognitive Load Theory and the Format of Instruction, Cognition and Instruction 8 (1991): 293–332, as referred to J. Holsanova, in ibid.

100. J. Holsanova, N. Holmberg and K. Holmqvist, above, 1–12, at 2–3. See also the following as referred to ibid, namely, J.M. Henderson and F. Ferreira, Scene Perception for Psycholinguists, in J.M. Henderson and F. Ferreira, eds., The Interface of Language, Vision and Action: Eye Movements and the Visual World (New York: Psychology Press, 2004), 1–58; K. Holmqvist, J. Holsanova, M. Barthelson and D. Lundqvist, Reading or Scanning? A Study of Newspaper and Net Paper Reading, in J. Hyona, R. Radach and H. Duebel, eds., The Mind's Eye: Cognitive and Applied Aspects of Eye Movement Research (Amsterdam: Elsevier Science, 2003), 657–670; J. Holsanova, H. Rahm and K. Holmqvist, Entry Points and Reading Paths on the Newspaper Spread: Comparing Semiotic Analysis with Eye–Tracking Measurements, Visual Communication 5 (2005) 65–93; H. –J. Jeung, P. Chandler and J. Sweller, The Role of Visual Indocators in Dual Sensory Mode Instruction, Educational Psychology 17 (1997) 329–343; R.E. Mayer, Multimedia Learning (Cambridge: Cambridge University Press, 2001); R.E. Mayer, Principles for Managing Essential Processing in Multimedia Learning: Coherence, Signalling, Redundancy, Spatial Continuity and Temporal Contiguity Principles, in R.E. Mayer, ed., Cambridge Handbook of Multimedia Learning (New York: Cambridge University Press, 2005), 183–200; and K. Scheiter, E. Wiebe and J. Holsanova, Theoretical and Instructional Aspects of Learning with Visualizations, in R. Zheng, ed., Cognitive Effects of Multimedia Learning, (Hershey, PA: IGI Global, 2009).

101. See, for example, S. Folker, L. Sichelschmidt and H. Ritter, Processing and Integrating Multimodal Material: The Influence of Color–coding, in B.G. Bara , L.W. Barsalou and M. Bucciarelli , eds., Proceedings of the 27th Annual Conference of the Cognitive Science Society (Mahwah, MJ: Erlbaum) 690–695.

102. C. Bundesen and T. Habekost, Principles of Visual Attention: Linking Mind and Brain (Oxford: Oxford University Press, 2008) 16–102.

103. Consider generally C.D. Wickens, M. Vincow and M. Yeh, Design Applications of Visual Spatial Thinking: The Importance of Frame of Reference, in P. Shah, P. and A. Miyake, above, 383–425.

104. Ibid, at 384.

105. Ibid, 418–419.

106. Ibid, 383–425, at 384.

107. Just one example of glasses with eye trackers is the EyeLock training system. See www.setcan.com/eyelock.html, accessed on June 12, 2010.

108. C.D. Wickens, M. Vincow and M. Yeh, above, at 384–385.

109. Ibid, 385.

110. Schmidt, H.C., above, 18.

111. A.T. Duchowski, above, 239.

112. R. Khosla, J. Simola, J. Salojarvi and I. Kojo, Using Hidden Markov Model to Uncover Processing States from Eye Movements in Information Search Tasks, Cognitive Systems Research 9 (2008): 237–251, at 249, and also J.K. O'Regan, Eye Movements and Reading, in E. Kowler, ed., Eye Movements and Their Role in Visual and Cognitive Processes (Amsterdam, The Netherlands: Elsevier, 1990), 395–453; and J.K. O'Regan, Optimal Viewing Position in

Words and the Strategy–tactics Theory of Eye Movements in Reading, in K. Rayner, ed., Eye Movements and Visual Cognition: Scene Perception and Reading (New York: Springer–Verlag, 1992), 333–354, each as referred to ibid.

113. To use the words of W. Sato and S. Yoshikawa, Detection of Emotional Facial Expressions and Anti–Expressions, Visual Cognition 18:3 (2010): 369–388.

114. R. Khosla, J. Simola, J. Salojarvi and I. Kojo, Using Hidden Markov Model to Uncover Processing States from Eye Movements in Information Search Tasks, Cognitive Systems Research 9 (2008): 237–251, at 249–250.

115. *Estes v Texas,* 381 US 532 (1965), at 611–612. Stewart, J. Minority opinion.

116. Ibid, at 616. White, J. Minority opinion.

117. Note that the Short Report in California did attempt to have observers in court to ascertain if the courtroom actors were effected by the cameras. However, they did not have the benefit of eye trackers, nor do they appear to have been tested for confidence. Indeed the test recording sheet does not appear to rate whether or how many times a particular courtroom actor is (a) distracted by and (b) focuses at the television camera. Schmidt used a press button system once the subject perceived a target effect. See H.C. Schmidt, above, at p. 30. Also note 38.

118. See example reference to same at www.eyetracker.co.uk/, accessed June 12, 2012.

119. One example of glasses with eye trackers is the EyeLock training system. See www.setcan.com/eyelock.html, accessed on June 12, 2010.

120. In terms of head mounted display applications see discussion in C.D. Wickens, M. Vincow and M. Yeh, above, at 406 et seq.

121. To use the words of W. Sato and S. Yoshikawa, Detection of Emotional Facial Expressions and Anti–Expressions, Visual Cognition 18:3 (2010): 369–388.

122. An example of one study using both eye tracking and content analysis, see V.M.G. Barrios, et al, AdELE: A Framework for Adaptive E–Learning Through Eye Tracking, www.iicm.tu–graz.ac.at/home/cguetl/publications/2004/Garcia%20et%20al.%202004%20–%20IKNOW.pdf, accessed June 12, 2012.

123. Referred to at An Affordable Future for Eye Tracking in Sight, www.physorg.com/news63294534.html, accessed April 30, 2012.

124. Ibid.

125. Ibid.

126. H.C. Schmidt, above, 74.

127. *Estes v Texas*, 381 US 532 (1965), 532–616.

128. See L.J. Ware, above, 11.

129. See www.prsresearch.com/prs–tools/, accessed May 25, 2010, accessed 12 June, 2010.

130. J. Hirschhorn, Cameras in the Courtroom? No, Barrister (7:3)(1980): 7 and 9.

Chapter Thirteen

The Location Challenge

INTRODUCTION

It has already been indicated by the author that location is an important issue for television courtroom broadcasting. In particular, the location of the courtroom participants and of the in-court television camera. Equally, the location of the in–court camera operator — when present — is important and must be gauged. Location issues have never been properly addressed in the body of general and empirical TCB research to date. It is important to point out also that the research to date is flawed and unreliable to the extent that location issues and location factors are ignored.

This is important because the location of the television camera and the camera operator, respective to the location of the courtroom participants, could influence the courtroom participants in the courtroom. These issues also potentially influence the viewing audience outside of the courtroom.

The locus of the camera, and operator, can influence the courtroom participants and what goes on in the courtroom (in–court effects). Indeed, we need to assess courts and trial procedures[1] in this research also. In addition, there can be effects outside of the courtroom too.

In making assessments about the effects of television courtroom broadcasting we need to be aware of where the camera is located. Therefore, research studies need to record and indicate where the camera was located. By way of background and context, we will now look at how the literature occasionally and implicitly refers to location. However, the body of the general and empirical research both avoid the location issue. It is not addressed. This is an issue beyond the Supreme Court challenge, but is equally important to research.

LOCATION AND THE RESEARCH LITERATURE

The general non–social science studies not unexpectedly refer very little to the location issue. They do not record the actual location of cameras in particular experiments. This is unfortunate, as it means we cannot properly consider and evaluate the efficacy of those experiments as influenced by location factors.

However, what is more disturbing is how seldom the television camera location is recorded even in the empirical studies. The instances where there is some recordal of location available in the literature are referred to below.

It must be pointed out, also, that it does not appear that any of the non–empirical or the empirical research studies refer to the camera operator issue. While it can be said that, for example, of course the camera operator will always be beside the television camera, this is an oversimplistic appraisal. If we are properly researching for in–court distraction effects, we need to record if there is a camera operator present, how many, where, are they moving, record exactly what they are doing, are there assistants, etc.

In terms of the empirical research the following references to location and or operators have been identified by the author.

Nevada is referred to as requiring camera operators to dress appropriately for court.[2] The camera locations are nor recorded.

In James L. Hoyt's study it was indicated that in the camera obtrusively present control condition, the camera was "in front" of and pointing "directly at" the subjects.[3] No recorded diagram or photograph is produced.

The Short Report does not address the camera location effect issue, but does attach diagrams of some of the courts which mark the location of the television camera.[4]

Donald Shores refers to one of his control groups where the camera operator noticeably adjusts the camera and also turn it on and off.[5] The location issue is not mentioned.

Saul M. Kassin indicates that in his study the camera was "directed at the jury box from the witness stand."[6] No diagram was attached. The location issue is not mentioned.

Eugene Borgida, Kenneth G. DeBono and Lee A. Buckman used a camera behind a one way mirror, approximately 17 feet from the witnesses.[7] They do not refer to the location issue.

Alan D. Punches does record and include a diagram of where the two cameras were, both facing the subject head on from left and right.[8] He does not, however, refer to the location issue.

Allen Bukoff in his research on video recording refers as follows, television "[c]amera *position* and angle, closeness of focus, lighting, and other video production techniques may be able to influence a juror's perception of the physical attractiveness of the witness and attorneys by recording them in a more or less visually appealing view."[9] In his study, he indicated that the cameras and equipment were set up "approximately ten feet from the witness."[10] No diagrams, layouts or photographs of the experiment environment marking the cameras are included.

S.L. Alexander refers to Paul Goldman and Richard Larson who produces a diagram of camera location in one actual experimental case study.[11] Also referred to is feedback from one media representative, who felt that the judge(s) had too much discretion in relation to where equipment (and presumably cameras too) would be located.[12] One case is referred to where the pooled camera was located at the rear of the courtroom.[13] The location issue is not referred to or documented.

Paul Thaler in his case study of the Steinberg case, indicated that in the pre–trial stages, cameras were permitted in the "well" of the courtroom, but during the trial they were located at the end of the jury box behind the lawyers, thus shooting over the lawyers' shoulders.[14] In fact the lawyers were asked to move on a number of occasions to permit line of sight access to witnesses.[15] The location issue is not referred to.

The first federal pilot study refers to media representatives, who indicate that single camera footage of a case can cause a problem for gavel to gavel (G2G) recording, as occasionally courtroom participants move and or block the camera line of sight.[16] No camera locations are recorded.

The following did not refer to nor record television camera location, nor refer to the separate location issue itself, namely, the first federal pilot experiment,[17] Kermit Netteburg,[18] Donald Shores,[19] Steve Pasternack,[20] Anna R. Paddon,[21] Steve Esposito,[22] William Petkanas,[23] Stephen Kohm,[24] Ruthie Elizabeth Reeves Stewart,[25] Jessica Ossinger,[26] the New York study,[27] Teresa Keller[28] and Roberta Entner.[29] Neither does Susanna Barber,[30] Warren Freedman,[31] Ronald Goldfarb,[32] or Marjorie Cohn and David Dow.[33] Even Daniel Stepniak in one of the more recent texts (2008) does not address this issue.[34] It appears that the author is the first to raise location issues as a significant consideration to be addressed in effects research in future.

The Supreme Court in the three camera cases, *Estes*, *Chandler* and *Hollingsworth*, does not refer at all to the camera and location issues. Neither does the Supreme Court research challenge refer to the location problem, nor recommend this as an empirical research issue. The author has previously made the point that while the Supreme Court challenge refers to many issues to be empirically researched, we should not assume that the Supreme Court has definitively referred to all such potential issues and effects.

The Cameras in the Court: A State-By-State Guide,[35] produced by Radio Television Digital News Association in the US, refers to local state laws in the US relating to television courtroom broadcasting. The issue of location and effects is not referred to at all. However, in many instances, particularly the Tier 1 category identified therein, judges are given wide discretion[36] and, therefore, at least in these instances should be able to specify where the television camera(s) will be put. Most states also provide a limit on the number of cameras and or camera operators.[37] In one instance (North Carolina) the camera and camera personnel must be behind a partition or booth, albeit this may be waived.[38] This is the only location reference. The impact of the location issue is not addressed in the law reviewed.

The Guidelines for Media Access to Judicial Proceedings in the Rhode Island experiment (1981 – 1982) specified that the location of the television camera would be as directed or designated by the judge.[39] The importance of the location issues is not identified however.

TRUTV (FORMERLY COURTTV)

TruTV generally uses a single camera, without an operator in–court.[40] It is unclear if camera location, camera operator location, etc. are ever recorded and documented. Given that TruTV undertakes so much of the TCB that occurs, it would be useful for researchers, both now and in the future, to have these details documented and made available. A further issue is that future experimental periods, including the second Federal pilot TCB experiment period there should be a requirement to properly record location issue data.

DISTRACTION

The research needs to properly address in-court distraction effects. This has long been voiced as one of the reasons militating against camera access.

Unfortunately, camera location and actor location, and their interplay have never been addressed. Take lawyers for example. Sometimes cameras are places somewhere in front on where they are seated or standing. Therefore, the camera is within their cone of vision. It is logical, therefore, that the camera may be a distraction. If there is a camera operator present, this possibility of distraction may be enhanced.

However, if the television camera is located somewhere in the courtroom that is behind the lawyers, then the possibility of distraction in the lawyers' cone of vision is less. It is important therefore, that in considering effect and research of effects, that we know which actor we are considering, what effect, what cause, and where the cause (camera) in this instance, was located.

While a camera in front of the lawyers would seem to enhance the possibility of distraction possibilities, one should not assume that a camera located behind the lawyers precluded distraction effects. Psychological concerns still arise. There have already been recorded instances where television cameras and operators have recorded (and attempted to record) discussions between lawyer and client, and also record documents and notes on the lawyers table. It appears that this is the reason why these concerns are explicitly addressed and prohibited in some of the US state laws regulating television courtroom broadcasting.[41] When a lawyer is in discussion with his or her client, or witness, or other lawyers or assistants, he or she is frequently altering their cone of vision sideways or backwards. The television camera is, therefore, potentially within focus, even if behind.

The cases and the literature recognise that lawyers may not be the only person in court who might be distracted. Take the jury for example. Depending on the layout of a courtroom, they may be seated along one side of the courtroom. Let us assume the jury box is on the right hand side of the courtroom. They might then have to turn to their right to see the lawyers, the judge and the witness box. If the television camera is located in the upper end of the courtroom, then the camera will be in the right facing cone of vision of the jury. It is a potential distraction. If the camera moves, tilts, pans, zooms, etc. then the possibility of jury distraction may be higher. If there are lights on the camera, or there is a camera operator, then potential distraction effects may be heightened.

Yet, the location issue, and the recording and linking of the actual location of the camera and the location of the courtroom participants are not addressed in the research literature. Therefore, because of this gap, there is always going to be a limit to our proper appraisal and consideration of much of the research to date. The author recommends that future research address this gap.

We also need to consider the other courtroom participants. If we take the judge and the official court personnel, they are always seated at the top of the courtroom and facing towards everyone else. Consider further that some of the literature commentary has suggested that while there may be effects of television cameras in the courtroom, the judges will not be affected or will be the least affected. The basis of this suggestion is that the judges are professionally trained (and one might add experienced). However, if we now interpose the camera location issue, we note that regardless of where the television camera is located, the judge will be facing the camera (and the camera operator, if present). Is it not the case, therefore, that they are the courtroom actor whose cone of vision is most frequently going to see and have the opportunity to be distracted by the television camera (and operator)? Let us leave the issue of professional training aside for the moment, and which issue has not in any event been empirically researched. Can we still say that judges are the least likely courtroom participants who will be distracted by in-court television courtroom broadcasting? The location issue suggests not. Admittedly, many other issues arise, such as training, professional experience, media experience, psychology, etc. While a judge will have his or her professional training, depending on the jurisdiction, they may or may not have additional specific judicial training. Even where such additional and express judicial training exists, the literature nor research address how many judges are trained in camera issues. It is clear that the judicial distraction issue needs far more in depth consideration than any of the literature and research has to date afforded.

The official courtroom personnel have been mentioned only briefly in the literature. However, the same concerns arise. Indeed, one might argue that the concerns are somewhat escalated given that they may have less professional training than a judge. From a location perspective, their cone of vision is most likely more directed towards the camera than any other courtroom actor — with the exception of judges.

Without going into attraction issues and concerns in detail, the location issue and the recoding of the camera location is also relevant to a review of attraction issues and effects.

AUDIENCE EFFECTS/CAMERA PERSPECTIVE BIAS

The research in relation to camera perspective bias and confessions highlights how important it is to record camera and media issues which impact upon the legal process, and which may have effects. Only by recording and examining the data, and carrying out research in relation to such data can we properly assess effects. Where adverse effects are identified, we can then factor this into policy decisions to ameliorate such adverse effects.

In terms of the camera perspective bias effect, as was already highlighted, G. Daniel Lassiter and Audrey A. Irvine [42] showed that the same interview recorded on different camera locations showing (1) suspect only, (2) police officer only, and (3) both equally focused. Research subjects then viewed one of the videos. Subjects who saw the suspect only video, felt that there was less coercion.[43] Other research confirmed that suspect focus only videos, yielded significantly higher ratings for perceived guilt and voluntariness.[44] This has already led to policy changes.[45]

In any proper assessment of audience effects, and more importantly in comparing effect as between different forms of television courtroom broadcasting, we need to be aware of the layout of the courtroom, the location of the courtroom participants and the location of the television camera(s). Potentially, different locations can mean different audience effects, as different locations and frames can have different biases and effects in the context of video confessions. We need to expand our research knowledge of relevant effect research avenues.

CONE OF VISION

The concept of a cone of vision of courtroom participants needs to be researched. It is important, the author argues, for all research of TCB and TCB effects to accurately record where each individual courtroom actor is located, and to indicate and record where the television camera is located. If the television camera moves and is in more than one location, the exercise of recording location is obviously more difficult, but nonetheless necessary. Only when these two specifics are recorded, can we then consider the direction and cone of vision of the individual courtroom actor in question.

That enables us to research and examine whether the television camera is feasibly within the cone of vision, whether it is proximate–central or proximate–peripherally. When such information is recordable, it allows us to then consider research and distraction effect issues properly and methodically. We are also better able to begin designing particular experiments with eye trackers. There is no point, for example, introducing an eye tracker to a mock lawyer subject (real or otherwise) standing at the front of the courtroom if the fixed tripod television camera is located at the back of the courtroom or on a balcony at the back of the courtroom. It is not within their cone of vision.[46] That is not to say that there can be no other effects, other than distraction.[47]

In designing experiments for distraction and eye tracking in actual court settings, we need to respect the actual use of a normal courtroom. We need to be cognizant of cone of vision and location issues. We need to record these and we need to incorporate this knowledge into our distraction effects eye tracking experiments in future.

OBSERVER LOCATIONS

Few studies, whether general or empirical have sought to use trained independent observers in court to watch for actual in–court camera effects, and to seek to gauge and measure these effects. The Short Report[48] is one of the few studies which used observers for part of its research.

However, no research, including the Short Report, records where the observers were located in each of the courtrooms being examined. While Short does provide some diagrams of courts and where the television cameras was located, it is important also that any parties looking at the Short Report subsequently, should also be able to consider and assess where the observers were viz a viz the cameras and the respective courtroom participants.

As pointed out elsewhere, the Short Report and most studies do not begin the data collection process prior to the cameras entering the court. The baseline for recording effects against, is absent.

It is noted elsewhere that there is increasing research in relation to camera perspective bias. This field of research has found that the camera focus, and who is in the focus of the camera, can influence viewers perceptions of recorded confession interviews. In terms of TCB effects, we need to consider camera focus and camera location.

There is further research separate from the camera perspective bias research[49] which may be relevant to TCB. There is also research which suggests that fixed versus moving cameras can have different effects on perception.[50] This is something which is not considered in terms of e.g. the wide disparity of camera footage shown in TCB.

These issues are also extremely relevant to the author's suggestion that eye trackers should be used for TCB effects research, in particular distraction effects. There is also related research other than eye tracking research.[51] Certain research also uses television cameras to measure movements.[52] While not directly considered presently, even this research should be investigated further to see if it could be applicable to TCB research. Helen L. Westcott found that variations in production factors and type/length of camera shot leads to different results and effects.[53]

One early non–TCB study used the terms "field of view," and incidentally found effects and decision errors relating to the television camera field of view and the size of the research targets in the view.[54]

The "design consideration"[55] and its relationship with in–court and out–of–court effects and potential effects is entirely lacking in the experiments and examples of television courtroom broadcasting to date. The author recommends that this as a significant area for future research. In addition, it is suggested that a framework of design considerations should be developed for future TCB experiments, pilots and rollouts – if and where permitted, of course.[56]

EYE TRACKING AND LOCATION

Generally, neither the general or empirical research of television courtroom broadcasting effects refers to the importance of the layout of the courtroom nor the recording of where the television camera is located in the courtroom. These are critical flaws in the research to date. These flaws need to be addressed. Just one of the implications of this gap is that it is not possible to compare the results of one study with another.

It is also not possible to assess the effects of the camera on any of the courtroom participants.

The research does not refer to or record the layout of the courtroom and the location of the television cameras. None of the empirical and general research reviewed includes a diagram addressing the layout and location issues. The relevant research such that it is, and the implications for future research are referred to below.

One exceptions is the Short Report. It does record the layout of some, but not all, of the courtrooms where research was undertaken. It included diagrams of seven courtroom and the camera locations.[57] However, even this empirical research is flawed as it does not do so for all cases researched. It is also typical of the general and empirical research by not appreciating the importance of recording details of the courtroom and cameras for comparative purposes. One of the remits of the report was also in relation to effects research. Height issues are also ignored.

The Short Report fails to appreciate that one cannot research and assess effects in–court without factoring in the location of the courtroom participants and the location of the television camera. This is the first research to identify this important point. In terms of communications in the courtroom, Tuula–Riitta Valikoski notes that the communicative situation is formed by the purpose of the activity and the environment.[58]

Let us consider an example of this point.

DISTRACTION EFFECTS

If we wish to research distraction effects we need to incorporate the courtroom actor location and camera location. The Short Report refers to location issues in seven cases. Diagrams for the seven cases below were included,

- *Burnett v National Enquirer*;
- *People v Bittaker* (Sentencing);
- *People v Parnell*;
- *People v Robbins* (Opening and closing arguments only);
- *People v McDermand*;
- *People v Snyder*;
- *Michel v Dillard* (EMC Layout).[59]

Let us assume that we wish to research for distraction effects on the lawyers in the respective cases. If we look at the diagram for the case of *Burnett v National Enquirer*, we note that the single television camera is located behind the rail, which itself is located behind the counsel table. The lawyers will be (generally) looking forward. Their cone of vision is forward. Therefore, the lawyers do not have the television camera within their cone of vision. They cannot be distracted visually by the television camera. While there can be other effects, there is no visual distraction effects. The situation is similar in *People v Parnell* and *People v Snyder*.

The situation is different in the case of *People v Bittaker*, where we note that the television camera is located in advance of the lawyers, to the left. While it is not in the core of the cone of vision, it is still visible in the peripheral cone of vision.

In *People v Robbins* the courtroom layout means that the television camera is central in the cone of vision of the lawyers. The courtroom layout and camera location in *Michel v Dillard* also means that (one of) the television camera(s) is directly in the lawyers cone of vision.

Therefore, only in three of the Short Report cases can we say that there is potential visual distraction effects on the lawyers causes by the television camera (and or operator) in the courtroom. Without the courtroom layout and the location of the cameras and courtroom participants being recorded, we would not know this. We would not know that we should be focusing on these three cases for distraction effects on lawyers, and seeking to compare these cases with the distraction research in other studies. Unfortunately, the research is currently not sufficient to allow us to do this. If we are considering eye tracking technology for researching distraction effects on lawyers, our research of the courtroom layout, courtroom actor location, and the location of the television cameras, would tell us to focus on these three cases and or courtrooms. A further point is that eye tracking research of in–court distraction effects on lawyers may be less applicable to courts with the layout in the other cases referred to above.

However, we may wish to research other in–court distraction effects. Take witnesses for example. If we examine the courtroom layouts and locations, we can see that there is a television camera in the cone of vision of the witness in all seven cases referred to above (albeit in *People v Bittaker*, *People v Robbins* and *Michel v Dillard* the camera is in the peripheral cone of vision). Therefore, distraction effects and effects research is a live issue in each of these cases. Eye tracking technology as a research tool is applicable in all of the cases to examine witness distraction effects.

While we only refer to lawyers and witnesses above, the layout and location issues are important in relation to all courtroom participants.

CONCLUSION

The location issue is clearly important. Recording the camera and courtroom actor location is also very important. We need to address this in order to be satisfied we are undertaking proper research. It is also critical as it is one of the markers which allows us to compare research results.

Future research also needs to cross reference location issues and eye tracking research.

A perhaps complicating issue for research is the suggestion that American courtrooms are increasingly changing their layout to place the jury in more strategic locations.[60] This would appear relevant to research on courtroom design, courtroom processes as well as TCB effects issues.

It is recommended that all effects research in future must record and document the courtroom layout, and in the case of research studies conducted in locations other than actual courtrooms, the layout of the research environment. Taking cognizance of the layout and location issues is also a prerequisite in planning any effects research. Without taking these issues into account, the research remains flawed individually. It is also flawed in that it precluded comparison and the buildup of a useful body of effects research in respect of each of the effects issues being examined in similar studies.

NOTES

1. See generally, C.E. Smith, Courts and Trials: A Reference Handbook, (Santa Barbara, California: ABC–CLIO, 2003).
2. As referred to in K.L. Netteburg, Cameras in the Courtroom: Is a Picture Worth a Thousand Words? (Ph.D diss., University of Minnesota, 1980), 43.
3. J.L. Hoyt, Courtroom Coverage: The Effects of Being Televised, Journal of Broadcasting (1977): 487–495, at 491.
4. E.H. Short, and Associates, Evaluation of California's Experiment with Extended Media Coverage of Courts, Submitted to The Administrative Office for the Courts, The Chief Justice's Special Committee on the Courts and the Media and The California Judicial Council, September 1981, see 57–63. (Short Report).
5. D. Shores, The Effects of Courtroom Camera on Verbal Behavior: An Analysis of Simulated Trial Witness Testimony in Courtrooms Using Television Cameras (Ph.D diss., The University of Florida, 1981), 59.
6. S. Kassin, TV Cameras, Public Self–Consciousness, and Mock Juror Performance, Journal of Experimental Social Psychology 20 (1984): 336–349, at 339–340.
7. E. Borgida, K. DeBona and L.A. Buckman, Cameras in the Courtroom, The Effects of Media Coverage on Witness Testimony and Juror Perceptions, Law and Human Behaviour 14:5 (1990): 489–508, at 495–496.
8. A.D. Punches, The Cognitive Effects of Camera Presence on the Recall of Testimony in a Simulated Courtroom Setting (Ph.D diss., Colorado State University, Fort Collins, 1991): 33–34, at 40–41.
9. A. Bukoff. The Effects of Video Camera Techniques on the Pre–Deliberation Judgements and Perceptions of Role–Playing Jurors (Ph.D diss., Kent State University, 1984), 22. Emphasis added.
10. Ibid, 58.
11. S.L. Alexander. "Mischievous Potentialities": A Case Study of Courtroom Camera Guidelines, Eight Judicial Circuit, Florida, 1989 (Ph.D diss., University of Florida, 1990), 65, referring to P. Goldman and R. Larson, News Cameras in the Courtroom During *State v Solorzano*: End to the Estes Mandate?, Southwestern–Nevada Law Review 10 (1978): 2001–2061.
12. Ibid, 129.
13. Ibid, 138.
14. P. Thaler, The Impact of the Television Camera on Courtroom Participants: A Case Study of the Joel Stenberg Murder Trial (Ph.D diss., New York University, 1990), 62.
15. Ibid.

16. M.T. Johnson and C. Krafka, Pilot Program Involving Electronic Coverage in Six US District Courts and Two Appeal Courts (Federal Judicial Centre, 1994): 37.
17. M.T. Johnson and C. Krafka, C. above.
18. K.L. Netteburg, Cameras in the Courtroom: Is a Picture Worth a Thousand Words? (Ph.D diss., University of Minnesota, 1980).
19. D. Shores, above.
20. S.R. Pasternack, The Effects of Perceived Community Pressure on Simulated Juror Guilt Attributions: An Experimental Study (Ph.D diss., The University of Tennessee, Knoxville, 1982).
21. A. R. Paddon, Television Coverage of Criminal Trials with Cameras and Microphones: A Controlled Experiment of Audience Effects (PhD diss., University of Tennessee, 1985).
22. S.A. Esposito, OJ TV: A Narrative Analysis of Television's Pretrial Coverage of the O.J. Simpson Case (Ph.D diss., Graduate School of Wayne State University, Detroit, Michigan, 1996).
23. W. Petkanas, Cameras on Trial: An Assessment of the Educational Affects of News Cameras in Trial Courts (Ph.D diss., New York University, 1990).
24. S.A. Kohm, I'm Not a Judge But I Play One On TV: American Reality Based Courtroom Television (PhD diss., Simon Fraser University, 2004).
25. R.E.R. Stewart, The Changing Relationship Between Camera and the Courts (MA diss., Florida Atlantic University, 1998): 1–2, and 32.
26. J. Ossinger, Electronic Access to Courtrooms: Television as an Educational Socializing Agent on the Judiciary (MA diss., The University of Maine, 2006).
27. New York State Committee to Review Audio–Visual Coverage of Court Proceedings, An Open Courtroom: Cameras in New York Courts (New York: Fordham University Press, 1997).
28. T.D. Keller, Cameras in Courtrooms: An Analysis of Television Court Coverage in Virginia (Ph.D diss., The University of Tennessee, 1992): 125.
29. R. Entner, The Image of the Judiciary: A Semiotic Analysis of Broadcast Trials to Ascertain its Definition of the Court System (Ph.D diss., New York University, 1993).
30. S. Barber, News Cameras in the Courtroom: A Free Press – Fair Trial Debate (Norwood, New Jersey: Ablex, 1987).
31. W. Freedman, Press and Media Access to a Criminal Courtroom (New York: Quorum Books, 1988).
32. R.L. Goldfarb, TV or Not TV: Television, Justice, and the Courts (New York: New York University Press, 1998), in particular 116 et seq.
33. Referring to M. Cohn, and D. Dow, Cameras in the Courtroom: Television and the Pursuit of Justice (New York: Rowman & Little, 2002).
34. D. Stepniak, Audio–Visual Coverage of Courts (Cambridge: Cambridge University Press, 2008).
35. Available at www.rtdna.org, accessed August 13, 2012.
36. Ibid.
37. Ibid.
38. Ibid.
39. Referred to and appended in J.R. Weisenberger, Cameras in the Courtroom: The Rhode Island Experience, Suffolk University Law Review (1983): 299–311, at 300 and 308.
40. D.A. Harris, The Appearance of Justice: Court TV, Conventional Television, and the Public Understanding of the Criminal Justice System, Arizona Law Review 35 (1993): 785–827, at 804.
41. See survey and summary of state laws at www.rtdna.org, accessed August 13, 2011.
42. G.D. Lassiter and A.A. Irvine (1986), above, 286–276. Referred to in H.C. Schmidt, above, 26.
43. Ibid.
44. See for example G.D. Lassiter, P.J. Munhall, R.J. Ploutz–Snyder and D.L Breitbecher, Illusory Causation: Why It Occurs, Psychological Science 13 (2002): 299–305, as referred to in H.C. Schmidt, above, 28.
45. See H.D. Schmidt, above, 31.

46. See Chapter 18.
47. Also see Chapter 18.
48. Short, Ernest H., and Associates, "Evaluation of California's Experiment with Extended Media Coverage of Courts, submitted to Administrative Office for the Courts; the Chief Justice's Special Committee on the Courts and the Media, and the California Judicial Council," (1981).
49. For instance, S.A. Koyama, Effects of Television Camera Angle, Locus of Control, and Two–sided/One–sides Persuasive Messages Upon Attitudes Toward Disabled People (diss., University of Washington, 1982).
50. For example, see, P. Kipper and C. Mills, Television Camera Movement as a Source of Perceptual Information, Journal of Broadcasting and Electronic Media 30 (1986) 295–307.
51. See for example, R.R. Mourant and R.J. Donaghue, Acquisition of Indirect Vision Information by Novice, Experienced, and Mature Drivers, Journal of Safety Research 9 (1977): 39–46.
52. A.P. Rudell, The Television Camera Used to Measure Movement, Behavior Research Methods and Instrumentation 11 (1979): 339–341.
53. H.L. Westcott, Children's Credibility on Camera: The Influence of Age and Production Factors, Children and Society 5 (1991): 254–265.
54. G. Rusis and H.L. Snyder, The Effects of TV Camera Field of View and Size of Targets Upon Air–to–ground Target Recognition, Human Factors, 7 (1965): 493–501.
55. To use the words of P. Baker, et al in another context. P. Baker, A. Fairchild, J. Pater, and A. Seavey, Community, Participation and Virtual Spaces: Design Considerations for Inclusivity, 10th European Conference on eGovernment, University of Limerick, June 17–18, 2010. Note also The Courtroom Design and Research Centre, http://coweb.cc.gatech.edu/courtnext/3 and related pages, accessed on August 13, 2011. This project does not appear to consider design, location and layout issues in terms of the influence and effects of TCB.
56. The author makes no recommendation whether for or against TCB per se.
57. E.H. Short and Associates, Evaluation of California's Experiment with Extended Media Coverage of Courts, Submitted to The Administrative Office for the Courts, The Chief Justice's Special Committee on the Courts and the Media and The California Judicial Council, September, 1981, see 57–63.
58. T–R Valikoski, The Criminal Trial as a Speech Communication Situation, (Tampere, Finland: University of Tampere, 2004): 116.
59. Short Report, above, 57–63.
60. As referred to in K.L. Netteburg, Cameras in the Courtroom: Is a Picture Worth a Thousand Words? (Ph.D diss., University of Minnesota, 1980), p. 167. Also, S.R. Hall and B.D. Sales, Courtroom Modifications for Child Witnesses: Law and Science in Forensic Evaluations (Washington, DC: American Psychological Association, 2008).

Chapter Fourteen

Education Effects Research

INTRODUCTION

Now we turn to one of the out-of-court issues, educational effects. We are familiar with the argument that television courtroom broadcasting will educate the public. However, is this correct? Does television courtroom broadcasting really educate? Has TCB, or any forms of TCB, been proven to educate? Is the research comprehensive? Is there a sufficient body of research?

The Supreme Court has not addressed how we should research the educational effects issues. The baseline and parameters for this empirical research was left unaddressed.

This chapter shall refer to the available empirical research, while the following chapter shall highlight some of the wider educational research issues, and many of which are not addressed in television courtroom broadcasting literature to date.

Some initial points arise. Firstly, there is no sustained body of empirical research of the educational effects of television courtroom broadcasting. Secondly, even the argument that (television) courtroom broadcasting is educational is grossly over simplistic. There are many issues which arise in any proper consideration of educational effects, even before conducting research and analysis for educational effects of television courtroom broadcasting. Additionally, the literature in discussing the educational argument does not even seek to distinguish educational television courtroom broadcasting from other educational courtroom broadcasting per se. Nor does it distinguish between different types of (educational) television courtroom broadcasting. Do some forms better educate than others?

Journalists and broadcasters frequently argue that television courtroom broadcasting will be educational and should therefore be permitted. However, they never say what the media will do to be educational nor what form, or forms, of television courtroom broadcasting the media will undertake to ensure educational television courtroom broadcasting and or educational effects. Nor do they indicate whether optimum educational courtroom broadcasting will be achieved nor what balance will be achieved as between education and, for example, ratings or news programming per se.

While we refer to some of these wider educational issues in the following chapter, it is worth pointing out how limited the debate and the research to date actually is. Susanna Barber in 1987, in the first book dedicated to courtroom broadcasting,[1] was not able to identify any empirical research on educational effects. Roberta Entner states that up until 1992, there was no research of how television used television courtroom broadcasting footage.[2] Ronald L. Goldfarb in 1998 did not find any educational research.[3] The Supreme Court in *Hollingsworth*[4] recently (2010) referred to Marjorie Cohen and David Dow,[5] yet those authors were also unable to refer to any empirical educational research whatsoever. Equally, Amanda Hiber in 2008 refers to no empirical educational research.[6] This is reflective of the literature generally.

EMPIRICAL RESEARCH REGARDING EDUCATIONAL EFFECTS

However, there is some empirical educational research and which the author identifies below. It will be seen that the number of such studies is small. Furthermore, the research is not complimentary, coordinated, replicated or verified. Almost entirely the research has ignored the need for initial baseline research. This is a major issue. It is important also because, if the opportunity is missed in a given jurisdiction, the window of opportunity does not (easily) repeat itself.

PETKANAS

William Petkanas undertook research of the educational affects of news cameras in trials.[7] He contextualises his research by referring to the New York State legislature's decision to permit experimentation with certain television courtroom broadcasting.[8] The legislature's decision was based on the belief that it would prove to be educational.[9]

Education is referred to as meaning that "public knowledge of the judicial system would rise and public confidence in the courts would be enhanced."[10] The Preamble to the law confirms that the purpose of the broadcasting was to educate and inform.[11] However, Petkanas points out that these educational effects have *not* been proven.[12] The mooted educational benefits were not shown in the research, which was conducted *before* and *after* the experiment.

Generally, the research where it exists tends be during or after the experiment, and gathers no baseline data *before* cameras are introduced.

Interestingly, the legislature went further than proponents, by expanded upon what it understood by "being educational." It gave four markers of what it meant by being educational. Educational courtroom broadcasting must increase public knowledge of the judicial system; increase public confidence; educate; and inform. (However, by referring to education, the definition becomes circular. It is also not clear if referring to "inform" means increasing awareness or, for example, increasing the mere "push" content available).

Petkanas defines the concepts of "audiovisual coverage," "confidence in the judicial system," "information sources," "enhancement," etc.[13] He also codes the television footage according to close up (CU), mid shot (MS), long short (LS), jump cut (JS), and title.[14] Television courtroom broadcasting general research and argument are not so exacting when dealing with television courtroom broadcasting.

Petkanas asks if the public's understanding of the judicial system was enhanced, when measured objectively? and also if public confidence was enhanced, when measured objectively?[15] One could also ask, and begin to test, whether the media increased their coverage of cases in order to increase education through the use of television courtroom broadcasting. Teresa Keller in one study (see below) found increasing television access does not increase the amount of legal news stories.

In relation to the New York experiment, Petkanas found that the

> television stations used pictures of courtroom proceedings as a substitute for the courtroom sketch artist. That is, there seemed to be little difference in most of the trial reporting with cameras and without them. However, ... [n]o comparative research has yet been done to determine if there are any differences, and if so, just what they are.[16] (See Anna R. Paddon).

It is sometimes said that as courtroom participants become more familiar with television cameras, the distraction effects diminish. (Implicitly, therefore, it is accepted that there are distraction effects). It is also frequently said that as the public see more television courtroom broadcasting, they will become more confident in the legal process. However, Petkanas did not find any correlation between reported familiarity with cases/judicial process and the confidence ratings of respondents.[17] There was no increased confidence.

Importantly, Petkanas undertook a study at the beginning and the end of the New York experiment. It, therefore, has an advantage over other studies. Petkanas found no statistically different answers at the end than at the beginning.[18] "Therefore, according to this measuring instrument, public knowledge and confidence in the courts did not increase or decrease after camera access was permitted in New York courts."[19] If "education" means mere "information," there was no increased educational effects demonstrated. "Public understanding of the judicial system and public confidence in the system were not enhanced as a result of allowing camera access to courtrooms, as measured by the survey conducted."[20]

Researching and recording baseline data at the very beginning is important. Unfortunately, generally the television courtroom broadcasting research does not do this. It is important to appreciate also, that the opportunity to do this is limited temporally in each courtroom.

A further result was that "[m]ost of the public either cannot remember when news reports include pictures from the courtroom, or cannot distinguish news reports made with cameras inside courtrooms from news reports made without camera coverage. The latter group increased over the period of this study."[21] This has a number of implications, not least in relation to how the media use television courtroom broadcasting footage and the forms of television courtroom broadcasting which predominates. Does educational television courtroom broadcasting need to be presented and differentiated from conventional television programming to be successful are education? Which forms of television courtroom broadcasting are (potentially) most efficient at achieving educational effects? Clearly significantly more research is needed.

Petkanas notes that initial examination of case transcripts suggests that there are differences between reports with and without cameras present.[22] This requires further research, he suggests.[23]

Another suggestion for research from the author, might be an assessment of effects on sentences before and after introducing television courtroom broadcasting. A further suggestion would be to research the length of cases with and without cameras. It should, however, be conducted after an extended baseline research period, and across a full range of cases.

PADDON

Anna R. Paddon[24] investigated certain audience effects by comparing a videotaped criminal trial and the same trial with a sketch artist. She tested recall of information, presentation appeal and willingness to be a juror.[25] Based on the results of this study, she states that "cameras enhance information gain but cause no attitude change that would imperil justice."[26]

In terms of the empirical audience effects research generally, she notes that such research "could give empirical support for the hopes or warn of the pitfalls expected from news cameras and microphones in the courtrooms, but unfortunately few of these have been done."[27] Empirical research is particularly important. Unfortunately, we need significantly more empirical research.

She refers to the various sides in the educational debate, one arguing that access will lead to an "increase in news about judicial matters and hence increased public understanding of the courts," while others argue that the judicial process is not designed or intended to educate.[28] However, Paddon does not examine whether media court reports increase as a result of access, nor whether there are any actual audience or public educational effects.

In terms of what it may mean to be educational, Paddon refers to W. Stone and S.G. Edlin[29] who refer to the hope that television courtroom broadcasting will act as a socializing agent and improve understanding of the judicial system, increase awareness of citizen rights and responsibilities, and increase judicial scrutiny – in turn leading to enhanced competence of lawyers and judges.[30] Neither the authors or Paddon deal with the issue of defining what "information" and "education" are, and how to measure these effects.

In terms of the social science effects research to date she refers to James Hoyt (1977) and K. Netterburg (1980).[31] She notes Hoyt's study as finding that reliability of testimony improved when witnesses were aware they were being televised, and Netterburg's study as over 50% incorrectly remembering the whole outcome of a highly publicised case, while 36% were not aware of the trial.[32] Hoyt's research, however, deals with in–court–effects, not out–of–court educational effects.

Paddon researches five hypotheses[33] several of which were not supported by her research findings.[34] The separate condition variables used are: courtroom with video camera; sketches and voice over; and talking head presenter.[35] However, while she concludes that there was better aided recall of factual information in the videotape group than the sketch or talking head groups,[36] this requires further research. Her other effects hypothesis which were not found to be supported. The basis for her conclusion that there is no attitude that would imperil justice[37] is relying upon only one finding. She notes the study comprised of one viewing only; the content was only of part of the case; and that "[e]ven though television viewers see only part of the courtroom testimony in the abbreviated coverage given by newscasts, their perceptions of a defendant's guilt or innocence is unlikely to be affected by what is seen on television." The latter statement in particular is open to question. There is a significant issue in terms of how different forms and frames can influence viewers perceptions and opinion. It is highlighted above how research in relation to how the manner of videotaping of false confession interviews can influence perceptions of guilt and voluntariness of confessions.[38] Paddon is also suggesting that television footage does not influence perceptions of guilt and voluntariness. Is this suggesting that television has no effects, even educational?

She comments on the data that persons were more willing to serve as jurors if assured they would not be recognised from photographs.[39] Paddon's comments that this supports the rationale for having guidelines and rules restricting the filming of jurors in court, and which she states most US states have in place.[40] She feels that the media is happy to accommodate these rules and furthermore that it is possible to cover a trial "without exposing jurors to the community pressure that could result if they become instantly recognizable."[41] But for regulations and restrictions, she accepts that there could be adverse effects on juries.

Paddon appropriately cautions against generalising this study, but agrees that "experiments are the best evidence for causal direction."[42] We need more empirical research. This is clear. Padden's research, and all of the empirical research, needs to be copied, replicated and validated. Only that way do we attain an acceptable body of research in relation to television courtroom broadcasting effects.

She concludes that more research is needed, particularly of the effect on trial fairness and the effects on public knowledge and attitudes.[43] It does not appear that she is distinguishing the viewing audience from the wider public, which also requires to be researched. There does not appear to be even an initial study on this issue yet.

The present author suggests that in addition to significantly more research, we also need ongoing and longitudinal research. Once cameras are permitting in a given jurisdiction, or that an experiment ends, should not mean that the research effort should immediately stop. There are ongoing issues and changes in the courts and in the media presentations that need to be monitored and researched as well as the audience and courtroom actor effects. Some effects may only appear after time. While Paddon does not say this, she does note that there is a need for continual and ongoing changes and adaptations.[44] Television courtroom broadcasting, and the related issues, will not remain fixed and constant, and hence there is a need for ongoing research and policy changes on foot of such research and as issues arise where such broadcasting is permitted.

NETTEBURG

Kermit Netterburg[45] examines one educational hypothesis in his six research hypotheses, namely, whether television courtroom broadcasting educates the public. While the proposition was not supported by the results, over the series of research questions for this proposition, it was found that the "low–coverage community [in the study] has significantly more knowledge about court procedures than [the] high–coverage community."[46] This appears to support the proposition that even increasing amounts of television courtroom broadcasting does not increase knowledge and or education of the audience and or the public.

OSSINGER

Jessica Ossinger[47] reviewed the educational issues in terms of television as an educational socializing agent of the judiciary. This is a narrow definition, or subset of what "education" means. She undertook an attitude and perception survey. The results were that residents in Maine do not watch a lot of courtroom [television] programmes and therefore base their "opinions and confidence levels in the judicial system on other factors"[48] and other media.

It would be interesting to research whether other sources of news and information on the courts are reduced or supplanted once television courtroom broadcasting is introduced. Do people use both sources or migrate over to television courtroom broadcasting? This study suggests that in Maine they do not move over. Further research is required however. How different forms interact with each other requires research. A separate and additional issue is the literature which says that people get most of their information and news from television. That does not mean they get all of or most of their information and news on particular issues from television. However, most information and or news on the courts come from other sources. Could television courtroom broadcasting diminish this? Greater research is needed. We also need greater granularity in terms of considering the educational issues.

KOHM

Stephen Arthur Kohm[49] carried out an extensive content analysis of reality based courtroom broadcasting programmes (Judge Judy and People's Court). He finds an increasing tendency to use court judgements as a form of entertainment and spectacle. His research leaves questions in terms of what form or forms of "telemediated courtroom"[50] programming we want, and for what particular purpose. If we seek to have educational television courtroom broadcasting, do we have choices and decisions to make in terms of the content, style and form of such broadcasting? This author suggests that the answer is yes. For example, how tenable is it to suggest, as proponents do, that all forms of television courtroom broadcasting will educate, and furthermore all will educate equally?

This research supports the forms of television courtroom broadcasting research of the author. It also highlights how court judgements are increasingly used for entertainment – not education.

KELLER

Teresa Keller found that during the period of her review, the number of courts open to television cameras did not increase the number of legal or court stories in the television media.[51]

The news editors in Virginia felt the public were more confused than educated by television courtroom broadcasting, due to disparities between what courts were shown in the Virginia and what out of state programming content was shown.[52] The issue of content, comparable and indigenous, is not researched. All issues influencing what affect television courtroom broadcasting programme content has, should be researched and considered.

ENTNER

Roberta Entner notes that up until 1992, there was no research of how television used television courtroom broadcasting footage.[53] She undertook a semiotic analysis of visual parts of a sample of television courtroom broadcasts. Amongst other things, she states that "the camera is not a neutral transmitter of information."[54] She states that television courtroom broadcasting research must not only examine the event being filmed, but also how it is filmed.[55]

She finds that generally defendants were not shown in a neutral aspect but rather in "tightly framed" and "unsympathetic shots."[56] A "suggestion of guilt was implied."[57] Closeups of the weapon and the defendant often occurs.[58] In another case the victim's weeping mother was juxtaposed with the defendant.[59] Some cases emphasised visuals which encouraged excitement.[60]

Television is also very different from traditionally understood education.[61] The audience does not progress from the start to finish of a course, nor always view in exact sequence.[62] "A real danger of televised trials, is the audience's acceptance of the visual assertion as an argument, allowing this use as a substitute for reasoning."[63]

Roberta Entner states that,

> [c]onsidering that the New York State Legislature's reason to permit cameras in the courts was to enhance public knowledge and confidence in the judicial system, it is unsettling to realize that several production requirements may not help achieve this aim. To begin with, time on network news is limited. Trials are reduced to seconds of visuals. In this form, complex ideas must be either ignored or treated simplistically.[64]

In addition, can there be other unintended effects? We must consider the view that television is not "neutral."[65] There can also be different kinds and levels of education, with the one intended not being the one achieved.[66] Also, television "may offer little control over educational messages."[67]

FIRST FEDERAL PILOT EXPERIMENT STUDY

The first federal pilot experiment study in 1994 was partly empirical, in that it carried out a public opinion survey and content analysis of television courtroom broadcasting reports.[68] However, it was not explicitly researching educational effects.

The content found that the footage that was submitted for analysis revealed that the news footage was not used directly, but had reporter voice-over, which provided only "basic" information on the facts of the cases, and provided little in terms of the legal process.[69] Content analysis was defined as "the objective and systematic description of communicative material."[70] However, the content analysis only involved certain cases, some of which were those chosen and furnished by the media.[71] The report, therefore, cautions against overreliance on the results.[72] Less than 58% of requests for footage were complied with, with a total of ninety reports being analysed.[73] There was an average of 56 seconds of courtroom footage per story.[74] Also, 63% of footage was narrated over by the broadcasters.[75] Most stations also used a mixture of footage from inside and outside the courtroom.[76] This latter point is not yet addressed in the empirical education effects research.

However, while educational effects research was not expressed as an aim of the research, the content analysis study did examine whether "basic educational information" was provided using information scales or codes.[77] The codes were (1) identification as a civil matter (95% of non first day stories did not); (2) identification of stage of proceeding covered (77% did not); (3) identification of whether jury present or not (74% did not); (4) description of day's proceedings; and (5) discussion of the next step in the proceedings.

Interestingly the research distinguishes single day and multi day proceedings,[78] which is not explicitly referred to in most educational effects research.

Overall, the stories did not provide a "high level" of legal process details, and furthermore, even when the proportion of courtroom footage used was increased, the legal process information did not actually increase.[79] This does not bode well for educational effects.

In addition, there was "considerable variation – across both stations and cases – of the following: amount of courtroom footage used and its integration with other elements of the story; the information conveyed about the facts of the case and the legal processes involved; and the degree to which both sides of the case were presented."[80] Most footage was dubbed over with narration, "thus, the visual information was typically used to reinforce a verbal presentation, rather than add new and different material to the report."[81] There appeared to be good information on the instant case but "poor" information on the legal process.[82] This begs the question, what are we seeking to "educate" about? What is the purpose? Is the purpose achieved successfully?

Most of the research above related to news reports. The researchers also sought to do some research in relation to extended coverage on Court TV (now TruTV) and C–SPAN. However, it appears no content analysis of this footage was undertaken, instead relying on information furnished by the networks.[83] One of the networks said that working with just a single camera makes gavel to gavel (G2G) coverage more difficult.[84] Both networks are said to have made the point that they provide "educational information."[85] This is not copied, defined or validated. Do they mean they "push" educational information? If so, why do they, proponents or researchers not research and show the educational effects achieved?

NEW ZEALAND

The New Zealand content analysis of television courtroom programming in its experiment, found that such programming "provided more information about court proceedings and the legal process than conventional coverage, which provided more information about the case. The degree of educative value was indexed to the commitment of television to the story." [86] This related to two cases in particular.[87] However, it is noted that when "the cameras were present throughout the trial providing regular coverage through to sentencing then a higher educative value was recorded than when only a few days of a trial were covered."[88] Gavel to gavel (G2G) coverage appears to be better. In addition, however, the cases "that were covered conventionally were judged to be more educative about the case in general."[89] Overall, plaintiffs received more airtime.[90] Therefore, we again need to consider the issue of what we mean by "educate." Is the purpose to educate generally on the legal process or on the specific case in question? Do we validate whether the purpose is achieved?

As regards the content and content use, the study found that "[n]one of the 149 stories evaluated contained film continuously shot in the court. Instead, stories were generally a mixture of visual film gathered inside the court, outside the court and re–cut with file footage."[91]

The authors of the related Final Report empirical content analysis study,[92] note that content analysis is "one of the most frequently used research methodologies in communications research" and furthermore that it is "reliable."[93] TCB content analysis seldom arises. In the instant research, there were six full cases and four sentencing hearings.[94] Unfortunately, there is too little content analysis and educational validation[95] of television courtroom broadcasting.

The Final Report notes that radio and print were "less competitive in nature than television" and were not "head to head."[96] This has implications to be considered in relation to forms of courtroom broadcasting.

One of the points of this work is that before carrying out television courtroom broadcasting experiments and empirical effects research, we should first carry out baseline research before cameras are introduced. This is absent from most research and is, therefore, a significant flaw in the research effort to date. This applies both in terms of in–court and out–of–court research.

The Final Report does not address the pre–experiment baseline issue. However, it does refer to comparison between what happens in court and what is ultimately broadcast. This is frequently absent from television courtroom broadcasting research. The Final Report states that,

> [a]ccuracy cannot be fully determined by content analysis as there needs to be some level of comparison between what occurred in court during the day and what was eventually broadcast on television that evening. Only someone who has sat in court for some/all of the proceedings is qualified to make this judgement. In some instances inaccuracies may be recounted through content analysis, for instance, if the charges are inaccuracy reported, or if legal counsel is improperly named. On the whole though, content analysis is not an appropriate means of measuring accuracy.[97]

This might well be an issue for future research.

While not an educational issue, there is a need for research and documentation of the process of television courtroom broadcasting stories from the start to final broadcast and out–of–court effects.

The Final Report also notes the complicating issue of balance, and measuring balance, in reports. For example, while a television report may be very accurate, due to the nature of certain legal systems, the prosecution side may be presented first, or the prosecutor may be the only side to speak on a particular day. If this is the only day covered by the media, then for "coverage to be balanced overall,"[98] must an equal dominance be given to the other side subsequently? Also, can a television report of a case only be fully balanced if it covers the whole of a case?

One of the New Zealand rules states, in part, that "[m]aterial obtained from expanded media broadcast ... is to be without editorial comment."[99] The research content analysis examined whether any narrative from the reports included subjective opinion. Of the seven cases referred to, the answer was yes in one case and "possibly" in three cases.[100]

In one set of interviews, fifteen of seventeen non–media participants felt that the television reports were selective and sensational.[101] In longitudinal interviews the main reasons of those opposed to the experiment "were the selective nature of the news reports and perceived negative effects of cameras in court on those involved in the proceedings, which was thought to detract from the judicial process."[102]

While a professional market research firm was engaged to undertake a study of public views to television courtroom broadcasting, there does not appear to have been any research of education audience effects or public opinion.[103]

Content analysis also examined the reports for sensationalism and misrepresentation (both of which were defined).[104] On the question of whether "[a]ny aspects of the stories was sensational," four of seven case reports were found to be sensational.[105] In relation to the degree to which the story provides information about the case on TV1, 35% provided only "basic" information, with 40% providing "relatively informative" information.[106] The figures were 35% and 27% for TV3.[107] On the issue of the degree to which the story provided information about court proceedings, 37% was basic and 25% relatively informative for TV1, and 37% and 7% for TV3.[108]

On the question of the degree to which the story provided information about the legal process, the figures for TV1 were 34% basic and 9% relatively informative.[109] The TV3 figures were 21% and 7%.[110]

While there was a two minute minimum footage requirement, none of the 149 stories evaluated were of continuous (or extended) courtroom film footage.[111] Instead, what was broadcast was a mix of courtroom footage, out of court footage and re–cut file footage.[112] There was also editing, splicing, re–ordering and a "mixture of visual elements."[113] Several counsel expressed concern at how the footage was used, for example, slowing down footage of the defendant, relying on the defendant and counsel for reaction shots, the repetition of dramatic footage and cutting audio or footage and using it with other audio or footage, some from out of court.[114] This is referred to as "mixed footage" and "mixed mode of visual elements" and it is suggested that the media would "resist" any amendments to this practice.[115] The research confirmed that there was,

> a difference in the framing of the news according to the visual elements available. When the story is dominated by courtroom film an emphasis is the actual trial process featuring courtroom routines and judicial processes. When there is an emphasis on file footage or outside court film the framing of the story is more likely to match other crime stories with in–court film acting as one visual ingredient only in the story's composition.[116]

The Final report adds that this "has implications if a purpose of the cameras in court pilot was to promote public understanding of the court procedure and the justice system."[117] Again, what do we mean by "education"?

In terms of the intended purposes, the report notes that "[o]ne of the hoped for outcomes of the pilot was that there be some kind of 'trade–off' that would see less intrusive media behaviour outside the courts in return for access inside the court."[118] This has not occurred,[119] the report concludes.

POGORZELSKI AND BREWER

Wendy Pogorzelski and Thomas W. Brewer[120] undertook a content analysis case study of television courtroom broadcasting of a particular case in New York. The case was particularly controversial (Amadou Diallo).

The researchers quote Barbara Corcoran who testified at the US Sunshine in the Courtroom proceedings on behalf of Radio–Television News Directors Association. She is quoted as saying that television courtroom broadcasting would allow "complete and direct observation of the demeanour, tone, credibility, contentiousness, and perhaps even the competency and veracity of the participants, [it] is the best means through which to advance the public's right to know."[121] However, these claims need closer examination and research. Considering even the camera perspective bias effect in police interrogation videos, it is far from clear if these sweeping claims are correct, whether they all apply, and whether they all apply equally across all forms of television courtroom broadcasting.

In the instant case study, it was noted that there was a pooling arrangement in place between the television stations.[122] It does not appear that this study, nor any other study thus far, has sought to compare the broadcast footage of different television stations from the same pooling feed, and the consequent potential educative effects as between the television stations.

In the instant study three items were coded in each newscast, namely, total time spent on the story; total in court video footage; and total in court audio used.[123] There were 201 stories the majority of which consisted of reporter or anchorperson voiceovers using out of court footage.[124] The in court footage was only used "in the form of soundbites."[125] They continue,

> The mean length of each newscast was 3.35 (215 seconds). On average, each story contained 47 seconds (22 percent of the total story) of audio coverage from inside the courtroom. For every ten minutes of news coverage, the public heard two minutes of actual court proceedings. Broadcasting audio from inside the courtroom is the purest form of communicating court proceedings to the public but was the least used. Producers tend to rely on the video feed from inside the courtroom rather than the audio footage. The mean length of video usage of a broadcast was 1:18 (78 seconds, 36 percent of the total time).[126]

Over the course of the twelve day trial, almost two thirds of the stories focused on non in–court video footage e.g. commentary, narration.[127] On average, 75% of the time was devoted to non in court audio, so the audience did not hear the judge, lawyers, witnesses or defendants for 75% of the time.[128]

In terms of policy, the research states that the "disparity between total story coverage and broadcasting what was being said in the courtroom speaks to the mismatch between how policy makers would like news stations to cover judicial proceedings and how the media actually covers them. These findings are from one case study and this limits its generalizability."[129] Again, more empirical research is needed.

The researchers raise a query as to whether television courtroom broadcasting are effective at increasing "perception."[130] They point out the almost two thirds of the footage was not in court footage, and that the in court footage was generally used to supplement regular traditional broadcasting.[131] We need to define what we mean by "education." They also point out that there is no apparent increase in public opinion of courts.[132] The audience does not get to see the courts "at work."[133] They further point out that the content analysis shows that this is as a result of media choices and not the courts or the applicable rules.[134] Media decisions and media forms need to be considered and analysed.

The Rhode Island experimental is referred to. After the first period the courts said that the media "had an obligation to further the goal of public education as a justification for the" additional court management burdens.[135] After reviewing the second experimental period, it was said that 45 seconds of courtroom footage "scarcely contributes to such public understanding."[136]

They also refer to S.L. Alexander's research which also found that media footage was generally using the in court footage to enhance traditional reporting only, and that this may not be what was intended by the courts or legislature.[137]

Referring to "news formats" they note research and content analysis which shows that selection and ordering of footage can "significantly alter [the] meaning."[138] They refer to Roberta Entner's research which found that the frame by frame analysis shows that new television "production bias" does not give adequate explanation of the courts nor does it enhance the image of the judiciary.[139] Will this differ between TCB forms?

They feel that the "assumption that courts are an exception to this pattern [of information/entertainment blurring] needs to be questioned and re–examined" particularly on the television courtroom broadcasting debate.[140] The present research parallels previous research regarding "how established news formats and editing decisions shape broadcast content."[141] Sustained research of other court forms needs to be undertaken.

They recommend wider research, including for example tracking how much judicial and court time is spent in relation to assisting and monitoring television courtroom broadcasting; monitoring media compliance with the rule; monitoring the party opponents time dealing with camera issues; and media effects.[142] Wider research is needed into how the judicial process is effected and "at what cost" in order to fully understand the various impacts.[143] They comment that the research has not altered much since the concerns voices in *Estes*.[144] More research, research funding and observational research is required.[145] Without increasing of research methodology and coding our knowledge continues to be shaped by "good intentions, rather than systematic evidence."[146]

They add,

> Nor is it evident that broadcasting brief, heavily edited clips of trial footage is an effective means of increasing the visibility of, or improving the perception of, the judiciary. The public has identified its concerns: unfair and unequal treatment in the justice system. The challenges faced by the judicial system are more complex than a lack of public awareness and a continued focus on cameras in court as a tool to improve public trust and confidence seems misdirected.[147]

If television courtroom broadcasting is educational and/or informative, and if one seriously wants to establish (or research) the points, one obvious place to examine is existing television courtroom broadcasting output. We can examine the current television courtroom broadcasting programmes and content. There is not enough content analysis and alternative research.

In initial interviews with non–media subjects, fourteen of seventeen people thought that there was no "actual" educational benefits[148] The final interview sets revealed thirteen of twenty eight interviewees indicating that there was no actual education.[149] The market research study did relate to some of the educational issues. Firstly, it assessed whether the public were aware of the ongoing experiment at all, and gauged responses at three different stages. The results were 69%, 57% and 65%.[150] Secondly, it sought to assess whether public awareness of how the court system operates actually improved. 23% thought that their awareness had improved while 67% felt it had not improved.[151]

The literature generally, when referring to the education arguments, does not separate non–media and media responses on the educational debate. This is an area which should be addressed, particularly as it is felt that differences may exist. It is also suggested that we should examine media education arguments in favour of courtroom access with how they see their actual roles. While positive educational effects is a media argument advanced, do the media see one of their primary news and process functions as being education? The New Zealand Final Report comments that "journalists themselves do not necessarily see their fourth estate role in terms of an educative value."[152]

The study appears to have only examined educative content analysis in two cases.[153] In terms of the research, it appear to show that educative potential effects are optimum the longer the footage and the more a case is shown in entirety.[154]

In an interesting finding regarding TV1 footage, the study found that there was more educative content regarding court proceedings and the legal process in camera cases than in conventional television reporting.[155] However, the conventional reporting was more educational in relation to the specific case.[156] It is speculated that this may be because "with no cameras in court footage, there is less visuals to drive the coverage of what actually went on in court (apart from textual graphics) and more visuals (such as file footage) to prompt further contextual coverage of the crime/case itself."[157] Again, the question arises as to what we want to educate about?

A factor relevant to educational effect was seen as the length of the story. In New Zealand there was a minimum requirement of two minutes duration for television courtroom broadcasting. These stories therefore "tend to have more information and hence are potentially more educative than the shorter conventional stories (which averaged 95 seconds in length).[158] This is from a push or content perspective, not actual testing of education effects. There are many effects research opportunities in relation to minimum broadcast requirements.

The Final Report refers to another issue which does not appear to have been canvassed in the general literature on television courtroom broadcasting. It notes that often the broadcast footage contains repeat materials and therefore "may not be truly educational after a series of repetitions."[159] This appears to be the first reference to this issue. Future research is required.

HARRIS

The legal information people tend to get from television is generally crime focused and comes in the "form of" news, entertainment and infotainment programming.[160] However, such information is frequently "misleading" and "wrong."[161] David A. Harris[162] compares the portrayal of criminal courts on TruTV (previously CourtTV) versus "conventional" television media. Conventional television is defined as "the combination of entertainment and informational programming offered by television since its beginnings, whether in cable or broadcast format."[163] He compliments TruTV as presenting more of the courtroom than news or entertainment programming, but notes that there are flaws nonetheless.[164] These are that it exclusively focused on trials, predominantly on criminal cases, and ignores the other parts and processes of the individual case in question, as well as being selective in the trials it chooses.[165]

Regardless of educational television courtroom broadcasting, the public gets and will continue to get the existing court portrayals in news, entertainment and infotainment. The "entertainment offerings"[166] may surpass any amount of educational programming. The question, therefore, arises as to whether (educational) television broadcasting can increase public confidence in the justice system or allay misunderstandings. How do we know television courtroom broadcasting makes a difference?

Harris refers to literature commenting on "heavy viewers"[167] which raises the interesting issue for research as to what the effect of television courtroom broadcasting forms are on, for example, habitual TCB viewers.

He also notes that,

> Since news programming would seem to aim at informing rather than providing dramatics, one would expect a more accurate portrayal of the criminal justice system than in entertainment programming. This is not always true. News coverage of crime and criminal justice can and often does suffer from incompleteness. Given the demands of the typical half–hour newscast, even top news stories on television seldom get more than 'tiny bites' of airtime. This almost guarantees oversimplification. Thus the public seldom sees more than a fraction of actual trial proceedings, if any. In these constraints, with perhaps ten or fifteen seconds to devote to film of the event itself, those producing television news programs naturally pick the most dramatic slice of the day's events that they can.[168]

Research is referred to where a trial video was shown to research subjects and their attitudes and knowledge tested before and after viewing the case.[169] Harris notes that that study showed that confidence did not "decrease."[170] However, importantly it appears that there was, therefore, no enhanced or increased confidence. The viewing of the footage did not increase the confidence levels. If confidence is a measure of education, then there was no increase.

In many respects, TruTV "offers a view of the criminal justice system that contrasts markedly with the less than accurate picture presented by conventional television. As such, it represents a chance for a better understanding of how the criminal justice process works."[171] "[TruTV] does not necessarily do a better job than conventional television [in the areas studied] ... indeed, [TruTV] does not address some of them in any way whatsoever, and may even help perpetuate some incorrect ideas."[172]

In considering the educational issue and the potential of each form of television courtroom broadcasting to educate, we should also bear in mind the comment of Harris, namely, that we must also consider the difficulties of the form aswell.[173] He additionally notes that both conventional and TruTV programming "transmit representation of the system. Neither conventional television not [TruTV] is the criminal justice system."[174] "The Fact remains, however, that [TruTV] must select and weave together its own story of the criminal justice system, its own narrative of what the system does, how it functions and why. This is where the potential to mislead arises."[175]

Even with TruTV "editing is necessary to make programming fit television's format and advertising requirements ... [TruTV] leans more heavily on edited programming."[176]

In terms of the best way of educating and the best forms of educational television broadcasting, Harris notes references to Alan Dershowitz who criticises TruTV and whom advocates public cable courtroom television broadcasting.[177] He favours a form of TCB, not TCB generally per se.

VINSON AND ERTTER

These authors[178] carried out content analysis research of television and newspaper court coverage. They say that "while not devoid of informative and even explanatory content, its subject matter and emphasis is on the most accessible facets of the judicial process appear to be driven by audience and market considerations ... cameras contribute to the dramatization of court reporting."[179]

They also point out that the literate on how the media cover the courts is "limited."[180] The existing literature and research to an extent refers to what is "reported," it does not "address whether court coverage is more explanation or entertainment."[181]

Their research found that the emphasis was on entertainment, the predominant focus on the defendant and that media interest was strongest at the beginning and the end of the case.[182] This all emphasised news media consideration rather than "educational concerns."[183] Seventy five percent of television news stories were less than one minute, as opposed to the equivalent of only one third for newspapers.[184]

They found in one case study that television courtroom broadcasting did not influence the "amount" of coverage, but that the substance, sources and how graphic the stories were did vary depending on whether cameras were in court or not.[185] Also, "there is unmistakable, if somewhat subtle, evidence that news organizations do prefer to report on what will interest us, regardless of its importance or implications for us, and they are partial to stories and sources that are most accessible and therefore easiest to cover."[186] They also said that,

> [A]lthough we would hesitate to make generalizations on the basis of our limited case studies, we do see evidence in the Bobbit trials [one broadcast, one not] that cameras in the courtroom shape coverage and encourage the broadcast media to highlight the more dramatic aspects of a case at the expense of discussing the wider significance of a judicial proceeding ... cameras in the court allow television more avenues for dramatic reporting than print

media have. Further, because of the limited news space in television, newspaper reporters may be better able than their television counterparts to incorporate more detailed information and point out the broader importance of seemingly isolated local cases even in the most dramatic reports.[187]

ROBERTS

Ralph E. Roberts[188] also carried out research, in particular a review of the polling and public opinion surveys regarding confidence in the judicial process and public opinion regarding television courtroom broadcasting.[189] He notes initially that there is "little research" examining television courtroom broadcasting "impact" and effects on the public.[190] He also states that there is little research on "whether the public's perception of the efficacy of the judicial system should factor into the debate about cameras in the courtroom."[191]

He also provides a definition. He defines "televised proceedings" as "any form of electronic media coverage, including television or radio broadcasts."[192]

He states that the television audience is "in the comfort of ... home" and are also denied "the sensory impressions associated with the dignity and solemnity of the courtroom."[193]

He cites the first federal pilot experiment study which found that two third of news footage was narrated while only one third used the actual in court audio footage.[194] The first federal pilot study is also referred to as finding that increasing the amount of courtroom footage did not significantly increase the information given about the legal process generally.[195]

Overall, there is a "paucity" of effects research and effects evidence.[196] The data referred to in the article is referred to as being "by no means complete or sophisticated, it is a first step in analyzing the impact of televised court proceedings on public opinion."[197] While there is some research "attempting" to research in court effects, there is "little" audience effects research.[198] In particular, there is little education effects research – which might partly be explained by the *Estes* case which concentrated on in court effects issues.[199]

Unfortunately, while there were a lot of polls carried out during and immediately after the Simpson (criminal) case, "few questions ... were asked by the same polling organization to the same group of respondents over time. Had this quality of information been available, it would have provided a valuable insight into the changes over time in the public's perception of Simpson's trial and the participants in the trial."[200]

In his concluding section he asks if "the risk of damaging the legitimacy of the courts worth the marginal benefits of televising the proceedings? The available evidence suggests that there is not a significant educational value to televising trials.[201] The polling data in the Simpson criminal case "seems to indicate the presence of some degree of risk that there is a correlation between televising trials and the loss of confidence in the judicial system. The Simpson data superficially indicate that significant numbers of the public lost confidence in defence attorneys, police, and jurors."[202] The "public believes that cameras in the courtroom so have some type of influence on the proceedings; however, the direction of the effect is not clear."[203]

He concludes that,

> [i]n the three decades since *Estes*, there has not been any systematic study that provides the courts or the legislatures with sufficient evidence to make an informed decision on the impact of televised legal proceedings on the public. The evidence that has been presented is either anecdotal, or is so limited that it cannot be generalized. Before going any further with a procedure that may imperceptibly affect a trial or lessen the public's confidence in the courts, rigorous empirical analysis should be performed. Until the effects, if any, of televised proceedings are known with any degree of certainty, the television camera should be turned off to protect the defendant and the courts.[204]

ADDITIONAL EMPIRICAL LITERATURE RELEVANT TO EDUCATIONAL EFFECTS

There is also some additional empirical literature which while not investigating educational effects, is still worthy of mention.

LASSITER

Christo Lassiter argues from his analysis and review that while there prejudicial potentials of television courtroom broadcasting, these outweigh the advantages of increased public awareness.[205]

The piece is important as it is one of the few references which identify the television courtroom broadcasting feedback loop. He points out that television courtroom broadcasting "created a feedback loop between the principal actors in a televised event and its audience, which potentially includes new witnesses and evidence, discovered through investigative journalism, and the significance of which is initially filtered through the television lens for entertainment appeal."[206] He adds that "[b]y virtue of this instantaneous and comprehensive information exchange, the electronic media has the potential to alter the very event televised in ways much beyond that of a much slower and much less comprehensive and therefore much less commercially resourceful print media."[207]

He continues,

> Television cameras ... creat[e] a comprehensive and instantaneous feedback loop between trial principles and the television audience. This feedback loop provides a medium by which the reactions of a remote public to the ongoings at trial become known to the trial principles. When the trial principles respond to the public reaction, the trial loses its judicial character.[208]

"The feedback loop empowers the remote public to prejudice the trial process ..."[209] Lassiter states that the Simpson criminal case was an example of the feedback loop whereby there was an "interplay between cameras in an out of court altering the trial process from the perspective of the jurors."[210] Television courtroom broadcasting "makes the public's reaction accessible to those inside the courtroom."[211] Paul Thaler also makes a similar feedback loop point in relation to the Steinberg case study he undertook.[212]

Lassiter feels that the Simpson (criminal) case was not a bad example of television courtroom broadcasting, but rather it provided the "blue print for [TruTV's] commercialized success."[213] He adds that "[w]hile proponents of cameras in the courtroom have artificial and limited surveys to support their position that cameras do not prejudice the proceedings, the O.J. Simpson criminal trial provides the most compelling empirical evidence of what the future of cameras in the courtroom holds."[214] He highlights in his footnote reference, the flawed and limited studies and surveys he refers to.[215]

SHORT REPORT

The California Short Report while referring to the rules permitting television courtroom broadcasting for educational use,[216] the research itself does not appear to have investigated for educational effects. Neither did it investigate effects or the actual media content produced. However, it does state that to their knowledge "only one extended coverage event of a purely educational nature took place. In Yolo County, a wrongful death civil suit was videotaped in its entirely for the University of California at Davis Law School. All other media requests were from media organizations or independent journalists."[217] This is interesting in that access applications appear to be separated between media access requests and educational access request. The literature since does not generally refer to such a separation, and neither apparently the access arguments. Since then the media access argument tent to say that granting media television access will result in positive educational effects. Hence, the educational argument may have merged. Interestingly, however, the media arguments generally do not appear to say that media access will enhance student/educational institution education. Rather, the media stress that the audience or public (variously) will be educated.

However, the report did note that during the experiment, the media showed little interest in appellate court footage.[218] Only two appeals were broadcast.[219] The predominant media interest in access requests was for criminal trials.[220] In addition, the "predominant purpose ... was for daily news stories on the particular case being covered. Relatively few 'feature stories' or purely educational applications ... occurred."[221] This would have implications, therefore, in relation to what types of cases were ultimately broadcast to the public.

The report and the research are acknowledged as not covering the publics' reaction to television courtroom broadcasting; the "immediate" public effects; whether the public feel better informed than with conventional coverage; are the public educated on the judicial process?[222] It notes that the answers to all of these issues are linked to how the media present the footage.[223]

While these issues were not reached and not queried with the various categories of respondents and interviewees, they were obviously covered as they volunteered replies nonetheless.[224] These were categorised into three groups of replies. One group were sceptical of the media's willingness to cover cases fairly and referred to the commercial nature of the media industry.[225] The second group were broadly in favour of television courtroom broadcasting.[226] The third group, the largest, are sympathetic to the media but point out that news style programming does not permit extended coverage, very little in–court footage is used, and some of that is dubbed over with voiceovers.[227] The report notes in a related footnote that the research found that the "overwhelming number of ... applications are for news stories. Very few 'gavel to gavel' broadcasts of trial occurred."[228]

The report notes the following,

> Public education in light of this highly selective editing cannot possibly take place, say the critics.
> This evaluation was not required to offer an opinion on the quality of television news coverage of judicial proceedings. Suffice it to say that highly selective editing does occur and that this necessary practice is one of the most controversial issues associated with cameras in the courts. Little scientific inquiry has been done to contribute knowledge to the debate. This issue and other long range effects on society at large represent the main frontier of 'cameras in the courts' research.[229]

Unfortunately, this frontier of debate and of research has not been systematically or comprehensively addressed since the Short Report in 1981.

It should be noted that the Short Report was presented to the California Chief Justice's Special Committee on the Courts and the Media. The Committee however, only accepted the report, it did not adopt or agree with the conclusions drawn.[230] Ephraim Margolin criticises the report. "[A]ny report which fails to evaluate or even consider the use made by the media of the coverage obtained from observation of the courts leaves us with only partial evaluation insufficient for a final determination of the wisdom of the project."[231] Margolin is also critical of any potential educative effects given media programming styles and editing.[232]

STEWART

Ruthie Elizabeth Reeves Stewart carries out research of what effect trials on television have on confidence in the justice system.[233] The research question addressed is whether broadcast coverage of courts has an impact on the public's perception of the justice system.[234]

While not researching educational issues *per se*, she states that the cameras are a "poor teacher" and that high profile and lurid cases are chosen without regard to educational value.[235] She is speaking in relation to TruTV (previously CourtTV). "The education of the masses on the court system is perhaps the most valid and noteworthy goal of [TruTV]. The drawback on making such a claim is that empirical support for this statement is tough to produce. ... [others] point to other ways to achieve the same goal without tampering with justice."[236] She refers to studies asking if the public watch television courtroom broadcasting, where the answer is a "resounding yes."[237] However, there is scant research of watching television courtroom broadcasting on the public opinion of the effectiveness of the justice system,[238] or confidence in the justice system. As we see from William Petkanas above, there was no increase in confidence found in the New York experiment. Anna R. Paddon, however, finds some "information gain." (See William Petkanas and Anna R. Paddon).

COMMENTS ON THE EMPIRICAL EDUCATION RESEARCH

The first point is that there is so little educational effects research. Secondly there is not validation and replication. Only Petkanas sought to carry out research at the beginning and at the end. However, the baseline issue appears wholly ignored in the general and empirical research and the literature generally. What is meant by "education" is not addressed and tested. None of the studies undertook exactly similar research or used identical methodologies.

William Petkanas[239] found that "confidence" did not increase as a result of television courtroom broadcasting. While Anna R. Paddon[240] found that there was some "information gain," there does not appear to have been any change in "attitude." Kermit Netteburg[241] did not find any educational effect, nor any enhanced knowledge about the court procedures. Jessica Ossinger did not find any enhanced usage of television courtroom broadcasting.

Steven Kohm[242] found evidence of television courtroom broadcasting being used or made for entertainment programming. Similarly so with C. Danielle Vinson and John S. Ertter.[243]

Theresa Keller[244] found that television courtroom broadcasting did not increase the number of legal and court stories.

Roberta Enter[245] in a detailed study found that thy type and style of courtroom broadcasting examined was biased and presented the defendant unfairly. Entertainment and excitement were emphasised.

The first federal pilot experiment study found that most courtroom footage was dubbed over and the audio from inside the court was not used. It also found that the footage was mostly used as short snippets. The federal experiment and the New Zealand study both found television courtroom broadcasting used in-court and out-of court footage in the same broadcasts. New Zealand found conventionally reported cases more educational.

Wendy Pogorzelski and Thomas W. Brewer found the average length of stories to be 215 second, of which 78 seconds (36%) was in–court footage, and 47 seconds (22%) was in–court audio. The first federal pilot experiment study found the average courtroom footage per story to be 56 seconds (N=90). [246] 95% of non first day stories did not identify cases as civil laws cases; 745 did not identify if a jury was present; 74% did not explain what transpired in the days proceedings.[247] The "stories did not provide a high level of detail about the legal process ... [and] increasing the proportion of courtroom footage used in a story did not significantly increase the information given about the legal process .... the coverage did a poor job of providing information to viewers about the legal process."[248] Pogorzelski and Brewer point out that almost two thirds of footage was out–of–court footage. Also, there was no increase of in public opinion.

S.L. Alexander[249] also found the court footage was mostly used to supplement conventional stories.

While D.A. Harris notes that TruTV carried more amounts of television courtroom broadcasting, he raises many questions of the broadcasts.[250] He also finds that confidence in the justice process did not increase.[251]

Ralph E. Roberts[252] finds no evidence of increase in education.

EDUCATIONAL

The New York experiment was predicated on the belief that television courtroom broadcasting permitted by the experiment would be educational.[253] Yet, no official research sought to verify whether there were educational effects. William Petkanas notes that since the New York experimental law was passed, no educational affects have been proven.[254] The first phase of the experiment was in 1987[255] and he was writing in 1990. No educational effects were researched.

That access and filming may be permitted does not always mean that the footage will be used for educational purposes, in the most educationally amenable form, or that it will not be re–used in less educationally amenable forms afterwards.[256]

Even assuming educational quality programming content is push out, various issues arise. Is it watched? What is the take up level? What is the quality if viewing? What is the impact? Is education achieved? How much? Is it significant? Is it sufficient? Is there a sufficient success rate compared to the effort (and risks) expended? Is pushing "educational" content by itself a sufficient tool to educate?[257] Is it a sufficient tool to increase (or restore) confidence in the judicial process? These are serious questions, and that is even before we address any issue of what it is exactly that we wish to educate about or communicate in the educational message pushed out to the assumed audience.

The consideration of it and how courtroom television broadcasting may educate is really only in its infancy. Considerable and more significant research is required, and over a longer period. In addition, we need to incorporate research of form (and format) issues which arise with television courtroom broadcasting. Our capacity for considered evaluation of the educational issues, and arguments, must not remain underscored by presumptions and soundbites.[258]

Another issue is that television courtroom broadcasting predominantly shows criminal trial. In addition, it ignores all of the legal process issues before and outside of the courtroom trial. Richard K. Sherwin states that 90% of civil and criminal cases end in negotiated outcomes.[259]

CONCLUSION

What does the empirical education research to date actually say? We can see that there is little empirical research of the so called educational effects. Clearly more empirical research is needed. Overall, the research does not demonstrate that education is achieved. There are no proper definitions in relation to educational TCB etiher.

A further criticism is that most studies do not carry out any baseline data research and measurements before the experiment with television courtroom broadcasting begins. It appears, as an example, that the New Zealand experiment, while aware of empirical issues it only engaged academic professional researchers at or near the end of the experiment.[260] This should be an essential first stage of any such experiment, and indeed should be carried out over an extended period, possibly a year or more. This includes the Supreme Court research challenge.

NOTES

1. S. Barber, News Cameras in the Courtroom: A Free Press – Fair Trial Debate (Norwood, New Jersey: Ablex, 1987).
2. R. Entner, The Image of the Judiciary: A Semiotic Analysis of Broadcast Trials to Ascertain its Definition of the Court System (Ph.D diss., New York University, 1993), see abstract.
3. R.L. Goldfarb, TV or Not TV: Television, Justice, and the Courts (New York: New York University Press, 1998), in particular 116 et seq.
4. *Hollingsworth v Perry*, 558 US _ 2010, www.supremecourt.gov/opinions/09pdf/09A648.pdf, accessed August 13, 2012.
5. M. Cohn and D. Dow, Cameras in the Courtroom: Television and the Pursuit of Justice (New York: Rowman & Little, 2002).
6. A. Hiber, ed., Should Cameras be Allowed in Courtrooms? (New York: Gale, 2008). While no research ad no empirical research is referred to, there is an article reproduced which argues that there are/will be educational effects. See S. Gale, Cameras in Courtrooms Would Lead to a More Educated Public, in A. Hiber, above, 61–65. No studies or research is referred to.
7. W. Petkanas, Cameras on Trial: An Assessment of the Educational Affects of News Cameras in Trial Courts (Ph.D diss., New York University, 1990).
8. Ibid, 2.
9. Ibid.
10. Ibid.
11. Referred to ibid, 3.
12. Ibid.
13. Ibid, 21.
14. Ibid, 68–69.
15. Ibid, 20.
16. Ibid, 63.
17. Ibid, 91.
18. Ibid, 110.
19. Ibid.
20. Ibid, 112.
21. Ibid.
22. Ibid, 117.
23. Ibid.
24. A.R. Paddon, Television Coverage of Criminal Trials with Cameras and Microphones: A Controlled Experiment of Audience Effects (Ph.D diss., University of Tennessee, 1985).
25. Ibid.
26. Ibid, see Abstract.
27. Ibid, 3.
28. Ibid, 4.
29. W. Stone and S.G. Edlin, TV or Not TV: Televised and Photographic Coverage of Trials, Mercer Law Review 29 (1978) 1119–1135.
30. A.R. Paddon, above, 5.
31. Ibid, 5. Referring to J.L. Hoyt, Courtroom Coverage: The Effects of Being Televised, The Journal of Broadcasting 21 (1977): 487–495; K. Netterburg, Does Research Support the Estes Ban on Cameras in the Courtroom?, Judicature 63 (1980): 467–475.
32. Ibid, 5–6.
33. Ibid, 6–7.
34. Ibid, 9 et seq.

35. Ibid, 7.
36. See ibid, 1 and 13.
37. See ibid, 1 and 13.
38. See Chapters 8 and 9 above, and for example, D.G. Lassiter, A.L. Geers, I.M. Handley, P.E. Weiland and P.J. Mulhall, Videotaped Interrogations and Confessions: A Simple Change in Camera Perspective Alters Verdicts in Simulated Trials, Journal of Applied Psychology 87 (2002): 867–874.
39. A. Paddon, above, 11.
40. Ibid, 13.
41. Ibid.
42. Ibid, 13.
43. Ibid, 14.
44. Ibid, 14.
45. K.L. Netteburg, Cameras in the Courtroom: Is a Picture Worth a Thousand Words? (Ph.D diss., University of Minnesota, 1980).
46. Ibid, 170.
47. J. Ossinger, Electronic Access to Courtrooms: Television as an Educational Socializing Agent on the Judiciary (MA diss., The University of Maine, 2006).
48. Ibid, see abstract.
49. S.A. Kohm, I'm Not a Judge But I Play One On TV: American Reality Based Courtroom Television (Ph.D diss., Simon Fraser University, 2004).
50. Ibid, 291.
51. T. Keller. T. Cameras in Courtrooms: An Analysis of Television Court Coverage in Virginia (Ph.D diss., The University of Tennessee, (1992), 125.
52. Ibid, 146.
53. R. Entner, The Image of the Judiciary: A Semiotic Analysis of Broadcast Trials to Ascertain its Definition of the Court System (Ph.D diss., New York University, 1993), see abstract.
54. Ibid, 25.
55. Ibid, 26.
56. Ibid, 157.
57. Ibid.
58. Ibid.
59. Ibid, 160.
60. Ibid, 161.
61. W. Petkanas, above, 8.
62. Ibid.
63. R. Entner, above, 167.
64. Ibid, 159. Note also the first Federal pilot experiment content analysis, M.T. Johnson and C. Krafka, Electronic Media Coverage of Federal Civil Proceedings, An Evaluation of the Pilot Program in Six District Courts and Two Courts of Appeal (Federal Judicial Centre, 1994).
65. W. Petkanas, above, 4.
66. Ibid., 7.
67. Ibid, referring to J. Fiske and J. Hartley, Reading Television (New York: Methuen, 1978), 81–82.
68. M.T. Johnson and C. Krafka, Electronic Media Coverage of Federal Civil Proceedings, An Evaluation of the Pilot Program in Six District Courts and Two Courts of Appeal (Federal Judicial Centre, 1994).
69. Ibid, 7.
70. Ibid, 32, n. 27.
71. Ibid, 33.
72. Ibid.
73. Ibid.
74. Ibid, 34.
75. Ibid.
76. Ibid, 34.

77. Ibid, 35.
78. See ibid, 36.
79. Ibid.
80. Ibid.
81. Ibid.
82. Ibid.
83. Ibid, 37.
84. Ibid.
85. Ibid.
86. Media Coverage of Court Proceedings Pilot Evaluation Committee, Media Coverage of Court Proceedings, Introduction and Research Findings (August, 1998), 8.
87. Ibid.
88. Ibid.
89. Ibid.
90. Ibid.
91. Ibid, p. 12.
92. K. Allan, J. McGregor and S. Fontaine, The Impact of Television, Radio and Still Photography Coverage of Court Proceedings, Final Report, A Report Prepared for the Department For Courts (Department of Human Resource Management, Faculty of Business Studies, Massey University, April, 1998): 2. (New Zealand).
93. Ibid.
94. Ibid, 4
95. For example, V. Stodden, Enabling Reproducible Research: Licensing for Scientific Innovation, International Journal of Communications Law and Policy 13 (2009): 1–25, at 2.
96. K. Allan, J. McGregor and S. Fontaine, above, 13.
97. Ibid, 26. In the original the word "inaccuracies" is emphasised in bold.
98. Ibid.
99. Ibid, 88, referring to Rule A1: Without editorial comment.
100. Ibid, 88.
101. Ibid, 32.
102. Ibid, 63.
103. See reference ibid, 67. There were some opinion queries on the potential to educate asked of judges, counsel and court staff, see ibid, 98 et seq.
104. Ibid, 89. Sensationalism was defined as "[c]oncentration on the unusual, shocking, bizarre or melodramatic aspects of, or associated with, a trial which are more than just dramatic real footage." Misrepresentation is defined as "[c]oncentration on aspects of the trial that distort the judicial system or are insignificant in terms of the trial in general."
105. Ibid, 89–90. No misrepresentation was found.
106. Ibid, 99. Author's calculations from data in report.
107. Ibid. Author's calculations from data in report.
108. Ibid, 99–100. Author's calculations from data in report.
109. Ibid,100. Author's calculations from data in report.
110. Ibid.
111. Ibid, 203.
112. Ibid.
113. Ibid.
114. Ibid, 203–204.
115. Ibid, 204.
116. Ibid.
117. Ibid.
118. Ibid, 205.
119. See ibid.
120. W. Pogorzelski and T.W. Brewer, Cameras in Court, How Television News Media Use Courtroom Footage, Judicature 91 (November–December 2007): 125.
121. Quoted ibid, 126.
122. Ibid, 128.

123. Ibid, 128–129.
124. Ibid, 129.
125. Ibid.
126. Ibid.
127. Ibid.
128. Ibid, 131.
129. Ibid.
130. Ibid, 132.
131. Ibid.
132. Ibid.
133. Ibid.
134. Ibid.
135. At ibid, referring to *In re Extension of Media Coverage for a Further Experimental Period*, 473 R.I. A.2d. 1232 (1984).
136. At ibid, referring to *In re Extension of Media Coverage for a Further Experimental Period*, 473 R.I. A.2d. 1232 (1984).
137. Ibid, 132, referring to S.L. Alexander, Cameras in the Courtroom: A Case Study, Judicature 74 (1991): 307–313.
138. Ibid, 132, referring to R. Entner, The Image of the Judiciary: A Semiotic Analysis of Broadcast Trials to Ascertain Its Definition of the Court System (New York: New York University Press, 1993), 197. They also refer to P. Thaler, above, S.J. Drucker, The Television Mediated Trial: Formal and Substantive Characteristics, Communications Quarterly 37 (1989) 305–318; V.P. Hans and J.L. Dee, Media Coverage and the Law: It's Impact on Juries and the Public, American Behaviour Scientist 35 (1991) 136–149; E.J. Epstein, News from Nowhere: The Selection of Reality in Television News Programs, (New York: Vantage, 1973); S.A. Esposito, Source Utilization in Legal Journalism: Network TV News Coverage of the Timothy McVeigh Oklahoma City Bombing Trial, Communications and Law 20 (1998): 15–33.
139. Ibid, 132, referring to R. Entner, above.
140. Ibid, 133.
141. Ibid.
142. Ibid.
143. Ibid.
144. Ibid.
145. Ibid, 134.
146. Ibid.
147. Ibid, 134.
148. Short Report, above, ibid, 102.
149. K. Allan, J. McGregor, and S. Fontaine, The Impact of Television, Radio and Still Photography Coverage of Court Proceedings, Final Report, A Report Prepared for the Department For Courts (Department of Human Resource Management, Faculty of Business Studies, Massey University, April, 1998): 134.
150. Ibid, 105.
151. Ibid, 105.
152. Ibid, 194.
153. See ibid, 195.
154. Ibid.
155. Ibid.
156. Ibid, 195–196.
157. Ibid, 196.
158. Ibid.
159. Ibid.
160. D.A. Harris, The Appearance of Justice: Court TV, Conventional Television, and Public Understanding of the Criminal Justice System, Arizona Law Review 35 (1993): 786.
161. Ibid, 786, 812 et seq.
162. Ibid, 785–837.
163. Ibid, 787, n. 24.

164. Ibid, 788.
165. Ibid, 788, 824.
166. Ibid, 797.
167. Ibid, 809, n. 191, referring to G. Gerbner and L. Gross, The Scary World of TV's Heavy Viewer, Psychology Today (April, 1976): 44.
168. Ibid, 811, footnote omitted.
169. Ibid, 817, referring to P. Raymond, The Impact of a Televised Trial on Individual's Information and Attitudes, Judicature 75 (1992): 204–208.
170. Ibid, referring to 208 in P. Raymond, above.
171. Ibid, 818.
172. Ibid.
173. Ibid, see 820–821.
174. Ibid, 821.
175. Ibid, 821.
176. Ibid, 825.
177. Ibid, 825–826.
178. C.D. Vinson and J.S. Ertter, Entertainment or Education, How Do Media Cover the Courts?, Press/Politics 7:4 (2002): 80–97.
179. Ibid, 80, 84.
180. Ibid, 81.
181. Ibid, 82.
182. Ibid, 86–87.
183. Ibid, 87.
184. Ibid, 88.
185. Ibid, 90.
186. Ibid, 94.
187. Ibid, 95.
188. R.E. Roberts, An Empirical and Normative Analysis of the Impact of Televised Courtroom Proceedings, SMU Law Review 51 (1998) 621–664.
189. Ibid, 622.
190. Ibid, 622.
191. Ibid.
192. Ibid, 621, n. 1.
193. Ibid, 627.
194. Ibid, 631.
195. Ibid, 631–632.
196. Ibid, 632.
197. Ibid.
198. Ibid, 634.
199. Ibid, and n. 105, 634.
200. Ibid, 635.
201. Ibid, 644.
202. Ibid, 645.
203. Ibid.
204. Ibid.
205. C. Lassiter, Cameras and the Infusion of Political Bias into the Courtroom, International Journal of Law and Information Technology, 5:1 (1997): 28–82.
206. Ibid, 29.
207. Ibid.
208. Ibid, 31.
209. Ibid, 55.
210. Ibid, 75.
211. Ibid, 81.
212. P. Thaler, The Impact of the Television Camera on Courtroom Participants: A Case Study of the Joel Stenberg Murder Trial (Ph.D diss., New York University, 1990).
213. Ibid, 57.

214. Ibid, 57–58. Footnote omitted.

215. These are: "Arizona – (untitled ('the Arizona Study'), which is at handwritten page 39 of the Information Service Memorandum IS 88.002, TV Cameras In the Courts, Evaluation of Experiments) (with Attachments)('Sample Survey'); California – Evaluation of California's Experiment With Extended Media Coverage of Courts, Submitted by Ernest H. Short and Associates, Inc. (Sept. 19810 ('the California Study'); see also Cameras In Court, 1983 report to the Governor And Legislature: Florida – (untitled)(the Florida Study); Louisiana – Report On Pilot Project On The Presence of Cameras And Electronic Equipment In The Courtroom (undated)(the Louisiana Study); Minnesota – Report Of The Minnesota Advisory Commission On Cameras In The Courtroom To The Supreme Court (Jan. 1982)(the Minnesota Study); Nevada – Final Statistical Report Cameras In The Courtroom In Nevada (1980)(the Nevada Study); New York – Report Of The Chief Administrator To The New York State Legislature The Governor And Chief Judge On The Effect Of Audio–Visual Coverage On The Conduct Of Judicial Proceedings, Matthew T. Crossan (March 1991)('the 1991 New York Study'); Report Of The Committee On Audio–Visual Coverage of Court Proceedings, Hon. Burton B. Roberts, Chair (May 1994)('the 1994 New York Study'); Washington, Cameras In The Courtroom – A Two–Year Review In The State of Washington, A Project Of The Washington State Superior Court Judges' Association Committee On Courts and Community (Sept. 1978)(the Washington Study). Most of these state studies, and studies from Hawaii, Kansas, Maine, Massachusetts, New Jersey, Ohio and Virginia, are described in Electronic Media Coverage of Courtroom Proceedings: Effects On Witnesses And Jurors, Supplemental Report of Federal Judicial Centre To The Conference Committee On Court Administration And Case Management (1994)." Referred to *ibid*, 57, n. 107.

216. E.H. Short and Associates, Evaluation of California's Experiment with Extended Media Coverage of Courts, Submitted to The Administrative Office for the Courts, The Chief Justice's Special Committee on the Courts and the Media and The California Judicial Council, September, 1981, see 1, 6, 9 and 55.

217. Ibid, 54 and 71.

218. Ibid, 44.

219. Ibid, 71.

220. Ibid, 220.

221. Ibid.

222. Ibid, 240.

223. Ibid.

224. Ibid.

225. Ibid, 240–241.

226. Ibid, 241.

227. Ibid.

228. Ibid, 241, footnote 37.

229. Ibid, 242.

230. See E. Margolin, Memorandum to the Members of the Chief Justice's Special Committee on the Courts and the Media, the Judicial Council of California, 16 October, 1981.

231. Ibid.

232. Ibid.

233. R.E.R. Stewart. The Changing Relationship Between Camera and the Courts (MA diss., Florida Atlantic University, 1998): 1–2, and 32.

234. Ibid, 21.

235. Ibid, 61–64.

236. Ibid, 65. She concludes that there "are many extensive and valid reasons to ban cameras from courtrooms. Their merits must be weighed against their negative factors in order to make a decision when determining if televising a trial is worthwhile. Each case needs to be decided on an individual basis because its framework and issues at hand are unique." Ibid.

237. Ibid, 1. However, the studies referred to are not cited at the reference made.

238. Ibid, 1–2, and 32.

239. W. Petkanas, Cameras on Trial: An Assessment of the Educational Affects of News Cameras in Trial Courts (Ph.D diss., New York University, 1990): 3.

240. A.R. Paddon, Television Coverage of Criminal Trials with Cameras and Microphones: A Controlled Experiment of Audience Effects, Radio–television Journalism Division, AEJMC Montreal, Que, Canada, August 7, 1992, p. 1. Also A. R. Paddon, Television Coverage of Criminal Trials with Cameras and Microphones: A Controlled Experiment of Audience Effects (Ph.D diss., University of Tennessee, 1985).

241. K. Netteburg, Does Research Support the Estes Ban on Cameras in the Courtroom, Judicature 63 (1980) 467–475.

242. S.A. Kohm, I'm Not a Judge But I Play One On TV: American Reality Based Courtroom Television (Ph.D diss., Simon Fraser University, 2004).

243. C.D. Vinson and J.S. Ertter, Entertainment or Education, How Do Media Cover the Courts?, Press/Politics 7:4 (2002): 80–97.

244. T. Keller, Cameras in Courtrooms: An Analysis of Television Court Coverage in Virginia (Ph.D diss., The University of Tennessee, 1992).

245. R. Enter. The Image of the Judiciary: A Semiotic Analyse of Broadcast Trials to Ascertain its Definition of the Court System (Ph.D diss., New York University, 1993).

246. M.T. Johnson and C. Krafka, Electronic Media Coverage of Federal Civil Proceedings, An Evaluation of the Pilot Program in Six District Courts and Two Courts of Appeal (Federal Judicial Centre, 1994): 34.

247. Ibid, 36.

248. Ibid.

249. S.L. Alexander, "Mischievous Potentialities": A Case Study of Courtroom Camera Guidelines, Eight Judicial Circuit, Florida, 1989 (Ph.D diss., University of Florida, 1990).

250. D.A. Harris, The Appearance of Justice: Court TV, Conventional Television, and the Public Understanding of the Criminal Justice System, Arizona Law Review 35 (1993): 785–827, as referred to in R.E.R. Stewart, The Changing Relationship Between Camera and the Courts (MA diss., Florida Atlantic University, 1998), 28.

251. Ibid.

252. R.E Roberts, An Empirical and Normative Analysis of the Impact of Televised Courtroom Proceedings, SMU Law Review 51 (1998): 621–664.

253. W. Petkanas. Cameras on Trial: An Assessment of the Educational Affects of News Cameras in Trial Courts (Ph.D diss., New York University, 1990), 3.

254. Ibid.

255. Ibid, 49.

256. Ronan Kennedy makes the point that scientific environmental statistics and data is often used for a purpose different to that which was originally intended. "Information and Communications Technology and Institutional Design for Climate Change," draft version, forthcoming, 13.

257. R. Kennedy, above asks that "[d]isclosure by itself is not a sufficient tool of governance," in relation to ICT and environmental issues, ibid, 39.

258. Notes comments in relation to rushing to judgements and the need for proper evaluated judgement in R.K. Sherwin, When Law Goes Pop: The Vanishing Line Between Law and Popular Culture (Chicago: The University of Chicago Press, 2000), 5.

259. Ibid, 245.

260. Media Coverage of Court Proceedings Pilot Evaluation Committee, Media Coverage of Court Proceedings, Introduction and Research Findings (August 1998), Introduction.

Chapter Fifteen

Education Effects Challenge

INTRODUCTION

When we look at television courtroom broadcasting research we see that most of the general research that does exist is confined to the answers and opinions of (some of) the courtroom participants – exactly those people who are not in a position to show whether or not television courtroom broadcasting is informative or educational.

The previous chapter highlighted, inter alia, the limited number of empirical educational effects studies thus far. Indeed, there is also some connection between the education issues and the media, communications and form issues referred to in Chapters 3 and 4 earlier. The research can also be criticised because it ignores a whole range of important issues and considerations in relation to the potential educational effects. Again, while the Supreme Courts concerns and the Supreme Court challenge refer to education issues briefly, there is no definition, scoping, baselines or any suggestions made in terms of how we might undertake the educational effects research. Some of the wider issues which need to be addressed and investigated are referred to below.

"The information television presents about the criminal justice system is often misleading and frequently wrong."[1] This work is not about the multiple portrayals of the legal system in the diverse facets of the media. However, we do need to pose questions. Obviously we need to ask whether TCB educates, and how we go about testing and researching the proposition that it educates. However, even beyond those issues is perhaps a more important question posed, for the first time, by the author. If TCB can educate, do we need to distinguish different forms of TCB to consider which form(s) educate best? Certainly there are policy implications.

FORMS

The debate and literature do not refer to television courtroom broadcasting form issues. Education and information effects/potential effects are not equal all of the time, and equal across all forms of television courtroom broadcasting. This should be investigated through research because educational issues and form issues are more sophisticated and complex than the superficial educational arguments to date. Clearly, different styles and forms of television courtroom broadcasting need to be considered in the research of educational effects.

When we undertake sustained research into the issues of television courtroom broadcasting, there may come a stage when proponents and opponents of television courtroom broadcasting, will have to state their preference for particular forms over others. The research thus far, and the level of consideration and depth of the research, has been far too limited (and in many instances flawed) thus far. Therefore, proponents and opponents have not had to consider the different forms of television courtroom broadcasting. This is a serious research gap.

We must also consider different forms because each form has different characteristics. Take the example of D.A. Harris where he states that a 60 second "news clip cannot properly educate the public on the workings of the system."[2] The audience effects from the various different "coverage and style[s]" of television courtroom broadcasting remain at issue."[3] How can a two minute television courtroom broadcasting news clip (without in–court audio), be the same as a full gavel to gavel (G2G) trial – whether civil or criminal?

While arguing that television can be used as an educational medium, Aliza Duby admits that "[o]nly if TV has more to offer educationally than other tools have, or if it makes a specific contribution to education, can its expensive use be justified."[4] The courtroom broadcasting arguments do not address or assess the benefits of one form of courtroom broadcasting over another. Neither do they distinguish between different forms of television courtroom broadcasting viz a viz education. There are gaps in the debate as well as the effects research.

So even if television courtroom broadcasting is educational (but which has not yet been verified to be the case), we also need to go beyond this. We need to examine the level and extent of this educational effect, and compare it with other potentially competing issues and methods of education.

Indeed, an interesting issue is therefore the extent to which we value the cost and balance to be achieved in attaining educational television courtroom broadcasting. This is perhaps a discussion for another time, and after we have first investigated the educational issues in greater depth.

OPPORTUNITY FOR VALIDATION OF EDUCATIONAL TELEVISION COURTROOM BROADCASTING

Television courtroom broadcasting is generally not permitted in Britain (with the exception of the England and Wales Supreme Court) or in Ireland. However, other countries exist where television courtroom broadcasting may be evaluated in terms of the educational effect. Despite the possibility of sustained empirical education research elsewhere, in particular the US, this has not occurred. Interestingly, proponents of TCB do not advocate educational research.

Should the argument for attaining access to courtrooms be to educate, one would think there should be examples and research of educational television courtroom broadcasting. If broadcasters wish to become educators in jurisdictions which have heretofore not permitted access, the strongest pillar in their argument might be to flag past courtroom broadcasting which has proved educational. Unfortunately, there is no sustained research thus far attempting to address this issue.

The standard to judge such broadcasting is arguably by its overall educative value. Therefore, there are policy issues in terms of deciding if we wish to educate generally, or educate in relation to a specific instant case.

Ruthie Elizabeth Reeves Stewart also refers to how trials are increasingly used as a profitable form of entertainment.[5] Entertainment and entertainment TCB require to be understood, researched, and compared to other TCB forms.

Of course, educational and entertaining courtroom broadcasting are not always distinct and clearly delineated. However, if one sets the benchmark by saying that television courtroom broadcasting *will* be educational or *is* already educational for the public at large, then one is arguably creating at least some responsibility for showing, or attempting to show, that people watching television courtroom broadcasting are actually educated by the broadcast/broadcasting.

Unfortunately, the educational argument is not validated, despite the ample opportunity to research the issue.

"INFORMATION" AND "EDUCATION"

In terms of addressing the gaps and raising the sophistication of the research debate regarding television courtroom broadcasting, we must begin to clarify and define whether we are referring to potential *information* effects or potential *educational* effects. It is also important to note that being informative may not always be educational. Being educational may be something quite different from being informative. These concepts should not always be referred to with exact equivalence or interchangeability. Television courtroom broadcasting in documentary or news broadcasting forms may be informative, but may not be educational. We need to begin defining what we are referring to, if we are serious about television courtroom broadcasting research and expanding meaningful audience effects research.

It is also the case that television courtroom broadcasting forms may be informative or educational, but this may not be the main aim, intention or actual effect. Effects may also be co–incidental or side effects. Does an unintended educational effect justify television courtroom broadcasting? The issue of multiple effects is not addressed. Research needs to be sophisticated enough to analyse and distinguish between a variety of effects and discern the main or predominant intentions and effects. If we are suggesting that television courtroom broadcasting is educational, then we need to devise ways to examine whether it is in fact educational, i.e. was the aim and purpose successfully achieved, and if so, to what extent? Again, we must start with proper definitions.

Overall, when television courtroom broadcasting has been permitted for educational reasons, it has not been validated at the end of the experiment period. Indeed, there is frequently no attempt to test for educational results and effects whatsoever.

A further complicating issue is that of examining what people may mean when justifying television courtroom broadcasting on the basis of being informative. What does this mean exactly? Is it identical with being educational, or does it mean something else entirely? Is imparting "information" to be considered a lower threshold than imparting "educational" effects? If so, what policy implications arise?

William Perkanas agrees that there is an issue as to what is meant and understood by the phrase "public understanding."[6] The author points out that significant issues need to be addressed in terms of defining what is meant by "information" and "educational" in the context of television courtroom broadcasting.

While television can inform, it is "informally allocated [a] role of public informer."[7] Educational television is generally associated and childrens' educational television.[8] Adult television programming is less frequently contemplated in terms of (information and or) educational effects. Television is also the largest channel for advertising.[9] So in terms of suggested educational effects of adult television courtroom broadcasting, we need to be more exacting in describing how we are saying it will educate.

We also need to start defining and expanding upon what is meant by educational adult television courtroom broadcasting. Indeed, without proper descriptors and definitions, how are we to test at all that there may be positive, or indeed significant, education effects being achieved by television courtroom broadcasting? Even the limited research to date, which is scant, needs to incorporate these points. The general debate in terms of television courtroom broadcasting policy issues, is therefore ill served and ill informed to date.

TESTING EDUCATION

We also need to define "education" so that there is agreement as to what actually is being tested. In addition, we need definitions so that we can compare results and build up a body of sustained empirical research. Such comparison needs to be across contemporaneous studies and also across studies longitudinally.

A further issue is, what are the tests used to prove that it does educate? Since there are a number of potential meanings that can be taken, it should not be automatically assumed (or claimed) that the meaning that is intended (education, for instance), is the one that will be assimilated by the viewer. There is research in terms of childrens' educational and childrens' educational television. We need to do a lot of research catch up in terms of adult educational television. In terms of the present topic we have substantial research to examine and test adults' educational television courtroom broadcasting. When is education achieved? Is there a minimum threshold? Is it sufficient to "push" educational content, assuming it will be used/received as intended?, or must there be a sufficient amount of pull and reception to be satisfied that education is achieved? Do we need to delve into how the audience use the programming before we consider whether there might be educational effects? Social learning occurs in the home and depends upon "patterns of viewing."[10] We need to test the content as well as examining how and where it is viewed.

EDUCATION AND MEANING

What does the footage of television courtroom broadcasting actually mean?[11] In many definitions of mass media the definition assumes a transmission model, where the mass media merely transfer a message to the audience. Other definitions focus on the process and making of the message within the media organisation. Some refer to what the audience recipients do once they receive the message.[12]

Robert Fiske refers to a media text as being the outcome of its reading and enjoyment by the recipient audience.[13] He refers to a plurality of meaning, so that there is not just one meaning or some automatic meaning that the (whole of the) audience will receive and understand.[14] This makes the proponents of transmission of education content in educational television courtroom broadcasting more difficult to accept.

EDUCATION AND TELEVISION USAGE

What does the audience do with the content and footage? What does the public do? What do the other (television and other) media do with other media affected by it? What happens television courtroom broadcasting and content after we have varied it? How do we use it after viewing it? This is another research gap. In one study, there was a greater degree of "learning" associated not with the footage but rather with the "increase in interpersonal communication about the legal system."[15]

In one survey in 1994, during a high level of television courtroom broadcasting, 66 percent felt they had a greater understanding of the legal system, with 33 percent saying they did not learn anything (N = 1,200).[16] However, surveys seem to suggest that while confidence in the system may increase, the actual amount learned is relatively little.[17] The interview section of William Petkanas's research revealed that there was scepticism in relation to the value of television courtroom broadcasting.[18]

A complicating factor for research and for education, is why the audience watches television courtroom broadcasting. Possibly, for example, an "interest, or base level of understanding, could lead to furthering this interest by seeking out specific programming, such as programs only found on [*TruTV*]."[19] However, there appears to be no relevant television courtroom broadcasting research on the motivation for watching. This is another research gap.

WHAT AMOUNT OF "EDUCATIONAL" EFFECT IS REQUIRED?

Assuming that television courtroom broadcasting is educational, will there be a significant amount of education in quantifiable or justifiable terms? Is this sufficient in terms of rights issues, and in the context of the effort and investment made, to justify television courtroom broadcasting? Is a particular policy course justified solely on the out–of–court educational issues?

One study has found that viewers asked to watch evening news broadcasts recalled significantly more news items than viewers who were not asked. However, neither group was able to recall more than 25 percent of the news items.[20] The same study concluded that both radio and television audiences do not recall many of the news items they see/hear.[21] Furthermore, changes in the medium or form do not increase the rate of overall recall.[22]

If this was repeated in the context of (even) the form(s) of television courtroom broadcasting potentially most amendable to educational effects, this could mean that there is no great recall rate. So, the level of information intake or educational effect could be minimal for the television courtroom broadcasting in different less amendable forms. Is there a minimum threshold of educational effects required in order to proceed with television courtroom broadcasting?

EDUCATE ABOUT WHAT? SPECIFIC VERSUS GENERAL EDUCATION

A separate, although perhaps more complicated issue, is differentiating case–specific educational motives from issue–specific educational motives. In some instances one may wish to educate the public about a specific case. One is permitting a specific case to be broadcast, hoping that the public are educated in relation to that case. This may well be the case when individual judges are asked to consider permitting television courtroom broadcasting. However, there is no research on this point i.e. is the motivation of judges who permit television courtroom broadcasting general or specific education? (or general or specific in terms of some other reason?).

In other instances, one may be less concerned with the specifics of the case being broadcast, but rather that the main issues and themes involved in the case are broadcast via television courtroom broadcasting. This may be the case when considering television courtroom broadcasting at the policy level, such as when creating procedures, codes or general court rules permitting and or regulating television courtroom broadcasting (or forms of television courtroom broadcasting).

Are we seeking to educate in relation to the legal and jury process or the specific instant case? It has been said that if broadcasters are to become educators "then the responsibility is to inform the public about the trial process in general, the administrative complexities of the justice system, and the daily routine of dealing with often overcrowded court dockets."[23] This suggests a general education, not education on a specific instant case. However, our testing and evaluation of educational television courtroom broadcasting will depend on what the end motivation is.

Susanna Barber[24] raises important points when she states that judges are less positive when they see biased courtroom broadcast reports and sensational broadcast reports. "[I]f, as many judges hope, broadcasters are to take on the role of educators as well as news gatherers, then their responsibility is to inform the public about the trial process in general, the administrative complexities of the justice system, and the daily routine of dealing with often overcrowded dockets."[25]

There is no extensive empirical research on what is being educated about, the case, the process, policy objectives (e.g. punishments, sentencing, society norms), etc. The gap in educational discussion, and educational research, needs to expand.

EFFECTIVE EDUCATION AND LEARNING

How do we decide that particular courtroom broadcasts are, to use the words of Denis McQuail, "communicating effectively."[26] Is television courtroom broadcasting successful at educating?

Television continues to change and evolve and "it would be risky to try and summarise its features in terms of communicative purposes and effects."[27] Having the aim of education or having push educational television courtroom broadcasting, does not mean that education is actually achieved.

Some of the features of television as a medium are that many events are relayed "live"; others are relayed "with the aim to create an illusion of ongoing reality"; and that it aims to create a sense of "intimacy and personal involvement."[28]

Social learning refers to,

> the numerous way in which television can be used to 'teach' values and aspirations. At the most general level this relates to ideas about discourse and representation, but more specifically [James] Lull[29] points to the active ways in which parents, for example, may comment upon particular representations to discuss the issues they raise with their children. The concept is closely related to the public sphere and working through.[30]

EDUCATIONAL ACCURACY

Is the media and media content fair? For example, does it offer equal access and hear both sides; is it true; is it objective? Denis McQuail[31] feels objectivity refers (not to truth but rather) a version of truth. It portrays neutrality, a lack of partisanship, accuracy criteria, and presumes a lack of ulterior motive. The main information "quality" requirement is that the media should furnish a comprehensive supply of relevant news as well as background information about society and world events.[32] The information must be balanced and fair (McQuail calls this "impartial"), report alternative perspectives and in a non–sensational unbiased manner.[33] The media must be responsible.[34]

Matt Briggs defines and refers to the "text" as follow:

> Any communicative form involves the production of text. In this sense there is little difference between texts which have a fixed material form, such as an episode of a soap opera, or ephemeral texts which unfold as audiences speculate and gossip as they watch or converse more generally. More radically we can threat our thoughts as texts insofar as they are semiotic in nature: responding to particular representations, discourses, memories, associations and experiences. While fixed material texts have boundaries and offer meanings, and

> must be analysed as such, this view of text stresses intertextuality and the fluid nature of semiosis.[35]

How accurate is television courtroom broadcasting and how well does it have to be in order to successfully educate.

EDUCATION AND BROADCASTING RULES

Andrea Biondi feels that substantive safeguards and restrictions can ensure that the "educational purpose of showing how the machinery of justice works can easily be satisfied by selecting and showing trials which do not involve particularly sensitive or private issues."[36] However, it would appear that celebrity, sensational and criminal trials are the ones that are the predominant focus of television courtroom broadcasting in the US. Equally, he feels that it is not proper that only criminal trials be televised.[37] Civil cases and trials can be educational.[38] Again, most US cases broadcast are criminal trials.

In terms of what is then broadcast, Andrea Biondi feels that trials should be broadcast in entirety, in particular to "avoid any interference in the editing stage."[39] He also appears to be against live televising on the basis of distortion and sensational effects.

Only when recognising and respecting precautionary safeguards "can television really 'contribute to the public understanding of the rule of law and to the comprehension of the functioning of the entire judicial system.'"[40] In many instances television courtroom broadcasting has been permitted without, or with very minimum, pre–defined rules. Sometimes there are safeguards. In the US, the rules also vary significantly between states.

Denis McQuail comments that "the distinction between message and meaning is a significant one." He adds that the,

> physical text of the message in print, sound or pictorial image is what we can directly observe and is in a sense 'fixed.' But we cannot simply 'read off' the meanings that are somehow 'embedded' in the texts or transmitted to audiences. These meanings are not self–evident and certainly not fixed. They are also multiple and often ambiguous.[41]

In terms of getting to an understanding the meaning of broadcasting (and other) messages, there is no one overall method. Instead there are a variety of methods "for different purposes and kinds of content and for a variety of media genres."[42]

To use the words of Dennis McQuail,[43] what is the "informational value" of media texts and courtroom broadcasting media texts. In terms of news we can measure the facts, density, breath, readability, etc.[44] The essence of meaning is described as the reduction of uncertainty,[45] however, are we aware yet of the information value of courtroom broadcasts or of how much uncertainty is reduced, and in relation to what issue or topic?

EDUCATION: CULTURAL AND COUNTRY DIFFERENCES

There are also cultural and country differences to consider. For example, not everyone spends the same amount of time viewing television and there appear to be marked differences between countries. Dennis McQuail refers to research of viewing in 1998.[46] This is set out in Table 15.1.

While television may be watched globally, some argue that there is no homogeneous global television market, particularly for many television genres.[47] Rather programming and viewing are generally segmented into national markets – in the first instance.[48] Indeed, there are many instances where individuals express their opinion that certain examples of television courtroom broadcasting in the US would not be desirable and or permitted in Europe, for example.

EDUCATION: THE AUDIENCE TO BE EDUCATED

Who is to be educated? This is not considered in the general courtroom broadcasting literature. To refer to the potential educational effects generally is simplistic and ignores the nature of the television media and the potential audiences.

Television is particularly concerned with attracting or focusing in on particular audience segments.[49] Teaching is also a conscious intentional function[50] with particular defined tasks and goals in focus. These may not be the same aims which a commercial television station or programme is focused upon. Alternatively, it may only be a sub–theme, while the more dominant themes are ratings and commercial success.

Table 15.1.

Country	Viewing minutes per day
United States	238
United Kingdom	235
Italy	217
France	193
Netherlands	157
Norway	144
Czech Republic	130

We have to date ignored the whole sector of out–of–court television courtroom broadcasting effects research. The audience for television courtroom broadcasting needs to be researched. We need to advance beyond mere ratings. There are some materials on ratings during particular popular broadcasts of celebrity or unusual criminal trials. However, there no research as to why audience member watching particular trials, nor why the courtroom broadcasting generally. There is no ethnography in situ research to research how people actually view television courtroom broadcasting, and what they may be doing at the time. This is not an impossible task. In fact there are a large number of studies and methodologies utilised in the existing study of the audience which can assist.

One reporter is quoted by Paul Thaler, as saying that television "increases [public] interest" and even people who do not use print coverage are engrossed in the television coverage.[51] The journalist also feels that many people watched the Steinberg case for its entertainment value, not its news value.[52]

Other research may also be applied to television courtroom broadcasting. What are the "needs" of the audience?[53]

What do we experience from media messages of courtroom television broadcasting?[54] Much depends on viewer activity, which is not yet researched.[55] Is the audience active or passive? Effects may depend also on what is referred to as active viewing.[56]

Our experience, prior knowledge and even expectations and assumptions also interpret the television text[57] and potentially impact upon the meaning of courtroom television broadcasting. Glen Creeber notes that,

> Understanding the meaning of television news has also led to researcher on audience on audiences. The influence of news on the way people think about the world has been a focus of media research for some time, and although questions of media influence were initially somewhat elusive, there is now a body of evidence to suggest that the news is influential on public opinion in a range of specific and measurable ways. So, for example, a number of studies have demonstrated that news clearly sets an agenda that I then reproduced in responses to surveys about people's priorities and opinions .... Overall, audience studies focusing on television news in particular (now a dominant news source for most people) indicate that people watch television news more inadvertently and with less attention than other forms of television ... This has led researchers to use various qualitative methods to explore in some detail the way in which television news does impact on viewers. So, for example, ... research suggests that what he calls the 'episodic' framing of most news stories (which focus on events themselves rather than the causes or history of those events) makes it difficult to understand the social causes of issues like crime or poverty, and instead to attribute blame only to the individuals themselves ... suggest that television news can be important in creating and reinforcing fairly simple associations ... that stick in people's minds.[58]

Other audience research can also be incorporated for television courtroom broadcasting research.

AUDIENCE CHOICE AND SELECTION

Increasingly, the media revolution means that the audience has more choice and options in terms of what they can access through mainstream media channels, but also through new communications technologies. In addition, many communications channels are no longer one way, but are rather interactive with communications and messages going both ways, whether alone or in addition to traditional one way messages. Furthermore, there is now an increase in private communications or private "media making" with the likes of camcorders, PCs, digital cameras, etc.[59] The internet is also very much a part of the media and communications revolution.[60] Dennis McQuail refers to the point that frequently the audience have a low salience for many communicators.[61] What are the potential impacts in relation to educational TCB?

AUDIENCE FRAGMENTATION

Audience consumption has become even more fragmented with increasing channel hopping, zapping and grazing, with for example the advent of satellite television, the ability to record programmes, cable channels, etc.[62] In addition, these developments have helped to,

> customise the consumption of programmes and genres alike, making it difficult (especially at a time when 'classic' television is increasingly being recycled) to align ritual or ideological readings of programmes and genres with contemporary audiences and viewing populations. At the same time, the proliferation of generic channels like Comedy Central, the Sci–Fi Channel, MTV, CNN News and TCM alongside alongside viewing practice such as zapping – which, as Feuer[63] points out …, entails the rapid deployment of genre–recognition skills – suggest that genre, in each of its facets and dimensions, remains central to television, its organisations, and its viewers and consumers.[64]

Even if television courtroom broadcasting is educational, is the educational effect quite limited? If there is a parallel with television parliamentary broadcasting, generally it does not have any significant audience. Other than content in news programming, most extended parliamentary broadcasting programming does not even rate on standards ratings barometers. These are low compared to other programmes. Increasing multiplication of broadcast channels[65] also raises the risk of smaller audiences for quality or educational television courtroom broadcasting.

EXPANDING LEGAL EDUCATION?

Brainerd Currie[66] refers to legal education and an increasing acceptance of non–legal materials for legal teaching and training. This is arguably more evident in certain countries. An example of this increasing reliance on non–traditional legal materials, is the development of law–psychology and law–psychiatry courses in law schools and or cross disciplinary courses. Many legal courses will now use established texts in the area of statistics, for example. Perhaps more familiar to those interested in the criminal legal process, is the increasing use of psychology and psychology experts in profiling, witness evaluation, eyewitness identification, jury selection, etc. Brainerd Currie writes that,

> The most significant development in American legal education since 1870 is the movement toward reorganization of courses along functional lines and toward the broadening of law school studies to include non legal materials, chiefly from the social sciences, which are relevant to legal problems.[67]

Perhaps the most striking thing about these comments is not how correct and self evident they appear today but rather that they were made in 1955. That a particular line of contemporary study relies on "social sciences," for example, using media and communications studies research and methodologies to study television courtroom broadcasting, which might be described by some as non conventional, does not mean that it should not be pursued. Rather the more important argument is that it would be overly conservative not to pursue such an avenue in the interests of expanding our knowledge and understanding of social and legal issues such as television courtroom broadcasting. A more recent example in Ireland is the use of sentencing statistics and databases.[68]

COMPETING ENVIRONMENT

In addition, future television courtroom broadcasting research which examines the content and effects, must also analyse the comparable or competing programmes available. This is necessary to properly examine the form and effects of particular television courtroom broadcasting programmes. Competing programmes help to define the form of a particular programme, as well as make statements in relation to the likely audience. Also, the times and scheduling arrangements at which such programmes are available, are also useful indicators in the study of television courtroom broadcasting.

When we talk of education and informative value, we must also consider definitions, different programming forms, different television courtroom broadcasting forms, different newspaper forms and different radio forms, and how these influence the type and level of educational and or informative value that can be expected.

Three realisms of television are described in the literature, namely, documentary, drama and actuality.[69] Meaning depends on the type of programme being presented.[70] As Pierre Sorlin describes it, "[c]onsumption is, in fact, determined by the context in which it occurs."[71] Therefore, the type/class of programme against which *TruTV,* for example, competes, helps to form public impressions. Arguably, the class of programme it competes against in the US is not what we traditionally identify as educational.[72] David A. Harris agrees that "[v]iewers choose whether to watch [TruTV], and the network must therefore compete with other programming sources." [73] This needs to be researched in future.

TELEVISION COURTROOM BROADCASTING CONTENT

The footage and content of television courtroom broadcasting has received little attention.[74] Of the empirical research studies highlighted in the previous chapter very few examined content. We need to examine in detail the content of particular television courtroom broadcasting programmes in *each* of the different forms. This will help us to understand courtroom broadcasting in each of these forms and also the different messages being carried in the respective forms. Comparative research is also required. We need to understand the message(s) in order to understand the effects on the audience, and the likely effects on the audience of different television courtroom broadcasting forms.

We do not know that television courtroom broadcasting is educational, as is so often claimed. First, the pictures that are presented have the capacity to form a variety of different meanings and impressions upon those who see them. No proper or sustained out–of–court audience research has yet been conducted nor sufficient educational effects research. Secondly, one must also remember that it is not just the pictures that are presented to the viewer that have an effect. Headlines, adverts and trailers that may precede or follow the programme have effects also. There is then the angle or line of the presenter and what they say (verbally and otherwise). Thirdly, there is not enough research. Of the research that exists, most that searched for educational effects did not find any (see previous chapter).

Ruth Elizabeth Reeves Stewart indicates that normally television news programmes cover stories in 15 – 30 second slots and tell the who, what and where of the story in question.[75] However, trial broadcasts "focus on the details of the crime being prosecuted, the strategy and approaches of the lawyers and the details surrounding the alleged criminal; practically no information is given on the how and why of the court proceedings."[76] TruTV coverage is much more extensive.[77]

CONTENT OBJECTIVITY

Have we yet measured and assessed the objectivity[78] of television courtroom broadcasting and the objectivity of different styles of television courtroom broadcasting? Are some styles more objective? How much courtroom broadcasting is news? How much courtroom broadcasting is factual, quality, accurate, complete, significant, relevant, impartial, neutral, etc.?[79]

Do "visuals and camera shots ... lead the viewer in certain evaluative directions"[80] ?

Could television courtroom broadcasting give disproportionate impressions or representations? Does it give a negative picture, or possibly misrepresent susceptibility to (certain types of) crime? Might it neglect or ignore particular points or issues, or favouring a particular issue?[81] Is violent crime and personal crime news over–represented on TCB?[82]

Non verbal communication[83] in television courtroom broadcasting also needs to be researched.[84]

Are "dramatising"[85] elements added to TCB? How much does it rely on "reconstructive" and added audiovisual content?[86]

What is the aim and the effect of voiceovers? Does re–created drama content appears to be "actual" footage? Even where real scenes are included, they appear brief, and "most of a documentary–drama will be the product of full directorial management of scripted action and speech."[87] How television cameras change and pan back and forth, or pan to and from footage of courtroom broadcasting requires analysis. Cutting, editing and montage[88] effects can also mean that what is presented is not the full and continuous actual footage of the courtroom. For example,

> Editing, or the techniques used to regulate the relationship between camera shots, moves the story forward, cutting the passage of time between actions and events when it is important dramatically that the viewer should not know what happens next or when events become irrelevant to the narrative … The omission of intervals of both story and plot duration in the *viewing time* is known as *ellipsis* or *elliptical editing*. Ellipsis also refer to the shortening of plot duration by omitting intervals of story duration.[89]

Editing or,

> stitching together of individual shots controls the timing and pace of the narrative. This is a powerful tool which can slow down or speed up the pace and rhythm of the narrative. Editing can help create suspense, curiosity or surprise. Television advertisements and pop music videos have a very fast paced edit-

> ing. 'Fly on the wall' documentaries, in contrast, may have very few cuts and present the action in long stretches of real time. Conventional film and television narratives use the techniques of 'continuity editing' to stitch shots together to create an apparently invisible, seamless flow, give the impression of a continuity of time and space, and knit the spectator into the narrative.[90]

The "*frequency* with which any one event is presented by the plot is another feature."[91] The scene includes settings, props, lights, costumes, make up, "figure movement", behaviour, acting.[92] To analyse the structure of a media narrative we must consider,

- Cause and effect logic connecting events;
- Characters and motives;
- Temporal order, duration and frequency of events and how time is represented;
- How the plot manipulates and communicates spatial information as well as how narrative space and movement in space are constructed and made meaningful.[93]

The climax is the "dramatic highpoint of conflict, excitement or tension, followed by release."[94] "Does the use of visual information or live footage lead towards a certain impression? So, for example, if two different interpretations are accompanied by visual information, does this make that interpretation seem more persuasive as an account?[95] " "Most of these forms of analysis demand not only a detailed examination of television news, they also require us to know more about the topics represented than we can glean from the newscast. In order to evaluate what is being represented, in other words, we need to know what information or perspective is being excluded from the story."[96] We need to be familiar with the original in-court trial.

A number of methodical issues and questions arise.[97] In order to generalise, we need to examine what is typical rather than the unusual.[98] A

> *sample* of news programmes ... large enough to establish clear patterns, and to minimise ... untypical ... news coverage as a whole. If we are looking at coverage of a particular event, it is helpful to look at coverage of other comparable events as a point of comparison. If we are looking at more general features of television news, then we need to ensure that our sample is spread across a reasonable period, so that the nature of the coverage will not be distorted by any one (possibly unusual) news content.[99]

In addition, "[o]nce we have chosen a sample, we need to establish a systematic procedure for analysis. This may involve developing a coding frame, which comprises a set of criteria for categorising each news item or news programme."[100] The coding categories should be relevant to the particular research question or issue.[101] Then the coding categories then need to be particularised.[102] When we consider someone being presented, we may categorise appearance according to,

- Quoted but not seen;
- Quoted next to photograph;
- Shown speaking on the camera;
- Etc.[103]

We must examine the media news text, and after that the wider context within which the news is produced.[104] Internally there are a number of levels of decision–making and a variety of institutional, professional or ideological pressures on programme–makers."[105] In addition, the other additional influences and pressures can be examined, such as ownership and control.[106]

Gillespie and Toynbee add "mapping narrative structures ... share[d] certain basic features ... we need to watch out for how stories can impose as well as create certain meanings – including ... cues [to] us."[107] We need to,

> "[a]nalys[e] narrative structure and narrational processes ... Analysing narrative structures requires an essentially static lens, while studying processes of narration captures the movement–by–movement activities in which viewers engage. In analysing film texts we also need to consider the use of specific film techniques.[108]

In reviewing, analysing and testing for effects and meanings, do we not have to examine specific examples of proposed educational programming and the text of such programming. We should not be just superficially referring to the existence of the programme per se, but rather to get into the content and details of the programme and its content and texts.

How much comment comes from the presenter, from first hand speakers, from commentators and from experts.[109] It is important to know and understand not just what is said (and not said) but also who is saying it. The empirical studies in the earlier chapter show that this seldom occurs thus far. Following on, we also need to understand whether one source predominates and predominates unduly.

We need a "close analysis of language to dig out the latent or hidden meanings … beneath media texts."[110] We need much more content analysis.[111] "[A]n effective claim or account concerning the media combines theory and evidence in a way that is *coherent*, *comprehensive* and *empirically adequate*."[112] In terms of educational television courtroom broadcasting, no one has shown and verified educational effects, nor explained how and when predefined educational effects will be achieved.

The "analysis of media texts is central to understanding the ways in which meanings are organised and circulated in society."[113] It is important to analyses programming, the media and texts because it is widely believed that media content can influence politics, individuals, groups and society generally.[114] The information explosion "has resulted in pressure to communicate information as efficiently and economically as possible, resulting in compression styles."[115] There is research into how newspaper texts are edited.[116] There has been no investigated of television courtroom broadcasting production processes.

NEWS USE OF TELEVISION COURTROOM BROADCASTING

One of the issues arising is whether most television courtroom broadcasting footage will be used predominantly for news footage. In addition, we need to assess whether it is used mostly in news programming as backdrop or whether pictures and in court audio is also used. Glen Creeber describes the backdrop and uses of television,

> Television news generally presents itself as a 'window on the world', in which the events of the day are transparently revealed for all to see. Although we may praise or criticise television fiction for being realistic or unrealistic, many people assume that, in the case of news, such judgements are unnecessary. Thus news is not merely seen as like reality but as unmediated reality itself, beamed directly into people's homes. If this were really so, it follows that there would be little reason for anyone to study television news, since to study it would merely be to study the world it reveals. For us to analyse the news is therefore to assume that, like other television genres, the news is a form of representation (or, as it is called in semiology, signification) and that the images and words it uses are, like TV drama, the result of creative and interpretative processes. It is to assert that making television news is … a matter of 'putting reality together.'[117]

Also, "[t]elevision news (and the news media in general) has been studied from a number of perspectives ... rang[ing] from ... social–science–based approaches ... to forms of analysis that come from the humanities (in which TV news is examined as a text)."[118] "In general sociological terms, we can identify three road frameworks that inform the analysis of the social role of television news."[119]

> The liberal pluralist model [sees] television news provid[ing] useful information and thus plays an important role in strengthening democracy and citizenship … Within this framework, more news is good news, both in the sense that a range of different news organisations is needed to guarantee a healthy diversity of providers, and because it is assumed that the presence of television

> news in TV schedules should be sufficient to guarantee wide access to serious news programming.[120]

We are also "accustomed" to news and news presentation and news routines.[121] We thus expect or have an expectation as regards the genre of news, news formats and news programming content.

An interesting point is the general agreement that news coverage should have some proportion and relation to the importance of event, there is little clear definition in terms of what "importance" actually is or what makes one event more important that other.[122] Does importance differ between the public's perception versus the media view? The media also make judgement in terms of what they perceive the audience will want or will see. TruTV does not go into any detail whether in terms of the importance of cases broadcast to the media and the audience.

We can look at what is included in television courtroom broadcasting (as we can with news programming content),

- We can also look at what items and event are not included in courtroom broadcasting, and similarly news programmes;
- We can consider and examiner "how stories are told"[123];
- Is there equal weight[124] between different news broadcasts and between news media generally;
- Who is quoted[125] and from where;
- What are the sources[126] for the stories;
- What are the wider implications of news stories, for example crime?[127];
- How is the story actually told, e.g. the narrative, visuals?[128];
- Is live footage used and if so, does this "lead towards a certain impression?"[129]

Journalists believe television news depict "objectivity."[130] Does increased news dumbing down and tabloid news values at the expense of "hard" news[131] undermine educational TCB?

Television news content has been examined both quantitatively and qualitatively, structure, narrative, news "text," news audiences,[132] textual analysis, content analysis.[133] This seldom occurred for TCB.

In terms of specific aspect of research of news programmes (and TCB), items to study may be found in tables 15.2, 15.3, and 15.4

NEWS ACCURACY

We trust the news to be accurate and truthful.[134] However, while "audiences *rely* upon television news, even if this *trust* is frequently betrayed by incomplete, incomprehensible and biased reporting."[135] Part of the reason news is

Table 15.2. Analysing Television News. Extract adapted from Glen Creeber (110, originally adapted from Hartley, Uses of Television (London and New York: Routledge), 229 – 231).

News as a generic form	Visual elements	Studio anchor and décor; graphics and design; actuality footage.
	Verbal/sound elements	Institutional voices (reporters, commentators, anchors); accessed voices ("real" people); effects (music, dubbed sounds).
	Narration	The "plot" of stories; characters ("we" and "they" personifications, heroes, villains, victims); action and dialogue within and between stories; sequence as a dramatisation of "our democracy today."
	Differentiation	How news is both like and unlike surrounding genres (advertising, talk shows, drama) and media (newspapers, radio, Internet).
News as a dramatisation of democracy	Our representatives	Talking heads (decision-making), visualised by location (reporters hanging around in doorways); celebrities (actions and comments), based on bodily recognition.
	Vox pop	"Ordinary" (i.e. anonymous) people's views – the grab and the sound bite as the chorus of politics.
	National identity	Myths of who "we" are; policing the boundary of the social ("we" have a government, "they" have a regime, "we" love children, "they" are paedophiles; "we" are free, "they" are illegal immigrants).
News as a regime of truth	Impartiality versus bias	How can you tell one from the other?

	Conflict	Truth as a product of "both" sides of a story; truth as violence.
	Eyewitness ideology	News stories are often based on reports, statistics, media releases. But trustworthy reporting is associated with being there in the thick of the action. In practice, the information comes from a "handout," while the reporter stands in front of something visually relevant.
	Fact versus fiction	News has eye contact but not music; drama has music but not eye contact.
Who wants to know?		What are you looking for that you do not already know? The research question will shape your findings, and your methods will determine your results.

trusted is because of the prime institutional and scheduling status given to the news bulletin and also because of the trust and familiarity with the news presenter.[136] David A. Harris comments of how news summaries of courts may be incomplete. "The whole event will be summarized in two minutes by a reporter with little or no knowledge of the legal process. Thus the person interested in a case depends on a highly derivative, filtered source of information." [137] He adds that "[b]y contrast, those who see [TruTV] can make up their own minds about the case and the evidence, [TruTV's] virtually uncut live coverage of trial testimony allows anyone to see the trial as if present. The viewer sees an almost unmediated version of the proceedings, rather than interpretations of the event."[138]

WHO EDUCATES?: THE TRUTV EXAMPLE

There is also the whole aspect of the broadcaster. For example, is the best broadcaster for courtroom broadcasting a public service broadcaster?[139] How might content and presentation differ?

TruTV, which began as CourtTV, started in 1991.[140] Why do people tune in to TruTV courtroom broadcasting? The answer may lie in one of the many ads in the US for TruTV at the time of the Simpson criminal case. One example was a newspaper advert three quarters of which was a picture of Simpson.[141] It contained the phrase "[w]atching the real life *drama* of jus-

Table 15.3.

Who?	Says what?	In which channel?	To whom?	With what effect?
Communicator	Message	Medium	Receiver	Effect

tice." (Emphasis added). Brill, the founder of TruTV,[142] contends that courtroom broadcasting has nothing to do with the insatiable media circus. Can TruTV be viewed as distinctly separate from other media, as it suggests?[143]

Ruthie Elizabeth Reeves Stewart finds that while TruTV makes a better effort than others to educate, "there are still gaps of information missing from this education."[144] TruTV is not educational programming, rather it is "infotainment programming," which she defines as "educational programming told through an entertainment medium."[145] Infotainment is the largest educational "outlet" but "infotainment programs are not immune to ratings and therefore need to appeal to a wide audience. This need to garner ratings often leads back to airing the sensational."[146]

Some of the other criticisms of TruTV are that it focuses exclusively on trials, which are atypical of the overall criminal justice system, and are only a small part of the justice system, and ignores civil cases completely.[147] The trials aired are invariably sensational trials.[148] The main content, such as murder, rape and theft in actuality only account for 10% of overall crimes.[149] Stewart also feels it necessary to remind us that TruTV is not a public service broadcaster.[150]

David A. Harris states that TruTV ,

> is not a public service venture or a broadcasting outlet devoted to educating the public without regard to profits. Rather it is a commercial venture, just like traditional broadcast and cable networks; it airs advertising. It differs from traditional networks in what it offers viewers – trials and other proceedings in rela courts. [It] may help to educate and inform the public, but it does so with the aim of selling of its advertisers' products.[151]

Commercial business influences[152] also cannot be ignored. In New Zealand's television courtroom broadcasting experiment court staff had to intervene between competing television stations in a dispute over footage and pooling.[153] In addition, court staff were also pressed by media representatives to indicate in advance whether a competing station was going to film a case and there also appeared to be competition for the best "visuals" in certain instances.[154]

"[C]ontemporary news ... is dominated by deadlines, urgency, live feeds, twenty–four–hour news channels, Internet news and new news consumption patterns, which facilitate instantaneity."[155] News values[156] of the organisation and the news policy[157] of the organisation. News value requires,

Table 15.4.

Who?	Says what?	In which channel?	To whom?	With what effect?
Control Studies	Content analysis	Media analysis	Audience analysis	Effect

- Good pictures;
- Short dramatic occurrences "which can be sensationalised";
- Novelty value;
- Open to simple reporting;
- Occur on a grand scale;
- Are negative, violent, crime, confrontation or catastrophe;
- Are highly unexpected or is what one would expect;
- It is relevant to the audience;
- There are similar events in the news;
- Contain elites or human interest.[158]

All of this poses "threats and risks to the accuracy of news journalism since being accurate in news that is often disseminated globally has to embrace and work with the constraints of new time pressures."[159] Europe arguably has a greater reliance on public service broadcasters than the US.[160] Public service broadcasting are meant to lean much more towards information and education.[161]

Many earlier models of communication and the audience referred to almost a single receptive non–critical audience More frequently this is expanded upon by greater research of the audience, different audience segments or groups and also research of individual audience members.[162] One example is ethnography research. We now also think of active readers and "active engagement," as opposed to passive spectators, when we consider the audience.[163] "[I]nfotainment" is often criticised.[164] Infotainment programming, for example reality television, is cheaper to produce than action programmes or studio based drama programmes.[165] Television genres are subject to market and commercial pressures – and influence, which can impact upon their content and texts.[166]

Television station of programme maker might classify, label or promote particular programme as being a particular genre does not mean that the audience should automatically accept the categorisation proffered. There should also be at least some element of "genre criticism."[167] In addition, a producer or television station may decide to foreground certain genre elements, such as educational or news, over other elements of genre which are also applicable to the particular programme itself. The television market is increasingly competitive.[168] How does this effect TCB forms?

ENTERTAINMENT

Clearly the reality courtroom programmes are primarily entertaining. However, is this what real cases must also compete against? Arguably reality programming, including reality courtroom programming, is becoming more "daring."[169]

Denis McQuail, a leading communications researcher, states that television is "primarily considered a medium of entertainment."[170] Creeber adds,

> At its most basic level, television is a scientifically managed institution for the mass production of entertainment ... that systematically produces permutations of the everyday and the spectacular. Those permutations are designed to capture audiences and deliver them to advertisers, in the case of commercial networks, or government, in the case of public stations. Genres combine the memorandum and the commodity; one ensures standardisation, the other marketability.[171]

One of the constraints of television is that it requires visuals.[172] Does this mean that TCB must be visually compelling? Context and contextualisation of courtroom broadcasting[173] require examination. Another feature of the mass communication process is that the "symbolic content or message of mass communication is typically 'manufactured' in standardized ways (mass production) and is reused and repeated in identical forms. It has generally lost its uniqueness and originality through reproduction and overuse."[174] Can television courtroom broadcasting differentiate itself?

SUMMARY

As Ruthie Elizabeth Reeves Stewart notes, if,

> television's portrayal of the courtroom is inaccurate or contrived for entertainment purposes, such as syndicated courtroom reality shows like *Judge Judy*, then the viewing public will have an unrealistic perception of the system. If the viewer only comes into contact with the justice system through unrealistic infotainment programming, the viewer will conclude that the programming excludes typical court behaviour. This will lead to low confidence in the system.[175]

The media undoubtedly do have (some) potential to educate but it remains, as of yet, uncertain whether the educational potential is outweighed by other media interests and indeed other competing rights such as constitutional rights). How such organisations go about educating (and measuring their success) has not been fully considered. How seriously they threat their role of education (particularly) in the context of television courtroom broadcasting is also questionable. There has been no analysis of what amounts to "educational" in the context of courtroom broadcasting. Arguably it will only be when this occurs that we can begin to properly evaluate which of the various *types and forms* of courtroom broadcasting come within the definition of "educational" – and which do not. Indeed it may be necessary also to attempt a definition of "educational" in this context. Only at that stage do the implications for the justice system become apparent. If we want to test for educational effects, we need to define what we mean by educational and also in terms of what audience and what forms of television courtroom broadcasting.

Overall, our research in investigating the television courtroom broadcasting issues and arguments is very basic indeed. Clearly is it limited, and clearly it is difficult to consider any of the arguments, in particular effects arguments, as having been justified or validated. On examination, there are many flaws and gaps in the arguments and research. Luckily, once we identify the gaps and flaws we can move to the next stage, which is to deal with these and begin to properly and methodically research all of the separate, and complex, issues. In Chapters 16 and 17 we look at how we may begin particular studies, and in Chapters 6, 7 and 10 we begin to see how important it is to have an overall framework to contextualize our research of individual issues and forms.

Clearly, we need to begin research of the argument that television courtroom broadcasting is educational, as this impacts so significantly on the courtroom broadcasting debates.

William Petkanas notes that the "ongoing debate is not resolved, but the legislatures of many states have agreed that informing the public via television news outweighs any risks that that the critics of television raise."[176] If one emphasises the word "any" does this mean that absolutely all risks are discounted or rather disregarded? Given the lack of extended research, it would seem that disregard is perhaps a better description than disregard of the risks. One could suggest that there is a case and need for a due diligence assessment of the risks and of the research at any given time, whenever deciding upon camera access issues. It would seem that there is no detailed due diligence in some instances, and a limited assessment in others. Again, the research and our consideration of the research needs to be more expansive.

The New York experiment was "prompted by a perceived need for educating the public and increasing public respect for, and confidence in, the judiciary."[177] The politician promoting the law states that he "would venture to say that 99 percent of the electorate have never seen a judge or prosecutor in action."[178] This is an example of debate and policy being decided on beliefs and without referencing the research in relation to effects; (generally) without mandating any particular effects research; and without referencing an identified problem which the introduction of television courtroom broadcasting may be the solution to.

While there are studies which tend to show public misconceptions about the legal and justice system,[179] or at least parts of it, there is seldom a deliberate effort to assess these before and after the introduction of television courtroom broadcasting. This applies equally to educational effects, informational effects and confidence effects.

Parliamentary broadcasting sometimes appears in debated in relation to permitting television courtroom broadcasting. However, there do not appear to be research studies referenced whereby greater educational, information and or confidence effect have been manifest after parliamentary broadcasting.

Petkanas also wonders why it is assumed that "if we increase familiarity we would necessarily increase confidence?"[180] Are the educational aspects of TCB programmes in the foreground[181] or background of the programme? What are the effects?

NOTES

1. D.A. Harris, The Appearance of Justice: Court TV, Conventional Television, and the Public Understanding of the Criminal Justice System, Arizona Law Review 35 (1993) 785–827, at 786.
2. Ibid.
3. R. Surette, Media, Crime and Criminal Justice: Images and Realities, (Belmont CA: Wadsworth Publishing Company, 1998), as referred to in R.E.R. Stewart. The Changing Relationship Between Camera and the Courts (MA diss., Florida Atlantic University, 1998): 31.
4. A. Duby, Using Television as an Educational Medium, Educational Media International 28 (1991) 190–198.
5. R.E.R. Stewart, The Changing Relationship Between Camera and the Courts (MA diss., Florida Atlantic University, 1998): iv.
6. W. Petkanas, Cameras on Trial: An Assessment of the Educational Affects of News Cameras in Trial Courts (Ph.D diss., New York University, 1990): 116.
7. D. McQuail, McQuail's Mass Communications Theory (London: Sage, 2005), 35.
8. Ibid, 35 and references throughout.
9. Ibid, 35.
10. M. Briggs, Television, Audiences and Everyday Life (Berkshire: McGraw Hill/OUP, 2010), 105.
11. See similar question regarding the meaning of video evidence in M. Gillespie and J. Toynbee, Analysing Media Texts (Maidenhead: Open University Press and McGraw Hill, 2006), 36.
12. See discussion in D. McQuail, above, 55 et seq. Also 63.
13. J. Fiske, Television Culture (London: Methuen, 1987), as referred to in D. McQuail, above, 118.
14. J. Fiske, Television Culture, ibid.
15. R.E.R. Stewart, The Changing Relationship Between Camera and the Courts (MA diss., Florida Atlantic University, 1998), 33, referring to D. Brown, J. Duane and B. Fraser, Media Coverage and Public Opinion of the OK Simpson Trial: Implications for the Criminal Justice System, Communications Law and Policy 2:2 (1997): 261–287.
16. Times Mirror telephone survey, referred to in A. Paul, Turning the Camera on CourtTV: Does Televising Trials Teach Us Anything About Real Law?, Ohio State Law Journal 58

(1997): 655–604, as referred to in R.E.R. Stewart, above, 34. The survey is available at http://people–press.org/reports/pdf/19940204.pfd , accessed by Stewart on October 26, 2005.

17. R.E.R. Stewart, above, 33–35.
18. W. Petkanas, above, 98.
19. R.E.R. Stewart, ibid, 57.
20. J. Stauffer, R. Frost and W. Rybolt, The Attention Factor in Recalling Network Television News, Journal of Communications, 33 (1983) 29.
21. Ibid.
22. Ibid.
23. S. Barber, News Cameras in the Courtroom: A Free Press – Fair Trial Debate (Norwood, New Jersey: Ablex, 1987): 88.
24. Ibid.
25. J. Stauffer, R. Frost and W. Rybolt, above.
26. D. McQuail, McQuail's Mass Communications Theory (London: Sage, 2005), 10.
27. Ibid, 34.
28. Ibid.
29. J. Lull, The Social Uses of Television, Human Communication Research 6:3 (1980): 197, as referred to in Briggs, above, 160.
30. See M. Briggs, above, 160.
31. See McQuail, D., above, 200.
32. Ibid, p. 202.
33. D. McQuail, 203.
34. See the "frame of public responsibility, D. McQuail, ibid, 213. Also see the "frame of professional responsibility," ibid, 214.
35. M. Briggs, above, 161.
36. A. Biondi, TV Camera Access in the Courtroom: A Comparative Note, Yearbook of Media and Entertainment Law (YMEL), (1996): 150.
37. Ibid.
38. Ibid.
39. Ibid.
40. Ibid.
41. D. McQuail, above, 340.
42. Ibid.
43. Ibid, 351.
44. Ibid, 351–352.
45. See ibid, 353.
46. Ibid, 35.
47. See M. Briggs, above, 122.
48. See ibid.
49. A. Hart, Understanding Television Audiences, Journal of Educational Television 18 (1992): 12.
50. S. Duby, Using Television as an Educational Medium, above, 192.
51. Pat Clark of The Daily News, in P. Thaler, The Impact of the Television Camera on Courtroom Participants: A Case Study of the Joel Steinberg Murder Trial (Ph.D diss., New York University, 1990), 185.
52. Ibid.
53. D. McQuail, above, 85.
54. See general discussion and references in D. McQuail, above, 126–127.
55. See M. Gillespie and J. Toynbee, Analysing Media Texts, (Maidenhead: Open University Press and McGraw Hill, 2006), 101 et seq.
56. See ibid, 102.
57. See ibid, 102.
58. G. Creeber, ed., above, 108 and references therein.
59. See generally D. McQuail, above, 39.
60. See ibid, 39–40.
61. Ibid, 295.

62. See G. Creeber, above, 6.
63. Feuer, "Genre and Television," in Allen, ed., Channels of Discourse, Reassembled: Television and Contemporary Criticism (London and New York: Routledge, 1992), 158, as referred to in G. Creeber, above, 6.
64. See G. Creeber, above, 6.
65. D. McQuail, above, 320.
66. See, for example, B. Currie, The Materials of Law Study, Journal of Legal Education 8:1 (1955)(8:1) 62 et seq.
67. Ibid, 1.
68. See http://irishsentencing.ie , accessed August 13, 2011. See also US Sentencing Commission, http://www.ussc.gov/ , accessed August 13, 2011.
69. P. Sorlin, Mass Media (London: Routledge, 1994), 43.
70. Ibid.
71. Ibid.
72. See M. Alvarado, R. Gutch and T. Wollen, Learning the Media: An lntroduction to Media Teaching (London: Macmillan, 1987), 41, 53, 105–118, 135 et seq.
73. D.A. Harris, The Appearance of Justice: Court TV, Conventional Television, and Public Understanding of the Criminal Justice System, Arizona Law Review 35 (1993): 817.
74. W. Pogorzelski and T.W. Brewer, Cameras in Court, How Television News Media Use Courtroom Footage, Judicature 91 (November–December, 2007): 125.
75. R.E.R. Stewart, above, 57.
76. Ibid.
77. Ibid.
78. See discussion in D. McQuail, above, 355–358.
79. See general discussion in ibid, 355–357.
80. Ibid, 358.
81. See generally, ibid, 358.
82. Ibid, 358–359.
83. See reference or Non Verbal Communication in D. McQuail, ibid, 362.
84. Ibid.
85. To use the words of G. Creeber, above, 44.
86. To also use the words of Creeber, ibid.
87. See ibid.
88. See M. Gillespie and J. Toynbee, Analysing Media Texts (Maidenhead: Open University Press and McGraw Hill, 2006), 94.
89. Ibid. Emphasis in original.
90. Ibid, 95.
91. See ibid. Emphasis in original.
92. See ibid, 96.
93. Gillespie and Toynbee, above, 96.
94. See ibid, 97, and references therein.
95. Creeber, ed., above, 109.
96. Ibid.
97. Ibid.
98. Ibid.
99. Ibid.
100. Ibid.
101. Ibid.
102. Ibid.
103. Ibid.
104. Ibid, 109.
105. Ibid.
106. Ibid.
107. Gillespie and Toynbee, Analysing Media Texts (Maidenhead: Open University Press and McGraw Hill, 2006), 115.
108. Ibid.

109. See comments in ibid, 132.
110. Ibid, 137.
111. See ibid, 138 et seq.
112. See ibid, 141. Emphasis in original.
113. Ibid, 187.
114. See ibid, 187.
115. A. Durant and M. Lambrou, Language and Media (London and New York: Routledge Taylor & Francis Group, 2009), 195.
116. For example T. van Dijk, News as Discourse (London: Lawrence Erlbaum Associates, 1988); A. Bell, The Language of News Media (Oxford: Blackwell, 1991), as referred to in A. Durant and M. Lambrou, ibid, 195, and indeed the discussion therein.
117. G. Creeber, above, 104.
118. Ibid.
119. Ibid.
120. Ibid, 104, bold emphasis in original.
121. See ibid, above, 108.
122. See ibid.
123. Ibid.
124. Ibid.
125. Ibid.
126. Ibid.
127. Ibid, 109.
128. Ibid.
129. See ibid.
130. See ibid, 106.
131. Ibid, 104.
132. Ibid, 106.
133. Ibid, 110.
134. M. Briggs, Television, Audiences and Everyday Life, (Maidenhead: Open University Press and McGraw Hill), 17.
135. Ibid, 29. Emphasis in original.
136. Ibid, 41.
137. D.A. Harris, The Appearance of Justice: Court TV, Conventional Television, and Public Understanding of the Criminal Justice System, Arizona Law Review 35 (1993) 819, footnotes omitted.
138. Ibid.
139. See discussion in relation to public service broadcasting in D. McQuail, above, 178 et seq.
140. D.A. Harris, above, 786.
141. New York Times, 19 July, 1994.
142. S. Brill, The Eye That Educates, New York Times, 15 July, 1994. Brill is the founder of US TruTV channel (then called CourtTV).
143. For other research concurring with this view read the account of the Steinberg case; the position of court cameras in the media; and also his reflection on American culture, P. Thaler, The Watchful Eye American Justice in the Age of the Television Trial (Westport, CT: Praeger Press, 1994).
144. R.E.R. Stewart, above, 1–2.
145. Ibid.
146. Ibid, 22.
147. See ibid, 30.
148. Ibid, 31.
149. Ibid.
150. Ibid, 31.
151. D.A. Harris, above, 801.
152. G. Creeber, above, 112.

153. K. Allan, J. McGregor, and S. Fontaine, The Impact of Television, Radio and Still Photography Coverage of Court Proceedings, Final Report, A Report Prepared for the Department For Courts (Department of Human Resource Management, Faculty of Business Studies, Massey University, April, 1998), 202. (New Zealand).
154. Ibid.
155. G. Creeber, above, 112.
156. Ibid.
157. Ibid.
158. Ibid.
159. Ibid.
160. See, for example, D. Creeber, ibid, 115.
161. Ibid.
162. See ibid, 14.
163. See ibid, 15.
164. See ibid, 115 et seq.
165. According to figures referred to in ibid, 24.
166. See ibid, 7.
167. To use the words of D. Creeber, ibid, 10.
168. See references and comments in D. Creeber, ibid, 33.
169. R.E.R. Stewart, above, p.1.
170. D. McQuail, above, 35.
171. D. Creeber, above, 159.
172. Ibid, 112.
173. Briggs refers to the point that there is a lack of contextualisation in relations to audience research and television viewing, M. Briggs, Television, Audiences and Everyday Life (Maidenhead: Open University Press and McGraw Hill), 15.
174. See D. McQuail, above, 55.
175. R.E.R. Stewart, above, 24.
176. W. Petkanas, above, 11.
177. Ibid, 11.
178. Ibid.
179. See references ibid, 12–13.
180. Ibid, 118–119.
181. See, for example, M. Gillespie and J. Toynbee, Analysing Media Texts (Maidenhead: Open University Press and McGraw Hill, 2006), 109.

Chapter Sixteen

TCB Effects: Meeting the Research Challenges

INTRODUCTION

The above analysis indicates how little effects research there is, and how there are numerous gaps in the effects research that does exist. The Supreme Court effects research challenge throughout the three cameras cases is not referred to in the discussion and debate. It is not catered for in research design issues. Indeed, there is little general empirical research of the impact of news coverage and, for example, juror behaviour. [1]

In all of the above suggested research avenues, and indeed any other research regarding TCB effects, we need to address a number of other problems which have afflicted the research generally to date. These are referred to below, and the general themes of which are referred to variously elsewhere throughout the work. (However, a detailed analyse of all such issues would require significantly greater resources than available for the current work. It is strongly recommended that future research collect (to the extent that they are still available), assess and compare the general research studies).

We need to address the Supreme Court effects research challenge. Any debate or policy discussion is diminished for its absence.

Importantly, the implications are international and not simply national to the US.

We have seen in the above chapters and research, that while significant effort is required in order to deal with the Supreme Court effects research challenge, such effort requires an interdisciplinary approach. A simple legal caselaw analysis is unable to address the Supreme Court challenge. It has also been highlighted above, that the Supreme Court has not delved into how to address the challenges and the effects concerns. This work has sought to identify the gaps and set out the definitions and baseline parameters which will enable sustained research of TCB effects, and which will assist in answering the Supreme Court challenge. Carrying out such research is the next stage. The author recommends such research and the funding of such valuable research.

This chapter now ties the above research and chapters together in terms of summarising the issues, challenges and recommendations for future TCB effects research.

At the beginning, we asked an important but overlooked question. What is television courtroom broadcasting? Indeed, a wider question also arises: what is courtroom broadcasting? The research effort, and indeed the overall Supreme Court effects research challenge have not addressed either of these definitional questions.

DEFINITIONS

The author provides the first considered definition of television courtroom broadcasting. It is defined as follows: *television courtroom broadcasting is television cameras in the courtroom, filming courtroom proceedings for live and or contemporaneous television push broadcast to the general public.*

This definition excludes relayed or closed circuit television courtroom broadcasting (in other courts or similar locations). It also excludes radio, pull internet, recording media, juryroom, still photography and archival recording courtroom broadcasting. The term *television courtroom broadcasting* is therefore used throughout in relation to this effects research work (and the abbreviation TCB).

Future research (and discussion) of the effects of television courtroom broadcasting need to work from specific definitions of what is be referred to and researched. Without control definitions, any such commentary and effects research is undermined.

DATA COLLECTION

The California Cameras in the Courtroom: Report on Rule 980 report of 2000 noted that all media applications contained incomplete information.[2] It also refers briefly to media education issues.[3] Any research going forward need to be rigorous in the collection of valuable data, all of which is required in order to properly research the many and varied effects issues.

HYPOTHESIS TO RESEARCH

In future, it is not sufficient for TCB research to simply begin as an afterthought after the experiment has concluded or after it has begun – as has happened in many instances previously.

Of fundamental importance, however, is that actual effect hypothesis for each of the areas of concern, are actually set out and methodically researched from there.

TIME TO BEGIN: THE BASELINE

Research must begin before the cameras enter the courtroom. Significant data is otherwise lost, and some of which cannot be gathered after the cameras have entered. The baseline data for effects research needs to begin before the potential effect changes which cameras may introduce.

SUBSTANTIATION AND THE BODY OF RESEARCH

A significant body of research must be developed for each effect hypothesis, so that we can then build up our knowledge on specific effect and also compare studies like for like. Without this, each study effectively remains isolated, stand alone and limited to its own facts. It can have no general applicability.

The mistaken generalisation of studies to date, many with flaws, is one of the most significantly disturbing aspects of the courtroom broadcasting debate. There is not enough valid and empirical research to make any generalisations. This flaw is not previously addressed in the literature.

METHODOLOGY

While we need to develop a hypothesis and then research that hypothesis in effects studies, we also need to adopt modern research methodologies. Some of the areas to be addressed and considered include research methods and methodologies,[4] interviewing,[5] content analysis,[6] meaning[7] and messages,[8] cross jurisdictional issues,[9] forms,[10] news narratives and framing,[11] real/factual television,[12] media research,[13] production and process issues,[14] audience,[15] audience groupings,[16] television uses and consumption,[17] education issues and research,[18] audience and memory,[19] research study comparisons and validation issues,[20] effects research,[21] influence[22] and agenda influences, and location.[23]

QUESTIONS TO BE ADDRESSED IN FUTURE RESEARCH

From the foregoing analysis it is clear that significant research already undertaken in other areas and related areas can be applied to television courtroom broadcasting issues. What is also clear is that even looking at the television courtroom broadcasting arguments, apart from the issue of there being no validations of any arguments, there has been no proper consideration of what each of the arguments actually means.

When properly considered, the various television courtroom broadcasting arguments lead to queries and consideration about the meaning and parameters of each argument. For example, some of these queries and parameters for some of the television courtroom broadcasting issues include:

Education and the television audience

- Is education possible through broadcasting of the courts?
- Is education a primary or secondary media interest?
- What effect on the potential educational value of television courtroom broadcasting will ensue if it is only a secondary or subsidiary interest?
- How does the educational potential differ amongst the various types of television courtroom broadcasting?
- At what stage is there a sufficient amount of educational potential/effect to make television courtroom broadcasting, or particular forms of television courtroom broadcasting, worthwhile?

Communication models

- Does courtroom broadcasting fit within an existing communications model?
- How does one construct a new communications model for television courtroom broadcasting, if this is necessary?
- How does television courtroom broadcasting communicate to the reader (audience)?
- What does it communicate?
- How are cases selected for broadcast and what are the various stages of this selection/gatekeeping?
- What influences viewers to watch television courtroom broadcasting?

The media audience

- How extensive is the television courtroom broadcasting audience?
- What forms of television courtroom broadcasting are watched?

- What influences selection of television courtroom broadcasting and why are particular selections made?
- Does the audience differ among the various types of television courtroom broadcasting?
- What, if anything, does the audience learn?
- Which forms of television courtroom broadcasting does the audience learn most from?
- How does the audience react to television courtroom broadcasting in news programmes, docu-dramas, documentaries, etc. and how does the audience react as between light entertainment and serious presentations within those categories?

Agendas

- Is television courtroom broadcasting reflective of the court process?
- Is television courtroom broadcasting reflective of the types of cases?
- Is television courtroom broadcasting reflective of the actual cases covered?
- Do agendas surface in any of the forms of television courtroom broadcasting as exists, and in which forms of television courtroom broadcasting in particular?
- Do others use what has been broadcast on television courtroom broadcasting to serve or enhance their own agendas?
- How does television courtroom broadcasting affect existing agenda setting?

Language

- What language or languages are used in television courtroom broadcasting and television courtroom broadcasting programmes?
- What are the consequences for meaning and understanding by using different languages and texts while ignoring others?
- When more than one language or text is present, what is the effect of one being subordinate to another?
- What other things within television courtroom broadcasting convey meaning apart from that which is said (i.e. the main text)?

Confidence

- Can self report studies of themselves accurately indicate the effects of television courtroom broadcasting?

- How does one overcome the limitations of the self report and confidence problems?

Weapons focus

- How can weapons focus and other psychological research, such as stress, impact upon the study of television courtroom broadcasting effects?
- How can existing studies be adapted to study courtroom broadcasting?
- How can existing studies form the basis for creating studies specific to television courtroom broadcasting?

Other issues

- What influence should the views of courtroom participants have on the decision to broadcast generally, and also upon the decision to broadcast individual cases in particular?
- What does the research so far reveal?
- Is the research adequate? If not, why not?
- Does an educational/entertainment distinction exist between the various forms of television courtroom broadcasting and what are the implications?
- What are the effects of television courtroom cameras on the courtroom participants?
- What are the effects of television courtroom broadcasting on the courtroom participants?
- What are the effects of television courtroom broadcasting on the audience?
- Should criteria or minimum guidelines be outlined for the content and process of television courtroom broadcasts and television courtroom broadcasting forms?

RESEARCH FORMS MAP/MATRIX

An obvious overall research point is to itemise all of the various issues at a headline level, particularly since this has not been undertaken before. This would help to given a proper and full impression of the full extent of the research effort that actually faces researchers and those involved with television courtroom broadcasting issues. Then in terms of specific types of research it will be possible to see what needs to be done to research the particular television courtroom broadcasting arguments. This will also assist in enhancing the sophistication and depth of the research carried out in future.

As mentioned already, a specific project involves identifying many of those studies, research and techniques from other disciplines which can be and which should be utilised for courtroom broadcasting research.

An understanding of proper research, the scientific and procedural methodologies, internal checks and balances, and validation and replication processes used for general and scientific research is a fundamental starting point for all future television courtroom broadcasting research.

In considering the suggested beneficial educational effects of television courtroom broadcasting the research which needs to be conducted has to incorporate existing research results and the methodologies used, to begin researching,

- Whether television, as opposed to print [journalism] better informs the public about a particular case;
- Then within television courtroom broadcasting forms we need to investigate which form(s) better inform the public about a particular case;
- What are the impacts of television courtroom broadcasting restrictions?;
- What effect do television courtroom broadcasting restrictions have on education?;
- What are the effects of and broadcasting content/text of each of the different forms of television courtroom broadcasting?;
- Which forms of television courtroom broadcasting are the most balanced?;
- What are the different effects of different courtroom filming forms and different television broadcasting forms?;
- What types of case predominate television courtroom broadcasting?;
- Can this lead us to any conclusions or better understanding of the issues and effects of television courtroom broadcasting?;
- What led the media not to take up the opportunity to undertake television courtroom broadcasting frequently, when permitted to do so in an extensive New York pilot scheme, and which was apparently one of the factors leading to the non–renewal of the scheme?
- How do courtroom actor effects differ between different television courtroom broadcasting forms?;
- How do courtroom actor effects differ between different courtroom participants per each of the different television courtroom broadcasting forms?;
- How do viewing audience effects differ between different television courtroom broadcasting forms?;
- How does television courtroom broadcasting differ between different jurisdictions?
- Where, and to what extent, does there exist (or support for such a right exist) for a general right to television courtroom broadcasting?
- Where do the boundaries of judicial discretion, both generally and individually, lie?

- Who else besides media interests are proactively in favour of television courtroom broadcasting?
- Does open justice and public access mean that courts have to use technology when a particular court cannot hold everyone who is interested in attending a particular case?

Even if potential effects may be difficult to gauge, does this mean the arguments about effects and potential effects are redundant. Clearly, however, because of the important issues at stake, we need more expansive research studies into television courtroom broadcasting.

DEFINITION OF COURTROOM BROADCASTING

The author has proposed the first comprehensive definition of television courtroom broadcasting (above). However, our future research needs to be defined and scoping all of the forms of courtroom broadcasting; forms of television courtroom broadcasting; and any sub–forms.

FORMS OF TELEVISION COURTROOM BROADCASTING

Specific cognisance needs to be taken of identifying and examining each of many and varied television courtroom broadcasting forms. It is likely that different forms will have different effects. While the list identified previously (and set out again below) is the authors own observations, specifically detailed research is required into the different forms and differentiations. Quite simply how can anyone seriously argue in favour of or against courtroom broadcasting without being clear on what form they are specifically referring to. Once the forms are identified sufficiently it will increasingly become evident where particular research can be carried out into, and comparatively between, the different forms.

PSYCHOLOGY AND EYEWITNESS RESEARCH

It has long been realised that eyewitness identification can be fallible, but sustained research is illuminating why this may be so and in what circumstances. Surely then, such evidence is pertinent to cases where there exists a strong reliance upon eyewitness identification.

Psychological research into the court process dates back at least to 1908.[24] More recently such research has centred upon eyewitness testimony and factors affecting eyewitness identifications, for example, Elizabeth Loftus in her book Eyewitness Testimony.[25]

There is evidence of the weapons focus effect, as already discussed. It has been hypothesised by the author,[26] that there might be a similar effect caused by television courtroom cameras, distracting (or attracting) the (full) attention of court participants. Loftus has empirical evidence of weapons focus[27] using a corneal reflection device[28] to discover where and for how long individuals focus their attention.

Such an experiment could also be constructed for television courtroom cameras. That the opportunity for such research has been left untapped is an indictment on those involved in such broadcasting.

When examined, however, one realises that such research could prove detrimental to these interests in continued television courtroom broadcasting. Indeed in anticipation of such research ever coming forth in the future, the networks are reported as already preparing to devalue and undermine the results of such studies.[29]

This area provides only one avenue of potential research into television courtroom broadcasting, others coming from the fields of psychology–law, media and communications studies.

SENTENCING EFFECTS

One avenue for future research, which may be interesting in terms gauging the effects of television courtroom broadcasting upon judges, is to study sentencing decisions where television courtroom broadcasting was present and where it was not present. Any discrepancies between the two study groups would also be an effect which would not be observable from limited self reports and questionnaires. It may also be useful to have a body of such studies from a variety of jurisdictions. One reason would be to compare different television courtroom broadcasting forms. A second reason is that some jurisdictions have more stringent sentencing guidelines than others. This may be a factor which would reduce the possibility of, for example, longer sentences where television courtroom broadcasting occurred. Therefore, if such an effect is present it may take a number of studies before it presents itself. This is particularly interesting point given that there are, to a large extent, more stringent sentencing guidelines in the US than elsewhere, and it is in the US where most television courtroom broadcasting occurs. A similar case for such research can be made in relation to conviction rates as has been made for television courtroom broadcasting sentencing research.

PARLIAMENTARY BROADCASTING

There is also considerable scope for comparative research between existing television courtroom broadcasting and television parliamentary broadcasting.

Little, if any, comparative research has been undertaken anywhere. Even where a particular jurisdiction does not permit courtroom broadcasting it may be possible to conduct research into existing parliamentary broadcasting (where permitted). Particular avenues include audience research, actor research and the generally fixed and/or restricted forms of television parliamentary broadcasting. Indeed given that generally television parliamentary broadcasting is so regulated and restricted, why are advocates of television courtroom broadcasting (a) not complaining about the restrictions placed on television courtroom broadcasting; and/or (b) advocated for such forms of television courtroom broadcasting which are significantly more liberal, and unrestricted, than is the case with television parliamentary broadcasting as it is generally understood and practised in most jurisdictions where it exists. Television parliamentary broadcasting also permits detailed research of education issues and the potential for educational effects and benefits. One of the particular areas of research obviously has to involve details study of the use and possibilities surrounding miniturised, fixed and rotating, and sliding cameras. Also interesting would be study of the restrictions on the end content use which apply to parliamentary broadcasting.

While the existence of parliamentary courtroom broadcasting is frequently used as an argument for permitting TCB, it is seldom noted what the effects of parliamentary broadcasting are. Also ignored is the actual content of parliamentary courtroom broadcasting. The actual audience for parliamentary broadcasting is also ignored. When one examines parliamentary broadcasting figures it is noted that the actual audience figures are comparatively low.

A research report in Ireland relating to these issues, which the author understands remains to be published, states as follows,

> Audience Projections
>
> In other countries where there is a parliamentary channel it is significant that even where access is almost universal, the hour–by–hour audiences (the "'share') for parliamentary channels is so small that it is often not measurable by standard industry methods and few countries even attempt to measure or estimate the size of their audience in this fashion.
>
> BBC Parliament uses an audience figure which represents the total number of viewers who tune in to the channel at any point, over an extended period of time (this is known as 'reach'). Taken over a month this estimate of 'reach' is approaching 1.3 million viewers from a total UK population 60.5 million.
>
> Just over half of the total TV audience for BBC Parliament comes from the Freeview DTT platform. This information may be contrasted with a viewing figure which is shown in the BBC annual report as being 0.0%.
>
> Using BBC Parliament as a comparator the audience 'reach' for the Oireachtas Channel might eventually rise to 100,000 viewers per month.[30]

In the UK, parliamentary broadcasting figures do not register on the normal programme ratings measures. In Ireland the main parliamentary broadcasting programme is called Oireachtas Report. Figures obtained from RTE (the main Irish broadcaster) reveal that during the period 19/1/2010 to 8/7/2010 indicate that the audience ratings varied between a low of 8,400 and high of 101,200 per programme.[31] These are low compared to other programmes. There has been some consideration on Oireachtas (i.e. Parliament) TV channel.[32]

Apparently a number of courts audio record their cases, including the Supreme Court.[33] A useful study would be to see the extent to which the media use these recordings (where permitted) or where third parties uses them, and for what purposes.

We also need to look at the make up of the television parliamentary and television courtroom broadcasting audiences.

Given the strong arguments put forward in favour of television courtroom broadcasting such as greater openness, understanding and educational effects, we should study in detail these specific effects arguments in the context of television parliamentary broadcasting. Equally, we should try to discover what misconceptions exist in relation to the political process and parliament, and to what extent this is clarified by television parliamentary broadcasting.

Television parliamentary broadcasting may prove a very useful tool for examining arguments into possible grandstanding effects by particular participants.

One of the most widely publicised and courtroom broadcast cases viewed was the Simpson criminal case. Yet the majority of the literature and books after the case did not seek to study or analysis the effects of television courtroom broadcasting.

We then also need to consider the different types of educational benefits. It is limited to assume there is only one for of being "educational" or one form of educational television courtroom broadcasting.

The content analysis and comparative programming analysis as referred to elsewhere above. This includes the types of cases, where and the actual presentation of these cases, the amount of time given to different types of cases.

We need also to consider which forms of television courtroom broadcasting are preferable and why. These are some of the issues which should and can be investigated.

There are so many different types of television courtroom broadcasting rules, restrictions, procedures that these should be examined and compared to understand their rationales and to recommend which rules and restriction should apply in any given case pursuant to the policy decisions being pursued.

We can also conduct research into the content of television courtroom broadcasting programmes to date.

Television courtroom broadcasting advocates feel that broadcasting is more accurate than newspaper reports. This could be tested to some extent in the context of parliamentary broadcasting effects.

There is significant research to be carried out into effects inside and outside the courtroom, both in terms of positive and negative effects.

Another area of research is to see what links or influences there may be between sentencing, courtroom broadcasting and conventional media reporting.

There is no general courtroom broadcasting in Ireland or the UK (other than the UK Suprem Court), yet on the very limited number of occasions where cameras have been permitted into Irish and UK courts, it appears that no empirical research or studies were contemplated or undertaken, either by the judiciary or the media themselves.

MEDIA AND COMMUNICATIONS

While worthwhile research, on a significant scale, into effects has yet to be undertaken, other pertinent areas should not be ignored. The whole issue of television courtroom television cameras should not be divorced from other facets of the media and communications field. The exact location of television courtroom broadcasting forms within the communications compendium is also awaiting definition.

BIAS

Another issue also arises in relation to the construction of effects type studies and questionnaires. Apart from the fact of other supporting research, it is common to seek to cross validate and cross compare results within a study itself. It appears that none of the studies to date have sought to do this in terms of, for example, issues of bias. Are courtroom participants more or less likely to indicate effects or non–effects if they are in favour of or alternatively not in favour of courtroom broadcasting? A courtroom actor who may have objected to television courtroom broadcasting may react differently to television courtroom broadcasting and may indicate an observable difference in their answers from other courtroom participants. A courtroom actor who may have their features digitally blocked may act, react or answer differently from other courtroom participants, or from identical courtroom participants in another case who may not have their features blocked. None of the many opportunities for internal comparison and validation have been utilised in the studies to date.[34] It is possible to construct studies in such a way as to test for pre–existing biases held by courtroom participants.

A supplementary point to the effects research issues is that at least some of the effects may not show up on or be possible to gauge and test for in questionnaires and self report studies (at least on their own). As a simple example a courtroom actor may react to, look at or be affected by television courtroom broadcasting without their realising it. It is not possible for self report studies or questionnaires alone to satisfactorily test for such effects. We need to carry out research under additional and other research methodologies. These are not necessarily new as they have been used for a long period in other areas of study.

Many other pertinent and relevant research areas and research methodologies appear not merely to have been ignored, but not even considered in conducting research into television courtroom broadcasting, both in terms of effects type research and also research into other areas of television courtroom broadcasting.

THE MEDIA AND RESEARCH

Television courtroom broadcasting is naturally an emotive issue. It also poses significant legal, social and ethical issues. It is because of this that there have been so many arguments and issues raised by those supporting and opposing television courtroom broadcasting. There are clearly many issues and concerns to be addressed and hopefully resolved. However, as Barber[35] highlighted the television courtroom broadcasting research carried out during the period 1975 – 1981 did not answer these questions. In fact most of the questions and issues were ignored completely in the research. The present author feels that nothing significant has changed in the research since that date. Therefore, the research and the media proponent of television courtroom broadcasting (and others) can be accused of not being serious in examining the effects of television courtroom broadcasting, or indeed any of the other issues which relate to this topic. As long as this remains the case, it appears that the media's concern, balance and public altruism may be less then sincere.

We also have to ask generally why there has been so little research, and also why the research is so limited and primitive. In terms of the media the accusation will remain, until such time as the media addressed the broader research opportunities, that it does not serve its commercial and entertainment aspiration to undertake or assist such research.

In terms of the courts themselves, they have on occasion sought to conduct research. Unfortunately, the court while legitimately and responsibly concerned about the issues involved with television courtroom broadcasting may not always be the best entity to conduct such research. Firstly, in many instances courts have been pushed into permitting access. Where they have permitted access they have not been provided with additional resources to properly achieve the research task. There has been no adequate separate budget to conduct a wide and meaningful study of effects, etc., particularly on an ongoing basis. Not every court or series of courts has been able to carry out research. Judges may not always be aware of the wider research opportunities, and it is clear that judges themselves are not professionally trained social scientists and researchers of many of the particular issues involved. Many of the studies require scientific, communications, psychological and statistical experience. In many instances media organisations will have experience or knowledge of some of these issues and research opportunities but have never volunteered their knowledge to the courts. Indeed, in some instances the media themselves are best placed to carry out some of this research.

EDUCATIONAL RESEARCH

One of the arguments used by proponents of courtroom broadcasting, particularly the media, is that it is or will be educational. None of the research to date bears this out, albeit partly because most of the research is not considered. In fact no proponent of television courtroom broadcasting has shown any study where television courtroom broadcasting has been shown to be educational. The media is well aware of media research, and media effects research methodologies and techniques. Why has the media not conducted research into the education effects of television courtroom broadcasting? One answer is that the media is simply and solely concerned with getting access to our courts for the purpose of television courtroom broadcasting. Another is that they feel that such research, if carried out, will not bear out their argument that television courtroom broadcasting proves educational for the viewing audience. A further reason may well be that they recognise that the extent to which such educational effect research will prove positive, it will show positive effects but only for certain forms of television courtroom broadcasting. Worse still, it may show no effects at all, thus undermining their arguments for access in the first instance. It may even show negative effects of certain forms of television courtroom broadcasting. This would also worry the media generally but also many forms of broadcasting in particular.

Also, when one accepts that there are different television courtroom broadcasting forms, we may have to make a value judgement as to whether we want to adopt a particular form of television courtroom broadcasting over another. We may, for example, wish only to support the most educational form(s) of television courtroom broadcasting, or the form(s) which offer the optimum potential for education. Critical thinking media commentators or scholars may question to what extent the media generally have a vested interest in preventing a recognition of or research into different forms of television courtroom broadcasting.

MORE ACCURATE REFLECTION OF COURTS

Certain television courtroom broadcasting proponents when arguing in favour of permitting television courtroom broadcasting indicate that it provides a greater and more accurate picture of what happens in the court. They say that because the pictures are actually shown that such broadcasting is therefore more accurate. In addition, because there are pictures shown this is clearly better than any possible reports in newspapers. Such arguments can be queried and the existing research criticised for not seeking to test these propositions. Research could quite easily be undertaken by building upon or following other relevant research, which seeks to show whether and which forms of television courtroom broadcasting are better and more accurate than particular forms of newspaper court reporting. Similar research could also seek to investigate which forms of television courtroom broadcasting show more of actual court proceedings, noting for example differences in voice-overs, reporting and commentary.

It is also implicit in television courtroom broadcasting arguments that because of the pictures, such broadcasting is more educational. Also implicit is that television courtroom broadcasting is more informative. Existing research is flawed to the extent that is has not sought to demonstrate or substantiate these propositions. This raises a number of questions, particularly of the media, as to why not.

None of the research to date, at least none of the research thus far reviewed, had ever sought to refer to the different television courtroom broadcasting forms, to describe the form of television courtroom broadcasting being studied, or to distinguish at a general level between the different television courtroom broadcasting forms. Surely, before we can make any decisions or conclusions in relation to television courtroom broadcasting and the various issues it raises we must have as much information, analysis and research as possible. Even if there is not as much as possible there must at least be such an amount as is necessary and proportionate to the issues and seriousness which exists with such an important topic as television courtroom broadcasting. This certainly has not been the case to date.

GATEKEEPING

There are many studies in existence which examine the form and content of particular media product/output, be it programming, print or radio. Some of this research also examines the personnel, processes and decisions through which information must go through before becoming the final report or broadcast content. No similar research has been conducted into the television courtroom broadcasting process and what stages, personnel, criteria and decisions influence and mould what television courtroom broadcasting cases and forms reach the ultimate viewing audience. If such studies have been and continue to be carried out for a whole variety of television and newspaper content, why can this not also been done for television courtroom broadcasting? The answer is that some of those who should be conducting or requesting such research may be unaware of it (e.g. courts), or alternatively those who are aware of and are familiar with such research (e.g. the media) are unwilling to carry it out or to assist others to carry it out.

The current research is flawed, as has already been pointed out because it is so confined and limited both in terms of its scope and methodologies. A related criticism is that much obvious published and available research and also existing research methodologies have been ignored. Whatever one can say about whether or not judges should be aware of such research avenues, certainly the media proponents of television courtroom broadcasting and at least some of the (academic) commentators who have published papers on the overall theme of television courtroom broadcasting should have averred to and carried out research using the supplementary research themes and methodologies. Therefore, this is not just a flaw of the research to date, but it is a criticism of most of those involved in and commenting upon television courtroom broadcasting and television courtroom broadcasting research.

MEDIA

Fairclough develops research into media discourse, and relies, amongst other things to media studies, social theory, linguistic and sociolinguistic analysis, conversation analysis, semiotic analysis, critical linguistic and social semiotics, social–cognitive analysis and cultural–generic analysis.[36]

In television courtroom broadcasting debates most effects–arguments focus on what effects occur with the main courtroom participants, namely the lawyers, judge, jury, etc. However, there are other participants or participants in courtroom broadcasting. These include reporters, court personnel, presenters, editors, experts, the audience(s), and other interested parties e.g. politicians, academics.[37]

Even after a particular case may be filmed, it may be significantly packaged and presented, especially where this is in a non live television courtroom broadcasting form. For example, a media television text may be mediated and worked on by journalists, presenters, various editors, and various technical staff.[38] It may also go through numerous drafts and versions, a news story may be amended eight times.[39]

PERSONALITY TYPE

The research to date in relation to television courtroom broadcasting does not take into account that effects can depend upon the personality type of the courtroom actor or viewer. Research in relation to other areas, sometimes including television,[40] takes into account the personality type of the individual research subjects *before* going on to examine the effects of particular stimuli.[41]

Without doing so, would be similar to saying that we are testing to see if a given potential effect, e.g. education in the context of TCB, was the same for every person.

Individual also vary in their individual backgrounds and experiences.[42] Again, while this is examined in other research, it is still ignored in the contest of TCB research. It is suggested that it is over simplistic to suggest or assume that TCB and cameras in the courtroom will have the exact same effect across all courtroom participants and across all categories of courtroom participants.

There is already suggestions in terms of introducing emotional intelligence issues into law school teaching.[43]

RESEARCH DESIGNS

Too many of the studies to date are undermined by their methodology.[44] Greater rigour and planning[45] needs to be adhered to in future. Studies need to state their methods. They need to be empirical and scientific,[46] otherwise it is difficult if not impossible to say that suggested results are anything other than supposition and opinion. It is also difficult if not impossible to justify a particular cause and effect if the effect is not disentangled and isolated from other possible effects or variables.[47] Court cases are complex events and processes, and therefore, require great particularity in terms of researching such effects.[48] We need proper data on effects, and not mere opinions and interpretations of effects and what occurred.[49]

GENERAL APPLICABILITY

Researchers need to advise those reading them if they feel that the particular study is generalisable.[50] The official studies in particular, especially opinion and self reports, do not consider whether the results can or should be applicable to other court cases and other courtroom participants. In terms of audience type issues, the general applicability is also ignored.

Unfortunately, unless all studies begin to incorporate proper assessments and qualification, commentators will continue to misinterpret the research findings, and also make generalisations which are not backed up by the actual research they cite or refer to.

WHAT IS BEING RESEARCHED?

The opinion reports and self reports are particularly prone to ignoring the basic first step of research, which is to identify the effect or effect hypothesis[51] being researched. It is the effect hypothesis that is being identified and tested.[52] The research question which is formulated becomes the "anchor" of the research.[53] The research question then needs to be even more refined before the research study can be prepared and begun.[54]

REVIEW

Research will undertake a review of the pre–existing literature and research as this scopes and assists the proposed research.[55] However, very few general studies will ever undertake a literature or prior art review. This is extraordinary, given that the Supreme Court challenge and the empirical research calling for further empirical research would have been identified. The knowledge that empirical methods and studies were being called for would in many instances influence the path and detail of the general (and empirical) research. However, this is something we can rectify with future research.

RELIABILITY AND VALIDITY OF THE RESEARCH

Frequently the research effort to date is ill planned, recorded and or implemented. A research study needs to reveal sufficient information and date in terms of the hypothesis, what is being measured (researched) and how in order for us to assess its credibility and reliability. We also need to be able to consider whether it can have wider general applicability and how it compares or supports other research results. "A reliable test gives the same score again and again when it is applied to the same situation ... reliable tests are characterized by consistency."[56]

The general research is often unclear what it is about. Why does most general research rely upon opinion and self report questionnaires? The literature indicates that if we wish to know why people do what they do or what they think, experimental designs should be used.[57] However, if we want to know what people think, we should use non experimental designs, such as survey research.[58] Unfortunately, by relying so heavily upon self report and opinion report questionnaires only, the general research assumes that questionnaire can answer and resolve all effect issues. There are many inherent limitations to these studies (e.g. bias, inaccurate replies, expected responses, unknown answers, etc.). In addition, survey designs do not allow the establishment of causality (cause and effect).[59]

Research studies, and the level of detail and description provided, needs to be as equivalent as possible in as many respects as possible in order for conclusions to support each other.[60] Predominantly, the research does not seek to justify itself or previous research.

Therefore, future research needs to address and reveal its methodology, reliability and validity[61] in terms of measuring the effects and variables being studied.

EFFECTS AND EFFECTS SENSITIVITY

There is not discussion in the research to date of the adequacy and sensitivity of the research measurements to find and measure any particular effects being researched.[62] In a given instance, it is possible that there are effects but that the methodology used, and or the research study design, is inadequate to find and gauge the effects.

Commentators, deliberately or inadvertently, have fallen into the mistake of assuming that because a study they are reading does not prove a particular effect hypothesis that therefore means that the effect is not there. This entirely depends on an assessment of the study in question and how adequate and sensitive it is. There are clear misrepresentations of many of the research studies – which may have occurred with or without motivation.

Policy makers, commentators and those designing research studies in future need to be very transparent in addressing and explaining the effect sensitivity issues. These are critical in good research, but equally importantly in third party understanding of the results achieved. An effect hypothesis, e.g. distraction caused by the courtroom camera, can be proven or not proven. Depending on design, we need to be cognisant that a finding of effect of hypothesis not found, does not mean in every instance that there is no actual effect.

A measuring technique may not be adequate or may not be sensitive enough in relation to a particular potential effect. We need to choose the best methods to test for effects.[63] Questionnaires which are opinion reports and self reports should not be assumed and relied upon as the best method for testing all effects on all courtroom participants in–court and all audience and public issues out–of–court. That is not to say not to do away with (better) questionnaires, but we need significant amounts of additional and complimentary research. In terms of in–court distraction effects, eye tracking is one such method. Where we do utilise self reports, we need to first ask if the self report (method) will provide accurate answers.[64] Also, the research should state the advantages and disadvantages[65] of the self report questionnaires e.g. reliability issues. Invariably this has not occurred.

A further issue not yet addressed either in the research to date, and across the research, is statistical significance.[66] Further research is needed to assess significance issues in general and empirical studies to date. Where this is not possible because of flaws and gaps, we need to learn lessons for future research. We also need to begin comparing effects studies, sometimes called meta–analysis.[67]

RECORDS

Unfortunately some general studies cited in the commentary and literature is not available, or not easily accessible. The bigger issue, however, is that in many general studies that are available, there is insufficient information and data incorporated into the study, and or included in the official report of the study. We, therefore, are not able to properly assess the validity of the study not fully accept is proffered results. It is also an inadequate basis for policy decision.

On occasion also, a particular study may not even indicate how many responses were received and what the questions were. It may also be unclear who the exact courtroom respondents were.[68]

Studies need as many scientific measurements as possible, need systematic record keeping, objectivity and scientific basis for assessment and generalising.[69] Just because questionnaires may be less expensive, easier and quicker,[70] does not mean that we should forego other complimentary and in many instances better research methods.

ADMINISTERING THE SURVEY

It is noted that many of the general questionnaire surveys are (designed and) administered by judges and or courts personnel. One of the problems with this is that they may have been participants in the instant case being examined themselves. Also, they would not be the best qualified to design the research instruments. However, there is also an issue in terms of the ability of judges particularly being in the best position alone to be able to undertake and administer[71] the survey. This also applies to court personnel.

This is an issue which requires very careful consideration.[72] Future research needs to investigate and address from this issue.

ANALYSIS AND RESULTS

It is not always transparent that a proper and where necessary professional level of analysis has been undertaken as part of the research studies. This is necessary.[73] It is required to properly come to conclusions in terms of a given set of results and also to draw comparisons and policy implications.

OVER TIME

There is no general or sustained empirical research which researched effects over and extended and ongoing period of time. Longitudinal research[74] of this type assists in assessing effect per se, but also in establishing that particular effects, or effect levels, are not dependent on other variables, such as a sensational case or personality, etc.

ESTABLISHING THE BASELINE

R.A. McQueen and C. Knussen,[75] writing about research and research methods, state that "any research involving changes or manipulations within an organisation runs the risk of interfering with and undermining normal organisational processes, practices and procedures." Yet in terms of television courtroom broadcasting, some people argue still that there are not and will not be *any* in–court effects whatsoever. McQueen and Knussen continue that there must be a strong rationale for the research and also that an ethics committee may be unlikely to approve the research if disruptive or unscientific.[76] However, cameras have been introduced into many courtrooms without any research beforehand nor a plan in relation to how to undertake subsequent research, where this is potentially envisaged. There is also strong legal rationale advanced[77] in terms of why courtrooms and court processed should be altered or affected in order to experiment with cameras. Such experiments are undertaken in live and often sensitive cases, and sometimes over the objections and wishes of courtroom participants. Decisions in relation to experiments are made without consideration of the different form issues. Should pilots and experiments be undertaken in non–live and non–real cases prior to real cases?

The research to date ignores a very important issue, namely, the lack of baseline research. Establishing a baseline is important.[78] Where experiments have been permitted there is no baseline research undertaken prior to the introduction of the cameras. We need to begin incorporating baseline research and data gathering prior to introducing television cameras to the courtroom. This data will then be used in assessing the effects of the cameras once they are subsequently introduced.

Part of the Supreme Court challenge is to properly research for the effects of introducing television cameras. However, if we do not collect data and measurements in the courtroom prior to the introduction of the cameras, we have lost many measurements against which to gauge the areas where there are potential effects caused as a result of introducing cameras and or camera operators.

This very significant gap in the effects research needs to be addressed. While the development of a forms map of TCB can assist in conceptualizing and developing models to begin gathering baseline research measurements, this is forecast to be a significant task. In addition to the forms map and wheels of justice models, we need to look beyond the courtroom broadcasting literature to date, in order to find and incorporate appropriate cross disciplinary knowledge and research.

This is the first research to highlight this significant research gap. This issue alone requires significant resources and development. This chapter can only hope to highlight the issue and point to some areas and literature which may assist in developing our knowledge, and future research, devoted to the baseline issue.

COMMUNICATIONS

The study of communications and communications processes is one area which can assist our development of baseline research of the in–court effects of TCB.[79] John H. Power provides one map of communications processes, tiers and research.[80] He also provides a description and diagram of the social foundation of human communications theory.[81]

The activities of the courtroom, the relationships and the matters communicated are all deserving of analysis prior to introducing television cameras. Many markers and features of communications research[82] assist this research.

COURTROOM DISCOURSE

Part of the process of gathering baseline research prior to introducing television cameras is the process of examining the discourse within the courtroom. Bryna Bogoch examines courtroom discourse in relation to gender issues.[83] This includes quantitative analyses of terms used for address, intrusions, judges taking over of examinations, challenging comments, etc.[84] Frans Viljoes also undertakes analysis of the language of the courtroom.[85] This indicates that it is feasible to begin the research of baselines in the courtroom before, during and after TCB.

There is also various research in relation to legal language and legal content from the perspective of making legal language more comprehensible and plain English.[86] This is another indication that research and coding of legal communication in the courtroom is possible.

Tuula–Riitta Valikoski undertook very detailed empirical in–court research of the criminal trial as a speech communication situation in Finland.[87] This research is very useful in considering how we might undertake pre–camera in–court research. For example, she refers to research or the principle of orality in the courtroom and how oral speech is used for achieving various goals.[88] We might, for example, record how these goals are achieved before, during and after the introduction of the television cameras. Does the process change? Is the process extended? In order to make these (and other) comparisons, we first need to make our baseline research recordings. As Valikoski points out, there are very few speech communication studies on the courtroom in Europe.[89] There are even less in terms of TCB effects research. It is, therefore, applicable to look widely at other fields. Research is needed to adapt the most applicable research to the baseline problem and the effects research gaps of TCB.

Valikoski provides a map of the macro and micro levels of communication in the courtroom.[90] The research utilizes observation and questionnaires of prosecutors.[91] In terms of considering the activities of prosecutors, reference is required to their role as provided in relevant law and legal procedural regulations.[92] Judicial action is additionally guided by constitutional principles.[93]

Related areas for studying communication speech comes from linguistics, psychology, sociology and social psychology.[94]

Some research has found that lawyers accommodate their language to meet the defendants language during courtroom questioning, but changed during the presentation of the plea stage.[95] Other judicial parties also changed their language to different stages of the trial.[96] We do not know if the media and or television cameras alter the actions and communications of those in the courtroom. In terms of beginning the process of such assessment research, we should establish baseline data research studies. "Trials have different tasks and phases of action which are accomplished through communication."[97] What phases are portrayed in TBC? If we undertake baseline research, what changes will we find in the respective phases which are associated with TCB?

Some of the measures used by Valikoski include length of speech,[98] length of case,[99] differentiating stages of case,[100] expectations, observation compared to expectations.[101]

The survey was to discover how the court activity as a speech communication situation was experienced by the prosecutors.[102] The two can then be compared. Interestingly, one of the items mentioned most frequently by prosecutors was eye contact and moving in the courtroom.[103] The results found that prosecutors pay attention to non verbal elements in the courtroom.[104]

One of the roles of the judge in a case is to "direct the discussions in the courtroom by regulating the content of the messages and ensuring that discussions keep to the point."[105] The role of the judge as baseline and when television cameras are introduced, and any changes and effects, have not been examined. It is argued that once it is decided to pilot TCB, then the courts in which it is to be introduced should be researches and examined in detail prior to the introduction of the cameras.[106]

In Valikoski's research she found that only 15 of the 58 prosecutors referred to a specific descriptions of taking the injured parties into consideration when speaking in the court.[107] It is noted previously in this research that the defendants are one of the least researched courtroom participants in terms of TCB effects.

Valikoski notes further research that found that habitual offenders preferred a formal and quick trial,[108] while witnesses preferred smooth and natural communication relationships in the court.[109]

Another issues is also raised. If a courtroom actor is changed or affected in their communication, this may then affect the communication etc. of others.[110]

Tuula–Riitta Valikoski also points out that the judicial process is wider than just the trial in the courtroom.[111] Tuula–Riitta Valikoski also points out the problems with the use of observers for analysing effects in the courtroom, for example, that it depends on the observer's understanding of courtroom activities.[112] If the observer is not familiar with courtroom activity or courtroom communication, they may not be able to gauge all effects before them.

The issue of emotional arousal also needs to be gauged and researched in future effects research.[113]

There is also little research of the lexical aspects cross examination and the meanings created for jurors.[114] One study begins to use corpus linguistic and discourse analytics to study of, inter alia, courtroom lexication.[115] While there is other research using hedges, intensifiers,[116] discourse analysis, ethnography, pragmatics, psychology, forensic linguistics, role perceptions and expectations, surveys, interviews, focus groups, experiments, etc., there is little research of the impacts upon the legal process.[117] Linguistics in the Courtroom: A Practical Guide[118] is another guide which may be useful in advancing in–court language effects research for TCB.

Sarah Elizabeth Lowndes undertakes research of barrister discourse, and its effects upon witness testimony.[119] She uses conversation analysis and discourse analysis techniques.

Isolda E. Carranza also examines courtroom discourse and the markers within the discourse.[120] In particular she researches attorney/judge discourse with witness, and closing argument discourse.[121] The Bloody Sunday Inquiry was examined how in–court activities were reported in the process in order to examined, *inter alia*, how key words were used and reported.[122]

Further research analyses witnesses expanded answers to yes/no questions during direct examination and cross examination, including narrative expansions where replies go beyond the ambit of the initial question.[123] An obvious area of research for television courtroom broadcasting is to examine a cross section of cases before TCB, and then one stream of cases where TCB is introduced, and a parallel stream which continues without broadcasting. This is just one option.

EYE TRACKING

There are various potential effects which can occur inside the courtroom. One of these is distraction of the courtroom participants which may be caused by the television cameras and or the operators of those cameras in the courtroom. The author's proof of concept demonstration research successfully shows how eye tracking technology is relevant to the Supreme Court challenge and how we may begin empirical and recorded research of distraction effects in court.

Such research can be undertaken for any one or more of the different courtroom participants. The author strongly recommends that such research be followed through and indeed associated funding to enable such research.

CONCLUSION

The above can serve as only a brief introduction to how we might begin the baseline research so that we have measures to compare in terms of effects before television cameras are introduced with data recoded when they are so introduced. Tuula–Riitta Valikoski carried out speech communication research which focused upon the criminal trial situation.[124]

We also need to assess the reliance on observations in the few studies where observation has been used as a method of effects research in terms of assessing its credibility, such as examining and comparing whether locations is a relevant factor.[125] Eye tracking research can be used to test the validity of observation for discovering TCB effects. As previously pointed out by the author, much of this suggested research would individually be deserving of an entire book in itself. Some of it will also require a variety of interdisciplinary skills.

NOTES

1. J.S. Carroll, Free Press and Fair Trial: the Role of Behavioral Research, Law and Human Behavior 10 (1986) 187–201.

2. Administrative Office of the Courts, Research and Planning Unit, Cameras in the Courtroom, Report on Rule 980 (May, 2000), 3. The report also says that "[e]very media request form received was missing at least one piece of requested information." Ibid, 13.

3. Ibid, p. 13

4. N. Gilbert, Researching Social Life (London: Sage, 2008); M. Garner, C. Wagner and B. Kawilich, eds., Teaching Research Methods in the Social Sciences (Surrey: Ashgate, 2009); D.J. Greenwood and M. Levin, Introduction to Action Research: Social Research for Social Change (Thousand Oaks: Sage, 2007); A. Crisell, A Study of Modern Television: Thinking Inside the Box (Hampshire: Palgrave MacMillan, 2006).

5. H.J. Rubin and I.S. Rubin, Qualitative Interviewing: The Art of Hearing Data (Thousand Oaks, CA: Sage, 2005).

6. R. Franzosi, ed., Content Analysis, Sage Benchmarks in Social Science Research Methods (Los Angeles: Sage, 2008); I. Hutchby, Media Talk: Conversation Analysis and the Study of Broadcasting (Oxford: OUP, 2006); I. Hutchby, Media Talk: Conversation Analysis and the Study of Broadcasting (Maidenhead, Berkshire: OUP, 2006).

7. A. Durant, Meaning in the Media: Discourse, Controversy and Debate (Cambridge, CUP, 2010).

8. B. Winston, Messages: Free Expression, Media and the West from Gutenberg to Google (London: Routledge, 2005); Chapter 8: How Are Messages Formulated? The Linguistics of Lines and Between the Lines, in J.P. Ginnekan, Understanding Global News: A Critical Introduction (London: Sage, 1998).

9. D. Newsom, Bridging the Gap in Global Communication (Malden, MA: Blackwell, 2007); S. Ting–Toomey and L.C. Chung, Understanding Intercultural Communication (Los Angeles: Roxbury, 2005); Chapter 2: Media Globalization, in E. Deveraux, Understanding the Media (Los Angeles: Sage, 2007); P. Golding and P. Harris, eds., Beyond Cultural Imperialism: Globalization, Communication and the New International Order (London: Sage, 1997); C. Barker, Global Television: An Introduction (Oxford, Blackwell, 1997); J.V. Ginnejan, Understanding Global News: A Critical Introduction (London: Sage, 1998); D.C. Hallin and P. Mancini, Comparing Media Systems: Three Models of Media and Politics (Cambridge: CUP, 2004); D.A. Cai, Intercultural Communication (Los Angeles: Sage, 2010).

10. N. Lacey, Narrative and Genre: Key Concepts in Media Studies (Hampshire: MacMillan, 2000).

11. K.S. Johnson–Cartee, News Narratives and News Framing, Constructing Political Reality (Lanham, MD: Rowman & Littlefield); H. Tumber, News: A Reader (Oxford: OUP, 1999); O. Boyd–Barrett and T. Rantanen, eds., The Globalization of News (London: Sage, 1998); R. Fowler, Language in the News: Discourse and Ideology in the Press (London: Routledge, 1991); J. Curran and M. Gurevitch, eds., Mass Media and Society (London: Hodder, 2005); A. Bell, The Language of News Media (Oxford: Blackwell, 1991).

12. A. Hill, Restyling Factual TV: Audiences and News, Documentary and Reality Genres (Oxon: Routledge, 2007); A. Hill, Reality TV: Audiences and Popular Factual Television (Oxon: Routledge, 2005).

13. I. Bertrand and P. Hughes, Media Research Methods, Audiences, Institutions, Texts (Houndmills, Basingstoke, Hampshire: Palgrave Macmillan, 2005); E.S. Herman and R.W. McChesney, The Global Media: The New Missionaries of Corporate Capitalism, (London: Continuum, 1997, reprinted 2004); E. Deveraux, Understanding the Media (Los Angeles: Sage, 2007); A. Hansen, ed., Mass Communication Research Methods (Los Angeles: Sage, 2009).

14. R.L. Nabi and M.B. Oliver, The Sage Handbook of Media Processes and Effects (Los Angeles: Sage, 2009); Chapter 4: Media Production and Media Professionals, in E. Deveraux, Understanding the Media (Los Angeles: Sage, 2007); D. Giles, Media Psychology (Mahwah, New Jersey: Lawrence Erlbaum, 2003); Chapter 1: Making the News, in G. Philo, Seeing and Believing: The Influence of Television (London: New York, 1990); Chapter 3: The Production of News Language, in A. Bell, The Language of News Media (Oxford: Blackwell, 1991).

15. B. Gunter and D. Machin, eds., Media Audiences (Los Angeles: Sage, 2009); S.E. Bird, The Audience in Everyday Life: Living in a Media World (New York: Routledge, 2003); M.A. Hogg, and G.M. Vaughan, Social Psychology (Edinburgh Gate, Harlow, Essex: Pearson, 2008); P.J. Schulz, ed., Communication Theory: Volume 1, General Approaches to Communication and the Processing of Communication on the Intra–Individual Level (Los Angeles: Sage, 2010); K. Ross and V. Nightingale, Media and Audiences: New Perspectives (Maidenhead, Berkshire: OUP, 2003); K. Schroder, K. Drotner, S. Kline and C. Murray, Researching Audiences (London: Arnold, 2003); W. Brooker and D. Jermyn, eds., The Audience Studies Reader (London: Routledge, 2003); C. Brunsdon and J. Caughie, eds., Television and New Media Audiences (Oxford: OUP, 1999); E. Seiter, Television and New Media Audiences (Oxford: Clarendon, 1999).

16. Chapter 3: Occupational Groups; Chapter 4: Special Interest Groups; and Chapter 5: Residential Groups, in G. Philo, Seeing and Believing: The Influence of Television (London: New York, 1990); I Ang, Desperately Seeking the Audience (London: Routledge, 1991); SM. Livingston, Making Sense of Television: The Psychology of Audience Interpretation (Oxford: Pergamon, 1990).

17. D. Gauntlett and A. Hill, TV Living: Television, Culture and Everyday Life (London: Routledge and British Film Institute, 1999); B. Mullan, Consuming Television: Television and Its Audience (Oxford: Blackwell, 1997); R.E. Frank and M.G. Greenberg, The Public's Use of Television: Who Watches and Why (Beverly Hills: Sage, 1980).

18. C. Lacey and D. Longman, The Press as Public Educator: Cultures of Understanding, Cultures of Ignorance (Luton: University of Luton Press, 1997); S.D. Stein, Learning, Teaching and Researching on the Internet: A Practical Guide for Social Scientists (New York: Longman, 1999).

19. C.C. Williams, Not All Visual Memories Are Created Equal, Visual Cognition 18 (2010) 201–228.

20. R.W. Preiss, B.M. Gayle, N. Burrell, M. Allen and J. Bryant, eds., Mass Media Effects Research: Advances Through Meta Analysis (Mahway, New Jersey: Lawrence Erlbaum, 2007).

21. J. Bryant and S. Thompson, Fundamentals of Media Effects (New York: McGraw Hill, 2002).

22. G. Philo, Seeing and Believing: The Influence of Television (London: New York, 1990).

23. L. Ewing and G. Rhodes, Have You the Look? Gaze Direction Affects Judgements of Facial Attractiveness, Visual Cognition 18 (2010): 321–330; H.J.V. Rutherford and J.E. Raymond, Effects of Spatial Cues on Locating Emotional Targets, Visual Cognition 18 (2010): 389–412; T.A. Brown and M.P. Munger, Representational Momentum, Spatial Layout, and Viewpoint Dependency, Visual Cognition 18 (2010) 780–800.

24. C. Hollin, Psychology and Crime (London: Routledge, 1989), n. 47, 152 et seq., 171–180. B. Hughes, Psychology in Court, An Overview, Galway Student Law Review 1 (1998). L.S. Wrightsman, The Psychology of the Supreme Court (Oxford, OUP: 2006).

25. E.F. Loftus, Eyewitness Testimony (Cambridge MA: Harvard University Press, 1979, 1996). See also, A. Heaton–Armstrong, E., Shepard, G.H., Gudjonsson and D. Wolchover, eds., Witness Testimony: Psychological, Investigative and Evidential Perspectives (Oxford: OUP, 2006).

26. P. Lambert, Cues, Cameras and Courtroom Actors: Resisting the Temptation of Courtroom Television Cameras, Irish Law Times (January, 1996): 13–17.

27. E. Loftus, G. Loftus and J. Messo, Some Facts About 'Weapon Focus,' Law and Human Behaviour 11:1 (1987): 55–62, at n. 43, 55.

28. As originally used by G.R. Loftus and N.H. Mackworth, Cognitive Determinants of Fixation Location during Picture Viewing, Journal of Experimental Psychology 4:4 (1978) 565–572.

29. R.L. Hughes, Chandler v Florida: Cameras Get Probation in Courtrooms, Journal of Broadcasting 26:1 (1982): 432–444, at n. 82, 442.

30. Details with author.

31. Details obtained on 11 August, 2010. On file with author.

32. See S. Hegarty, Drama and Intrigue, Vanity and Hysteria – It's 'Oireachtas Report,' Irish Times, 20 February, 2010.

33. See the Oyez Project, www.oyez.org, accessed August 13, 2011. Generally, note, J. Goldman, Multimedia for Research and Training – The Oyez Oyez Oyez and the History and Politics Out Loud Projects, Social Science Computer Review 16 (1998) 30–39.

34. Obviously, many of these studies will draw the simple and obvious comparison between courtroom actors of X% of lawyers being in favour of courtroom broadcasting as compared to Y% of judges.

35. S. Barber, above, 92–93.

36. N. Fairclough, Media Discourse (London: Edward Arnold, 1995), 20–34.

37. Some of these are referred to by Norman Fairclough when he refers to the media generally. Ibid, 39.

38. Parts of which are referred to in N. Fairclough, ibid, 3. See also above, 48.

39. Referred to ibid, 48.

40. D. Zillman, Television Viewing and Psychological Arousal, chapter in J. Bryant and D. Zillman, Responding to the Screen: Reception and Reaction Processes (Hillside, NJ: Erlbaum, 1991). Also, R.A. McQueen and C. Knussen, Introduction to Research Methods and Statistics in Psychology, (Edinburgh: Pearson, 2006), 16.

41. Other examples refer to emotional issues, for example, K. Klein and A. Boals, Expressive Writing Can Increase Working Memory Capacity, Journal of Experimental Psychology: General 130 (2001) 520–533.

42. As an example, see S. Wortley and J. Hagan, Just Des(s)erts? The Racial Polarization of Perceptions of Criminal Injustice, Law and Society Review 31 (1997): 637–676. Also, P.J. Dean, H.E. Lombard, and S. Wilkes, Committal of a Patient Due to Media Influence? A Case Report, Australian and New Zealand Journal of Psychiatry 35 (2001): 129–130.

43. P.J. Cain, A First Step Toward Introducing Emotional Intelligence into the Law School Curriculum: The 'Emotional Intelligence and the Clinic Student' Class, Legal Education Review 14 (2003–2004): 1–18.

44. In relation to research methods, see R.A. McQueen and C. Knussen, Introduction to Research Methods and Statistics in Psychology (Edinburgh: Pearson, 2006); G.M. Breakwell, S. Hammond., C. Fife–Schaw and J.A. Smith, Research Methods in Psychology (London: Sage, 2006); F.J. Gravetter and L–A.B. Forzana, Research Methods for the Behavioral Sciences (Belmond, CA: Wadsworth/Thomson Learning, 2003).

45. M. Mitchell and J. Jolley, Research Design Explained (London: Wadsworth, Thomson Learning, 2001), 469–470. Also, R.A. McQueen and C. Knussen, above, Part 3.

46. See comments on scientific method in R.A. McQueen and C. Knussen, above, 5.

47. See ibid, 56 regarding variables.

48. See comments ibid, 7.

49. Note comments in ibid, 12 et seq.

50. On generalisability issues see M. Mitchell and J. Jolley, ibid, 26; and R.A. McQueen and C. Knussen, C., above, 8.

51. Ibid, 47 et seq. Also, R.A. McQueen and C. Knussen, above, 229 et seq, 6, 344. Also, K.F. Punch, Developing Effective Research Proposals (Los Angeles: Sage, 2006).

52. C. Spatz and E.P. Kardas, Research Methods in Psychology (Boston: McGraw Hill, 2008), see chapter on measurement, 93–124.

53. R.A. McQueen and C. Knussen, above, 19.

54. Ibid, 20. Also, Part II Research Designs, Methodological Issues, and Analytic Procedures, in S.F. Davis, Handbook of Research Methods in Experimental Psychology (Oxford: Blackwell, 2003), 39 et seq.

55. Ibid, 22, 335.
56. C. Spatz and E.P. Kardas, above, 107.
57. R.A. McQueen and C. Knussen, above, 469.
58. Ibid.
59. Ibid, 474.
60. R.A. McQueen and C. Knussen, above, 66.
61. M. Mitchell and J. Jolley, above, 71 et seq. Note, there are also different types of questionnaires models, see ibid, 477, and 488. Also, R.A. McQueen and C. Knussen, above, 15, 58; W.J. Ray, Methods Toward A Science of Behavior and Experience (Belmont, CA: Wadsworth/Thomson Learning, 2003), 300–301; D. Langdridge, Introduction to Research Methods and Data Analysis in Psychology (London: Pearson, 2004), 31–36.
62. R.A. McQueen and C. Knussen, C., above, 139.
63. See ibid, 120 et seq.
64. Ibid, 474.
65. See for example, ibid, 477. Also R.A. McQueen and C. Knussen, above, 361.
66. See C. Spatz and E.P. Kardas, above, 263. S.F. Davis, Handbook of Research Methods in Experimental Psychology (Oxford: Blackwell, 2003), 83 et seq.
67. S.F. Davis, ibid, 98. Also, D. O'Sullivan, Meta–analysis, in G.M. Breakwell, S. Hammond., C. Fife–Schaw and J.A. Smith, Research Methods in Psychology (London: Sage, 2006), 466 et seq.
68. On sample size issues see M. Mitchell and J. Jolley, J., above, C–6. Also, W.J. Ray, Methods Toward A Science of Behavior and Experience (Belmont, CA: Wadsworth/Thomson Learning, 2003), 299–300.
69. See ibid, 426–435; C–9.
70. Ibid, 479.
71. Ibid, 499.
72. W.J. Ray, Methods Toward A Science of Behavior and Experience, (Belmont, CA: Wadsworth/Thomson Learning, 2003), 289 et seq.
73. M. Mitchell and J. Jolley, above, 500.
74. R.A. McQueen and C. Knussen, above, 61.
75. In relation to research methods, see ibid, 14.
76. Ibid.
77. Note discussion in R. O'Malley, A Change to the Scheduled Viewing: Does Ireland Need to Change Its Approach to Courtroom Television or Does the Camera Really Add Ten Years?, Trinity College Law Review 2 (1999): 57–72.
78. D. Barlow, M. Nock and M. Hersen, Single Case Experimental Designs, Strategies for Studying Behaviour for Change (Boston: Pearson, 2009), 65–72.
79. John H. Powers provides one example of research and descriptions of communications research. See J.H. Power, On the Intellectual Structure of the Human Communication Discipline, Communication Education 44 (1995): 191–222.
80. Ibid.
81. Ibid, 205.
82. See ibid, 205.
83. B. Bogoch, Courtroom Discourse and the Gendered Construction of Professional Identity, Law and Social Inquiry (1999): 329–375.
84. Ibid, 329.
85. F. Viljoen, Look Who's Talking, In the Courtroom, Too! South African Law Journal 109 (1992): 64–76. A separate stream of research includes J.W. Wright, II and L.A. Hosman, Language Style and Sex Bias in the Courtroom: The Effects of Male and Female Use of Hedges and Intensifiers on Impression Information, Southern Communications Journal 48 (1983): 137–152.
86. For one example, see R.C. Wydick, Plain English for Lawyers, California Law Review 66 (1978): 727–765.
87. T–R Valikoski, The Criminal Trial as a Speech Communication Situation (Tampere, Finland: University of Tampere, 2004).
88. Ibid, 13.

89. Ibid, 24.
90. Ibid, 16–17, and in particular Figure 1.
91. Ibid, 17.
92. Ibid, 19–21.
93. Ibid, 24.
94. Ibid, 24, 26.
95. Ibid, 28, referring to K. Aronsson, L. Jonsson, L. and P. Linell, The Courtroom Hearing as a Middle Ground: Speech Accommodation by Lawyers and Defendants, Journal of Language and Social Psychology 2 (1987) 99–115.
96. Ibid.
97. Ibid, 36.
98. Ibid, 69–70.
99. Ibid, 70–72.
100. Ibid, for example, 75 et seq.
101. Ibid, 123.
102. Ibid, 98.
103. Ibid, 102–104.
104. Ibid.
105. Ibid, 119
106. Ibid, 136.
107. Ibid, 127.
108. Ibid, referring to K. Aronsson, L. Jonsson and P. Linell, The Courtroom Hearing as a Middle Ground: Speech Accommodation by Lawyers and Defendants, Journal of Language and Social Psychology 2 (1987): 99–115.
109. Ibid, referring to J. Haapasalo, Types of Offence Among the Cleckley Psychopaths, International Journal of Offender Therapy and Comparative Criminology 38 (1994): 59–67; and T–R. Valikoski, The Communicative Nature of Finnish Criminal Trials from the Perspective of the Witness, Paper presented at the annual convention of National Communication Association (NCA), Seattle, Washington (November 9–12, 2000).
110. Ibid, 204.
111. T–R. Valikoski, The Criminal Trial as a Speech Communication Situation (Tampere, Finland: University of Tampere, 2004): 18.
112. Ibid, 105.
113. Ibid, 46.
114. J. Cotterill, Collocation, Connotation, and Courtroom Semantics: Lawyers' Control of Witness Testimony Through Lexical Negotiation, Applied Linguistics 25 (2004) 513–537. The authors undertook research of cross examinations in assault cases in the UK.
115. Ibid.
116. J.W. Wright, II and L.A. Hosman, Language Style and Sex Bias in the Courtroom: The Effects of Male and Female Use of Hedges and Intensifiers on Impression Information, Southern Communications Journal 48 (1983) 137–152.
117. S. Hale, Themes and Methodological Issues in Court Interpreting Research, Linguistica Antverpiensia 5 (2006): 205–228. In relation to psychology research issues see, for example, B.E. Bell and E.F. Loftus, Trivial Persuasion in the Courtroom: The Power of (A Few) Minor Details, Journal of Personality and Social Psychology 56 (1989): 669–679. Note also, K.A. MacFarlane, Understanding Justice: Criminal Courtroom Interpretation in Eighteenth–Century London and Twenty–First–Century Toronto, TTR 20 (2007): 271–299; D. Archer, Questions and Answers in the English Courtroom (1640 – 1760): A Sociopragmatic Analysis (Amsterdam: Benjamins, 2005).
118. R.R. Butters, Linguistics in the Courtroom: A Practical Guide, Language and Society 37 (2008) 300–304.
119. S.E. Lowndes, Barristers on Trial: Comprehension and Misapprehension in Courtroom Discours (Queens University, Belfast, 2004), available at Dissertation Abstracts international.
120. I.E. Carranza, Discourse Markers in the Construction of the Text, the Activity, and the Social Relations: Evidence from Courtroom Discourse, Current Trends in the Pragmatics of Spanish (2004): 203–227.

121. Ibid.
122. M. Bondi, Key–Words and Emotions: A Case Study of the Bloody Sunday Inquiry, Linguistic Insights – Studies in Language and Communication 54 (2007): 407–432.
123. R. Galatolo and P. Drew, Narrative Expansions as Defensive Practices in Courtroom Testimony, Text & Talk 26 (2006): 661–698.
124. T–R. Valikoski, above, 15.
125. In relation to observation research, note R.A. McQueen and C. Knussen, Introduction to Research Methods and Statistics in Psychology (Edinburgh: Pearson, 2006): 9 et seq. Also ibid, 355–357.

Chapter Seventeen

The First TCB Eye Tracking Demonstration

INTRODUCTION

The Supreme Court has discussed some of the issues and concerns which arise in relation to television courtroom broadcasting on three occasions. The cases were *Estes*[1] (1965), *Chandler*[2] (1981) and most recently in *Hollingsworth*[3] (2010). The Supreme Court is aware that there are substantial research gaps, and has set a challenge that more social science and empirical research be carried out to address the research gaps. Unfortunately, the research challenge has not been properly or fully tackled.

One of the issues and concerns with TCB is that the courtroom participants may be distracted by the television cameras and or the camera operators. The relevant research is TCB distraction effects research.

One of the problems with the distraction hypothesis is that if there are effects, they may be different for different courtroom participants. Also, the research to date is undermined to the extent that it almost solely relies on self reports from courtroom participants, as to whether they themselves were affected or not. Other reports of effects on others are also opinions. Typically, the general research to date is questionnaire based only. The empirical research is relation to in-court distraction effects is very minimal.

EYE TRACKING AND THE LAW

Eye tracking has not been used for in-court research before. It certainly has not been applied to the TCB research problems. The author is novel in linking TCB and eye tracking, and in making the suggestion that eye tracking can apply to TCB distraction effects research. In terms of advancing, it is a useful, if not a necessary, first step to undertake a proof of concept demonstration of eye tracking in-court (see below).

By way of background and context, it is useful to refer to eye tracking generally. Regardless of TCB research, eye tracking is used widely across many fields. Some of the fields where eye tracking is used include medicine, psychology, advertising, marketing and design. Legal-psychology research into eyewitness identification and witness memory also used eye tracking.[4]

Eye trackers examine how eyewitness recognise suspects in photograph lineups.[5] They are used for examining the weapons focus effect,[6] e.g. a corneal reflection device[7] to discover where and for how long individuals focus their attention. This is one of the types of eye tracker.[8]

Eye tracking is also used to research effects of cameras and camera perspective in recorded police confessions.[9] The interview camera can alter significantly how viewers of such film footage rate the genuiness and voluntariness of the recorded "confessions." The manner in which the evidence is filmed, i.e. the confession footage, can influence judgements of guilt.[10] Mock jurors have been found to be influenced by the camera angle from which the interrogation is filmed.[11] This is now known as *camera perspective bias*. This is additionally significant since the creation of the Innocence Project.[12]

G. Daniel Lassiter and Audrey A. Irvine [13] used the same interview recorded on different cameras to show suspect only, police officer only, and both equally focused. The research study subjects then viewed one of the videos, depending on which group they were in. Subjects who saw the suspect only video, perceived less coercion.[14] Other research also confirmed that suspect focus only videos, yielded significantly higher ratings for perceived guilt and voluntariness.[15] As a result of the Lassiter and Irvine study, police practice in New Zealand was changed to ensure that there are no suspect only video recordings, and that suspect and questioner were always in frame.[16] Lezlee J. Ware [17] also examined camera perspective bias and used eye trackers to monitor visual attention. She also refers to studies and the literature which show that suspect focus only camera perspective, creates a bias for judgements of voluntariness and guilt.[18] Pressure is increasing to change policies elsewhere also.

Eye trackers have also been used in another novel legal context, but not in-court. Philip Smith[19] refers to tobacco effects litigation in the US, and enquires about the effect of different forms and formats of court mandated health advertisements. Smith also used baseline[20] research, which is one of the earlier points of the author, namely, that TCB research generally ignores the gathering of important baseline data in effects research.

THE SUPREME COURT CHALLENGE AND DISTRACTION

The author recommends the use of eye tracking technology for addressing part of the Supreme Court challenge. As far as the author can ascertain, eye tracking has never been considered in any courtroom on any issue. Certainly it has not been addressed, nor considered, in any of the Supreme Court TCB cases nor the related TCB effects research. The literature on (television) courtroom broadcasting has not considered or referred to the utility of eye tracking technology.

PROOF OF CONCEPT DEMONSTRATION

The author sought permission from the Courts Service in Ireland to undertake the first ever recorded demonstration of eye tracking technology inside a courtroom as a proof of concept for TCB effect research.

THE NECESSITY OF AN ACTUAL COURTROOM

By way of explanation again, an eye tracker is a double miniature camera which is affixed to a person's head, one focused in the direction that the person is looking, and the other focused on the person's eye.

Eye trackers allow us to track and record where an individual is actually looking and for how long. This is relevant to research of "distraction" effects of courtroom participants caused by television cameras/operators in mock and non-live court settings. There has been no courtroom broadcasting research as of yet which incorporates eye tracking technology. Therefore, this is very novel.

It is necessary to undertake same in an actual court environment as it is difficult to replicate an actual courtroom layout without great expense; the demonstration is less valid and less real if undertaken in a room or environment which does not in any way look like a courtroom; no environment sufficiently similar to a courtroom is actually available; the results of the demonstration are more valid and more useful to researchers and other interested parties for having been undertaken in a real court environment. The demonstration should allow greater insights in relation to the actual detailed practicalities and methodologies required for undertaking an actual empirical in-court eye tracking mock trial experiment.

The author also undertook certain research and review work at the new criminal court complex in Dublin, and which included some of the new layouts and technology incorporated into these courts.[21] There is also a roll-out of a digital audio recording system in courts.[22] It would certainly appear to offer many research opportunities, both on its own and also in terms of potential basesline research in case TCB were ever to be considered in Ireland. As pointed out previously by the author, baseline research needs to begin *prior to* the introduction of TCB.

THE DEMONSTRATION

A full eye tracking experiment is complex and costly. For the moment the author wished to demonstrate the technology in an actual (non live) court environment. It would hopefully demonstrate as a proof of concept that it can be used to address in-court effects research as referred to in the Supreme Court challenge.

This would be a necessary first step before carrying out a full eye tracking experiment. It would be the first such demonstration of eye tracking in a courtroom environment for courtroom broadcasting effects research anywhere.

The author requested access to an empty courtroom for two hours with an eye tracker, laptops, audio visual equipment, still camera, related equipment and technical experts. It was also suggested by the author that it would be useful to get access to more than one courtroom, as the layout of courtrooms can vary. In the end, one courtroom was used. It was a criminal courtroom.

It is useful also to take still photographs, which would be of necessary assistance in designing an actual eye tracking effects experiment, and also in choosing which particular effect to study, and how to do so.

The research, as well as requiring the author's legal knowledge and experience, also required technical assistance to operate the eye tracker and to compile the data. The author gratefully acknowledges the kind assistance of Anarta Ghosh and Mirko Arnold, both (at that time) researchers in Trinity College, Dublin. The author also acknowledges the kind permission of the computer science department in Trinity College for the use of its eye tracker.

RESEARCH AIM

The research aim was to undertake and record the use of an eye tracker in an actual non-live real court environment and to demonstrate and record what someone might see from different courtroom actor positions in the court – both with and without the television camera.

RESEARCH METHOD

The demonstration was conducted to undertake and record the use of an eye tracker in an actual non-live real court environment and including the use of a static non working camera as an example distractor.

One of the research assistants had the eye tracker placed upon them. The eye tracker was then calibrated to the individual. This is an exercise necessary with most eye trackers. The subject then positioned themselves in a number of directed positions within the courtroom which would be used as the normal locus of different courtroom participants within a courtroom.

The subject wearing the eye tracker then looked about in various directions simulating what a person in that position might see. The purpose was to demonstrate what is available in the immediate cone of vision for the person to see. The eye tracker recorded what they could see and what they could look at.

This exercise was undertaken with and without the television audiovisual equipment present and visible.

The eye tracker and laptop equipment tracked and recorded what the person saw and where they looked.

This is not, for the avoidance of doubt, an actual eye tracking effects experiment. It is only a demonstration of an eye tracker in a non live court environment.

THE FIRST PROOF OF CONCEPT DEMONSTRATION

The author was concerned to undertake a proof of concept demonstration of eye tracking in-court for research of in-court distraction effects caused by television broadcast cameras and operators. This demonstration research exercise was carried out in a real court in Dublin, Ireland on October 29, 2010.[23]

Incidentally, this is also understood to be the first use and demonstration of eye tracking technology for any purpose in a real courtroom anywhere. The courtroom used was a District (lower level) criminal arraignment and criminal trial court. The courtroom was empty of lawyers and the public.

EQUIPMENT

An Ergoneer[24] Dikabilis Cable (wired) head mounted eye tracker system was used for conducting the demonstration.[25]

In addition, a Sony DVCAM Model DSR 1P television camera and Sachler tripod was used as a distraction foil. It was not plugged in or operating.

A number of still photographs were also taken on a Sony Cyber-shot 14.1 mega pixel camera.

PROCEDURE

One of the technical assistants wore the eye tracker (the "subject"). The subject took up the following courtroom actor positions using the eye tracker, namely,

- Judge;
- Court Clerk:
- Witness;
- Sitting solicitor[26] ;
- Standing solicitor/barrister.

The tripod mounted television camera was located in four different positions within the courtroom. It was intended to identify the different television camera position and actor positions on an accurate map of the courtroom. At the time of writing, this map is still being awaited from the Courts Service.

Prior to the actual demonstration, the author briefly met officials and was shown the proposed courtroom. There were four different Camera positions for the subject in the witness box position. It is intended to identify the different positions once the courtroom map drawing is obtained from the Court Service. Unfortunately, no sufficiently detailed official map was available.

It was also intended to record the eye tracker subject from a public seated position but this was not technically or logistically possible in this instance. However, it should be possible in future demonstrations and or experiments.

RESULTS

The eye tracker used for the demonstration was successful for the demonstration and proof of concept. The demonstration was a success. However, the eye tracker used, like many eye trackers, is very conspicuous and would be very obvious to the courtroom actor wearing it, aswell as to other courtroom participants. This would, therefore, not be the best type of eye tracker to use for any in-court experiment.

In addition, these types of eye trackers offer less flexibility to the wearer, again hindering the authenticity of an actual eye tracking experiment for in-court TCB effects.

There were two video files created and close to 20,000 still images created and recorded from the eye tracker. In addition there were a number of still camera photographs taken. The later were mainly to record some background and environment photographs of the subject courtroom. In addition, they also recorded the markers for the four different television tripod position in the courtroom.

Samples of the witness eye tracker still images are presented below. The marked "+" on the still images (and relevant video) marks where the subject courtroom actor is actually looking.

WITNESS: JUDGE

Figure 17.1 has the eye tracker "+" cross marker shows that the witness is looking at the judge's position.

WITNESS: BARRISTER/LAWYER

Figure 17.2 shows solicitor sitting and barrister standing. The eye tracker "+" cross marker shows that the witness is looking at the barrister. There is no television camera distractor.

Figure 17.1.

Figure 17.3 shows solicitor sitting. The eye tracker "+" cross marker shows that the witness is looking at the solicitor. The television camera is focused on the witness. The television distractor is in Position 1.

Figure 17.4 shows solicitor sitting. The eye tracker "+" cross marker shows that the witness is looking at the television camera.

Figure 17.5 shows solicitor sitting. The eye tracker "+" cross marker shows that the witness is looking at the solicitor. The television camera is focused on the witness. The television distractor is in Position 1. The camera operator is also present. It is noted that the camera position is directly in the witness cone of vision, and also directly behind the solicitor position. It is highly visible even when the witness is looking at the solicitor. It could, therefore, still be a distraction.

Figure 17.6 is similar but shows the witness looking at the television camera.

It would also seem to be clear that in this demonstration, the subject witness can look at the various courtroom lawyers and the distractor television camera in Position 2, without having to tilt one's head left or right. What is the implication of this? If the limited self reports, opinion reports and in some limited instances observer reports in previous research, rely upon an

Figure 17.2.

Figure 17.3.

expressive visual cue such as courtroom actor head tilting or turning, this may be flawed. The current demonstration would appear to indicate that the subject witness can look at or be distracted by the television camera without turning, or visibly turning, their head. There is, therefore, a real possibility that there are effects which no previous research has gauged. Indeed, it can also be said that no previous television courtroom broadcasting research has sought to research for such subtle or non head tilt effects. This is a significant research gap.

FUTURE RESEARCH

The author recommends that research be undertaken culminating in a body of eye tracking television courtroom broadcasting effects research. Eye tracking has been demonstrated to be possible for in-court research, and in particular in-court television courtroom broadcasting distraction effects. It is recommended that the next stage, an actual eye tracking effects experiment, be undertaken. The present demonstration (and the Supreme Court challenge) can form the basis for planning and designing such an experiment.

Figure 17.4.

Such an experiment could involve any one of the courtroom participants referred to above in a single television courtroom broadcasting eye tracking experiment. Ultimately, all courtroom participants should be the focus of research.

In addition, a mock trial could be constructed, or the relevant portion of the trial, relevant to the particular courtroom actor being tested. Let us take one example.

We could take the case of a witness and distraction research hypotheses. Other actor subjects would act as actor facilitators for the experiment, acting as normal. Therefore, a realistic courtroom scene is created for the witness distraction research experiment. The same case would be re-run for new witness test subjects who would attend and act as the witness in the case which would be re-run for each test subject. Therefore, by repeating the experiment, we build up a statistically relevant body of test subjects in the experiment. Obviously, as pointed out above, research of this type then needs to be replicated in further studies, and in particular third party research studies.

The group of test witness subjects could, for example, be split into one group with no television camera present, and a second group with a televi-

Figure 17.5.

sion camera present. Each group of test subject would wear an eye tracker. Thus, in this briefly described experiment, we are able to test via eye tracking whether (subject) witnesses are distracted or change their cone of vision or what they look at and or for how long when a television camera is present.

Variations of this type of experiment could include, for example, varying the camera location, varying the type and size and camera, varying between camera only and camera plus camera operator.

Further variation and experiment can be designed for all of the courtroom participants.

A further layer of experimentation involves carrying out self reports and eye tracking, and comparing the results. Are the self reports verified, or are there discrepencies between them? If there are differences, and significant differences, what are the implications for the general research previously conducted? Can we rely upon it?

There is also a further issue to be considered. Obviously the individual actor wearing the eye tracker is aware that they are wearing it, and also have to have it individually calibrated to their eyes. However, there are different types of eye trackers which may not have to be so calibrated and or which do not have to be "worn" by the subject courtroom actor. It may be possible to

Figure 17.6.

design an experiment where a non-conspicuous non wearable eye tracker and subsequently a wearable eye tracker are used. If such an experiment is possible, this would go some way to measuring eye tracker effects separate from the television camera distraction effect.

Eye tracking experiments such as those above could be used to test for distraction effect of television cameras. Fundamentally, they can also be used to research and measure location issues and camera size/type issues. These are important issues and issues which have never been researched to date.

CONCLUSION AND FUTURE RESEARCH

This is the first in-court demonstration of eye tracking anywhere. It was a success and proved the concept of eye tracking for television courtroom broadcasting effects research. Yet, this is only the first step. The next stage is to design and undertake an actual eye tracking television courtroom broadcasting effects experiment (and ultimately experiments). It is important to note, however, that as with previous research problems, one experiment on its own is not sufficient to prove or decide any individual effect. A body of television courtroom broadcasting eye tracking research and experiments must be built up. Only at that stage are we beginning to seriously address the Supreme Court challenge.[27]

We can be optimistic, however, in that the insights of the author and the eye tracking demonstration offer a bright future for television courtroom broadcasting effects research, which has thus far been lacking.

"If we don't like the way courtrooms look on camera, the solution is to change the courtrooms, not toss out the cameras. At least that's how a free and open society ought to work."[28] However, with respect, should it not be that if we decide to have television courtroom broadcasting, and we do not like some aspect of it, we can alter and change the *form of* television courtroom broadcasting where necessary?[29]

H.C. Schmidt states that the current research in psychology into videotaped confessions is motivated by the Supreme Court treatment of confession evidence cases.[30] It is surprising that more research has not been undertaken into the effects of television courtroom broadcasting, given that the Supreme Court first called for empirical research studies as far back as the *Estes*[31] case.

Judge Kozinski concluded with the suggestion that "[w]e must consider the issue [of TCB] again, in light of the world today."[32] However, the present author suggests that we must also do so in light of our recognition of current research and current research methods. Indeed, we should not be blinkered in our approach. If other research is relevant, whether comparative or even unrelated, we must still embrace it. This includes technologies such as eye tracking and fields such as psychology.

Researchers use eye tracking for research across a wide variety of fields and applications. Why should we not use eye tracking in addressing the many TCB effects gaps and the Supreme Court challenge? The author recommends eye tracking to examine some of the effects of television courtroom broadcasting. Eye tracking provides a direct measure of eye focus.[33] It permits testing and direct observation of eye fixation, focus and attention.[34] Eye tracking research also has the advantage that is tracks and records exactly what people see.[35] It also overcomes the limits of opinion reports and self reports. It can also test, and validate, opinion reports and self reports. "[E]ye movements are a direct indicator of overt attention" and provides "a highly direct measure of visual attention, eye systems also allow continuous measurement of eye movements."[36] Eye tracking is the future of television courtroom broadcasting distraction (and attraction) effects research.

The time has come to address the research challenge set by the Supreme Court and also to ensure that the research effort into the effects of television courtroom broadcasting advances beyond the criticism that "[s]ocial scientists measure the intelligence of monkeys more effectively than courts have attempted to ascertain the effects of television in the courtroom."[37] It is time to move beyond limited self reports and opinion reports and embrace modern empirical research, including eye tracking technology.

The author commends eye tracking research to examine the distraction of witnesses in television courtroom broadcasting. Quite simply, eye tracking research is part of the future of television courtroom broadcasting research.

The author recommends that research be undertaken culminating in a body of eye tracking TCB effects research. Eye tracking has been demonstrated to be possible for in-court research, and in particular in-court TCB distraction effects. It is recommended that the next stage, an actual eye tracking effects experiment, be undertaken. The present demonstration (and the Supreme Court) can form the basis for planning and designing such an experiment.

Such an experiment could involve any one of the courtroom participants referred to above in a single TCB eye tracking experiment. In addition, a mock trial could be conducted, or the relevant portion of the trial, relevant to the particular courtroom actor being tested. We could take the example of a witness. Other actor subjects would act as actor facilitators for the experiment, acting as normal. The same case would be re-run for a test subjects who would attend and act as the witness in the case which would be re-run for each test subject. The group of test witness subjects could, for example, be spit into one group with no television camera present, and a second group with a television camera present. Each group of test subject would wear an eye tracker. Thus, in this briefly described experiment, we are able to test via eye tracking whether (subject) witnesses are distracted or change their cone of vision or what they look at and or for how long when a television camera is present.

Variations of this type of experiment could include, for example, varying the camera location, varying the type and size and camera, varying between camera only and camera plus camera operator.

Further variation and experiment can be designed for all of the courtroom participants.

A further layer of experimentation involves carrying our self reports and eye tracking, and comparing the results. Are the self reports verified, or are there discrepancies between them? If there are differences, and significant differences, what are the implications for the general research previously conducted?

There is also a further issue to be considered. Obviously the individual actor wearing the eye tracker is aware that they are wearing it, and also have to have it individually calibrated to their eyes. However, there are different types of eye trackers which may not have to be so calibrated and or which do not have to be "worn" by the subject courtroom actor. It may be possible to design an experiment where a non-conspicuous non wearable eye tracker and subsequently a wearable eye tracker are used. If such an experiment is possible, this would go some way to measuring eye tracker effects separate from the television camera distraction effect.

Eye tracking experiments such as those above could be used to test for distraction effect of television cameras. Fundamentally, they can also be used to research and measure location issues and camera size/type issues. These are important issues and issues which have never been researched to date.

CONCLUSION

This is the first in-court demonstration of eye tracking anywhere. It was a success and proved the concept of eye tracking for TCB effects research. Yet, this is only the first step. The next stage is to design and undertake an actual eye tracking TCB effects experiment (and ultimately experiments).

It is important to note, however, that as with previous research problems, one experiment on its own is not sufficient to prove or decide any individual effect. A body of TCB eye tracking research and experiments must be built up. Only at that stage are we beginning to seriously address the Supreme Court challenge.[38]

We can be optimistic, however, in that the insights of the present eye tracking demonstration offer a bright future for TCB effects research, which has thus far been lacking.

NOTES

1. *Estes v Texas*, 381 US (1964), 532 – 616.
2. *Chandler v Florida*, 449 US (1981), 560 – 589.
3. *Hollingsworth v Perry*, 558 US _ 2010, available at www.supremecourt.gov/opinions/09pdf/09A648.pdf, accessed August 13, 2012. See "US Judge Overturns Gay Marriage Ban," Irish Times online, www.irishtimes.com, accessed August 13, 2012, regarding ultimate trial decision.
4. For one recent example, see J.Y. Kwak, Remembering Faces: Using Eye Movement Measures to Investigate Differences Between True and False Memory (Ph.D diss., University of California, 2009).
5. An example is S. Josephson and M. Holmes, Have You Seen Any of These Men? Looking at Whether Eyewitnesses Use Scanpaths to Recognize Suspects in Photo Lineups, ETRA, Proceedings of the 2010 Symposium on Eye-Tracking Research & Applications, Austin, Texas (March 22-14, 2010).
6. E. Loftus, G. Loftus, and J. Messo, Some Facts About 'Weapon Focus,' Law and Human Behaviour 11:1 (1987): 55-62, n. 43 at 55. More recently, see for example, J.Y. Kwak, Remembering Faces: Using Eye Movement Measures to Investigate Differences Between True and False Memory (Ph.D diss., University of California, 2009).
7. As originally used by G.R. Loftus and N.H. Mackworth, Cognitive Determinants of Fixation Location During Picture Viewing, Journal of Experimental Psychology 4:4 (1978): 565-572.
8. See description in L.J. Ware, Monitoring Visual Attention in Videotaped Interrogations: An Investigation of the Camera Perspective Bias (MSc diss., Ohio University, 2006), 34-35.
9. This is also noted by L.J. Ware, ibid, 35.

10. H.C. Schmidt, Effects of Interrogator Tactics and Camera Perspective Bias on Evaluations of Confession Evidence (MSc diss., Ohio University, 2006), 3.

11. G.D. Lassiter and A.A. Irvine, Videotaped Confessions: The Impact of Camera Point of View on Judgements of Coercion, Journal of Applied Social Psychology 16 (1986): 286-276. Referred to in H.C. Schmidt, above, 9-10.

12. See www.innocenceproject.org, and as referred to in H.C. Schmidt, above, 11.

13. G.D. Lassiter and A.A. Irvine, above, 286-276. Referred to in H.C. Schmidt, above, 26.

14. Ibid.

15. See for example G.D. Lassiter, P.J. Munhall, R.J. Ploutz-Snyder and D.L. Breitbecher, Illusory Causation: Why It Occurs, Psychological Science 13 (2002): 299-305, as referred to in H.C. Schmidt, above, 28.

16. See H.D. Schmidt, above, 31.

17. Ware, L.J., above.

18. W.A. Geller, Police Videotaping of Suspect Interrogations and Confessions: A Preliminary Examination of Issues and Practices, A Report to the National Institute of Justice (Washington, DC: US Department of Justice, 1992); S.M. Kassin, The Psychology of Confession Evidence, American Psychologist 52 (1997): 221-233; and G.D. Lassiter, Illusory Causation in the Courtroom, Current Directions in Psychological Science 11 (2002): 204–208; each as referred to in Ware, above, 10.

19. P. Smith, Evaluating the Corrective Statements Proposed in the Court Case *US Department of Justice vs. Philip Morris U.S.A. Inc., et al* (M.S. diss., State University of New York at Buffalo, 2009).

20. Ibid.

21. Undertaken on December 20, 2010. The author also acknowledges the kind assistance and information furnished by a certain senior barrister whom shall remain nameless.

22. Referred to in C. Coulter, Judiciary Signals Support for Setting Up Judicial Council, Irish Times, May 10, 2010, www.irishtimes.com, accessed August 13, 2011.

23. The author acknowledges the kind assistance and permission afforded by the Courts Service. In addition, extensive gratitude is expressed to Anarta Ghosh and Mirko Arnold, researchers at Trinity College, Dublin, each of whom provided invaluable technical expertise in relation to the use, operation and recording of proof of concept demonstration results with the eye tracker.

24. See www.ergoneers.com, accessed August 13, 2011.

25. The system comprises the ergonomic head unit with EyeCam, nasal fitting, elastic band and infrared diode for illumination of the eye. See Dikabil Manual, Section 2.1., 5.

26. In certain courtrooms, including the instant courtroom, this position could have also been a senior prosecuting Garda (police officer).

27. Of course, eye tracking is only one of many methods for researching TCB effects. Many methods need to be used in conjunction in order to build up the body of research knowledge required.

28. A. Kozinski and R. Johnson, above, 1119.

29. This is not to suggest that we experiment willy nilly, or that we make and remake rules on the hoof. Separately, the wide disparity between the length and consent of the rules that do exist is also illuminating on the disparity of forms of television courtroom broadcasting.

30. H.C. Schmidt, above, 74.

31. Estes v Texas, above, 532-616.

32. A. Kozinski and R. Johnson, above, 112.

33. T. Armstrong and B.O. Olatunji, What They See Is What You Get: Eye Tracking of Attention in the Anxiety Disorders, American Psychological Society, March, 2009, www.apa.org/science/about/psa/2009/03/science-briefs.aspx, accessed April 30, 2010.

34. See L.J. Ware, above, 11.

35. See www.prsresearch.com/prs-tools/. Accessed August 13, 2012.

36. Ibid.

37. J. Hirschhorn, Cameras in the Courtroom? No, Barrister 7:3 (1980): 7 and 9.

38. Of course, eye tracking is only one of many methods for researching TCB effects. Many methods need to be used in conjunction in order to build up the body of research knowledge required.

Chapter Eighteen

Conclusion

Is the TCB effects research to date sufficient? Do we know the effects of television courtroom broadcasting (TCB)? Has the Supreme Court challenge been adequately addressed? It has been demonstrated, unfortunately, that the answer to these questions is no.

The author highlights that the research effort of the effects of television courtroom broadcasting (and by implication the policy discussion and legal arguments), is not sufficiently developed. The research effort and results fall far short of what we should expect. Only by critically examining the research to date is it possible to fully appreciate this. Any extensive review and examination of the general research and empirical research effort to date reveals this. The Supreme Court challenge has not been analysed until now. Unfortunately, the body of empirical research needed to meet the Supreme Court challenge is still absent. All proper research of the effects of television courtroom broadcasting must meet certain minimum research standards. Unfortunately, the standard of the general and some of the empirical research to date can be criticised. Significant further research deserves to be carried out. We are, unfortunately, still unaware of the full effects of television courtroom broadcasting.

The author has advances the international discussion and policy considerations of TCB, by identifying the Supreme Court TCB effects research challenge.

The author sets out for the first time a fundamental and significant research problem, as yet unaddressed in the literature and indeed in the Supreme Court cases. No one asks the founding question: What is television courtroom broadcasting? So much stems from this question. Tackling this question directs our research effort into the effects.

The author therefore provides the first considered definition of television courtroom broadcasting. It is defined as follows: television courtroom broadcasting is television cameras in the courtroom, filming courtroom proceedings for live and or contemporaneous television push broadcast to the general public. This definition needs to be expanded upon in order to provide a comprehensive understanding of *courtroom broadcasting* and *television courtroom broadcasting* categories and concepts. We need these in order to move our policy discussion and research efforts forward.

The New Zealand study found, through reports and opinion research, that most judges were distracted by the television cameras.[1] It also found that 58% of the public would be less willing to testify as witnesses if there was TCB.[2] The New Zealand research also found that 67% of the public felt that the TCB experiment was not educational.[3]

The author's research is significant internationally, not just in the US. This work paves the way for addressing the Supreme Courts issues, concerns and challenges and in a manner which is structured, defined, understandable and comparable across the respective research. In future, we should be able to compare effects studies and verify the results of effects studies. We also need to start gathering baseline data and research *prior to* television cameras being introduced to a given courtroom. The research effort must begin before television courtroom broadcasting experiments go live.

Let us hope that the current federal experiment will advance the effects research. The Supreme Court research challenge needs to be dealt with. Let the empirical research roll.

NOTES

1. Referred to in UK Department of Constitutional Affairs, Justice Rights and Democracy, Broadcasting Courts, Consultation Paper, CP 28/04 (November 2004): 109. Referring to the UMR Insight Surveys and Massey University research in New Zealand.
2. Referred to *ibid.*
3. Referred to *ibid*, p. 110.

Appendix 1

Select General Literature on Courtroom Broadcasting

COMMENTARY

Svenson, E. Cameras in the Courtroom? Between Lawyers, July 18, 2006, available at http://betweenlawyers.corante.com, accessed May 15, 2009; Thompson, E. Courtroom Cameras: Issue Moves in and Out of Focus. Quill Magazine (September, 2004): 7–9; Brust, R. From Term Limits to Circuit Riding to Cameras in the Courtroom, Rethinking, Reforming and Re–engineering the Top Bench. ABA Journal 94 (2008): 39–43; Mulgrew, I. Cameras in the Courtroom Put Risks to Justice in Focus, Vancouver Sun, March 19, 2010; Fisher, L. Through the Camera Lens: When Justice is Not Seen to be Done. Australian Law Journal 69 (1995): 477–480; Chicago Judges Adopt Rule Barring Cameras from Court Rooms. Judicature (1925): 18–19; Lawyers Aren't Convinced that TV Belongs in Courtrooms. American Bar Association Journal (X): X–X; Editorial, Cameras Out of Courtroom? American Bar Association Journal (1979): 304; Whisenend, J.D. Florida's Experience with Cameras in the Courtroom. American Bar Association Journal (1978): 1860–1864; Shall We Dance? The Courts, the Community, and the News Media, An Edited Transcript of a Panel Discussion at the American Judicature Society's 1996 Midyear Meeting. Judicature (1996): 30–42; Carter, C.A., Television in the Courts. State Court Journal 5 (1981): 6–21; Abrahams, S. New Efforts in 17 States to Expand Camera Coverage of Courts. Judicature 65 (1981): 116–118; Goodwin, A.T. A Report on the Latest Rounds in the Battle Over Cameras in the Courts. Judicature (1979): 74–77; Hoyt, J.L. Prohibiting Courtroom Photography: It's Up to the Judge in Florida and Wisconsin. Judicature 63 (1980): 290–295; Von Hoene, W.A.

Jr., Cameras in the Courtroom: An Overview. Communications Law 13 (1995): 1, 18; Sloviter, D.K. If Courts Are Open, Must Cameras Follow? Hofstra Law Review 26 (1998): 873–889; Heflin, H.T. Fair Trial v Free Press: Time for a Rehearing? Judicature (1977): 154–155; Hirshhorn, J. and Stern, C. Does Television Make a Fair Trial Impossible? – A Debate. Judicature (1980): 145–146; Sellers, D.A. The Circus Comes to Town: The Media and High–Profile Trials. Law and Contemporary Problems, 71 (2008): 182–199; State Courts Are Flirting With TV and Cameras. ABA Journal 63 (1977): 473–474; Owles, D. Cameras in the Courtroom. New Law Journal (October 21, 1982): 985; Bender, D., Leone, B. and Roleff, T.L. Legal System: Opposing Viewpoints. San Diego, CA: Greenhaven Press, 1996; Cameras in Court. New Law Journal (December 4, 1980): 1136; Editorial, Tele–justice. New Law Journal (May 26, 1989): 705; In Camera, New Law Journal, 16 March, 1990, 382; Reske, H.R. Rally for Court Cameras Falls Short. ABA Journal (March, 1995): 30; Spann, W.B. Jr. Cameras in the Courtroom – for Better or for Worse. American Bar Association Journal 64 (1978): 797; Roschwalb, S. Does Television Belong in the Courtroom? USA Today (November, 1994), available at http://findarticles.com/p/articles/mi_m1272/is_n2594_v123/ai_15897248/, last accessed on August 23, 2010; Puxley, C. Man May Allow Cameras in Courtrooms, London Free Press, March 18, 2009, available at www.lfpress.ca/newsstand/News/Cnada World/2009/03/18/8794766.html, last accessed on April 15, 2009; Florek, E., Daugherty R. and Mitchell, K.B. "Camera Controversy in Courtrooms Continues," News Media and the Law, February 1, 2005, available at www.rcfp.org/newsitems/index.php?i=6183, last accessed on April 22, 2009.

HISTORICAL

Strickland, R.A. and Ricjter, H.M. Jr. Cameras in State Courts: A Historical Perspective. Judicature 78 (1994); 128–137; Trossman, M.S. Tuning in to the Courtroom: A Brief History of Television and Criminal Trials. Justimages (1995): 4–12; McCoy, P. The Judge and Courtroom Publicity. Judicature (1954): 167–181; Cleveland Publicity–Cleveland Paper Defies Photo Ban. Judicature (1958): 188–189; LCJ's 'No' to Court TV. New Law Journal, 1 March, 1996, X; Trossman, M.S. Tuning in to the Courtroom: A Brief History of Television and Criminal Trials. Update on L. Related Education 23 (1999–2000): 21–X; ABA Adopts New Cameras Rule. Judicature (1983): 250; Hoyt, M. Steven Brill Builds and Empire, First Came The American Lawyer. Then Ten More Law Journals. Now, the Volatile Editor is Breaking into TV. Columbia Journalism Review (September/October 1990): X; Kielbowicz, R.B. The Story Behind the Adoption of the Ban on Courtroom Cameras. Judicature 63 (1979): 14–23; Hatch, D. Focus is on Courtroom

Cameras. Electronic Media 19 (2000): 2; Ehite, J.G. III. Celebrating the 30th Anniversary of Cameras in the Courtroom. Florida Bar Journal (April, 2009): 4 – 6; Middleton, M. Delegates Broaden Rules on Cameras in Court. ABA Journal 68 (1982): 1199–1200; Hedges, C.L. Teddy Roosevelt Faces the Cameras. ABA Journal (July, 1992): 1792; White, F.W. Cameras in the Courtroom: A US Survey. Journalism Monographs No. 60 (1979).

DESCRIPTION

Graves, D. Cameras in the Courts: the Situation Today. Judicature 63 (1979): 24–27; O'Connor, J.M. Cameras in Maine's Courts: Has the Time Come? Will it Ever? Maine Law Review 42 (1990): 483–513; Corbett, M.A. Lights, Camera, Trial: Pursuit of Justice or the Emmy? Seton Law Review 27 (1996–1997): 1542–1548; Sasaki, L.M. Electronic Media Access to Federal Courtrooms: A Judicial Response. University of Michigan Journal of Law Reform (1990): 769–811; Reske, H.J. Cameras in Federal Courts Vote Delayed: US Judicial Conference Instead Focuses on Long–Range Plan Recommendations. ABA Journal 81 (1995): 16; Reske, H.J. A Repeat Performance: Judicial Conference Allows Cameras Back in Appeals Courts. ABA Journal 82 (1996): 38; Carter C.A. et al. Media Coverage and the State Courts: An Update. State Court Journal 6 (1982): 26–31; Starcher, L.V. Cameras in the Courts – A Revival in West Virginia and the Nation. West Virginia Law Review 84 (1982): 267–300; Carlisle, J.C. An Open Courtroom: Should Cameras be Permitted in New York State Courts? Pace Law Review 18 (1998): 297–307; Epstein J.R. and Fogel, P.D California's Experience with Cameras Suggests the Need for Change to the New Federal Rule. Communications Lawyer 9 (1991): 9–11, and 31; Marcotte, P. Courts on Cable: Two Companies Vie for Viewers with Live Trials, Commentators. ABA Journal (1990): 19; News Cameras in the Alaska Courts: Assessing the Impact. Judicature 71 (1988): 356; Krygier, K.M. The Thirteenth Juror: Electronic Media's Struggle to Enter State and Federal Courtrooms. CommLaw Conspectus 3 (1995): 71 – X; Televising Coverage in the State Courts: An Update. State Court Journal 7 (1983): 13–15; McEwan, S.J. Jr. TV or Not TV: The Telecast of Appellate Arguments in Pennsylvannia. Journal of Appellate Practice and Process 2.2 (2000): 405–410; TV Jury, Have Cameras in the Courtroom Undermined the US Justice System? PBS.org, January 20 1998, available at www.pbs.org.newshour/forum/january98.tvcourts_1–19.html, last accessed on May 15, 2009; Cameras in the Courtroom. Time online, July 23, 1979, available at www.time.com/time/magazine/article/0,9171,947079,00.html, last accessed on May 15, 2009; Zelezny, J.D. Communications Law, Liberties, Restraints, and the Modern Media. Belmont, CA: Thomson/Wadsworth, 2004, 280–285; Moore R.L. and Murray, M.D.

Media Law and Ethics. New York: Erlbaun, 2008; Towers–Romero, S. Media and Entertainment Law. Clifton Park, NY: Delmar Cengage, 2009; O'Brien, R.J. , Mattson, E.S. and Healey, B.J. Chapter Eight: Cameras in the Courts, in Media Law Handbook, available at www.isba.org/newscenter/medialawhandbook/, last accessed on April 15, 2009.

COMPARATIVE

Ball, M. Coming Attractions: TV in Court: Would It Lead to Sensationalism or Better Understanding? Law Society Journal (September, 1996): 45–48; Metz, S.A. Justice Through the Eyes of a Camera: Cameras in the Courtrooms in the United States, Canada, England, and Scotland. Dick. Journal of International Law (1995–1996): 673–X; Cunningham, N. Lights, Cameras, Action. Justice Report 11 (1995): 18–21; Ramsay, I. Televising Court Proceedings, Current Affairs Bulletin 70 (1993): 16 – 22; Nettheim, G. Cameras in the Courtroom, (December, 1981): 855–861; Linton, J.M. Camera Access to Courtrooms: Canada, U.S., and Australian Experiences. Canadian Journal of Communications 18 (1993): 1–13; Stephens, M. OJ – What Price for UK Law? The Lawyer (October 10, 1995): 15; Piccus, T. Demystifying the Least Understood Branch : Opening the Supreme Court to Broadcast Media. Texas Law Review (1992–1993): 1053–1098; Hodgkins, E.M. Throwing Open a Window on the Nation's Courts by Lifting the Ban on Federal Courtroom Television. Kansas Journal of Law and Public Policy 4 (1994–1995): 89–X; Lanzara, G.F. and Patriotta, G. Technology and the Courtroom: An Inquiry into Knowledge Making in Organizations. Journal of Management Studies 38 (2001): 943–971; Lepofsky, D. Cameras in the Courtroom – Not Without My Consent. National Journal of Constitutional Law 6 (1996): 161–232; Kataria, S. and Sharma, A. Cameras in Indian Courtrooms: A Bliss or a Misery? – Learning from the American Experience. NUJS Law Review (2008): 345–358; Tate E.G. and Trach, L.F. The Effects of United States Television Programs Upon Canadian Beliefs About Legal Procedure. Canadian Journal of Communication (1980): 1–17; French, J. Radio and Television Broadcasting in the Magistrates' Court – Is There a Future? Federal Judicial Scholarship (2006), available at www.austlii.edu.au, last accessed on October 16, 2006; Olausson, U., Towards a European Identity? The News Media and the Case of Climate Change. European Journal of Communications 25 (2010): 138–152.

ARGUMENTATIVE/ADVOCATING FOR OR AGAINST COURTROOM BROADCASTING

Martinez, M.T. Cameras in the Courts: A Case for Increased Judicial Transparency. American Journalism Historians Association, Birmingham, Alabama, October 7–11, 2009; Hutton, E., Cameras in the Courtroom: A Comprehensive Examination. Internet Journal of Criminology (2009), available at www.internetjournalofcriminology.com, last accessed on September 25, 2010; Verniero, P.G. Supreme Court TV. Wall Street Journal, October 21, 2007, A.20; Tuma, C. Open Courts: How Cameras in Courts Help Keep the System Honest. Towards More Reliable Jury Verdicts? Law, Technology, and Media Developments Since the Trials of Dr. Sam Sheppard. Cleveland State Law Review 49 (2001): 417–420; Ramsay, I. Televising Court Proceedings. Current Affairs Bulletin 70 (1993); Lassiter, C. Cameras and the Infusion of Political Bias into the Courtroom, International Journal of Law and Information Technology 5 (1997): 28–82; Mason, P. Lights, Camera, Justice? Cameras in the Courtroom: An Outline of the Issues. Crime Prevention and Community Safety: An International Journal 2 (2000): 23 – 34; Kollin, J. Reporter Says Let's Ban Cameras from Courtroom. Editor & Publisher 128 (1995): 48–X; Brill, S. Courtroom Cameras. Notre Dame Law Review 72 (1997): 1181–1192; Stillman, C.A. Adversary System: Cameras in the Courtroom After O.J.? – No. New York Law Journal (16 October, 1995): 2; Emery, R.D. Cameras in the Courtroom After O.J.? – No. New York Law Journal (October 16, 1995): 2; Weiner, D.C. Courtroom Cameras. Litigation 21 (1994–1995): 1–X; Hodgkins, E.M. Throwing Open a Window on the Nation's Courts by Lifting the Ban on Federal Courtroom Television. Kansas Journal of Law and Public Policy 90 (1994–1995): 89–103; Stepniak, D. Why Shouldn't Australian Court Proceedings be Televised?" UNSW Law Journal 17 (1994): 345–382; Holland, T. Counting the Couch Potato – the Court TV Experience Leads to Sharpened Legal Knowledge, Not Square Eyes. Law Society Gazette (1995): 92–93; Graham, F. and Fretz, D.R. Cameras in the Courtroom: A Dialogue. ABA Journal 64 (1978): 545–550; Zemans, F.K. Public Access, The Ultimate Guardian of Fairness in Our Justice System, Edited Testimony of Francis Kahn Zemans Before the Judicial Counsel of California Task Force to Review Photographing, Recording and Broadcasting in the Courtroom, January 8, 1996. Judicature (1996): 173–175; D'Alemente, T. The Case for an Open Judicial System. Judicature (1974): 61–118; Sutro, J.A. A Lawyer's View of Courtroom Broadcasting. Journal of Broadcasting XXI (1967 – 1968): 19–22; Ripley, J.M. An Argument for Television in the Civil Courtroom. Journal of Broadcasting XII (1967 – 1968): 23–31; Dickstein, M. Cameras in the Courtroom. Bench & Bar of Minnesota 7 (2008): 4; No Lights, No Camera, No Action. Bench & Bar of Minessota 6 (2008): 23–27; Wieland, L.A. Cameras in the Courtroom,

6 (2007): 4, also available at www.mncourts.gov/district/4/?page=1995, last accessed on January 2, 2011; Televising Courts. New Law Journal (16 February, 1990): 194; Cedarquist, W.B. Televising Court Proceedings, A Plea for Order in the Court. Notre Dame Lawyer 36 (1961): 147–157; Bar Recommends TV in Courts. New Law Journal (May, 1989): 706; McConnell, B. Cameras in Court. New Law Journal (November, 1990): 1622; Flashlight in the Courtroom. Saturday Evening Post (13 November, 1937): 1; Lepofsky, D. Cameras in the Courtroom – Not Without My Consent. National Journal of Constitutional Law 6 (1996): 161–232; Schleiff, H. Cameras Have a Place in the Supreme Court, Television Week 22 (2003): 8; Dyk, T. and Donald, B. Cameras in the Supreme Court: Should Supreme Court Proceedings be Televised? ABA Journal (March, 1989): 34–35; Alridge, R. McVeigh Trial Cries Out for Cameras in Court. Electronic Media 16 (1997): 22; Reske, H.J. Courtroom Cameras Face New Scrutiny, Critics Say Simpson Case Demonstrated Why Trials Should Not be Televised. ABA Journal (November, 1995): 48d; Hernandez, D.G. Courtroom Cameras Debated. Editor & Publisher 129 (1996): 11; Weinstein, J.B. and Zimmerman, D.L. Let the People Observe Their Courts. Judicature 61 (1977): 156–165; Kirtley, J. Forget O.J.: Cameras Belong in Court. American Journalism Review 17 (1995); Editorial, Cameras Belong in Court. Broadcasting & Cable. June 20, 2005, 36; Tomkins, A. A Case for Cameras in the Courtroom. Poynter Online, November 28, 2000, available at www.poynter.org.content.content_view.asp?id=5132, last accessed on May 15, 2009; Light from Courtroom Cameras. New York Times. February 6, 1989; Rose, N. Camera–shy Prosecutor Hits Out, American Bar Association Conference. Law Society Gazette 8 (2002): X; Mason, P. Justice Seen to be Done – Electronic Broadcast Coverage of the International Criminal Tribunal for the Former Yugoslavia. American Society of International Legal Process 95 (2001): X – X; Cohn, M. Let the Sun Shine on the Supreme Court. Hastings Constitutional Law Quarterly 35 (2007 – 2008): 161 – 169.

TYPES OF COURTROOM BROADCASTING

Pritchard. Should Cameras be Allowed in the Courtroom? Legal Business (January – February, 1992): 3–5; Pritchard. Televising the Courts: Some Second Thoughts. Legal Business (May, 1995): 11–12; Marcotte, P. Cameras in Federal Courts? Judicial Conference Considers New Evidence. ABA Journal 76 (1990): 15; Kiesel, D. No to Cameras: Federal Court Ban Remains. ABA Journal 70 (1984): 29; Why Right to Switch Off Cameras is Central to Granting Court TV, LexisNexis News Analysis, available at www.lexisnexis.com, last accessed on May 9, 2009; Wieland, L.A. Cameras in the Courtroom. Bench & Bar of Minnesota 64 (2007): 4D; Judges Bring

History to Naturalization Ceremonies. The Third Branch, Newsletter of the Federal Courts 40 (2008).

SPECIFIC CASES OR APPLICATIONS

Hentoff, N. Judge: No Cameras in SLA Bomb Trial. The Recorder, January 11, 2000; Sarner, J. Justice, Take Two: The Continuing Debate Over Cameras in the Courtroom. Seton Hall Constitutional Law Journal 10 (1999 – 2000): 1053–1084; Ares, C.E. Chandler v Florida: Television, Criminal Trials, and Due Process. Supreme Court Review (1981): 157–192; Hughes, R.L. Candler v Florida: Cameras Get Probation in Courtrooms. Journal of Broadcasting 26 (1982): 431–444; Indiana Court Allows Cameras. Editor and Publisher 38 (1996): 3; Ramo, R.C. [interview], GL&B in Conversation with ABA President Roberta Cooper Ramo. Global Law & Business (October, 1995): 54, 55; Simpson and Cameras. Editor & Publisher 128 (1995): 8; Cameras in the Courtroom: A Dialogue. ABA Journal 64 (1978): 545–559; Editorial. Kobe Bryant Case Points to Need for Cameras in Court. Television Week 22 (2003): 9; Winter, B. Cameras in the Courtroom: What Next After Chandler? ABA Journal 67 (1981): 277–278; Alexander, S.L. The Impact of California v Simpson on Cameras in the Courtroom. Judicature 79 (1995–1996): 169 – X; Stein, M.L. Appeal Court Allows Cameras in Courtrooms. Editor & Publisher 129 (1996) 11; Sallon, C. OJ Simpson – Justice on Trial. Counsel May – June (1995): 8, 10; Pizza, W.T. The OJ Simpson Trial and the American Legal System. New Law Journal (1995): 990–991; Pugsley, R.A. Symposium: The Sound of Silence: Reflections on the Use of the Gag Order: This Courtroom is Not a Television Studio: Why Judge Fujisaki Made the Correct Call in Gagging the Lawyers and Parties, and Banning the Cameras from the O.J. Simpson Civil Case. LA Entertainment Law Journal 17 (1997): 369 – X; Chance, S.F. Considering Cameras in the Courtroom, Journal of Broadcasting and Electronic Media 39 (1995) 555–561; Loux, A.C., Jury Nullification, Andrea C. Loux Argues that It's A Lawful Verdict in the OJ Simpson Trial. New Law Journal (1995): 1522; Voboril, M. Cameras on Trial. Columbia Journalism Review (1980): 9–10; Electronic Public Access to Court, regarding British Columbia, Canada and the Case of R v Clark, available at www.adidem.org/Electronic_Public_Access_to_Court, last accessed on December 6, 2009, the case being available at www.courts.gov.bc.ca; Smolowe, J. and Cohen, A. TV Cameras on Trial: The Unseemly Simpson Spectacle Provokes a Backlash Against Televised Court Proceedings. Time 146 (1995): 38; Strand, M. Cameras in the Courtroom: Will Illinois be Next? available at www.lib.nui.edu/1981/ii810408.html, last accessed on May 15, 2009; Osterreicher, M.H. New York Court of Appeals Hears Arguments in Court TV v State of New York. National Press Photographers Association, available at www.nppa.org/news_and_events/news/2005/04//ny_cameras_court.html, last accessed on April 22, 2009; Perrotta, T. N.Y. Law Banning Cameras in State Courts Found Constitutional. Law.com, July 16, 2003; Hughes, R.L. Chandler v Florida: Cameras Get Probation in Courts. Journal of Broadcasting 26 (1982): 431 – 444; Murphy, M. Supreme Court, Nassau County, Coleman v O'Shea. Touro Law Review 17 (2000 – 2001): 53–60; People v Boss and Others. Albany Law Review (1999–2000): 1051–X; Gilbert, P. Annual New York State Constitutional Decisions: 2004 Compilation: Freedom of Speech: Supreme Court of New York Appelate Division, First Department: Courtroom Television Network LLC v New York. Touro Law Review (2005): 21; Wall, B.V. Ban on Cameras in Courtroom Unconstitutional, New York Court Rules, Gannett, available at www.gannett.com/go/newswatch/2000/february/nw0225–3.htm, last accessed on April 22, 2009; Court of Appeals of New York: Courtroom Television Network, LLC v New York. Touro Law Review 22 (2006 – 2007): 191; Lithwick, D. How the Supreme Court Managed to Insult Both the Law and the Public, Sodahead, January 16, 2020, available at www.sodahead.com, last accessed on February 24, 2010.

PARTICULAR COURTROOM PARTICIPANTS

Carter, T. Lawyers Fade Away to Grey, US Journalist Terry Carter Looks at the Frequently Bizarre Conduct of the Lawyers in the Simpson Case. Law Society Gazette 93: 36 (1995): 16; Green Paper on Procedural Safeguards for Suspects and Defendants in Criminal Proceedings Throughout the European Union, IP/03/245, February 19, 2003; Podlas, K. Please Adjust Your Signal: How Television's Syndicated Courtrooms Bias Our Juror Citizenry. American Business Law Review 39 (2001): 1–24.

RELATED LAWYERS

Kula, G.V. Trial Judges v Trial Lawyers: Mutual Expectations. New York State Bar Journal (March/April, 1998): 6–11; Langbein, J.H. The Criminal Trial Before the Lawyers, University of Chicago Law Review 45 (1978): 263–316.

JUDGES

Goldstein, A.S. and Marcus, M. The Myth of Judicial Supervision in Three 'Inquisitorial' Systems: France, Italy, and Germany. Yale Law Journal 87 (1977) 240–283; Anderson, S. Judicial Accountability: Scandinavia, California & the USA. American Journal of Comparative Law 28 (1980): 393–422;

Kirby, The Hon. Justice M, AC, CMG. The Globalisation of Media and Judicial Independence. Communications Law 1 (1996): 115–122; Barak, A. Judicial Discretion. New Haven: Yale University Press, 1996; Mason, K. The Inherent Jurisdiction of the Court. Australian Law Journal 57 (1983): 449–459; Harris, B. Appointments to the Bench – Role of a Judicial Services Commission. Adelaide Law Review 15 (1993): 191–207; Ison, T.G. The Sovereignty of the Judiciary. Adelaide Law Review 10 (1985–1986): 1–31; Stevens, R.B. The Independence of the Judiciary: The View from the Lord Chancellor's Office. Oxford Journal of Legal Studies 8 (1988): 222–248; Dawson, D. The Honourable Sir, Judges and the Media. University of New South Wales Law Journal 10 (1987): 17–31; Fiss, O.M. The Bureaucratization of the Judiciary. Yale Law Journal 92 (1983): 1442–1468.

VICTIMS

Pizza W.T. and Perron, W. Crime Victims in German Courtrooms: A Comparative Perspective on American Problems. Stanford Journal of International Law 40 (1996): 37–64; Kidd, R.F. and Chayet, E.F. Why Do Victims Fail to Report? The Psychology of Criminal Victimization, Journal of Social Issues 40 (1984): 39–50; Wakshlag, J.J., Bart, L., Dudley, J., Groth, G., McCutcheon, J. and Rolla, C. Viewer Appreciation About Victimization and Crime Drama Programs. Communication Research 10 (1983): 195–217; Weaver, J. and Wakshlag, J. Perceived Vulnerability to Crime, Criminal Victimization Experience, and Television Viewing. Journal of Broadcasting and Electronic Media 30 (1986): 141–158; Hosh, H.M., Leippe, M.R., Marchioni, P.M. and Cooper, D.S. Victimization, Self Monitoring, and Eyewitness Identification. Journal of Applied Psychology 69 (1984): 289–299; Doob, A.N. and Macdonald, G.E. Television Viewing and Fear of Victimisation: Is the Relationship Causal? Journal of Personality and Social Psychology 37 (1979): 170–179; Feldman–Summers and Ashworth, Factors Related to Intentions to Report a Rape. Journal of Social Issues 37 (1981): 53–70; Riger, S. and Gordan, M.T. The Fear of Rape: A Study in Social Control. Journal of Social Issues 37 (1981): 71–92; Toseland, R.W. Fear of Crime: Who is Most Vulnerable? Journal of Criminal Justice 10 (1982): 199–209.

PROSECUTORS

Uviller, H.R. The Virtuous Prosecutor in Quest of an Ethical Standard: Guidance from the ABA. Michigan Law Review 71 (1973): 1145–1168.

JURY

Erskine, D.H. An Analysis of the Legality of Television Cameras Broadcasting Juror Deliberations in a Criminal Case. Akron Law Review 39 (2006): 701–738; Doyle, D. Juries, How Do You Plead? Guilty of Bias, Your Honour: Lawyers Are Despairing of the Decisions Made by Juries. Sunday Tribune, May 10, 1998; Swaine, E.T. Pre–deliberations Juror Misconduct, Evidential Incompetence, and Juror Responsibility. Yale Law Journal 98 (1988): 187–206; The Psychology of Juror and Jury Decision Making, chapter in Hastie, R. Penrod, S. and Pennington, N. Inside the Jury. Cambridge: Harvard University Press, 1983: 15–36; Adler, S.J. Trial and Error in the American Courtroom. New York: Times Books, 1994.

POLICE

B. Mitchell, Confessions and Police Interrogation of Suspects, Criminal Law Review (1983): 596–604; Cops and Cameras: Why TV is Slow to Cover Police Brutality, Columbia Journalism Review (CJR) (September/October, 1991): 15–16.

DEFENDANTS

Langbein, J.H. Torture and Plea Bargaining, University of Chicago Law Review 46 (1978): 3–22; Cohen, L. Kids, Courts, and Cameras: New Challenges for Juvenile Defenders (The Juvenile Justice Counter–Reformation: Children and Adolescents as Adult Criminals). QLR 18 (1999): 701–731; Greenhut, J. Lights ... Cameras ... Action!!! It's Trial Time. Library: National Centre for State Courts, VA., (May, 1996): 33–34.

RIGHTS

Pequignot, M. From Estes to Chandler: Shifting the Constitutional Burden of Courtroom Cameras to the States. Florida State University Law Review 9 (1981): 315–350; Martin, S. Cameras in the Courtroom: A Denial of Due Process? Baylor Law Review 30 (1978): 853–864; Tushnet, M. Supreme Court and Its First Amendment Constituency. Hastings Law Journal 44 (1992–1993): 881–900; Denbeaux, M.P. The First Word of the First Amendment. Northwestern University Law Review 80 (1986): 1156–1220; Geis, G. and Talley, R.E.L. Cameras in the Courtroom. Journal of Criminal Law, Criminology, and Police Science 47 (1957): 546–560; Hansen, M.L. Camera Access to Our Public Courtrooms. San Francisco Law Review 7 (1997): X –

X; Winograde, A. Cameras in the Courtroom: Whose Right Is It Anyway? Sw. J. L. and Trade Am. 4 (1997) (4): 23–X.

MEDIA RIGHTS/RIGHT OF ACCESS

Smallman, D. Cameras in courtrooms: Revisiting the Experiment. IRE Journal (May/June, 2001): 15, 32; Anderson, D.A. Democracy and the Demystification of Court: An Essay, Review of Litigation 14 (1995): 627–655; Platte, M.K. TV in the Courtroom: Right of Access. Communications and the Media 3 (1981): 11–29; Lofton, J. The Press as Guardians of the 1st Amendment. Carolina: University of St. Carolina, 1980; Beloff, M.J. Fair Trial – Free Press? Reporting Restrictions in Law and Practice. Public Law (1992): 92–101; Kuriyama, D.N. The Right 'Right of Information Triangle': A First Amendment Basis for Television Judicial Proceedings. University of Hawaii Law Review 4 (1982) 85–138; Sager, K.L. and Frederiksen, K.N. Televising the Judicial Branch: In Furtherance of the Public's First Amendment Rights. Southern California Law Review 69 (1995 – 1996)(69): 1519–1550; Broyles, D.K. New Rules for Open Courts Progress or Empty Promise? Tulsa Law Journal 18 (1982): 147–158; Carter, S.L. Technology, Democracy, and the Manipulation of Consent. Yale Law Journal 93 (1984)(93): 581–609, a book review regarding Yudof, M.G. When Government Speaks: Politics, Law, and Government Expressions in America. Berkeley: University of California Press, 1983 and Ithiel de Sola Pool, Technologies of Freedom. Cambridge: Belknap/Harvard Press, 1083; Dyk, T.B. Newsgathering, Press Access, and the First Amendment. Stanford Law Review 44 (1992): 927–960; Kiesel, D. Cameras in Court: Media Appeal for Easing Rule. ABA Journal, (X): 576; Access to Courts and Videoconferencing in Immigration. Harvard Law Review 122 (2009): 1181–1192; Lee, D. Cameras in the Courtroom, First Amendment Centre, available at www.firstamendmentscenter.org/Press/topic.aspx?topic=cameras_courtroom, last accessed on April 15, 2009; Braber, L. Self–Government Before the Judiciary and a First Amendment Standard That Protects the Content of Courtroom Argument. First Amendment Law Review 3 (2004–2005): 252–300; Cook, T.E. Ed. Freeing the Presses, The First Amendment in Action. Baton Rouge: Louisiana State University Press, 2005.

DEFENDANT OR PARTY ISSUES

Halonen, D. High Court Shuts Door on Cameras. Electronic Media 18 (1999): 4; Easton, S.D. Cameras in Courtrooms: Contrasting Viewpoints: Whose Life if it Anyway?: A Proposal to Redistribute Some of the Economic Benefits of Cameras in the Courtroom from Broadcasters to Crime Victims.

South Carolina Law Review 49 (1997): 1–54; Morse, L. Eye–Witness: Television's Expanding Coverage of the Courts. DePaul–LCA Journal of Art and Entertainment Law 3 (1992–1993): 68–X.

TCB RULES, REGULATIONS AND EXCEPTIONS

Cameras in the Courts: A State–by–State Guide, Radio Television, Digital News Association, available at www.rtdna.org; Lassiter, C. An Annotated Descriptive Summary of State Statutes, Judicial Codes, Canons, and Court Rules Relating to Admissibility and Governance of Cameras in the Courtroom. Journal of Criminal Law and Criminology 86 (1996): 1019–1095; Dyer, C.S. and Hauserman, N.R. Electronic Coverage of the Courts: Exceptions to Exposure. Georgia Law Review 75 (1986 – 1987): 1633– 17XX; Killian, D.P. Propriety of Restrictive Guidelines for Cameras in the Court. Communications and the Law 9 (1987): 27–43; McNeil, C.B. Public Access and Media Rules for Administrative Adjudications in High–Profile Hearings. Judicature 91 (2008): 298–303.

FACILITATION/ADAPTATION FOR COURTROOM BROADCASTING

Helwig, G.J. Should Special Facilities be Provided for Courtroom Photography and Broadcasting? Judicature 50 (1967): 163–167; Kogan, G., Weisberg, S. and Klieman, R. Television Coverage of State Criminal Trials. St. Thomas Law Review 9 (1996–1997): 505–516.

PERIPHERAL BUT RELATED ISSUES

Lederer, F. The Potential Use of Courtroom Technology in Major Terrorism Cases. William & Mary Bill of Rights 12 (2004): 887–X; Flynn, K.H. General Provisions: Establishing Factors for Courts to Consider When Determining Whether to Allow Filming or Videotaping in the Courtroom; Allow for Citations When Court Orders Related to Media Cameras in the Courtroom are Violated, accessible at http://dspace.gsu:8080/dspace/handle/2197/531, last accessed on November 30, 2009; Carney, C.P. The Accused, the Jury and the Media. New Law Journal (January 13, 1995): 12–30; Sodos, N.S. The Ethical Considerations of Televising Federal Courtroom Proceedings. Georgetown Journal of Legal Ethics 5 (1992): 915–937; Alschuler, A.W. Courtroom Misconduct by Prosecutors and Trial Judges. Texas Law Review 50 (1972): 629–X; Gilmore, W.H. Arraignment by Television: A New Way to Bring Defendants to the Courtroom. Judicature (1980): 396–401; P.J.B [initials only given]. Recent Cases: Contempt of Court – Extent of Liability of Members of Legal Profession. Australian Law Journal 52 (1978): 151–154; Barrera, L. Law Review Editing and Choe v Fordam University School of Law: Is the Courtroom the New Front for the Resolution of Publishing Disputes? Wayne Law Review 42 (1995–1996): 2183–X; Rogers, S. Smith Bernal Courts Legal IT Market. The Lawyer (September 20, 1994): 6; Harris, J. 'OJ' on the Computer Screen. The Eagle 14 (1995): 48–49; Sodos, N.S. The Ethical Considerations of Televising Federal Courtroom Proceedings. Geo. J. Legal Ethics 5 (1991–1992): 915–X; Burcham, D.W. High Profile Trials: Can Government Sell the Right to Broadcast the Proceedings? UCLA Law Review 3 (1995–1996): 169–X; Easton, S.D. Cameras in Courtrooms: Contrasting Viewpoints: Whose Life if it Anyway?: A Proposal to Redistribute Some of the Economic Benefits of Cameras in the Courtroom from Broadcasters to Crime Victims. South Carolina Law Review 49 (1997): 1–X; Jeff, A. Televising California's Death Penalty: Is There a Constitutional Right to Broadcast Executions? Hastings Law Review 43 (1991–1992): 1489–X; Howard, W. Televised Trials: Can the Government Market Electronic Access. SC Law Review 49 (1997–1998): 55–X; Rotunda, R.D. Dealing with the Media: Ethical, Constitutional, and Practical Parameters. Illinois Bar Journal 84 (1996): 614–621; Hardy, K.A. Order in the Courtroom, Silence on the Courthouse Steps: Attorneys Muzzled by Ethical Disciplinary Rules. Seton Hall Law Review 22 (1991 – 1992): 1401–X; Elffers, H., Keijser, J.W. de, Koppen, P.J. van and Haeringen, L. van. Newspaper Juries: A Field Experiment Concerning the Effect of Information on Attitudes Towards the Criminal Justice System. Journal of Experimental Criminology 3 (2007): 163–182; Dowler, K. Sex, Lies and Videotape: The Presentation of Sex Crime in Local Television News. Journal of Criminal Justice 34 (2006): 383–392; Hanks, W. and Longini, Television Access: A Pittsburgh Experiment. Journal of Broadcasting 18 (1974): 289–297 (regarding public access broadcasting); Posey, A. and Dahl, A.J. Beyond Pretrial Publicity: Legal and Ethical Issues Associated with Change of Venue Surveys. Law and Human Behaviour 26 (2002): 107–125; Edwards, D.L. If It Walks, Talks and Squawks Like a Trial, Should it be Covered Like One? The Right of the Press to Cover INS Deportation Hearings. Communication Law and Policy 10 (2005): 217–239; Gnisci, A. and Bonaiuto, M. Grilling Politicians: Politicians' Answers to Questions in Television Interviews and Courtroom Examinations. Journal of Language and Social Psychology 22 (2003): 385–413; Greene, E. Media Effects on Jurors. Law and Human Behaviour 14 (2005): 439–450; Troscianko, T., Holmes, A., Stillman, J., Mirmehdi, M., Wright, D. and Wilson, A. What Happens Next? The Predictability of Natural Behaviour Viewed Through CCTV Cameras. Perception 33 (2004): 87–101; Hochberger, R.S. Ethical Issues in Covering Courts. Syracuse Law Review, 56 (2006): 443–457.

GENERAL EFFECT ISSUES

Reske, H.J. Panelists Differ Over TV's Impact on Trials. ABA Journal (October, 1992): 44.

MEDIA REPORTING ISSUES

Bennun, M.E. Publicity for Criminal Trials, Chapter 13, in Bridge, J.W. Lasok, D. Plender, R.O. and Perott, D.L. eds. Fundamental Rights, London: Sweet and Maxwell, 1973, pp. 175–188; Schlesinger, P. Tumber, H. and Murdock, G. The Media Politics of Crime and Criminal Justice. British Journal of Sociology 42 (1991): 397–420; Isralowitz, J.P. The Reporter as Citizen: Newspaper Ethics and Constitutional Values, University of Pennsylvania Law Review 141(1992): 221–281; Bennett, R.R. and Wiegand, R.B. Observations on Crime Reporting in a Developing Nation. Criminology 32 (1994): 135–148; Shaw, D. Media Coverage of the Courts: Improving But Still Not Adequate. Judicature 65 (1981): 18–24; McCormack, G. Corrupting the Criminal Process. Irish Law Times 1 (1985): 6–8; Evans, K., The Publicity is the Problem. New Law Journal (7 July, 1995): 992–1004; Bonnington, A.J. Press and Prejudice. New Law Journal (3 November, 1995): 1623; Blume, P. Law, Communications and Publication. Scandinavian Studies in Law 35 (1991): 9–28; Greenhouse, L. Telling the Court's Story: Justice and Journalism at the Supreme Court. Yale Law Journal 105 (1996): 1537–1561; Gibbons, T. Freedom of the Press: Ownership and Editorial Values. Public Law (1992): 279–299; Gillmor, D.M. Free Press Versus Fair Trial: A New Era? Journalism Quarterly Review (1964): 27–37; Brechner, J.L. News Media and the Courts. Journal of Broadcasting (1967–1968): 3–17; Jensen, K.B. Television Politics of Polysemy: Television News, Everyday Consciousness and Political Action. Media, Culture and Society 12 (1990): 57–77; Bennett, W.L., Gressett, L.A. and Haltom, W. Repairing the News: A Case Study of the News Paradigm. Journal of Communication 35 (1985): 50–68; Chibnall, S. Introduction section, sub–heading Law–and–order–news, in Chibnall, S. Law and Order News: An Analysis of Crime Reporting in the British Press. London: Tavistoch Publications, 1977: ix–226; McManus, J. Local TV News: Not a Pretty Picture. Columbia Journalism Review (CJR) (May/June, 1990): 42–43; Berger, A.A. Media Analysis Techniques. London: Sage, 1982, 1998; Thakker J. and Durrant, R. News Coverage of Sexual Offending in New Zealand, 2003. New Zealand Journal of Psychology 35 (2006): 28–35; Mauro, T. Five Ways Appellate Courts Can Help the News Media. Journal of Appelate Practice and Process (2007): 311–X.

GENERAL MEDIA EFFECTS OTHER THAN TCB

Fedler, F. and Jordan, D. How Emphasis on People Affects Coverage of Crime. Journalism Quarterly (1982): 474–478; McLeod, D.M. Communicating Deviance: The Effects of Television News Coverage of Social Protest. Journal of Broadcasting & Electronic Media 39 (1995): 4–19; McRobbie, A. and Thornton, S.L. Rethinking 'Moral Panic' for Multi–mediated Social Worlds. BJS 46 (1995): 559–574; Heath, L. Impact of Newspaper Crime Reports on Fear of Crime: Multimethodological Investigation. Journal of Personality and Social Psychology 47 (1984): 263–276.

PRE–TRIAL PUBLICITY

Studenbaker, C.A. and Penrod, S.D. Pretrial Publicity and Its Influence on Juror decision Making, in Williams, N. and Williams, K.D., eds., Psychology and Law: An Empirical Perspective. New York: Guildford Press, 2005; Kerr, N.L. Social Psychology in Court: The Case of the Prejudicial Pretrial Publicity, in Brannigan, G.G. and Merrens, M.R. The Social Psychologists: Research Adventures. New York: McGraw–Hill, 1995; Kaplan M.F. and Miller, L.E. Reducing the Effects of Juror Bias, in Wrightsman, L.S., Kassin S.M. and Willis, C.E. In the Jury Box: Controversies in the Courtroom. Thousand Oaks, CA: Sage, 1987; [author not given], Prejudicial Publicity in Trials of Public Officials. Yale Law Journal 85 (1978): 123–135; Dixon, T.L. and Linz, D. Television News, Prejudicial Retrial Publicity, and Depiction of Race. Journal of Broadcasting & Electronic Media 46 (2002): 112–136; Bruschke, J.and Loges, W.E. The Effect of Pretrial Publicity on Trial Outcomes, available at http://commfaculty.edu/jbruschke/PTP%20revision%20as%20of%205–22–98.htm, last accessed on August 23, 2010.

IMAGES AND PORTRAYAL OF LAW

Macauley, S. Images of Law in Everyday Life: the Lessons of School, Entertainment, and Spectator Sports. Law and Society Review 21 (1987–1988): 185–218; Lorenzo–Dus, N. Real Disorder in the Court: An Investigation of Conflict Talk in US Television Courtroom Shows. Media, Culture and Society 30 (2008): 81–107; McNeely, C.L. Perceptions of the Criminal Justice System: Television Imagery and Public Knowledge in the United States. Journal of Criminal Justice and Popular Culture 3 (1995): 1–20; Felcher, P.L. and Ruin, E.L. Privacy, Publicity, and the Portrayal of Real People by the Media. Yale Law Journal 88 (1979): 1577–1622; Davis, A. Media and the Courts, available at http://kenmentor.com/courses/liberties/media.html, last accessed on August 23, 2010, referring to courts, CSI, Law & Order, etc.; Thakker, J. and Durrant, R. News Coverage of Sexual Offending in New Zealand, 2003. New Zealand Journal of Psychology 35 (2006): 28–35; Bergman, P. and Asimov, M. Reel Justice: the Courtroom Goes to the Movies. Riversdale, NJ: Andres McMeel, 2006.

LEGAL DOCUMENTARIES AND RECONSTRUCTIONS

Glatt, D.M. Trial by Docudrama: Fact or Fiction? Cardoza Arts and Entertainment Law Journal 9 (1990): 201–230; Reith, M. Viewing of Crime Drama and Authoritarian Aggression: An Investigation of the Relationship Between Crime Viewing, Fear, and Aggression. Journal of Broadcasting & Electronic Media 43 (1999): 211–221.

Appendix 2

Summary and Categorisation of Supreme Court Effects Issues and Concerns

(Note: The categorisations and headings are from the author, while the concerns are from the three Supreme Court camera cases)

Lawyers

- Effective counsel;
- Lawyers will look to see if they can confer with their client without, or out of, close-ups.
- Adverse psychological effects on lawyers.

Juries (In-Court)

- Jury awareness;
- Jury influence;
- Juror television viewing during trial;
- Jury prejudice by media;
- Jury ability to judge fairly;
- Voting decisions [presumably jury decisions];
- Adverse psychological effects on jurors.

Prospective Juries (Out-of-Court)

- Prejudice of actual and potential jurors;

- Make an impartial jury for a re–trial impossible.

Judges

- Judge effects;
- Duties of the trial judge;
- Politics and elected judges;
- Adverse psychological effects on jurors.

Defendants

- Defendant effects;
- Objection by defendant;
- Prejudicial conditions not experienced by other defendants;
- Singling out certain defendants;
- Coerced confession (see camera perspective bias issues below).

Parties

Parties generally not mentioned (other than criminal defendants above).

Witnesses

- Witness effects;
- Witnesses awareness;
- Effect of increasing public awareness of witnesses;
- Reasonable or feasible for witnesses to object;
- Witness security;
- Witness TV viewing;
- Public recognition/harassment of witnesses;
- Effect of witness testimony chilling [potentially in-court and out-of-court];
- Adverse psychological effects on witnesses.

Court Personnel

Not mentioned.

Courtroom Participants Effects Generally

- Attention;
- Awareness;
- Undivided attention;

- Diversion;
- Effects on courtroom participants;
- Conscious or unconscious effects;
- Courtroom actor objections ignored;
- Accuracy;
- Over dramatization;
- Amending testimony;
- Apprehension;
- Reluctance;
- Quality of the testimony;
- Frightening;
- Cocky;
- Personal acting up;
- Interruptions;
- Rulings ;
- Concentration;
- Harassment;
- Sensibilities;
- Concentration;
- Acting up;
- Dividing actor efforts;
- Subtle effects;
- Effect on timid or reluctant witness;
- Unconscious effects;
- Act differently;
- Acting up;
- Adverse effects from presence of camera;
- Altered testimony;
- Unwillingness to testify;
- Qualitative differences;
- Playing to audience;
- Playing to potential clients;
- Trial management;
- Peer pressure;
- Pre-trial publicity;
- Community pressure;
- Focus;
- TV viewing;
- No longer calm;
- Emphasising that the case is special;
- Popular verdicts;
- Pre–trial publicity;
- Bias;

- Extraneous influence;
- Knowledge of being televised;
- Aggravation/escalation;
- Attitude to testifying;
- Impact of being filmed and broadcast;
- Demoralized;
- Overstatement;
- Public speaking;
- Additional responsibility;
- Direct news media pressure;
- Influence of public opinion by news media;
- P sychological effects and reactions.

Other In-Court Issues

- General distraction;
- Actor distraction;
- Changing behaviour because of awareness;
- Awareness of being televised;
- Increasing nervousness;
- Increasing tension;
- Acting differently;
- Not giving full attention;
- Distortion;
- Disruptive;
- Psychological considerations;
- Influence on verdicts;
- Highly publicised trials;
- Criminal trials;
- Prejudice;
- Diverting the trial;
- Impacting on all participants;
- Opportunism;
- Effort of trying not to be effected;
- Noise of cameras;
- Appearance of cameras;
- Undercutting reliability of the trial process;
- Probable hazards;
- Criminal trial with notoriety versus a routine trial;
- Effects on the normal detached atmosphere;
- The integrity of judicial process;

- Distorting the trial process. [Neither baseline pre-camera nor with-camera courtroom processes have yet been researched to compare and examine effects].

Audience

- Emotional audience;
- Effects of commercials and intervals;
- Editing;
- Commentary;
- Close ups;
- Entertainment;
- Commercial objectives;
- Effects in re education;
- Television as the most accurate and comprehensive means of conveying to the public;
- Only selected trials;
- Only courts with amenable layouts selected;
- Sensational cases predominate;
- Television cannot cover everything and all actions in court, only where [television cameras are] focused.

Public

- Conditioning the public;
- Prejudicing the public;
- Educational by acquainting with the judicial process;
- Educational institutions;
- Influence on public opinion;
- Giving the public the wrong impression about the trial process;
- Conditioning the public against the defendants;
- Edited and selected programming;
- Influencing opinions before verdict;
- Effect of the audience who may become jurors or witnesses;
- Change [public] attitudes.

Other Effects Issues

- Limited and non scientific research;
- Further studies;
- Body of reliable factual data;
- Experience effects research;

- Techniques of public communication;
- Future technology;
- Process of televising;
- Detracting from the trial, justice and constitutional functions;
- Undermining or effecting the serenity, calm and decorum of the court;
- Decorum;
- Increasing publicity;
- Inadmissible evidence leakage;
- Re-trial effects;
- Pre-trial effects;
- Psychology research;
- Various effects;
- Inconsistency;
- Dignity;
- Wide publicity;
- Heightened publicity;
- Intrusions;
- Restrictions;
- Prejudice;
- [Television] developing the personalities of the courtroom participants;
- Dramatisation;
- Undermining fairness;
- Diverting the process;
- Leading to suspicions concerning integrity of trial process;
- Undercutting integrity of trial process;
- Dignity and calmness;
- Effects on other media;
- More lenient;
- Editing;
- Biasing editing;
- Effects even on unedited film footage;
- Wrong impression;
- Unfairness;
- Educate as to nature of judicial process;
- Personality, famous and celebrity;
- Kind of case;
- Non-notorious trial;
- Effect of television performance;
- Effects of constitutional dimensions;
- Prejudice;
- Prejudice;
- Something more than juror awareness;
- Threats;

- Harassment;
- Death threats [which has now occurred in the *Hollinsworth* case];
- Irreparable harm;
- Live streaming;
- Internet;
- Adequate remedies to effects through an appeal?;
- Unwillingness to cooperate with future cases;
- Integrity of trial process;
- High profile trials;
- Considered standards and guidelines;
- Non high profile cases;
- Cases with witnesses;
- Cases without witnesses;
- Sensitive issue cases;
- All or parts of cases being broadcast;
- Good and bad cases for television courtroom broadcasting experiments;
- High profile publicly divisive cases;
- Effects of harm in non jury cases;
- All harm rectifiable on appeal;
- Integrity of trial;
- Protective measures;
- Actual prejudice;
- Subtle prejudice;
- Slippery slope.

THE ACTUAL WORDS OF THE SUPREME COURT ON EFFECTS ISSUES AND CONCERNS TAKEN FROM THE CAMERA CASES

- Distraction;
- Distortion;
- Disruptive;
- General distraction;
- Actor distraction;
- Psychological considerations;
- Adverse psychological effects on judges, lawyers, witnesses, jurors;
- Duties of the trial judge;
- Influence on public opinion;
- Influence on verdicts;
- Further studies;
- Body of reliable factual data;
- Experience effects research;
- The integrity of judicial process;

- Highly publicised trials;
- Criminal trials;
- Prejudice;
- Diverting the trial;
- Impacting on all participants;
- Giving the public the wrong impression about the trial process;
- Singling out certain defendants;
- Prejudicial conditions not experienced by other defendants;
- Changing behaviour because of awareness;
- Increasing nervousness;
- Increasing tension;
- Opportunism;
- Acting differently;
- Effort of trying not to be effected;
- Not giving full attention;
- Noise of cameras;
- Appearance of cameras;
- Awareness of being televised;
- Undercutting reliability of the trial process;
- Techniques of public communication;
- Future technology;
- Process of televising;
- Probable hazards;
- Criminal trial with notoriety versus a routine trial;
- Effects on the normal detached atmosphere;
- Distorting the trial process;
- Effects of commercials and intervals;
- Detracting from the trial, justice and constitutional functions;
- Undermining or effecting the serenity, calm and decorum of the court;
- Decorum;
- Witnesses and jury awareness;
- No longer calm;
- Increasing publicity;
- Conditioning the public;
- Prejudicing the public;
- Prejudice of actual and potential jurors;
- Inadmissible evidence leakage;
- Juror television viewing during trial;
- Editing;
- Commentary;
- Peer pressure;
- Courtroom actor objections ignored;
- Conscious or unconscious effects;

- Voting decisions;
- Pre-trial publicity;
- Community pressure;
- Awareness;
- Focus;
- Attention;
- TV viewing;
- Re-trial effects;
- Pre-trial effects;
- Emphasising that the case is special;
- Popular verdicts;
- Pre-trial publicity;
- Bias;
- Extraneous influence;
- Knowledge of being televised;
- Emotional audience;
- Aggravation/escalation;
- Jury prejudice by media;
- Witness effects;
- Witness TV viewing;
- Amending testimony;
- Attitude to testifying;
- Apprehension;
- Reluctance;
- Quality of the testimony;
- impact of being filmed and broadcast;
- demoralized;
- Frightening;
- Cocky;
- Overstatement;
- Public speaking;
- Accuracy;
- Over dramatization;
- Public recognition/harassment of witnesses;
- Judge effects;
- Additional responsibility;
- Undivided attention;
- Politics and elected judges;
- Diversion;
- P sychological effects and reactions;
- Direct news media pressure;
- Influence of public opinion by news media;
- Psychology research;

- Various effects;
- Personal acting up;
- Interruptions;
- Rulings ;
- Inconsistency;
- Concentration;
- Defendant effects;
- Harassment;
- Close ups;
- Sensibilities;
- Dignity;
- Concentration;
- Wide publicity;
- Heightened publicity;
- Effective counsel;
- Intrusions;
- Acting up;
- Restrictions;
- Objection by defendant;
- Acting up;
- Awareness;
- Prejudice;
- Out-of-court effects;
- Entertainment;
- Commercial objectives;
- Developing the personalities of the courtroom participants;
- Dramatisation;
- Conditioning the public against the defendants;
- Edited and selected programming;
- Make an impartial jury for a re-trial impossible;
- Influencing opinions before verdict;
- Undermining fairness;
- Effects on courtroom participants;
- Effect of the audience who may become jurors, witnesses;
- Effects in re education;
- Entertain;
- Diverting the process;
- Leading to suspicions concerning integrity of trial process;
- Dividing actor efforts;
- Undercuting integrity of trial process;
- Television as the most accurate and comprehensive means of conveying to the public;
- Educational by acquainting with the judicial process;

- Educational institutions;
- Only selected trials;
- Only courts with amenable layouts selected;
- Sensational cases predominate;
- Dignity and calmness;
- Effects on other media;
- Act differently;
- Acting up;
- More lenient;
- Playing to audience;
- Playing to potential clients;
- Change attitudes;
- Editing;
- Biasing editing;
- Effects even on unedited film footage;
- Wrong impression;
- Television cannot cover everything and all actions in court, only where focused;
- Lawyers will look to see if they can confer with their client without, or out of, close-ups;
- Unfairness;
- Educate as to nature of judicial process;
- Personality, famous and celebrity;
- Kind of case;
- Non-notorious trial;
- Subtle effects;
- Effect on timid or reluctant witness;
- Unconscious effects;
- Effect of television performance;
- Effects of constitutional dimensions;
- Prejudice;
- Jury ability to judge fairly;
- Limited and non scientific research;
- Prejudice;
- Something more than juror awareness;
- Threats;
- Harassment;
- Death threats;
- Harm irreparable harm;
- Live streaming;
- Internet;
- Effect of witness testimony chilling;
- Unwillingness to testify;

- Qualitative differences;
- Adequate remedies to effects through an appeal?;
- Altered testimony;
- Unwillingness to cooperate with future cases;
- Integrity of trial process;
- High profile trials;
- Considered standards and guidelines;
- Witness security;
- Non high profile cases;
- Cases with witnesses;
- Cases without witnesses;
- Sensitive issue cases;
- All or parts of cases being broadcast;
- Good and bad cases for television courtroom broadcasting experiments;
- High profile publicly divisive cases;
- Effects of harm in non jury cases;
- Adverse effects from presence of camera;
- All harm rectifiable on appeal;
- Effect of increasing public awareness of witnesses;
- Reasonable or feasible for witnesses to object;
- Trial management;
- Integrity of trial;
- Protective measures;
- Actual prejudice;
- Subtle prejudice;
- Slippery slope;
- Coerced confession (see camera perspective bias issues below);
- Jury influence.

Appendix 3

General (Non Social Science) Research Literature

BARBER

The seventeen (17) non scientific or non–social science research studies listed by Susanna Barber are[1]

- Washington Bench Bar Press Committee;
- Report to the Supreme Court of Florida Re. Conduct of Audio–visual Trial Coverage, State v Zamora, (1977);
- Report to the Supreme Court of Florida Re.: Audio–visual Trial Coverage, State v Herman, (1978);
- Judge Mounts, Report to the Supreme Court of Florida Concerning Audio–visual Trial Coverage, State v Martin;
- Goldman and Larson, News Cameras in the Courtroom During *State v Solorzana*: End to the Estes Mandate? Southwestern University Law Review 10 (1978): 2001;
- Humphries, Judge Guy, Report on Pilot Project on the Presence of Cameras and Electronic Equipment in the Courtroom, Louisianna (1979);[2]
- Wisconsin Supreme Court Committee;
- Hawaii State Bar Association;
- Massachusetts Advisory Committee;
- J.R. Weisberger, Cameras in the Courtroom, the Rhode Island Experience, SUF–Folk University Law Review 17:2 (1983): 299;
- Connecticut Chief Court Administrator;

- Florida Conference of Circuit Court Judges, Report in Re: Petition of Post–News–Week Stations, Florida, Inc., For Change in Code of Judicial Conduct (1978);
- D. Strawn, R. Buchanan, M. Meeske and B. Prior, Report to the Florida Supreme Court In Re: Petition of Post–Newsweek Stations, Florida, Inc., For Change in Code of Judicial Conduct (1978);
- Florida State Courts Administrator, Florida Conference of Circuit Judges Report In Re: Petition of Post–News–Week Stations, Florida, For Change in Code of Judicial Conduct (1978);
- Washington State Superior Court Judges' Association Committee on Courts and Community, Cameras in the Courtroom – A Two Year Review in the State of Washington (1978);
- K. Netteburg, Does Research Support the Estes Ban on Camera in the Courtroom? Judicature 63: 10 (May, 1980): 467;
- Cleveland Bar Association Study.

(Note, not all references furnished in original).

STRICKLAND AND MOORE

They refer to[3] :

- [Judicial Planning Coordination Unit;]
- Office of the State Courts Administrator, A Sample Survey of Attitudes of Individuals Associated with Trials Involving Electronic Media and Still Photography Coverage in Selected Florida Courts Between July 5, 1977 and June 30, 1978 (November, 1979);
- Short and Associates, Evaluation of California's Experiment with Extended Media Coverage of Courts, Administrative Office of the Courts (September, 1981);
- Cameras in the Courtroom – A Two–Year Review in the State of Washington released by the Washington State Superior Court Judge's Association Committee on Courts and Community in 1978;
- X. Raker, An Evaluation of the Experiment (1983) examines cameras and recorders in Arizona's trial courts;
- Report of the Committee on Audio–Visual Coverage of Court Proceedings (New York, May 1994);
- X. Ellsworth, Start of Year Long Experiment in R.I. Went Well, Presiding Judge Says, Providence Journal (R.I.) (2 October, 1981);
- X. McCollum, Extension is Urged for Cameras in Court, Hartford (Conn.) Courant (February 27, 1983);

- X. Schechet, Supreme Court Extends Trial of News Cameras in Courtrooms, Wicheta–Eagle Beacon (December 27, 1985);
- X. Sherman, Court Cameras: A Gain, Times–Argus (Barre, Vt.) (December 3, 1983).

(Note, not all references furnished in original).

RESEARCH CITED BY COURTROOM VIEW NETWORK (2009)

The studies listed on behalf of Courtroom View Network[4] are:

- Florida pilot program begun in 1977 and approved in *In re Petition of Post–Newsweek Stations*, 370 So.2d 764 (Fla. 1979);
- California experiment permitted in 1980 resulting in the Short and Associates Report;
- California Task Force on Photographing, Recording and Broadcasting in the Courtroom (May 10, 1996);
- Alaska Judicial Council, News Cameras in the Alaska Courts: Assessing the Impact (January, 1988);
- Judicial Information Officer, Superior Court of Maricopa County, Cameras and Recorders in Arizona's Trial Courts (February, 1983);
- Hon. Maurice J Sponzo, Report of the Chief Court Administrator on the "Cameras–In–The–Court" Experiment in the State of Connecticut (May 1, 1983);
- C Robert Taylor, *et al*, Report of the Bar–Bench–Press Conference of Delaware on Television in the Courtroom (March 16, 1981);
- Howard Schwartz, Memo[randa] to Justices of [Kansas] Supreme Court, (October 3, 1984 (5 November, 1985);
- Hon Guy E. Humphries, Jr., District Judge, State of Louisiana, Report on Pilot Project on the Presence of Cameras and Electronic Equipment in the Courtroom, ("dated on or about 1979");
- Supreme Judicial Court of the State of Maine, Administrative Order: Cameras in the Courtroom, Dkt No. SJC–228 (July 11, 1994);
- Maryland Judicial Conference, Official Transcript of Proceedings, Murphy CJ, presiding (May 8, 1980);
- Herbert F Travers, Justice, Mass. Superior Court, *et al*, The Advisory Committee to Oversee the Experimental Use of Cameras and Recording Equipment in Courtrooms to the Supreme Judicial Court (July 16, 1982);
- Report of the Minnesota Advisory Commission on Cameras in the Courtroom (undated);
- Administrative Office of the Courts of Nevada, Final Statistical Report: Cameras in the Courtroom in Nevada (May 7, 1981);

- Norman W. Shibley et al., Report and Recommendations of the Ad Hoc Committee of the Bar Association of Greater Cleveland on the Effect of Cameras in the Courtroom on the Participants in Such a Trial, Cleveland Bar Journal (May 1980): 172–177 (transmitted to the Ohio Supreme Court);
- Hon. Ralph B. Hodges, Chief Justice, Oklahoma Supreme Court, *et al*, Recommended Proposal of the Committee on Radio and Television in the Courtroom (undated);
- Hon. James A. Noe, Cameras in the Courtroom – A Two Year Review of the State of Washington (September 11, 1978);
- Committee of the Supreme Court of the State of Wisconsin, Report of the Supreme Court Committee to Monitor and Evaluate the Use of Audio and Visual Equipment in the Courtroom (April 1, 1979).

(Note, not all references furnished in original).

Table 18.1. Table A3.1. Summary of Main Courtroom Broadcasting Studies (General). General Non Social Science Studies of Courtroom Broadcasting

Author (if given)	*Title*	*Year (if any)*	*Cited*	*Official (O) / Private (P) Research*
X	Washington Bench Bar Press Committee	1975	B	O
Baker, Judge	Report to the Supreme Court of Florida Re. Conduct of Audio–visual Trial Coverage, *State v Zamora*	1977	B	O
Sholts, Judge	Report to the Supreme Court of Florida Re.: Audio–visual Trial Coverage, *State v Herman*	1978	B	O
Mounts, Judge	Judge Mounts, Report to the Supreme Court of Florida Concerning Audio–visual Trial Coverage, *State v Martin*	1978	B	O
Goldman and Larson	News Cameras in the Courtroom During *State v Solorzana*: End to the Estes Mandate? Southwestern University Law Review	1978	B	P
Humphries, Judge Guy	Report on Pilot Project on the Presence of Cameras and Electronic Equipment in the Courtroom, Louisianna	1979	B	O

Wisconsin Supreme Court Committee	Report of Wisconsin Supreme Court Committee to Monitor and Evaluate the Use of Audio and Visual Equipment in the Courtroom, 1/4/1979	1979	B	O
Florida Conference of Circuit Court Judges	Report in Re: Petition of Post–News–Week Stations, Florida, Inc., For Change in Code of Judicial Conduct	1978	B	O
Strawn, D., and Buchanan, R., Meeske, M. and Prior, B.,	Report to the Florida Supreme Court In Re: Petition of Post–Newsweek Stations, Florida, Inc., For Change in Code of Judicial Conduct	1978	B	O
Florida State Courts Administrator	Florida Conference of Circuit Judges (1978) Report In Re: Petition of Post–News–Week Stations, Florida, For Change in Code of Judicial Conduct	1978	B	O
Washington State Superior Court Judges' Association Committee on Courts and Community	Cameras in the Courtroom – A Two Year Review in the State of Washington	1978	B S&M	O
Office of the State Courts Administrator	A Sample Survey of Attitudes of Individuals Associated with Trials Involving Electronic Media and Still Photography Coverage in Selected Florida Courts Between July 5, 1977 and June 30, 1978, November, 1979	1979	S&M	
Netteburg, Kermit	Does Research Support the Estes Ban on Camera in the Courtroom? Judicature (1980): 467	1980	B	P
Cleveland Bar Association Study	Report and Recommendations of the Ad Hoc Committee of the Bar Association of Greater Cleveland on the Effects of Cameras in the Courtroom on the Participants in such a Trial	1980	B	

Ellsworth	Start of Year Long Experiment in R.I. Went Well, Presiding Judge Says, Providence Journal (R.I.), 2 October, 1981	1981	S&M	
X	Hawaii State Bar Association	1982	B	
Massachusetts Advisory Committee	Report of the Advisory Committee to Oversee the Experimental Use of Cameras and Recording Equipment in Courtrooms to the Supreme Judicial Court of Massachusetts, July 16, 1980	1982	B	O
J.R. Weisberger,	Cameras in the Courtroom, the Rhode Island Experience, SUF–Folk University Law Review (1983): 299	1983	B	P
Connecticut Chief Court Administrator	Report of the Chief Court Administrator on the "Cameras–in–the–Courtroom " Experiment of the State of Connecticut	1983	B	O
Raker	An Evaluation of the Experiment (1983) examines cameras and recorders in Arizona's trial courts	1983	S&M	
McCollum	Extension is Urged for Cameras in Court, Hartford (Conn.) Courant (February 27, 1983)	1983	S&M	
Sherman	Court Cameras: A Gain, Times–Argus (Barre, Vt.), (Dec 3, 1983)	1983	S&M	
Schechet	Supreme Court Extends Trial of News Cameras in Courtrooms, Wicheta–Eagle Beacon (December 27, 1985)	1985	S&M	
Burull, Jeanne Rowley	An Analysis of First Amendment Cable Television Cases in the Federal and State Courts, 1969 – 1989 (Ph.D diss., University of Wisconsin, Madison, 1990)	1990	L	G
Kumar, Korni Swaroop	Murder and the News Media (Ph.D diss., Temple University, 1993)	1993	P	

	Report of the Committee on Audio–Visual Coverage of Court Proceedings (New York) (May 1994)	1994	S&M
Elizabeth Reeves Stewart, Ruthie	The Changing Relationship Between Cameras and the Courts (MA diss., Florida Atlantic University, 1998)	1998	L

B: Barber
G: Goldfarb
C&D: Cohen and Dow
L: Lambert (herein)
S&M: Strickland and Moore
CVN: Court View Network

NOTES

1. S. Barber, News Cameras in the Courtroom: A Free Press – Fair Trial Debate (Norwood, New Jersey: Ablex, 1987): 71.
2. Unavailable from Louisianna courts service, correspondence with author.
3. R.A. Strickland and R.H. Moore, Cameras in State Courts: A Historical Perspective Judicature 78 (1994):128.
4. Boies, Schiller and Flexner LLP, Memorandum, Prepared for the Committee on Court Administration and Case Management (Hon. John R Tunheim, Chair), The Judicial Conference of the United States, Submitted on Behalf of Courtroom View Network, June 6, 2009. Available at www.google.ie/url?sa=t&source=web&cd=1&ved=0CBMQFjAA&url=http%3A%2F%2Fwww.courtroomview.com%2Fnews%2FCVN%2520White%2520Paper%2520(6%2520 6%252009)%2520(with%2520exhibits).pdf&ei=Gb2MTOuSFMOV4gbL2uWnCg&usg=AF QjCNEdysCcE_qaIlKgbw3EvomZW_7DTg&sig2=UJyaEtrpo493UfAhGO9kSw, last accessed on August 21, 2012.

Bibliography

AB v BBC [1981] AC 303.
ABA Adopts New Cameras Rule. Judicature (1983): 250.
Abrahams, S. New Efforts in 17 States to Expand Camera Coverage of Courts. Judicature 65 (1981): 116.
Adler, S.J. Trial and Error in the American Courtroom. New York: Times Books, 1994.
Access to Courts and Videoconferencing in Immigration. Harvard Law Review 122 (2009): 1181.
Administrative Office of the Courts of California, Task Force on Photographing, Recording and Broadcasting in the Courtroom, Report Summary (1996), and Administrative Office of the Courts, Cameras in the Courtroom: Report on Rule 980 (May 2000).
Administrative Office of the Courts, Research and Planning Unit, Cameras in the Courtroom. Report on Rule 980, (May, 2000).
AG v Channel 4, referred to in Contempt: Prohibition of TV Broadcast – Inherent Power of Court. Criminal Law Review (1988): 237.
AG v Times [1974] AC 273.
Aho, K. TV and the Supreme Court: Broadcasters Want Access, But Will They Deliver Serious Coverage? Columbia Journalism Review (September/October, 2003): 63.
Alden. Televising of Federal Hearing Is Permitted: Judge Allows First Use of Cameras Since 1994. New York Law Journal (March, 1996).
Alexander, S.L. 'Mischievous Potentialities': A Case Study of Courtroom Camera Guidelines, Eight Judicial Circuit, Florida. Ph.D diss., University of Florida, 1990.
——— Cameras in the Courtroom: A Case Study. Judicature 74 (1991): 307.
——— The Impact of *California v Simpson* on Cameras in the Courtroom. Judicature 79 (1995–1996): 169.
Allan, K., McGregor, J., and Fontaine, S. The Impact of Television, Radio and Still Photography Coverage of Court Proceedings, Final Report, A Report Prepared for the Department For Courts, (Department of Human Resource Management, Faculty of Business Studies, Massey University, April, 1998).
Allowing Cameras and Electronic Media in the Courtroom, Wednesday, September 6, 2000, US Senate, Subcommittee on Administrative Oversight and the Courts, Committee on the Judiciary, Washington, DC.
Alridge, R. McVeigh Trial Cries Out for Cameras in Court. Electronic Media 16 (1997): 22.
Alschuler, A.W. Courtroom Misconduct by Prosecutors and Trial Judges. Texas Law Review 50 (1972): 629.
Altheide, D.L., and Snow, R.P. Media Logic. Beverly Hills: Sage, 1979.
Altheide, D.L. Media Power. Beverly Hills, CA: Sage, 1979.

Alvarado, M., Gutch, R., and Wollen, T. Learning the Media: An lntroduction to Media Teaching. London: Macmillan, 1987.

Anderson, D.A. Democracy and the Demystification of Court: An Essay. Review of Litigation 14 (1995): 627.

Anderson, S. Judicial Accountability: Scandinavia, California & the USA. American Journal of Comparative Law 28 (1980): 393.

Ang, I. Desperately Seeking the Audience. London: Routledge, 1991.

Appeals Courts Can Let Cameras Cover Arguments. The Legal Intelligencer. (March, 1996): 4.

Archer, D. Questions and Answers in the English Courtroom (1640 – 1760): A Sociopragmatic Analysis. Amsterdam: Benjamins, 2005.

Ares, C.E. Chandler v Florida: Television, Criminal Trials, and Due Process. Supreme Court Review (1981): 157.

Aronsson, K., Jonsson, L., and Linell, P. The Courtroom Hearing as a Middle Ground: Speech Accommodation by Lawyers and Defendants. Journal of Language and Social Psychology 2 (1987): 99.

Atwater, T. News Format in Network Evening News Coverage of the TWA Hijacking. Journal of Broadcasting and Electronic Media 33 (1989): 293.

A Sample Survey of the Attitudes of Individuals Associated with Trials Involving Electronic Media and Still Photography Coverage in Selected Florida Courts between July 5, 1977 and June 30, 1978, available from the Florida Supreme Court, as referred to in Netteburg, K. Does Research Support the Estes Ban on Cameras in the Courtroom. Judicature 63 (1980): 467.

Altman, R. Cinema and Genre, in Nowell–Smith, G., Ed. The Oxford History of World Cinema. Oxford: Oxford University Press, 1996, 280, as referred to in Creeber, G., at 3.

An Open Courtroom, Cameras in New York Courts.

Armstrong, T., and Olatunji, B.O. What They See Is What You Get: Eye Tracking of Attention in the Anxiety Disorders. American Psychological Society. (March, 2009).

Bacik, I., and O'Connell, M. Crime and Poverty in Ireland. Dublin: Round Hall Sweet and Maxwell, 1998.

Bagdikian, B., "The Empire Strikes Back," 153–157, in Hiebert, R.E., Ed., The Impact of Mass Media: Current Issues. New York: Longman, 1995.

Bagdikian, B. The New Media Monopoly. Boston: Beacon Press, 2004.

Baker, P., Fairchild, A., Pater, J., and Seavey, A. Community, Participation and Virtual Spaces: Design Considerations for Inclusivity. 10th European Conference on eGovernment, University of Limerick, June 17–18, 2010.

Baksi, C. News: Starmer Wades Into TV Trials Debate. Law Society Gazette (January 15, 2009): 2.

——— Court on Camera. Law Society Gazette 13 (2008): 50.

Ball, M. Coming Attractions: TV in Court: Would It Lead to Sensationalism or Better Understanding? Law Society Journal (September, 1996): 45.

Banaszak, R., Ed. Fair Trial Rights of the Accused. London: Greenwood, 2002.

Barber, S. News Cameras in the Courtroom: A Free Press – Fair Trial Debate. Norwood, New Jersey: Ablex, 1987.

Barendt, E. Broadcasting Law: Comparative Analysis. Oxford: Claredon Press 1995.

Barlow, D., Nock, M., and Hersen., M. Single Case Experimental Designs, Strategies for Studying Behaviour for Change. Boston: Pearson, 2009).

Bar Recommends TV in Courts. New Law Journal (May 26, 1989): 706.

Bar Paves Way for TV Courts. Law Society Gazette (1990): 87.

Barker, C. Global Television: An Introduction. Oxford, Blackwell, 1997.

Barak, A. Judicial Discretion. New Haven: Yale University Press, 1996.

Barrera, L. Law Review Editing and *Choe v Fordam University School of Law*: Is the Courtroom the New Front for the Resolution of Publishing Disputes? Wayne Law Review 42 (1995–1996): 2183.

Barron, J.A., Creating a New First Amendments Right: Miami Herald Publishing Co. v Tornillo and the Story of Access to the Media, chapter in Russomanno, J., Ed. Defending the First: Commentary on the First Amendment Issues and Cases. Mahwah, NJ: Erlbaum, 2005.

Bell, A. The Language of News Media. Oxford: Blackwell, 1991.
Bell, B.E., and Loftus, E.F. Trivial Persuasion in the Courtroom: The Power of (a Few) Minor Details. Journal of Personality and Social Psychology, 56 (1989): 669.
Beville, H.M., Jr. Audience Ratings: Radio, Television, and Cable. Hillside, NJ, Erlbaum, 1988.
Beloff, M.J. Fair Trial – Free Press? Reporting Restrictions in Law and Practice. Public Law (1992): 92.
Bender, D., Leone, B., and Roleff, T.L. Legal System: Opposing Viewpoints. San Diego, CA: Greenhaven Press, 1996.
Bennett, R.R., Wiegand, R.B. Observations on Crime Reporting in a Developing Nation. Criminology 32 (1994): 135.
Bennett, W.L., Gressett, L.A., and Haltom, W. Repairing the News: A Case Study of the News Paradigm. Journal of Communication 35 (1985): 50.
Bennun, M.E. Publicity for Criminal Trials. Chapter 13, in Bridge, J.W., Lasok, D., Plender, R.O., and Perott, D.L., Eds. Fundamental Rights. London: Sweet and Maxwell, 1973, 175.
Berger, A.A. Media Analysis Techniques. London: Sage, 1982, 1998.
Bergman, B.E. Written Statement of Barbara E. Bergman, on Behalf of the National Association of Criminal Defense Lawyers, Before the Senate Committee on the Judiciary, Re: 'Cameras in the Courtrooms,' November 9, 2005.
Bergman, P., and Asimov, M. Reel Justice: the Courtroom Goes to the Movies. Riversdale, NJ: Andres McMeel, 2006.
Bertrand, I., and Hughes, P. Media Research Methods, Audiences, Institutions, Texts. Houndmills, Basingstoke, Hampshire: Palgrave Macmillan, 2005.
Biondi, A. TV Cameras Access into the Courtroom: A Comparative Note. Yearbook of Media and Entertainment Law (YMEL) (1996): 133.
Bird, S.E. The Audience in Everyday Life: Living in a Media World. New York: Routledge, 2003.
Biskupic, J. Justice Pleads with Senate: No Cameras in High Court. USA Today (February 15, 2007).
Blashfield, A.E. The Case of the Controversial Canon. American Bar Association Journal 48 (1962): 429 – 434, as referred to in Shores, D. The Effects of Courtroom Camera on Verbal Behavior: An Analysis of Simulated Trial Witness Testimony in Courtrooms Using Television Cameras. Ph.D. (The University of Florida, 1981): 19.
Blume, P. Law, Communications and Publication. Scandinavian Studies in Law 35 (1991): 9.
Bogoch, B. Courtroom Discourse and the Gendered Construction of Professional Identity. Law and Social Inquiry (1999): 329.
Boies, Schiller and Flexner LLP. Memorandum, Prepared for the Committee on Court Administration and Case Management (Hon. John R Tunheim, Chair), The Judicial Conference of the United States, Submitted on Behalf of Courtroom View Network (June 6, 2009).
Bondi, M. Key–Words and Emotions: A Case Study of the Bloody Sunday Inquiry. Linguistic Insights – Studies in Language and Communication 54 (2007): 407.
Bonnington, A. J. Press and Prejudice. New Law Journal (November 3, 1995): 1623.
Borgida, E., DeBona, K., and Buckman, L.A. Cameras in the Courtroom, The Effects of Media Coverage on Witness Testimony and Juror Perceptions. Law and Human Behaviour 14 (1990): 489.
Borrie, G., and Lowe, N. The Law of Contempt. London: Butterworths, 1996).
Boyd–Barrett, O., and Rantanen, T., Eds. The Globalization of News. London: Sage, 1998.
Braber, L. Self–Government Before the Judiciary and a First Amendment Standard That Protects the Content of Courtroom Argument. First Amendment Law Review 3 (2004–2005): 252.
Breakwell, G.M., Hammond., S., Fife–Schaw, C., and Smith, J.A. Research Methods in Psychology. London: Sage, 2006.
Brechner, J. L. News Media and the Courts. Journal of Broadcasting (1967–1968): 3.
Briggs, M. Television, Audiences and Everyday Life. Maidenhead: Open University Press and McGraw Hill, 2010.
Brill, S. Courtroom Cameras. Notre Dame Law Review 72 (1997): 1181.

Broadcasting Courts, Response to Consultation. CP(R) 28/04, 30/06/2005. Response to Consultation Carried Out by the Department for Constitutional Affairs.

Broadcasting the Courts. JUSTICE Submission to Consultation by the Department of Constitutional Affairs (February, 2005): 2.

Brooke, Lord Justice in Poor [IT] Technology 'Lets Down' UK Courts. BBC News (June 20, 2002).

Brooker, W., and Jermyn, D., Eds. The Audience Studies Reader. London: Routledge, 2003.

Broomhall, B. International Justice and the International Criminal Court: Between Sovereignty and the Rule of Law. Oxford: OUP, 2003.

Brown, C. Garda Public Attitudes Survey 2008. Garda Research Unit: Research Report No 1/08.

Brown, D., Duane, J., and Fraser, B. Media Coverage and Public Opinion of the OK Simpson Trial: Implications for the Criminal Justice System. Communications Law and Policy 2 (1997): 261.

Brown, R.L. Essay: Just A Matter of Time?, Video Cameras at the United States Supreme Court and the State Supreme Courts. Journal of Appellate Practice and Process 9 (2007): 1.

Brown, T.A., and Munger, M.P. Representational Momentum, Spatial Layout, and Viewpoint Dependency. Visual Cognition 18 (2010): 780.

Broyles, D.K. New Rules for Open Courts Progress or Empty Promise? Tulsa Law Journal 18 (1982): 147.

Brunsdon, C., and Caughie, J., Eds. Television and New Media Audiences. Oxford: OUP, 1999.

Brust, R. From Term Limits to Circuit Riding to Cameras in the Courtroom, Rethinking, Reforming and Re–engineering the Top Bench. ABA Journal 94 (2008): 39.

Bryant, J., and Thompson, S. Fundamentals of Media Effects. New York: McGraw Hill, 2002.

Bukoff, A. The Effects of Video Camera Techniques on the Pre–Deliberation Judgements and Perceptions of Role–Playing Jurors. Ph.D. (Kent State University, 1984).

Bundesen, C., and Habekost, T. Principles of Visual Attention: Linking Mind and Brain. Oxford: Oxford University Press, 2008.

Butler, J.G. Television: Critical Methods and Applications. New York: Routledge, 2006.

Butters, R.R. Linguistics in the Courtroom: A Practical Guide. Language and Society 37 (2008): 300.

Burcham, D.W., High Profile Trials: Can Government Sell the Right to Broadcast the Proceedings? UCLA Law Review 3 (1995–1996): 169.

Cai, D.A. Intercultural Communication. Los Angeles: Sage, 2010.

Cain, P.J. A First Step Toward Introducing Emotional Intelligence into the Law School Curriculum: The 'Emotional Intelligence and the Clinic Student' Class. Legal Education Review 14 (2003–2004): 1.

California Rules of Court (Revised January 1, 2009).

Calvo–Goller, K.N. The Trial Proceedings of the International Criminal Court, ICTY and ICTR Precedents (Leiden: Martinus Nijhoff, 2006).

Cameras in the Courts: A State–by–State Guide. Radio Television, Digital News Association, available at www.rtdna.org .

Cameras in Court. New Law Journal (December 4, 1980): 1136.

Cameras in the Courtroom: A Dialogue. ABA Journal 64 (1978): 545.

Camp, A.F. Cameras, Courts, and the Constitution. Pepperdine Law Review 9 (1981): 165.

Caplan, J. Televising the Courts – Case For Reform. Media Law and Practice 13 (1992): 176.

Caplan, J., Kalisher, M., and Speaight, A.. Televising the Courts: Report of a Working Party of the Public Affairs Committee of the General Council of the Bar [of England and Wales], (London: Bar Council of England and Wales, 1989).

Card, R., Gillespie, A., and Hirst, M. Sexual Offences. Bristol: Jordans, 2008.

Carlisle, J.C. An Open Courtroom: Should Cameras be Permitted in New York State Courts? Pace Law Review 18 (1998): 297.

Carey, G. The Performative Character of Media Presentation of Crime. Irish Criminal Law Journal 9 (1999): 47.

Carney, D.P. The Accused, the Jury and the Media. New Law Journal (13 January, 1995): 12.

Carney, W.B. Prime Time Law in America. New Law Journal 147 (1997): 1845.
Carranza, I.E. Discourse Markers in the Construction of the Text, the Activity, and the Social Relations: Evidence from Courtroom Discourse. Current Trends in the Pragmatics of Spanish (2004): 203.
Carroll, J.S. Free Press and Fair Trial: the Role of Behavioral Research. Law and Human Behavior 10 (1986): 187.
Carter, C.A. Television in the Courts. State Court Journal 5 (1981): 6.
Carter, C.A., Ito, J.E. Media Coverage and the State Courts: An Update. State Court Journal 6 (1982): 26.
Carter, T. Lawyers Fade Away to Grey, US Journalist Terry Carter Looks at the Frequently Bizarre Conduct of the Lawyers in the Simpson Case. Law Society Gazette 93 (1995): 16.
Carter, S.L. Technology, Democracy, and the Manipulation of Consent. Yale Law Journal 93 (1984): 581–609, a book review regarding Yudof, M.G. When Government Speaks: Politics, Law, and Government Expressions in America. Berkley: University of California Press, 1983.
Catliff, N. On Camera Not In Cameras. New Law Journal 144 (1994): 1597.
Cedarquist, W.B. Televising Court Proceedings, A Plea for Order in the Court. Notre Dame Lawyer, 36 (1961): 147.
Chance, S.F. Considering Cameras in the Courtroom. Journal of Broadcasting and Electronic Media 39 (1995): 555.
Chandler v Florida, 449 US, (1981), 560.
Chandler, P., and Sweller, J. Cognitive Load Theory and the Format of Instruction. Cognition and Instruction 8 (1991): 293, as referred to Holsanova, J.
Chang, B. Deconstructing Communication. Minnesota: 1996, Minnesota University Press.
Chapter 8: How Are Messages Formulated? The Linguistics of Lines and Between the Lines, in Ginnekan, J.P. Understanding Global News: A Critical Introduction. London: Sage, 1998.
Chapter 2: Media Globalization, in Deveraux, E. Understanding the Media. Los Angeles: Sage, 2007.
Chapter 4: Media Production and Media Professionals, in Deveraux, E. Understanding the Media. Los Angeles: Sage, 2007.
Chapter 1: Making the News, in Philo, G. Seeing and Believing: The Influence of Television. London: New York, 1990.
Chapter 3: The Production of News Language, in Bell, A. The Language of News Media. Oxford: Blackwell, 1991.
Cherif Bassiouni, M. The Legislative History of the International Criminal Court. New York: Transnational Publishers, 2005.
Chibnall, S. Introduction section, sub–heading "Law–and–order–news," in Chibnall, S. Law and Order News: An Analysis of Crime Reporting in the British Press. London: Tavistoch Publications, 1977, ix.
Chicago Judges Adopt Rule Barring Cameras from Court Rooms. Judicature (1925): 18.
Christie, N. Crime Control as Industry. London: Routledge, 1993.
Clawson, R.A., Strine, H.C.N. IV, Waltenburg, E.N. Frame Supreme Court Decisions: The Mainstream Versus the Black Press. Journal of Black Studies 33 (2003): 784.
Cleveland Publicity–Cleveland Paper Defies Photo Ban. Judicature (1958): 188.
Cohen, J. Cameras in the Courtroom and Due Process: A Proposal for a Qualitative Difference Test. Washington Law Review 57 (1982): 277, as referred to in Alexander, S.L., 69.
Cohen, L. Kids, Courts, and Cameras: New Challenges for Juvenile Defenders (The Juvenile Justice Counter–Reformation: Children and Adolescents as Adult Criminals). QLR 18 (1999): 701.
Cohen, S. Folk Devils and Moral Panics. Herts: Paladin, 1973.
Cohn, M. Let the Sun Shine on the Supreme Court. Hastings Constitutional Law Quarterly 35 (2007 – 2008): 161.
Cohn, M., and Dow, D. Cameras in the Courtroom: Television and the Pursuit of Justice. New York: Rowman & Little, 2002.
Cook, T.E., Ed. Freeing the Presses, The First Amendment in Action. Baton Rouge: Louisiana State University Press, 2005.

Comstock, G., *et al.* Television and Human Behaviour (New York: Columbia University Press, 1978), as referred to in McQuail, D., and Windahl, S.

Conference on Criminal Jurisdiction in November 2002 related to The Criminal Trial Process. See the Judicial Studies Institute Journal 3 (2002): 39–71.

Cops and Cameras: Why TV is Slow to Cover Police Brutality. Columbia Journalism Review (CJR) (September/October, 1991): 15.

Corbett, M.A. Lights, Camera, Trial: Pursuit of Justice or the Emmy? Seton Law Review 27 (1996–1997): 1542.

Cornett, J.M. The Ethics of Blawging: Genre Analysis. Loyola University Chicago Law Journal 41 (2009): 221.

Cotterill, J. Collocation, Connotation, and Courtroom Semantics: Lawyers' Control of Witness Testimony Through Lexical Negotiation. Applied Linguistics 25 (2004): 513.

Court TV Deterrent. New Law Journal 138 (1988)(138): 906.

Court of Appeals of New York: Courtroom Television Network, LLC v New York. Touro Law Review 22 (2006 – 2007): 191.

Courtroom Cameras: Appeals Court to Decide. Pennsylvania Law Weekly (March, 1996): 8.

Courts Service. Personal correspondence with the Courts Service during December 2010 – January 2011, correspondence with author.

Courtney, C., Newell, D., and Rasaiah, S. The Law of Journalism. London: Butterworths, 1995.

Craig v R. Craig v The King, High Court, Australia. *Craig v R* [1933] HCA 41; [1933] 49 *CRL* (1933)(49) (29 August, 1933); available atwww.austlii.edu.au, last accessed on 30 January, 2011.

Cranston, R. The Rational Study of Law: Social Research and Access to Justice. In Zuckerman, A.A.S., and Cranston, R. Reform of Civil Procedure: Essays on Access to Justice. Oxford: Clarendon, 1995, 31.

Crawford, A., and Goodey, J. Integrating a Victim Perspective Within Criminal Justice, International Debates. Burlington: Ashgate, 2000.

Creeber, G., Ed. The Television Genre Book. London: Palgrave MacMillan, 2008).

Creech, K. Electronic Media Law and Regulation. Burlington, MA: Focal Press/Elsevier, 2007.

Cripe, K.L. Empowering the Audience: Television's Role in the Diminishing Respect for the American Judicial System. UCLA Entertainment Law Review 6 (1998–1999): 235.

Criswell, A. A Study of Modern Television: Thinking Inside the Box. Hampshire: Palgrave MacMillan, 2006.

Cross and Tapper on Evidence. Oxford: OUP, 2007.

Cullen v Toibin and Magill [1984] ILRM 577.

Cunningham, N. Lights, Cameras, Action. Justice Report 11 (1995): 18.

Cutler, Brian L., Penrod, Steven D., and Martens, T.K. The Reliability of Eyewitness Identifications: The Role of System and Estimator Variables. Law and Human Behavior 11 (1987): 223.

Cutler, B., and Penrod, S. Mistaken Identification: The Eyewitness, Psychology and the Law. New York: Cambridge University Press, 1995.

Curran, G. Journalists and Judges: Tension and Distortion. Judicial Studies Institute Journal 2 (2001): 11.

Curran, J., and Gurevitch, M., Eds. Mass Media and Society. London: Hodder, 2005.

Currie, B. The Materials of Law Study. Journal of Legal Education 8 (1955)(8:1): 62.

D'Alemente, T. The Case for an Open Judicial System. Judicature (1974): 61.

Dahlgren, P. What's the Meaning of This? Viewers' Plural Sense–Making of TV News. Media, Culture and Society 10 (1988): 285.

Dawson, D. The Honourable Sir. Judges and the Media. University of New South Wales Law Journal 10 (1987): 17.

Davidson, W.P. The Third Person Effect in Communication. Public Opinion Quarterly 47 (1983): 1–15, referred to in Innes, J.M., and Zeitz, H. The Public View of the Impact of the Mass Media: a Test of the 'Third Person' Effect. European Journal of Social Psychology 18 (1988): 437.

Davies, G., and Griffiths, L. Eyewitness Identification and the English High Courts: A Century of Trial and Error. Psychiatry, Psychology and Law 15 (2008): 435.

Davies, G.M., Smith, S., and Blincoe, C. A 'Weapon Focus' Effect in Children. Psychology, Crime and Law 14 (2008): 19.

Davis, N. Television in Our Courts: The Proven Advantages, The Unproven Dangers. Judicature 64 (1980): 85.

Davis, S.F. Handbook of Research Methods in Experimental Psychology. Oxford: Blackwell, 2003.

Dayan, D., and Katz, E. Media Events: The Live Broadcasting of History. Cambridge: Harvard University Press, 1992.

Dean, P.J., Lombard, H.E., and Wilkes, S. Committal of a Patient Due to Media Influence? A Case Report. Australian and New Zealand Journal of Psychiatry 35 (2001) 129.

DeBenedictis, D.J. Cameras Banned, Pens Allowed: San Francisco Judge Refuses TV Station's Request to Tape Inmate Execution. ABA Journal (August, 1991): 16.

Deffenbacher, K.A., and Loftus, E.F. Do Jurors Share a Common Understanding Concerning Eyewitness Behaviour? Law and Human Behaviour, 6 (1982): 26.

DeFleur, M.L., Davenport, L., Cronin, M., and DeFleur, M. Audience Recall of News Stories Presented by Newspaper, Computer, Television and Radio. Journalism Quarterly 69 (1992): 1010.

Denbeaux, M.P. The First Word of the First Amendment. Northwestern University Law Review 80 (1986)(80): 1156.

Department of Constitutional Affairs [UK]. Broadcasting Courts, Consultation Paper. CP 28/04 (November, 2004).

Department of Constitutional Affairs. Broadcasting Courts, Response to Consultation, CP(R) 28/04, 30/06/2005, Response to Consultation Carried Out by the Department for Constitutional Affairs.

Department for Constitutional Affairs in Great Britain consultation "Broadcasting Courts," (2004).

Department of Constitutional Affairs, Justice Rights and Democracy, *Broadcasting Courts*, Consultation Paper, CP 28/04, November 2004, p. 109. Referring to the UMR Insight Surveys and Massey University Research in New Zealand.

Department of Constitutional Affairs [UK]. Broadcasting Courts, Consultation Paper. CP 28/04 (November, 2004).

Department of Constitutional Affairs, Broadcasting Courts, Response to Consultation. CP(R) 28/04, June 30, 2005. Response to Consultation Carried Out by the Department for Constitutional Affairs.

Dershowitz, A. Reasonable Doubts: The Criminal Justice System and the O.J. Simpson Case. New York: Touchstone, 1996, 1997.

Deutacher. What We Say/What We Do (Glenview, IL: Scott, Foresman, 1973), referred to in Jensen, K.B., and Jankowski, N.W., Eds. A Handbook of Qualitative Methodologies for Mass Communication Research. London: Routledge, 1991, n. 15, at 61.

Deveraux, E. Understanding the Media. Los Angeles: Sage, 2007.

Dickstein, M. Cameras in the Courtroom. Bench & Bar of Minnesota 7 (2008): 4.

Dikabil Manual, Section 2.1., at 5.

Dimbelby, R., and Burton, G. More Than Words, An Introduction to Communication. London: Routledge, 1998.

Dixon, T.L., Linz, D. Television News, Prejudicial Retrial Publicity, and Depiction of Race. Journal of Broadcasting & Electronic Media 46 (2002): 1[illegible]2.

Dockray, M. Cameras at the Door of the Court. New Law Journal 20 (1990) 548.

Doob, A.N., and Macdonald, G.E. Television Viewing and Fear of Victimisation: Is the Relationship Causal? Journal of Personality and Social Psychology 37 (1979): 170.

Dowler, K. Sex, Lies and Videotape: The Presentation of Sex Crime in Local Television News. Journal of Criminal Justice 34 (2006): 383.

Downing, J., Mohammadi, A., and Sreberny–Mohammadi, M.A. Questioning the Media. London: Sage, 1995.

Drucker, S.J. The Television Mediated Trial: Formal and Substantive Characteristics. Communications Quarterly 37 (1989): 305.

Drummond, P., and Paterson, R. Television and Its Audience: International Research Perspectives: A Selection of Papers from the Second International Television Studies Conference. London: British Film Institute, 1986.

Duby, A. Using Television as an Educational Medium. Educational Media International 28 (1991): 190.

Duchowski, A. Eye Tracking Methodology, Theory and Practice. London: Springer, 2007.

Durant, A. Meaning in the Media: Discourse, Controversy and Debate. Cambridge: CUP, 2010.

Durant, A., and Lambrou, M. Language and Media. London and New York: Routledge Taylor & Francis Group, 2009.

Dyer, C.S., and Hauserman, N.R. Electronic Coverage of the Courts: Exceptions to Exposure. Georgia Law Review 75 (1986 – 1987): 1633.

Dyk, T.B. Newsgathering, Press Access, and the First Amendment. Stanford Law Review 44 (1992): 927.

Dyk, T., and Donald, B. Cameras in the Supreme Court: Should Supreme Court Proceedings be Televised? ABA Journal (March, 1989): 34.

Eady, D., Sir, and Smith, A.T.H. Arlidge, Eady & Smith on Contempt. London: Sweet & Maxwell, 2005.

Easton, S.D. Cameras in Courtrooms: Contrasting Viewpoints: Whose Life if it Anyway?: A Proposal to Redistribute Some of the Economic Benefits of Cameras in the Courtroom from Broadcasters to Crime Victims. South Carolina Law Review 49 (1997): 1.

Editorial, Cameras Out of Courtroom? American Bar Association Journal (1979): 304.

Editorial. Cameras Belong in Court. Broadcasting & Cable (June 20, 2005): 36.

Editorial. Kobe Bryant Case Points to Need for Cameras in Court. Television Week 22 (2003): 9.

Editorial. Tele–justice. New Law Journal (May 26, 1989): 705.

Edwards, D.L. If It Walks, Talks and Squawks Like a Trial, Should it be Covered Like One? The Right of the Press to Cover INS Deportation Hearings. Communication Law and Policy 10 (2005): 217.

Ehite, J.G. III. Celebrating the 30th Anniversary of Cameras in the Courtroom. Florida Bar Journal (April, 2009): 4.

Einsiedel, E. Television in the Courtroom: An Ohio Experiment. Association for Education in Journalism, Seattle (1978), as referred to in Alexander, S.L. 'Mischievous Potentialities': A Case Study of Courtroom Camera Guidelines, Eight Judicial Circuit, Florida, (1989). Ph.D. (University of Florida, 1990): 87.

– Television in the Courtroom: An Ohio Experiment, paper presented to the Association for Education in Journalism, (August, 1978), as referred to in Netteburg, 470.

"Electronic Public Access to Court," regarding British Columbia, Canada and the case of *R v Clark*, available at www.adidem.org/Electronic_Public_Access_to_Court , last accessed on December 6, 2009, the case being available at www.courts.gov.bc.ca .

Elffers, H., de Keijser, J.W., van Koppen, P.J., and van Haeringen, L. Newspaper Juries: A Field Experiment Concerning the Effect of Information on Attitudes Towards the Criminal Justice System. Journal of Experimental Criminology 3 (2007): 163.

Emery, R.D. Cameras in the Courtroom After O.J.? – No. New York Law Journal (October 26, 1995): 2.

Entner, R. The Image of the Judiciary: A Semiotic Analysis of Broadcast Trials to Ascertain its Definition of the Court System. Ph.D diss., New York University, 1993.

Entner, R. The Image of the Judiciary: A Semiotic Analysis of Broadcast Trials to Ascertain Its Definition of the Court System. New York: New York University Press, 1993.

Epstein, E.J. News from Nowhere: The Selection of Reality in Television News Programs. New York: Vantage, 1973.

Epstein, J.R., and Fogel, P.D. California's Experience with Cameras Suggests the Need for Change to the New Federal Rule. Communications Lawyer, 9 (1991).

Ergun, D., Deason, G., Borgida, E., and Charles, G–U. Race and Redirecting: What the Print Media Conveys to the Public About the Role of Race. Journal of Social Issues 64 (2008): 619.

Ericson, R.V., Baranek, P.M., and Chan, J.B.L. Representing Order: Crime Law and Justice in the News. Oxford: OUP, 1991.
Erjavec, K., and Kovacic, P. A Discursive Approach to Genre, Mobi News. European Journal of Communication 24 (2009): 147.
Erskine, D.H. An Analysis of the Legality of Television Cameras Broadcasting Juror Deliberations in a Criminal Case. Akron Law Review 39 (2006): 701.
Esposito, S.A. OJ TV: A Narrative Analysis of Television's Pretrial Coverage of the O.J. Simpson Case. Ph.D diss., Graduate School of Wayne State University, Detroit, Michigan, 1996.
Esposito, S.A. Source Utilization in Legal Journalism: Network TV News Coverage of the Timothy McVeigh Oklahoma City Bombing Trial. Communications and Law 20 (1998): 15.
Estes v Texas, 381, US 533 (1965).
Evaluation of California's Experiment with Extended Media Coverage (1981), and available from the National Centre for State Courts.
Evans, A. Lawyers' Perceptions of Their Values: An Empirical Assessment of Monash University Graduates in Law 1980–1998. Legal Education Review 12 (2001): 209.
Evans, K. The Publicity is the Problem. New Law Journal (July 7, 1995): 992.
Ewing, L., Rhodes, G., and Pellicano, E. Have You Got the Look? Gaze Direction Affects Judgements of Facial Attractiveness. Visual Cognition 18 (2010): 321.
*E*Trade Financial Corp.* v *Deutsche Bank AG*, 582 F. Supp. 2d 528, 535 (SDNY 2008).
Fairclough, N. Media Discourse. London: Edward Arnold, 1995.
Falconer Close to Rejecting TV Trials as Sky Breaks New Ground in Jenkins Case. Law Society Gazette (7 July, 2005), available at www.lawgazette.co.uk , last accessed on 24 October, 2010.
Faludi, S. Backlash. The Undeclared War Against American Women. New York: Anchor, 1991.
Fang, I.E. Television News, Radio News. (St. Paul, MN: Rada Press, 1985).
Fatzer, H.R. Cameras in the Courtroom: The Kansas Opposition. Washburn Law Journal (1978–1979): 230, quoted in Tongue, T.H., and Lintott, R.W. The Case Against Television in the Courtroom. Williamette Law Review 16 (1980): 790.
Fatzer, J., former Chief Justice of Kansas Supreme Court, in Fatzer, H.R. Cameras in the Courtroom: The Kansas Opposition. Washburn Law Journal, 18 (1978): 230, as referred to in Shores, D., 38.
Fedler, F., and Jordan, D. How Emphasis on People Affects Coverage of Crime. Journalism Quarterly (1982): 474.
Felcher, P.L., and Ruin, E.L. Privacy, Publicity, and the Portrayal of Real People by the Media. Yale Law Journal 88 (1979): 1577.
Feldman–Summers, and Ashworth, C.D. Factors Related to Intentions to Report a Rape. Journal of Social Issues 37 (1981): 53.
Fennell, C. The Law of Evidence in Ireland. Dublin: Butterworth, 1992.
Fennell, C., and Ryan, A. A Cork Study on 'Domestic' Violence and the Criminal Process: Tentative Conclusions from the Policing Perspective. Judicial Studies Institute Journal 4 (2004): 79.
Feuer. Genre and Television, in Allen, Ed. Channels of Discourse, Reassembled: Television and Contemporary Criticism. London and New York: Routledge, 1992), at 158, as referred to in Creeber, G., at 6.
Findahl, B., and Hoijer, O. Some Characteristics of News Memory and Comprehension. Journal of Broadcasting and Electronic Media 29 (1985): 379.
Findlay, P., and Duff, M. The Jury Under Attack. London: Butterworths, 1988.
Fionda, J. Public Prosecutors and Discretion, A Comparative Study. Oxford: Clarendon, 1995.
Fisher, L. Through the Camera Lens: When Justice is Not Seen to be Done. Australian Law Journal 69 (1995): 477.
Fiske, J., and Hartley, J. Reading Television. New York: Methuen, 1978.
Fiske, J. Television Culture. London: Methuen, 1987, as referred to in McQuail, D., at 118.
Fiss, O.M. The Bureaucratization of the Judiciary. Yale Law Journal 92 (1983): 1442.
Flashlight in the Courtroom, Saturday Evening Post (November 13, 1937): 1.

Florek, E., Daugherty, R., Mitchell, K.B. Camera Controversy in Courtrooms Continues. News Media and the Law (February 1, 2005), available atwww.rcfp.org/newsitems/index.php?i=6183, last accessed on April 22, 2009.

Flynn, K.H. General Provisions: Establishing Factors for Courts to Consider When Determining Whether to Allow Filming or Videotaping in the Courtroom; Allow for Citations When Court Orders Related to Media Cameras in the Courtroom are Violated, accessible at http://dspace.gsu:8080/dspace/handle/2197/531 , last accessed on November 30, 2009.

Folker, S., Sichelschmidt, L. and Ritter, H. Processing and Integrating Multimodal Material: The Influence of Color–coding, in Bara, B.G., and Bucciarelli, Eds. Proceedings of the 27th Annual Conference of the Cognitive Science Society. (Mahwah, MJ: Erlbaum): 690.

Fowler, R. Language in the News: Discourse and Ideology in the Press. London: Routledge, 1991.

Frank, R.E., Greenberg, M.G. The Public's Use of Television: Who Watches and Why. Beverly Hills: Sage, 1980.

Franklin, M.A., Anderson, D.A., and Lidsky, L.B. Mass Media Law, Cases and Materials. New York: Foundation Press, 2005.

Franzosi, R., Ed. Content Analysis, Sage Benchmarks in Social Science Research Methods. Los Angeles: Sage, 2008.

Freckelton, I.R.L., Research Paper No. 4. Prejudicial Publicity and the Courts (Australian Law Reform Commission, 1986).

Freedman, W. Press and Media Access to the Criminal Courtroom. New York: Quorum, 1988.

French, J., Radio and Television Broadcasting in the Magistrates' Court – Is There a Future? Federal Judicial Scholarship (2006), available at www.austlii.edu.au , last accessed on October 16, 2006.

Gallant, S., and Epsorth, J. Media Law, A Practical Guide to Managing Publication Risks. London: Sweet and Maxwell, 2001.

Galatolo, R., and Drew, P. Narrative Expansions as Defensive Practices in Courtroom Testimony. Text & Talk 26 (2006): 661.

Gale, S. Cameras in Courtrooms Would Lead to a More Educated Public, in Hiber, A., 61.

Galligan, D.J. Due Process and Fair Procedures, A Study of Administrative Procedures. Oxford: Clarendon, 1996.

Garner, M., Wagner, C., and Kawilich, B., Eds. Teaching Research Methods in the Social Sciences. Surrey: Ashgate, 2009.

Gardner, N.T. Cameras in the Courtroom: Guidelines for State Criminal Trials. Michigan Law Review, 84 (1985): 475.

Gauntlett, D., and Hill, A. TV Living: Television, Culture and Everyday Life. London: Routledge and British Film Institute, 1999.

Geis, G., and Talley, R.E.L. Cameras in the Courtroom. Journal of Criminal Law, Criminology, and Police Science 47 (1957): 546.

Geller, W.A. Police Videotaping of Suspect Interrogations and Confessions: A Preliminary Examination of Issues and Practices. (A Report to the National Institute of Justice, Washington, DC: US Department of Justice, 1992).

Gerbner, G., *et al.* TV Violence Profile No. 8: The Highlights. Journal of Communication, 27 (Spring 1977), as referred to in Mowlana, H., 73.

Gerbner, G., and Gross, L. The Scary World of TV's Heavy Viewer. Psychology Today (April, 1976): 44.

Gerber, G., Courtroom TV Makes for Low–budget Entertainment. Interview on NPR Morning Edition on 12 July, 1994, referred to in Lassiter, C. Put the Lens Cap Back on Cameras in the Court Room: A Fair Trial in at Stake. Law and Justice (1994): 111, referred to at 119.

——— Trial by Television: Are We At The Point Of No Return? Judicature 63 (1980):416, as referred to in Keller, T., 70.

Gibbons, T. Freedom of the Press: Ownership and Editorial Values. Public Law (1992): 279.

Gibney, I. Trial by Media. Law Society Gazette (August/September, 1997): 12.

Gilbert, N. Researching Social Life. London: Sage, 2008.

Gilbert, P. Annual New York State Constitutional Decisions: 2004 Compilation: Freedom of Speech: Supreme Court of New York Appelate Division, First Department: *Courtroom Television Network LLC v New York*. Touro Law Review 21 (2005)(21): 21.

Giles, D. Media Psychology. (Mahwah, New Jersey: Lawrence Erlbaum, 2003).

Gillespie, M., and Toynbee, J. Analysing Media Texts. Maidenhead: Open University Press and McGraw Hill, 2006).

Gillmor, D.M. Free Press Versus Fair Trial: A New Era? Journalism Quarterly Review (1964): 27.

Gillmor, D.M., Barron, J.M., and Simon, T.F. Mass Communication Law, Cases and Comment. Belmont, CA: Wadsworth, 1998.

Gilmore, W.H. Arraignment by Television: A New Way to Bring Defendants to the Courtroom. Judicature (1980): 396.

Ginnejan, J.V. Understanding Global News: A Critical Introduction. London: Sage, 1998.

Glatt, D.M. Trial by Docudrama: Fact or Fiction? Cardoza Arts and Entertainment Law Journal 9 (1990): 201.

Gnisci, A., Bonaiuto, M. Grilling Politicians: Politicians' Answers to Questions in Television Interviews and Courtroom Examinations. Journal of Language and Social Psychology 22 (2003): 385.

Goldberg, D., Sutter, G., and Walden, I. Media Law and Practice (Oxford: OUP, 2009).

Goldfarb, R.L. TV or Not TV: Television, Justice, and the Courts. New York: New York University Press, 1998.

Goldfarb, R., in Statement of Ronald Goldfarb, Allowing Cameras and Electronic Media in the Courtroom, US Senate Subcommittee on Administrative Oversight and the Courts, Committee on the Judiciary, Washington DC, Wednesday, September 6, 2000, 55.

Golding, P., and Harris, P., Eds. Beyond Cultural Imperialism: Globalization, Communication and the New International Order. London: Sage, 1997.

Goldman, J. Multimedia for Research and Training – The Oyez Oyez Oyez and the History and Politics Out Loud Projects. Social Science Computer Review 16 (1998): 30.

Goldman, P. and Larson, R. News Cameras in the Courtroom During *State v Solorzano*: End to the Estes Mandate? Southwestern–Nevada Law Review 10 (1978): 2001.

Goldschmidt, J. 'Order in Court!': Constitutional Issues in the Law of Courtroom Decorum Hamline Law Review 31 (2008): 1.

Goldstein, A.S., and Marcus, M. The Myth of Judicial Supervision in Three 'Inquisitorial' Systems: France, Italy, and Germany. Yale Law Journal 87 (1977): 240.

Goldstein, M. US Judicial Conference Votes to Allow Cameras Into Appelate Courts. New York Law Journal (March, 1996): 1.

Goode, E., and Ben–Yehuda, N. Moral Panics: the Social Construction of Deviance. Oxford: Blackwell, 1994.

Goodenough, O.R., Retheorising Privacy and Publicity, Intellectual Property Quarterly 1 (1997): 37.

Goodman, G.S., and Hahn, A. Evaluating Eyewitness Testimony in Weiner, I., and Hess, A. Handbook of Forensic Psychology. New York: Wiley, 1987, 258.

Goodwin, A.T. A Report on the Latest Rounds in the Battle Over Cameras in the Courts. Judicature (1979): 74.

Grady, S. Cameras in Courtrooms Would Lead to a More Educated Public, in Hiber, A., 61.

Graham, F., and Fretz, D.R. Cameras in the Courtroom: A Dialogue. ABA Journal 64 (1978): 545.

Graham, R., Friesen, C.K., Fichtenholtz and LaBar. Modulation of Reflexive Orienting to Gaze Direction by Facial Expressions. Visual Cognition 18 (2010): 331–368.

Granhad, P.A., Stromwall, L.A., and Hartwig, M. Eyewitness Testimony: Tracing the Beliefs of Swedish Legal Professionals. Behavioral Sciences and the Law 23 (2005): 709–727.

Graves, D. Cameras in the Courts: the Situation Today. Judicature 63 (1979): 24–27.

Gravetter, F.J., and Forzana, L–A.B. Research Methods for the Behavioral Sciences. Belmond, CA: Wadsworth/Thomson Learning, 2003.

Greek, C.E. Lecture 9, Shadow Justice: Courts and the Media (1996), atwww.fsu.edu/~crimdo/lecture9.html, 7.

Green v Broadcasting Corporation of New Zealand [1989] RPC 469; and appeal at [1989] RPC 700.
Green, M. Social Contexts and Uses of Research: Media, Education and Communities, in Jensen, K.B., and Jankowski, N.W., Eds. Handbook of Qualitative Methodologies for Communication Research. London: Routledge, 1991.
Green, L. Australian Law Journal 69 (1995): 477.
Greene, E. Media Effects on Jurors. Law and Human Behavior 14 (2005): 439.
Greenfleld, P.M. Minds and Media: The Effects of Television, Computers and Video Games. Fontana, 1984).
Greenhut, J. Lights ... Cameras ... Action!!! It's Trial Time. Library, National Centre for State Courts, VA. (May, 1996): 33.
Greenhouse, L. Telling the Court's Story: Justice and Journalism at the Supreme Court. Yale Law Journal 105 (1996): 1537.
Green Paper on Broadcasting, (Dublin: Government Publications, 1995).
Green Paper on Procedural Safeguards for Suspects and Defendants in Criminal Proceedings Throughout the European Union. IP/03/245 (February 19, 2003).
Greenwood, D.J., and Levin, M. Introduction to Action Research: Social Research for Social Change. Thousand Oaks: Sage, 2007.
Groner, J., and Barbieri, R. Federal Judiciary Opens Window to Cameras in Court. The Recorder (March, 1996): 1.
Groner, J. Who Rule? Which Rules, Cameras in Court Decision Tests Power of Judicial Conference. Legal Times (March, 1996).
Gunter, B., and Machin, D., Eds. Media Audiences. Los Angeles: Sage, 2009.
Haapasalo, J. Types of Offence Among the Cleckley Psychopaths. International Journal of Offender Therapy and Comparative Criminology 38 (1994): 59.
Hale, S. Themes and Methodological Issues in Court Interpreting Research. Linguistica Antverpiensia 5 (2006): 205.
Haldar, P. The Evidencer's Eye: Representations of Truth In the Laws of Evidence. Law and Critique 2 (1991): 171.
Hall, E., introduction to McDonnell Bodkin. Famous Irish Trials. Dublin: Blackhall Printing, 1997, vii.
Hall., M. Victims of Crime, Policy and Practice in Criminal Justice. Devon: Willan, 2009.
Hall, S. The Determination of News Photographs, in Cohen, C., and Young, J. The Manufacture of News: a Reader. Beverly Hills: Sage, 1983, referred to in Schudson, M. The Sociology of News Production. Media, Culture and Society 11 (1989): 263.
Hall, S.R., and Sales, B.D. Courtroom Modifications for Child Witnesses: Law and Science in Forensic Evaluations. Washington, DC: American Psychological Association, 2008.
Hallin, D.C., and Mancini, P. Comparing Media Systems: Three Models of Media and Politics. Cambridge: CUP, 2004.
Halonen, D. High Court Shuts Door on Cameras. Electronic Media 18 (1999): 4.
Hamelink, C.J. Information Imbalance Across the Globe, in Downing *et al*, 293.
Hamilton, C. Moral Panic Revisited: Part One. Irish Criminal Law Journal 15 (2005): 8 (part 1), and 15 (part 2).
Hahn, D.F. Political Communication, Rhetoric, Government, and Citizens. Pennsylvania: Strada, 2003.
Hanks, W., and Longini. Television Access: A Pittsburgh Experiment. Journal of Broadcasting 18 (1974): 289.
Hansen, A., Ed. Mass Communication Research Methods. Los Angeles: Sage, 2009.
Hansen, M.L. Camera Access to Our Public Courtrooms. San Francisco Law Review 7 (1997): X.
Hans, V.P., and Dee, J.L. Media Coverage and the Law: It's Impact on Juries and the Public. American Behaviour Scientist 35 (1991): 136.
Harbage, W., Q.C. Camera in Court. Counsel (February, 2005): 13.
Harris, D.A. The Appearance of Justice: Court TV, Conventional Television, and the Public Understanding of the Criminal Justice System. Arizona Law Review 35 (1993): 785.
Hart, A. Understanding Television Audiences. Journal of Educational Television 18 (1992): 12.

Hatch, D. Cameras in Court. Electronic Media 17 (1998): 38.
——— Focus is on Courtroom Cameras. Electronic Media 19 (2000): 2.
Hatfield, G. Perception and Cognition: Essays in the Philosophy of Psychology. Oxford: Clarendon Press, 2009.
Henderson, J.M.., and Ferreira, F., Scene Perception for Psycholinguists, in Henderson, J.M., and Ferreira, F., Eds. The Interface of Language, Vision and Action: Eye Movements and the Visual World. New York: Psychology Press, 2004: 1.
Hill, A. Restyling Factual TV, Audiences and News, Documentary and Reality Genres. Abington, Oxon.: Routledge, 2007.
Hallin, D. Whatever Happened to the News?, in Hiebert, R.E., Ed. The Impact of Mass Media: Current Issues. New York: Longman, 1995, n. 18, 159.
Harris, B. Appointments to the Bench – Role of a Judicial Services Commission. Adelaide Law Review 15 (1993): 191.
Harris, D.A. The Appearance of Justice: Court TV, Conventional Television, and the Public Understanding of the Criminal Justice System. Arizona Law Review 35 (1993)(35): 785.
Harris, J. 'OJ' on the Computer Screen. The Eagle 14 (1995): 48.
Hartley, Uses of Television. London and New York: Routledge.
Hatch, D. Focus is on Courtroom Cameras. Electronic Media 19 (2000): 2.
Hawes, W. Television Performing: News and Information. Boston, Mass.: Focal, 1991.
Heath, L. Impact of Newspaper of Newspaper Crime Reports on Fear of Crime: Multimethodological Investigation. Journal of Personality and Social Psychology 47 (1984): 263.
Heaton–Armstrong, A., Shepard, E., Gudjonsson, G.H., and Wolchover, D., Eds. Witness Testimony: Psychological, Investigative and Evidential Perspectives. Oxford: OUP, 2006.
Hedges, C.L. Teddy Roosevelt Faces the Cameras. ABA Journal (July, 1992): 1792.
Heffernan, L. Evidence: Cases and Materials. Dublin: Thomson Round Hall, 2005.
——— Scientific Evidence: Fingerprints and DNA. Dublin: First Law, 2006.
Heflin, H.T. Fair Trial v Free Press: Time for a Rehearing? Judicature (1977): 154.
Herman, E.S., and McChesney, R.W. The Global Media: The New Missionaries of Corporate Capitalism. London: Continuum, 1997, 2004.
Herman, J., and Kawamoto, D. Memorandum, Prepared for the Committee on Court Administration and Case Management (Hon. John R. Tunheim, Chair), the Judicial Conference of the United States, submitted on Behalf of Courtroom View Network (June 6, 2009): 22.
Helwig, G.J. Should Special Facilities be Provided for Courtroom Photography and Broadcasting? Judicature 59 (1967): 163.
Henderson, J.M., Ed. Real–world Scene Perception. New York: Psychology Press, Taylor and Francis, 2005.
Hentoff, N. Judge: No Cameras in SLA Bomb Trial. The Recorder (January 11, 2000).
Hiber, A., Ed. Should Cameras be Allowed in Courtrooms? New York: Gale, 2008.
Hiebert, R.E., Ed. The Impact of Mass Media: Current Issues. New York: Longman, 1995.
Hill, A. Restyling Factual TV: Audiences and News, Documentary and Reality Genres. Oxon: Routledge, 2007.
——— Reality TV: Audiences and Popular Factual Television. Oxon: Routledge, 2005.
Hirschhorn, J. Cameras in the Courtroom? No. Barrister, 7 (1980): 7 and 9.
Hirschhorn, J., and Stern, C. Does Television Make a Fair trial Impossible? – A Debate. Judicature (1980): 145.
Hochberger, R.S. Ethical Issues in Covering Courts. Syracuse Law Review 56 (2006): 443.
Hodgkins, E.M. Throwing Open a Window on the Nation's Courts by Lifting the Ban on Federal Courtroom Television. (The Impact of the Mass Media Revolution). Kansas Journal of Law & Public Policy (1995): 89.
Hogan, G., and Whyte, G. JM Kelly: The Irish Constitution. Dublin: Lexis Nexis, Butterworths, 2003.
Hogg, M.A., and Vaughan, G.M. Social Psychology. Edinburgh Gate, Harlow, Essex: Pearson, 2008.
Holland, T. Counting the Couch Potato – the Court TV Experience Leads to Sharpened Legal Knowledge, Not Square Eyes. Law Society Gazette (1995): 92.

Hollin, C. Psychology and Crime: An Introduction to Criminological Psychology. London: Routledge, 1989.

Hollingsworth v Perry, 558 US _ 2010.

Holmqvist, K., Holsanova, J., Barthelson, M., and Lundqvist, D. Reading or Scanning? A Study of Newspaper and Net Paper Reading, in Hyona, J., Radach, R., and Duebel, H., Eds. The Mind's Eye: Cognitive and Applied Aspects of Eye Movement Research. Amsterdam: Elsevier Science, 2003: 657.

Holsanova, J., Holmberg, N., and Holmqvist, K. Reading Information Graphics: The Role of Spatial Contiguity and Dual Attention Guidance. Applied Cognitive Psychology 22 (2008): 1.

Holsanova, J., Rahm, H., and Holmqvist, K. Entry Points and Reading Paths on the Newspaper Spread: Comparing Semiotic Analysis with Eye–Tracking Measurements. Visual Communication 5 (2005) 65.

Holtenson, O.P. The Admission of Expert Evidence of Opinion as to the Potential Unreliability of Evidence of Visual Identification. Melbourne University Law Review 16 (1988) 521.

Hope, L., and Wright, D. Beyond Unusual? Examining the Role of Attention in the Weapon Focus Effect. Applied Cognitive Psychology 21 (2007): 951.

Horgan, J. Irish Media: A Critical History Since 1922. London: Routledge, 2001.

Horgan, J., O'Connor, B., and Sheehan, H., Eds, Mapping Irish Media, Critical Explorations. Dublin: University College Dublin Press, 2007.

Horgan, R. Domestic Violence and Civil Harassment: Some Issues Which Arise When the Case Comes to Court. Judicial Studies Institute Journal 4 (2004): 79 – 107.

Hosh, H.M., Leippe, M.R., Marchioni, P.M., and Cooper, D.S. Victimization, Self Monitoring, and Eyewitness Identification. Journal of Applied Psychology 69 (1984): 289–299.

Howard, W. Televised Trials: Can the Government Market Electronic Access. SC Law Review 49 (1997–1998): 55.

Hoyt, J. Courtroom Coverage: the Effects of Being Televised. Journal of Broadcasting 21 (1977): 487.

Hoyt, M. Steven Brill Builds and Empire, First Came The American Lawyer. Then Ten More Law Journals. Now, the Volatile Editor is Breaking into TV. Columbia Journalism Review (September/October 1990): X.

Hoyt, J.L. Prohibiting Courtroom Photography: It's Up to the Judge in Florida and Wisconsin. Judicature 63 (1980): 290.

Hoult, P. Press Round–Up: OJ Ko As Pilot Allows Cameras Into Court of Appeal. Law Society Gazette (September 9, 2004): 10.

HO. Report of the Working Group on the Fear of Crime. London HO: Standing Conference on Crime Prevention, December 1, 1989.

Hudson, B.A. Understanding Justice, An Introduction to Ideas, Perspectives and Controversies in Modern Penal Theory. Buckingham: OUP, 2003.

Hughes, B. Psychology in Court, An Overview. Galway Student Law Review 1 (1998).

Hughes, R.L. Chandler v Florida: Cameras Get Probation in Courtrooms. Journal of Broadcasting 26 (1982): 432.

Hutchby, I. Media Talk: Conversation Analysis and the Study of Broadcasting. Maidenhead, Berkshire: OUP, 2006.

Hulse, L.M., and Memon, A. Fatal Impact? The Effect of Emotional Arousal and Weapon Focus on Police Officer's Memories for a Simulated Crime. Legal and Criminal Psychology 11 (2006): 313.

Hutchins, B., and Rowe, D. Reconfiguring Media Sport for the Online World: An Inquiry Into 'Sports News and Digital Media.' International Journal of Communication 4 (2010)(4): 696.

Hutton, E. Cameras in the Courtroom: A Comprehensive Examination. Internet Journal of Criminology (2009).

In Camera. New Law Journal (March 16, 1990): 382.

Indiana Court Allows Cameras. Editor and Publisher 38 (1996): 3.

In re Post –Newsweek Stations, 370 Southern Reporter, 2nd Series, 766.

In Re R Ltd [1989] IR 126.

In re Murchison, 349, US 133 (1955).

In Re R Ltd [1989] IR 126.
In re R Limited [1989] IR 126.
In re Murchison, 349, US 133 (1955); *In re Petition of Post–Week Stations, Florida, Inc.*, 370 So. 2d, 764, 781 (1979).
In re Extension of Media Coverage for a Further Experimental Period, 473 R.I. A.2d. 1232 (1984).
Inadmissible. Texas Lawyer (March, 1996): 3.
Infield, P., and Platford, G. The Law of Harassment and Stalking. London: Butterworths, 2000.
Irons, P., and Guitton, S., Eds. May It Please The Court. New York: The New Press, 1993.
Irvine, L. Reporting the Courts: The Media's Rights and Responsibilities. JUR 34 (1999): 1.
Ison, T.G. The Sovereignty of the Judiciary. Adelaide Law Review 10 (1985–1986): 1.
Isralowitz, J.P. The Reporter as Citizen: Newspaper Ethics and Constitutional Values. University of Pennsylvania Law Review 141 (1992): 221.
Jackson, J.D. Law's Truth, Lay Truth and Lawyers' Truth: The Representation of Evidence in Adversary Trials. Law and Critique III (1992): 29.
Jacob, R.J.K., and Karn, K.S. Eye Tracking in Human–Computer Interaction and Usability Research: Ready to Deliver the Promises, in Hyona, J, Radach, R., and Deubel, H., Eds The Mind's Eye: Cognitive and Applied Aspects of Eye Movement Research. Amsterdam: The Netherlands: Elsevier Science (2003): 573.
Jacoby, J. Survey and Field Experimental Evidence, in Kassin, S., and Wrightsman, L., Eds. The Psychology of Evidence and Trial Procedure. Beverly Hills: Sage, 1985, 194.
Jeff, A. Televising California's Death Penalty: Is There a Constitutional Right to Broadcast Executions? Hastings Law Review 43 (1991–1992): 1489.
Jensen, K.B. Television Politics of Polysemy: Television News, Everyday Consciousness and Political Action. Media, Culture and Society 12 (1990) 57.
Jensen, K.B., and Jankowski, N.W., Eds. Handbook of Qualitative Methodologies Mass Communication Research. London: Routledge, 1991.
Jeung, H. –J., Chandler, P., and Sweller, J. The Role of Visual Indicators in Dual Sensory Mode Instruction. Educational Psychology 17 (1997): 329.
Ji, Q., and Yang, X. Real–Time Eye, Gaze, and Face Pose Tracking for Monitoring Driver Vigilance. Real–Time Imaging 8 (2002): 357.
Johnson, M.T., and Krafka, C. Electronic Media Coverage of Federal Civil Proceedings, An Evaluation of the Pilot Program in Six District Courts and Two Courts of Appeal. (Federal Judicial Centre, 1994).
Johnson, M.T., and Krafka, C. Pilot Program Involving Electronic Coverage in Six US District Courts and Two Appeal Courts. (Federal Judicial Centre, 1994).
Johnson–Cartee, K.S. News Narratives and News Framing, Constructing Political Reality. Lanham, MD: Rowman & Littlefield.
Josephson, S., and Holmes, M. Have You Seen Any of These Men? Looking at Whether Eyewitnesses Use Scanpaths to Recognize Suspects in Photo Lineups. ETRA, Proceedings of the 2010 Symposium on Eye–Tracking Research & Applications, Austin, Texas, March 22–24, 2010.
Journalism Department at the University of Arizona. New Law Journal (30 November, 1987): 13, as referred to in Freedman, W., 46.
Joy, P.A., and McMunigal, K.C. Clients, Lawyers, and the Media. Criminal Justice 19 (2004 – 2005): 77.
Judicial Conference of the United States. Statement of the Honourable John R. Tunheim, Judge, United States District Court for the District of Minnesota, For the Committee on the Judiciary of the United States House of Representatives, Hearing on Cameras in the Courtroom: The 'Sunshine in the Courtroom Act of 2007.' H.R. 2128, September 27, 2007: 6.
Jury Deliberations To Air? The National Law Journa (19 February, 1996): A8.
Kahan, D.M., Hoffman, D.A., and Braman, D. Whose Eyes Are You Going to Believe? *Scott v Harris* and the Perils of Cognitive Illiberalism. Harvard Law Review 122 (2008–2009): 837.
Kaplan, M.F., and Miller, L.E. Reducing the Effects of Juror Bias, in Wrightsman, L.S., Kassin, S.M., and Willis, C.E. In the Jury Box: Controversies in the Courtroom. Thousand Oaks, CA: Sage, 1987.

Kassin, S., TV Cameras, Public Self–Consciousness, and Mock Juror Performance. Journal of Experimental Social Psychology 20 (1984): 336.

Kassin, S.M. The Psychology of Confession Evidence. American Psychologist 52 (1997): 221.

Kataria, S., and Sharma, A. Cameras in Indian Courtrooms: A Bliss or a Misery? – Learning from the American Experience. NUJS Law Review (2008): 345.

Katz, J. Guilty. Wired. September, 1995: 130, quoted in Greenhouse, L. Telling the Court's Story: Justice and Journalism at the Supreme Court. Yale Law Journal 105 (1996):1548.

Katz, J. What Makes Crime 'News'? Media Culture and Society 9 (1987): 47.

Katzman v. *Victoria's Secret Catalogue*, 923 F. Supp. 580, 586–587 (SDNY 1996).

Keane, A. The Modern Law of Evidence. Oxford: OUP, 2008.

Keller, T. Cameras in Courtrooms: An Analysis of Television Court Coverage in Virginia. Ph.D. (The University of Tennessee, 1992).

Kelly, M.J., and O'Connor, B. Media Audiences in Ireland: Power and Cultural Identity. Dublin: University College Dublin Press, 1997.

Kennedy, R. Extra–Judicial Comment by Judges. Judicial Studies Institute Journal 5 (2005): 199.

Kennedy, R. Information and Communications Technology and Institutional Design for Climate Change. Draft version, forthcoming, 13.

Kerr, N.L. Social Psychology in Court: The Case of the Prejudicial Pretrial Publicity, in Brannigan, G.G., and Merrens, M.R. The Social Psychologists: Research Adventures. New York: McGraw–Hill, 1995.

Khosla, R., Simola, J., Salojarvi, J and Kojo, I. Using Hidden Markov Model to Uncover Processing States from Eye Movements in Information Search Tasks. Cognitive Systems Research 9 (2008): 237.

Khosla, R., *et al.* Reading Information Graphics: The Role of Spatial Contiguity and Dual Attention Guidance. Applied Cognitive Psychology 22 (2008): 1.

Kidd, R.F., and Chayet, E.F. Why Do Victims Fail to Report? The Psychology of Criminal Victimization. Journal of Social Issues 40 (1984): 39.

Kielbowicz, R.B. The Story Behind the Adoption of the Ban on Courtroom Cameras. Judicature 63 (1979): 14.

Kiesel, D. No to Cameras: Federal Court Ban Remains. ABA Journal 70 (1984): 29.

——— Cameras in Court: Media Appeal for Easing Rule. ABA Journal (XXXX): 576.

——— Federal Court Ban Requests. ABA Journal (November, 1984): 29.

Killian, D.P. Propriety of Restrictive Guidelines for Cameras in the Court. Communications and the Law 9 (1987): 27.

Kipper, P., and Mills, C. Television Camera Movement as a Source of Perceptual Information. Journal of Broadcasting and Electronic Media 30 (1986): 295.

Kirby, M., The Hon. Justice, AC, CMG. The Globalisation of Media and Judicial Independence. Communications Law 1 (1996): 115.

——— The Globalisation of Media and Judicial Independence. Communication Law 1 (1996): 115.

Klausner, Speaking at Forum, Says More Judges in County are Barring Cameras From Courts, Metropolitan News Company, March 22, 1996, 1.

Klein, K., and Boals, A. Expressive Writing Can Increase Working Memory Capacity. Journal of Experimental Psychology: General 130 (2001): 520.

Kogan, G., Weisberg, S., and Klieman, R. Television Coverage of State Criminal Trials. St. Thomas Law Review 9 (1996–1997): 505.

Kollin, J. Reporter Says Let's Ban Cameras from Courtroom. Editor & Publisher 128 (1995): 48.

Kohm, S.A. I'm Not a Judge But I Play One On TV: American Reality Based Courtroom Television. Ph.D. (Simon Fraser University, 2004).

——— The People's Law Versus Judge Judy Justice: Two Models of Law in American Reality–Based Courtroom TV. Law and Society Review 40 (2006): 693.

Koyama, S.A. Effects of Television Camera Angle, Locus of Control, and Two–sided/One–sides Persuasive Messages Upon Attitudes Toward Disabled People. (University of Washington, 1982).

Kozinski, A. Judge, and Johnson, R. Of Cameras and Courtrooms. Fordham Intellectual Property Media & Entertainment Law Journal 20 (2010): 1107.

Kramer, T.H., Buckhout, R., and Eugenio, P. Weapons Focus, Arousal, and Eyewitness Memory, Attention Must be Paid. Law and Human Behaviour 14 (1990): 167, as referred to in Pickel, K.L., Ross., S.J., and Truelove, R.S. Do Weapons Automatically Capture Attention. Applied Cognitive Psychology 20 (2006): 871.

Kraus, K., and Davis, D. The Effects of Mass Communication on Political Behaviour. (London: Pennsylvania State University Press, 1980).

Krupp, K., Journalism Meets Art. Media Studies Journal (1998): 71.

Krygier, K.M. The Thirteenth Juror: Electronic Media's Struggle to Enter State and Federal Courtrooms. CommLaw Conspectus 3 (1995): 71.

Kula, G.V. Trial Judges v Trial Lawyers: Mutual Expectations. New York State Bar Journal (March/April, 1998): 6.

Kuriyama, D.N. The Right 'Right of Information Triangle': A First Amendment Basis for Television Judicial Proceedings. University of Hawaii Law Review 4 (1982): 85.

Kwak, J.Y. Remembering Faces: Using Eye Movement Measures to Investigate Differences Between True and False Memory. Ph.D. University of California, 2009.

Lacey, N. Narrative and Genre: Key Concepts in Media Studies. Hampshire: MacMillan, 2000.

Langbein, J.H. The Criminal Trial Before the Lawyers. University of Chicago Law Review 45 (1978): 263.

Langbein, J.H. Torture and Plea Bargaining. University of Chicago Law Review 46 (1978): 3.

Langdon–Down, G. Cameras In Court: American Lawyers Switch On To Living Life Through A Lens. Law Society Gazette (30 September, 2004): 24.

Lanzara, G.F., and Patriotta, G. Technology and the Courtroom: An Inquiry into Knowledge Making in Organizations. Journal of Management Studies 38 (2001): 943.

Lassiter, C. An Annotated Descriptive Summary of State Statutes, Judicial Codes, Canons, and Court Rules Relating to Admissibility and Governance of Cameras in the Courtroom. Journal of Criminal Law and Criminology 86 (1996): 1019.

Lassiter, C. Cameras and the Infusion of Political Bias into the Courtroom. International Journal of Law and Information Technology 5 (1997): 28.

Lassiter, G., Geers, A., Munhall., P., Handley, I., and Beers, M. Videotaped Confessions: Is Guilt in the Eye of the Camera?, in Zanna, M., Ed. Advances, in Experimental Social Psychology, Vol. 20. (San Diego, CA: Academic Press, 2001): 189.

LCJ's 'No' to Court TV. New Law Journal (March 1, 1996): X.

Lederer, F. The Potential Use of Courtroom Technology in Major Terrorism Cases. William & Mary Bill of Rights 12 (2004): 887.

Lepofsky, D. Cameras in the Courtroom – Not Without My Consent. National Journal of Constitutional Law 6 (1996): 161.

Lindsay, R.C.L., Ross, D.F., Read, J.D., and Toglia, M.P., Eds. The Handbook of Eyewitness Psychology. Mahwah, NJ: Erlbaum, 2007.

Linton, J.M. Camera Access to Courtrooms: Canada, U.S., and Australian Experiences. Canadian Journal of Communications 18 (1993): 1.

Lofton, J. The Press as Guardians of the 1st Amendment. Carolina: University of St. Carolina, 1980.

Loftus, E., Loftus, G., and Messo, J., referred to in Cutler, B., and Penrod, S. Mistaken Identification: The Eyewitness, Psychology and the Law. New York: Cambridge University Press, 1995, 101.

Lorenzo–Dus, N., Real Disorder in the Court: An Investigation of Conflict Talk in US Television Courtroom Shows. Media, Culture and Society 30 (2008): 81.

Loux, A.C. Jury Nullification, Andrea C. Loux Argues that It's A Lawful Verdict in the OJ Simpson Trial. New Law Journal (1995): 1522.

Lacey, C., and Longman, D. The Press as Public Educator: Cultures of Understanding, Cultures of Ignorance. Luton: University of Luton Press, 1997.

Lacey, N., Narrative and Genre, Key Concepts in Media Studies. London: MacMillan Press, 2000.

Lambert, P., Effects Research Issues in Television Courtroom Broadcasting: Getting Past Monkey. 10th European Conference on eGovernment, University of Limerick, June 17–18, 2010

Lambert, P. Time to Leave the Monkey Behind?: How Eye Tracking and Psychology Can Contribute to Television Courtroom Broadcasting Effects Research, British Psychological Society, BPS Cognitive Psychology Section Annual Conference, 27th Annual Cognitive Psychology Section Conference, Cardiff University, September 6–8, 2010.

Lambert, P. Eye Tracking Technology and Television Courtroom Broadcasting. Computers and Law, August 11, 2010.

Lambert, P. TCB Effects: Eye Tracking and Camera Distraction in Court. Irish Association of Law Teachers Annual Conference, Strand Hotel, Limerick, November 26–28, 2010.

Lambert, P., Monkey Magic: Problems With Effects Research of Television Courtroom Broadcasting. Irish Law Times 18 (2010): 278.

Lambert, P. In Camera: the Case Against Courtroom TV. Law Society Gazette (June 1998): 6.

Lambert, P. Cameras in the Courtroom: Incitement to Act Up? Law Society Gazette (April, 2000): 4.

Lambert, P. A Candid Camera, Eye Tracking Technology Could Transform Courtroom Broadcasting. New Law Journal (December 10, 2010): 169.

Lambert, P. Courtroom Television Broadcasting. Communications Law 2 (1997): 180.

Lambert, P. Courtroom Television Cameras and the Media. Journal of Media Law and Practice 16 (1995): 139.

Lambert, P. Judicial Questionnaire on Courtroom Broadcasting. Irish Law Times 15 (1997): 50.

Lambert, P. Cues, Cameras and Courtroom Actors: Resisting the Temptation of Courtroom Television Cameras. Irish Law Times (January, 1996): 13.

Lambert, P. Confessions and Camera Perspective Bias. Bar Review (December, 2010): 128.

Lambert, P. Effects Research Issues in Television Courtroom Broadcasting: Getting Past Monkey, 10th European Conference on eGovernment, University of Limerick, June 17–18, 2010.

Lambert, P. Eye Tracking Technology and Television Courtroom Broadcasting. Computers and Law, August 11, 2010.

Lambert, P. Eyeing the Supreme Court's Challenge: A Proposal to Use Eye Tracking to Determine the Effects of Television Courtroom Broadcasting. 1:3 Reynolds Courts and Media Law Journal, (2011).

Lambert, P. Television Courtroom Broadcasting Research: The Problem, the Challenge and Eye Tracking. Elsa Malta Law Review, (forthcoming).

Lambert, P. Courting Publicity, Twitter and Television Cameras in Courts. West Sussex: Bloomsbury, 2011.

Lambert – Merrion Legal – RedC Courts Public Survey, September 8, 2010. Survey results with author.

Langdon–Down, G. Cameras In Court: American Lawyers Switch On To Living Life Through A Lens. Law Society Gazette (September 30, 2004): 24.

Langdon–Down, Grania. Lights, Cameras, Law. Law Society Gazette (September 30, 2004).

Landstrom, S., Hjelmsater, E., and Granhag, P. The Camera Perspective Bias: A Case Study. Journal of Investigative Psychology and Offender Profiling 4 (2007): 199.

Langbein, J.H. The Criminal Trial Before the Lawyers. University of Chicago Law Review 45 (1978): 263.

Langbein, J.H. Torture and Plea Bargaining. University of Chicago Law Review 46 (1978): 3.

Langdridge, D. Introduction to Research Methods and Data Analysis in Psychology. London: Pearson, 2004.

Lanzara, G.F., and Patriotta, G. Technology and the Courtroom: An Inquiry into Knowledge Making in Organizations. Journal of Management Studies 38 (2001): 943.

Lassiter, G., Geers, A., Munhall., P., Handley, I., and Beers, M. Videotaped Confessions: Is Guilt in the Eye of the Camera?, in Zanna, M., Ed. Advances, in Experimental Social Psychology. San Diego, CA: Academic Press, 2001: 189.

Lassiter, G.D., and Irvine, A.A. Videotaped Confessions: The Impact of Camera Point of View on Judgements of Coercion. Journal of Applied Social Psychology 16 (1986): 286.

Lassiter, G.D. Illusory Causation in the Courtroom. Current Directions in Psychological Science 11 (2002): 204–208; referred to in Ware, 10.

Lassiter, G.D., Munhall, P.J., Ploutz–Snyder, R.J., and Breitbecher, D.L., Illusory Causation: Why It Occurs. Psychological Science 13 (2002): 299, as referred to in Schmidt, H.C., 28

Lassiter, D.G., Geers, A.L., Handley, I.M., Weiland, P.E., and Mulhall, P.J. Videotaped Interrogations and Confessions: A Simple Change in Camera Perspective Alters Verdicts in Simulated Trials. Journal of Applied Psychology 87 (2002): 867.

Lassiter, C. Cameras and the Infusion of Political Bias into the Courtroom. International Journal of Law and Information Technology 5 (1997): 28.

——— An Annotated Descriptive Summary of State Statutes, Judicial Codes, Canons, and Court Rules Relating to Admissibility and Governance of Cameras in the Courtroom. Journal of Criminal Law and Criminology 86 (1996): 1019.

Laughlin, A. Sky News Calls for Courtroom TV Cameras. Digital Spy, 6 December, 2010, last accessed on January 18, 2010.

Law Reform Commission. Consultation Paper on Contempt of Court. Dublin: Government Publications, 1991.

Law Reform Commission. Report on Contempt of Court. Dublin: Government Publications, 1994.

Law Reform Commission. Consultation Paper on the Consolidation and Reform of the Courts Acts. Dublin: Government Publications, 2007.

Law Reform Commission. Report on Spent Convictions. Dublin: Government Publications, 2007.

Law Reform Commission. Jury Service. Dublin: Official Publications, 2010.

Law Reform Commission. Consultation Paper on the Consolidation and Reform of the Courts Acts. Dublin: Government Publications, 2007.

Lawyers Keep It Real in Court Battle. Law Society Gazette, April 28, 2005, available at www.lawgazette.co.uk , last accessed on 24 October, 2010.

LCJ's 'No' to Court TV. New Law Journal, March 1, 1996, X.

Lederer, F. The Potential Use of Courtroom Technology in Major Terrorism Cases. William & Mary Bill of Rights 12 (2004): 887.

Lemert, J.B. Criticising The Media – Empirical Approaches. London: Sage, 1989.

Lepofsky, D. Cameras in the Courtroom – Not Without My Consent. National Journal of Constitutional Law 6 (1996): 161.

Linton, J.M. Camera Access to Courtrooms: Canada, U.S., and Australian Experiences. Canadian Journal of Communications 18 (1993): 1.

Livingston, S.M. Making Sense of Television: The Psychology of Audience Interpretation. Oxford: Pergamon, 1990.

Lofton, J. The Press as Guardians of the 1st Amendment. Carolina: University of St. Carolina, 1980.

Loftus, G.R., and Mackworth, N.H. Cognitive Determinants of Fixation Location During Picture Viewing. Journal of Experimental Psychology 4 (1978): 565.

Loftus, E. A 30–year Investigation of the Malleability of Memory. Learning and Memory 12 (2005): 361.

——— Eyewitness Testimony. Cambridge MA: Harvard University Press, 1979, 1996.

——— Reconstructing Memory: the Incredible Eyewitness. Psychology Today 8 (1974): 116.

Loftus, E., Loftus, G., and Messo, J. Some Facts About 'Weapon Focus.' Law and Human Behavior 11 (1987) 55.

Loftus., E.F., and Ketcham, K. The Malleability of Eyewitness Accounts, in Lloyd–Bostock, S., and Clifford, B.R., Eds. Evaluating Eyewitness Testimony. New York: Wiley (1985): 159.

Loftus, E.F., and Doyle, J.M., Eyewitness Testimony: Civil and Criminal (New York: Kluwer, 1987), Chapter 2. Note also second edition/supplement published in 1994 by Lex Law Publishing.

Lord Irvine of Lairg, the then Lord Chancellor, Reporting the Courts: The Media's Rights and Responsibilities. 4th RTE/UCD Media Lecture, University College Dublin, April 14, 1999.

Lorenzo–Dus, N. Real Disorder in the Court: An Investigation of Conflict Talk in US Television Courtroom Shows. Media, Culture and Society 30 (2008), 81.
Lowery, S., and DeFleur, M.L. Milestones in Mass Communication Research: Media Effects. New York: Longman, 1985.
Loux, A.C. Jury Nullification, Andrea C. Loux Argues that It's A Lawful Verdict in the OJ Simpson Trial. New Law Journal (1995): 1522.
Lovegrove, A. The Framework of Judicial Sentencing, A Study in Legal Decision Making. Cambridge: CUP, 1997.
Lowndes, S.E., Barristers on Trial: Comprehension and Misapprehension in Courtroom Discourse, Queens University, Belfast (2004), available at Dissertation Abstracts international.
Luhmann, N. The Reality of the Mass Media (Cambridge: Polity, 2000), as referred to in McQuail, D. McQuail's Mass Communication Theory. London: Sage, 2005, 97.
Lull, J. The Social Uses of Television. Human Communication Research 6 (1980): 197.
Luus, C.A., and Wells, G.L. The Malleability of Eyewitness Confidence: Co–witness and Perseverance Effects. Journal of Applied Psychology 79 (1994): 714.
MacFarlane, K.A. Understanding Justice: Criminal Courtroom Interpretation in Eighteenth–Century London and Twenty–First–Century Toronto. TTR 20 (2007): 271.
McCraty, R.T., Atkinson, M., and Sundram, J. Impact of the HeartMath Self–Management Skills Program on Physiological and Psychological Stress in Police Officers (Boulder Creek, CA: Institute of HeartMath), HeartMath Research Centre Publications No. 99–075)(1999).
McConnell, B. Cameras in Court. New Law Journal 16 (1990): 1622.
McCormack, G. Corrupting the Criminal Process. Irish Law Times 1 (1985): 6.
McCoy, P. The Judge and Courtroom Publicity. Judicature (1954): 167.
McCombs, M.E., Picard, R.G., Winter, J.P., and Lacy, S., Eds. Press Concentration and Monopoly. New Jersey: Ablex, 1988.
McEwan, S.J., Jr. TV or Not TV: The Telecast of Appellate Arguments in Pennsylvannia. Journal of Appellate Practice and Process 2 (2000): 405.
McGonagle, M. A Textbook on Media Law. Dublin: Gill and MacMillan, 1997, and the follow up Media Law. Dublin: Sweet and Maxwell, 2006. (New edition forthcoming);
McHugh, D. Public Relations and Corporate Communications Law in Ireland. Dublin: Firstlaw, 2006.
McKeone, M. Defeat for TV Courts Bill. Law Society Gazette (1991): 88.
McLeod, J.M. Community Deviance: the Effects of Television News Coverage of Social Protest. Journal of Broadcasting and Electronic Media 39 (1995): 4.
McManus, J. Local TV News: Not a Pretty Picture. Columbia Journalism Review (CJR) (May/June, 1990): 42.
McNeely, C.L., Perceptions of the Criminal Justice System: Television Imagery and Public Knowledge in the United States. Journal of Criminal Justice and Popular Culture 3 (1995): 1.
McNeil, C.B. Public Access and Media Rules for Administrative Adjudications in High–Profile Hearings. Judicature 91 (2008): 298.
McRobbie, A., and Thornton, S.L. Rethinking Moral Panic for Multi–Mediated Social Worlds. British Journal of Sociology 46 (1995): 559.
McQuail, D., and Windahl, S. Communications Models: For the Study of Mass Communication. London: Longman, 1993.
McQuail, D. Western European Media, The Mixed Model Under Threat, in Downing, J., *et al*, 147.
——— McQuail's Mass Communications Theory. London: Sage, 2005.
McQueen, R.A., and Knussen, C. Introduction to Research Methods and Statistics in Psychology. Edinburgh: Pearson, 2006.
Maass, A., and Kohnken, G., Eyewitness Identification: Simulating the Weapon Effect. Law and Human Behavior 13 (1989) 379.
Macauley, S. Images of Law in Everyday Life: the Lessons of School, Entertainment, and Spectator Sports. Law and Society Review 21 (1987–1988): 185.
Mahon, E., and Moore, E. Post Separation Parenting: A Study of Separation and Divorce Agreements Made in the Family Law Circuit Courts in Ireland and their Implications for

Parent–Child Contract and Family Lives, January 2011, Office of the Minister for Children and Youth Affairs, available at www.omc.gov.ie .
Malcolm, J. The Journalist and the Murderer. London: Boomabury, 1991.
Maletzke, G. Psychologie der Massenkommunikation. Hamburg: Verlag Hans Bredow–Institut, as referred to in McQuail, D., and Windahl, S., 46.
Mamber, S. Cinema Verite in America. Screen 13 (1972): 79, as referred to in Creeber, G., 128.
Management/IT: Court on Camera. Law Society Gazette (March, 2007): 13.
Mannheim, K. Ideology and Utopia. London: Routledge and Keegan Paul, 1936.
Marisol A. v *Giuliani*, 929 F. Supp. 660, 661 (SDNY 1996).
Margolin, E. Memorandum to the Members of the Chief Justice's Special Committee on the Courts and the Media, the Judicial Council of California, 16 October, 1981.
Martin, D., and Macrae, C.N. Processing Style and Person Recognition: Exploring the Face Inversion Effect. Visual Cognition 18 (2010): 161.
Matsch, R.P. Television in the Courtroom: Mightier Than The Pen? Michigan Law Review 97 (1999): 2037.
Marxist Institute for Public Opinion Poll, December, 1996, contained in the New York Cameras in New York Courtrooms report, New York State Committee to Review Audio–Visual Coverage of Court Proceedings, An Open Courtroom: Cameras in New York Courts, (New York: Fordham University Press, 1997).
Marcotte, P. Courts on Cable: Two Companies Vie for Viewers with Live Trials, Commentators. ABA Journal (1990): 19.
Marcotte, P. Cameras in Federal Courts? Judicial Conference Considers New Evidence. ABA Journal 79 (1990): 15.
Martin, S. Cameras in the Courtroom: A Denial of Due Process? Baylor Law Review 30 (1978): 853.
Martin, D., and Macrae, C.N. Processing Style and Person Recognition: Exploring the Face Inversion Effect. Visual Cognition 18 (2010): 161.
Martinez, M.T. Cameras in the Courts: A Case for Increased Judicial Transparency. American Journalism Historians Association, Birmingham, Alabama, October 7–11, 2009.
Mason, K. The Inherent Jurisdiction of the Court. Australian Law Journal 57 (1983): 449.
Mason, P. Justice Seen to be Done – Electronic Broadcast Coverage of the International Criminal Tribunal for the Former Yugoslavia. American Society of International Legal Process 95 (2001): X.
Mason, P. Lights, Camera, Justice? Cameras in the Courtroom: An Outline of the Issues. Crime Prevention and Community Safety: An International Journal 2 (2000): 23.
Mason, P. Court on Camera: Electronic Broadcast Coverage of the Legal Proceedings, available at www.usfca.edu/pj/camera–mason.htm. Last accessed on April 15, 2009.
Mauro, T. Five Ways Appellate Courts Can Help the News Media. Journal of Appelate Practice and Process (2007): 311.
Mayer, E.E. Multimedia Learning: Guiding Visuospatial Thinking with Intructional Animation. 477.
Maynard, R. Television Formats in Johnston, D.H., Ed. Encyclopaedia of International Media and Communications 4 (2003): 409.
Mayer, R.E. Multimedia Learning. Cambridge: Cambridge University Press, 2001.
——— Principles for Managing Essential Processing in Multimedia Learning: Coherence, Signalling, Redundancy, Spatial Continuity and Temporal Contiguity Principles, in Mayer, R.E., Ed. Cambridge Handbook of Multimedia Learning. New York: Cambridge University Press, 2005: 183.
Media Coverage of Court Proceedings Pilot Evaluation Committee, Media Coverage of Court Proceedings, Introduction and Research Findings, (August, 1998): 8.
Memorandum to Members of the Court Management Committee from Administrative Office of the Courts, Michael A. Fisher, Attorney regarding Cameras in Court Experiment (Rule 980.2), 11.
Metz, S.A. Justice Through the Eyes of a Camera: Cameras in the Courtrooms in the United States, Canada, England, and Scotland. Dick. Journal of International Law (1995–1996): 673.

Millerson, G. The Technique of Television Production. London: Focal, 1989, 1990.
Middleton, M. Delegates Broaden Rules on Cameras in Court. ABA Journal 68 (1982): 1199.
Mitchell, B. Confessions and Police Interrogation of Suspects. Criminal Law Review (1983): 596.
Mittell, J. Genre and Television: from Cop Shows to Cartoons in American Culture. London and New York, Routledge, 2004, as referring to in Creeber, G., 12.
Mitchell, M., and Jolley, J. Research Design Explained. London: Wadsworth, Thomson Learning, 2001.
Moores, S. Interpreting Audiences: the Ethnography of Media Consumption. London: Sage, 1993.
Moy, P., Pfau, M., and Kahlor. Media Use and Public Confidence in Democratic Institutions. Journal of Broadcasting & Electronic Media 43 (1999) 137.
Montgomery, M., 26, as referred Durant, A., and Lambrou, M. Language and Media. London and New York: Routledge Taylor & Francis Group, 2009: 78.
Montgomery, M., Durant, A., Fabb, N., Furniss, T., and Mills, S. London: Routledge, 2006, as referred to in Durant, A. and Lambrou, M., 23.
Montgomery, M. The Discourse of Broadcast News: A Linguistic Approach. London: Routledge, 2007, 145, as reprinted in Durant, A. and Lambrou, M., 201.
Moore, R.L., and Murray, M.D. Media Law and Ethics. New York: Erlbaun, 2008.
Morimoto, C., and Mimica, M.R.M. Eye Gaze Tracking Techniques for Interactive Applications. Computer Vision and Image Understanding 98 (2005): 4.
Morse, L. Eye–Witness: Television's Expanding Coverage of the Courts. DePaul–LCA Journal of Art and Entertainment Law 3 (1992–1993): 68.
Morton, J. Court TV – the Cameras Are Switched on Again. Criminal Law Legislation Update 68 (2004) 451.
Mourant, R.R., and Donaghue, R.J. Acquisition of Indirect Vision Information by Novice, Experienced, and Mature Drivers. Journal of Safety Research, 9 (1977) 39.
Mowlana, H. Global Information and World Communication. London: Sage, 1997.
Mullan, B. Consuming Television: Television and Its Audience. Oxford: Blackwell, 1997.
Murphy, M. Supreme Court, Nassau County, *Coleman v O'Shea*. Touro Law Review 17 (2000 – 2001): 53.
Murphy, Y. Journalists and the Law. Dublin: Round Hall Sweet & Maxwell, 2000.
Myers, L.J. *Hollingsworth v Perry*: The Supreme Court's Renewed Hostility Toward Cameras in the Courtroom. Michigan State University College of Law (Spring 2010).
O'Malley, R. A Change to the Scheduled Viewing: Does Ireland Need to Change Its Approach to Courtroom Television or Does the Camera Really Add Ten Years? Trinity College Law Review 2 (1999) 57.
Nabi, R.L., and Oliver, M.B. The Sage Handbook of Media Processes and Effects. Los Angeles: Sage, 2009.
National Crime Forum, Lambert, P. Submission to the National Forum on Crime Reporting. Dublin, March 5, 1998, (references omitted). Details on file with author.
Nebraska Press Assn. v *Stuart*, 427 U. S. 539.
Nelson, T.E., Clawson, R.A., and Oxley, Z.M. Media Framing of a Civil Liberties Conflict and Its Effect on Tolerance. American Political Science Review 91 (1997) 567.
Nessmann, K. Media Education in Leisure Time. Journal of Educational Television 11 (1985): 33.
Nettheim, G. Cameras in the Courtroom (December, 1981): 855.
Netterburg, K. Does Research Support the *Estes* Ban on Cameras in the Courtroom? Judicature 63 (1980): 467.
——— Cameras in the Courtroom: Is a Picture Worth a Thousand Words? Ph.D, (University of Minnesota, 1980).
——— Does Research Support the *Estes* Ban On Cameras in the Courtroom?, in Wrightsman, L.S., Willis, C., and Kassin, S.M., Eds. On The Witness Stand: Controversies in the Courtroom. London: Sage, 1987: 287.
——— Cameras in the Courtroom: Is a Picture Worth a Thousand Words?, Ph.D, (University of Minnesota, 1980).

——— Does Research Support the Estes Ban on Cameras in the Courtroom. Judicature 63 (1980): 467.

Newcomb. Media Institutions: The Creation of Television Drama, in Jensen, K.B., and Jankowski, N.W., Eds. A Handbook of Qualitative Methodologies for Mass Communication Research. London: Routledge, 1991: 93.

New Hampshire Supreme Court, Petition of WMUR Channel 9, (December 13, 2002), at www.courts.state.nh.us/opinions/2002/0212/wmur156.htm as referred to in Stepniak, D., above, 101. Accessed by author on June 8, 2010.

New York State Committee to Review Audio–Visual Coverage of Court Proceedings, An Open Courtroom: Cameras in New York Courts. New York: Fordham University Press, 1997.

Newenham, P. Televising the Courts: An Exploration of Opinions of Irish Media and Legal Professions. Masters in Journalism, DCU, 2008.

Newsom, D. Bridging the Gap in Global Communication. Malden, MA: Blackwell, 2007.

News Cameras in the Alaska Courts: Assessing the Impact. Judicature 71 (1988): 356.

Neuman, P. Patterns of Recall Among Television News Viewers. Public Opinion Quarterly 40 (1976–7): 115.

Nevas, S. Case for Cameras in the Courtroom. Judges Journal (Winter 1981), 22, and 49, as referred to in Alexander, S.L., 66, but title and page range ommited.

Nicholson, S.P., and Howard, R.M. Framing Support for the Supreme Court in the Aftermath of *Bush v Gore*. Journal of Politics 65 (2003) 676.

Nielsen, J., and Pernice, K. Eyetracking Web Usablility. Berkely, CA: New Riders, 2009.

No Lights, No Camera, No Action. Bench & Bar of Minessota 6 (2008): 23.

Norowzian v Arks (No 2) [2000] FSR 363.

O'Connor, J.M. Cameras in Maine's Courts: Has the Time Come? Will it Ever? Maine Law Review, 42 (1990): 483.

O'Donnell, D. Some Reflections on the Law of Contempt. Judicial Studies Institute Journal 2 (2002) 87.

O'Donnell, I., Dr. Trial Venue and Process: the Victim and the Accused. Judicial Studies Institute Journal 3 (2003) 103.

O'Regan, J.K. Eye Movements and Reading, in Kowler, E., Ed. Eye Movements and Their Role in Visual and Cognitive Processes. Amsterdam, The Netherlands: Elsevier, 1990: 395.

O'Regan, J.K. Optimal Viewing Position in Words and the Strategy–tactics Theory of Eye Movements in Reading, in Rayner, K., Ed. Eye Movements and Visual Cognition: Scene Perception and Reading. New York: Springer–Verlag, 1992: 333.

O'Scannlain, J., (Exhibit 4) Statement of Judge Diarmuid O'Scannalain On Behalf of The Judicial Conference of the United States Regarding S.892 As Applied to Federal Courts.

O'Scannlain, D.F. Some Reflections on Cameras in the Appellate Courtroom. Journal of Appellate Practice and Process (2007): 323.

O'Scannlain, D.F. Statement of Judge Diarmuid O'Scannlain on Behalf of the Judicial Conference of the United States Regarding S. 829 as Applied to Federal Trial Courts, 9 November, 2005, Exhibit 4, 48.

O'Sullivan, D. "Meta–analysis," in Breakwell, G.M., Hammond., S., Fife–Schaw, C., and Smith, J.A. Research Methods in Psychology. London: Sage, 2006, 466.

Ogden, C.K., and Richards, I.A. The Meaning of Meaning. London: Keegan Paul, 1946, referred to in Hoijer, B., 31

Olausson, U. Towards a European Identity? The News Media and the Case of Climate Change. European Journal of Communications 25 (2010): 138.

Open University. The Barristers, About the Series, atwww.open2.net/about_the_barristers.html. Last accessed on April 4, 2009.

Oskanp, A., Lodder, A., and Apistola, M., Eds. IT Support of the Judiciary, Australia, Singaport, Venezuala, Norway, The Netherlands and Italy. The Hague: Asser Press, 2004.

Ossinger, J. Electronic Access to Courtrooms: Television as an Educational Socializing Agent on the Judiciary. MA, (The University of Maine, 2006).

Oue, W., Hakoda, Y., Onuma, N. The Effects of Visual Features of a Weapon on Eyewitnesses' Cognitive Processing. Japanese Journal of Psychology 77 (2006) 443.

Owles, D. Cameras in the Courtroom. New Law Journal. October 21, 1982: 985.

Oyez, atwww.oyez.org. Last accessed on September 18, 2010.

Paddon, A.R. Television Coverage of Criminal Trials with Cameras and Microphones: A Laboratory Experiment of Audience Effects. Ph.D, University of Tennessee, Knoxville, 1985.

——— Television Coverage of Criminal Trials with Cameras and Microphones: A Controlled Experiment of Audience Effects, Radio–television Journalism Division, AEJMC Montreal, Que, Canada, August 7, 1992, 1.

Parker, C. What Do They Learn When They Learn Legal Ethics? Legal Education Review 12 (2001): 175.

Part II Research Designs, Methodological Issues, and Analytic Procedures, in Davis, S.F. Handbook of Research Methods in Experimental Psychology. Oxford: Blackwell, 2003, 39.

Pasternack, S.R. The Effects of Perceived Community Pressure on Simulated Juror Guilt Attributions: An Experimental Study. Ph.D, The University of Tennessee, Knoxville, 1982.

People (AG) v Casey (No 2) [1963] IR 33.

People (AG) v Stafford [1983] IR 165.

People (DPP) v Courtney, reported in Irish Times, January 28, 1993. But note report of permission granted to CBS in the US to film actual jury deliberations,

People (DPP) v Christo, Court of Criminal Appeal, January 31, 2005.

People v Boss and Others. Albany Law Review (1999–2000): 1051.

Pequignot, M. From Estes to Chandler: Shifting the Constitutional Burden of Courtroom Cameras to the States. Florida State University Law Review 9 (1981): 315.

Perrotta, T. N.Y. Law Banning Cameras in State Courts found Constitutional. Law.com, July 16, 2003.

Peterson–Manz, J.G. Copycats: Homicide and the Press. Dissertation Abstracts International: Section B: The Sciences and Engineering 63 (2002): 591.

Domke, D. The Press, Race Relations and Social Change. Journal of Communication 51 (2001): 317.

Petkanas, W. Cameras on Trial: An Assessment of the Educational Affects of News Cameras in Trial Courts, Ph.D (New York University, 1990).

Philo, G. Seeing and Believing: The Influence of Television. London: New York, 1990.

Piccus, T. Demystifying the Least Understood Branch: Opening the Supreme Court to Broadcast Media. Texas Law Review (1992–1993): 1053.

Pickel, K.L., French, T.A., and Betts, J. A Cross–modal Weapon Focus Effect: The Influence of a Weapon's Presence on Memory for Auditory Information. Memory 11 (2003): 27.

Pickel, K.L., Ross, S.J., and Truelove, R.S. Do Weapons Automatically Capture Attention? Applied Cognitive Psychology 20 (2006): 871.

Pickel, K.L., Narter, D.B., Jameson, M.M., and Lenhardt, T.T. The Weapon Focus Effect in Child Eyewitnesses. Psychology, Crime and Law 14 (2008): 61.

Pickel, K.L. Unusualness and Threat as Possible Causes of Weapon Focus. Memory 6 (1998): 277.

Pizza, W.T., and Perron, W. Crime Victims in German Courtrooms: A Comparative Perspective on American Problems. Stanford Journal of International Law 40 (1996)(40): 37.

Pizza, W.T. The OJ Simpson Trial and the American Legal System. New Law Journal (1995): 990.

P.J.B [initials only given]. Recent Cases: Contempt of Court – Extent of Liability of Members of Legal Profession. Australian Law Journal 52 (1978): 151.

Platte, M.K. TV in the Courtroom: Right of Access. Communications and the Media 3 (1981) 11.

Podlas, K. Please Adjust Your Signal: How Television's Syndicated Courtrooms Bias Our Juror Citizenry. American Business Law Review 39 (2001): 1.

Pogorzelski, W. and Brewer, T.W. Cameras in Court, How Television News Media Use Courtroom Footage. Judicature 91 (November–December, 2007): 125.

Pool, Ithiel de Sola. Technologies of Freedom. Cambridge: Belknap/Harvard Press, 1983.

Posey, A., and Dahl, A.J. Beyond Pretrial Publicity: Legal and Ethical Issues Associated with Change of Venue Surveys. Law and Human Behavior 26 (2002): 107.

Post –Newsweek Stations, Florida, Inc. v US (370 So2d 764 (Fla., 1979).

Power, J.H. On the Intellectual Structure of the Human Communication Discipline. Communication Education 44 (1995): 191.

Pradao, E.C., and Hyman, L.S. Technological Advances in the Courtroom. Issues in Democracy: The Changing Face of U.S. Courts 8 (2003): 32.

Preiss, R.W., Gayle, B.M., Burrell, N., Allen, M., and Bryant, J., Eds. Mass Media Effects Research: Advances Through Meta Analysis. Mahway, New Jersey: Lawrence Erlbaum, 2007.

Prejudicial Publicity in Trials of Public Officials, [author not given]. Yale Law Journal 85 (1978): 123.

Price, M.E., and Raboy, M., Eds. Public Service Broadcasting in Transition: A Documentary Reader. London: Kluwer, 2003.

Primus, R.A. The American Language of Rights, Cambridge: CUP, 1999.

Pritchard, J. Editorial. Should Cameras be Allowed in the Courtroom? Legal Business magazine, (1992), 3, referred to in Biondi, A., 146.

——— Should Cameras be Allowed in the Courtroom? Legal Business (January – February, 1992): 3.

Pritchard, J. Televising the Courts: Some Second Thoughts. Legal Business (May, 1995): 11.

Pryor, B., Strawn, D., Buchanan, R., and Meeske, M. The Florida Experiment: An Analysis of the On–the–Scene Responses to Cameras in the Courtrooms. Southern Speech Communications Journal 45 (1979): 12, as referred to in Shores, D., 22.

Pugsley, R.A. Symposium: The Sound of Silence: Reflections on the Use of the Gag Order: This Courtroom is Not a Television Studio: Why Judge Fujisaki Made the Correct Call in Gagging the Lawyers and Parties, and Banning the Cameras from the O.J. Simpson Civil Case. LA Entertainment Law Journal 17 (1997): 369.

Punch, K.F. Developing Effective Research Proposals. Los Angeles: Sage, 2006.

Punches, A.D. The Cognitive Effects of Camera Presence on the Recall of Testimony in a Simulated Courtroom Setting. Ph.D, Colorado State University, Fort Collins, 1991.

Puxley, C. Man. May Allow Cameras in Courtrooms. London Free Press, 18 March, 2009.

Quinn, F. Law for Journalists. London: Pearson Longman, 2007.

Rafter, N., and Hahn, C.A. Courtroom Files, in Rafter, N. Shots in the Mirror: Crime Films and Society. Oxford: Oxford University Press: 2000.

Rahaim, G.L., and Brodsky, S.L. Empirical Evidence Versus Common Sense: Juror and Lawyer Knowledge of Eyewitness Accuracy. Law and Psychology Review7 (1982): 1.

Ramsay, I. Televising Court Proceedings. Current Affairs Bulletin 70 (1993): 16.

Rawlings, P. 'A Complete System of Knavery': Folk Devils, Moral Panics and the Origins of Financial Regulation. Current Legal Problems 61 (2008): 325.

Ray, W.J. Methods Toward A Science of Behavior and Experience. Belmont, CA: Wadsworth/ Thomson Learning, 2003.

Raymond, P. The Impact of a Televised Trial on Individual's Information and Attitudes. Judicature 75 (1992): 204.

Reality Television. Criminal Law and Justice Weekly (2003): 917.

Re, L. Eyewitness Identification: Why So Many Mistakes? Australian Law Journal 58 (1984): 519.

Re Learho [1990] 2 AC 165.

Reddy. The Conduit Metaphor – A Case of Frame Conflict in Our Language About Language, quoted in Erickson *et al.* Representing Order Crime, Law and Justice in the News. Oxford: OUP, 1991, n. 15, at 43.

Reddy, M.J. The Conduit Metaphor – A Case of Frame Conflict in Our Language About Language, in Metaphor and Thought, Ortony, A., Ed., Cambridge: Cambridge University Press, 1993: 164.

Reith, M. Viewing of Crime Drama and Authoritarian Aggression: An Investigation of the Relationship Between Crime Viewing, Fear, and Aggression. Journal of Broadcasting & Electronic Media 43 (1999): 211.

Report of the Commission on the Newspaper Industry (Dublin: Government Publication, 1996).

Report of the Advisory Committee to Oversee the Experimental Use of Cameras and Recording Equipment in Courtrooms, indicated as being available from the National Centre of the State Courts, Williamsburg, Virginia.

Report Summary of the California Judicial Task Force on Photographing, Recording and Broadcasting in the Courtroom.

Report of the Commission on the Newspaper Industry, (Dublin: Government Publications, 1996).

Report Summary of the California Judicial Task Force on Photographing, Recording and Broadcasting in the Courtroom.

Report of the Supreme Court Committee to Monitor and Evaluate the Use of Audio and Visual Equipment in the Courtroom (April 1, 1979), as referred to in Netteburg, 472.

Re Learho [1990] 2 AC 165.

R v Parke [1903] 2KB 432, at 438.

Reske, H.J. Ground–Breaking But Boring: Few Cameras Expected in Federal Courts as Broadcast Experiment Gets Underway. ABA Journal (September, 1991): 26.

——— No More Cameras in Federal Courts: Judicial Conference Ends Experiment Despite Few Complaints from Judges. ABA Journal (November, 1994): 28.

——— Rally for Court Cameras Falls Short: Judicial Conference Committee Rejects Judge's Plea to Keep Broadcasting. ABA Journal (March, 1995): 30.

——— Cameras Experiment One Year Old: Retired Justice Marshall Among the Judges Who Refused Broadcast Requests. ABA Journal (July, 1992): 28.

——— A Repeat Performance: Judicial Conference Allows Cameras Back in Appeals Courts. ABA Journal 82 (1996) 38.

——— Cameras in Federal Courts Vote Delayed: US Judicial Conference Instead Focuses on Long–Range Plan Recommendations, ABA Journal 81 (1995): 16.

——— Courtroom Cameras Face New Scrutiny, Critics Say Simpson Case Demonstrated Why Trials Should Not be Televised. ABA Journal (November, 1995): 48d.

Hernandez, D.G. Courtroom Cameras Debated. Editor & Publisher 129 (1996): 11.

——— Panelists Differ Over TV's Impact on Trials. ABA Journal (October, 1992): 44.

Richardson, D., and Spivey, M. Eye Tracking: Research Areas and Applications, in Bowlin G., and Wnek, G. Encyclopedia of Biomaterials and Biomedical Engineering, August 31, 2004.

Rideau v Louisiana, 373, US 723 (1963).

Riger, S., and Gordan, M.T. The Fear of Rape: A Study in Social Control. Journal of Social Issues 37 (1981) 71.

Rimmer, T. Electronic Media in the Courtroom: Legal and Social Science Perspectives. Portland OR: American Association for Education in Journalism and Mass Communication, 1988.

Ripley, J.M., An Argument for Television in the Civil Courtroom, Journal of Broadcasting XII (1967 – 1968): 23.

Roberts, A. Eyewitness Identification and Expert Insight: *R v Forbes*. International Journal of Evidence & Proof 14 (2010)(14): 57.

Roberts, R.E. An Empirical and Normative Analysis of the Impact of Televised Courtroom Proceedings. SMU Law Review 51 (1998): 621.

Rogers, E.M., foreword in Lower, S.A., and Defer, M.L. Milestones in Mass Communication Research: Media Effects. New York: Longman, 1985.

Robertson, G. Freedom, the Individual and the Law. London: Penguin, 1989, 1993.

Rogers, E.M. foreword in Lowery, S.A., and DeFleur, M.L. Milestones in Mass Communication Research: Media Effects. New York: Longman, 1985.

Rogers, S. Smith Bernal Courts Legal IT Market. The Lawyer, September 20, 1994, 6.

Rolph, C.H. In Camera. New Law Journal 16 (1990): 382.

Rooney, J.F. Panel OK's Cameras in US Appeals Courts; Seen as Unlikely Here. Chicago Daily Law Bulletin, 13 March, 1996, 1.

Roper Starch 1995 Global Consumer Survey, as referred to in Creeber, G., 131.

Ross, K., and Nightingale, V., Media and Audiences: New Perspectives, (Maidenhead, Berkshire: OUP, 2003).

Rose, N. Camera–shy Prosecutor Hits Out, American Bar Association Conference. Law Society Gazette 8 (2002): X.
Rothwell, R. Lights, Camera, Court. Law Society Gazette 18 (2004): 5.
Rotunda, R.D. Dealing with the Media: Ethical, Constitutional, and Practical Parameters. Illinois Bar Journal 84 (1996): 614.
Hardy, K.A. Order in the Courtroom, Silence on the Courthouse Steps: Attorneys Muzzled by Ethical Disciplinary Rules. Seton Hall Law Review 22 (1991 – 1992): 1401;
Rotunda, R.D. Reporting Sensational Trials: Free Press, a Responsible Press, and Cameras in the Courts. Communications Law and Policy 3 (1998): 295.
Rozenberg, J. Sending the Right Message. Law Society Gazette 25 (2008): 8.
Rudell, A.P. The Television Camera Used to Measure Movement. Behavior Research Methods and Instrumentation 11 (1979): 339.
Rusis, G., and Snyder, H.L. The Effects of TV Camera Field of View and Size of Targets Upon Air–to–Ground Target Recognition. Human Factors 7 (1965): 493.
Rubin, H.J., and Rubin, I.S. Qualitative Interviewing: The Art of Hearing Data. Thousand Oaks, CA: Sage, 2005.
Rutherford, H., and Raymond, J. Effects of Spatial Cues on Locating Emotional Targets. Visual Cognition 18 (2010): 389.
R v Dunne (English Court of Appeal) 4 October 1976, (unreported), referred to in Re, L.
R v Turnbull [1976] 3 All ER 549.
Re Barber v Lloyds Underwriters [1987] 1 QB 103, 105.
R v Loveridge, Lee and Loveridge [2001] 2 Cr. App. Rep. 29, CA.
Re R Limited [1989] IR 126.
Sadler, R.L. Electronic Media Law. Thousand Oaks, CA: Sage, 2005.
Safer, M., Christianson, S–A, Autry, M., and Osterlund, K. Tunnel Memory for Traumatic Events. Applied Cognitive Psychology 12 (1998): 99.
Sager, K.L., and Frederiksen, K.N. Televising the Judicial Branch: In Furtherance of the Public's First Amendment Rights. Southern California Law Review 69 (1995 – 1996): 1519.
Sallon, C. OJ Simpson – Justice on Trial. Counsel (May – June, 1995): 8, 10.
Sarner, J. Justice, Take Two: The Continuing Debate Over Cameras in the Courtroom. Seton Hall Constitutional Law Journal 10 (1999–2000): 1053.
Sasaki, L.M. Electronic Media Access to Federal Courtrooms: A Judicial Response. University of Michigan Journal of Law Reform (1990): 769.
Sato, W., and Yoshikawa, S. Detection of Emotional Facial Expressions and Anti–Expressions. Visual Cognition 18 (2010): 369.
Saunders, J. Memory Impairment in Weapon Focus Effect. Memory and Cognition 37 (2009): 326.
Schleiff, H. Cameras in Courts. New Law Journal (2004)(154): 1745.
Schlesinger, P., and Tumber, H. Reporting Crime: the Media Politics of Criminal Justice. Oxford: Clarendon, 1994.
Schlesinger, P., Tumber, H., and Murdock, G. The Media Politics of Crime and Criminal Justice. British Journal of Sociology 42 (1991): 397.
Scheiter, K., Wiebe, E., and Holsanova, J. Theoretical and Instructional Aspects of Learning with Visualizations, in Zheng, R., Ed. Cognitive Effects of Multimedia Learning. Hershey, PA: IGI Global, 2009.
Schoeps v *Museum of Modern Art*, 599 F. Supp. 2d 532, 534 (SDNY 2009).
Schudson, M. The Sociology of News Production. Media, Culture and Society 11 (1989): 263.
Schmidt, H.C. Effects of Interrogator Tactics and Camera Perspective Bias on Evaluations of Confession Evidence, MSc thesis, Ohio University (2006).
Schleiff, H. Cameras in Courts. New Law Journal 154 (2004): 1745.
——— Cameras Have a Place in the Supreme Court, Television Week 22 (2003): 8.
Schlesinger, P., and Tumber, H. Reporting Crime: the Media Politics of Criminal Justice. Oxford: Claredon, 1994.
Schroder, K., Drotner, K., Kline, S., and Murray, C. Researching Audiences. London: Arnold, 2003.

Schulz, P.J., Ed. Communication Theory: Volume 1, General Approaches to Communication and the Processing of Communication on the Intra–Individual Level (Los Angeles: Sage, 2010).

Seiter, E. Television and New Media Audiences. Oxford: Clarendon, 1999.

Sellers, D.A. The Circus Comes to Town: The Media and High–Profile Trials. Law and Contemporary Problems 71 (2008): 182.

Shah, P., Freedman, E., and Vekiri, I. The Comprehension of Quantitative Information in Graphical Displays, in Shah, P., and Miyake, A. The Cambridge Handbook of Visuospatial Thinking. Cambridge: Cambridge University Press, 2005, 426.

Shah, P., and Miyake, A. The Cambridge Handbook of Visuospatial Thinking. Cambridge: Cambridge University Press, 2005.

Shall We Dance? The Courts, the Community, and the News Media, An Edited Transcript of a Panel Discussion at the American Judicature Society's 1996 Midyear Meeting. Judicature (1996): 30.

Shattuc, J.M. The Talking Cure: TV Talk Shoes and Women. New York: Routledge, 1997.

Shaughnessy, H., and Fuente–Coba, C. The Cultural Obligations of Broadcasting. European Institute for the Media, 1990.

Shaw, D. Media Coverage of the Courts: Improving But Still Not Adequate. Judicature 65 (1981): 18.

Shaw, D.L., and McCombs, M.E. The Agenda Setting Function of the Media. Public Opinion Quarterly 36 (1972): 176.

Shaw, J.S., III, McClure, K.A., and Dykstra, J.A. Eyewitness Confidence from the Witnessed Event Through Trial, chapter in Toglia, M., Read, J.D., Ross, D.F., Lindsy, R.C.L., Eds. The Handbook of Eyewitness Psychology, Vol 1: Memory for Events. Mahwah, NJ: Erlbaum, 2007, 371.

Sherman, J., and Kawamoto, D., Boies, Schiller & Flexner LLP, Memorandum: Prepared for the Committee on Court Administration and Case Management (Hon. John R. Tunheim, Chair), The Judicial Conference of the United States, submitted on behalf of Courtroom View Network, June 6, 2009, at 9.

Sherwin, R.K. When Law Goes Pop: The Vanishing Line Between Law and Popular Culture. Chicago: The University of Chicago Press, 2000.

Sherwin, R.K. The Jurisprudence of Appearances. New York Law School Law Review 43 (1999–2000) 821.

Shores, D. The Effects of Courtroom Camera on Verbal Behavior: An Analysis of Simulated Trial Witness Testimony in Courtrooms Using Television Cameras. Ph.D, The University of Florida, 1981.

Short, E.H., and Associates. Evaluation of California's Experiment with Extended Media Coverage of Courts, Submitted to The Administrative Office for the Courts, The Chief Justice's Special Committee on the Courts and the Media and The California Judicial Council, September 1981.

Shugart, H.A. Ruling Class: Disciplining Class, Race, and Ethnicity in Television Reality Court Shows. Howard Journal of Communications 17 (2006): 79.

Simpson and Cameras. Editor & Publisher 128 (1995): 8.

Skowronski, J.J.., Betz, A.L., Thompson, C.B., and Shannon, L. Social Memory in Everyday Life: Recall of Self–Events and Other–Events. Journal of Personality and Social Psychology 60 (1991): 831.

Slater, book review. JOBEM 31 (1987): 479.

Slater, D., and Hans, V.P., Methodological Issues in the Evaluation of 'Experiments' with Cameras in the Courts," Communications Quarterly 30 (1982): 376.

Slotnick, E.E., and Segal, J.A. Television News and the Supreme Court: All the News That's Fit to Air? Cambridge: Cambridge University Press, 1998.

Sloviter, D.K. If Courts Are Open, Must Cameras Follow? Hofstra Law Review 26 (1998): 873.

Smallman, D. Cameras in Courtrooms: Revisting the Experiment. The IRE Journal (May/June, 2001): 15.

Smith, C.E. Courts and Trials: A Reference Handbook. Santa Barbara, California: ABC–CLIO, 2003.
Smith, P. Evaluating the Corrective Statements Proposed in the Court Case *US Department of Justice vs. Philip Morris U.S.A. Inc., et al*, M.S., State University of New York at Buffalo, 2009.
Smolla, R.A. Suing the Press, Libel, Media and Power. Oxford: OUP, 1986.
Snow, referred to in Kirby, J. The Globalisation of Media and Judicial Independence. Communications Law 1 (1996): 115.
Sodos, N.S. The Ethical Considerations of Televising Federal Courtroom Proceedings. Georgetown Journal of Legal Ethics 5 (1992): 915.
Solomon, G., and Cohen, A.A. Television Formats, Mastery of Mental Skills, and the Acquisition of Knowledge. Journal of Educational Psychology 69 (1977): 612.
Sony, Warner, Atlantic, Arista and UMG, Court of Appeals For the First Circuit, No. 09–1090, Amicus Brief, 29 January, 2009.
Sorlin, P. Mass Media. London: Routledge, 1994.
Spacapan, S., and Cohen, S. Effects and After Effects of Stressor Expectations. Journal of Personality and Social Psychology 45 (1983): 1243.
Spann, W.B., Jr. Cameras in the Courtroom – for Better or for Worse. American Bar Association Journal 64 (1978): 797.
Spatz, C., and Kardas, E.P. Research Methods in Psychology. Boston: McGraw Hill, 2008.
Spector, J.M. Handbook of Research on Educational Communications and Technology. New York: Lawrence Erlbaum Associates, Taylor and Francis, 2008.
Spence, G. Justice: The New Commodity. ABA Journal (March, 1992) 46, as referred to in Stewart, R.E.R. The Changing Relationship between Cameras and Courts, MA, Florida Atlantic University (1998): 34.
Sporer, S., Penrod, S., Read, D., and Cutler, B., Choosing, Confidence and Accuracy: A Meta–analysis of the Confidence–Accuracy Relation in Eyewitness Identification Studies. Psychological Bulletin 118 (1995): 315.
Spreaight, A. Let the Cameras In. Law Society Gazette 38 (2001):16.
Court TV Deterrent. New Law Journal 16 (1988): 906.
Starcher, L.V. Cameras in the Courts – A Revival in West Virginia and the Nation. West Virginia Law Review 84 (1982): 267.
State Courts Are Flirting With TV and Cameras. ABA Journal 63 (1977): 473.
State of Connecticut Judicial Branch, protocol for Broadcasting, Televising, Recording or Photographing Appellate Court Oral Arguments, available atwww.jud.state.ct.us/EXTERNAL/supapp/protocol_ap_oral_argu.htm. Last accessed on October 31, 2010.
State v Langley, 214 Ore. 445, 323 P.2d 301 (1958), as referred to in The Special Committee on Radio and Television of the Association of the Bar of the City of New York. Radio, Television, and the Administration of Justice: A Documented Survey of Materials. New York and London: Columbia University Press, 1965, 99.
State v Manley (1962), as referred to in Freedman, W. Press and Media Access to a Criminal Courtroom. New York: Quorum Books, 1988, 42.
State v Manley, Docket Number 22092, Oklahoma County District Court, as referred to in Freedman, W., 42.
Stauffer, J., Frost, R., and Rybolt, W., "The Attention Factor in Recalling Network Television News," Journal of Communications 33 (1983): 29.
Stebley, N.M. A Meta–Analytic Review of the Weapon Focus Effect. Law and Human Behaviour 16 (1992): 413.
Stein, M.L., "Appeal Court Allows Cameras in Courtrooms," Editor & Publisher 129 (1996): 11.
Stein, S.D. Learning, Teaching and Researching on the Internet: A Practical Guide for Social Scientists. New York: Longman, 1999.
Stephens, M. OJ – What Price for UK Law? The Lawyer (October 10, 1995): 15.
Stenson, D., and Cowell, K. The Politics of Crime Control. London: Sage, 1991.
Stepniak, D. Audio–Visual Coverage of Courts. Cambridge: Cambridge University Press, 2008.

——— Why Shouldn't Australian Court Proceedings be Televised? UNSW Law Journal 17 (1994): 345.

Stevens, R.B. The Independence of the Judiciary: The View from the Lord Chancellor's Office. Oxford Journal of Legal Studies 8 (1988): 222.

Stewart, R.E.R. The Changing Relationship Between Camera and the Courts MA, (Florida Atlantic University, 1998).

Stillman, C.A. Adversary System: Cameras in the Courtroom After O.J.? – No. New York Law Journal (16 October, 1995): 2.

Stodden, V. Enabling Reproducible Research: Licensing for Scientific Innovation. International Journal of Communications Law and Policy 13 (2009): 1.

Stone, W., and Edlin, S.G. TV or Not TV: Televised and Photographic Coverage of Trials. Mercer Law Review 29 (1978): 1119.

Strickland, R.A., and Moore, R.H. Cameras in State Courts: A Historical Perspective. Judicature 78 (1994): 128.

Studenbaker, C.A., and Penrod, S.D. Pretrial Publicity and Its Influence on Juror Decision Making, in Williams, N., and Williams, K.D., Eds. Psychology and Law: An Empirical Perspective. New York: Guildford Press, 2005.

Summers, R.S. The Jurisprudence of Law's Form and Substance. Brookfield: Ashgate, 2000.

Surette, R. Media, Crime and Criminal Justice: Images and Realities. Belmont CA: Wadsworth Publishing Company, 1998, as referred to in Stewart, R.E.R., The Changing Relationship Between Camera and the Courts. MA, Florida Atlantic University, 1998.

Sutro, J.A. A Lawyer's View of Courtroom Broadcasting. Journal of Broadcasting XXI (1967 – 1968): 19.

Svenson, E. Cameras in the Courtroom? Between Lawyers, July 18, 2006.

Swaine, E.T. Pre–deliberations Juror Misconduct, Evidential Incompetence, and Juror Responsibility. Yale Law Journal 98 (1988): 187.

Tate, E.G., and Trach, L.F. The Effects of United States Television Programs Upon Canadian Beliefs About Legal Procedure. Canadian Journal of Communication (1980) 1.

Television Cameras in the Courts, A Survey of New York State, December, 1996. Marist Institute for Public Opinion Poll, as contained in New York State Committee to Review Audio–Visual Coverage of Court Proceedings. An Open Courtroom, Cameras in New York Courts. New York: Fordham, 1997.

Televising Courts. New Law Journal (16 February, 1990): 194.

Televising Coverage in the State Courts: An Update. State Court Journal 7 (1983): 13.

Teun A. van Dijk. The Interdisciplinary Study of News as Discourse, in Jensen, K.B., and Jankowski, N.W., 108.

TerBeek, C. A Call or Precedential Heads: Why the Supreme Court's Eyewitness Identification Jurisprudence is Anachronistic and Out–of–Step with the Empirical Evidence. Law & Psychology Review 31 (2007): 21.

Terry, H.B. Electronic Journalism in the Colorado Courts. Journalism Quarterly 34 (1957): 341.

Thakker, J., and Durrant, R. News Coverage of Sexual Offending in New Zealand, 2003. New Zealand Journal of Psychology 35 (2006): 28.

Thaler, P., The Impact of the Television Camera on Courtroom Participants: A Case Study of the Joel Stenberg Murder Trial, Ph.D (New York University, 1990).

——— The Watchful Eye American Justice in the Age of the Television Trial. Westport, CT: Praeger Press, 1994.

The Psychology of Juror and Jury Decision Making, chapter in Hastie, R., Penrod, S.D., and Pennington, N. Inside the Jury. Cambridge: Harvard University Press, 1983, 15.

The Thoughts of Sir Thomas. New Law Journal 144 (1994): 593.

The Special Committee on Radio and Television of the Association of the Bar of the City of New York. Radio, Television, and the Administration of Justice: A Documented Survey of Materials. New York and London: Columbia University Press, 1965.

The Verdict Is In: And You're Out. Law Society Gazette, August 4, 2006, available at www.lawgazette.co.uk , last accessed on October 24, 2010.

Ting–Toomey, S., and Chung, L.C. Understanding Intercultural Communication. Los Angeles: Roxbury, 2005.
Toseland, R.W. Fear of Crime: Who is Most Vulnerable? Journal of Criminal Justice 10 (1982): 199.
Tongue, C. Report on the Tole of Public Service Television in a Multi–media Society. Committee on Culture, Youth, Education and the Media, A4–0243/96.
Troscianko, T., Holmes, A., Stillman, J., Mirmehdi, M., Wright, D., and Wilson, A., "What Happens Next? The Predictability of Natural Behaviour Viewed Through CCTV Cameras." Perception 33 (2004): 87.
Trossman, M.S. Tuning in to the Courtroom: A Brief History of Television and Criminal Trials. Update on L. Related Education 23 (1999–2000)(23): 21.
Trossman, M.S. Tuning in to the Courtroom: A Brief History of Television and Criminal Trials. Justimages (1995): 4.
Tuchman, G. Objectivity as Strategic Ritual: Examination of Newsmen's Notions of Objectivity. American Journal of Sociology 77 (1972): 660.
Tuggle, C.A., and Huffman, S. Live Reporting in Television News: Breaking News or Black Holes? Journal of Broadcasting & Electronic Media 45 (2001): 335.
Tuma, C. Open Courts: How Cameras in Courts Help Keep the System Honest. Towards More Reliable Jury Verdicts? Law, Technology, and Media Developments Since the Trials of Dr. Sam Sheppard. Cleveland State Law Review 49 (2001) 417.
Tumber, H. News: A Reader. Oxford: OUP, 1999.
Tumey v Ohio, 273, US 510 (1927).
Tunhein, J., Judicial Conference of the United States, Statement of the Honorable John R. Tunheim, Judge, United States District Court for the District of Minnesota, For the Committee on the Judiciary of the United States House of Representatives, Hearing on Cameras in the Courtroom: The 'Sunshine in the Courtroom Act of 2007,' HR 2128, September 27, 2007, (Washington: Administrative Office of the US Courts, 2007).
Turner v Louisiana, 379, US 466 (1965).
Tushnet, M. Supreme Court and Its First Amendment Constituency. Hastings Law Journal 44 (1992–1993): 881.
Twining, W. Rethinking Evidence, Exploratory Essays (Oxford: Blackwell, 1990).
——— Identification and Misidentification in Legal Processes: Redefining the Problem, in Lloyd–Bostock, S., and Clifford, B.R., Eds., 255.
UMR Insight Limited, Media Coverage of Court Proceedings: A Summary Report, (February 1998).
US v Amaral, 488 F.2d 1148 (1973).
UMR Insight Ltd. Media Coverage of Court Proceedings: Summary Report, (February 1998) and The Impact of Television, Radio and Still Photography on Coverage of Court Proceedings – Final Report, A Report Prepared for the Department of Courts by a research team from the Department of Human Management, Massey University, (April, 1998). (The New Zealand research).
Uviller, H.R. The Virtuous Prosecutor in Quest of an Ethical Standard: Guidance from the ABA. Michigan Law Review 71 (1973): 1145.
Van Dijk, T. News as Discourse. London: Lawrence Erlbaum Associates, 1988.
Van Gorp, B., Vettehen, P.H., and Beentjes, J.W.J. Challenging the Frame in the News, The Role of Issue Involvement, Attitude, and Competing Frames. Journal of Media Psychology 21 (2009): 161.
VAB Assessment Report to the [Virginia] Supreme Court, 1989, as referred to in Keller, T., 12.
Valentine, T., Pickering, A., and Darling, S. Characteristics of Eyewitness Identification that Predict the Outcome of Real Lineups. Applied Cognitive Psychology 17 (2003): 969.
Valikoski, T–R. The Criminal Trial as a Speech Communication Situation, (Tampere, Finland: University of Tampere, 2004).
Valikoski, T–R. The Communicative Nature of Finnish Criminal Trials from the Perspective of the Witness. Paper presented at the annual convention of National Communication Association (NCA), Seattle, Washington, 9–12 November, 2000.

Vane, E.T., and Gross, L.S. Programming for TV, Radio and Cable. Boston, MA and London: Focal Press, 1994.

Verkaik, R. Cameras Cross the Atlantic: The USA's Trial Broadcasters Are Making A Pitch to Televise UK hearings. Gazette (May 17, 1995): 14.

Viljoen, F. Look Who's Talking, In the Courtroom, Too! South African Law Journal 109 (1992): 64.

Vinson, C.D., and Ertter, J.S. Entertainment or Education, How Do Media Cover the Courts? Press/Politics 7 (2002): 80.

Vismann, C., and Ogger trans, S. Tele–Tribunals: Anatomy of a Medium. Grey Room 32 10 (2003): 5.

Vo, M. L–H., and Schneider, W. A Glimpse is Not a Glimpse: Differential Processing of Flashed Scene Previews Leads to Differential Target Search Benefits. Visual Cognition 18 (2010): 171.

Von Hirshe, A., and Ashworth, A. Proportionate Sentencing, Exploring the Principles. Oxford: OUP, 2005.

Von Hirsch, A., Ashworth, A., and Roberts, J. Principled Sentencing, Readings on Theory and Policy. Oxford: OUP, 2009.

Von Hoene, W.A., Jr. Cameras in the Courtroom: An Overview. Communications Law 13 (1995): 1.

Voboril, M. Cameras on Trial. Columbia Journalism Review (1980): 9.

Wakshlag, J.J., Bart, L., Dudley, J., Groth, G., McCutcheon, J., and Rolla, C. Viewer Appreciation About Victimization and Crime Drama Programs. Communication Research 10 (1983): 195.

Walker, L., Thibaut J., and Andreoli, V. Order of Presentation at Trial. Yale Law Journal 82 (1972): 216.

Ward, S. Fights, Cameras, Action. Law Society Gazette 18 (2001): 22.

Warden, K.P. Canon 35: Is There Room for Objectivity? Washburn Law Journal 4 (1965): 211.

Ware, L.J. Monitoring Visual Attention in Videotaped Interrogations: An Investigation of the Camera Perspective Bias, MSc thesis, Ohio University, (2006).

Weaver, J., and Wakshlag, J. Perceived Vulnerability to Crime, Criminal Victimization Experience, and Television Viewing. Journal of Broadcasting and Electronic Media 30 (1986) 141.

Weber, S., and Dixon., Eds. Growing Up Online: Young People and Digital Technologies. New York: Palgrave Macmillan, 2007.

Wedel, M., and Pieters. Eye Tracking for Visual Marketing. Hanover, MA: now Publisher, 2008, Foundations and Trends in Marketing, vol. 4.

Weiner, D.C. Courtroom Cameras. Litigation 21 (1994–1995): 1.

Weinstein, J.B., and Zimmerman, D.L. Let the People Observe Their Courts. Judicature 61 (1977): 156.

Weisberger, J.R. Cameras in the Courtroom: The Rhode Island Experience. Suffolk University Law Review XVII (1983): 299.

Wells, G. Applied Eyewitness–testimony Research: System Variables and Estimator Variables. Journal of Personality and Social Psychology 12 (1978): 1546.

Wells, G.L., *et al*, Accuracy, Confidence, and Juror Perceptions in Eyewitness Identification. Journal of Applied Psychology 64 (1979): 440.

Wells, G.L, and Bradfield, A.L. 'Good, You Identified the Suspect': Feedback to Eyewitnesses Distorts Their Reports of Witnessing Experience. Applied Psychology 83 (1998): 360, as referred to in TerBeek, C. A Call or Precedential Heads: Why the Supreme Court's Eyewitness Identification Jurisprudence is Anachronistc and Out–of–Step with the Empirical Evidence. Law & Psychology Review 31 2007): 21.

Wells, G.L., and Murray, D.M. Eyewitness Confidence, in Wells, G.L., and Loftus, E.F., Eds. Eyewitness Testimony: Psychological Perspectives. Cambridge: Cambridge University Press, 1984, 165.

Wells, G.L., and Loftus, E.F., Eds. Eyewitness Testimony: Psychological Perspectives. Cambridge: Cambridge University Press, 1984.

Westcott, H.L. Children's Credibility on Camera: The Influence of Age and Production Factors. Children and Society 5 (1991): 254.

Whisenend, J.D. Florida's Experience with Cameras in the Courtroom. American Bar Association Journal (1978): 1860.
White, F.W. Cameras in the Courtroom: A US Survey. Journalism Monographs, No. 60 (1979).
White, R. Courts Web–Cam Call. Law Society Gazette 10 (2007): 4.
Wickens, C.D., Vincow, M., and Yeh, M., Design Applications of Visual Spatial Thinking: The Importance of Frame of Reference, in Shah, P., and Miyake, A. The Cambridge Handbook of Visuospatial Thinking. Cambridge: Cambridge University Press, 2005, 383.
Wieland, L.A. Cameras in the Courtroom. Bench & Bar of Minnesota 64 (2007): 4D.
Williams, C.C. Not All Visual Memories Are Created Equal. Visual Cognition 18 (2010): 201.
Winston, B. Messages: Free Expression, Media and the West from Gutenberg to Google. London: Routledge, 2005.
Winter, B. Cameras in the Courtroom: What Next After Chandler? ABA Journal 67 (1981): 277.
Winograde, A. Cameras in the Courtroom: Whose Right Is It Anyway? Sw. J. L. and Trade Am. 4 (1997): 23.
Wisenand, J.. Florida's Experiment. American Bar Association Journal 64 (1978): 1860.
Wober, J.M. Case on Camera: An Audience Verdict. IBA Research Department, February 1986.
Woolnough, P. and MacLoud, M. Watching the Birdie Watching You: Eyewitness Memory for Actions Using CCTV Recordings of Actual Crimes. Applied Cognitive Psychology 15 (2001): 395.
Wood, K. Recent Judgement Could Lead to TV Cameras in the Court Rooms. Law Society Gazette, (May 1998) 7.
Wood, K. Televising the Courts: A Radio Telefis Eireann Discussion Paper, (Dublin: RTE, 1995). Prepared by Kieron Wood, the then RTE Legal Affairs Correspondent.
Would Cameras Change the Court? The News Media & The Law, May 1, 2006, 22.
Wortley, S., and Hagan, J. Just Des(s)erts? The Racial Polarization of Perceptions of Criminal Injustice. Law and Society Review 31 (1997): 637.
Wright, J.W. II, and Hosman, L.A. Language Style and Sex Bias in the Courtroom: The Effects of Male and Female Use of Hedges and Intensifiers on Impression Information. Southern Communications Journal 48 (1983): 137.
Wrightsman, L.S. The Psychology of the Supreme Court. Oxford, OUP: 2006.
Wydick, R.C. Plain English for Lawyers. California Law Review 66 (1978): 727.
Yaffe, D. TV Trial Restrictions Urged: Task Force Nixes Call for Outright Ban, Even Though Most Judges Want It. The Recorder. February 26, 1996.
Yarmey, A.D., and Jones, H.P.T. Is Eyewitness Identification a Matter of Common Sense?, in Lloyd–Bostock, S., and Clifford, B.R., Eds. Evaluating Witness Evidence. London: Wiley, 1993, as referred to in Loftus, E., Loftus, G., and Messo, J. Some Facts About 'Weapon Focus." Law and Human Behaviour 11 (1987): 55.
Yuille, J., Davies, G., Gibling, F., Marxsen, D., and Porter, S. Eyewitness Memory of Police Trainees for Realistic Role Plays. Journal of Applied Psychology 79 (1994): 931.
Yuille, J., and Cutshall, J. A Case Study of Eyewitness Memory of a Crime. Journal of Applied Psychology 71 (1986): 291.
Zamora v Florida, 372 So. 2d 473, 1979.
Zelezny, J.D. Communications Law, Liberties, Restraints, and the Modern Media. Belmont, CA: Thomson/Wadsworth, 2004.
Zemans, F.K. Public Access, The Ultimate Guardian of Fairness in Our Justice System, Edited Testimony of Francis Kahn Zemans Before the Judicial Counsel of California Task Force to Review Photographing, Recording and Broadcasting in the Courtroom, January 8, 1996, Judicature (1996): 173.
Zillman, D. Television Viewing and Psychological Arousal, chapter in Bryant, J., and Zillman, D. Responding to the Screen: Reception and Reaction Processes. Hillside, NJ: Erlbaum, 1991.

Index